FEAST

FEAST

FOOD *of the* ISLAMIC WORLD

ANISSA HELOU

An Imprint of HarperCollins*Publishers*

For my late father, who
would have preferred me
to follow my first ambition
to be the Arab Marie Curie
but was then perfectly
happy to see me switch to
art, and later to food!

CONTENTS

INTRODUCTION VIII

BREAD
1

THE WHOLE BEAST
90

RICE, GRAINS, PASTA & LEGUMES
194

THE SEA
308

SPICES, SPICE MIXTURES & SPICE PASTES
354

FRESH PRODUCE
374

A SWEET TOOTH
438

ACKNOWLEDGMENTS 508
GLOSSARY 512
INDEX 518

INTRODUCTION

Islam was born at the beginning of the seventh century in one of the world's harshest climates, in Mecca in Saudi Arabia around the year 610 AD, when the Prophet Muhammad began receiving divine revelations from the angel Gabriel. However, it wasn't until the year 622 AD or 1 AH (after Hijrah, or exile) that the Islamic calendar marks the official start of the religion when, after a dispute with his tribe, the Prophet Muhammad fled Mecca to the city of Yathrib, now known as Medina.

Medina was and still is an oasis in the desert, but though there was water, there wouldn't have been much variety available to the early Muslims in terms of food, and their diet was mainly limited to dates from the palm trees growing in the oasis; meat and dairy from their flocks of sheep, camel, and goat; and bread from grain they either grew or imported in their trade caravans from the fertile countries of the Levant and beyond. The Prophet's favorite meal is said to have been *tharid*, a composite dish made of layers of dry bread topped with a stew of meat and vegetables, which still exists in one form or another, under different names, throughout the Middle East and North Africa, and even as far as Indonesia, where some curries are served over roti.

The Arabs have always been great traders, from even before the advent of Islam. They controlled lucrative trade routes along the Silk Road, and in the early days of Islam, they spread their religion not only through war conquests but also by peacefully converting the people they traded with. The goods they traded included spices as well as dry ingredients such as rice and legumes, although it is unlikely that they traded any fresh produce given how long the camel caravans took to cross the desert from lands where fruits and vegetables grew in abundance.

Even today the Muslim world whose recipes I have included follows the same arc more or less as that of the conquests during the expansion of Islam: Morocco, Algeria, Tunisia, and Egypt in North Africa, finishing in Afghanistan, Bangladesh, Pakistan, and India in South Asia, and Xinjiang province and Uzbekistan in Central Asia. In between are Lebanon, Syria, Palestine, Jordan, Turkey, and Iran in the Levant; the United Arab Emirates, Oman, Saudi Arabia, and Qatar in the Arabian Gulf. On the fringes are countries where the influences are more diffuse, such as Zanzibar, Somalia, Senegal, Nigeria, Malaysia, and Indonesia, the world's most populous Muslim country.

After the Prophet Muhammad died in 632, the Rashidun (wise guides) established a caliphate, with Medina as its capital, to continue spreading the Prophet's word. They took Islam to the Levant and North Africa to the west and Persia, Afghanistan, and Iraq to the east, but it wasn't until the Ummayads founded their own dynasty (661–750 AD), moving the capital to Damascus in Syria, that Muslims began to live in splendor. They expanded their culinary repertoire because of easy access to more varied produce—part of Syria is desert but much of the country is fertile with the fruit growing around Damascus famous throughout the Middle East and beyond; as are the pistachio and olive groves around Aleppo. The Muslims also acquired new culinary knowledge from the locals they ruled over, which they absorbed into their own cuisine.

The Ummayads established one of the largest empires the world had yet seen, continuing Islamic conquests further west onto the Iberian peninsula, and east into Central Asia to create the fifth-largest contiguous empire ever. However, it wasn't until the Abbasid Caliphate (750–1258 and 1261–1517), when the capital moved to Baghdad, that Muslims started to develop a rich culinary tradition.

The Abbasid caliphs favored Persian chefs—the Persians already had splendid courts and a rich culinary tradition—who brought a whole new culinary knowledge with them, which they then adapted to the taste of their new masters.

Food became an important element of Abbasid culture and, in the tenth century, a scribe named Abu Muhammad ibn Sayyar wrote the first Arab cookbook, *Kitab al-Tabikh* (*The Book of Cooking*) for an unnamed patron who may have been Saif al-Dawlah al-Hamdani, a cultivated prince of Aleppo. The book contained a collection of recipes from the court of ninth-century Baghdad. The scribe himself descended from the old Muslim aristocracy and, as such, he was in a good position to faithfully transcribe the court's recipes, which he gleaned from the personal collection of individual caliphs, such as al-Mahdi, who died in 785 AD, and al-Mutawakkil, who died in 861 AD, among others.

Many of the dishes that are today typically associated with Arab, Persian, or North African cooking, such as hummus, tabbouleh, kibbeh, baklava, pilaf, or couscous, do not appear in this book. Still, there are dishes from that time such as *hariisah* (meat and grain "porridge") or *qataa'if* (pancakes folded over a filling of nuts, fried, and dipped in syrup) that are prepared today even if slightly differently and with different names. The medieval lavish use of herbs continues to this day.

The Abbasids allowed several autonomous caliphates like the Fatimids in the Maghreb and Egypt and the Seljuks in Turkey to prosper, and each developed its own distinct cuisine based on local know-how and ingredients, but all remained rooted in the tradition of Persian cooking. It was also during the reign of the Abbasids that Sufism rose as a mystical trend with a particular emphasis on the kitchen as a place of spiritual development.

The next great Muslim empire was that of the Ottomans (1299–1922/1923) who established Istanbul as the capital; and with them, a new culinary influence was born. Ottoman cooks introduced many innovations and were among the first to quickly adopt New World ingredients.

They took inspiration from the different regional cuisines of the empire, which they refined in the Topkapi Palace kitchens in Istanbul where hundreds of chefs cooked for up to four thousand people. Each group of chefs concentrated on one specialty with some groups, like the sweets-makers, having their own separate kitchens. All the chefs were hired on the basis of one test, which was how well they cooked rice, a simple task but a good indicator of skill. Eventually, the Ottoman palace cuisine filtered to the population during Ramadan events when food from the palace was distributed to the poor, and through the cooking in the yalis of the pashas, which was directly influenced by palace cooking.

The Mughals were the last great Muslim dynasty and, at the height of their reign in the seventeenth century, their empire spread over large parts of the Indian subcontinent and Afghanistan. The Mughal emperors belonged to the Timurid dynasty, direct descendants of both Genghis Khan and Timur. The former in particular was famous for his pitiless conquests, destroying conquered cities such as Damascus and Baghdad, with mass slaughter of the citizens. But the Mughals founded a refined dynasty that owed a debt to Persian culture. This was evident in their art and literature and in their cooking, which they made their own by using local ingredients and techniques, and using an impressive number of spices, which they almost always toasted before use.

The recipes I have included in this book are mostly from countries where these three great culinary traditions have developed. There are more than three hundred recipes, but even with this number, I have had to limit the selection to classics as well as personal favorites. For a comprehensive selection, I would have needed more than one volume. And I have divided the book into chapters concentrating on ingredients or types of food that are essential to the foods of Islam, with the two largest chapters devoted to the two main staples of the Muslim world—bread and rice.

(*continues on page xii*)

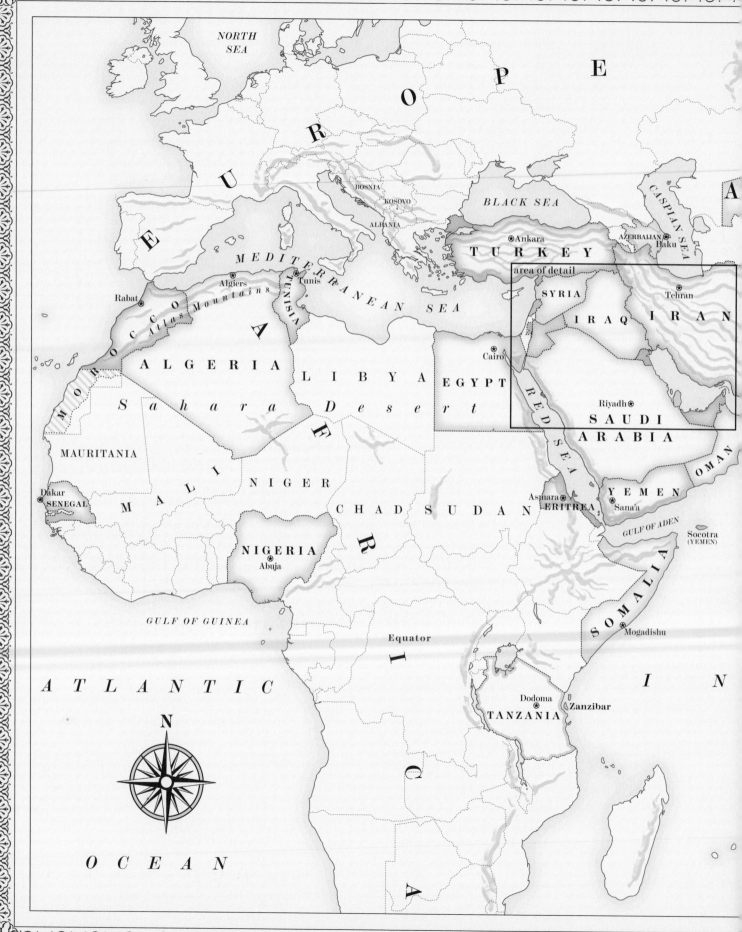

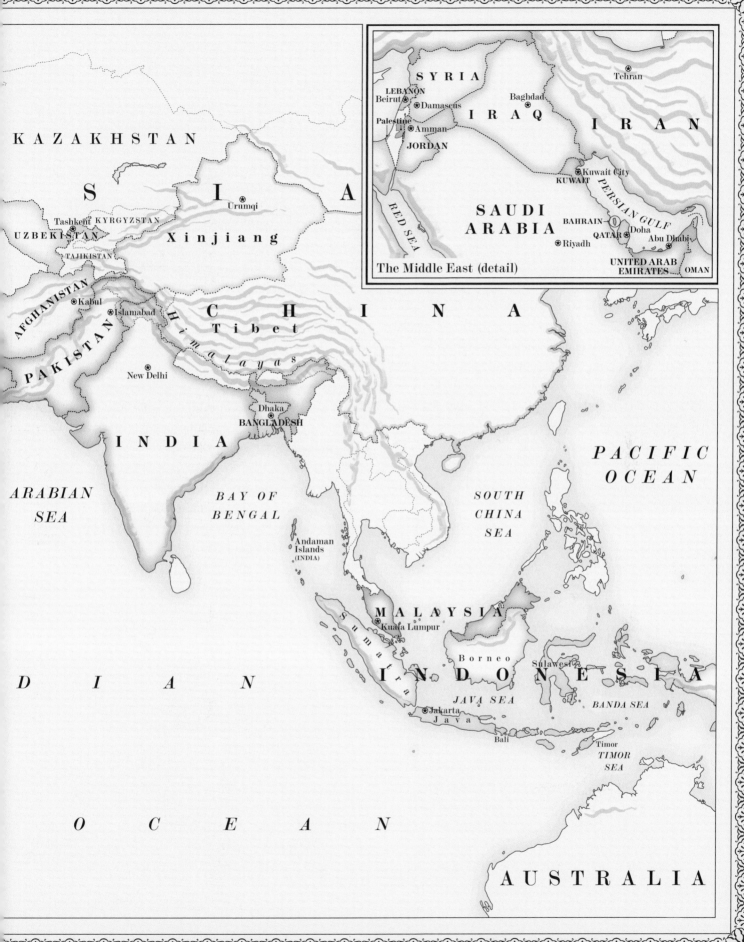

KAZAKHSTAN

A S I A

Urumqi

Tashkent KYRGYZSTAN

UZBEKISTAN

Xinjiang

TAJIKISTAN

AFGHANISTAN

Kabul

Islamabad

C H I N A

Himalayas

Tibet

PAKISTAN

New Delhi

Dhaka

BANGLADESH

I N D I A

ARABIAN
SEA

BAY OF
BENGAL

PACIFIC
OCEAN

Andaman
Islands
(INDIA)

SOUTH
CHINA
SEA

D I A N

MALAYSIA

Kuala Lumpur

Sumatra

I N D O N E S I A

Borneo

Sulawesi

JAVA SEA

BANDA SEA

Jakarta
Java

Bali

Timor

TIMOR
SEA

O C E A N

AUSTRALIA

SYRIA

LEBANON

Beirut

Damascus

Palestine

Amman

JORDAN

IRAQ

Baghdad

Tehran

IRAN

Kuwait City

KUWAIT

PERSIAN GULF

RED SEA

SAUDI
ARABIA

BAHRAIN

QATAR

Doha

Abu Dhabi

Riyadh

UNITED ARAB
EMIRATES

OMAN

The Middle East (detail)

(continued from page ix)

THE DATE

The date is the most important fruit in Islam. It was important in the early days of Islam and it remains important today, at least in the parts of the Islamic world where it grows, which is mainly the Middle East and North Africa. In many places, the date palm is known as the tree of trees, also known as "the mother and aunt of Arabs," as their lives depended on it. Long before oil riches, dates were the main staple of Gulf Arabs, both in terms of diet and trade (the date palm sap is used to make palm sugar), as well as construction (its wood, although not very hard, is used in building), and they were also Gulf Arabs' main sustenance along with bread, meat, and milk. Dates were a commodity used to barter with neighboring tribes.

It is not easy to pinpoint the exact origins of the date palm. According to one myth, the tree was first planted in Medina by the descendants of Noah after the Flood. But if not in Medina, then in an equally hot place with plenty of water. As the Arabs say: "The date palm needs its feet in water and its head in the fire of the sky." It is therefore probable that the date palm first appeared in the oases of the Arabian desert. And that is still where most date palms are grown. Saudi Arabia is the second largest grower in the world after Iraq, and the Saudi's coat of arms is a date palm over crossed swords.

The date palm is also grown on the coasts of Africa, in Spain—in the east, a reminder of the time of Muslim rule—in western Asia, and in California. The soldiers of Alexander the Great are said to have introduced it to northern India by spitting the pits from their date ration around the camp, so that, over the course of time, palm groves grew there.

There are three main types of date: soft, hard, and semi-dry. The semi-dry is most popular in the West, commonly sold in long boxes with a plastic stem between the rows of fruit as they do in Tunisia. Soft dates are grown in the Middle East mainly to eat fresh, although they are also dried and compressed into blocks to be used in a range of sweets. As for hard dates, also called camel dates, they are dry and fibrous even when fresh. When dried, they become extremely hard and sweet and keep for years. They remain the staple food of Arab nomads.

The fruit goes through different stages of ripening, with each stage described by an Arabic term that is used universally in all languages. *Khalal* describes the date when it is full size and has taken on its characteristic color depending on the variety—red or orange for Deglet Noor, dull yellow for Halawi, greenish for Khadrawi, yellow for Zahidi, and rich brown for Medjool. *Rutab* is the stage at which the fruit softens considerably and becomes darker, and *tamr* is when it is fully dry and ready for packing.

The date still figures prominently in the diet of Gulf Arabs. It is the first food people eat when they break the long day's fast during the month of Ramadan, the tradition being to eat only three, to emulate the Prophet Muhammad who broke his fast with three dates. The date's high sugar content makes it an ideal breakfast after so many hours without any food or water, supplying the necessary rush of energy while being easy on the empty stomach. Some people eat it plain, others dip it in tahini, and others have it with yogurt or cheese, and particularly a homemade curd called *yiggit*.

The date also features prominently in the Gulf Arabs' regular diet, both in savory and sweet dishes; and date syrup is used to make a drink called *jellab*, which is sold on the street packed with crushed ice and garnished with pine nuts and golden raisins.

RAMADAN AND OTHER IMPORTANT OCCASIONS IN ISLAM

From the birth of a child to the circumcision of boys to marriage to burying the dead, every occasion in Islam is marked with special dishes that celebrate, commemorate, or comfort, as the case may be.

The month of Ramadan is the most important time of the year for Muslims, a time for fasting and feasting when Muslims throughout the world change their ways to show their devotion to God. No food or drink is allowed to pass their lips from sunrise to sundown, but as soon as the sun sets, people gather with family and friends to break their fast, whether at home or in restaurants and cafés, or simply on the street if they happen to be working and have nowhere to go to break the fast. The menu changes according to where you are. In the Arabian Gulf the fast is first broken with dates and water before moving on to the main meal, known in Arabic as *iftar*. Then people pray before sitting at the table to partake of their first meal of the day. In the Levant, people break their fast with apricot leather juice, fattoush (a mixed herb and bread salad), and/or lentil soup. In the Maghreb, soup is the first thing people eat after sunset, whereas in Indonesia they break their fast (called *buka puasa* there) with sweet snacks and drinks known as *takjil*. During Ramadan, Indonesian restaurants serve their whole menu at each table and charge diners only for the dishes they consume before taking away those that remain untouched to stack them again in the restaurant window.

Lailat al-Bara'a (the night of innocence), on 15 Sha'ban, is the night of the full moon preceding the beginning of Ramadan, when sins are forgiven and fates are determined for the year ahead and when mosques are illuminated and special sweets are distributed.

The two main feasts in Islam are Eid el-Fitr (the feast of breaking the fast), which celebrates the end of Ramadan, and Eid al-Adha (the feast of the sacrifice), which signals the end of Hajj (Muslim pilgrimage to Mecca) and is the most important festival in Islam. Eid al-Adha is also known as Baqri-Eid (the "Cow Festival") because its most important feature is the sacrifice of an animal in commemoration of the ram sacrificed by Abraham in place of his son. In Muhammad's time, a camel normally would have been sacrificed.

Ashura, which falls on the tenth day of the month of Muharram (which means "forbidden"), is a time of mourning for Shi'ite Muslims to commemorate the massacre of Muhammad's grandson Hussain and his band of followers at Karbala. A perfect place to witness the rituals associated with Ashura is Iran, which is predominantly Shi'ite, as well as South Lebanon, the stronghold of Shi'ite Hezbollah (the party of God).

Most Shi'ites follow the ancient Persian tradition of *nazr* (distributing free foods among the people) and cook *nazri* (charity food) during the month.

Turkey is one of the places to witness the holy nights called *kandili*: Mevlid Kandili (the birth of Prophet Muhammad), Regaip Kandili (the beginning of the pregnancy of Prophet Muhammad's mother), Miraç Kandili (Prophet Muhammad's ascension into heaven and into the presence of God), Berat Kandili (when the Qur'an was made available to the Muslims in its entirety), and Kadir Gecesi (the Qur'an's first appearance to Prophet Muhammad). The word *kandil* (from the Arabic *kindil*) means candle in Turkish, and some trace the application of this word to the five holy nights back in the reign of the Ottoman sultan Selim II (1566–1574) who gave orders to light up the minarets of the mosques for these occasions.

Saints' days are also widely observed in the Muslim world, but the two Eids and the holy nights are the great festivals, and they are the only ones universally observed by all Muslims without any question as to the worthiness of the occasion.

And there are of course the celebrations for important life occasions such as circumcision and marriage, with rich Gulf Arabs roasting whole baby camels for weddings while Moroccans prepare lavish feasts called *diffa* (hospitality) where pretty much the whole of the Moroccan repertoire is served, starting with b'stilla, a sweet-savory pigeon pie, and finishing with a seven-vegetable couscous to make sure no guest is left hungry. In between are the *mechoui* (whole roasted lamb), a selection of tagines (both savory and sweet-savory), and salads. Moroccan and Indian weddings last up to three days, although the latter can, in some cases, last up to a week, with biryani, a multilayered rice dish, taking pride of place at the wedding buffet, in particular on the night of the wedding.

I had planned to devote a separate chapter to celebratory dishes, but I feared this would be repetitive, not to mention confusing. Instead, I single out these dishes in the chapters they belong to, explaining in the headnote which special occasion they are associated with.

BREAD

PITA BREAD

KHOBZ

Pita bread is often described as pocket bread in the West because the dough puffs and separates into two layers as it bakes. It is the most common bread throughout the Levant and as far as Egypt, where it is made thicker and smaller and in two versions, one with white flour and the other with whole wheat. Also, the dough for Egyptian pita is a lot softer and the loaves are put to rest on a coarse flour called *radda* (probably wheat germ), which also prevents sticking. Egyptian pita is called *aysh*—which means "life," signaling the importance of bread in Egypt—and the whole wheat version is called *aysh baladi*, which means "local bread." The Lebanese, Syrian, and Jordanian pita is thinner and larger, and mostly made with white flour. These days, bakeries also make medium-size pita and tiny ones to be filled with a variety of savory fillings and served as canapés.

Making pita at home is fairly easy and definitely worth trying, even if the result will not be as perfect as that made professionally. Homemade pita is closer to Egyptian pita than Lebanese/Syrian/Jordanian because it comes out thicker. If you decide to make the pita with whole wheat, be sure to increase the hydration of the dough by using 2 cups (500 ml) water instead of the amount indicated below; and once you have mixed the dough, let it rest for 30 minutes instead of 15 minutes before kneading again.

MAKES 10 INDIVIDUAL LOAVES

Just over 4 cups (500 g) unbleached all-purpose flour, plus more for kneading and shaping

1 heaping teaspoon instant (fast-acting) yeast

2 teaspoons fine sea salt

¼ cup (60 ml) extra-virgin olive oil

1. Mix the flour, yeast, and salt in a large bowl and make a well in the center. Add the oil to the well and, with the tips of your fingers, rub the oil into the flour. Gradually add 1⅓ cups (325 ml) warm water, bringing in the flour as you go along. Knead until you have a rough, rather sticky ball of dough.

2. Transfer the dough to a lightly floured work surface. Sprinkle a little flour on the dough and knead for 3 minutes. Roll the dough into a ball, invert the bowl over the dough, and let rest for 15 minutes. Knead for 3 more minutes, or until the dough is smooth and elastic and rather soft. Shape the dough into a ball and place in an oiled bowl, turning it to coat all over with oil. Cover with plastic wrap and let rise in a warm, draft-free place for 1 hour, until nearly doubled in size.

3. Transfer the dough to your work surface. Divide into 10 equal portions, each weighing just under 3 ounces (80 g). Roll each portion of dough into a ball. Cover with a very damp kitchen towel and let rest for 45 minutes.

4. Roll each ball of dough into rounds 6 to 7 inches (15 to 17.5 cm) in diameter, flouring your work surface and the dough every now and then to prevent the dough from sticking. Make the rounds as even as possible. This will help the breads puff out evenly

in the oven. A good way to achieve a perfect round is to give the disk a quarter turn between each rolling out. Cover the rounds of dough with a floured couche (baker's linen), or use clean kitchen towels sprinkled with flour. Let rest for 15 to 20 minutes.

5. Preheat the oven to 500°F (260°C), or to its highest setting. For a perfect result, set your baking sheet in the oven to heat up.

6. Use a floured peel to slide the breads onto the baking sheet (or simply lay the rounds of dough on the sheet) and bake for 6 to 8 minutes, or until well puffed and very lightly golden. The baking time will vary depending on how hot your oven is. I suggest you start checking the breads after 5 minutes. You will probably have to bake them in separate batches unless you have a very large oven.

7. Homemade pita is best served immediately or while still warm. Alternatively, you can let it cool on a wire rack and freeze it for later use. When you are ready to serve the bread, simply thaw it in the bag and reheat.

SAJ BREAD
MARKOUK OR YUFKA

You can make *yufka* and *markouk* with the same dough, but with different shaping techniques. *Markouk* is thinner and flattened by passing the disk of dough from one hand to the other until the round of dough is paper thin and almost as wide as your arm, a feat that requires tremendous skill and much practice. *Yufka*, on the other hand, is flattened with a long thin rolling pin called *oklava*. Both are baked on a large round metal plate called a *saj*, which is flat in Turkey and concave in Lebanon, Syria, Jordan, and Palestine. In the old days (and still today in remote rural areas), the *saj* was heated over a wood fire. In Lebanon and Syria, *saj* bread is known as *markouk*, while in Jordan and Palestine, where it is made a little thicker, it is known as *shraaq*. In Turkey, the bread is known as *yufka* unless it is filled and folded in half, in which case it becomes *saj borek*. When used to make *boreks*, *yufka* is made thinner to be stuffed with a variety of fillings ranging from spinach to cheese to meat. I cannot roll out my *yufka* or *saj* bread as thinly as they do in Turkey or in Lebanon, either using an *oklava* or passing it from one hand to the other as they do in the Lebanese mountains. Still, it comes out thin enough and making it at home gives me great satisfaction.

MAKES 10 SMALL SAJ OR YUFKA BREADS

2 cups (240 g)
  unbleached all-purpose
  flour, plus more
  for kneading and
  rolling out
1 teaspoon fine sea salt

1. Mix the flour and salt in a large bowl. Add ¾ cup plus 1 tablespoon (200 ml) water. Mix until you have a rough ball of dough.

2. Transfer the ball of dough to a lightly floured work surface and knead for 3 minutes. Shape into a ball and invert the bowl over the dough and let rest for 15 minutes. Then knead for 3 more minutes until you have a smooth firm dough.

3. Divide the dough into 10 portions, each weighing about 1½ ounces (40 g). Shape each into a small ball, rolling the dough in between the palms of your hands. Then roll the ball of dough against your work surface—which should not be floured—keeping the side with the seam against the work surface to seal it. Sprinkle a tray or part of your work surface with flour and place the balls of dough on the floured surface. Cover with a damp kitchen towel. Let rest for 30 minutes.

4. Roll out each ball of dough—here it is a good idea to use a thin rolling pin like the Turkish *oklava*—sprinkling with flour every now and then, until you have a round 7 to 8 inches (17.5 to 20 cm) in diameter. Place the rounds of dough in between floured couches (baker's linen)—or simply use floured kitchen towels.

5. Heat a large nonstick pan over medium heat and until very hot. Add the dough rounds, one at a time, and cook for a minute or so on each side. They should be lightly

golden with small burned spots where they have bubbled up. Stack in between clean kitchen towels. You can serve these immediately or use them to make wraps. Or you can do what the Turks do and stack them in a dry place where they will keep for weeks.

6. When you are ready to serve, sprinkle each bread with a little water to soften, fold it in half, and wrap in a clean kitchen towel. Let rest for 30 minutes so that it becomes soft and pliable and ready to serve.

TANNUR: *Tannur* is a flatbread that is eaten throughout rural Syria, thicker than either *saj* or *yufka* and named for the oven in which it is baked. *Tannur* ovens are found in Iran, India, and Pakistan, as well as Central Asia. To make *tannur*, divide the dough into 6 equal portions and flatten the bread a little thicker. Bake in the same way.

MAKES 6 TANNUR BREADS

SOMALI PANCAKES
ANJERO

Anjero is similar to Ethiopian injera although a little thicker, and it is used in lieu of cutlery to scoop up food. Unless, that is, it is eaten for breakfast, in which case it is spread with butter and sprinkled with sugar or drizzled with honey. Another way to have *anjero* at breakfast is to tear it in pieces and pile them in a bowl, sprinkle with sugar, drizzle with olive oil, and drench the whole lot with tea. I can't imagine ever wanting to have *anjero* this way, either for breakfast or any other time for that matter, but it is lovely with stews or simply spread with butter and honey. This kind of fluffy bread is closer to a pancake and it is found with slight variations all over the Muslim world. The Yemeni variation is known as *lahoh*. It is very close to *anjero* while the Zanzibari version, known as *chila*, can be made with ground rice. Moroccan *beghrir* is another take on *anjero,* while Lebanese/Syrian *qatayef* are similar but are used as in sweets, filled with either clotted cream or walnuts or eaten plain or fried, drenched in sugar syrup.

MAKES 8 MEDIUM PANCAKES

FOR THE SOURDOUGH
½ cup (70 g) white corn flour
¼ cup (35 g) sorghum flour
1½ teaspoons superfine sugar
1½ teaspoons instant (fast-acting) yeast

FOR THE PANCAKES
2 cups (240 g) self-rising flour
¼ teaspoon salt
2 tablespoons superfine sugar

1. To make the sourdough: Mix the corn flour, sorghum flour, sugar, and yeast in a bowl, then add ½ cup (125 ml) water. Mix well and let ferment for at least 2 hours. Some people let the sourdough ferment for 2 days.

2. To make the pancakes: Mix the self-rising flour, salt, and sugar in a large bowl, then add the sourdough. Add 1 cup (250 ml) water to the mixture and mix well. Add another ¾ cup (180 ml) water and once the water is absorbed by the dough, start slapping the dough, raising it with your hand, at least a dozen times—you can also do this with a whisk. This will aerate the dough and will help it become smooth. Then add another ½ cup (125 ml) to ¾ cup (180 ml) water to have a pancake batter. Mix until the batter is smooth. Cover and let ferment for at least 2 hours or even overnight.

3. Heat a nonstick skillet over medium heat. Once the pan is hot, pour a ladleful of batter into the middle of the pan and spread the batter with the back of the ladle from the center in a circular motion. You should aim for a round that is about the size of a dinner plate with a circular swirl inside it where the batter should be thinner. Cook until the surface is full of tiny holes and the bottom is golden.

4. Remove from the pan and place on a plate lined with parchment paper. Keep cooking the remaining *anjero* in the same way until you have made eight pancakes. Serve with a stew or for breakfast.

IRANIAN FLATBREAD
BARBARI

Barbari is probably the most common bread in Iran. It is the bread that most people eat for break-fast and it can be baked in a *tannur* oven, although most *barbari* bakeries I have seen in Iran bake the bread on a very interesting rotating hot plate, which as it rotates moves the bread into the oven under the oven doors (set high enough so as not to scrape the loaves). The baker starts by shaping the loaves on a large table in front of the oven doors, making deep indentations in thin lines down the long *barbari* loaves. He then lifts and lays these on the rotating plate, which car-ries them into the oven, where they bake quickly, and then out again the other side of the doors, crisp and golden. In the morning *barbari* bread is served with eggs scrambled with tomatoes, feta cheese, and butter while at other meals it is served with a platter of herbs, cheese, and walnuts before the rest of the meal.

MAKES 2 MEDIUM LOAVES

3⅓ cups (400 g) unbleached all-purpose flour, plus more for kneading and shaping
½ teaspoon instant (fast-acting) yeast
2 teaspoons fine sea salt

1. Mix the flour, yeast, and salt in a large bowl and make a well in the center. Gradually add 1 cup (250 ml) water, bringing in the flour as you go along. Knead until you have a rough dough.

2. Transfer the dough to a lightly floured surface and knead for 3 minutes. Shape the dough into a ball, invert the bowl over it, and let rest for 15 minutes. Knead for 3 more minutes. Shape the dough into a ball and place in a lightly floured bowl. Cover with plastic wrap and let rise in a warm, draft-free place for 1 hour, or until doubled in size.

3. Divide the dough in half and shape each half into a ball. Place on a lightly floured work surface. Cover with a damp kitchen towel and let rest for 20 minutes.

4. Flatten the dough into a long oval loaf about ½ inch (1 cm) thick and using the tips of your fingers, make deep indentations about ½ inch (1 cm) from the edge and the top down the long side and stop about the same distance from the bottom. Make a few more lines of deep indentations at equal intervals. Do the same to the other loaf, then gently pick up one end of one loaf with your fingers, while still holding on to the other end, and stretch the loaf to elongate the bread. Repeat at the other end, being mindful not to tear the dough.

5. Let rest while you preheat the oven to 475°F (250°C).

6. Bake for 10 to 12 minutes, or until golden brown all over. The top should be darker than the bottom. Remove to a wire rack to cool. Serve at room temperature or reheat to serve hot.

TURKISH FLATBREAD

PIDE

Pide is a thicker, softer version of *barbari* bread (Iranian Flatbread, page 9). Like *barbari*, it is long and oval, but smaller; and whereas *barbari* is crisp and holey inside, pide is soft and spongy with an even crumb. Pide dough is also used with a variety of toppings to make long, boat-shaped filled breads, also called pide but with the name of the topping preceding pide to differentiate them from the plain bread such as *patlicanli pide* (with an eggplant topping; see page 58) or *etli pide* (with a ground meat filling; see page 58).

SERVES 4

3¾ cups (450 g) unbleached all-purpose flour, plus more for kneading and shaping

1 packet (7g/ 2¼ teaspoons) instant (fast-acting) yeast

2 teaspoons baker's sugar or superfine sugar

2 teaspoons fine sea salt

2 tablespoons extra-virgin oil, plus more for greasing the bowl and baking sheet

Egg wash: 1 egg whisked with ½ teaspoon water

2 tablespoons sesame seeds

1. Mix the flour, yeast, sugar, and salt in a large bowl and make a well in the center. Add the oil and with the tips of your fingers rub the oil into the flour. Gradually add 1 cup (250 ml) warm water, bringing in the flour as you go along. Knead until you have a rough ball of dough.

2. Transfer the dough to a lightly floured work surface and knead for 3 minutes. Shape the dough into a ball, invert the bowl over it, and let rest for 15 minutes. Knead for 3 more minutes, or until the dough is smooth and elastic. Shape the dough into a ball and place in a large oiled bowl, turning it to coat all over with oil. Cover with plastic wrap and let rise in a warm, draft-free place for 1 hour, or until doubled in size.

3. Transfer the dough to a work surface. Shape into a ball. Place on a nonstick baking sheet (or a baking sheet lined with parchment paper or a silicone baking mat). Cover with a very damp kitchen towel. Let rest for 15 minutes.

4. With your hands, flatten the dough into a long oval loaf about ½ inch (1 cm) thick. Cover with the damp towel and let rise for 45 minutes.

5. About 20 minutes before the dough is ready, preheat the oven to 425°F (220°C).

6. Uncover the dough 5 to 10 minutes before baking to let the surface dry. With the tips of your fingers, make deep dimples all over the top. Brush with the egg wash and sprinkle with the sesame seeds. Bake for 30 minutes, or until golden all over. Let cool on a wire rack before serving at room temperature or reheat to serve warm.

MOROCCAN BREAD

K'SRA

MOROCCO

Morocco is one of those rare countries where bakeries are not so much a place where professional bakers bake and sell bread, but rather a resource for the neighborhood: Dough is prepared and proofed at home and the risen loaves taken to the local bakery to bake. Each neighborhood has at least one bakery. The lady of the house will not be the one to take the bread to the bakery, however. She will be too busy cooking the meal at home. Instead it will be one of her offspring or one of the grandparents who will carry out the bread and bring it back home once baked. That moment of the day, just before lunch, when a procession of boys, girls, and old men and women files through the narrow lanes of the medina, each carrying a tray either in their arms or on their head where they have the family's loaves ready to be taken to the bakery, is quite magical. And if you venture inside a bakery, you will inevitably find the baker feeding the loaves into the hot oven, being careful not to mix them up from one tray to another. He usually knows which loaves belong to whom by the order he places them in the oven, or by the mark the home baker will have made on the loaf, or simply by the cloth they have used to cover the dough. The trays with the baked breads are lined up on shelves by the entrance of the bakery to be taken away by those who brought them in. During Ramadan, the bakeries will start baking later in the day shortly before *iftar* (the breaking of the fast). During Eid (the Muslim feast, one at the end of Ramadan and the other a month or so later), they will work double time as everyone will be feasting and receiving family and friends.

In the countryside, people bake their own bread, usually in a large round shallow earthenware bowl called a *g'saa* placed over an open fire. The dough can be mixed with anise and sesame seeds (see Variation, below) for special occasions or even just for breakfast, and, depending on the region, that same bread can be made with barley or whole wheat flour. The usual flour used here is semolina.

MAKES 1 LOAF

2¾ cups (450 g) fine semolina (also known as semolina flour), plus all-purpose flour for kneading and shaping
1 packet (7g/ 2¼ teaspoons) instant (fast-acting) yeast
1 teaspoon fine sea salt

1. Mix the semolina, yeast, and salt in a large bowl and make a well in the center. Gradually add 1¼ cups (310 ml) warm water, bringing in the flour as you go along. Knead until you have a rough ball of dough.

2. Transfer the dough to a lightly floured work surface and knead for 3 minutes. Shape the dough into a ball, invert the bowl over it, and let rest for 15 minutes. Knead for 3 more minutes, or until the dough is smooth and elastic. Shape into a ball. Cover with a damp kitchen towel and let rest for 30 minutes.

Recipe continues

3. Line a baking sheet with parchment paper or a silicone baking mat (or use a nonstick pan). Flatten the dough into a disk ¾ inch (2 cm) thick and place on the baking sheet. Cover with a floured kitchen towel and let rise in a warm, draft-free place for about 1 hour, or until well risen.

4. About 20 minutes before the dough is ready, preheat the oven to 400°F (200°C).

5. Carefully brush any excess flour off the dough and bake for 30 to 40 minutes, or until golden all over. Let cool on a wire rack and serve at room temperature (if you want to serve the bread hot, reheat it). It is always a good idea to let breads cool completely before serving them as they continue to develop as they cool outside the oven. The only breads to which this does not apply are the totally flat breads.

VARIATION: For an anise/sesame seed version, add ½ tablespoon anise seeds and 1 tablespoon sesame seeds when you mix together the semolina, yeast, and salt.

NORTH AFRICAN MULTILAYERED BREADS

M'HAJJIB

MOROCCO | ALGERIA | TUNISIA

M'hajjib are typical North African street food that are made either plain or filled with a variety of stuffings. The name changes from country to country. In Algeria, they are called *m'arekk* or *m'hajjib*, in Morocco they are known as *r'ghayef*, and in Tunisia as *m'lawi*. The plain version of Tunisian *m'lawi* is used to make wraps, whereas *r'ghayef*, also known as *m'semmen*, are eaten as a snack or a quick meal on the go.

MAKES 8 INDIVIDUAL MULTILAYERED BREADS

1 cup (120 g) unbleached all-purpose flour, plus more for kneading
1 cup (165 g) semolina flour
½ teaspoon instant (fast-acting) yeast
1 teaspoon fine sea salt
Vegetable oil, for shaping the dough and greasing the pan

1. Mix the flours, yeast, and salt in a large bowl and make a well in the center. Add a generous ¾ cup (190 ml) warm water to the well and gradually mix with the flours until you have a rough, sticky dough.

2. Transfer the dough to a lightly floured work surface. Sprinkle the dough with a little flour and knead for 3 minutes. Shape into a ball and invert the bowl over the dough and let rest for 15 minutes. Knead for 3 more minutes, or until the dough is smooth and elastic. Cover with a damp kitchen towel and let rest for 30 minutes.

3. Divide the dough into 8 equal portions, each weighing about 2 ounces (60 g). Roll each piece into a ball. Smear your work surface and hands with oil. Place a ball of dough

Recipe continues

on the oiled surface and flatten it into a very thin round with your fingers, greasing your hands and work surface with more oil if necessary. Fold in one-third of the round, then fold the other third over to make a long rectangle. Fold one-third of the long end of the rectangle of dough, then fold over the other third to make a 5-inch (12.5 cm) square. Let rest while you make 3 more squares of dough.

4. Flatten the squares of dough with your fingers as thinly as you can without tearing them.

5. Grease a large nonstick skillet with a little oil and place over medium-high heat. Place 1 square in the hot pan (or 2 if they fit). Dip your fingers in a little oil and drizzle over the bread. Cook for 1½ to 2 minutes, or until the bottom is lightly golden. Turn over, drizzle with a little more oil, and cook for another 1½ to 2 minutes. Remove to parchment paper or a wire rack. Cook the remaining 3 breads in the same way. Then form and cook the remaining 4 breads in the same manner, making sure to oil your hands, work surface, and pan in between each bread. Serve warm.

REGAG

QATAR | UNITED ARAB EMIRATES | BAHRAIN

Regag is a very thin crisp bread from the Arabian Gulf that is made by rolling a ball of very loose dough over a hot plate to leave a thin film that is scraped off as soon as it becomes crisp and golden. Some of the older ladies who make it seem oblivious to the intense heat of the plate so close to their hand and are very adept at rolling the dough, but younger ones use a flat plastic panel (or sometimes a DVD case) to roll the dough over the hot plate. The bread can be spread with cheese and/or egg or with *mehyawa* (Iranian/Arabian Fish Sauce, page 331) as it bakes and then eaten as a snack, or it can be baked plain and used in Tharid (page 85), the Prophet's favorite dish. *Regag* is delicious but rather difficult to make, not unlike *warqa* (see page 516) or *brik*, both of which use the same principle of leaving a thin film of dough on a hot plate. The difference is that *regag* is crisp and eaten on its own or broken up and used as a bed for a stew, while *warqa* is soft and pliable and used to make a variety of savory filled pastries.

ARABIAN PANCAKES

KHOBZ AL-JBAB

A few years ago, I filmed a TV series in the United Arab Emirates called *Al Chef Yaktachef* (meaning "the chef discovers") where I was taken around the Emirates by a delightful poet named Tarek Al-Mehyass to learn about local delicacies, after which I would try to re-create them in the show's open-air kitchen. I am still in touch with many of those I met or worked with on the series, including Tarek and a wonderful woman caterer, Mariam Al-Subousi, also known as Umm Saeed, in whose kitchen I learned how to prepare many Emirati dishes including the pancakes below. *Jbab* are served for breakfast or as a sweet finish to a meal, drizzled with date syrup. And it was in Mariam's kitchen that I finally got to have my first taste of camel hump (see "Roasting a Camel Hump," page 100).

MAKES EIGHT 6-INCH (15 CM) PANCAKES

1⅔ cups (200 g) unbleached all-purpose flour

¾ tablespoon whole milk powder

¼ teaspoon instant (fast-acting) yeast

¼ teaspoon baking powder

Pinch of salt

1 organic egg

¼ cup (50 g) raw cane sugar

Pinch of saffron threads

Unsalted butter, melted, for the skillet

½ cup (65 g) sesame seeds

Date syrup or maple syrup, for serving

1. Mix the flour, milk powder, yeast, baking powder, and salt in a bowl and make a well in the center.

2. Whisk together the egg, sugar, saffron, and 1¼ cups (310 ml) warm water in a bowl until the sugar is dissolved.

3. Add the sweet egg mixture to the flour mixture and gradually whisk it in until you have a batter that is thicker than crepe batter but thinner than pancake batter. Cover with plastic wrap and let sit for about 45 minutes to let the batter ferment.

4. Brush a large nonstick skillet with a little melted butter and place over medium heat. When the pan is hot, scoop out a ladleful of the batter and pour into the pan, tilting the pan to spread the batter evenly. Sprinkle with some sesame seeds and cook for 2 minutes, or until the bottom is golden. Flip the *jbab* and cook the other side for 2 minutes, or until it is the same color. You may want to slip a knob of butter underneath the *jbab* after you flip it. Sprinkle the top with some more sesame seeds.

5. Cook the remaining *jbab* the same way, and serve hot or warm drizzled with date or maple syrup.

YEMENI BREAD

BINT EL-SAHN

This slightly sweet bread when made as one large loaf is known as *bint el-sahn*, which in Arabic means "the daughter of the plate." If made into individual squares, it's known as *m'lawwah* (see variation). The recipe here is for the large version and the bread is baked in a round dish. Cut into wedges and serve with hard-boiled eggs and *z'houg* (Yemeni Cilantro Chutney, page 369) for a savory snack, or with honey or jam for a sweet snack or breakfast. SERVES 8

3 cups (360 g) unbleached all-purpose flour, plus more for kneading and rolling out

½ teaspoon instant (fast-acting) yeast

¾ teaspoon fine sea salt

2 organic eggs

6 tablespoons (90 g) unsalted butter, melted, plus more for the pan

Egg wash: 1 egg yolk whisked with 1 teaspoon water

1 tablespoon nigella seeds

1. Mix the flour, yeast, and salt in a bowl and make a well in the center. Add the eggs and 2 tablespoons (30 g) of the melted butter to the well and with your fingers mix them before gradually adding ¼ cup (60 ml) water and bringing in the flour to mix with the liquid until you have a rough dough.

2. Transfer the dough to a lightly floured work surface and knead for 3 minutes. Shape into a ball, invert the bowl over the dough, and let rest for 15 minutes. Knead for 3 more minutes, or until the dough is smooth and elastic. Divide into 8 equal portions and roll each into a ball. Line the balls up on a floured sheet or a floured work surface. Cover with a damp kitchen towel and let rest for 30 minutes.

3. Preheat the oven to 400°F (200°C). Brush a nonstick round baking dish about 13 inches (33 cm) in diameter with a little melted butter. Keep the remaining 4 tablespoons (60 g) melted butter at hand for when you start rolling out the dough.

4. Place one ball of dough on a lightly floured work surface. Sprinkle with a little flour and roll out as thinly as you can into a round about 11 inches (28 cm) in diameter, turning the round of dough over, lightly sprinkling it with flour if it is sticking. Lay the round of dough smoothly onto the buttered baking dish and gently brush the dough with a little melted butter. Roll out the remaining balls of dough, stacking the rounds of dough and brushing each with melted butter except for the top one. Brush the top round of dough with the egg wash and sprinkle with the nigella seeds.

5. Bake for 20 to 25 minutes, or until slightly risen and golden brown on top.

M'LAWWAH: To make individual breads, roll out a ball of dough into a large circle about ¼ inch (0.5 cm) thick, brush it with melted butter, then fold into a long rectangle before folding into a square to make 9 layers. Flatten the square with your hand, brush both sides of the dough with melted butter, and cook in a hot skillet over medium heat, 2 to 3 minutes on each side, until golden all over.

ARABIAN DATE BREAD

KEIKAT AL-TAMR

A rather luxurious sweet bread flavored with saffron, cardamom, and rose water and sweetened with dates. It provides a subtle, sweet note when eaten with savory food, but it is also lovely on its own, spread with good butter or labneh.

MAKES 10 ROUND BREADS ABOUT 6 INCHES (15 CM) IN DIAMETER

1 cup (150 g) pitted dates

1¼ cups (310 ml) boiling water

2 tablespoons rose water

Good pinch of saffron threads

5 cups (600 g) unbleached all-purpose flour, plus more for kneading

1½ teaspoons instant (fast-acting) yeast

¼ cup (50 g) raw cane sugar plus 1 tablespoon

2 teaspoons ground cardamom

1 organic egg, beaten

⅓ cup (80 ml) date syrup

2 tablespoons (30 g) unsalted butter, melted, plus more for the bowl

Vegetable oil, for the work surface and rolling pin

FOR THE TOPPING

2 tablespoons vegetable oil

¼ cup (50 g) raw cane sugar

¼ cup (30 g) sesame seeds

1½ tablespoons coarsely ground cardamom

1. Soak the pitted dates in the boiling water. Put the rose water in a small bowl and add the saffron threads. Let steep for 15 minutes.

2. Whizz the dates with their soaking water in a blender.

3. Mix the flour, yeast, ¼ cup sugar, and cardamom in a large bowl and make a well in the center. Add the date puree, saffron rose water, egg, date syrup, and melted butter. Mix the ingredients in the well as much as you can before bringing in the flour to make a rough ball of dough.

4. Transfer the dough to a lightly floured surface and knead for 3 minutes. Shape the dough into a ball, invert the bowl over the dough, and let rest for 15 minutes. Knead for 3 more minutes, or until the dough is smooth and elastic.

5. Scrape the bowl clean and brush it with a little melted butter. Place the ball of dough into the bowl, turning it over to coat all over with the butter. Cover with plastic wrap and let rise in a warm, draft-free place for 1 hour 30 minutes, or until doubled in size.

6. Preheat the oven to 425°F (220°C).

7. Remove the risen dough to your work surface and divide into 10 portions. Roll each into a ball. Line up on a lightly floured work surface and cover with a damp kitchen towel.

8. Grease your work surface and rolling pin with a little oil. Dissolve the 1 tablespoon sugar in ¼ cup (60 ml) water and keep it at hand.

9. Take a ball of dough and roll it into a round about 6 inches (15 cm) in diameter and ¼ inch (0.5 cm) thick. Dip your hand in the sugar water and smooth the flattened dough with your wet hand, pressing in the center to make a dip and push the gas bubbles to the edges.

10. Transfer the round of dough to a nonstick baking sheet. Brush the dough with vegetable oil, and sprinkle with a little sugar, sesame seeds, and cardamom. Shape and top the remaining balls of dough in the same way.

11. Bake for 12 minutes, or until golden and puffed up. Serve hot or warm.

PARATHA

The classic technique for forming paratha (see "Multilayered Breads," page 23) results in the most layers, but it is not so easy to master, so I use a much simpler method of folding the dough into squares, although it produces fewer layers. If you'd prefer to make your parathas round (see photographs below), flatten the dough the same way as directed in the recipe, but roll the round a little thinner. Fold the round into thin strips or roll it into a thin cylinder, taking care to brush the dough with the fat of your choice in between each step. (If you use tahini as the fat of choice, you will be making the Turkish *tahinli katmer* but with whole wheat flour.) Coil the folded strip into a small disk. Let it rest for 10 minutes, then flatten it out and cook the same way as for the square paratha.

Paratha are either baked in a *tannur* oven or cooked on a large hot plate or in a tawa, a very shallow skillet used in India and Pakistan. If you don't have a tawa, just use a regular skillet. I use a nonstick one. Serve the parathas hot with curry or cheese or instead of bread with your meal.

MAKES 8 INDIVIDUAL PARATHAS

2 cups (225 g) whole wheat flour, plus all-purpose flour for kneading and shaping
¼ teaspoon fine sea salt
2 teaspoons vegetable oil

FAT (CHOOSE ONE)
Unsalted butter, melted
Vegetable oil
Ghee

1. Mix the flour and salt in a bowl and make a well in the center. Add the oil and ¾ cup (180 ml) water to the well and gradually bring in the flour until you have a rough dough.

2. Transfer the dough to a lightly floured work surface and knead for 3 minutes. Shape into a ball, invert the bowl over the dough, and let rest for 15 minutes. Knead for 3 more minutes, or until the dough is smooth and elastic. Shape into a ball. Cover with a damp kitchen towel and let rest for 30 minutes.

Recipe continues

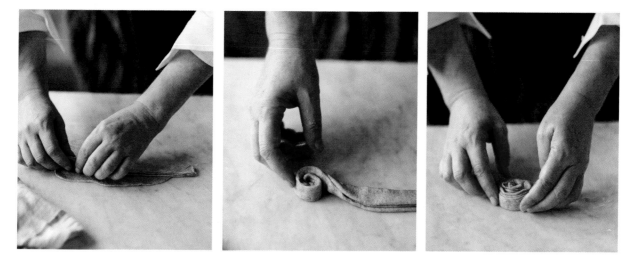

3. Divide the dough into 8 equal portions. Roll each portion into a ball and set the balls of dough to the side on a floured surface, covered with a damp towel. Place one ball on a lightly floured work surface and roll out to a round about ⅛ inch (3 mm) thick. Brush the round with the fat of your choice—the last ones I had in Pakistan were brushed with buffalo ghee and they were amazing—then fold one-third of the round over, then the other third over the folded side. Brush again with fat and fold one-third of the rectangle over, then fold in the other third to make a square (see page 15). Flatten the dough to make a 6-inch (15 cm) square. Continue to make 3 more parathas.

4. Place a tawa or large skillet over medium heat and when the pan is hot, slip a paratha into the pan. Slip a little fat of choice under the paratha and cook until the dough starts bubbling, about 3 minutes. Flip the paratha over and cook until golden all over, another 3 minutes, slipping a little more of the fat of choice underneath it. Remove to a plate. Repeat with the remaining 3 parathas. Keep this first batch warm while you layer and cook the remaining 4 parathas.

SHEERMAL: Turn your paratha into sheermal, a northern Indian bread colored red with saffron water (although nowadays most bakers use turmeric water or, worse, colored water). Sheermal is usually round and I first had it at a nihari place in Hyderabad where, like most street-food stalls in India and Pakistan, they had a baker making breads to order. I got started talking with my neighbor and ordered sheermal so that I could try it. It was amazing, mainly because the bright-red color of the crust made a stunning contrast with the white insides. To turn paratha into sheermal, soak a couple of good pinches of saffron in ½ cup (125 ml) water for about 30 minutes. Shape the dough as directed and once it's in the pan, brush the top with the saffron water to color it a reddish yellow.

MULTILAYERED BREADS

The specific technique used to produce a multilayered bread varies according to the type of bread and the country in which it's made, but the principle is the same for all: You first have to flatten the dough, grease and/or flour it, and use one of several rolling or folding methods to create layers. In one method, the dough is rolled into a cylinder and then the cylinder is twisted as you flatten the dough again to create the layers. In another method, after flattening the dough you fold it into a rectangle and then into a square, or sometimes into a square or a triangle. There are also variations on the cylinder method, but the one I find most fascinating is that used in India to make paratha: The dough is rolled into a round, folded in half, and then rolled into a cone shape with the tip end folded inside the cone. The cone is then stood up on its fat end and twisted down before being flattened to produce the multilayered paratha, and all the time it is greased so that the layers separate as the paratha bakes.

NAAN

INDIA | PAKISTAN

From the Persian word for bread, naan is found throughout South Asia, and further afield in Central Asian countries. Naan is baked in a *tannur* oven, but because I doubt many home cooks have access to that, I suggest baking it on a pizza stone or preheated baking sheet in the oven or in a pan on top of the stove, then sliding it under a hot broiler to get the charred effect on the bubbling bits of the bread that you would get in a *tannur*. The most interesting and most delicious naan I have ever had was from a baker in Hyderabad, India, who made his naans square. They were thicker than normal, and flakier, perhaps because he made his dough with both milk and yogurt. I give his version of the dough in the recipe for *keema naan* (page 69) but am keeping it simple for the plain naan below. I suggest a round bread here, but you can easily make yours square by dividing the dough in half, then flattening each piece into a long rectangle, which you then cut into three medium-size squares before baking. Serve hot with the curry or kebabs of your choice.

MAKES 6 INDIVIDUAL NAANS

3½ cups (420 g) unbleached all-purpose flour

1½ teaspoons fine sea salt

1 packet (7g/ 2¼ teaspoons) instant (fast-acting) yeast

Scant ½ cup (120 ml) organic whole milk, at room temperature

Vegetable oil, for the bowl

2 to 4 tablespoons (30 g to 60 g) unsalted butter or ghee, melted

1. Mix the flour, salt, and yeast in a bowl and make a well in the center. Add the milk along with ¾ cup (180 ml) water and gradually bring in the flour to create a rough dough.

2. Transfer the dough to a lightly floured work surface and knead for 3 minutes. Shape the dough into a ball, invert the bowl over it, and let sit for 15 minutes. Knead for 3 more minutes, or until the dough is smooth and elastic. Shape the dough into a ball and place in an oiled bowl. Cover with plastic wrap and let rest for 1 hour, or until well risen.

3. Divide the dough into 6 equal portions and shape each portion into a ball. Brush the balls of dough with the melted butter and let rest for 20 minutes while you preheat the oven.

4. Preheat the oven to 475°F (250°C). If you have a pizza stone, place it on the bottom rack of the oven to preheat. Failing that, preheat a sturdy baking sheet. It is best to bake the naans directly on a hot surface.

5. Flatten one ball of dough into a round 6 to 7 inches (15 to 17.5 cm) in diameter, or you can flatten and stretch it in length to make an oblong naan, 8 to 9 inches (20 to 22.5 cm) long and 4 inches (10 cm) wide at its widest. Quickly transfer to the hot pizza stone or baking sheet and bake for 4 to 5 minutes, until it has bubbled up in parts and has gone golden brown where it has puffed up. Take out of the oven and brush with butter or ghee. Repeat with the other balls of dough until you have made all 6 naans.

STOVETOP NAAN: You can also "bake" the naan in a tawa or a broilerproof skillet. Heat the tawa or pan over medium heat and heat your broiler to the maximum. Transfer the flattened dough to the tawa or pan. Cook on one side for 2 to 3 minutes, or until the naan has puffed up in parts and is golden on the bottom. Slide the pan under the broiler for a minute or so to color the top. Transfer to a rack and brush with butter or ghee. Repeat for all the dough.

ZANZIBARI SAVORY DOUGHNUT

MANDAZI

ZANZIBAR

Mandazi is a delicious sweet-savory doughnut with a heady flavor of cardamom. It reminds me of Tunisian *fricassee* (a fried bread used to make sandwiches). *Mandazi* is eaten on its own for breakfast or as a street snack. The classic shape is a triangle, but you can make *mandazi* square or even round. If you opt for the round shape, use a pastry cutter, otherwise a sharp knife or dough scraper is all you need to shape the triangles or squares. I have had them in Zanzibar, both very fluffy with a strong cardamom flavor and rather dense with hardly any flavor at all. The quality depends on the vendor's skill at spicing and at making the dough with just the right amount of hydration for the texture of the doughnuts to be light.

MAKES 12 MANDAZI

2 cups (240 g)
  unbleached all-purpose
  flour, plus more for
  shaping
½ teaspoon fine sea salt
1 packet (7g/
  2¼ teaspoons) instant
  (fast-acting) yeast
5 tablespoons (65 g) raw
  cane sugar
Seeds from a few green
  cardamom pods,
  cracked open, the seeds
  extracted and ground
  to yield 1 teaspoon
¾ cup (190 ml) coconut
  cream
Olive oil, for deep-frying

1. Put the flour, salt, yeast, sugar, and cardamom in a bowl and mix well. Make a well in the center and add the coconut cream. Gradually bring in the flour until you have a rough dough.

2. Transfer the dough to a lightly floured work surface and knead for 3 minutes. Shape into a ball, invert the bowl over the dough, and let rest for 15 minutes. Knead the dough for 3 more minutes. Divide into 3 equal portions and shape each portion into a ball. Cover with a damp kitchen towel and let sit for 30 minutes.

3. Sprinkle your work surface with a little flour and place one ball of dough on it. Roll out the dough to a circle about ¼ inch (0.5 cm) thick and cut with a sharp knife into 4 quarters. To shape these into squares instead, roll out the dough into a rectangle. Place on a lightly floured board and cover with a damp towel. Roll out and cut the other 2 balls of dough and let rise for about 1 hour, or until doubled in size.

4. About 10 minutes before the dough is ready, pour 2 inches (5 cm) olive oil into a large deep skillet. Heat the oil over medium heat to 350°F (180°C). If you don't have a thermometer, drop a piece of bread in the oil—if the oil immediately bubbles around it, it is ready for frying. Place a wire rack over a rimmed baking sheet and have it at the ready.

5. Working in batches, slip in as many triangles (or squares) of dough into the oil as can fit comfortably in the pan and spoon a little hot oil over the surface of each—this will help the dough puff up. When the dough has puffed but not colored, turn it over and fry on one side until golden brown. Turn again and fry until golden brown on the other side. Remove the *mandazi* with a slotted spoon and place on the rack on the baking sheet to drain any excess oil. Serve warm or at room temperature. These are best served soon after they have been fried or reheat for a few minutes in a hot oven.

ZANZIBARI SESAME BREAD
MKATE WA UFUTA

This sesame bread is a typical Ramadan bread, served at *futari* or *iftar*, the daily breaking of the fast at sunset. It is usually baked at home, although you also see it for sale in markets, where it will have often been made at home by the women selling it. While walking through the narrow streets of Stone Town in Zanzibar, I came across a mother and daughter cooking right on their doorstep. The mother was frying various goodies such as *kaimati* or *l'geimat* (Saffron-Flavored Fritters, page 486) and *bhajis* while the daughter was making sesame bread, having put her young child in charge of brushing the baked loaves with vegetable oil once they were done. Both women were supremely unfriendly and would not let me photograph them or even the food they were cooking until they finally relented when I went back the next day with Farid Bawazir, a wonderful guide, who knew everyone in Stone Town. He talked them into letting me snap the daughter as she was baking the bread.

The way the daughter was kneading the dough was fascinating. She beat it really hard and for quite a long time, every now and then stretching the dough up with her fingers and letting it drop until it became smooth.

The way she baked the bread was also very interesting. She had a special aluminum pan that she only used for this bread. She first heated the pan over the charcoal fire then sprinkled it with a little water before thickly spreading the very wet dough over the bottom of the pan with her moistened fingers. She then placed the pan over the embers and left it for a few minutes until the bottom of the bread was done, after which she lifted the pan and turned it over the fire to expose the top of the bread to the heat. There was no danger of the bread falling off as it was stuck to the pan and she needed to loosen it off the sides and bottom with the help of a knife. It is a little like how pizza is made, where the pizzaiolo moves the top of the pizza along the roof of the oven to blister the sides, but instead she was moving the inverted pan over the embers until the top crust of the bread became charred in places and golden in others. She then set about loosening the loaf off the pan and placed it on a cloth where her child brushed it with a little oil.

I don't think many cooks will have either the right aluminium pan or the possibility of cooking this bread over embers, so this recipe uses a heavy cast-iron pan on the stovetop to cook the bottom of the bread, and then goes under a hot broiler to color and crisp the top of the bread. Serve with stews or drizzled with honey for a sweet snack.   MAKES EIGHT 8-INCH (20 CM) LOAVES

3⅓ cups (400 g)
   unbleached all-purpose
   flour
1 teaspoon fine sea salt
1 teaspoon instant (fast-
   acting) yeast
1½ cups (375 ml)
   coconut cream
2 organic eggs, beaten
Toasted sesame seeds,
   for sprinkling over the
   breads
Vegetable oil or ghee, for
   brushing the breads

1. Mix the flour, salt, and yeast in a large bowl and make a well in the center. Add the coconut cream and eggs to the well and gradually bring in the flour until you have a loose, sticky dough. Hold the bowl with one hand while you start beating the dough with the other, quite hard, stretching the dough up every now and then until the dough is smooth. You can also do this with a whisk. Either way it will take a few minutes. Cover with a clean kitchen towel and let rest for 30 to 45 minutes, until the dough has risen. Some people beat or whisk the dough again and let it rise one more time but the Zanzibari ladies I watched making the bread didn't.

2. Preheat the broiler to high. Place an 8-inch (20 cm) cast-iron skillet over medium heat. When it is hot, sprinkle the bottom with a little water, which should sizzle as soon as it touches the pan. With your wet hand, grab enough dough to spread thickly over the pan. Sprinkle some toasted sesame seeds over the top of the bread and leave over the heat for 3 to 5 minutes, or until the bottom has crisped up and become golden—the top of the bread will cook better if you cover the pan. Quickly slip the pan, uncovered, under the broiler and move it around to color the top all over. Don't worry if a few spots char. Use a spatula to loosen the bread off the pan and lay it on a clean kitchen towel. Brush the bread with a little oil or ghee.

3. Scrape the pan clean and return to the heat. Sprinkle with a little water and repeat to make the remaining breads. In Zanzibar, the women (it is almost always women who cook) use two or three pans, but they make industrial quantities, either to sell or to feed large families. This recipe yield 8 loaves, so you can manage with the one pan. Stack the cooked breads and keep warm—they have wonderful pointed straw "hats" in Zanzibar to keep the food both warm and away from the flies. You can throw a kitchen towel over the breads to keep them both warm and soft.

INDIAN FLATBREAD
CHAPATI

INDIA | ZANZIBAR | ARABIAN GULF

Probably the most common bread of South Asia, chapatis are freshly made everywhere—at home, on the street, and in restaurants. In India, they start cooking the bread on a hot tawa (skillet) before moving it to an open flame (usually charcoal) for the bread to puff up like a balloon and separate into two layers. And for those of you who cannot make charcoal fires, simply put the bread over an open gas flame, which will produce the same result. Chapatis are also common in Zanzibar and the Arabian Gulf, but there they just cook the bread on a hot plate. Either way, it is a great bread that is very simple to make. You can make the dough a day ahead and keep it in the fridge for when you need it. This is what most cooks do in India. If you refrigerate the dough for later use, it is a good idea to remove it about an hour ahead of time. Serve the chapatis with any of the curries or stews on pages 154 to 163.   MAKES TWELVE 6-INCH (15 CM) ROUND BREADS

2 cups (225 g) whole wheat or 2 cups (240 g) unbleached all-purpose flour, plus more all-purpose flour for kneading and rolling out

½ teaspoon fine sea salt

1 tablespoon vegetable oil, plus more for brushing the dough and frying the bread

1. Mix the flour and salt in a large bowl and make a well in the center. Add the oil along with ¾ cup (180 ml) warm water. Gradually bring in the flour and mix with the liquid until you have a rough dough.

2. Transfer the dough to a lightly floured work surface and knead for 3 minutes. Shape the dough into a ball, invert the bowl over the dough, and let rest for 15 minutes. Knead for 3 more minutes. Let rest for a few minutes, then roll out the dough to a circle about ¼ inch (0.5 cm) thick. Brush with a little vegetable oil.

3. Roll the flattened dough into a cylinder, then stand the cylinder on end and flatten it before shaping the dough into a ball. Brush with oil. Cover with plastic wrap and let sit for 30 minutes.

4. Roll the ball of dough into a log about 2 inches (5 cm) thick, then cut crosswise into 12 pieces, each ¼ inch (0.5 cm) thick. Working with 4 pieces of dough, roll into rounds about 6 inches (15 cm) in diameter, keeping the other pieces of dough covered with a damp kitchen towel.

5. Place a large heavy skillet over medium heat and brush the bottom of the pan with vegetable oil. When the pan is hot, place a round of dough in it. Cook for 2 to 3 minutes on one side, then flip over and cook for another 2 to 3 minutes on the other side, pressing on the edge to let the chapati puff up. Both sides should be crisp on the edges and golden all over. Remove to a plate and stack the cooked chapatis one on top of the other to keep them warm. Cook the remaining 3 chapatis. Roll out and cook two more batches of 4 chapatis each. Serve hot or warm.

SAVORY PANCAKES

CHILA

ZANZIBAR

Another Ramadan specialty, *chila* is a fluffy pancake with one side smooth and the other pock-marked with a thousand and one holes, not unlike *anjero* (Somali Pancakes, page 8). These *chila* are savory and slightly spicy, but they can also be made sweet, depending on the occasion. If you want to make it sweet, omit the spices and herbs and use ¼ cup (50 g) raw cane sugar instead. You can make *chila* with either chickpea flour or by soaking rice then grinding it; I give both formulas below (both versions are gluten-free). Obviously, the chickpea flour is the quicker one but it is worth trying the rice flour one, too. The ingredients for each version may be different but the method remains the same. Serve as a side to curries or stews, or serve for breakfast with coconut cream (page 516) or butter and honey.   MAKES FOUR 8-INCH (20 CM) PANCAKES

FOR THE CHICKPEA FLOUR CHILA
2 cups (175 g) chickpea flour
1 teaspoon instant (fast-acting) yeast
¼ teaspoon cayenne pepper
¼ teaspoon ground turmeric
½ teaspoon fine sea salt

FOR THE RICE FLOUR CHILA
1 cup (200 g) long-grain rice, soaked overnight
1 packet (7g/ 2¼ teaspoons) instant (fast-acting) yeast
¼ cup (50 g) superfine sugar
1¼ cups (310 ml) coconut cream
½ teaspoon ground cardamom

TO FINISH
Vegetable oil, for frying the pancakes

1. To make the chickpea flour chila: Mix the chickpea flour, yeast, spices, and salt in a bowl. Add ½ cup (125 ml) water and mix until you have a smooth batter. Cover with plastic wrap and let sit for 1 hour.

2. To make the rice flour chila: Drain the rice and put in a food processor. Add the yeast, sugar, coconut cream, and cardamom and process until you have a smooth batter. Transfer to a bowl. Cover with plastic wrap and let sit for 1 hour.

3. To make the pancakes: Brush a nonstick skillet with a little vegetable oil and place over medium-high heat. Pour a ladleful and a half of batter in the pan and look out for the bubbles starting to pop up on the side. As soon as they do, reduce the heat, cover the pan, and cook for about 10 minutes, or until the top is completely pockmarked with tiny holes and the bottom is golden brown. Remove the pancake to a plate and make the others. Serve warm.

UZBEK FLATBREAD

NON

Uzbeks are famous for their bread and you see it all over the markets, different types with wonderful patterns stamped into them using an implement called a *chekish* (hammer in Arabic), which is a type of wooden mallet spiked with sharp metal nails arranged in different patterns. The *chekish* serves two purposes—one is to make lovely patterns on the bread and the other is to puncture the dough so it doesn't puff up while baking. It is not so easy to find *chekish* in the West, but you can use a fork or a sharp skewer to make the pattern of your choice. Uzbeks, along with most Muslims, consider bread sacred and they have lovely customs to show their reverence for bread, such as placing it under the head of a newborn baby to wish him or her a long, healthy life or in between the legs of a child taking her first steps to bless her endeavor. You find many types of bread in Uzbekistan, both plain and filled. This recipe is for the most common and plainest.

MAKES TWO 8-INCH (20 CM) ROUND BREADS

3¼ cups (390 g) unbleached all-purpose flour, plus more for kneading and shaping

1 teaspoon instant (fast-acting) yeast

1 teaspoon raw cane sugar

1 teaspoon fine sea salt

2 tablespoons (30 g) unsalted butter, at room temperature

FOR THE TOPPING

1 small onion (3½ ounces/100 g), very finely chopped

1 teaspoon sesame seeds

1 teaspoon nigella seeds

1. Put the flour, yeast, sugar, and salt in a large bowl and mix well. Slowly add 1¼ cups (310 ml) water, bringing in the flour as you go along. Mix until you have a rough dough.

2. Transfer the dough to a lightly floured work surface and knead for 3 minutes. Invert the bowl over the dough and let sit for 15 minutes. Knead for 3 more minutes, or until you have a smooth, soft dough. Shape into a ball.

3. Grease a clean bowl with the softened butter and also use some of it to smear the dough. Place the ball of the dough in the buttered bowl. Cover with plastic wrap and let rise in a warm, draft-free place for 1½ hours, or until doubled in size.

4. Divide the dough in half. Shape each piece into a ball and let rest on your work surface for 15 minutes. Then roll out each into a round 8 inches (20 cm) in diameter and ½ inch (1 cm) thick, making sure you raise the edges to have a good rim. Brush with water. Cover with a damp kitchen towel and let rest for 30 minutes.

5. During this time, preheat your oven to as high as you can and place a pizza stone inside if you have one.

6. Uncover the rounds of dough. Brush again with cold water and make a deep indentation in the middle with the heel of your hand. Then, using a fork—or a *chekish*, the traditional Uzbek bread stamp—prick the bread everywhere inside the raised edges. Transfer to a large nonstick baking sheet (or a regular baking sheet lined with parchment paper or a silicone baking mat). Or if you have preheated a pizza stone in the oven, transfer the dough to a floured peel.

7. To make the topping: Mix the chopped onion, sesame seeds, and nigella seeds in a bowl. With your hand, spread the mixture all over both breads.

8. Bake for 12 to 15 minutes, or until golden all over and risen around the edges. Check on the breads after about 12 minutes to see they are not baking too fast. Transfer to a wire rack to cool. Bread is always best left to cool as it continues developing. You can always reheat it to serve hot.

KASHGAR
MULTILAYERED NON

NON

CHINA

This bread is made with the same dough and topping as the regular *non*, but the shaping is different.

MAKES TWO 8-INCH (20 CM) ROUND BREADS

Uzbek Flatbread
  (page 32)
Vegetable oil, for shaping

1. Prepare the flatbread through the first rise (step 3) and divide the dough in half, shape into balls, and let rest 15 minutes.

2. Smear your work surface with oil and place one ball of dough over the oiled surface. Flatten the dough into a disk to about ½ inch (1 cm) thick and generously smear with oil. Roll the disk of dough into a cylinder and lightly squeeze it with both hands to thin it and stretch it further. Repeat with the other ball of dough. Hold the cylinder upright on your work surface and twist the bottom before you start pressing it down onto the work surface while twisting the cylinder. Keep twisting the cylinder of dough and pressing it down until you have a kind of multilayered pyramid. Repeat with the other cylinder. Cover with plastic wrap and let rest for 15 minutes. During this time, preheat your oven to as high as you can.

3. Take one of the dough pyramids and with the heel of your hand, press down the middle to flatten it in the middle. Then curl your fingers and with your curled fingers, keep pressing inside the slightly raised edges as you rotate the dough to flatten it further, until you have a round about 7 inches (17.5 cm) in diameter. Then pick up the round of dough and with your fingers raise the edge a little more as you turn it around in your hands. Lightly flour your work surface and place the round of dough down, raised edges up, and with your curled fingers keep flattening it inside the edges while turning it round to keep it an even round. Now you will need a short rolling pin with handles or a straight glass or soda/beer bottle to flatten the round further without squashing the edges. As you flatten the round, keep rotating it so that it is stays evenly round. Once you have flattened it to about 9 inches (22.5 cm), use both palms to stretch it further. You should end up with a round loaf that is 10 inches (25 cm) in diameter. If you have a *chekish*—an Uzbek bread stamp—stamp the bread inside the edges, starting all around the edge and finishing in the middle.

4. Spread the onion and seed mixture all over the bread and bake as directed in the flatbread recipe.

FILLED and TOPPED
BREADS and PIES

MOROCCAN PIGEON PIE
B'STILLA

MOROCCO

B'stilla is one of those classic sweet-savory Moroccan dishes that is an absolute must at any celebration, whether religious or secular. It is the first course served at a *diffa* (which means "reception" and describes a celebratory meal). One of the seasonings in the filling is *ras el-hanout*, possibly the most complex of all Islamic spice mixtures and usually used with game or in sweet-savory tagines. *Ras el-hanout* means the "head of the shop," signaling how precious the spice blend is, both because of its price and the fact that the blend is made with up to thirty different spices. The mixture once included Spanish fly before it was made illegal. I like to think it was banned because of its reputation as an aphrodisiac, but it is probably because it can be noxious if used liberally.

B'stilla is traditionally cooked on top of the stove, in a *tobsil* (a large, flat hand-beaten iron pan). Then, once the pie is cooked, the top is sprinkled with powdered sugar and decorated with crisscrossed lines of ground cinnamon. I still like to prepare the pie the traditional way, in three separate layers: one of ground almonds, another with the stewed pigeons (quartered and left on the bone; Moroccan pigeons are very small), and another with the eggs that have been scrambled in the sauce of the pigeons. Each layer is separated from the other by a couple of sheets of *warqa* and the whole is wrapped in more *warqa*. And I like to eat it with my hand the way Moroccans do by first breaking open the edge of the crisp pastry, then pulling out a piece of pigeon and sucking the meat off the bone before daintily pinching off more pastry, this time with a little of the almond and egg filling. Sadly fewer and fewer people, in Morocco or outside, will make b'stilla this way. They use chicken instead of pigeon and mix it with the scrambled eggs and almonds to make a single layer. It is a faster and simpler way to prepare b'stilla. If you don't want to go to the trouble of building the pie the way I describe below, simply mix all the filling ingredients and make the pie in one layer using the sheets of *warqa* in between each layer on the bottom of the pie.   SERVES 6 TO 8

FOR THE FILLING
2 squabs or 3 quail
2 medium onions (10½ ounces/300 g total), grated on the coarse side of a grater (about 1 cup)
½ cup (30 g) finely chopped flat-leaf parsley

1. To make the filling: Put the squabs in a heavy pot. Add the onions, parsley, cilantro, cinnamon, ginger, ras el-hanout, cayenne, saffron, and a little salt. Add 1¾ cups (430 ml) water and bring to a boil over medium-high heat. As the water comes to a boil, add the 4 tablespoons (60 g) butter. Cover and cook for 20 minutes, then reduce the heat to medium-low, turn the birds in the sauce, and simmer for 10 more minutes, or until the birds are done.

Recipe continues

½ cup (30 g) finely
   chopped cilantro
1½ teaspoons ground
   cinnamon
1½ teaspoons ground
   ginger
1 teaspoon ground ras el-
   hanout (see page 363)
¼ teaspoon cayenne
   pepper
2 good pinches of saffron
   threads
Sea salt
4 tablespoons (60 g)
   unsalted butter, plus
   more for greasing the
   baking dish
⅔ cup (100 g) blanched
   almonds

2. Put the almonds in the hot oven and toast them for about 7 minutes, or until golden brown. Take out of the oven and keep the oven on. Let the almonds cool before grinding them coarsely in a food processor.

3. Remove the squabs to a plate and let cool. The sauce should be very thick. If it isn't, let it bubble over high heat, stirring regularly, until completely reduced and silky. Once this is done, reduce the heat to low, then whisk the eggs into the sauce and scramble them, whisking all the time, for about 5 minutes, or until set but still creamy. Take off the heat.

4. Take the squab meat off the bone, discarding the skin. Tear into small pieces. Mix the ground almonds with the powdered sugar.

5. Preheat the oven to 450°F (230°C).

6. To assemble the pie: Lay one sheet of phyllo over the bottom of a shallow 12-inch (30 cm) round nonstick baking dish. If you don't have one, brush the bottom and sides of a normal one with a little of the melted butter. Brush with some melted butter

10 organic eggs, lightly
   beaten
2 tablespoons powdered
   sugar

FOR THE PIE
16 sheets phyllo dough
   (12½ x 7 inches/32 x 18
   cm), or 11 sheets warqa
1 stick (120 g) unsalted
   butter, melted
Powdered sugar, for
   garnish
Ground cinnamon, for
   garnish

and lay another sheet across the first one. Brush with butter and lay 4 more sheets, overlapping them as you go along so that you have pastry overhanging all around the edges. (If you are using *warqa*, cover the bottom of the dish with one sheet. Then fan 4 sheets in a rosette, half inside the dish and half outside. Cover the bottom of the dish with another sheet—you do not need to brush the *warqa* with butter as it is already lightly oiled.)

7. Spread the ground almonds evenly over the pastry. Lay 2 phyllo sheets (or one *warqa*) over the almonds and brush with melted butter. Spread the squab meat over the pastry and cover with another 2 phyllo sheets (or one *warqa*) and brush with melted butter. Spread the scrambled eggs all over the pastry and lay another phyllo (or *warqa*) sheet over the eggs. Fold the loose pastry over the eggs and lay the remaining 5 sheets of phyllo (or 2 *warqa*) over the filling, again overlapping them and brushing each with butter, and carefully tuck in the loose ends inside the pie dish and under the pie, as if you were tucking in a sheet under a mattress. If the *warqa* is too thick—some western commercial brands are—trim the inside layers and just lay the top 2 sheets over the pie without tucking them under the pie. Brush the top with butter.

8. Bake the b'stilla for 20 to 30 minutes, or until golden brown all over. Let sit for 2 to 3 minutes, then dust the top with powdered sugar. Make a square or diamond pattern by sprinkling thin lines of ground cinnamon at about 1-inch (2.5 cm) intervals. Serve immediately.

EGG BRIOUATS
BRIOUAT BEL BEID

Briouats are the Moroccan version of the Turkish *boreks* or the Lebanese/Syrian *fatayer*, or the Indian/Pakistani samosas. They are simple and quick to make, and in this version the filling is wonderfully moist, making a scrumptious contrast with the crunchy pastry. The subtle hint of saffron elevates the eggs. You could also serve the scrambled eggs and herb filling on toast as a quick starter or a light meal. The trick here is to cook the eggs just right: If undercooked, they'll sog up the pastry; if cooked too much, they will continue to cook inside the pastry and become rubbery. In Morocco they deep-fry the *briouats,* but I prefer to bake them.   MAKES 16 PASTRIES

FOR THE SCRAMBLED EGGS

¼ cup (60 ml) extra-virgin olive oil

3 medium onions (1 pound/450 g total), finely chopped (about 3 cups)

2 ounces (60 g) cilantro, most of the bottom stems discarded, finely chopped

1. To make the scrambled eggs: Heat the olive oil in a large skillet over medium heat. Add the onions and sauté, stirring regularly, until soft and transparent. Add the herbs and spices. Reduce the heat to low and cook for 5 more minutes.

2. Meanwhile, beat the eggs with salt to taste.

3. When the onions are completely soft, add the eggs and scramble for 7 to 10 minutes, or until just set. Don't let them stay too runny or they will sog up the pastry. Taste and adjust the seasoning if necessary. Let cool.

4. To make the *briouats*: Fold a sheet of phyllo in half lengthwise and brush with melted butter. Place 1½ tablespoons filling at the end nearest to you and slightly in from the edges. Fold a bottom corner of the pastry over the egg filling to form a triangle, then

2 ounces (60 g) flat-leaf parsley, most of the bottom stems discarded, finely chopped

Good pinch of saffron threads

¼ teaspoon finely ground black pepper

½ teaspoon ground cinnamon

8 organic eggs

Sea salt

FOR THE BRIOUATS

16 sheets phyllo dough (12½ x 7 inches/32 x 18 cm)

7 tablespoons (105 g) unsalted butter, melted

Vegetable oil, for deep-frying (optional)

continue folding to maintain the triangle shape until you reach the other end. The filling should be completely encased. If there is a little phyllo still loose, either cut it or fold it to be on the bottom of the pastry. Brush with butter and make the other *briouats* in the same way.

5. To bake the *briouats*: Preheat the oven to 450°F (230°C). Bake the *briouats* for 15 to 20 minutes, or until golden brown. Place on a wire rack to cool a little. Serve warm.

6. To deep-fry the *briouats*: Place a wire rack over a rimmed baking sheet. Pour 2 inches (5 cm) of oil into a large deep skillet. Heat the oil over medium heat until hot (if you drop a piece of bread in the oil, the oil should immediately bubble around it). Drop as many briouats as will fit comfortably in the pan and fry for 3 to 4 minutes on each side, or until golden brown all over. Transfer to a wire rack to let the excess oil drain off. Serve hot or warm.

SOUTHERN LEBANESE ZA'ATAR "PIZZA"

MANAQISH JREESH

Manaqish are the quintessential Lebanese breakfast, a sort of Lebanese "pizza" that comes with a variety of toppings. The most common topping is a mixture of za'atar (a dried herb mixture) and olive oil, and you can have these za'atar *manaqish* either plain or wrap them around lab-neh, fresh mint, olives, and tomatoes. In southern Lebanon, which is mostly Shi'ite, *manaqish* are often made with the same dough as that for *mishtah*, a regional flatbread that is made with added cracked wheat and is seasoned with a mixture of spices, which gives it an intriguing flavor and texture. I had never tasted *mishtah* or even knew about it when I lived in Lebanon, which is strange given how small the country is. But despite its size, Lebanon has distinctive and often hid-den regional specialties; and now that I have discovered *mishtah*, thanks to my friend Nayla Audi whose family comes from the south, it has become my favorite Lebanese bread and I often use *mishtah* rather than pita dough to make my *manaqish*. You can use either. The recipe below was given to me by a baker in South Lebanon who makes his *mishtah* in individual round loaves—other bakers make them very long, a little like Roman pizza, which they then cut and sell by the slice. You can replace the za'atar with thin slices of Halloumi cheese or even lay the sliced Halloumi over the za'atar (about 6 thin slices of cheese for each round of dough); it is a good idea to rinse the cheese to make it less salty.   MAKES 6 INDIVIDUAL "PIZZAS"

FOR THE DOUGH
3⅓ cups (375 g) whole wheat flour, plus all-purpose flour for kneading and shaping
1 packet (7g/ 2¼ teaspoons) instant (fast-acting) yeast

1 teaspoon fine sea salt
3 tablespoons sesame seeds
3 tablespoons anise seeds
½ teaspoon ground mahlep
½ teaspoon ground anise seeds

½ teaspoon daqqat kaak (a special spice mixture from the south; optional)
¾ cup (125 g) King Arthur's organic cracked wheat (jreesh), soaked for 1 hour in cold water, drained

Extra-virgin olive oil, for the bowl

FOR THE TOPPING
6 tablespoons za'atar
½ cup (125 ml) extra-virgin olive oil

1. To make the dough: Mix the flour, yeast, salt, sesame seeds, and spices in a large bowl. Stir in the cracked wheat and make a well in the center. Gradually add 1¼ cups (310 ml) warm water, bringing in the flour as you go along. Mix until you have a rough ball of dough.

2. Transfer the dough to a lightly floured work surface and knead for 3 minutes. Shape into a ball, invert the bowl over the dough, and let rest for 15 minutes. Knead for 3 more

minutes, or until the dough is smooth and elastic. Grease a large bowl with a little olive oil. Shape the dough into a ball and place in the bowl, turning it to coat all over with oil. Cover with plastic wrap. Let rise in a warm, draft-free for 1 hour, until more or less doubled in size.

3. Transfer the dough to your work surface. Divide into 6 equal portions. Shape each into a ball. Cover with a very damp kitchen towel. Return to rise for 45 minutes.

4. Flatten each ball with your hands or a rolling pin into a round 7 to 8 inches (17.5 to 20 cm) in diameter. Transfer to a nonstick baking sheet (or a regular baking sheet lined with parchment paper or a silicone baking mat).

5. To make the topping: Mix the za'atar and olive oil in a bowl. Dividing evenly, spread the za'atar mixture on the dough rounds, making sure you oil the edges. Let rest for 10 to 15 minutes.

6. Preheat the oven to 500°F (260°C) degrees, or to its highest setting.

7. Bake for 10 to 12 minutes, or until lightly golden. Serve warm or let cool on a wire rack to serve at room temperature.

RAMADAN BREAD

KHOBZ RAMADAN

The date shines during Ramadan, the Muslim month of fast, even more so than at any other time of the year. Apart from the fact that many Arabs break their fast by eating dates, there are many breads and sweets that are made with them during that time, including this one that you find in the souks of Tripoli in North Lebanon, as well as those of Damascus and also, in the past before they were destroyed, the souks of Aleppo. They are usually sold off street carts or in bakeries. They are also made at home. You can shape them small or very large, and in the case of the latter they are pricked all over to achieve a decorative effect. I got the following recipe from a charming baker in Byblos, Lebanon, who also explained to me all about the making of ka'keh (a sesame bread that looks like a handbag). He fills his with dates as described below, and also makes them plain as a sort of brioche-like bread. These breads freeze very well and I often make a batch to freeze and have for breakfast whenever I feel like it.   MAKES 6 INDIVIDUAL BREADS

FOR THE DOUGH
3⅓ cups (400 g)
   unbleached all-purpose
   flour, plus more for
   kneading and shaping
1 packet (7g/
   2¼ teaspoons) instant
   (fast-acting) yeast
⅛ teaspoon fine sea salt
½ teaspoon whole milk
   powder
¾ teaspoon baking
   powder
¼ cup (50 g) baker's
   sugar or superfine
   sugar
½ tablespoon (7 g)
   unsalted butter, at
   room temperature
1½ tablespoons extra-
   virgin olive oil

1. To make the dough: Mix the flour, yeast, salt, milk powder, baking powder, and sugar in a large bowl and make a well in the center. Add the softened butter and oil to the well and, with the tips of your fingers, rub into the flour until well incorporated. Gradually add 1 cup plus 2 tablespoons (280 ml) warm water, bringing in the flour as you go along. Knead until you have a rough ball of dough.

2. Transfer the dough to a lightly floured work surface and knead for 2 to 3 minutes. Shape the dough into a ball and invert the bowl over the dough. Let rest for 15 minutes. Knead for 3 more minutes, or until the dough is smooth and elastic. Shape into a ball and place in a clean, lightly floured bowl. Cover with plastic wrap. Let rise in a warm, draft-free place for 2 hours. Fold after the first hour: Take the dough out of the bowl. Gently flattening it with the palm of your hands, fold it over into a rectangle, then fold the rectangle into a square. Return to the bowl with the folded side down. Cover and let rise for 1 more hour.

FOR THE FILLING
9 ounces (250 g) pitted
  dates (10 to 12 Medjool
  dates)
4 tablespoons (60 g)
  unsalted butter

TO FINISH
Toasted sesame seeds
Egg wash: 1 egg yolk
  whisked with
  1 teaspoon water

3. To make the filling: Process the dates in a food processor until coarsely chopped. Add the butter and process until you have a fine paste. Roll into a ball. Wrap in plastic wrap and refrigerate while the dough is rising.

4. Transfer the dough to your work surface. Divide into 6 equal portions, each weighing about 4 ounces (125 g). Roll each into a ball. Cover with plastic wrap and let rest for 15 minutes.

5. Divide the date paste into 6 equal portions. Roll each into a ball.

6. Roll out one ball of dough to a round 6 inches (15 cm) in diameter. Flatten a ball of date paste to a 4-inch (10 cm) disk. Place the date disk in the middle of the disk of dough and fold the dough over, gently pulling and stretching until you completely cover the date filling. Pinch the edges to seal and, with your hands, flatten further to make an even disk.

7. Scatter sesame seeds all over a nonstick baking sheet (or a regular baking sheet lined with parchment paper or a silicone baking mat). Transfer the filled bread to the baking sheet, placing it seam side down. Cover with plastic wrap. Make the other breads the same way and transfer to the baking sheet. Cover with a wet, but not dripping, kitchen towel. Let rise for 30 to 45 minutes.

8. Twenty minutes before the breads are ready to bake, preheat the oven to 450°F (230°C).

9. Brush the breads with the egg wash and sprinkle sesame seeds all over the tops. Bake for 12 to 15 minutes, or until golden brown all over. Let cool on a wire rack. Serve at room temperature.

SAUDI MEAT PIES

AISH BIL-LAHM

Very simple to make and totally delectable, these meat pies from Saudi Arabia are eaten as a snack or part of a meal spread. I make them in individual portions but you can also make one large pie. The crumbly flaky pie dough makes for a nice crisp casing for the meat. It is also flavored with an intriguing Arabian spice mixture called *b'zar*. Serve with *duggus* or with an arugula and tomato salad.

MAKES 8 INDIVIDUAL PIES

FOR THE DOUGH
1¼ cups (160 g) unbleached all-purpose flour
1⅓ cups (150 g) whole wheat flour
¼ cup (30 g) whole milk powder
1 teaspoon b'zar (Arabian Spice Mixture, page 366)
1 packet (7g/ 2¼ teaspoons) instant (fast-acting) yeast
1 teaspoon baking powder
1½ teaspoons fine sea salt
1 teaspoon raw cane sugar
3½ tablespoons (50 g) ghee or unsalted butter
2 tablespoons sunflower oil
1 organic egg

FOR THE FILLING
3 tablespoons sunflower oil
2 medium onions (10½ ounces/300 g total), finely chopped
14 ounces (400 g) ground lamb or beef
1¼ teaspoons finely ground black pepper
1 medium leek, very thinly sliced
3 tablespoons tahini
1 tablespoon black vinegar
Fine sea salt
A few sprigs cilantro, most of the stems discarded, finely chopped

TO FINISH
Egg wash: 1 egg whisked with 1 teaspoon water
Toasted sesame seeds, for garnish

1. To make the dough: Mix the flours, milk powder, *b'zar*, yeast, baking powder, salt, and sugar in a large bowl and make a well in the center. Add the ghee and oil to the well and with the tips of your fingers, rub into the flour. Add the egg and gradually add ⅓ cup plus 1 tablespoon (100 ml) water. Mix until you have a rough dough.

2. Remove the dough onto a lightly floured work surface. Knead for 3 minutes. Shape the dough into a ball, invert the bowl over the dough, and let rest for 15 minutes. Knead for 3 more minutes. Roll into a ball. Place in a lightly floured bowl. Cover with plastic wrap and let rest for 1½ hours.

3. To make the filling: Heat the oil in a large skillet over medium heat. Add the onions and cook, stirring regularly, until caramelized and golden brown, about 10 minutes. Add the ground meat and cook, stirring until the meat is no longer pink and all excess liquid has evaporated. Season with the pepper and salt to taste. Remove from the heat and let

Recipe continues

cool. Transfer the meat to a bowl. Add the leeks and mix well. Mix the tahini, vinegar, and 1 tablespoon water in a bowl. Mix in the cilantro. Add to the meat and mix well. Taste and adjust the seasoning if necessary.

4. Preheat the oven to 425°F (220°C). Grease 8 shallow pie dishes measuring 5 inches (12.5 cm) in diameter and 1 inch (2.5 cm) deep with a little oil (or use nonstick ones).

5. Divide the dough into 8 equal portions. Shape each into a ball, cover with a damp kitchen towel, and let rest for 15 minutes. Roll out one ball of dough on your work surface into a round large enough to cover the bottom and sides of the oiled pie dish. Lift the dough onto the pie dish and tuck the corners in making sure it is equally high all along the sides.

6. Dividing evenly, spread the filling in the pie shells. Brush the high edges of the dough and the filling with the egg wash. Sprinkle a little sesame seeds all over.

7. Bake for 20 to 30 minutes, depending on how hot your oven gets. The crust should be golden brown and the top of the meat golden.

BERBER MEAT BREAD
MEDFOUNA

Medfouna, which means "buried" in Arabic, is a confusing name for this filled bread as it also describes a Moroccan dish where stewed pigeons are buried under a mound of steamed vermicelli. I am not sure why both dishes share the name. All I know is that this bread is a southern specialty. I initially saw the recipe on a postcard while browsing through a rack of them in Marrakesh. The name of the bread also refers to the fact that the bread is baked on a hot stone, buried under hot ashes—which is how it's done in most southern areas, although in other, more northern areas, the bread is baked in regular wood-fired ovens. You can use ground lamb as in the recipe below, or if you can get it, use *knlii* (dried strips of spiced beef that are simmered in clarified butter, or *smen* as it is known in Morocco) for a much stronger flavor. Some cooks add chopped or sliced hard-boiled eggs to the filling. I prefer the bread without.

SERVES 6 TO 8

FOR THE FILLING
1 pound 6 ounces (650 g) well-trimmed lamb shoulder (from about 2¼ pounds/1 kg), cut into tiny dice (see Note)

1 large onion (7 ounces/200 g), very finely chopped

A few sprigs flat-leaf parsley, finely chopped

1 tablespoon ground coriander

½ teaspoon ground cumin

½ teaspoon ground cinnamon

1 teaspoon finely ground black pepper

1 teaspoon fine sea salt, or to taste

¼ cup (60 ml) extra-virgin olive oil

1. To make the filling: Mix together the lamb, onion, parsley, spices, and oil in a large bowl. Let marinate, stirring occasionally, while you prepare the dough.

2. To make the dough: Mix the flour, semolina, yeast, and salt in a large bowl and make a well in the center. Gradually add 1⅓ cups (325 ml) warm water, bringing in the flour as you go along. Knead until you have a rough ball of dough.

3. Transfer the dough to a lightly floured work surface and knead for 3 minutes. Shape the dough into a ball, invert the bowl over the dough, and let rest for 15 minutes. Knead for 3 more minutes, or until the dough is smooth and elastic. Shape into a ball and place in a clean, lightly floured bowl. Cover with plastic wrap and let rise in a warm, draft-free place for 1½ to 2 hours, or until doubled in size.

4. Transfer the dough to a lightly floured work surface. Divide into 2 pieces, one slightly larger than the other. Roll each piece into a ball and place on a floured surface. Sprinkle a little flour over the balls. Cover with a clean kitchen towel and let rest for 15 minutes.

5. Roll out the smaller piece of dough to a round 12 inches (30 cm) in diameter. Be sure to sprinkle your work surface and the top of the dough with flour every now and then so it doesn't stick. Transfer the round of dough to a large nonstick baking sheet (or a regular baking sheet lined with parchment paper or a silicone baking mat). Prick with a fork here and there. Spread the meat filling evenly all over, leaving about ¾ inch (2 cm) free around the edges. Brush the edges with water. Roll out the other piece of dough

Recipe continues

FOR THE DOUGH

2 cups (240 g) unbleached all-purpose flour, plus more for kneading and shaping

1⅓ cups (220 g) fine semolina or semolina flour

1½ teaspoons instant (fast-acting) yeast

1½ teaspoons fine sea salt

to a slightly larger round. Carefully lay over the filling, making sure you align the edges. Press on the edges slightly to seal. Prick the dough in a few places. Cover with a damp kitchen towel and let rise for 30 to 45 minutes, depending on how warm your kitchen is. If too warm, go for the shorter rise time.

6. Preheat the oven to 375°F (190°C).

7. Uncover the bread 5 to 10 minutes before putting in the oven to let the top dry out. Place in the oven and bake for 45 minutes, until golden all over. Remove from the oven and let the bread rest for 5 minutes before transferring to a wire rack to cool slightly— you may have to drain off the excess juice that will have seeped out from the meat. Serve hot or warm. You can let the bread cool on the rack completely and freeze it for later use. Keep the bread wrapped as it is thawing. Once thawed, reheat in a 400°F (200°C) oven for 10 to 15 minutes and serve.

NOTE: *You can chop the meat in a meat grinder, but the texture is much nicer if you hand-cut it.*

LEBANESE/SYRIAN SAVORY PASTRIES

FATAYER

In Lebanon, *fatayer* are made in triangles, large or small, with the pastry completely encasing the filling, while in Syria, *fatayer* are made small, and shaped like boats with the pastry folded over part of the filling to let some of it show in the middle. They are the quintessential street food in both countries, sold in bakeries that make them throughout the morning. They are also served in restaurants as part of a mezze spread. Home cooks also make them, although many will only prepare the filling at home, which they then take to the local baker for him to use with his own dough to make the *fatayer*. Lebanese *fatayer* are made with an unleavened dough enriched with olive oil, while the dough for Syrian *fatayer* is leavened, and made slightly sweet with milk. A pinch of mahlep (a bitter, fragrant nut found inside the pit of the wild cherry) is added to give the *fatayer* an intriguing flavor. The filling can be greens (spinach, purslane, fresh thyme—the long-leaved one used in salads or pickles—or Swiss chard), dairy (such as cheese or labneh), or eggs, to name but a few of the choices. You can use the fillings I give below with either the Lebanese or Syrian dough and shape the *fatayer* accordingly. You can also use the dough for Pita Bread (page 4) to make *fatayer*, which is what Lebanese commercial bakers do.

FOR THE LEBANESE FATAYER

MAKES ABOUT 20 SMALL FATAYER OR 4 LARGE ONES

1¼ cups (160 g) unbleached all-purpose flour, plus more for shaping

¼ teaspoon fine sea salt

2 tablespoons extra-virgin olive oil

Filling of choice (recipes follow)

1. Mix the flour and salt in a bowl and make a well in the center. Add the oil to the well and with the tip of your fingers rub the oil into the flour. Gradually add ⅓ cup (80 ml) warm water, bringing in the flour as you go along. Mix until you have a rough dough.

2. Transfer the dough to a lightly floured work surface and knead for 3 minutes. Shape the dough into a ball, invert the bowl over the dough, and let rest for 15 minutes. Knead for 3 more minutes, or until the dough is smooth and elastic. Shape into a ball and cover with a damp kitchen towel. Let sit on your counter while you prepare the filling.

3. Preheat the oven to 450°F (230°C).

Recipe continues

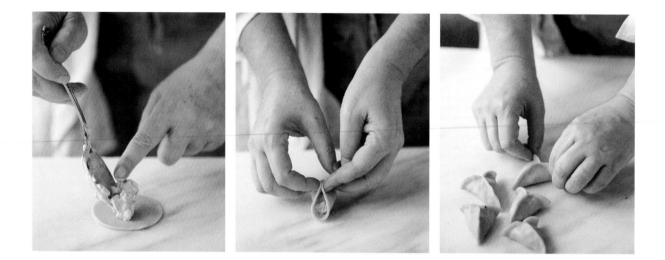

4. To shape small triangles: Divide the dough in half and flatten each slightly. Dip one ball of dough into flour on both sides. Shake off the excess flour and roll out into a large thin round about ⅒ inch (2 mm) thick, turning the dough over regularly. Using a 3-inch (7.5 cm) round pastry cutter, cut the sheet of dough into as many rounds as you can, minimizing waste. Start from the edge and work your way around the outside before moving into the inside. If you do not have pastry cutters, use a thin-rimmed glass. Gather up the scraps, knead them together, and let rest.

5. Turn the rounds over. Place 1½ to 2 teaspoons of the filling of your choice in the center of each round. To shape the triangles, lift two sides of the round of dough, each about one-third of the round, and with your thumb and index finger pinch the edges together, halfway down, making a thin raised joint. Lift the open side of the dough and pinch it equally to both loose ends in order to form a triangle that completely encases the filling and that has a thin raised inverted "Y" in the middle. Make sure you pinch the dough tightly together so that it does not open during baking. Transfer the filled pastries to a nonstick baking sheet (or a regular baking sheet lined with parchment paper or a silicone baking mat) and continue until you have used up all the dough and filling. You should end up with about 20 pieces.

6. Bake for about 10 minutes, or until golden. Serve hot, warm, or at room temperature.

LARGE TRIANGLES: If you make the triangles large, they will be a lot quicker to assemble, although the presentation will not be as dainty. Divide the dough into 4 pieces and roll each into a ball. Flatten each ball of dough into a large round and follow the same instructions for making the small triangles, using one-quarter of the filling for each triangle.

FOR THE SYRIAN FATAYER

1¾ cups (210 g) unbleached all-purpose flour, plus more for kneading and shaping

1 packet (7g/ 2¼ teaspoons) instant (fast-acting) yeast

1 teaspoon baker's sugar or superfine sugar

½ teaspoon fine sea salt

⅛ teaspoon ground mahlep

1 organic egg

¼ cup (60 ml) organic whole milk, at room temperature

Filling of choice but not labneh (recipes follow)

1. Mix the flour, yeast, sugar, salt, and mahlep in a large bowl and make a well in the center. Add the egg, milk, and 2 tablespoons water to the well. Mix the egg with the milk and water before slowly bringing in the flour. Knead until you have a rough ball of dough.

2. Transfer the dough to a lightly floured work surface. Knead for 2 to 3 minutes. Shape into a ball. Invert the bowl over the dough and let rest for 15 minutes. Knead for a few more minutes, or until the dough is smooth and elastic. Shape into a ball. Place in a clean, lightly floured bowl. Cover with plastic wrap and let rise in a warm, draft-free place for 1 hour, until more or less doubled in size.

3. Transfer the dough to your work surface. Divide into 8 equal portions, each weighing just under 2 ounces (50 g). Shape each piece into a ball. Cover with a very damp kitchen towel. Let rest for 30 minutes.

4. Preheat the oven to 450°F (230°C).

5. Using your fingers, flatten each ball into a thin round 6 inches (15 cm) in diameter. Stretch the round into an oval. Spread 1 to 2 tablespoons filling down the middle. Fold one-third of the oval over the filling. Then fold the other third to leave a narrow strip of the filling showing in the middle. Gently press the dough into the filling. Transfer to a large nonstick baking sheet (or a regular baking sheet lined with parchment paper or a silicone baking mat). Form the remaining *fatayer* in the same way and transfer to the baking sheet.

6. Bake for 10 to 12 minutes, or until golden brown all over. Serve hot, warm, or at room temperature.

FILLINGS

SPINACH

1 small onion
  (3½ ounces/100 g),
  very finely chopped
Sea salt
¼ teaspoon finely ground
  black pepper
1 tablespoon ground
  sumac
7 ounces (200 g) spinach,
  thinly sliced
1 tablespoon pine nuts
Juice of ½ lemon, or to
  taste
1 tablespoon extra-virgin
  olive oil

1. Combine the onion, a little salt, pepper, and sumac in a bowl and mix with your fingers, rubbing the seasonings into the onion to soften it.

2. Put the sliced spinach in a large bowl and sprinkle with a little salt. Rub the salt in with your hands until the spinach is wilted. Squeeze the spinach very dry. Transfer to a clean bowl and break up the clumps to separate the leaves as much as you can. Obviously not one by one!

3. Add the seasoned onion to the spinach, together with the pine nuts, lemon juice, and olive oil. Mix well. Taste and adjust the seasoning if necessary—the filling should be very tart to offset the rather bland dough. Place the filling in a sieve to drain off the excess juices.

LABNEH YOGURT

1 large onion (7 ounces/
  200 g), very finely
  chopped
½ teaspoon ground
  cinnamon
½ teaspoon ground
  allspice
¼ teaspoon finely ground
  black pepper
Pinch of red pepper flakes
  (optional)
Sea salt
1 medium tomato
  (3½ ounces/100 g),
  finely diced
1½ cups (375 g) strained
  yogurt
1 teaspoon unsalted
  butter, at room
  temperature

1. Place the onion, cinnamon, allspice, black pepper, pepper flakes (if using), and a little salt in a bowl. With your fingers, rub the seasonings into the onion to soften it.

2. Add the tomato, yogurt, and butter and mix well. Taste and adjust the seasoning if necessary.

CHEESE AND PARSLEY

The cheese filling for *fatayer* is traditionally made with *qarish*, a typical Lebanese/Syrian curd cheese that is not so readily available in the West, so I give akkawi or mozzarella as alternatives. You can make your own *qarish* by boiling yogurt with a little lemon juice and a little salt until it separates after which you drain the curds of all excess liquid and salt the cheese to taste. If you make it, use the same amount as stated in the recipe.

9 ounces (275 g)
akkawi or fior di latte
mozzarella cheese,
chopped very small
1 organic egg, beaten
1 tablespoon (15 g)
unsalted butter
¼ cup (15 g) finely
chopped flat-leaf
parsley
Fine sea salt and finely
ground black pepper

Mix together the cheese, egg, butter, parsley, and salt and pepper to taste.

SPICY CHEESE

9 ounces (275 g) feta
cheese
1 teaspoon Aleppo pepper

Mix the feta cheese with the Aleppo pepper.

GROUND MEAT PIDE

ETLI PIDE

Pide is the ultimate Turkish snack or light meal, both on the street or in cafés/restaurants. You can have them with a variety of toppings such as eggplant, spinach and eggs, or cheese, to name but a few. This recipe is for a meat-topped pide that is also known as *etli ekmek* (meaning meat bread) and what follows is an eggplant-topped variation called *patlicanli pide*. You can also use the rich, flaky dough with a topping of your choice.

MAKES 4 INDIVIDUAL PIDE

FOR THE DOUGH
2 cups (240 g) unbleached all-purpose flour, plus more for rolling out
½ teaspoon fine sea salt
½ teaspoon superfine sugar
1½ teaspoons instant (fast-acting) yeast
1 organic egg
1½ tablespoons vegetable oil
¼ cup (60 g) Greek whole-milk yogurt

FOR THE TOPPING
2 tablespoons extra-virgin olive oil
1 small onion (3½ ounces/100 g), finely chopped
1 small green chili pepper, sliced into medium thin rings
½ red bell pepper, finely diced
7 ounces (200 g) ground meat
1 tablespoon tomato paste
1 tablespoon mild Turkish red pepper paste
1 small tomato, diced
1 teaspoon Aleppo pepper or pul biber
Sea salt
1 tablespoon unsalted butter

TO FINISH
Enough grated fior di latte mozzarella to sprinkle all over the top or 2 organic eggs, beaten

1. To make the dough: Mix the flour, salt, sugar, and yeast in a large bowl and make a well in the center. Add the egg, vegetable oil, yogurt, and ⅓ cup (80 ml) lukewarm water and mix those in the well before gradually bringing in the flour. Mix until you have a rough ball of dough.

2. Transfer the dough to a lightly floured work surface and knead for 3 minutes. Shape the dough into a ball, invert the bowl over it, and let rest for 15 minutes. Knead for 3 more minutes, or until the dough is smooth and elastic. Cover with a very damp kitchen towel. Let rise in a warm, draft-free place for 30 to 45 minutes while you prepare the topping.

3. To make the topping: Heat the olive oil in a skillet over medium heat. Add the onion, chili pepper, and bell pepper and sauté until the onion is golden and the peppers have softened. Add the meat and stir, breaking up any lumps, until the meat is no longer pink. Add the tomato paste, pepper paste, the diced tomato, Aleppo pepper, and salt to taste. Cook, stirring regularly, until the tomato has reduced and there is no excess liquid in the pan, about 5 minutes. Stir in the butter and take off the heat.

4. Preheat the oven to 400°F (200°C).

5. Divide the dough into 4 equal portions. Roll each into a ball. Cover with the damp towel and let rest for 15 minutes. With your hands, flatten each ball to a 5-inch (12.5 cm) round. Then stretch the rounds into ovals and flatten further. Transfer to a large nonstick baking sheet (or a regular baking sheet lined with parchment paper or a silicone baking mat).

6. Spread one-quarter of the topping down the center, leaving enough edge on the dough to fold over the filling, but without covering the topping completely—you want to leave a narrow strip of the topping showing in the middle. Press on where they meet at the top and bottom ends to stick them together. If using mozzarella, sprinkle the filling with the grated mozzarella; if you are using beaten egg, spoon it over.

7. Bake in the hot oven for 10 to 15 minutes, or until crisp and golden. Serve hot or warm.

EGGPLANT PIDE

Dough from Ground Meat Pide (opposite)
3 tablespoons extra-virgin olive oil
½ pound (225 g) globe eggplant (1 medium), diced into small cubes

½ red bell pepper, finely chopped
Sea salt and finely ground black pepper
1 clove garlic, finely minced

Half of a 14-ounce (400 g) can whole peeled tomatoes, drained and chopped
1 teaspoon Aleppo pepper

A few sprigs flat-leaf parsley, most of the stems discarded, finely chopped (about ¼ cup)
A few sprigs cilantro, most of the stems discarded, finely chopped (about ¼ cup)

1. Make the dough through the first rise as directed.

2. Put the olive oil, eggplant, and bell pepper in a saucepan and place over low heat. Season with salt and black pepper to taste. Cook, covered, for 15 minutes, stirring regularly. Add the garlic, tomatoes, and Aleppo pepper and cook, covered, for another 15 minutes, stirring occasionally, or until the vegetables are tender and the sauce is very thick. Add the herbs and cook, uncovered, for another minute or so. Take off the heat and let cool.

3. Shape, top, and bake the pide as directed.

TURKISH MEAT BOREKS
BAKLAVA YUFKASIYLA KIYMALI MUSKA BÖREGI

Most people know baklava as a sweet nut-filled pastry dripping with sugar syrup. However, baklava can also describe savory pastries such as the *boreks* below, which can be made in different shapes as in the photo opposite. Before World War I, elegant households in Istanbul kept two phyllo makers, one to make the thinner sheets for sweet baklava and the other to make sturdier sheets for *boreks*. Sadly, this custom has died and it is rare nowadays for phyllo to be made at home. As for the origin of phyllo dough, it is undoubtedly of Turkish origin despite the Greeks' claim to it.

MAKES 8 INDIVIDUAL BOREKS

FOR THE FILLING
1½ tablespoons extra-virgin olive oil
½ teaspoon cumin seeds
1 large onion (7 ounces/ 200 g), finely chopped
2 tablespoons pine nuts
1 clove garlic, minced to a fine paste
½ cup finely diced red bell pepper

Scant 1 tablespoon finely chopped fresh chili pepper
½ pound (225 g) lamb shoulder, trimmed of fat and minced
Half of a 14-ounce (400 g) can whole peeled tomatoes, finely chopped

1½ tablespoons golden raisins
A few sprigs flat-leaf parsley, most of the stems discarded, finely chopped
2 tablespoons finely chopped fresh dill
½ teaspoon ground allspice

Sea salt and finely ground black pepper

FOR THE BOREKS
8 sheets phyllo dough (9 x 14 inches/22.5 x 35 cm)
5½ tablespoons (80 g) unsalted butter, melted

1. To make the filling: Heat the oil in a large skillet over medium-high heat. Add the cumin seeds and stir until fragrant. Add the onion and pine nuts and cook, stirring regularly, until lightly golden. Stir in the garlic.

2. Add the peppers and lamb and stir, breaking up any lumps, until the meat is no longer pink. Add the tomatoes, golden raisins, herbs, and allspice. Season with salt and pepper to taste. Cook, stirring occasionally, for a few minutes until there is no longer any liquid in the pan. Let cool.

3. Preheat the oven to 400°F (200°C).

4. To make the boreks: Lay one phyllo sheet on your work surface. Keep the others covered with plastic wrap and a kitchen towel so that they don't dry out. Brush the sheet of phyllo with melted butter. Fold it lengthwise in half. Put one-eighth of the meat filling at the end of the strip nearest to you and fold the pastry over the filling to form a triangle. Brush the strip of phyllo with butter and continue folding, keeping the triangle shape and brushing with butter every two folds or so, until you have encased the filling

entirely and made a neat triangle—trim any excess. Brush with butter on both sides and transfer to a nonstick baking sheet (or a regular baking sheet lined with parchment paper or a silicone baking mat), seam side down. Repeat to make 8 triangles total.

5. Bake for 20 to 25 minutes, or until golden all over. Serve hot or warm.

COILED BOREKS: For coiled *boreks,* fold a sheet of phyllo in half lengthwise and brush with butter. Spread one-eighth of the filling in a line over the length of the folded pastry, leaving about ½ inch (1 cm) clear at the edges. Roll the phyllo over the filling and continue rolling until you have encased the filling in a long log, then coil the log into a spiral (see photo). Brush with butter on both sides and bake as directed.

FAT FINGERS: To make fat fingers, fold a sheet of phyllo in half lengthwise and brush with butter. Spread one-eighth of the filling across the end nearest to you, leaving ½ inch (1 cm) free at the sides. Fold the sides over the filling and all the way down the strip of phyllo, then roll the phyllo up over the filling and continue rolling until you have completely encased the filling. Brush with butter all over and bake as directed.

TURKISH "CALZONE"

SAJ BOREK

TURKEY

Saj boreks are one of my favorite Turkish street foods. They are very thin flatbreads folded around a filling of spiced potatoes or spinach and cheese, baked over a *saj* (a large, flat metal sheet heated over woodfire or gas), then brushed with butter and served on paper to eat piping hot. The *boreks* are made by women who sit on low stools in the corner of a café or in small huts in parks with a large round low table in front of them, the *saj* to one side and the dough and fillings to the other. They spend their whole time rolling out large paper-thin sheets of dough, which they half cover with the client's filling of choice. They then flap the plain half of the dough over the filling and deftly transfer the *borek* to the *saj* where they cook it on both sides. Once done, they brush the *borek* with a little butter and use a short knife with a wide curved blade to cut the *borek* before they serve it. It is very simple to make and absolutely exquisite.   MAKES 4 INDIVIDUAL BOREKS

Dough for Saj Bread
   (page 6)
All-purpose flour, for
   shaping the dough
Spinach and Cheese
   Filling or Potato Filling
   (recipes follow)
4 tablespoons (60 g)
   unsalted butter, melted

1. Make the dough, kneading and letting it rest as directed. Divide the dough into 4 equal portions. Roll each into a ball and let rest covered with a damp cloth while you prepare the filling of choice.

2. Flour your work surface. Dip one ball of dough in the flour on both sides, shake off the excess flour, then roll it out as thinly as you can, sprinkling it with flour every now and then to stop it from sticking. You should end up with a round 10 inches (25 cm) in diameter.

3. If using cheese and spinach filling, sprinkle one-quarter of the feta-parsley mixture over half the dough leaving a border free. Then sprinkle one-quarter of the spinach over the feta. If using the potato filling, spread one-quarter of it over half the dough. Fold the dough over the filling to make a half-moon. Press on the edges to seal them. Repeat to make a total of 4 *saj boreks*.

4. Heat a nonstick griddle or skillet over medium heat. Lift one filled *saj borek* onto the hot pan. Cook for a minute or so on one side, then flip and cook on the other until lightly crisp and golden on both sides. Transfer to a plate, brush with melted butter and serve immediately. Repeat with the remaining *saj boreks* and serve immediately. You can also make them ahead and reheat them in a very hot oven to crisp them up, but they are best eaten straightaway.

FILLINGS

SPINACH AND CHEESE

MAKES ENOUGH FOR 4 INDIVIDUAL BOREKS

4½ ounces (125 g) crumbled feta cheese
A few sprigs flat-leaf parsley, most of the stems discarded, finely chopped
3½ ounces (100 g) spinach, finely shredded
Sea salt and finely ground black pepper

Mix the feta with the parsley in a bowl. Put the spinach in a separate bowl and sprinkle it with a little salt. Rub the salt into the spinach with your fingers to soften it, then squeeze it dry. Loosen the shredded spinach to separate the strips as much as you can. Season with pepper to taste. Keep the spinach and cheese in separate bowls.

POTATO

MAKES ENOUGH FOR 4 INDIVIDUAL BOREKS

1 pound 2 ounces (500 g) potatoes
1 bunch (2 ounces/60 g) scallions, thinly sliced
1 teaspoon Aleppo pepper
⅓ cup (80 ml) extra-virgin olive oil
Sea salt

Boil the potatoes and mash them. Add the sliced scallions, Aleppo pepper, and olive oil. Season with salt to taste and mix well.

NORTH AFRICAN FILLED BREAD
R'GHAYEF

This is the filled version of the plain *m'hajjib* (North African Multilayered Breads, page 15). The two fillings I give below are traditional, but you can improvise and use potatoes or grated cheese or whatever takes your fancy. These are quite irresistible and I never fail to stop at stalls that sell them whenever I am in Morocco or Tunisia. I always ask for mine to be cooked a little longer than they would normally, as I like them quite crisp.   MAKES 8 INDIVIDUAL BREADS

Dough for North African
Multilayered Breads
(page 15)
Vegetable oil, for shaping
the dough and greasing
the pan
Herb Filling or Meat
Filling (recipes follow)

1. Make the dough as directed, kneading and resting. Divide the dough into 8 equal portions, each weighing about 2 ounces (60 g). Roll each piece into a ball. Let the balls of dough rest while you prepare the filling of your choice.

2. Working with 4 balls of dough at a time, with oiled hands and on an oiled work surface, flatten the balls of dough into thin rounds as directed. Spread one-eighth of the filling of your choice over the middle. Fold one-third of the round over the filling, then fold the other third over to make a rectangle. Fold one-third of the rectangle over and the other under to end up with a 5-inch (12.5 cm) square. The reason for folding one side up and the other down is to enclose the filling evenly. Let rest while you make 3 more squares.

3. Flatten the squares of dough with your fingers as thinly as you can, being careful not to tear the dough and expose the filling. Grease a large nonstick skillet with a little oil and place over medium-high heat. Place 1 square in the hot pan (or 2 if they fit). Dip your fingers in a little oil and drizzle over the bread. Cook for 1½ to 2 minutes, or until the bottom is lightly golden. Turn over, drizzle with a little more oil, and cook for another 1½ to 2 minutes. Remove to parchment paper or a wire rack. Cook the remaining 3 breads in the same way. Then form and cook the remaining 4 breads in the same manner, making sure to oil your hands, work surface, and pan in between each bread. Serve immediately.

FILLINGS

HERB

MAKES ENOUGH FOR 8 FILLED BREADS

1 medium onion
  (5 ounces/150 g),
  grated on the coarse
  side of a grater
A few sprigs flat-leaf
  parsley, most of the
  stems discarded, very
  finely chopped
1 teaspoon paprika
½ teaspoon ground
  cumin
½ teaspoon Aleppo
  pepper
Sea salt

Mix the onion, parsley, paprika, cumin, Aleppo pepper, and salt to taste in a bowl. Taste and adjust the seasoning if necessary.

MEAT

MAKES ENOUGH FOR 8 FILLED BREADS

1 tablespoon
  sunflower oil
1 small onion
  (3½ ounces/100 g),
  finely chopped
½ red bell pepper, finely
  chopped
1 small tomato, finely
  diced
7 ounces (200 g) lean
  ground lamb or beef
1 teaspoon paprika
½ teaspoon ground
  cumin
¼ teaspoon finely ground
  black pepper
Sea salt

1. Heat the oil in a large skillet over medium heat. Add the onion and bell pepper and sauté until softened. Add the tomato and cook until all the excess liquid has evaporated.

2. Add the meat, paprika, cumin, black pepper, and salt to taste and cook, breaking up any lumps, until the meat is cooked through, about 5 minutes. Make sure you finely break up the meat so you can spread the filling evenly inside the dough. Taste and adjust the seasoning if necessary.

INDONESIAN MULTILAYERED BREAD

MARTABAK

Indonesian shallots are very small. In the recipe below I call for ten, but if you can only find medium shallots, use five.

MAKES 8 INDIVIDUAL MARTABAK

FOR THE DOUGH
2½ cups (300 g) unbleached all-purpose flour
½ teaspoon fine sea salt
1 tablespoon vegetable oil, plus more for soaking the dough

FOR THE FILLING
3 tablespoons vegetable oil
10 small shallots (7 ounces/200 g total), halved and cut lengthwise into thin wedges
10½ ounces (300 g) finely ground lean lamb or goat
1 bunch scallions (2 ounces/60 g), thinly sliced
2 teaspoons curry powder
½ teaspoon finely ground white pepper
½ teaspoon raw cane sugar
Sea salt
3 organic eggs, beaten with salt and pepper

1. To make the dough: Mix the flour and salt in a bowl and make a well in the center. Add the vegetable oil and ¾ cup (180 ml) water. Gradually bring in the flour and mix until you have a rough dough.

2. Transfer the dough to a lightly floured work surface and knead for 3 minutes. Shape into a ball, invert the bowl over the dough, and let rest for 15 minutes. Knead for 3 more minutes, or until the dough is smooth and elastic. Divide the dough into 8 equal portions and roll each portion into a ball. Place the balls of dough in a shallow bowl and pour enough vegetable oil to barely cover them—soaking the dough will make it more supple and will help flatten it out very thinly. Don't worry about wasting the oil: you will be using it later to fry the *martabak*.

3. To make the filling: Heat the oil in a skillet over medium heat. Add the shallots and sauté until golden, about 10 minutes. Add the meat and sauté, breaking up any lumps, until it has lost all traces of pink. Add the scallions and season with the curry powder, white pepper, sugar, and salt to taste. Cook for a couple more minutes and take off the heat. Let cool slightly before mixing in the beaten egg.

4. To make the dipping sauce: Combine the palm sugar, cane sugar, and 1¼ cups (310 ml) water in a saucepan. Bring to a boil over medium heat, then add the garlic and chilies and let bubble gently until the sauce has thickened. Add the lemon juice and salt to taste and take off the heat. Pour into a serving bowl and set aside.

5. To make the *martabak*: Drain the oil from the dough into a skillet in which you will fry the *martabak*—ideally the oil should be to a 2-inch (5 cm) depth. Take one ball of dough and flatten it with your hands as thinly as you can (see Note). Once you have flattened your dough, spread one-eighth of the filling in the center. Fold one side over the filling, then the other side. Then, fold the top and bottom over the filling so that you have a square with the filling encased evenly. Fill the other *martabaks* in the same way.

Recipe continues

FOR THE DIPPING SAUCE

2½ ounces (75 g) palm sugar

2 tablespoons raw cane sugar

1 large clove garlic, thinly sliced

4 bird's eye chilies, thinly sliced

Juice of ½ lemon, or to taste

Sea salt

6. Set a wire rack in a rimmed baking sheet. Place the skillet with the vegetable oil over medium heat and when the oil is hot (you can judge by dropping a piece of bread into the oil; if the oil bubbles around it, then it is ready), flatten one *martabak* slightly with your hands, making sure not to tear the dough, and slide it into the hot oil. Fry for 2 to 3 minutes on each side, or until crisp and golden. Remove to the wire rack to drain off the excess oil. Fry the remaining *martabaks*. Serve hot with the dipping sauce.

NOTE: *Martabak vendors first flatten the dough with their hands into a large round that they then pick up and flap in a circular motion before slapping it against the greased work surface; with each flap the round gets larger and thinner until it is paper-thin, at which point they slap it against the work surface and stretch it even further. I am not suggesting you do it this way, as it requires a lot of practice.*

INDIAN MEAT BREADS

KEEMA NAAN

INDIA | PAKISTAN

The dough for this filled naan is slightly different from that for the plain Naan (page 24) in that it uses both milk and yogurt instead of milk and water. You can also use the dough for the plain naan to make *keema naan*. And you can replace the *keema* filling with potatoes (by substituting an equal amount of mashed potatoes for the meat), or grated cheese, or shredded coconut mixed with a little sugar for a slightly sweet naan. The only filling you need a recipe for is the meat filling; for the other filling ideas you just need about a cup. And again, even though the ultimate naan is that baked in a *tannur* oven, you get excellent results by baking yours on a pizza stone or hot baking sheet in the oven or cooking it on a tawa (shallow, flat skillet).

MAKES 6 INDIVIDUAL FILLED NAANS

FOR THE DOUGH
3 cups (360 g)
   unbleached all-purpose
   flour, plus more for
   kneading and shaping
1 teaspoon sugar
1 packet (7g/
   2¼ teaspoons) instant
   (fast-acting) yeast
½ teaspoon salt
¼ cup (60 ml) organic
   whole milk, at room
   temperature
½ cup (125 g) plain
   yogurt
2 tablespoons vegetable
   oil, for greasing the
   bowl and dough

FOR THE FILLING
1 tablespoon
   vegetable oil
1 small shallot, very
   finely chopped
1 small fresh green chili,
   seeded and very thinly
   sliced
2 cloves garlic, minced to
   a fine paste
8 ounces (225 g) ground
   lamb

1. To make the dough: Mix the flour, sugar, yeast, and salt in a large bowl and make a well in the center. Add the milk and yogurt to the well. Mix lightly together before gradually bringing in the flour. Mix until you have a rough ball of dough.

2. Transfer to a lightly floured work surface and knead for 3 minutes. Roll the dough into a ball, invert the bowl over it, and let rest for 15 minutes. Knead for 3 more minutes or until smooth and elastic. Roll into a ball and place in an oiled bowl. Brush the dough with a little oil, cover the bowl with plastic wrap, and let rise in a warm, draft-free place for 1 hour, or until well risen and more or less doubled in size.

3. To make the filling: Heat the oil in a skillet over medium heat. Add the shallot and chili and sauté until the shallot is golden, then add the garlic. Stir for a minute or so, then transfer to a bowl. Add the meat, tomato paste, spices, and salt to taste to the bowl and mix well.

4. To make the naans: Divide the dough into 6 equal portions. Roll each into a ball. Place on a lightly floured surface and cover with a damp kitchen towel. Divide the filling into 6 equal portions and roll each into a ball. Take one ball of dough and flatten it slightly. Put the filling in the center and bring in the dough to cover the filling. Seal the edges and roll into a ball, then flatten with your hands until you have a thick disk. Using a rolling pin and flouring the dough slightly, roll out into a disk 6 to 7 inches (15 to 17.5 cm) in diameter. Press the tips of your fingers into the dough here and there to make indents and stop the bread from puffing up during baking.

Recipe continues

1 tablespoon tomato
    paste
1 teaspoon ground cumin
1 teaspoon ground
    coriander
½ teaspoon paprika
Sea salt

TO FINISH
2 tablespoons (30 g)
    unsalted butter, melted

5. To cook the naan on the stovetop: Heat a tawa or a griddle or a skillet over medium heat. Add the naan and cook for 2 to 3 minutes on each side.

6. To bake the naan: Preheat the oven to 475°F (250°C). Also preheat a pizza stone or a sturdy baking sheet. Slide the naan onto the hot stone or baking sheet and bake for 5 to 6 minutes, or until golden all over.

7. Brush with melted butter and serve immediately.

UIGHUR SCALLION PANCAKES

BING

CHINA

Uighur Chinese are Muslims, and their food reflects the restrictions of their religion and also the fact that they are Turkic people with a diet that includes wheat products such as noodles, pancakes, and bread. These pancakes have been adopted by the wider Chinese population and you find them on menus of Chinese restaurants that are not owned by Muslims. I had them first in a wonderful Muslim Chinese restaurant in Milpitas, California, where I was taken by Carolyn Phillips, the author of the wonderful *All Under Heaven*, and where I also tried hand-shaved noodles for the first time. I would have given a recipe for those here if they weren't so difficult to make—unless you have been making them forever.

MAKES 6 INDIVIDUAL PANCAKES

FOR THE DOUGH
2¼ cups (270 g) unbleached all-purpose flour, plus more for kneading and shaping
1¼ cups (150 g) cake flour
Vegetable oil, for greasing the bowl

FOR THE FILLING
1 teaspoon sea salt
½ teaspoon ground toasted Sichuan peppercorns (optional)
¼ cup (60 g) chicken fat or melted ghee
3 tablespoons peanut oil or vegetable oil
4 scallions, very finely chopped (about ⅔ cup)

TO FINISH
Vegetable oil, for frying

1. To make the dough: Mix the flours in a bowl. Measure out ½ cup (60 g) of the flour mixture and set aside. Make a well in the center of the flour left in the bowl. Gradually add 1¼ cups (310 ml) warm water to the well, bringing in the flour as you go along until you have a rough ball of dough.

2. Transfer the dough to a lightly floured work surface. Dust both hands with a little flour and gently knead the dough for 3 minutes. Shape the dough into a ball, invert the bowl over it, and let rest for 15 minutes. Knead for 3 more minutes, or until the dough is very soft but manageable. Brush a clean bowl with a little oil and place the dough in the bowl. Cover with plastic wrap or a damp towel and let the dough rest for 20 to 30 minutes.

3. To make the filling: Put the reserved ½ cup (60 g) flour mixture in a bowl. Add the salt, Sichuan peppercorns (if using), chicken fat, and oil and mix well. Keep the scallions next to the flour mixture.

4. To shape the pancakes: Divide the dough into 6 equal portions and roll each portion into a smooth ball. Take one ball—keep the others covered so that they do not dry out—and with a Chinese or regular rolling pin, roll out the ball into a strip, as thin as you can without tearing the dough, about 18 inches (45 cm) long. Smear one-sixth of the flour mixture over the strip and sprinkle one-sixth of the scallions along the long side

Recipe continues

of the strip. Roll up the strip over the scallions to form a log, then pull this log gently to stretch it to 24 inches (60 cm) long. Coil the log into a round, a little like a cinnamon roll. Shape the rest of the dough in the same way until you have 6 coiled rounds. Roll out each coiled round until it is 8 inches (20 cm) in diameter. Traditionally these are made thicker but I like them thin and crisp.

5. To finish: Heat a skillet over medium-high heat and brush the bottom with a little oil. As soon as the oil is hot, place a pancake in the pan. Cook until the bottom is golden, 2 to 3 minutes. Flip, cover, and cook until the second side turns golden too. Remove to a plate lined with paper towels and keep the bread warm in a 250°F (120°C) oven for up to 20 minutes. Serve warm.

BREAD-BASED
DISHES

SENEGALESE BREAD ROLLS
PETITS PAINS SENEGALAIS

Senegal was a French colony until the country gained its independence in 1960, but one relic left over from the French occupation is their predilection for crusty bread, be it their own version of the French baguette, which they call *tapalapa* and make with a mixture of different flours, or these gorgeous rolls, which are pretty straightforward and very simple to make.

MAKES 8 INDIVIDUAL BREADS

Just over 4 cups (500 g) unbleached all-purpose flour, plus more for kneading and shaping

1 packet (7g/ 2¼ teaspoons) instant (fast-acting) yeast

1 teaspoon fine sea salt

¼ cup (60 ml) extra-virgin olive oil

1. Mix the flour, yeast, and salt in a large bowl and make a well in the center. Add the oil to the well and, with the tips of your fingers, rub the oil into the flour. Gradually add 1⅓ cups (325 ml) warm water, bringing in the flour as you go along. Knead until you have a rough, rather sticky ball of dough.

2. Transfer the dough to a lightly floured work surface. Sprinkle a little flour on the dough and knead for 3 minutes. Shape into a ball, invert the bowl over the dough, and let rest for 15 minutes. Knead for 3 more minutes, or until the dough is smooth and elastic and rather soft. Shape the dough into a ball and place in an oiled bowl, turning it to coat all over with oil. Cover with plastic wrap and let rise in a warm, draft-free place for 1 hour, or until more or less doubled in size.

3. Transfer the dough to your work surface. Divide into 8 equal portions, each weighing about 3½ ounces (100 g). Roll each portion of dough into a ball. Cover with a very damp kitchen towel and let rest for 45 minutes.

4. Preheat the oven to 450°F (230°C).

5. Roll one ball of dough into a log about 18 inches (45 cm) long and ¾ inch (2 cm) thick. Coil the log into a spiral and transfer to a nonstick baking sheet (or a regular baking sheet lined with parchment paper or a silicone baking mat). Make the other rolls the same way.

6. Bake for 20 to 25 minutes, or until golden brown. Let cool on a wire rack. Serve as is or reheated.

ARABIAN "PASTA" with MEAT and VEGETABLES

MARGUGA

Marguga means "thinned" or "rolled out," and traditionally the dish is made with thin strips of dough. I like to call it Arabian "pasta," because it was traditionally made with dough. However, most home cooks nowadays no longer use fresh dough. Instead they make *marguga* with already baked bread, such as Iranian *barbari* or lavash, which they cut into long thin strips. All of those I have spoken to have assured me that the dish is just as good made with baked bread and I am happy to take their word for it as, like them, I am all for saving time in the kitchen. You find this dish in Qatar, the United Arab Emirates, and Bahrain as well as in Saudi Arabia where it goes by the name of *mataziz*. I have had both the Qatari and Emirati versions and they differ only slightly, with the spicing of the Qatari version being a little stronger than that of the Emirati version.

SERVES 4 TO 6

1 whole organic chicken (3 pounds 5 ounces/ 1.5 kg), skinned and cut into 8 pieces

1 cup (250 ml) sunflower oil, plus more for deep-frying

2 medium onions (10½ ounces/300 g total), finely chopped

1 whole star anise

8 whole cloves

3 fresh curry leaves

3 cloves garlic, minced to a fine paste

½ teaspoon minced fresh ginger

1 green chili, slit lengthwise halfway down the middle

5 green cardamom pods

1 cinnamon stick

1 tablespoon b'zar (Arabian Spice Mixture, page 366)

1 tablespoon ground turmeric

1 tablespoon paprika

1 teaspoon ground coriander

1 teaspoon ground cumin

½ teaspoon ground cardamom

½ teaspoon ground cinnamon

½ teaspoon ground fennel

¼ teaspoon red pepper flakes

Sea salt

4 large tomatoes (7 ounces/200 g total), peeled and processed in a food processor until completely pureed

½ cup (125 g) tomato paste

2 large zucchini (7 ounces/200 g total), cut into large chunks

2 large potatoes (7 ounces/ 200 g total), cut into large chunks

2 large carrots (7 ounces/ 200 g total), cut into large chunks

1¼ pounds (550 g) peeled pumpkin, cut into large chunks

½ green bell pepper, cut into chunks

3 large or 6 small black dried limes, pierced in a few places

4 cups (1 liter) boiling water

2 tablespoons finely chopped fresh cilantro

2 tablespoons finely chopped fresh flat-leaf parsley

2 tablespoons finely chopped fresh dill

½ to 1 very large Iranian Flatbread (page 9), cut into long narrow strips

1 large globe eggplant, sliced into medium-thick rounds

1. Put the chicken pieces in a skillet and place over medium heat to dry-roast them and get rid of any excess liquid and smell. (I doubt you will need to do this in the West, but this step is considered essential in Qatar.)

2. Heat the oil in a large pot over medium heat. Add the onions and fry until golden, about 10 minutes. Add the star anise, cloves, and curry leaves. Then add the chicken, garlic, ginger, and whole green chili. Sauté for a couple of minutes.

3. Add the whole spices, ground spices, salt to taste, the tomato pulp, tomato paste, zucchini, potatoes, carrots, pumpkin, bell pepper, and dried limes and stir for a couple of minutes. Add the boiling water, cover, and let bubble gently for 40 minutes.

4. Add the fresh herbs and another 2 cups (500 ml) water. Cover and cook for 30 minutes. Add the bread (to taste depending on how silky you like your stew) and cook, covered, for 15 minutes, or until the bread has softened and is somewhat dissolved in the sauce.

5. Meanwhile, deep-fry the eggplant. Set a wire rack in a rimmed baking sheet. Pour 2 inches (5 cm) sunflower oil into a deep frying pan. Heat the oil over medium heat until hot (if you drop a piece of bread in the oil, the oil should immediately bubble around it). Add the eggplant and fry until golden brown. Remove to the wire rack to drain the excess oil.

6. Transfer the *marguga* to a large shallow serving dish and arrange the fried eggplant all over. Serve very hot.

SAUDI EGGPLANT FATTEH

FATTET BATENJAN ASSWAD

The word *fatteh* comes from the Arabic verb *fatta*, meaning "to break up" or "to crumble," and it refers to the bread element of this composite dish made of bread, meat (lamb, chicken, or sheep's trotters), and/or chickpeas and yogurt and topped with toasted pine nuts. The bread is toasted or fried, then broken up and spread on the plate before being covered with the other ingredients. The recipe varies from country to country, and within each country there are different ways of making *fatteh*. The Arabian Gulf version is known as *tharid* (page 85) and it is reputed to have been the Prophet Muhammad's favorite dish. The Egyptian version is somewhat more complex, with added rice and tomato sauce, while the Saudi version below is made with fried vegetables. Most versions of *fatteh* are main courses, but when made with chickpeas alone, it becomes a breakfast dish in both Lebanon and Syria.

SERVES 4

2 tablespoons extra-virgin olive oil
1 small onion (about 3½ ounces/100 g), thinly sliced
1 medium tomato (about 3½ ounces/100 g), cut into small dice

½ teaspoon finely ground black pepper
Sea salt
½ cup plus 1 tablespoon (140 ml) sunflower oil
3 medium zucchini (about 10½ ounces/300 g in total), cut into sticks as for French fries

2 small Japanese eggplants (about 5 ounces/150 g in total), cut into sticks as for French fries
2 cups (17 ounces/500 g) Greek yogurt
3 cloves garlic, minced to a fine paste

2 medium pita breads, split horizontally into 4 disks, or 4 Turkish durum breads, toasted in a medium oven until golden brown
¼ cup (50 g) pine nuts, toasted in a hot oven for 5 minutes

1. Heat the olive oil in a large skillet over medium heat. Add the onion and sauté until golden, about 10 minutes. Add the tomato, black pepper, and salt to taste and cook until the tomatoes have softened but have not turned completely mushy.

2. Set a fine-mesh rack over a rimmed baking sheet or line it with paper towels. Heat the sunflower oil in another large skillet over medium heat. Fry the zucchini until cooked through, crisp and golden. Place on the rack to drain or drain on paper towels. Sprinkle with salt to taste. Repeat with the eggplants.

3. Mix the yogurt with the garlic and season with salt to taste.

4. To assemble the *fatteh*: Put a disk of toasted bread on a plate. Arrange twice as much zucchini as eggplant in a nice pile in the center of the bread. Top with one-quarter of the onion-tomato mixture. Drizzle one-quarter of the yogurt over the vegetables without entirely covering them. Garnish with one-quarter of the pine nuts. Quickly make the other 3 plates in the same way. Serve immediately.

SAUDI MEAT FATTEH

LUHUH

In this variation on the Saudi Eggplant Fatteh (opposite), the bread element is pancakes similar to *anjero* (Somali Pancakes, page 8) or the sweet hand pies, or *qatayef* (page 474), rather than toasted bread. Usually the pancakes are bought from specialist makers but I sometimes use English crumpets that I cut in half. And instead of the vegetables, there is a layer of ground meat cooked in a tomato sauce. In the Syrian town of Hama, they have a similar meat and yogurt dish that is served without the bread element.   SERVES 6

¼ cup (60 ml) vegetable oil
2 small onions (7 ounces/200 g total), halved lengthwise and cut into thin wedges

4 cloves garlic, minced to a fine paste
1 pound 2 ounces (500 g) ground lamb shoulder
1½ teaspoons finely ground black pepper
½ teaspoon ground cumin

Pinch of ground cinnamon
Two 14-ounce (400 g) cans whole peeled tomatoes, drained and finely chopped

Sea salt
1¾ pounds (800 g) small pancakes (see headnote)
2 cups (17 ounces/500 g) Greek yogurt
Cumin seeds, for garnish

1. Heat the oil in a large skillet over medium heat. Add the onions and sauté, stirring occasionally, until golden. Add the garlic and sauté until fragrant.

2. Add the ground meat and cook, breaking up any lumps, until it is no longer pink, about 5 minutes. Add the spices, tomatoes, and salt to taste and cook until the sauce has thickened.

3. Spread out the *qatayef* on a serving platter. Spoon the meat mixture all over, leaving some of the edges showing. Cover with yogurt, leaving bits of meat showing to break the white. Sprinkle with cumin seeds and serve immediately.

LEBANESE LAMB FATTEH

FATTET GHANAM

This is the Levantine version of *tharid* (page 85). Of all the versions of *fatteh*, it is the lightest, especially if you toast the bread as I do instead of frying it.   SERVES 4

¾ cup (150 g) dried chickpeas, soaked overnight in water to cover by 1 inch (2.5 cm) with ¾ teaspoon baking soda

2¼ pounds (1 kg) lamb leg or shoulder, trimmed of fat, cut into medium chunks

2 cinnamon sticks

Coarse sea salt

2 ounces (60 g) pine nuts

1 large pita bread, split into 2 disks and toasted

1 clove garlic, minced to a fine paste

3½ cups (28 ounces/ 875 g) Greek yogurt

Fine sea salt

1.   Drain and rinse the chickpeas. Put in a pot and with fresh water to cover by about 1 inch (2.5 cm) and bring to a boil over medium heat. Cover, reduce the heat to low, and simmer for 1 hour, or until they are tender.

2.   Meanwhile, put the meat in a pot, add 4 cups (1 liter) water, and place over medium heat. As the water is about to boil, skim the froth from the surface, add the cinnamon sticks and salt to taste. Cover the pan and let bubble gently for 45 minutes, or until the meat is tender.

3.   Take the meat out of the broth and cut into bite-size pieces. Strain the broth into a clean shallow pot and add back the pieces of meat. Remove the chickpeas with a slotted spoon and add to the meat. (At this point you can set the meat and chickpeas aside until you are ready to serve the *fatteh*. I often prepare the meat and chickpeas the day before and reheat and assemble the dish just before serving.)

4.   Preheat the oven to 425°F (220°C).

5.   Spread the pine nuts on a baking sheet and toast in the hot oven for 5 to 6 minutes, or until golden brown. Lay the pita disks on another baking sheet and toast in the oven until golden brown. Let the nuts and bread cool.

6.   Mix together the garlic, yogurt, and salt to taste.

7.   Break the toasted pita into bite-size pieces and spread over the bottom of a serving platter. Spread the meat and chickpeas over the bread. Sprinkle 2 or 3 tablespoons lamb broth over the meat and chickpeas and cover with the yogurt. Scatter the sautéed pine nuts all over the yogurt. Serve immediately.

EGYPTIAN FATTAH
FATTAT LAHM

Fattah, as it is pronounced in Egypt, is quite different from the Lebanese, Syrian, or Saudi *fatteh*. It is often made with sheep's trotters and has added layers of boiled rice and tomato sauce, making for a much more substantial version. It is prepared for Eid al-Adha (the feast of the sacrifice) as well as to celebrate the arrival of a new baby as part of an *'Aqeeqah*, which is a banquet prepared for family and friends to celebrate a newborn. In Islam the *'Aqeeqah* is the animal sacrifice that is offered on behalf of the newborn on the seventh day after birth. The custom was practiced by Arabs before the advent of Islam.

SERVES 4 TO 6

4 lamb shanks (3 pounds 5 ounces/1.5 kg total)

2 cups (400 g) short-grain rice, Egyptian if you can find it

2 tablespoons (30 g) unsalted butter

Sea salt

FOR THE TOMATO SAUCE

1 tablespoon (7 g) unsalted butter

2 cloves garlic, minced to a fine paste

One 14-ounce (400 g) can chopped tomatoes

2 teaspoons tomato paste

2 tablespoons vinegar

Sea salt and finely ground black pepper

3 cups (24 ounces/750 g) Greek yogurt

4 cloves garlic, minced to a fine paste

Sea salt

4 medium pita breads, split into 8 disks and toasted or fried in vegetable oil until golden

¼ cup (40 g) pine nuts, toasted in a hot oven for 5 minutes

1. Put the meat in a large pot and cover well with water. Place over medium heat and skim froth that rises to the surface as the water is about to boil. Reduce the heat to low, then cook, covered, for 1 hour 30 minutes, or until the meat is very tender. Take the meat off the bone and return to the broth to keep hot.

2. Rinse the rice under cold water and put in a pan. Add 4 cups (1 liter) water, the butter, and salt to taste and bring to a boil over medium heat. Reduce the heat, cover, and simmer for 15 minutes, or until the water is fully absorbed. Wrap the lid with a clean kitchen towel, replace over the pan and take off the heat.

3. To make the tomato sauce: Melt the butter in a saucepan over medium heat. Add the garlic and sauté until fragrant. Add the chopped tomatoes, tomato paste, and vinegar and season with salt and pepper to taste. Cook for another 15 minutes, stirring regularly, until the sauce thickens.

4. Mix the yogurt with the minced garlic and season with salt to taste.

5. To assemble the *fattah*: This should be done just as you are ready to serve it. Spread the toasted bread over the bottom of a shallow serving bowl. Cover with the rice. Scoop the lamb out of the broth with a slotted spoon and scatter over the rice. Drizzle with the tomato sauce. Cover with the yogurt mixture and sprinkle the toasted pine nuts all over. Serve immediately.

SYRIAN FATTEH
FATTET AL-MAKDUSS

The first time I tasted this *fatteh* was at Naranj, a large, glitzy restaurant converted from an old house just off Straight Street in Damascus with a delightful roof terrace. The waiters wore elegant modern takes on the traditional *'abaya* (long robe-like garment) and the menu also offered a modern take on regional specialities including this *fatteh* that is my favorite among all the variations. The bread is traditionally fried in olive oil but I prefer to brush it with olive oil and toast it in the oven. As for the meat element here, it is minced and stuffed inside baby eggplants that are cooked in a lamb broth before being layered in between the bread and the yogurt.   SERVES 4

FOR THE LAMB BROTH
1 pound 1 ounce
    (500 g) lamb from
    the shanks, cut into
    medium-size chunks
1 cinnamon stick
1 large onion (7 ounces/
    200 g), peeled and
    quartered
Sea salt
3 large ripe tomatoes,
    peeled, deseeded and
    finely chopped

**FOR THE STUFFED
EGGPLANTS**
6½ tablespoons (100 g)
    ghee or unsalted butter
⅓ cup (50 g) pine nuts
10½ ounces (300 g)
    freshly minced lean
    lamb, from the
    shoulder or neck (either
    ask your butcher to
    mince the lamb or do it
    yourself using the fine
    attachment on a meat
    grinder)
½ teaspoon ground
    allspice
½ teaspoon ground
    cinnamon

1. For the lamb broth: Put the meat from the shanks in a large saucepan and cover with water. Place over medium heat and bring to a boil, skimming any froth that rises to the surface. Add the cinnamon stick, onion, and salt to taste. Reduce the heat to medium low. Cover the pan and let simmer for 30 minutes or until the meat is half done. Add the chopped tomatoes and let simmer for 30 more minutes, or until the meat is done. Keep hot in the pan.

2. To make the stuffed eggplants: Put half the ghee in a frying pan and place over medium heat. Add the pine nuts and sauté, stirring constantly, until the nuts are golden brown. Remove with a slotted spoon onto a plate. Add the minced lamb. Cook, stirring the meat and mashing it with a wooden spoon to break up any lumps, until all traces of pink are gone. Add the allspice, cinnamon, and salt and pepper to taste. Return the toasted pine nuts to the pan, keeping some for garnish, and mix well. Let the meat and nut mixture cool before using to stuff the eggplants.

3. Cup your hand around a cored eggplant, holding it upright, and scoop a little stuffing with your other hand or using a very small spoon, and push the stuffing inside the eggplant, using either the narrow spoon or your finger to force it down. Shake the eggplant downward halfway through to make sure the stuffing has gone to the bottom of the eggplant. Stuff the remaining eggplants in the same way.

4. Put the remaining butter in a saucepan and place over medium heat. When the butter has melted, add the stuffed eggplants and sauté until they turn pale in color. Add 1½ cups (375 ml) of the meat broth to the pan. Turn the heat to medium low and let simmer for about an hour, or until the eggplants are done. Keep them hot while you prepare the rest of the dish.

Sea salt and finely ground
   black pepper
2 pounds 2 ounces (1 kg)
   Japanese eggplants,
   trimmed and cored

TO FINISH
3 medium pita breads
Extra-virgin olive oil to
   brush the bread
3 cups (24 ounces/750 g)
   Greek yogurt
2 tablespoons tahini
2 cloves garlic, peeled,
   minced into a fine paste
A few sprigs mint, leaves
   only, finely chopped

5. Preheat the oven to 400°F (200°C).

6. Tear the pita breads open at the seam, brush with a little olive oil, and toast in the oven until golden brown. Remove onto a wire rack to cool.

7. Mix the yogurt with the tahini, garlic, and mint. Spread out the toasted bread over the bottom of a deep serving dish. Remove the meat from the hot broth and spread over the bread. Then arrange the stuffed eggplants over the bread and meat and cover with the yogurt. Garnish with the reserved toasted pine nuts and serve immediately.

ARABIAN MEAT and VEGETABLE STEW over CRISPY BREAD

THARID

Tharid is the Arabian Gulf version of the Levantine *fatteh*, made with a lot more bread and topped with a hearty meat and vegetable stew. It is said to have been the Prophet Muhammad's favorite dish, and is a staple during Ramadan, being an essential part of the *iftar* meal. Whereas bread is an equal component of *fatteh*, the whole point of *tharid* is that bread be a substantial part of the dish. In the Gulf, the bread used is *regag* (page 16) but this is not readily available in the United States. The nearest you can get to it is by toasting *markouk* ("handkerchief bread") or very thin lavash until it is completely crisp, then breaking it up and using it as with *regag*. Both *markouk* and lavash will use more broth to soften, so make sure you add enough broth to soften the bread before topping it with the meat and vegetables. The cooking time and the amount of water needed will change depending on the meat you use. Last time I made *tharid*, I used the meat from a young ewe, which needed longer cooking.

SERVES 4 TO 6

4½ pounds (2 kg) boneless lamb shoulder or leg, or neck fillets (see Note)

2 ounces (60 g) caul fat, chopped

2 large tomatoes (14 ounces/400 g)

4 inches (10 cm) fresh ginger, peeled and cut into chunks

2 cloves garlic, peeled

1 medium onion (5 ounces/150 g), peeled and quartered

2 tablespoons tomato paste

4 black dried limes, pierced in a few places

2 bay leaves

2 dried chilies

2 tablespoons b'zar (Arabian Spice Mixture, page 366)

1 tablespoon ground cumin

1 teaspoon finely ground black pepper

¼ teaspoon ground cardamom

¼ teaspoon whole cloves

18 baby carrots

18 baby potatoes

18 baby zucchini

8 regag breads (or 2 to 3 handkerchief breads, toasted until crisp but not browned)

---

1. Put the meat, caul fat, and 2½ quarts (2.5 liters) water in a large pot and bring to a boil over medium heat. Drain the broth and pour the same amount of clean water over the meat. This will ensure you have a clean-tasting broth.

2. Put the tomatoes, fresh ginger, garlic, and onion in a food processor and process until completely pureed.

Recipe continues

3. Add the tomato puree to the lamb broth along with the tomato paste, dried limes, bay leaves, chilies, and spices and let bubble for 1 hour, until the lamb is tender (see Note).

4. Add the carrots and potatoes and cook for 10 minutes. Add the zucchini and cook for 10 more minutes.

5. Break up 2 sheets of *regag* or 1 sheet of toasted handkerchief bread in a shallow serving dish. Pour enough lamb broth over the bread to let it become soft but not soupy. Spread another layer of broken bread and add more broth. Make another layer, softening the bread with broth until you have a fairly thick layer of moistened bread, about 2 inches (5 cm) deep. Arrange the meat and vegetables over the bread and serve immediately.

NOTE: *You could also make this with veal or ewe (same cuts as above). If you do, increase the water in the broth to 3 quarts (3 liters), and cook the meat for 2 hours as it will need longer cooking to become tender.*

SWEET RECIPES
using BREAD

THE BREAD of the HAREM
AYSH EL-SARAYA

The name of this Lebanese sweet is somewhat confusing. *Saraya* and *seraglio* mean both harem and a sultan's palace. I am going for the harem translation as I cannot imagine a bread pudding being a sweet for kings, given what a modest ingredient bread is. It makes more sense to think of it as a sweet for concubines. I am being facetious here as I don't know much about the origins of this dessert apart from the fact that it is totally luscious despite its being made from pretty simple, basic ingredients such as bread and sugar. The cream makes it luxurious and the slivered pistachios add a welcome crunch.

SERVES 4 TO 6

One day-old 8-inch (20 cm) round loaf white bread (about 14 ounces/400 g)

1¼ cups (250 g) raw cane sugar

1 teaspoon lemon juice

¾ cup (180 ml) boiling water

1 tablespoon orange blossom water

1 tablespoon rose water

1¼ cups (300 g) Arabic clotted cream (see page 516) or English clotted cream

2 tablespoons slivered pistachios, for garnish (see Note)

1. Trim off and discard the crusts of the bread (or reserve it for making breadcrumbs). Tear the bread into rough 1-inch (2.5 cm) pieces.

2. Combine ¼ cup (60 ml) water, the sugar, and lemon juice in a medium saucepan. Bring to a boil over medium heat and cook, stirring constantly so that the sugar does not recrystallize in places, until the syrup has caramelized to a golden brown color, about 15 minutes; be careful not to burn it. Gradually add the boiling water, stirring with a long-handled wooden spoon; the syrup will splatter when you add the water, so make sure you do this very slowly and cautiously. Take off the heat and add the orange blossom water and rose water.

3. Add the bread to the syrup and cook over medium heat, pressing down on the bread with the back of the spoon to mash it up and help it soak up the syrup, for 5 to 10 minutes, or until it has absorbed the syrup.

4. Spread the bread into an even layer in an 8-inch (20 cm) round serving platter. If there is any syrup left in the pan, pour it over the bread. Let cool for about 20 minutes. Then, spread the cream over the bread, leaving a little of the edge showing. Garnish with the slivered pistachios and serve straightaway. If you want to refrigerate it, reserve the pistachio garnish until just before serving.

NOTE: *Pistachios are used as a garnish, for both sweet and savory dishes, throughout the Middle East. In the Levant they are used in mostly ground form, whereas in Iran they are slivered into beautiful green sticks to add color and crunch to both rice dishes and desserts. You can, of course, cut whole ones into slivers, but it is much easier to source ready-slivered pistachios from Persian or Middle Eastern stores.*

EGYPTIAN BREAD "PUDDING"

UMM ALI

Umm ali is the classic Egyptian dessert, an Arab version of bread pudding made with layers of very thin crisp flatbread and toasted nuts soaked with sweetened milk. I use a larger quantity of nuts than most people to give the pudding more crunch and I omit the melted butter. I also add a little orange blossom water to the milk to add an intriguing flavor note. Egyptians use *reqaq* (which means "flattened very thin") bread, which is not widely available in the West, so I suggest using toasted *markouk* ("handkerchief bread") or the thinnest lavash you can find, although I find it ironic that you first toast bread in order to then soak it in milk. *Umm ali* is best served freshly baked so that the bread retains a slight crunch, and it is a good idea to time it so that it can be served straight out of the oven.

SERVES 4 TO 6

7 ounces (250 g) markouk (handkerchief bread), about 1¾ sheets

2⅓ cups (350 g) mixed nuts (pistachios, hazelnuts, peanuts, cashews, almonds, and walnuts)

3 cups (750 ml) organic whole milk

½ cup (100 g) raw cane sugar

1 tablespoon orange blossom water

¼ cup (50 g) golden raisins, soaked for about 1 hour in water

Crème fraîche, for serving

1. Preheat the oven to 400°F (200°C).

2. Lay one sheet of *markouk* over a large baking sheet and toast for about 8 minutes, until golden. Remove from the baking sheet and lay the remaining sheet on the baking sheet. Toast until crisp and golden. Keep the oven on.

3. Break the toasted bread into medium pieces and arrange half of the toasted bread in a 2½-inch (6 cm) deep oval baking dish about 11 x 6 inches (27.5 x 15 cm).

4. Spread the nuts on a large baking sheet and toast in the oven for 10 to 12 minutes, or until golden brown. Remove from the oven and let cool.

5. Put the milk and sugar in a saucepan and bring to a boil over medium heat, stirring every now and then. Remove from the heat and add the orange blossom water.

6. Drain the golden raisins and spread half of them over the bread. Spread half the nuts over the raisins and cover with the remaining bread. Pour the hot milk over the bread and scatter the remaining raisins and nuts all over the top.

7. Bake for about 20 minutes, or until the milk is almost completely absorbed and the bread is a little crisp around the edges. Serve immediately with crème fraîche for each diner to dollop over their *umm ali*.

THE WHOLE BEAST

Eid al-Fitr (the feast of breaking the fast) marks the end of Ramadan and it is when Muslims all around the world, at least those who can afford it, buy a whole sheep or goat, or even a baby camel, to slaughter and give thanks to Allah for having marked the end of another year's fast. Some families will use part of the animal for their own festive meals and distribute the rest to those less fortunate, while others will distribute the whole animal, or more than one animal, depending on their means.

Eid al-Adha (the feast of the sacrifice), which comes about two months after Eid al-Fitr, is another occasion for buying whole animals, but this time, the meat is usually feasted upon by family and friends, although many will also share some with those in need.

In the early days of Islam, when the Prophet Muhammad lived in Mecca, an oasis in the Arabian desert, his diet and that of those around him consisted of mostly meat, dairy, and dates. The meat they ate daily would have been cuts that they grilled, stewed, or boiled, but when they celebrated special occasions or received important guests, they roasted whole lamb, goats, or baby camels.

Serving a whole animal, whether it is milk-fed or fully grown, is still very much a part of Muslim culinary tradition, whether to honor guests, to welcome family members returning from long trips abroad, or to celebrate religious or special occasions. Whole animals are also on the menu for large family gatherings on weekends—in the Arabian Gulf, Friday is the day when the whole family gathers to eat together and enjoy each other's company. In cities, it will be lamb or goat, but in the desert, the weekend family meal of Gulf Bedouins will often consist of a whole roast baby camel served on a bed of rice.

The way whole animals are cooked varies from one country to another. In the Emirates, the animal is marinated in a mixture of spices, rose water, saffron, and lemon juice, then wrapped in a wet straw mat and buried in a pit oven to roast slowly until the meat falls off the bone. Another spectacular way of cooking whole animals, which is reserved for grand occasions such as weddings or state occasions, is to roast whole baby

camels in the seated position, usually by burying them in a very large pit oven to let them slow-roast overnight. The seated roast animals are then carefully lifted and placed on huge platters of rice that are laid on large tables in the *majliss* (reception area) or banquet hall. Guests gather around each roast camel and tear pieces of meat with their hands to eat with the rice. Once they have had their fill, they will make way for other guests (usually less important) and will go to wash their hands, and so on until all the guests have eaten. The leftovers are then taken back to the kitchens for the staff to also enjoy the occasion.

My first-ever experience of being served a whole animal was in Sharjah, one of the seven United Arab Emirates (UAE), where Sheikha Bodour al-Qasimi, the daughter of the Emir, had invited me to introduce me to the Emirates' culinary delights. On my first day there, she had kindly arranged for a group of women to prepare a veritable feast in Sharjah's Heritage Center. I still remember the roast baby goat, served on a bed of fluffy rice, and garnished with a wonderful sweet-savory mixture of caramelized onions, yellow split peas, and raisins. Absolutely exquisite! A few years later, I was invited to another amazing meal in Doha, Qatar, by Mrs. Al-Fardan, a member of a preeminent Qatari merchant family. She also served a roast baby goat, but hers was laid on a bed of fluffy saffron rice with only a plain garnish of crisp caramelized onions. Less complex but just as exquisite!

Domestic ovens are not large enough to take whole animals, even when they are small, so I have scaled down most of the recipes for whole animals to a shoulder, a leg, or a quarter animal. The dish may not look as spectacular but it will be just as delicious and will still impress your family and friends. And I have, of course, included recipes for many meat dishes using a variety of cuts, which people eat on normal days.

I have also included in this chapter recipes that use dairy, a direct product of the whole animal and an essential part of the diet of most Muslims. There are recipes for how to prepare various dairy products as well as recipes for using them in various dishes, yogurt being an important ingredient in the Middle East, Central Asia, and the Indian subcontinent.

BABY GOAT ROAST

AL-MASHWI OR AL-MADFUN

Here is the home version of the Emirati *madfun*. Traditionally, the lamb was wrapped in a wet straw mat and cooked in a pit oven, with the mat placed directly on the embers. Obviously, the taste of *mashwi* roasted in a home oven is going to be different, but short of building a pit oven in the garden (if you have a garden), this recipe will be the closest you will get to a traditional *madfun* in a contemporary kitchen. The marinade is a heady mixture of rose water, saffron, spices, garlic, and lemon juice, which gives the meat a wonderfully exotic flavor without overpowering it. I often serve this roast with the Emirati Biryani on page 208.   SERVES 8 TO 10

1 baby goat or baby lamb (10 to 12 pounds/4 to 5 kg), a large leg of lamb, or a shoulder of lamb with part of the rib cage still attached
Juice of 2 to 3 lemons
Sea salt

FOR THE MARINADE
1 tablespoon b'zar (Arabian Spice Mixture, page 366)

1 tablespoon ground turmeric
1 teaspoon ground cardamom
1 teaspoon ground coriander
1 teaspoon ground cumin
1 teaspoon ground ginger
1 teaspoon ground dried lime

1 teaspoon finely ground black pepper
4 large cloves garlic, minced to a fine paste
Juice of ½ lemon
Good pinch of saffron threads, soaked for 15 minutes in ½ cup (125 ml) rose water
Emirati ghee or regular ghee or unsalted butter

FOR THE BASTING SAUCE
⅓ cup (60 g) seedless tamarind paste, soaked in 1 cup (250 ml) water
½ cup (125 ml) rose water
Good pinch of saffron threads
1 tablespoon b'zar (Arabian Spice Mixture, page 366)
Juice of 1 lemon
Sea salt

1. Rinse the goat and the head (if you were given one) under cold water—it is a good idea to soak the head for a few hours, changing the water regularly to get rid of all the blood. Pat dry with paper towels and rub both with the lemon juice and a little salt. If you are using other cuts, just pat them dry.

2. To make the marinade: Mix all the spices, the crushed garlic, lemon juice, and saffron rose water in a bowl. Brush the goat inside and out with the marinade. Brush a large roasting pan with a little ghee and place the goat in it. Cover loosely with foil and let sit for at least 1 hour to absorb the flavors.

3. Thirty minutes before the goat is ready, preheat the oven to 450°F (230°C).

4. To make the basting sauce: Strain the tamarind water into a clean bowl, pressing on the pulp to extract as much flavor as you can. Stir in the rose water, saffron, b'zar, lemon juice, and salt to taste.

5. Roast the goat uncovered for 2 hours to 2 hours 30 minutes, or until the meat is golden and falling off the bone—if you are using a leg or shoulder, roast for 1 hour 30 minutes. After the first 20 minutes, baste the meat with the basting sauce and add water if the roasting pan is getting too dry, then baste again every 15 minutes or so. If you think it is coloring too quickly, cover loosely with foil.

6. Let sit for about 15 minutes before serving. Serve hot.

IRANIAN STUFFED WHOLE LAMB

BARREH TU POR

This recipe may look daunting, but it is fairly simple to prepare. The only drawback is that most domestic ovens are too small to take in a whole lamb, even when it is a small one—you need to use a lamb that is between 20 to 30 days old. One way to get around this is to ask your butcher to bone the legs so that you can fold them against the rib cage. In any case, it is well worth making as it is one of Iran's most festive dishes, served on large platters on a bed of rice at weddings and other celebrations, and it is bound to impress both your family and friends as you bring it to table, either on a bed of extra rice or simply as is—the rice stuffing will be enough to serve with the meat. The glistening crisp saffron-colored skin is beautiful, and once you tuck into the meat and the sweet-savory stuffing that goes with it, you will be seduced by the rich yet subtle flavors and wonderful contrasting textures. One word of advice: When you order your whole lamb from your butcher, be sure to ask him or her to also give you the offal, as you will need it in the stuffing.

SERVES 8 TO 12

FOR THE STUFFING
2½ cups (500 g) long-grain rice (basmati or Iranian)
Sea salt
¼ cup (60 ml) vegetable oil
4 medium onions (1 pound 5 ounces/600 g total), finely chopped
2 teaspoons ground turmeric
Offal from the lamb (liver, heart, and kidney), trimmed of any fat and outer layer, finely diced

2 bunches scallions (3½ ounces/100 g total), thinly sliced
1 bunch cilantro (7 ounces/200 g), most of the bottom stems discarded, finely chopped
1 bunch flat-leaf parsley (7 ounces/200 g), most of the bottom stems discarded, finely chopped
A few sprigs tarragon, leaves stripped off the stems

1 cup (150 g) walnuts, coarsely chopped
¾ cup (125 g) slivered almonds
½ cup (60 g) slivered pistachios
1⅔ cups (250 g) dried apricots, coarsely chopped
⅓ cup (50 g) dried barberries (zereshk), soaked for 15 minutes in room temperature water and drained
Finely ground black pepper

FOR THE LAMB
Sea salt
2 medium onions (10½ ounces/300 g total), grated on the fine side of a grater
1 whole young lamb (about 15 pounds/7 kg)
1 stick (120 g) unsalted butter, melted
2 good pinches of saffron, steeped in ¼ cup (60 ml) water

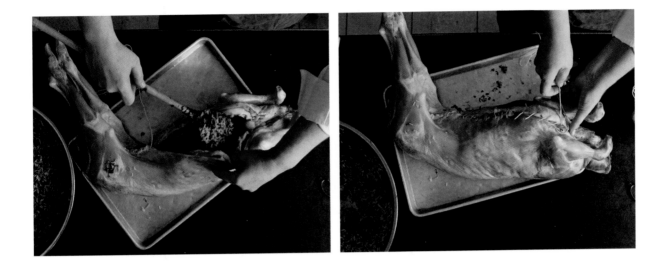

1. To make the stuffing: Rinse the rice under cold water. Fill a large pot with water and add 2 to 3 tablespoons of salt. Bring to a boil over medium heat. Drop the rice into the boiling water and let bubble for 5 minutes. Drain the rice. Rinse under cold water and set aside.

2. Heat the oil in a large skillet over medium heat. Add the onions and cook, stirring regularly, until the onion is golden, about 10 minutes. Stir in the turmeric. Add the offal, scallions, herbs, nuts, apricots, barberries, and salt and pepper to taste. Cook, stirring regularly, for 5 minutes, or until the offal is just cooked through. Add the cooked rice and mix well. Taste and adjust the seasoning if necessary. Take off the heat and let cool.

3. Preheat the oven to 450°F (230°C).

4. To prepare the lamb: Sprinkle a little salt over the grated onion and mix well. Rub the lamb with the salted onion, inside and out. Then use a sturdy needle and thick thread to sew part of the lamb belly shut before pushing the stuffing inside it, spreading it evenly in the belly cavity. Sew the rest of the opening shut.

5. Line a large baking sheet with enough foil to wrap the lamb. Lay the lamb on the foil and brush it all over with the melted butter. Close the foil over the lamb and place in the hot oven. Roast for 30 minutes, then open the foil and baste the lamb with half the saffron water. Close the foil again, return to the hot oven, and roast for 1 hour. Uncover the lamb and baste with the rest of the saffron water and the juices that have come out of the lamb. Cover the lamb, return to the oven, and roast for 30 minutes. Baste the lamb one more time with the lamb juices, then leave uncovered to roast and color for the last 30 minutes.

SAUDI ROAST LAMB SHOULDER
on a Bed of FRAGRANT RICE
MESHWI LAHM 'ALA ROZZ

SAUDI ARABIA

Lamb and goat—and baby camel for special occasions!— are the meats of choice in the Arabian Gulf. Here, in this Saudi version of roast lamb, the shoulder (you can also use the leg) is marinated in a luxurious saffron yogurt marinade and served on a bed of fragrant rice. Simple to prepare and absolutely exquisite to serve and eat.

SERVES 4

1 lamb shoulder on the bone (about 4½ pounds/2 kg)
1½ cups plus 1 tablespoon (14 ounces/400 g) Greek yogurt
3 cloves garlic, minced to a fine paste

2 good pinches of saffron threads
Sea salt
2½ cups (500 g) basmati rice, soaked for 30 minutes in lightly salted water
1 teaspoon finely ground black pepper
1 teaspoon ground galangal

½ teaspoon ground cardamom
½ teaspoon ground coriander
¼ teaspoon ground cinnamon
5 whole cloves
Juice of 1 lemon
1½ tablespoons rose water

FOR THE GARNISH
¼ cup (40 g) blanched almonds, toasted in a hot oven for 7 minutes
2 tablespoons pine nuts, toasted in a hot oven for 5 minutes

1. Trim the lamb of all excess fat. Place in a large roasting pan.

2. Mix the yogurt and minced garlic in a large bowl. Add half the saffron and salt to taste and mix well. Let the yogurt sit for 15 to 30 minutes, stirring it every now and then, until it has turned a lovely yellow color from the saffron.

3. Pour the yogurt over the lamb shoulder and coat it well. Cover with plastic wrap and let sit for a couple of hours.

4. Thirty minutes before the shoulder is ready, preheat the oven to 450°F (230°C).

5. Add 2 cups (500 ml) water to the roasting pan. Mix well with the yogurt and loosely cover the lamb shoulder with foil. Roast until done to your liking—if you like your meat pink, calculate 20 minutes per pound, and if you prefer it well done, calculate 30 minutes per pound or a little longer.

6. About 20 minutes before the meat is ready, drain the rice and put it in a saucepan. Take the meat out of the oven and uncover. Drain the juices and add to the rice together

with the spices, lemon juice, and salt to taste. You may need to add a little water (up to 1 cup/250 ml). Return the meat to the oven, leaving it uncovered so that it browns.

7. Bring the rice to a boil, then reduce the heat to medium-low, cover, and simmer for 10 to 15 minutes, or until the rice is tender and has absorbed all the liquid. Check on the level of liquid and if the rice looks too dry, add a little more if needed. When done, take the rice off the heat. Uncover and sprinkle the top of the rice with the rose water. Then wrap the lid with a clean kitchen towel and place back over the rice. Let sit for 5 minutes.

8. Transfer the rice to a large serving platter, making space in the middle to place the shoulder of lamb. Garnish with the toasted almonds and pine nuts and serve.

ROASTING A CAMEL HUMP

UNITED ARAB EMIRATES

A few years ago, I was co-presenting a travel/cookery show in the United Arab Emirates with a delightful poet, Tariq Al-Mehyass, who, unlike many Emirati men, was interested in cooking and not afraid to show it. One day when we were shooting in Al-Ayn, a relatively lush emirate near Abu Dhabi, the producer announced that a local grandee had invited us all to a lavish feast, where camel hump would be the centerpiece of the meal.

We finished our morning filming and got into our respective cars to drive up to the grandee's compound—a collection of villas for him and his children, as well as a separate *majliss* (reception quarters that are very common in the Gulf). As I got out of my car, the producer led me to a different place from where Tariq and the rest of the male crew were headed. When I asked why I was being separated, he explained that our host was very conservative and that, as a woman, I was not allowed into his *majliss*. Instead, I would be dining in the main house, where the women were waiting for me. I was assured, they would bring us food as soon as it was served to the men. I reluctantly accepted the situation, and I could barely muster enough grace to greet my charming hostesses, the grandee's beautiful wife and her mother. I resignedly sat with them in a large dark drawing room, chatting over Arabic coffee while waiting for the food.

After an excruciating wait, several servants arrived with a large covered platter. I eagerly looked on as they uncovered the dish to reveal a pile of large chunks of dark, gristly meat sitting atop a bed of rice. Nothing that looked like a hump. I politely asked if we were going to get any hump. They explained that it was reserved for the men. The offering before us was positively nasty, the meat both tough and tasteless. The camel must have been too old. Most of the time, only baby camels (*h'war* or *qo'ood*; the

latter being slightly older) are served. The rice was good though.

We left soon after lunch—Emirati people don't linger once they've eaten. The traditional sign that it's time to leave is when someone brings out burning incense called *'otoor*. You perfume yourself by fanning the scented smoke toward your hair and clothes, and then you hightail it. As we drove back to the hotel, I sulked, wondering if I would get another chance to taste hump. To obtain one, you need to buy a whole camel—preferably a baby—and have it killed for you. And even if I were prepared to spend the thousand or so dollars it would cost to buy the camel, I had nowhere to cook it.

But the very next day, I was standing in a catering kitchen where I'd come to learn to cook Emirati dishes. As I was being shown around the kitchen, I noticed a chef rubbing a big lump of fat with a yellow marinade. I tried to temper my excitement, thinking that it might just be the tail from a fat-tail lamb. I stopped dead in my tracks and asked nervously if it was a hump. It was. The chef explained that a local man was celebrating the return of his brother from a long job posting abroad, and he had sent them a whole baby camel to cook for the feast. I told the chef my sad story of being denied a taste of the hump because of my gender. He immediately offered to remedy the situation even if the camel in question belonged to someone else. I just had to wait a couple of hours for the camel and a couple of baby goats to roast in a massive covered cauldron topped with glowing charcoal, and set atop a huge gas burner. When the meat was ready, he carefully cut a piece of the fatty hump from the bottom before arranging the rest of the meat over rice. It was better than any camel meat I had eaten—not exactly tender but not stringy either and beautifully seasoned with saffron, rose water, and a complex mixture of spices that is typical to the Emirates called *b'zar*—but, to be honest, still not the camel nirvana I had built up in my mind.

For that, I had to wait another couple of years. When I was staying with my brother in Dubai for the Emirates Literary Festival, I saw my wonderful friend Sheikha Bodour al-Qasimi at the opening of the festival. She had been instrumental in introducing me to the pleasures of Emirati food, and if anyone could help me get a camel hump it was she. So I asked her how I could lay my hands on a camel hump, explaining that I was writing an article about it. With her customary grace and generosity, Sheikha Bodour asked lovely Amani who runs her executive office to help arrange it for me. The very next day, Amani called to give me the choice of just having the hump or going to the camel market to choose the baby camel and have it killed there and then. The market was too far in an area called Maleha, but I did want to see the slaughter, so we decided to have the baby camel brought to Sharjah (a smaller emirate about 30 minutes' drive from Dubai) to the slaughterhouse behind the live animal market—Emiratis often cook whole animals and usually buy them live to have them killed especially for them.

The baby camel arrived alive in the back of a van, sitting quite placidly with his legs folded and tied so that he could not move. A group of immaculate-looking butchers arrived, sporting long white plastic aprons and wellington boots and carrying their knives in white plastic sheaths hanging from one hip with the sharpener hanging on the other. The camel must have realized his fate, because he began braying as soon as the van backed onto the ramp. The men in white dragged him off the van and untied his legs so they could walk him to the killing chamber.

Once they had seated the baby camel in the middle of the chamber, one of the men opened the mouth of the camel and showered it with water. The animal did not resist, nor did it resist when one of the butchers said "Allah Akbar" and slit its throat. After letting the body relax a little, they proceeded to first skin, then butcher it, and finally I could claim my very own camel hump.

I thanked the butchers and carried my prize home to my brother's house. There, I massaged it with saffron, rose water, and *b'zar* (page 366) before roasting it. I followed the same principles as the caterer in Al-Ayn, putting the oven on high and cooking the hump for 2 hours, covering it part of the time with foil so that the top wouldn't burn. The hump looked gorgeous as it came out of the oven, crisp and golden. Both the fat and meat were scrumptious—the baby camel must have been milk-fed. The meat was pale and tender and the fat very soft and not at all fatty if you get my meaning. Some fats coat the tongue in an unpleasant manner but not this one. It was almost the same as lamb's tail fat, which in Lebanon we eat raw with raw liver. Apparently, people also eat the fat from the hump raw. I will have to try it next time around.

Finally, I'd secured the prize that had eluded me for so long. When you want the good stuff, sometimes you have to take matters into your own hands. And now that I'd broken through the camel-cooking barrier, I would be planning a baby camel feast on my brother's terrace, overlooking the Arabian Gulf. I would serve the whole animal, with the hump as the centerpiece, and there would be no one to tell me to go to the women's quarters. To be honest, I never did manage the camel feast because I have not been back to Dubai since, but my advice to you, now that camel milk is in vogue, is to look for a camel farm or a supplier of camel meat (there are a few) and see if they can supply you with the hump, still on the bone as the meaty parts are the two fillets nestled between the rib cage and the spine. And if you manage to get one, follow the recipe for Baby Goat Roast (page 94) to roast your camel hump.

SAUDI CAMEL MEATBALLS

KABAB EL MIRO

The first time I tasted camel was some twenty-five years ago in Damascus, Syria. A friendly taxi driver had driven me to Midan (a working-class neighborhood that sadly has been decimated by the regime as they tried to clear it of rebels) because I had told him I was researching street food. As I walked down the main street—full of street vendors selling all kinds of scrumptious specialties—I came face-to-face with a hairy camel's head. Hanging by its fleshy lips outside a butcher shop, the head was the butcher's rather gruesome shop sign indicating he specialized in camel meat. Like most butchers in Damascus, he had a charcoal grill on which he cooked meat to order for patrons to take away or to eat at a rickety table set to one side of his store. I had never tried camel and I didn't want to pass up the chance, despite the stall's noticeable lack of hygiene. I sat down and asked the butcher to grill me some meat. He suggested I have it ground rather than cubed as it would be too tough otherwise. It was not a gastronomic marvel. The meat was dry with a slightly gamey taste, but I was excited to have tried it. In this recipe, which also uses ground meat, the meatballs are made more interesting by adding millet grains, which provide a nice crunch, and the dipping sauces temper the dryness of the meat. If you can't get camel meat, simply use lamb or beef, or a mixture of both.

SERVES 6 TO 8

FOR THE TAHINI DIP
½ cup plus 2 tablespoons (150 ml) tahini
Juice of 1½ lemons, or to taste
1 clove garlic, minced to a fine paste
Sea salt

FOR THE TAMARIND DIP
1 cup (200 g) seedless tamarind paste
½ teaspoon ground coriander
½ teaspoon finely ground black pepper
A few sprigs cilantro, most of the bottom stems discarded, finely chopped
Sea salt

1. To make the tahini dip: Put the tahini in a bowl and, alternating them, gradually add the lemon juice and ⅓ cup plus 1 tablespoon (100 ml) water, stirring all the time. The tahini will thicken at first even though you are adding liquid, but do not worry; it will soon thin out again. Taste the dip before you use up all the lemon juice to adjust the tartness to your liking. If you decide to use less lemon juice, add a little more water to make up for the lost liquid. Stir until the sauce has the consistency of sour cream. Add the garlic and salt to taste. Mix well.

2. To make the tamarind dip: Put the tamarind paste in a bowl. Add 1⅓ cups (325 ml) hot water and let steep for 15 minutes, then mash the pulp in the water. Line a fine-mesh sieve with cheesecloth and set over a bowl. Strain the tamarind mixture in the sieve, pressing on the pulp to extract as much tamarind as you can. Add the coriander, pepper, and cilantro. Season with salt to taste and mix well.

3. To make the meatballs: Combine the meat, millet, garlic, coriander, pepper, and salt to taste and mix well. Shape the meat into small balls, each the size of a walnut, and place on a baking sheet. Refrigerate for 15 minutes while you heat the oil.

FOR THE MEATBALLS

1 pound 2 ounces (500 g) ground lean camel (or lamb) meat

Scant 1 cup (150 g) uncooked millet

6 cloves garlic, minced to a fine paste

1 teaspoon ground coriander

½ teaspoon finely ground black pepper

Sea salt

Sunflower oil, for deep-frying

4. Set a fine-mesh rack in a rimmed baking sheet or line the baking sheet with several layers of paper towel. Pour 2 inches (5 cm) sunflower oil into a large deep skillet. Heat over medium heat to 350°F (180°C). If you don't have a thermometer, test by dropping a piece of bread into the oil—if the oil immediately bubbles around it, it is ready. Drop in as many meatballs as will fit comfortably in the pan. Fry, stirring the meatballs every now and then, until the millet is golden and the meatballs are cooked through, 3 to 5 minutes. Drain on the wire rack or the paper towels. Serve with the tahini dip and the tamarind dip.

MOROCCAN MECHOUI
MECHOUI

Mechoui in Arabic means "grilled," but in Morocco it means a whole lamb, roasted in a pit oven with twenty or more other lambs, each trussed to a pole and the poles arranged all around the oven leaning against its walls, until the meat is so tender you can pull it off the bone with your hand without the help of any cutlery. You will find *mechoui* stalls in the Medina of Marrakesh and by the slaughterhouse in Casablanca, as well as in the weekly souks. Each will have one large, round clay pit oven where the *mechoui* vendor can bake up to twenty-five whole lambs in one go. Once done the roast lambs are taken out, one at a time, and placed on a large counter onto the street where people gather to buy their chosen cuts, which they carry off wrapped in paper to eat on the go or in a nearby café with mint tea. The meat is not seasoned when it is roasted and it is eaten dipped in a 50/50 mixture of salt and cumin. Often they will take the meat home for an impromptu meal. When you are offered *mechoui* in someone's home, it will usually be a quarter of the lamb as they can roast only quarters (usually the shoulder, ribs, and neck) in their home ovens. You can do the same or simply roast a shoulder as I suggest here.   SERVES 4

1 lamb shoulder on the
   bone (4½ pounds/2 kg)
3½ tablespoons (50 g)
   unsalted butter, at
   room temperature
Sea salt
Ground cumin

1. Preheat the oven to 350°F (180°C).

2. Rub the lamb all over with the softened butter and place on a rack in a roasting pan. Roast for 2 hours to 2 hours 30 minutes, basting the meat every 15 minutes with a little water, until the meat is very tender and the skin is crisp and completely browned.

3. Let the lamb sit for about 20 minutes before serving. Serve with a mixture of salt and cumin in a 1:1 ratio.

MOROCCAN MEAT KEBABS
QOTBANE L'HAM

Kebabs are a constant throughout the Muslim world. From satay to *kefta* to *koobideh* to *galawat* kebabs to *firin* kebabs, there isn't a Muslim country that doesn't offer an amazing array of kebabs, either grilled over charcoal or seared in huge metal pans over wood fires or roasted in large copper baking dishes in wood-fired ovens. The marinades and seasonings, as well as the size of the kebabs, vary from country to country. In Lebanon and Syria, the meat is diced into medium chunks and marinated in a mixture of minced garlic, lemon juice, olive oil, and fairly mild spices whereas in Morocco, the meat is cut small and marinated in a dry mixture of onion, fresh herbs, and spices. In Indonesia, the meat for satay is often left fairly plain with the flavor supplied by the accompanying sauce whereas in Uighur country, it is all about coating the pieces of meat in a mixture of egg and potato starch, for a crisp outside, and seasoning the meat as it grills with cumin and chili. The recipe below is for Moroccan lamb kebab. You can use beef if you want, but choose a tender cut such as filet, sirloin, or rib eye. Even if Moroccans dice their meat very small, I like my grilled meat on the rare side so I am suggesting here to cut the meat in slightly bigger chunks. Serve with a small bowl of salt and cumin (in a 1:1 ratio), Moroccan Bread (page 11), and Mint Tea (page 503).

SERVES 4 TO 6

2¼ pounds (1 kg) tender boneless lamb, cut into into 1-inch (2.5 cm) cubes

1 medium onion (5 ounces/150 g), halved and cut into thin wedges

A few sprigs flat-leaf parsley, most of the bottom stems discarded, finely chopped

1 teaspoon ground cumin

½ teaspoon paprika

1 teaspoon finely ground black pepper

Sea salt

1. Put the cubed meat in a bowl. Add the onion, parsley, cumin, paprika, and pepper. Season with salt to taste (see Note, page 115) and mix well. Let marinate in a cool place or the refrigerator for at least 2 hours.

2. Start a charcoal fire in an outdoor grill or preheat the broiler to high.

3. Thread the meat onto 8 or 12 long skewers depending on how many you want to serve. Cook on the grill or under the broiler for 2 to 3 minutes on each side, or until the meat is done to your liking. Serve hot.

TURKISH KEBABS

SHISH KEBABI

Grilled meats or kebabs are a mainstay of the Muslim world, from Turkey to Iran to India and Pakistan to Muslim China to Indonesia (where kebabs are known as satay), and each country has its own way of preparing the meat or fish and marinating it for grilling. One of the earliest references to kebabs is found in an eleventh-century Turkish dictionary, which describes men as having "competed against each other in skewering meat." It was the Turks who disseminated kebabs all over the Middle East and North Africa during the Ottoman Empire. The recipe below is for classic Turkish meat kebabs, with a marinade that includes tomato paste and a mix of spices for an intense flavor.

SERVES 4

FOR THE MARINADE
3 cloves garlic, minced to a fine paste
3 tablespoons extra-virgin olive oil
1 tablespoon tomato paste
½ teaspoon paprika
¼ teaspoon cayenne pepper
¼ teaspoon ground cinnamon
¼ teaspoon ground cumin
2 tablespoons fresh thyme leaves
Sea salt and finely ground black pepper

FOR THE KEBABS
1¾ pounds (800 g) boneless lamb leg, trimmed of most of the fat and cut into 1-inch (2.5 cm) chunks
24 cherry tomatoes
Flatbread, for serving

1. To make the marinade: Mix together the garlic, olive oil, tomato paste, spices, thyme, and salt and pepper to taste.

2. To prepare the kebabs: Add the meat to the marinade and toss. Let marinate for at least 2 hours.

3. Prepare a charcoal fire in an outdoor grill, switch on the gas if you have an outdoor gas grill, or preheat the broiler to high.

4. Thread the meat onto 7 long skewers and the tomatoes onto an eighth one. Grill over high heat or broil for 3 to 4 minutes on each side, or until the meat and tomatoes are done to your liking. Slip the meat and tomatoes off the skewers onto flatbread and serve immediately.

Lebanese Kebabs (page 108)
and Turkish Kebabs

LEBANESE KEBABS

LAHM MESHWI

Sunday is grilling day in Lebanon. Whether in the city or in the countryside, people will take out their *manqal* (a low grill made of a rectangular metal box set on short legs) to put on their balcony, in the garden, in the courtyard, or simply outside their front door and make a charcoal fire for their grilled meat, chicken, or even fish if they live near the sea. My grandmother lived in Beirut, and every Sunday she would take her *manqal* out onto the balcony where my uncles built the fire while she was in the kitchen seasoning whatever was going on the grill that day. In high summer and autumn, it would often be little birds, which my uncles would have shot in the mountains that morning—during bird season, they often woke up very early to drive out-side of the city to shoot the little birds known as *becfigues* in French because they feed on figs. People are forbidden from shooting them in the West, but the Lebanese still happily feast on these little birds when in season. And I have to admit to forgetting my principles when I am back home during this season and joining in the feasting. My grandmother also grilled fish that used to be brought to her doorstep by door-to-door fishmongers. However, both birds and fish were reserved for special days and, more often than not, she would have chicken wings, other pieces of chicken, or simply the kebabs in this recipe on the grill. The same marinade can be used for both chicken wings and boneless chicken. The kebabs made with chicken are called *shish tawuk*, and the wings *jawaneh*.

SERVES 4 TO 6

FOR THE MARINADE
5 cloves garlic, minced to a fine paste
2 tablespoons extra-virgin olive oil
Juice of 1 lemon, or to taste

1 teaspoon Aleppo pepper, or to taste
½ teaspoon ground allspice
½ teaspoon Lebanese 7-Spice Mixture (page 358)

¼ teaspoon ground cinnamon
Sea salt and finely ground black pepper

FOR THE KEBABS
1¾ pounds (800 g) boneless lamb leg,

trimmed of most of the fat and cut into 1-inch (2.5 cm) chunks
16 baby onions, peeled

Flatbread, for serving

1. To make the marinade: Mix together the garlic, olive oil, lemon juice, spices, and salt and black pepper to taste.

2. To prepare the kebabs: Add the meat to the marinade and mix it well. Let marinate for at least a couple of hours, or longer if you can.

3. Prepare a charcoal fire in an outdoor grill or preheat the broiler to high.

4. Thread the meat onto 8 skewers, inserting a baby onion in between every two or three pieces of meat. Grill over high heat or broil for 3 to 4 minutes on each side, or until the meat and onions are done to your liking. Serve very hot wrapped in flatbread.

LEBANESE KAFTA

KAFTA

LEBANON

When I lived in Beirut, I often went with my mother to the butcher's. As a child, I had a morbid fascination with severed sheep's heads, carcasses, and knives. I was fascinated by how our butcher would wield his knife, slicing meat off carcasses, then chopping it by hand before chopping herbs and onions and adding it to the chopped meat to make *kefta*. In those days, even though my mother pounded her own meat for kibbeh in a mortar with a heavy wooden pestle, she asked the butcher to make the *kefta;* but she insisted on being there to watch the whole process to make sure the butcher was giving her the meat she wanted and not another cheaper cut. I would stand next to her, mesmerized by the butcher's dexterity with his very large and very sharp knife. I make my *kefta* at home, grinding the meat in a meat grinder and chopping the parsley and onion in a food processor. If you don't have a meat grinder, I suggest you do as my mother did and buy the cut you want from your butcher (either shoulder or leg), then ask him to grind it for you. This way you will make sure you have the best-quality ground meat—store-bought preground meat is too fatty and often made from off-cuts. Serve on a bed of Onion and Parsley Salad (page 387) and with flatbread.

SERVES 4

2 medium onions (7 ounces/200 g total), quartered

1 ounce (30 g) fresh flat-leaf parsley leaves
1 pound 2 ounces (500 g) ground lamb, from the shoulder

½ teaspoon ground allspice
½ teaspoon ground cinnamon

¼ teaspoon Lebanese 7-Spice Mixture (page 358)
Sea salt and finely ground black pepper

1. Put the onions and parsley in a food processor and process until finely chopped. Transfer to a bowl. Add the ground meat, spices, and salt and pepper to taste and mix well with your hands. Pinch a little off and sear in a hot pan. Taste and adjust the seasoning if necessary. Divide the meat into 12 equal portions.

2. Prepare a charcoal fire in an outdoor grill or preheat the broiler to high.

3. Roll each portion of meat into a ball. Put one in the palm of your hand, take a long, flat skewer—the meat will hold better on a flat one—and start wrapping the meat around the skewer, squeezing it upward, then downward to bind it to the skewer in the shape of a long flat sausage. Taper the ends and place on a rack ready to grill or broil. Shape the rest of the meat on the remaining skewers the same way.

4. Grill or broil the meat for 2 to 3 minutes on each side, or until it is done to your liking. Serve hot.

MOROCCAN KEFTA

KEFTA

Moroccan *kefta* is a lot more intense in flavor than the Lebanese one. One of its main seasonings is the complex ras el-hanout, a mixture of more than twenty spices, including cardamom, nutmeg, ginger, the now-illegal aphrodisiac Spanish fly, and dried roses, and the meat is mixed with even more herbs. You can mold it around skewers as with the Lebanese *kefta* (page 109) or simply shape it into patties and pan-fry it. These are traditionally served with a tomato and onion salad and Moroccan Bread (page 11).   SERVES 4 TO 6

1 medium onion
  (5 ounces/150 g),
  quartered
A few sprigs cilantro,
  most of the bottom
  stems discarded
A few sprigs flat-leaf
  parsley, most of
  the bottom stems
  discarded
A handful of mint leaves
2 small handfuls of
  marjoram leaves
2¼ pounds (1 kg) lean
  lamb, finely ground
1 teaspoon ground cumin
1 teaspoon paprika
½ teaspoon ground
  allspice
½ teaspoon cayenne
  pepper
½ teaspoon ras el-
  hanout (see page 363;
  optional)
Sea salt

1. Put the onions and herbs in a food processor and process until very finely chopped. Transfer to a bowl and add the ground lamb, spices, and salt. Mix with your hands until evenly blended.

2. Divide the meat into 24 equal portions. Roll each portion into a ball and wrap each tightly around a skewer (preferably flat), squeezing the meat up and down, to form a sausage 4 or 6 inches (10 to 15 cm) long. Pinch it quite thin at each end.

3. Prepare a charcoal fire in an outdoor grill or preheat the broiler to high.

4. Grill or broil the skewers for 2 to 3 minutes on each side, or until done to your liking. Serve immediately.

MEAT SATAY
SATE DAGING

Satay or sate could be considered the national dish of Indonesia, found everywhere from the humblest street stall to an upmarket restaurant to the most elegant of celebrations. Satay is basically skewered meat, fish, poultry, or even tofu. Traditionally the skewers themselves were made from the center of palm fronds, but most people nowadays use bamboo skewers, which need to soak before they are put on the fire. I love watching satay street vendors in Indonesia ply their trade. Some will set up shop right outside their homes. Others will wheel carts filled with half-cooked skewers and at the front of the cart they will have a charcoal fire on which they will finish cooking the skewers to give them to you piping hot, served on a leaf, either already dipped in a sauce kept hot in a pot on the side or with sauce on the side for you to dip your skewers into. Those sellers who have access to electricity will use a fan to keep their fires going, while others will use a fan woven from palm leaves. The dipping sauce for these meat skewers is made with peanuts.   SERVES 4

FOR THE PEANUT SAUCE
Vegetable oil, for deep-frying
About 1 cup (5 ounces/ 150 g) raw peanuts
2 shallots (2 ounces/ 60 g), finely chopped
1 fresh chili pepper, seeded and finely chopped
1 clove garlic, minced to a fine paste
1 medium tomato (3½ ounces/100 g), peeled, seeded, and finely chopped
1 teaspoon soy sauce
Sea salt
Juice of 1 lime

FOR THE MEAT
1 pound 10 ounces (750 g) tender boneless beef or lamb, cut into smallish cubes or sliced into strips ¼ inch (0.5 cm) thick

1. Soak 16 medium bamboo skewers for 30 minutes in cold water.

2. To make the sauce: Pour 1 inch (2.5 cm) oil into a deep skillet and heat over medium heat until hot (if you drop a piece of bread in the oil, the oil should immediately bubble around it). Add the peanuts and deep-fry for 3 to 4 minutes, or until lightly golden. Remove with a slotted spoon to a sieve to drain off any excess oil. Let cool, then grind finely in a mortar or a food processor.

3. Drain off most of the oil, leaving about 1 tablespoon in the skillet. Add the shallots and chili and fry for a couple of minutes before adding the garlic. Fry for 1 minute more before adding the tomato, soy sauce, and the ground peanuts. Add 1 cup (250 ml) water and salt to taste and let bubble gently for 10 minutes. Add the lime juice. Take off the heat and let cool.

4. Prepare a charcoal fire in an outdoor grill or preheat the broiler to high.

5. To prepare the meat: Thread the cubes or strips of meat onto the bamboo skewers and grill or broil for 3 minutes on each side, or until the meat is done to your liking. Serve immediately with the peanut sauce.

CHICKEN SATAY

SATE AYAM

INDONESIA

Here is the chicken version of satay with a slightly different nut sauce, where the peanuts are mixed with candlenuts. If you can't find the latter, use cashews or almonds. The dipping sauce here is also used as a marinade to give the meat a more intense flavor. The same sauce can also be used with meat or fish. There are many different dipping sauces, including a quick version made by simply mixing soy sauce with scallions and chili. SERVES 4

FOR THE MARINADE/ SAUCE

5 candlenuts or cashews, or 10 blanched almonds
5 cloves garlic
2 fresh red chilies, cut into medium chunks
Sea salt
1 tablespoon ground coriander
Finely ground black pepper
½ teaspoon cayenne pepper
2 tablespoons vegetable oil
½ cup (75 g) raw peanuts, finely ground
1 tablespoon kecap manis (or 1 teaspoon sugar), plus more for the sauce

FOR THE SATAY

1 pound 10 ounces (750 g) boneless, skinless dark chicken meat, cut into long strips ¼ inch (0.5 cm) thick

1. Soak 14 medium bamboo skewers for 30 minutes in cold water.

2. To make the marinade: Put the candlenuts, garlic, chilies, and a little salt in a mortar and grind with a pestle until you have a fine paste—you can also do this in a food processor. Transfer to a bowl. Add the coriander, black pepper, and cayenne and mix well.

3. Heat the vegetable oil in a skillet over medium heat. Add the candlenut-garlic mixture and fry until lightly colored, 2 to 3 minutes. Add the peanuts and kecap manis and fry for another couple of minutes. Let cool.

4. Prepare a charcoal fire in an outdoor grill or preheat the broiler to high.

5. To prepare the satay: Marinate the chicken in the sauce for at least 30 minutes or longer, then scrape the marinade off the chicken before threading it equally onto the skewers. Grill or broil for 3 minutes on each side, or until completely cooked through.

6. Meanwhile, scrape the leftover marinade into a small saucepan. Add ½ cup (125 ml) water and a little more kecap manis (or a little sugar) and bring to a boil over medium heat. Transfer to a small bowl and serve as a dipping sauce with the grilled chicken.

INDIAN GALAWATI KEBABS
GALAWAT KEBAB

The texture of these Indian kebabs is unlike anything I have had before—very smooth, almost melting, and softer than any minced meat kebab I have ever tasted. The way to achieve this is by first asking your butcher to pass the meat twice through the fine disk of the meat grinder—you can also do this yourself if you have a meat grinder—then at home, to process the meat in a food processor until it becomes silky. Then, after adding the seasonings, you need to lightly wet your hands and work very quickly as you shape the kebabs. In the kebab shops I have been to in India, they pinch off a little of the ground meat mixture and slap it into the pan and it somehow shapes itself. Anyhow, as long as you lightly wet or oil your hand you will be fine shaping such a smooth mixture. Green papaya is used in India to tenderize the meat, but meat in the United States is tender enough so if you can't find it, don't worry about using it. These are normally served hot with *sheermal*, a thin flatbread baked in a *tannur* oven, but I often serve them with ready-baked naan.

SERVES 6 TO 8

2 tablespoons small chunks green papaya, both skin and flesh (optional)
1 pound 5 ounces (600 g) lean ground lamb, from the shoulder or leg
Sea salt
Vegetable oil, for deep-frying and pan-frying

4 medium onions (1 pound 5 ounces/ 600 g total), halved and cut into thin wedges
1 cup (125 g) chickpea flour, lightly toasted in a nonstick pan
2 teaspoons Kashmiri chili powder

2 teaspoons Garam Masala 3 (page 361)
1½ teaspoons ground cardamom
1½ teaspoons ground mace
½ teaspoon lazzat e-taam
½ teaspoon finely ground black pepper

3 tablespoons kewra (pandanus flower extract; see page 513)
2 tablespoons clotted cream
2 tablespoons heavy cream
Naan (page 24), for serving

1. Process the green papaya with about ¼ cup (60 ml) water in a small food processor until you have a very fine paste.

2. Process the meat in a food processor until very smooth. Transfer to a large bowl. Add the papaya paste and salt and mix well. Let sit for 1 hour or so.

3. Pour ½ inch (1 cm) vegetable oil into a large deep skillet and heat over medium heat until hot (if you drop a piece of bread in the oil, the oil should immediately bubble around it). Add the onion and fry until golden brown but be careful not to burn it. Remove with a slotted spoon and drain on several layers of paper towel.

4. Transfer the fried onion to a food processor and process into a fine paste. Add to the meat. Add the chickpea flour, spices, kewra, clotted cream, and heavy cream and mix well with your hands. Taste and adjust the seasoning (see Note).

5. Brush a large skillet with a little vegetable oil and put over medium-high heat. When the pan is hot, start to shape the meat into small patties about 2 inches (5 cm) in diameter and immediately drop as many as will fit comfortably in the hot pan. Cook for 2 to 3 minutes on each side—wipe the pan clean before brushing the pan again with oil in between the batches if necessary. Serve hot with naan.

NOTE: *I don't mind tasting raw meat but if you don't like doing this, sear a little meat in a hot pan and taste to adjust the seasoning if need be.*

HYDERABADI KEBAB

Kebabs in India are sometimes made with already cooked meat instead of raw—strange, given that you don't necessarily need to cook meat twice. This said, cooking the meat before grinding it and grilling it makes for a different texture, and these kebabs are quite delicious, and typical of Hyderabadi cuisine, so they're definitely worth the trouble to make.   SERVES 4

6 tablespoons ghee or
  vegetable oil
1 teaspoon black cumin
  seeds
1-inch (2.5 cm) fresh
  ginger, peeled and
  minced to a fine paste
2 cloves garlic, minced
  to a fine paste
2 green chilies, thinly
  sliced
3 medium-hot dried
  chilies
½ teaspoon ground
  turmeric
2 tablespoons chana dal
  (yellow split peas)
9 ounces (250 g) lean
  ground lamb
1 tablespoon yogurt
Leaves from 2 sprigs
  mint, finely chopped
Sea salt
2 small shallots
  (1½ ounces/45 g total),
  halved and cut into
  wedges
A few sprigs cilantro,
  most of the bottom
  stems discarded, finely
  chopped
1 organic egg, beaten
  with a pinch of salt

1. Heat 2 tablespoons of the ghee in a medium pot over medium heat until hot. Add the black cumin seeds and let them sizzle for a few seconds, then add the ginger, garlic, and green chilies. Stir until fragrant, then add the dried chilies and the turmeric. Stir for another minute or so, then add the chana dal and sauté for a minute or so. Add the lamb, yogurt, mint, and salt to taste and cook, stirring to break up any lumps, until the meat is no longer pink, about 5 minutes. Add 1 cup (250 ml) water and let bubble for 30 minutes, or until the water is completely absorbed and the chana dal is very soft. Adjust the salt if necessary.

2. Meanwhile, heat 2 tablespoons of the ghee in another skillet over medium heat. Add the shallots and sauté until golden brown, about 10 minutes.

3. Transfer the cooked meat mixture to a food processor and process with the fried shallots until you have a smooth paste. Transfer to a bowl. Add the cilantro and half the beaten egg. Mix with your hand and check if the mixture can be easily shaped. If it is still a little stiff, add a little more egg. The whole egg may make it too soft to shape. Once you have the right consistency, shape the mixture into 8 medium patties or into 8 fat fingers.

4. Wipe the skillet in which you fried the shallots and heat the remaining 2 tablespoons ghee over medium heat. When the ghee is hot, add the meat patties or fingers and fry until browned on all sides. Serve hot.

GRILLED LAMB'S LIVER

KOUAH

MOROCCO

These kebabs are typical street food in Morocco and I usually have them at butchers who have a grill within their stall so that I can be sure of the freshness of the liver. Those butchers who do not have a grill within their premises are often located next to grill stalls or cafés, and all you have to do is to buy the meat from the butcher and take it to the grill man for him to season and grill it. Obviously this kind of setup does not exist in the West, so just make sure you source very fresh liver from a good butcher to season and grill at home. Serve with a salad.   SERVES 4 TO 6

1¾ pounds (800 g) lamb's liver, cut into 1-inch (2.5 cm) cubes

3 cloves garlic, minced to a fine paste

A few sprigs flat-leaf parsley, most of the bottom stems discarded, finely chopped

1 teaspoon ground cumin

1 teaspoon paprika

Sea salt

Lemon wedges and flatbread, for serving

1. Mix the liver, garlic, parsley, cumin, paprika, and salt to taste in a bowl. Let marinate for at least 2 hours in a cool place or in the refrigerator.

2. Prepare a charcoal fire in an outdoor grill or preheat the broiler to high.

3. Thread the liver onto 8 or 12 long skewers depending on how many you want to serve. Grill or broil for 1 to 2 minutes on each side, or until done to your liking. Don't overcook or the liver will go rubbery. Serve hot with the lemon wedges and flatbread.

INDIAN "SCOTCH EGG"

NARGISI KEBAB

Last time I was in India, I stayed nearly three weeks, traveling to different cities once ruled by the Mughals. Throughout this time, friends or acquaintances would rave about *nargisi kebab* as being one of the great Mughal culinary achievements, except that it seemed to be an elusive dish. Even when I saw it on a menu, it would not be available. Finally, when I got to Delhi, I was introduced to Vir Sanghvi, India's top food critic and a star journalist, and his delightful wife, Seema, by my great friends Bobby and Bipasha Gosh—Bobby is the editor in chief of the *Hindustan Times* and Bipasha is vice president of international marketing at NBCUniversal. Vir and Seema took me to Dum Pukht restaurant, and as Vir was ordering our meal, including a stupendous biryani, I lamented that I had not been able to taste *nargisi kebab* anywhere I'd been because it was never available. Vir, being totally wonderful, called chef Gulam Qureshi and explained to him my desperation at not having yet had the chance to try *nargisi kebab*, and he asked him if he could make us some. And he did! Finally, I was able to try the Mughal Indian dish that is at the origin of the Scotch egg, (a large meatball with a boiled egg inside it, rolled into breadcrumbs, fried and eaten at room temperature). I am so glad I did as, not surprisingly, it is far superior to the English version. You can serve *nargisi kebab* plain, which is how we had it at Dum Pukht, or you can serve it in a sauce for which I give a recipe below. If you want to serve it plain, just fry the kebab and serve.

SERVES 6

FOR THE NARGISI KEBABS

6 organic eggs

1 pound 5 ounces (600 g) boneless lean lamb shoulder or leg, cut into small pieces

1 small piece fresh ginger, peeled and finely minced

1 clove garlic, minced to a fine paste

1¼ teaspoons Garam Masala 2 (page 361)

1¼ teaspoons Kashmiri chili powder

½ teaspoon finely ground black pepper

¼ teaspoon ground turmeric

4 small green chilies, seeded and coarsely chopped

A handful of cilantro leaves

A few fresh mint leaves

2 tablespoons fine breadcrumbs

1 tablespoon vegetable oil, plus more to oil your hands

Sea salt

FOR THE CURRY SAUCE

3 tablespoons vegetable oil

3 large onions (1 pound 5 ounces/600 g total), finely chopped

1 small piece ginger, peeled and finely minced

1 clove garlic, minced to a fine paste

½ teaspoon Garam Masala 1 (page 361)

½ teaspoon Kashmiri chili powder

½ teaspoon finely ground black pepper

¼ teaspoon ground turmeric

6 medium tomatoes (1 pound 5 ounces/ 600 g total), processed to a fine puree (or an equal amount of canned peeled whole tomatoes)

12 cashews or 20 blanched almonds, soaked for 1 hour in hot water, then drained and processed until finely ground

Sea salt

TO FINISH

Vegetable oil, for deep-frying

A few sprigs cilantro, most of the stems discarded, finely chopped, for garnish

Recipe continues

1. To make the kebabs: Put the eggs in a pan full of water and bring to a boil over medium heat. Take off the heat and let sit for 5 minutes, then discard the hot water, let the eggs cool, and peel them.

2. Process the lamb in a food processor until finely ground. Add the ginger, garlic, spices, chilies, herbs, breadcrumbs, oil, and salt to taste and process until very finely ground. Transfer to a bowl and divide into 6 equal portions.

3. Put a little oil in a bowl, which you will use to oil your hands to shape the kebabs. Lightly oil your hands, then flatten one portion of the meat mixture into a medium-thin round that is large enough to wrap around a hard-boiled egg. Place the egg in the middle of the meat patty and wrap the meat around the egg. Smooth the seams and place on a plate. Make the other kebabs in the same way and refrigerate until it is time to fry them.

4. To make the curry sauce: Heat the oil in a pot over medium heat. Ad the onions and when they start sizzling, reduce the heat to low and sauté until golden brown, about 10 minutes. Add the ginger, garlic, and spices and stir for a minute or so. Add the pureed tomatoes and let bubble for about 10 minutes, or until you see the oil rise to the surface. Add the ground nuts and a little water if the sauce is too thick and salt to taste. Stir for a couple of minutes.

5. Set a wire rack in a rimmed baking sheet. Pour 2½ inches (6 cm) vegetable oil into a deep skillet and heat over medium heat until very hot (if you drop a piece of bread in the oil, the oil should immediately bubble around it). Working in batches of 1 or 2, drop the kebabs into the oil and fry for 2 to 3 minutes, turning them so that they crisp up and color evenly. Remove with a slotted spoon to the rack to drain the excess oil. At this point you can either serve them plain, or with the curry sauce on the side, or you can drop them into the sauce and let them cook in the sauce for a couple of minutes before serving them garnished with the chopped cilantro.

CHICKEN MISHKAKI

MISHKAKI DEJAJ

Mishkaki (*mishkak* in Oman) are the quintessential street food in Oman as well as in Zanzibar, once part of the Sultanate of Oman. They are basically grilled kebabs sold from stalls by the roadside or in the famous Forodhani Gardens in Stone Town, Zanzibar. You can identify the stalls from far away by the smoke rising over the charcoal grills, and as you get closer, by the smell of the grilling meat. *Mishkaki* make a great snack eaten on their own or a lovely quick meal wrapped in warm flatbread, garnished with herbs and sliced tomatoes and onions. You can use chicken as below, or meat or even shrimp. The marinade and sauce remain the same. SERVES 4 TO 6

FOR THE MARINADE
1 medium tomato (about 3½ ounces/100 g), cut into quarters
1 inch (2.5 cm) fresh ginger, peeled
4 cloves garlic, peeled
½ cup (125 g) labneh
2 tablespoons extra-virgin olive oil
1 tablespoon Aleppo pepper
½ teaspoon ground turmeric
½ teaspoon finely ground black pepper
Sea salt

FOR THE CHICKEN
2¼ pounds (1 kg) boneless chicken meat, both dark and white, cut into bite-size pieces

FOR THE ZANZIBARI SAUCE
1 tablespoon unbleached all-purpose flour
¼ teaspoon ground turmeric
¼ teaspoon cayenne pepper
Juice of 1 lemon, or to taste
Sea salt

1. To make the marinade: Put the tomato, ginger, and garlic in a food processor and process until completely pureed. Transfer to a bowl and add the labneh, oil, spices, and salt to taste. Mix well.

2. To prepare the chicken: Add the chicken to the marinade and mix to coat well. Let marinate for at least 2 hours in a cool place, preferably longer in the refrigerator.

3. Prepare a charcoal fire in an outdoor grill or preheat the broiler to high. Soak 8 medium bamboo skewers for 30 minutes in cold water.

4. Thread the chicken pieces onto the skewers and grill or broil for 5 minutes on each side, or until the meat is crisp on the outside, and cooked through but still juicy on the inside.

5. Meanwhile, to make the Zanzibari sauce: Put 2 cups (500 ml) water in a small saucepan. Add the flour, turmeric, and cayenne and whisk until completely blended. Bring to a boil over medium heat, whisking all the time. Let simmer for a few minutes, or until the sauce has thickened. Add the lemon juice and salt to taste and take off the heat.

6. Serve the chicken *mishkaki* with the sauce.

KASHGAR KEBABS

KASHGAR KAWAP

I was given this recipe, which comes from Kashgar, an oasis city in Xinjiang, by Fuchsia Dunlop, one of the foremost experts and writers on Chinese cuisine. Kashgar is the westernmost Chinese city, located near the border with Pakistan, Afghanistan, Kyrgystan, and Tajikistan in Muslim China. The marinade is interesting in that it is almost like a batter, made with potato starch and egg, which makes for a different texture compared with other kebabs, such as those from Turkey or Lebanon.

SERVES 4

1 pound (450 g) boneless lamb shoulder, cut into 1-inch (2.5 cm) chunks
1 organic egg, beaten
3 tablespoons potato starch
Sea salt and finely ground black pepper
Ground cumin
Red pepper flakes
Uzbek Flatbread (page 32), for serving

1. Put the lamb in a bowl. Combine the beaten egg with the potato starch in a small bowl and add to the lamb. Season with salt and pepper to taste and mix well. Let sit for 30 minutes.

2. Meanwhile, prepare a charcoal fire in an outdoor grill or preheat the broiler to high.

3. Thread the lamb chunks onto 4 metal skewers (preferably flat) or 8 presoaked bamboo skewers. Grill or broil the kebabs for 2 to 3 minutes on each side, or until done to your liking. I like to keep my kebabs pink in the middle, so I grill them for just under 2 minutes on each side. As the kebabs are grilling, season them with a little more salt, cumin, and pepper flakes. Serve hot on flatbread, either on or off the skewers.

AFGHANI SIKH KEBABS

SIKH KABAB

Unlike the Iranians who always serve their kebabs with rice, in Afghanistan kebabs are always served with flatbread with a garnish of fresh vegetables and herbs. They are typical restaurant or street food fare and the meat is either lamb or chicken. The marinade here is made with yogurt and a little oil, which would be replaced with melted lamb tail fat in Afghanistan. Small pieces of tail fat would also be used on the skewers alternating with the meat to provide extra moisture. Although it is nearly impossible to get tail fat outside the Middle East, both marinade and kebabs will still be good and moist without.

SERVES 4 TO 6

FOR THE MARINADE
⅔ cup (180 g) whole-milk yogurt
4 cloves garlic, minced to a fine paste
Juice of 1 lemon, or to taste
1 teaspoon ground coriander
Sea salt and finely ground black pepper

FOR THE KEBABS
2¼ pounds (1 kg) boneless lean lamb from the leg or the fillet, cut into 1-inch (2.5 cm) cubes
2 tablespoons vegetable oil
4 small onions (13 ounces/400 g total), quartered (optional)

FOR SERVING
Flatbread
Quartered raw onions
Tomato slices
Lemon wedges
Aleppo pepper

1. To make the marinade: Put the yogurt in a large bowl. Stir in the garlic and lemon juice. Stir in the coriander and salt and pepper to taste and mix well. Taste and adjust the salt and spices if necessary.

2. To prepare the kebabs: Add the lamb and oil to the marinade and mix well. Let marinate for at least 2 hours, preferably overnight in the refrigerator.

3. Prepare a charcoal fire in an outdoor grill or preheat the broiler to high.

4. Thread the cubes of lamb onto 8 or 12 flat metal skewers, depending on how many you want to serve. You could alternate quartered onions in between the meat. Grill or broil for 3 to 5 minutes on each side, or until done to your liking. Serve immediately, on or off the skewers, on flatbread with raw onions, tomatoes, and lemon wedges. Have Aleppo pepper available for those who want to lightly spice up their kebabs.

IRANIAN GROUND MEAT KEBABS

KABAB KOOBIDEH

The texture of the ground meat for these kebabs needs to be very fine. You can achieve this by first grinding it twice through the fine disk of a meat grinder and then kneading it with the seasonings. Or you can skip the kneading and pulse the ground meat in a food processor a few times.

To form the kebabs, be sure to use flat skewers, otherwise the meat will spin around as it shrinks away from the skewer during grilling. In Iran, people who are serious about their kebabs—like my friend Feridoonjan, who taught me how to make these—carry their own set of skewers inside a metal cylindrical case that is like a fishing rod case.

Kabab koobideh are absolutely delicious and probably the best known Iranian kebabs. They are served on flatbread with pickles (*torshi*), fresh herbs, and sumac, the latter an essential seasoning for grilled meat in Iran. You can also serve the kebabs on Plain Iranian Rice (page 242) instead of bread together with the yogurt and cucumber on page 192.   SERVES 4

1 pound 2 ounces (500 g) boneless lamb shoulder, trimmed of some of the fat, finely minced
1 medium onion (5 ounces/150 g), finely grated
1 teaspoon fine breadcrumbs
¼ teaspoon ground turmeric
Sea salt and finely ground black pepper
Flatbread, for serving

1. Put the minced meat in a bowl. Add the onion, breadcrumbs, turmeric, and salt and pepper to taste and knead, dipping your hand in a bowl of lightly salted cold water every now and then until you have a homogenous paste.

2. Prepare a charcoal fire in an outdoor grill or preheat the broiler to high.

3. Divide the meat into 8 equal portions. Wrap each portion around a flat skewer, pressing the meat up and down the skewer and making indentations with your thumb and index finger every inch or so until you end up with a kind of wavy flat sausage. Grill or broil for a couple of minutes on each side, or until done to your liking. Serve hot with flatbread.

CHICKEN KEBABS

JOOJEH KABAB

There are different marinades for chicken kebabs. The *joojeh kebab* is made with a simple marinade but there are other yogurt-based variations that are similar to the Afghani Sikh Kebabs (page 123). When I was in my friend Feridoonjan's village, watching him cook a veritable feast for us, he used pieces of chicken breast, but I like using poussin joints for a prettier presentation. Serve with Plain Iranian Rice (page 242) or flatbread, together with the Iranian Pickled Eggplant (page 422), fresh herbs, and sumac.

SERVES 4

1 small onion
(3½ ounces/100 g),
finely grated
Juice of ½ lemon, or to
taste
Sea salt and finely ground
black pepper
2 poussins or Cornish
hens, each jointed into
8 pieces
Pinch of saffron threads

1. Mix the onion, lemon juice, and salt and pepper to taste in a container big enough to hold the poussin pieces. Add the chicken and mix well. Let marinate for at least 2 hours.

2. Prepare a charcoal fire in an outdoor grill or preheat the broiler to high.

3. Steep the saffron in 1 tablespoon water.

4. Thread the poussin pieces onto 4 long, flat metal skewers. Mix the saffron water with what is left of the marinade in the bowl. Grill or broil the poussin for about 10 minutes on each side, or until the pieces are crisp on the outside and cooked through but still juicy on the inside. While the poussin is cooking, baste it with the saffron-marinade mixture. Serve hot.

LAMB SHAWARMA SANDWICH
SHAWARMA LAHMEH

Before Syria descended into the tragic situation in which it has been since shortly after the uprising, I visited often, and when I went to Damascus, I never failed to go to Siddiq, a restaurant specializing in shawarma grilled over charcoal, no easy feat given that the shawarma grill is vertical. They had that on the menu, plus a few select mezze items. You just sat down and waited for the mezze plates to be served, before the sensational shawarma was brought to the table, very thinly sliced, with some bits crisp and others very moist, depending on whether they were sliced from the first layer or the second inner one, all piled on pita bread and covered with more pita to keep the meat warm. Siddiq's was and still is the best shawarma I have ever had. I suspect the restaurant is still there as Damascus has been untouched by the civil war, and hopefully it will still be there once the war is over and I can return to visit.

The word *shawarma* comes from the Turkish *çevirme*, which means "to turn or rotate," describing how it cooks, slowly rotating in front of a fire. Shawarma is basically a very large, fat "kebab" that can be made with lamb or chicken. The meat is sliced into wide, thin pieces, marinated overnight, and threaded onto a long skewer. Lamb shawarma has slices of tail fat in between every few layers of meat to keep the meat moist during grilling. For chicken shawarma, the skin is kept on the meat to keep it moist and tender. The skewer is fixed in front of a vertical grill and left to rotate over a moderate heat for 2 to 3 hours, or until the meat is cooked through. Even before the meat is cooked through, the shawarma vendor starts slicing the outer, cooked layer to order, piling the thin slivers of meat onto pita bread to make a sandwich with tomatoes, onions, pickles, herbs, and tahini sauce if it is lamb shawarma or garlic sauce (*toum*) if it is chicken. Shawarma is basically street food and it is not usually prepared at home, but here is a great adaptation I learned from my Lebanese butcher in London. You can substitute chicken, both dark and white meat, for the lamb, and use *toum* (see Note) instead of the tahini sauce.

SERVES 4 TO 6

FOR THE LAMB
1¾ pounds (800 g) boneless lamb shoulder, thinly sliced
2 medium onions (10½ ounces/300 g total), thinly sliced
Juice of 1 lemon, or to taste

1. To prepare the lamb: Put the meat in a large bowl and add the onions, lemon juice, olive oil, spices, thyme, and salt and pepper to taste and mix well. Let marinate in the refrigerator for 2 to 4 hours, stirring occasionally.

2. Meanwhile, make the tahini sauce: Put the tahini in a bowl. Alternating between the lemon juice and 6 tablespoons (90 ml) water, gradually whisk in the liquids—this is to make sure that you get the right balance of tartness while keeping the consistency of the sauce like that of creamy yogurt. The tahini will first thicken to a puree-like

Recipe continues

¼ cup (60 ml) extra-
virgin olive oil
½ teaspoon ground
allspice
½ teaspoon ground
cinnamon
¼ teaspoon Lebanese
7-Spice Mixture (page
358)
A few sprigs fresh thyme,
leaves only
Sea salt and finely ground
black pepper

FOR THE TAHINI SAUCE
½ cup (125 ml) tahini
Juice of 1 lemon, or to
taste
2 cloves garlic, minced to
a fine paste
Sea salt

FOR THE SANDWICHES
2 to 3 round pita breads
(about 8 inches/20 cm
in diameter) or 4 to
6 oval ones
4 to 6 small firm-ripe
tomatoes, thinly sliced
1 small red onion, halved
and cut into very thin
wedges
4 to 6 gherkins, thinly
sliced lengthwise
Handful of mint leaves
A few sprigs flat-leaf
parsley, leaves only

consistency before starting to loosen up again. If you decide to use less lemon juice, make up for the loss of liquid by adding a little more water or vice versa. Add the garlic and salt to taste. Taste and adjust the seasoning if necessary.

3. When the meat is ready, place a large sauté pan over medium-high heat. When the pan is very hot, add the meat and sauté for a couple of minutes, or until the meat is done to your liking.

4. To make the sandwiches: You can make 4 or 6 sandwiches depending on how generously filled you want them to be.

IF YOU ARE USING ROUND PITA BREADS: Tear them open at the seam to split them into separate disks—you can also use markouk or handkerchief bread like in the photo. Arrange equal quantities of meat down the middle of each disk. Garnish with equal quantities of tomato, onion, gherkins, and herbs and drizzle as much tahini sauce as you like, bearing in mind it will sog up the bread if you go heavy. Roll each sandwich tightly. Wrap the bottom half with a paper napkin and serve immediately.

IF YOU ARE USING OVAL PITA BREADS: Open them at one wide end to create a large pocket. Drizzle tahini sauce inside the bread, then fill with equal amounts of sandwich ingredients. Drizzle with more tahini if you want—oval pita is a lot thicker and can take it. Serve immediately.

NOTE: *For an alternative to the tahini sauce, make* toum *by mincing 3 cloves garlic and grinding them to a fine paste with a little salt. Then drizzle in ⅓ cup (80 ml) extra-virgin olive oil the way you would with mayonnaise. To make this pungent dip a little milder, add 2 tablespoons labneh.*

BAKED KIBBEH
KIBBEH BIL-SANIYEH

Kibbeh in Lebanon, Syria, Jordan, and Palestine, and *kofte* in Turkey, is a mixture of ground lamb and bulgur that can be shaped as a pie, balls, or disks and cooked in endless variations. The recipe below is for *kibbeh bil-saniyeh,* which is meat, onion, and nut stuffing spread in between two layers of kibbeh to make a pie. It is one of Lebanon's grandest dishes, almost always present at special-occasion meals and big family reunions; and it is my go-to dish when I have friends coming over for a Lebanese meal. It is also one of the dishes that I like to demonstrate when I am teaching Lebanese cuisine. The last time I was teaching at Central Market, in Texas, together with Karen who runs the schools, we decided to do supper-club nights rather than straightforward cooking classes. We settled on a Lebanese menu with mezze to start, then *kibbeh bil-saniyeh* for the main course. I sent my recipes and arrived on the day to the usual warm welcome from everyone. But as I went through the ingredients for the dinner, I found they had purchased store-bought ground lamb for the kibbeh, which was far too fatty. So, when you make kibbeh, be sure not to buy preground meat! Ask your butcher to grind the lamb from the leg for you, or if you have a meat grinder, grind the meat yourself, after trimming it. Traditionally this kibbeh is made in a round baking dish, but my instructions are for a rectangular one as I am assuming that more cooks will have that shape than the more traditional round one. Sprinkle with rose petals and serve with the Yogurt and Cucumber Dip (page 192).   SERVES 6 TO 8

FOR THE STUFFING
Heaping ¼ cup (60 g) pine nuts
5 tablespoons (75 g) unsalted butter
1 pound (450 g) onions, finely chopped
7 ounces (200 g) lean ground lamb
2 teaspoons ground allspice
2 teaspoons ground cinnamon
½ teaspoon finely ground black pepper
Sea salt
1 teaspoon pomegranate molasses

1. Preheat the oven to 450°F (230°C).

2. To make the stuffing: Spread the pine nuts on a baking sheet and toast in the hot oven for 5 to 7 minutes, or until golden brown. Reduce the oven to 400°F (200°C).

3. Melt the butter in a deep skillet over medium heat. Add the onions and sauté until very soft and slightly caramelized, about 15 minutes. Stir in the lamb and cook, mashing and stirring with a wooden spoon or fork so that it separates well and does not form lumps, until it loses all traces of pink, 5 to 7 minutes. Take off the heat and season with the allspice, cinnamon, pepper, salt to taste, and pomegranate molasses. Stir in the toasted pine nuts. Taste and adjust the seasoning if necessary.

4. To prepare the kibbeh: Put the grated onion in a bowl. Add the ground lamb, spices, and salt to taste. Prepare a bowl of lightly salted water and have it at hand to use when you start mixing the meat with the bulgur.

Recipe continues

FOR THE KIBBEH

1 small onion
 (3½ ounces/100 g),
 grated on the fine side
 of a grater
1 pound 2 ounces
 (500 g) boneless lamb
 leg, trimmed of fat and
 passed twice through
 the fine disk of a meat
 grinder
2 teaspoons ground
 allspice
2 teaspoons ground
 cinnamon
½ teaspoon Lebanese
 7-Spice Mixture (page
 358)
½ teaspoon finely ground
 black pepper
Sea salt
1 cup (200 g) fine bulgur
6 to 8 teaspoons (30 g to
 70 g) unsalted butter

5. Rinse the bulgur in two or three changes of cold water. Drain and add to the meat. Mix together with your hand, dipping your hand every now and then in the salted water to moisten both your hand and the kibbeh. Knead the mixture for 2 to 3 minutes, or until the mixture is fairly smooth. Taste and adjust the seasoning if necessary.

6. Grease a 2-inch (5 cm) deep baking dish about 12 x 9 inches (30 x 22.5 cm) with a knob of butter (or use a nonstick baking dish). Divide the kibbeh in half. Moisten your hands in the salted water and pinch off a handful of kibbeh from one piece. Flatten it between your palms, to a thickness of about ½ inch (1 cm), and place it on the bottom of the baking dish starting from one corner. Smooth it down evenly with your fingers, pinch off another handful from the same half, flatten and lay next to the first piece, slightly overlapping it. Dip your fingers in water and smooth the pieces together until the seam disappears—make sure you connect the kibbeh pieces well so they do not come apart during cooking. Continue until you have covered the bottom of the pan with the first half of kibbeh. Go over the whole layer with moistened fingers to even it out.

7. Spread the stuffing evenly over the bottom layer of kibbeh. With the other half of kibbeh, make a top layer over the stuffing in the same way as you made the bottom layer. Spreading the top layer over the stuffing will prove slightly more difficult as you will be laying the kibbeh over the loose stuffing instead of the smooth surface of the baking dish, but you will soon get the hang of it.

8. With a sharp knife, cut through the kibbeh pie to divide it into 6 squares, then with the same knife, wiped clean, make shallow incisions to draw a geometric pattern across the top of each section, wiping the knife clean every now and then to make a neat pattern. The decoration work is time-consuming and can be either omitted altogether or simplified into larger diamond patterns, but the presentation will not be as impressive. After you finish decorating the kibbeh, make a hole in the center of the

kibbeh with your finger, and put a teaspoon of butter over the hole and one over each quarter. Insert a round-ended knife between the edge of the pie and the side of the pan and slide it all along the pie to detach the meat from the sides—you won't need to do this if you use a nonstick pan.

9. Bake for 15 to 20 minutes, or until the kibbeh has shrunk slightly and the meat is just done. Let sit for a few minutes before cutting into squares. Transfer carefully to a serving dish. Serve hot or warm.

KIBBEH in SUMAC SAUCE
KIBBEH SUMMAQIYEH

SYRIA

The first time I had this Syrian kibbeh was many years ago, long before the sad destruction of Aleppo, at the home of Joumana Kayali. In those days, the city was the ultimate destination for anyone visiting Syria, not only because of its historic monuments and medieval souks, the most enchanting of the Middle East, but also for its unrivaled culinary heritage, having earned the title of gastronomic capital of the Middle East from as far back as the eleventh century. The city's supremely sophisticated cuisine is quite distinct from that of Damascus, the capital, having been influenced by a succession of occupiers as well as refugee communities such as Armenians who fled there from neighboring Turkey at the beginning of the twentieth century. Also, the cooking of Aleppo's Christian communities is different from that of the city's Muslim ones. Joumana is Muslim and this kibbeh is one of her specialties. Once I discovered it and fell in love with it, I made a point of trying it in other places, such as one of my favorite restaurants then, Bazar el-Sharq—set in what had been the armory of the Aleppo Governorate in Ottoman times—where Chef Emad had it on the menu. The recipe below is a combination of Joumana's and Chef Emad's. It is a time-consuming dish, but well worth trying. It is one of the more intriguing and tastier kibbeh variations.

SERVES 4 TO 6

FOR THE STUFFING
Heaping ¼ cup (30 g) pine nuts
2 tablespoons (30 g) unsalted butter, plus more for greasing
3 medium onions (1 pound/450 g total), finely chopped
3½ ounces (100 g) boneless lamb leg, trimmed of fat and finely ground (see Note)
1 teaspoon ground allspice or Lebanese 7-Spice Mixture (page 358)
1 teaspoon ground cinnamon
¼ teaspoon finely ground black pepper

Sea salt
½ teaspoon pomegranate molasses
1 tablespoon finely chopped walnuts

FOR THE KIBBEH
9 ounces (250 g) boneless lamb leg, trimmed of fat and finely ground (see Note)
1 small onion (3½ ounces/ 100 g), grated on the fine side of a grater
½ cup (100 g) fine bulgur, rinsed under cold water and drained
1 teaspoon ground allspice or Lebanese 7-Spice Mixture (page 358)

1 teaspoon ground cinnamon
¼ teaspoon finely ground black pepper
Sea salt

FOR THE SAUCE
¼ cup (50 g) dried sumac berries
2¼ pounds (1 kg) lamb from the shanks, cut into medium chunks
3 medium onions (1 pound/450 g total), peeled, 1 kept whole and 2 halved lengthwise and cut into thin wedges
Coarse sea salt
¼ cup (60 ml) extra-virgin olive oil

1 teaspoon ground cinnamon
¼ teaspoon finely ground black pepper
Sea salt

3 cups (750 ml) tomato puree (passata)
2 tablespoons (30 g) unsalted butter
¾ pound (350 g) Japanese eggplants or 1 large globe eggplant, peeled lengthwise in stripes (if using a big eggplant, quarter it lengthwise, then cut across into medium-thick chunks)
2 teaspoons dried mint
5 cloves garlic, minced to a fine paste
Juice of 1 lemon, or to taste
½ teaspoon finely ground black pepper
Bread, for serving

1. Preheat the oven to 425°F (220°C).

2. To make the stuffing: Spread the pine nuts on a nonstick baking sheet and toast in the oven for 5 to 7 minutes, or until golden brown. Let cool.

3. Meanwhile, melt the butter in a large skillet over medium heat. Add the chopped onions and sauté, stirring regularly, until lightly golden, about 10 minutes. Add the ground lamb and cook, mashing and stirring it with a wooden spoon or fork to break up the lumps, until it loses all traces of pink. Season with the spices and salt to taste. Add the pomegranate molasses and mix well, then stir in the toasted pine nuts and the walnuts. Take off the heat and let cool.

4. To make the kibbeh: Prepare a bowl of lightly salted cold water and have it at hand. Put the ground meat in a large bowl. Add the grated onion, bulgur, spices, and salt to taste and mix together with your hand, dipping it every now and then in the salted water to moisten your hand and add a little water to the kibbeh to soften it. Knead for about 3 minutes, or until you have a fairly smooth, malleable mixture. Pinch off a little of the kibbeh and either taste raw to adjust the seasoning if need be, or sear it in a hot pan to taste.

5. Divide the kibbeh into 20 equal portions and roll them into balls, each the size of a large plum. Lightly moisten your hands in the salted water and place a kibbeh ball in the palm of one hand. With the index finger of your other hand burrow a hole into the kibbeh ball while rotating it—this makes the hollowing out easier and more even. You should produce a thin meat shell resembling a topless egg. Be careful not to pierce the bottom or sides of the kibbeh shell.

6. Put 1½ to 2 teaspoons of stuffing inside the kibbeh shell, gently pushing the stuffing in with a finger. Pinch the open edges together and gently mold back into a fully rounded shape—Syrians make their kibbeh balls round rather than oval like the Lebanese, Jordanians or Palestinians. Put the finished kibbeh ball on a nonstick baking

Recipe continues

sheet. Continue making the kibbeh balls until you have used up both the kibbeh mixture and stuffing. Place in the fridge or freezer to firm them up.

7. To make the sauce: Put the sumac berries in a small saucepan. Add 1½ cups (375 ml) water and bring to a boil. Take off the heat and let infuse while you prepare the rest of the ingredients for the sauce.

8. Put the meat and the whole peeled onion in a large saucepan and add 4 cups (1 liter) water. Bring to a boil over medium heat, skimming any froth that rises to the surface as the water comes to the boil. Add 1 tablespoon coarse sea salt, then reduce the heat, cover, and let bubble gently for 1 hour, or until the meat is very tender. Discard the onion.

9. Heat the olive oil in a wide pot over medium heat. Add the onion wedges and fry until lightly golden. Strain the lamb broth, reserving the meat, and add to the onions, followed by the passata. Strain the sumac liquid and add it to the pot. Bring back to a boil and adding the butter. Reduce the heat to low and let the sauce bubble gently for 15 minutes.

10. Add the eggplants and stewed lamb and cook for 15 more minutes, or until the eggplants are nearly done. Then add the mint, garlic, and lemon juice and drop the kibbeh balls into the sauce. Season with the black pepper and more salt if necessary and simmer for another 5 minutes, or until the meatballs are done. Taste and adjusting the seasoning if needed. Serve very hot in soup bowls with good bread.

NOTE: *Either have your butcher finely mince the lamb, or if you have a meat grinder, grind it once through the fine disk.*

GRILLED SYRIAN KIBBEH

KIBBEH SAJIYEH

SYRIA

The classic *kibbeh sajiyeh* is stuffed with seasoned lamb tail fat. The fat melts inside as the kibbeh grills over charcoal and oozes out as soon as you cut into it as it comes off the grill—it needs to be served very hot and eaten before the fat cools. I have had *kibbeh sajiyeh* stuffed with labneh and herbs in northern Lebanon and I have had it filled with the same stuffing as that of Kibbeh bil-Saniyeh (page 129). I like both, but neither is as luxurious as kibbeh suffused with tail fat. Having it straight off my Syrian aunt's charcoal grill remains one of my favorite childhood food memories, and in the days before the uprising, when I visited Syria, I never failed to order it in whatever restaurant I happened to dine in. For those of you living outside the Middle East, you can replace the lamb tail fat with the fat surrounding lambs' or calves' kidneys.   SERVES 4

1 cup (200 g) fine bulgur, rinsed under cold water and drained

1 pound 2 ounces (500 g) boneless lean lamb, very finely minced

1 medium onion (about 5 ounces/150 g), grated on the fine side of a grater

1 teaspoon ground allspice

½ teaspoon finely ground black pepper

Sea salt

5 ounces (150 g) sheep's tail fat (or fat from around the kidney), finely diced by hand

2 teaspoons ground cumin

2 teaspoons Aleppo pepper

1 teaspoon Lebanese 7-Spice Mixture (page 358)

Unsalted butter, melted, for shaping and serving

1. Put the bulgur in a bowl. Add the lamb, onion, allspice, black pepper, and salt to taste and mix well. Put some cold water in a small bowl and add a little salt. Wet your hands with the salt water, and add a little of it to the kibbeh and knead until you have a smooth mixture.

2. Put the diced tail fat in another bowl and season with the cumin, Aleppo pepper, and 7-spice mixture. Add salt to taste and mix well.

3. You are now ready to shape the domed kibbeh disks, and you can do this by hand or use shallow bowls to shape it. Divide the kibbeh into 8 equal portions of 4 ounces (125 g) each. Flatten each piece to a round about 4 inches (10 cm) in diameter. Take 4 shallow bowls measuring about 4 inches (10 cm) in diameter and line each with plastic wrap. Lightly grease the wrap with melted butter and lay a round on each bowl and flatten the meat a little more so it very slightly rises above the rim of the bowl. Spoon one-quarter of the seasoned fat into each bowl and cover with the remaining rounds of kibbeh. Seal the edges and brush with melted butter.

4. To grill the kibbeh: Prepare a charcoal fire in an outdoor grill. Invert the bowl molding the kibbeh onto your slightly greased palm, peel the wrap off the kibbeh, and gently slide the kibbeh onto the grill. Grill for 3 to 5 minutes on each side.

5. To bake the kibbeh: Preheat the oven to 450°F (230°C). Invert the kibbeh onto your palm then slide it onto a nonstick baking sheet. Bake for 15 minutes.

6. Serve hot, brushed with more butter.

KIBBEH BALLS with QUINCE in a FRESH POMEGRANATE SAUCE

KIBBEH SFARJALIYEH

SYRIA

Here is a typical autumn kibbeh variation with a very delicate sweet-sour flavor. This kibbeh dish is more like a thick soup than a stew and needs to be served in soup plates. And because quince are still totally seasonal, you cannot prepare this kibbeh unless quince are in season. You can easily freeze pomegranate juice with hardly any loss of flavor, but quince will go too soft if frozen, so plan on making it as soon as the fruit come into season. Again, it is a little time-consuming but worth the effort for its unusual, delicate flavor.

SERVES 4 TO 6

FOR THE SAUCE
Seeds from 2¼ pounds (1 kg) sweet-sour pomegranates
¼ cup (50 g) raw cane sugar
3 pounds 5 ounces (1.5 kg) quince, cored, peeled, and cut into wedges

FOR THE KIBBEH BALLS
1½ sticks plus 2 tablespoons (200 g) very cold unsalted butter, cut into ¾-inch (2 cm) cubes
½ teaspoon ground cinnamon

½ teaspoon ground allspice
Raw kibbeh mixture from Kibbeh in Sumac Sauce (page 132)

TO FINISH
9 ounces (250 g) lamb meat from the shanks

5 green cardamom pods
1 cinnamon stick
5 black peppercorns
1 medium onion (5 ounces/150 g), peeled and studded with 4 cloves
Sea salt

1. To make the sauce: Put the pomegranate seeds in a food processor and process until the seeds are completely pulverized, then strain the juice pressing on the pulp to extract as much as you can.

2. Put the sugar and ½ cup (125 ml) water in a large pot. Add the quince and place over medium heat. Cover and cook for 15 minutes, shaking the pan every now and then to coat the quince in the syrup. Add the pomegranate juice, reduce the heat to medium-low, and simmer for 1 hour, or until the quince is tender. By then, it should have turned a beautiful pink color.

3. To make the kibbeh balls: Put the butter cubes in a bowl, add the cinnamon and allspice, and gently toss to evenly coat the butter with the spices. Prepare a bowl of lightly salted cold water and have it at hand.

4. Divide the kibbeh into 20 equal portions and roll each into a ball the size of a walnut. Lightly moisten your hands in the salted water and place one kibbeh ball in the palm of one hand. With the index finger of your other hand burrow a hole into the kibbeh ball while rotating it—this makes the hollowing out easier and more even—taking care not to pierce the bottom or sides of the kibbeh shell.

5. Place a cube of seasoned butter into the kibbeh shell and seal the meat around the butter. Gently roll the kibbeh to create a round ball a little smaller than a Ping-Pong ball. Finish making the kibbeh balls and refrigerate or put in the freezer to firm them up.

6. To finish: Put the lamb in a pot and cover with water. Bring to a boil over medium heat, skimming the froth from the surface as the water is coming to the boil. Add the spices, onion, and salt to taste. Reduce to a simmer, cover the pan, and let bubble for 1 hour, or until the meat is tender. Reserving the broth, drain the meat. Discard the spices and onion.

7. Put the cooked lamb in a clean pot. Add the strained broth and the cooked quince and their juices, and set over medium-low heat. When the broth starts bubbling, gently drop in the kibbeh balls and taste the broth, adding a little more sugar if it is too sour. Adjust the salt, if necessary, and let bubble gently for 5 minutes, or until the kibbeh balls are just done. Serve very hot in soup plates, making sure each diner gets equal amounts of lamb, quince, and kibbeh.

NOTE: *Sweet-sour or sour pomegranates, which are known as* Abu-Leffan *in Arabic, are juiced and their juice is boiled down to make pomegranate syrup (or molasses) or used fresh in cooking as in the recipe above to add an intriguing sweet-savory flavor.*

MEATBALLS in SOUR CHERRY SAUCE

KABAB KARAZ

If there is a dish that symbolizes the cooking of Aleppo, this has to be it. Maria Gaspard Samra, a rare Syrian woman chef who gave cooking classes before the destruction of the city, grinds the cherries before cooking them, while my friends Lena Toutounji (famous for having one of the best tables in Aleppo) and May Mamarbachi (creator of the first boutique hotel in Damascus, Beit Mamlouka) both leave the cherries whole. May very kindly gave me cherries from her frozen stock so I could test the recipe. If you can't find fresh or frozen sour cherries, use dried.

SERVES 4

FOR THE MEATBALLS
1 pound (450 g) lean
    ground lamb, from the
    leg or shoulder
½ tablespoon sea salt
½ teaspoon Lebanese
    7-Spice Mixture (page
    358) or allspice
1 tablespoon (15 g)
    unsalted butter

FOR THE CHERRY SAUCE
2¼ pounds (1 kg) fresh
    or frozen pitted sour
    cherries (see Note)
1 tablespoon raw cane
    sugar
1 tablespoon
    pomegranate molasses

FOR ASSEMBLY
2 to 3 pita breads, split
    into 2 disks and cut into
    medium triangles
1 tablespoon (15 g)
    unsalted butter, melted
A few sprigs flat-leaf
    parsley, most of

the bottom stems
    discarded, finely
    chopped
¼ cup (50 g) pine nuts,
    toasted in a hot oven
    for 5 to 7 minutes, until
    lightly golden

1. To make the meatballs: Mix the lamb, salt, and spice mixture (or allspice) and shape into small balls, the size of large marbles. Melt the butter in a large skillet over medium heat and sauté the meatballs until lightly browned.

2. Put the cherries, sugar, and pomegranate molasses in a pot large enough to eventually hold the meatballs and bring to a bubble over medium heat. Reduce the heat to medium-low and simmer for 15 minutes, or until the sauce has thickened. Add the meatballs and simmer for another 15 minutes, until tender.

3. To assemble the dish: Arrange the pita bread triangles all over a serving platter, coarse side up, making sure the pointed ends are nicely arranged on the outside. Drizzle the melted butter all over the bread. Spoon the meat and sauce over the bread. Sprinkle the chopped parsley all over, then the toasted pine nuts. Serve immediately.

NOTE: *If you can't find fresh sour cherries, use dried sour cherries and simply rehydrate them by soaking them overnight in water: 2 cups (500 ml) water for 14 ounces (400 g) pitted dried sour cherries. Add the soaking water along with the cherries when you make the sauce.*

CHICKEN TAGINE with OLIVES and PRESERVED LEMONS

D'JAJ M'CHERMEL

MOROCCO

There are four different types of Moroccan tagines: *m'qalli* in which the sauce is flavored with saffron, ginger, and pepper; *m'hammar* where the only seasonings are cumin and paprika (*m'hammar* means "reddened" or "toasted," and I guess that here it alludes to the red color of paprika); *k'dra* with only saffron and black or white pepper as seasoning and lots of onions in the sauce; and finally *m'chermel*, which is the recipe I give below, made with lots of herbs and all the spices used in the other versions. Tagines are basically stews, and the interesting thing about Moroccan tagines is that instead of browning the meat at the beginning as with most other stews, the browning is done at the end after the meat has cooked and the cooking liquid has evaporated to leave only a silky sauce. You can cook tagines in the traditional earthenware tagine that gives its name to the dish. Or do as many Moroccan home cooks do and cook the tagine in a pot, then transfer it to a beautifully decorated ceramic tagine dish to serve at table. It is mostly street food vendors and rural folk who cook their tagines in earthenware tagines. I personally follow the example of city Moroccan home cooks and cook my tagine in a heavy stainless steel or cast-iron pot.   SERVES 6 TO 8

1 clove garlic, finely chopped
1 teaspoon ground ginger
½ teaspoon ground cumin
½ teaspoon paprika
Good pinch of saffron threads
¼ teaspoon finely ground black pepper
Sea salt

4 poussins or Cornish hens
2 medium onions (10½ ounces/300 g total), grated on the fine side of a grater
¼ bunch flat-leaf parsley (2 ounces/50 g), most of the bottom stems discarded, very finely chopped

¼ bunch cilantro (2 ounces/50 g), most of the bottom stems discarded, very finely chopped
1 cinnamon stick
2 tablespoons extra-virgin olive oil
2 tablespoons (30 g) unsalted butter
Juice of ½ to 1 lemon, to taste

1 large preserved lemon, peel only, cut lengthwise into medium-thin julienne
7 ounces (200 g) unpitted green or Kalamata olives, or a mixture of the two
Moroccan Bread (page 11), for serving

1. Mix together the garlic, ginger, cumin, paprika, saffron, pepper, and a little sea salt in a large pot. Add the poussins and rub well inside and out with the spice mixture.

2. Add the onions, herbs, cinnamon stick, and 3 cups (750 ml) water. Bring to a boil over medium-high heat. Add the oil and butter. Cover the pan and cook for 45 minutes, or until the poussins are cooked through and the broth has become very concentrated, and reduced down to about a quarter.

3. Add the lemon juice, preserved lemon peel, and olives. Carefully turn the poussins in the sauce. Simmer for 10 more minutes. Taste the sauce and adjust the seasoning if necessary.

4. Transfer the poussins to a serving dish. Spoon the sauce and olives all over. Serve very hot with Moroccan bread.

POUSSIN TAGINE with CARROTS, OLIVES, and PRESERVED LEMON

D'JAJ BKHIZÜ

MOROCCO

This tagine made with baby carrots is delightful served with Moroccan Bread variation made with anise and sesame seeds (page 12). The sweet flavor of the carrots is exquisitely offset by the tart preserved lemons and salty olives, and the added flavoring in the bread makes it even more delicious when dipped in the sauce. Instead of the poussins or Cornish hens suggested here, you can also make this tagine with quail (use 4) or squab (use 2), or simply with a whole chicken.

SERVES 2 TO 4

- 2 tablespoons extra-virgin olive oil
- 1 medium onion (about 5 ounces/150 g), grated on the fine side of a grater
- 3 cloves garlic, finely chopped
- ¼ bunch flat-leaf parsley (2 ounces/50 g), most of the bottom stems discarded, finely chopped
- ¾ teaspoon ground ginger
- ½ teaspoon finely ground black pepper
- A good pinch of saffron threads
- Sea salt
- 2 poussins or Cornish hens
- 1 pound 2 ounces (500 g) Chantenay or baby carrots, trimmed and brushed clean
- A few sprigs cilantro, most of the bottom stems discarded, finely chopped
- Juice of 1 lemon, or to taste
- 3½ ounces (100 g) unpitted Kalamata olives
- ½ preserved lemon, peel only, sliced into thin julienne
- Moroccan Bread variation (page 12), for serving

1. Put the olive oil, onion, garlic, parsley, spices, and a little sea salt in a large pot. Mix and spread all over the bottom. Lay the poussins on their backs over the oil-parsley mixture. Add 2 cups (500 ml) water and bring to a boil over medium-high heat. Reduce the heat to medium, cover, and let bubble gently for 30 minutes, stirring occasionally to make sure the poussins are not sticking to the bottom of the pan.

2. Add the carrots, cilantro (reserving some for garnish), lemon juice, olives, and preserved lemon. Reduce the heat to medium-low and let simmer for 15 more minutes, or until both poussins and carrots are done and the sauce has thickened.

3. Transfer the poussins to a serving dish. If the sauce is still too liquid, increase the heat and let it bubble uncovered until it thickens and becomes somewhat silky. Arrange the carrots and olives around the poussins and spoon the sauce all over. Garnish with the reserved chopped cilantro and serve hot with Moroccan bread.

LAMB TAGINE
with POTATOES and PEAS
L'HAM BEL B'TATA WA JEBLANA

MOROCCO

Tagines are typical street food in Morocco, and this is the one that is most commonly found, except that street vendors cut the potatoes into small dice and I prefer to use new potatoes, which I leave whole if they are very small or halve if they are medium. I also use frozen petits pois, which I blanch in boiling water and then add to the tagine at the very end so that they stay a bright green color.

SERVES 4 TO 6

4 lamb shanks (3 pounds 5 ounces/1.5 kg total)
2 medium onions (10½ ounces/300 g total), halved and cut into thin wedges
2 cloves garlic, finely chopped
1 teaspoon paprika

½ teaspoon ground cumin
½ teaspoon ground ginger
½ teaspoon finely ground black pepper
Good pinch of saffron threads
Sea salt
¼ cup (60 ml) extra-virgin olive oil

¼ bunch flat-leaf parsley (2 ounces/50 g), most of the bottom stems discarded, finely chopped
¼ bunch cilantro (2 ounces/50 g), most of the bottom stems discarded, finely chopped

1 pound 2 ounces (500 g) new potatoes, scrubbed clean and left whole if very small or halved if medium
9 ounces (250 g) fresh or thawed frozen petits pois (see Note)
Moroccan Bread (page 11), for serving

1. Put the shanks, onions, garlic, spices, and a little salt in a large pot. Add water to barely cover, about 4 cups (1 liter) and bring to a boil over medium-high heat. Add the oil, then reduce the heat to medium-low. Cover and cook for 30 minutes. Turn the shanks over in the sauce and cook for another 15 minutes. Turn the meat again and cook for another 15 minutes, or until the meat is tender. If the shanks are not tender after an hour, cook for 15 to 30 minutes longer, adding a little more water.

2. When the meat is tender, add the herbs (reserving a little cilantro for garnish) and potatoes and cook for another 15 minutes, stirring occasionally, until the potatoes are just done. Add the peas and cook uncovered for another few minutes, until the peas are cooked. Taste and adjust the seasoning if necessary. If the sauce is still runny, let it bubble hard uncovered until the sauce has thickened.

3. Transfer the meat and vegetables to a serving dish. Garnish with the reserved cilantro and serve very hot with Moroccan bread.

NOTE: *Quick-thaw the frozen petits pois by plunging them into boiling water.*

LAMB TAGINE with EGGPLANT

L'HAM B'BOUDENJAL

MOROCCO

Eggplants are ubiquitous in Morocco but they are not indigenous, at least not until the Arabs brought them there in the eighth century, which is when they began to be incorporated into the cuisine. As for the Arabs, they were introduced to eggplants by the Persians who in turn found them in India. For this tagine, you can mash the eggplants into the sauce, in which case use large globe eggplants and chop them into chunks; or you can use Japanese eggplants and keep them whole—a prettier presentation. If you choose the latter, be careful when you stir them, and when you transfer them to a serving dish, so as not to mash them up.   SERVES 4

1 small leg of lamb on the bone (about 4½ pounds/2 kg)

1 medium onion (about 5 ounces/150 g), grated on the fine side of a grater

¼ bunch flat-leaf parsley (2 ounces/50 g), most of the bottom stems discarded, finely chopped

¼ bunch cilantro (2 ounces/50 g), most of the bottom stems discarded, finely chopped

5 tablespoons (75 ml) extra-virgin olive oil

Good pinch of saffron threads

1 teaspoon ground ginger

½ teaspoon finely ground black pepper

1 cinnamon stick

Sea salt

1 pound 5 ounces (600 g) small Japanese eggplants or 2 large globe eggplants

Moroccan Bread (page 11), for serving

1. Put the leg of lamb in a wide pot. Add the onion, herbs (reserving a little cilantro for garnish), oil, spices, and a little sea salt. Add 4 cups (1 liter) water and bring to a boil over medium-high heat. Cover the pan. Reduce the heat to medium-low and cook for 1 hour to 1 hour 30 minutes, or until the meat is completely done and the cooking broth has reduced to a thick sauce.

2. Meanwhile, peel the caps off the tops of the eggplants, keeping the stems on. Peel the eggplant in vertical stripes, leaving some of the skin on. If you are using globe eggplants, trim the top off, cut in half lengthwise, then quarter the halves lengthwise and slice crosswise into medium chunks. Sprinkle with salt and let sweat for 30 minutes before rinsing under cold water and patting dry.

3. When the meat is done, discard the cinnamon stick. Taste the sauce and adjust the seasoning if necessary. Add the eggplants and cook for another 10 to 15 minutes, or until they are very soft.

4. Carefully remove the leg of lamb to a large serving platter, then gently remove the eggplants and arrange them around the meat. If the sauce is still too runny, boil it hard uncovered until reduced. Spoon the sauce all over and garnish with the reserved cilantro. Serve very hot with Moroccan bread.

MOROCCAN MEATBALLS
with RICE
KEFTA BIL REZZ

When I was first given this recipe by a lovely Moroccan lady I met while shopping in the medina in Tangiers many years ago, I was doubtful about how raw rice mixed with minced meat would cook given that I wasn't going to be boiling the meatballs. Still, I liked the sound of the recipe and decided to give it a go, and to my surprise, it worked perfectly, with the rice expanding properly as it absorbed the cooking sauce, making the meatballs moister than they would have been if made plain.

SERVES 4 TO 6

¾ of the kefta mixture from Moroccan Kefta (page 110)

½ cup (100 g) short-grain rice

1 medium onion (about 5 ounces/150 g), thinly sliced

Good pinch of saffron threads

¼ teaspoon red pepper flakes, or to taste

A few sprigs flat-leaf parsley, most of the bottom stems discarded, finely chopped

4 tablespoons (60 g) unsalted butter

A few sprigs cilantro, most of the bottom stems discarded, finely chopped

Juice of 1 lemon, or to taste

1. Prepare the kefta mixture as directed.

2. Rinse the rice in several changes of cold water, then add to the kefta and mix with the meat using your hand to make sure the rice is evenly blended.

3. Put 3 cups (750 ml) water in a large sauté pan. Add the onion, saffron, pepper flakes, and parsley and bring to a boil over a medium-high heat. Add the butter and let bubble for a few minutes. Take off the heat.

4. Shape the kefta and rice mixture into small balls, moistening your hands with lightly salted water every now and then. Return the pan to the heat and drop the meatballs into the broth. Cook covered for 20 minutes, stirring occasionally toward the end, until they are cooked through with the rice completely tender. If the sauce is still too runny, increase the heat and let bubble hard for a few minutes, gently stirring occasionally until it thickens.

5. Add the cilantro (reserving some for garnish) and lemon juice and let bubble uncovered for a couple of minutes. Taste and adjust the seasoning if necessary. Serve immediately garnished with the reserved cilantro.

LAMB STEWED with CUMIN

TANGIA

Tangia is a supremely simple dish in which you put meat and seasonings in a pot, without any liquid, to simmer on very low heat until done. It takes just a few minutes to prepare but the whole night to cook, at least the traditional way in the ashes of the *hammam* (communal baths). The dish is a specialty of Marrakesh, and it is named after the tall earthenware jar in which it is cooked. It is probably the only dish that is specifically cooked by men in Morocco. Tradition has it that men prepare their *tangia* at home on Thursday afternoon, then take it to their local *hammam* where the man in charge of the fire will bury the jars in the hot ashes until it is time to move them to the cooler ashes, where they will stay warm until the owners are ready to pick them up to take to their Friday picnic. I was given the recipe below by the late Boujemaa Mars, who was head chef at the Mamounia, one of Marrakesh's fanciest hotels. Initially, I wondered if the meat would cook without any added water or broth, but lamb releases a fair amount of liquid during slow-cooking, and the end result is among the most succulent, flavorful stewed meats I have ever tasted. Don't skip on adding the preserved lemon to the pot, even though the recipe asks for a small amount. Adding it makes all the difference to the flavor and if you cannot find it in the stores, it's easy to make your own (see Note). Traditionally, the preserved lemons used in *tangia* are aged for at least 6 months in a cool, dark place.

SERVES 4

½ cup (125 ml) extra-virgin olive oil
1 large clove garlic, peeled, finely chopped
1 teaspoon ground cumin
1 teaspoon freshly grated nutmeg

1 teaspoon finely ground white pepper
¼ teaspoon ground ginger
Good pinch of saffron threads

Sea salt
2 pounds 10 ounces (1.2 kg) lamb meat from the shanks or shoulder, trimmed of fat and cut into big chunks

¼ preserved lemon, preferably a well-aged one, rind only
Moroccan Bread (page 11), for serving

Put the oil, garlic, spices, and a little salt in a heavy pot. Mix well, then add the meat. Stir the meat with the seasoned oil, then add the preserved lemon rind. Cover and place over low heat. Simmer for 1 hour 15 minutes, stirring occasionally, until the meat is very tender and the sauce thickened. Taste and adjust the seasoning if necessary. If the sauce is runny, increase the heat to high and boil for a few minutes until the excess liquid has evaporated. Serve very hot with good bread, preferably Moroccan bread.

NOTE: *To make preserved lemons, quarter unwaxed lemons lengthwise without cutting all the way through, leaving them attached at one end. Spread 1 teaspoon sea salt inside each of 2 quarters for a total of 2 teaspoons per lemon. Pack the lemons tightly in a canning jar and seal tight. Let sit for at least 3 to 4 weeks.*

SWEET-SAVORY LAMB TAGINE for EID EL-KBIR

M'RUZIYAH

MOROCCO

M'ruziyah is the Moroccan dish for Eid el-Kbir, when all those who can afford it will slaughter one or more sheep to use for their festive meal. They will also distribute some to family and friends as well as to those less fortunate. The traditional division is one-third for the household, one-third for relatives and friends, and one-third for the needy. In Morocco, meat is generally cooked on the bone, and for this specific recipe, the cut used is the shoulder. I have also used shanks, and I have used neck fillets, but when I want the dish to look really impressive, I use a whole leg of lamb. You can use beef if you want, but it is rare for Moroccans to do this. They normally use lamb or goat.

SERVES 6

1 small leg of lamb on the bone (4½ pounds/2 kg)
⅓ cup (80 ml) extra-virgin olive oil
4 tablespoons (60 g) unsalted butter

Good pinch of saffron threads, soaked in 2 tablespoons rose water
1 medium onion (5 ounces/150 g), halved lengthwise and cut into thin wedges

1 teaspoon ras el-hanout (see page 363)
Sea salt
1½ cups plus 2 tablespoons (400 g) good honey
3⅓ cups (500 g) golden raisins, soaked for 1 hour in warm water

1 cup (150 g) blanched almonds, toasted in a hot oven for 7 minutes, until golden brown
Moroccan Bread (page 11), for serving

1. Put the leg of lamb in a heavy pot and add 4 cups (1 L) water. Bring to a boil over medium heat, skimming the froth that rises to the surface. Add the olive oil, butter, and saffron-rose water. Add the onion, ras el-hanout, and salt to taste, then reduce the heat to medium-low and simmer, covered, for 2 hours, turning the leg every 15 minutes to make sure it is not sticking and is coloring evenly, until the meat is cooked through.

2. Add the honey. Reduce the heat to as low as you can have it and let simmer, this time without disturbing the meat, for another 30 minutes.

3. Drain the golden raisins and add to the pot. Let simmer until the sauce is completely concentrated and silky, 5 to 10 more minutes.

4. Transfer the cooked leg of lamb to a serving dish. Scoop the raisins with a slotted spoon and scatter over it, then drizzle the sauce all over. Garnish with the toasted almonds and serve immediately with Moroccan bread.

AWADHI CHICKEN KORMA

MURG AWADHI KORMA

INDIA

When I was in Indonesia, I learned to make a chicken *gulai* using kenari nuts instead of coconut cream. The sauce was really interesting, concentrated and creamy yet light. It was incredibly delicious, and the dish was fairly simple to make if you don't plan on using the typical Indonesian flat mortar and horizontal pestle that Indonesians use to grind their ingredients. The sauce for this Indian curry is also made with nuts (almonds or cashews), but it is rather different from the Indonesian *gulai* because of the complexity of the spicing. The word *Awadhi* means the dish is from Awadh, a region of northern India, once ruled by the Nawabs—fine gourmets whose cooks, the *bawarchis*, prepared supremely sophisticated dishes that were very much influenced by the cooking of the Mughal court. The *bawarchis* of Lucknow, once the capital of Awadh but now the capital of Utar Pradesh, were famous for their kebabs, kormas, biryanis, and many other elaborate dishes. This particular korma is a classic of Lucknow. The amount of nuts is a little extravagant, but the final result is definitely worth it. This said, you can use less without making the dish any less delicious.

SERVES 4 TO 6

Vegetable oil, for frying
1 small onion
   (3½ ounces/100 g),
   halved and cut into thin
   wedges
3⅓ cups (500 g)
   blanched almonds
2 bay leaves
3 whole cloves
3 green cardamom pods
2 black cardamom pods
1 cinnamon stick
3 cloves garlic, minced to
   a fine paste

1 inch (2.5 cm) fresh
   ginger, peeled and
   finely minced
2¼ pounds (1 kg)
   boneless, skinless
   chicken meat, both
   white and dark, cut into
   medium chunks
½ cup (60 g) chickpea
   flour, toasted in a
   dry pan until lightly
   browned
¼ teaspoon finely ground
   black pepper

Sea salt
1 tablespoon ground
   yellow pepper
   (optional)
½ teaspoon Garam
   Masala 2 (page 361)
½ cup (125 g) yogurt,
   whisked
½ cup (125 ml) heavy
   cream
Good pinch of saffron
   threads
¼ teaspoon ground
   cardamom

¼ teaspoon freshly
   grated nutmeg
1 teaspoon kewra
   (pandanus flower
   extract)

FOR SERVING
A few sprigs cilantro,
   most of the stems
   discarded, finely
   chopped
Cooked basmati rice
   or Naan (page 24) or
   other good flatbread

1. Cover the bottom of a skillet with a thin film of oil and add the onion. Sauté until golden brown. Remove with a slotted spoon to a sieve to drain off excess oil. Process into a fine paste.

2. Add a little more oil to the pan and sauté the almonds until golden. Pour into a sieve. Let cool, then grind in a food processor until very fine.

3. Heat 3 tablespoons oil in a pot over medium heat. Add the bay leaves, cloves, green and black cardamom pods, and cinnamon stick and sauté until the spices start crackling. Add the garlic and ginger and stir for a few seconds, then add the chicken pieces. Sauté for a few minutes, then add the caramelized onion paste. Add the chickpea flour, pepper, and salt to taste. Stir in 1 cup (250 ml) water. Reduce the heat to low and cook for 25 minutes, or until the chicken is almost done.

4. Add the yellow pepper (if you have it), garam masala, and yogurt and simmer for a minute or so. Add the ground almonds, cream, saffron, cardamom, nutmeg, *kewra*, and 1 cup (250 ml) water and simmer for 5 minutes or so.

5. Transfer to a shallow serving bowl. Garnish with the chopped cilantro and serve immediately with rice or bread.

QUAIL TAGINE
with SWEET POTATOES
D'JAJ BEL BATATA LEH'LOUA

MOROCCO

In every medina or souk in Morocco, there is a section where they sell live birds, usually chickens and pigeons. The customer chooses the birds he or she wants. The vendor then takes them out of the cage, slits their throat, and throws them in a barrel to thrash out their last breath. Once completely dead, he lifts them out and plucks them by holding them against an antiquated rotating machine that removes the feathers in seconds. After that he dunks the birds in water that looks as if it is teeming with a million germs—he changes it only once a day—before putting them in a bag for the customer to take home where he or she not surprisingly will wash them carefully before cooking. This particular tagine is one of my favorite sweet-savory ones. I like to make it with quail instead of the more traditional chicken. You can also use squab or poussin.   SERVES 6

6 quail
1 medium onion (about 5 ounces/150 g), grated on the fine side of a grater
1 teaspoon ground ginger
¾ teaspoon finely ground black pepper
½ teaspoon ras el-hanout (see page 363)
Good pinch of saffron threads
Sea salt
3 tablespoons extra-virgin olive oil
1 pound 10 ounces (750 g) sweet potatoes, peeled, quartered lengthwise, and cut into medium chunks
1¼ cups (200 g) golden raisins
3 tablespoons good-quality honey
Moroccan Bread (page 11), for serving

1. Put the quail, onion, spices, and a little salt in a large pot. Add 2 cups (500 ml) water and bring to a boil over medium-high heat. Add the oil, then reduce the heat to medium-low. Cover the pan and let bubble gently for 30 minutes, or until the quail are done and the sauce is reduced by three-quarters.

2. Remove the quail to a serving platter and keep warm.

3. Add the sweet potatoes and golden raisins to the sauce. Reduce the heat to low and simmer, covered, for 10 to 15 minutes, or until the potatoes are tender and the golden raisins have plumped. If the sauce is too runny, increase the heat and boil it hard uncovered for a few minutes, until you have a silky sauce. Carefully stir in the honey, making sure you don't mash up the potatoes. Let bubble, uncovered, for a few more minutes. Taste and adjust the seasoning if necessary.

4. Arrange the sweet potatoes and golden raisins all around the quail and spoon the sauce all over. Serve very hot with Moroccan bread.

IRANIAN CHICKEN in WALNUT and POMEGRANATE SAUCE

KHORESHT-E FESENJÂN

IRAN

Possibly Iran's most famous dish, this *khoresht* is traditionally made with duck, but I make it with chicken because it is less fatty. The ducks that are bred in Iran are leaner than their Western equivalent. You can also use squab, quail, or poussin or Cornish hen if you want to serve individual birds. Pheasant is also a good choice. Use one pheasant to serve two—hen pheasants have more fat on them and they would work better here. Be sure to buy walnuts from a reputable source as they have a tendency to go rancid if poorly stored or if they have been around for too long.

SERVES 4

4 tablespoons extra-virgin olive oil

1⅔ cups (250 g) walnuts, finely ground

1 medium onion (about 5 ounces/150 g), finely chopped

1 whole chicken (about 3 pounds 5 ounces/ 1.5 kg), quartered

2 cups (500 ml) organic chicken stock

¼ cup (60 ml) pomegranate molasses

1 tablespoon raw cane sugar

Sea salt

Plain Iranian Rice (page 242), for serving

1. Heat 2 tablespoons of the olive oil in a small skillet over medium heat. Add the walnuts and sauté for 5 to 8 minutes, or until they start changing color. Be careful not to burn them.

2. Heat the remaining 2 tablespoons oil in a large sauté pan over medium heat. Add the onion and cook, stirring regularly, until lightly golden, about 5 minutes. Add the chicken and brown lightly on each side.

3. Remove the chicken pieces to a plate. Discard the skin and return the chicken to the pan. Add just enough stock to cover the chicken (save the remainder for adding in the next step) and let bubble gently, covered, for 15 minutes.

4. Add the walnuts and the remaining stock and cook for another 15 minutes. Add the pomegranate molasses and sugar. Season with salt to taste and cook for another 10 to 15 minutes, or until the sauce has thickened and the chicken is very tender. Serve hot with the rice.

ACEH-STYLE GOAT CURRY
GULAI KAMBING ACEH

Ramadan is big all over the Islamic world, but in some countries like Oman people hardly venture out during fasting. As a result if you visit the country during that time, as I did, you will not get to see much life on the street, even in the markets. But in other countries like Indonesia, the atmosphere is very festive with markets full of food for those fasting and not wanting to cook for their *buka puasa* (*iftar*, or breaking the fast). And in restaurants, huge curries are put to simmer on charcoal fires in the afternoon so that they can be ready for when the fast is broken at sunset. This goat curry is a speciality of Aceh, a province at the northern end of Sumatra with the largest concentration of Muslims in Indonesia, where they live by Sharia law, a religious law derived from the religious precepts of the Qu'ran.

SERVES 4 TO 6

FOR THE SPICE PASTE
3 tablespoons unsweetened shredded coconut
2 tablespoons coriander seeds
2 teaspoons white peppercorns
½ teaspoon fennel seeds
1 tablespoon white poppy seeds (kas-kas)
½ nutmeg, grated
½ teaspoon ground cumin

2 inches (5 cm) fresh ginger
2 inches (5 cm) fresh turmeric
1¼ inches (3 cm) fresh galangal
4 small shallots (3 ounces/85 g total), peeled
2 cloves garlic, peeled but whole
1 fresh red chili, trimmed
4 candlenuts, macadamia nuts, or cashews
Sea salt

FOR THE MEAT
2¼ pounds (1 kg) goat meat, preferably on the bone, cut into medium chunks
Juice of 2 limes or 1 lemon

FOR THE CURRY
¼ cup (60 ml) vegetable oil
4 medium shallots (3½ ounces/100 g total), halved and cut into thin wedges
2 fresh curry leaves

3 tablespoons mild chili powder mixed with 1 tablespoon water
2-inch (5 cm) cinnamon stick
2 star anise
4 whole cloves
2 green cardamom pods, smashed
4 stalks lemongrass, white part only, smashed
2½ cups (600 ml) coconut cream
Sea salt
Boiled fragrant jasmine rice, for serving

1. To make the spice paste: Put the shredded coconut, coriander seeds, white peppercorns, fennel seeds, white poppy seeds, and nutmeg in a nonstick skillet and place over medium heat. Toast, stirring all the time, until fragrant. Add the ground cumin and stir for a few seconds. Transfer to a food processor. Wipe the pan clean and put the fresh ginger, turmeric, and galangal in it and toast until lightly golden. Add the galangal to the food processor, then peel the ginger and turmeric and add to the food processor. Add the shallots, garlic, chili, nuts, and salt to taste and process until you have a fine paste.

2. To marinate the meat: Put the goat meat in a bowl and add the lime or lemon juice. Mix well, then rub the spice paste into the meat. Let marinate for at least 2 hours, or preferably overnight in the refrigerator.

3. To make the curry: Heat the vegetable oil in a large pot over medium heat. Add the shallots and cook, stirring occasionally, until lightly golden, about 3 to 5 minutes. Stir in the curry leaves and chili paste. Add the marinated goat, cinnamon, star anise, cloves, cardamom, and lemongrass and cook, stirring regularly, until the goat is lightly browned. Reduce the heat to medium-low, cover, and cook for a few minutes, or until the meat browns a little more. Add the coconut cream and salt to taste and mix well. Reduce the heat to low and let simmer 45 minutes, stirring regularly to make sure the sauce is not sticking, or until the sauce is thick and some of the oil has risen to the surface. Taste and adjust the seasoning if necessary. Serve hot with rice.

PAKISTANI CHICKEN CURRY

CHICKEN KARAHI

When I was in Lahore for the Lahore Literary Festival, I was invited to stay with Razi Ahmed, the founder of the festival, and his family; and every morning I would meet his mother in the kitchen for a *desi* breakfast and a chat that often revolved around *desi* food, which I adored, not to mention that I also loved being with the Ahmed family, whose hospitality and generosity reminded me so much of both my countries, Lebanon and Syria. I also remember my first home-cooked lunch, at Nuscie Jamil's beautiful home. Nuscie, who is also very involved with the festival, became a firm friend, and even though this recipe is not hers, I am pretty sure she served a similar curry at that lunch. It is simple to make and I love the concept of cooking the sauce before adding the chicken, which ensures a beautiful consistency not to mention an intense, irresistible flavor.

SERVES 4

¼ cup (60 ml) vegetable oil, plus more if needed
3 medium onions (1 pound/450 g total), finely chopped
2 medium tomatoes (7 ounces/200 g total), processed with a little water to a smooth puree

1-inch (2.5 cm) piece fresh ginger, peeled and minced to a fine paste
2 cloves garlic, minced to a fine paste
1 teaspoon Kashmiri chili powder
2 teaspoons ground coriander
1½ teaspoons ground cumin

1 teaspoon curry powder
½ teaspoon ground turmeric
Sea salt
1 tablespoon tomato paste
1 whole chicken (3 pounds 5 ounces/ 1.5 kg), skinned and jointed into 8 pieces

¼ bunch cilantro (2 ounces/50 g), most of the bottom stems discarded, coarsely chopped
½ teaspoon Garam Masala 1 (page 361)
Cooked basmati rice or Naan (page 24), for serving

1. Heat the oil in a medium pot over medium heat until hot. Add the onions and cook, stirring occasionally, until golden brown.

2. Add half the pureed tomatoes and mix well. When the tomatoes start bubbling, add the ginger, garlic, the chili powder, coriander, cumin, curry powder, turmeric, and salt to taste and mix well. Cook, stirring regularly, until fragrant.

3. Add the remaining pureed tomatoes and mix well, then stir in the tomato paste. If you find that the sauce is sticking at this stage, add 1 tablespoon more vegetable oil. Stir until the oil rises. Use a hand blender to process the sauce into a puree. (Or transfer to a food processor to puree, then return to the pot.)

4. Add the chicken pieces to the pot and cook until the meat is no longer pink. Add ¼ cup (60 ml) water and continue to cook until the water has evaporated and the sauce or masala is thick again with some of the oil rising to the surface. Then add 1 cup (250 ml) water and bring to a boil. Reduce the heat to low, cover the pan, and let simmer for 30 minutes, or until the chicken is cooked through and the sauce is concentrated; check on the chicken halfway through to make sure the sauce is not drying out.

5. Uncover and stir. Add the cilantro and garam masala and let simmer, covered, for a few more minutes. Serve immediately with rice or bread.

IRANIAN YELLOW SPLIT PEA STEW

KHORESHT-E GHEIMEH

Khoresht-e gheimeh is one of the most common *khoreshts* in Iran, mainly because it is economical and can be prepared all year round, given that it does not call for any fresh produce. My first taste of *gheimeh* was on my last trip to Iran. I was in Isfahan on the day of 'Ashura, the day of mourning for Shi'ite Muslims to commemorate the martyrdom of Hussein (the Prophet Muhammad's grandson), his companions, and members of his family in Karbala. I was staying in a charming boutique hotel near a large mosque and both places were an extraordinary scene of frenzied cooking. In the hotel, the cook was preparing a *khoresht-e gheimeh* for two hundred people, and at the mosque, the cooks were making a chicken *kohresht* for *three thousand*! And of course they were also cooking gigantic quantities of rice to serve with the stews. During 'Ashura food is distributed and old and young men process through the town and flagellate themselves to share in the suffering of their saint. I first went to the mosque's kitchens to watch the cooks soak huge quantities of rice in enormous vats before draining and boiling it, as well as wash hundreds of chickens to make the *khoresht*. It was an astonishing spectacle with the mammoth pots filling the kitchen, each placed over a low gas fire with either the stew or the rice cooking in it. I missed out on the killing of the lambs that were tied together in a tiny room across the courtyard from the kitchen.

Within the mosque, the cooks had laid long plastic sheets on the carpet to serve the meal they had cooked to those coming in after the procession. I then walked back to the hotel to watch the people from the neighborhood filing into the hotel to pick up their share of *khoresht-e gheimeh* and rice. The hotel cook garnished the *gheimeh* with chips, but in homes, the garnish would be either French fries or cubes of fried potatoes. Some people replace the potato garnish with fried eggplant.

SERVES 4

3 tablespoons vegetable oil, plus more for deep-frying the potatoes

4 lamb shanks (3 pounds 5 ounces/1.5 kg total)

2 medium onions (10½ ounces/300 g total), halved and cut into thin wedges

1 teaspoon ground turmeric

Finely ground black pepper

2 tablespoons (30 g) tomato paste

4½ teaspoons ground dried limes

1 pound (450 g) yellow split peas, rinsed

4 pale dried limes, pierced in several places

Juice of 1 lemon, or to taste

Sea salt

9 ounces (250 g) potatoes, cut for French fries

Plain Iranian Rice (page 242)

1. Heat the 3 tablespoons oil in a heavy pot over medium heat until hot. Add the shanks and brown them all over, about 10 minutes. Remove to a plate then add the onions and cook, stirring regularly, until golden brown. Add the turmeric and pepper to taste and mix well.

2. Return the browned shanks to the pot and add 4 cups (1 liter) water. When the water starts bubbling, add the tomato paste and ground dried limes. Reduce the heat to medium-low, cover, and let bubble gently for 45 minutes, stirring every now and then.

3. Add the split peas, whole dried limes, lemon juice, and salt to taste and continue cooking for another 40 to 45 minutes, or until the peas are soft but not mushy and the meat is tender. If the sauce is watery, uncover the pan, increase the heat, and let it boil hard until it has thickened.

4. Meanwhile, place a fine-mesh wire rack in a rimmed baking sheet or line with paper towels. Pour 1 inch (2.5 cm) vegetable oil in a deep skillet and place over medium heat. To test the temperature of the oil, drop in a piece of bread. If the oil immediately bubbles around it, it is ready. Fry the potatoes until golden and drain on the paper towels or set on the rack—the latter will keep them even more crisp. Lightly salt the fried potatoes.

5. Transfer the *khoresht* to a shallow serving bowl. Scatter the fried potatoes all over, or pile them in the middle. Serve immediately with the rice.

IRANIAN MIXED-HERB LAMB STEW

KHORESHT-E GHORMEH SABZI

Sabzi means "mixed herbs" in Iranian and this *khoresht* is made with an amazing number of different herbs, greens, and scallions—a mixture that people often buy ready-made in the bazaars in Iran, which they then have the seller chop in a special machine a little like a meat grinder but with a much wider rotating blade so as not to bruise the herbs. You can make this *khoresht* with fresh herbs, but if not available, you can use a packaged mix of dried *sabzi* available in Persian groceries. Obviously the dried mix will not be as vibrant as fresh *sabzi,* but it is more than acceptable. If you do use dried herbs, you will need 8 ounces (225 g), which is half the weight of the quantities of fresh *sabzi* I give below. I remember going into the courtyard of a refuge for the disabled in Isfahan and finding a group of women in black chadors chopping a huge mound of *sabzi* to freeze so they could use it in the winter months. It was an impressive sight, to say the least. Their grinder was quite different from those I had seen in the bazaars. Perhaps it was a cheaper version as it was giving them a lot of trouble, jamming with every batch, whereas the guys in the bazaars were operating theirs for client after client without any problem!

SERVES 4

2 tablespoons extra-virgin olive oil

FOR THE SABZI
1 ounce (30 g) fresh fenugreek leaves, finely chopped, or 2 tablespoons dried
¾ bunch flat-leaf parsley (5 ounces/150 g), most of the bottom stems discarded, finely chopped

½ bunch cilantro (3½ ounces/100 g), most of the bottom stems discarded, finely chopped
1 small bunch dill (1 ounce/30 g), most of the bottom stems discarded, finely chopped

FOR THE KHORESHT
1 tablespoon extra-virgin olive oil

4 bunches scallions or baby leeks (7 ounces/200 g total), white and green parts, thinly sliced
1 pound (450 g) boneless lamb meat from the shank meat, cut into medium chunks
⅔ cup (130 g) dried red kidney beans or black-eyed peas, soaked overnight in plenty of water with ½ teaspoon baking soda

2 tablespoons ground dried limes
4 pale dried limes, rinsed and pricked in several places with a sharp knife
Juice of 2 lemons, or to taste
Sea salt
Plain Iranian Rice (page 242), for serving

1. Heat the olive oil in a large skillet over medium heat. Add the *sabzi* and fry for about 30 seconds, stirring constantly, until the herbs begin to darken. Set aside.

2. To make the khoresht: Heat the olive oil in a large pot over medium-high heat. Add the scallions and cook, stirring regularly, until soft and lightly golden, 3 to 5 minutes. Add the lamb and sauté until browned.

3. Drain and rinse the beans. Add to the pot along with the fried *sabzi*, ground limes, and whole dried limes. Add water to barely cover. Reduce the heat to medium-low, cover, and simmer for 1 hour.

4. Stir in the lemon juice and salt to taste. Let simmer for another 15 minutes, or until the sauce is reduced and the meat and beans are tender. Taste and adjust the seasoning if necessary. Serve with rice.

IRANIAN LAMB and EGGPLANT STEW

KHORESHT-E BÂDENJÂN

IRAN

This khoresht is similar to the Moroccan Lamb Tagine with Eggplant (page 146), except that the eggplant is fried and added to the lamb at the end. As for the sauce, it is made with tomatoes and not with a lamb stock reduction. Both are delicious, though, and a wonderful way to combine meat with eggplants in the summer when they are at their best.   SERVES 4 TO 6

4½ pounds (2 kg) globe eggplants, peeled lengthwise in stripes and cut crosswise into 2-inch (5 cm) disks
Sea salt
Vegetable oil, for deep-frying

3 tablespoons extra-virgin olive oil
2 medium onions (10½ ounces/300 g total), halved and cut into thin wedges
1 teaspoon ground turmeric
1 pound 2 ounces (500 g) boneless lamb

leg or neck fillets, cut into medium chunks
3 tablespoons tomato paste
One 14-ounce (400 g) can whole peeled tomatoes, drained, seeded, and coarsely chopped

Juice of 1 lemon, or to taste
Finely ground black pepper
Pomegranate seeds, for garnish
Plain Iranian Rice (page 242), for serving

1. Salt the eggplant slices and let them sweat for 30 minutes. Rinse and pat dry.

2. Set a fine-mesh wire rack in a rimmed baking sheet or line with paper towels. Pour 1 inch (2.5 cm) vegetable oil into a deep skillet and heat over medium heat until hot (if you drop a piece of bread in the oil, the oil should immediately bubble around it). Working in batches, fry the eggplant until golden brown on both sides. Transfer to the rack or paper towels to drain.

3. Heat the olive oil in a wide pot over medium heat. Add the onions and fry until lightly golden, about 5 minutes. Stir in the turmeric and add the meat. Sauté until the meat is browned all over. Stir in the tomato paste, chopped canned tomatoes, and lemon juice. Add water to barely cover the meat. Season with salt and pepper to taste and let bubble gently for 30 minutes.

4. Add the fried eggplant slices and a little more water if the sauce seems too dry. Reduce the heat to medium-low and let simmer for 10 more minutes.

5. Carefully transfer to a serving platter, making sure you do not mash up the eggplant slices. Serve very hot, sprinkled with pomegranate seeds, alongside the rice.

QUINCE STEW

KHORESHT-E BEH

Here is quite a wonderful stew that can be made only when quince are in season as no self-respecting Iranian would consider using frozen or canned quince. I always look forward to the fall when I start seeing quince in the market, as this is one of the first quince dishes I rush to make. It is also very simple to prepare. I have made it with lamb and I have made it with veal. The latter takes longer to cook, so adjust the cooking times according to what kind of meat you are using.

SERVES 4 TO 6

¼ cup (60 ml) vegetable oil
4 medium onions (1 pound 5 ounces/ 600 g total), cut into thin wedges

1 pound 10 ounces (750 g) boneless lamb leg or neck fillets, or boneless veal breast, cut into medium chunks
½ cup (100 g) yellow split peas, rinsed

1 teaspoon ground turmeric
Good pinch of saffron threads
3 tablespoons raw cane sugar
Sea salt and finely ground black pepper

3 large quince (1 pound 10½ ounces/750 g total), peeled, cored, and cut into medium-thick wedges
Plain Iranian Rice (page 242), for serving

1. Heat the oil in a pot (large enough to eventually hold the meat, split peas, and quince) over medium heat. Add the onions and cook, stirring occasionally, until golden brown, about 10 minutes. Add the meat and sauté, stirring regularly, until browned.

2. Add the split peas, turmeric, saffron, sugar, salt and pepper to taste, and 2 cups (500 ml) water. Bring to a boil, then reduce the heat to low and simmer for 1 hour. Add the quince and simmer, covered, for another 30 minutes, or until the meat, split peas, and quince are tender. Taste and adjust the seasoning if necessary.

3. Transfer to a shallow serving bowl and serve with the rice.

DAIRY

YOGURT

I can still see my mother making yogurt in our kitchen in Beirut, how she wrapped a thick blanket around the pot in which she mixed the yogurt culture with the hot milk and then slowly and carefully pushed the pot to the back of the counter before sternly turning around to me—I was her kitchen pest and always hovered around her when she was cooking—to warn me not to touch the pot, otherwise we wouldn't have any yogurt. Hardly anyone makes yogurt at home nowadays. The choice in the supermarkets is vast, with goat, sheep, or cow's milk yogurt; organic, nonorganic; made with live culture; fat-free; and so on. Still, there is nothing more satisfying than making your own the old-fashioned way. Also, the yogurt made at home with live cultures will curdle more easily if you want to make fresh cheeses or ghee from scratch. And you can experiment and make dried yogurt products such as Lebanese *kishk* or Jordanian *jameed*, or Iranian *kashk,* or Turkish *tarhana,* which unlike the others comes in different versions.

Yogurt has been an important part of the diet of Arab Muslims from the time of the Prophet Muhammad. Their flocks of sheep, goats, or camels provided milk, and yogurt kept better than milk. It is still an important part of the diet of Muslims throughout western, southern, and central Asia as well as in the north and east of Africa. Here, I give a brief description of the different ways of preserving yogurt, followed by recipes that make use of both fresh and dried yogurt. Yogurt is also consumed on its own or served as a side with stuffed vegetables or freekeh, but more important, it is used in cooking a whole range of dishes (see pages 171 to 193).

LABNEH

Also known as *chaka* in Afghanistan, labneh is basically strained yogurt. Many call it "yogurt cheese," but it is not really a cheese. Labneh is made by simply draining the whey off yogurt. Helen Saberi also explains in her book *Afghan Cookery* that by straining yogurt, you get rid of the acidity or sourness that whey can impart to the yogurt. In the Levant, labneh is usually eaten on its own, drizzled with olive oil, or made into dips together with other ingredients. It can also be used in fillings for savory pastries.

KISHK

Kishk is made by mixing bulgur with part regular yogurt and part labneh, then fermenting and drying the mixture before grinding it to produce an ivory white powder that resembles flour. The time to prepare *kishk* is in late summer and early fall after the wheat has been harvested and processed into bulgur. Traditionally, *kishk* was prepared in mountain villages as a winter provision to be used during the cold months with *qawarma* (a kind of minced lamb confit) and garlic to make a hearty breakfast porridge. My mother's family, when they still made *kishk* at home, used one portion of bulgur to eight of salted yogurt. They placed all the bulgur in a wide crock and covered it with two parts regular yogurt. They let it soak in the yogurt for twenty-four hours, during which time they salted and strained the rest of the yogurt by putting it in a cloth bag to let the whey drain off. The next day, they divided the strained yogurt into three parts, and mixed one with the bulgur-yogurt mixture. They saved the other two to be added on successive days. Once all the yogurt was used, they let the mixture ferment for a week, kneading it every day, until it became quite sour. Then they pinched off small lumps, spread them on clean sheets laid over straw mats, and put them to dry in the sun. Once completely dried, my grandmother, mother, her sister, and a couple of neighbors gathered around a large tub and rubbed the lumps of *kishk* between the palms of their hands until they broke them all down into a coarse powder. My grandmother then sifted the *kishk* through a fine steel mesh into a fine powder, which she stored in canvas bags. She used the bigger pieces that were left with *qawarma*, and sometimes labneh to make a filling for savory pastries. *Kishk* is mostly made commercially nowadays and ground by machine. The result is a very fine powder with a uniform ivory color, whereas homemade *kishk* is speckled with golden flecks of bulgur. You can also mix *kishk* with onion, tomatoes, sesame seeds, walnuts, and olive oil to make a topping for *manaqish* (page 42).

KASHK

Kashk is the Iranian equivalent of the Levantine *kishk* but is made without any grain. It's simply dried salted yogurt that you can buy shaped into hard balls or reconstituted into a thick spread in jars or cartons. It is added to dips and soups, and is also used as a garnish. *Kashk* has a sour-salty flavor that is very pleasing and the spread has a thick texture that adds body to both soups and dips.

JAMEED

Also known as *quroot* in Afghanistan, Jordanian *jameed* is basically salted and dried yogurt. The yogurt is put in cheesecloth and salted daily. During that time, the outside of the cloth is rinsed daily to get rid of all the whey. When the yogurt has become very dense, it is unmolded and rolled into balls, either round or with a pointed top and put to dry outside. If left in the sun the balls will turn rather yellow, whereas if they are dried in the shade they will remain pristine white. It is important to dry the balls to the core so that they keep well. *Jameed* is used in the national dish of Jordan, *mansaf* (page 177).

TARHANA

Tarhana is the Turkish version of the Levantine *kishk*, which can be made simply with a grain and yogurt, with added tomatoes, or added vegetables. It comes in different shapes and forms, such as coarsely ground or as flakes or lacy chips, and it is mainly used in soups.

SHANKLISH

Shanklish is the Syrian version of blue cheese, with its own unique, rather pungent flavor. The way the cheese was traditionally made, and in some cases still is, was by first extracting some of the butterfat from the yogurt by shaking it in an earthenware jar and skimming off the fat bit by bit, after which the semi-skimmed yogurt was brought to a boil. Once curdled, it was strained to get *qarisheh*. When the *qarisheh* had cooled down, it was salted, seasoned with Aleppo pepper, then kneaded until it became quite smooth. At this stage it was rolled into rounds the size of tennis balls. These were put to dry in the sun first—my aunt put hers to dry on a white sheet on the flat roof of her house in Mashta el-Helou. After the balls of cheese had dried, they were put to ferment, traditionally in the same earthenware jars year after year so that the cheese could be innoculated by the same spores to grow the same mold (although nowadays it is more likely that those still making *shanklish* at home would ferment it in glass jars). The mold takes at least two weeks to develop and cover the outside of the balls; the longer it is left to ferment, the stronger the flavor and the creamier the cheese. The mold is then washed or scraped off and the cheese is rolled in dried thyme, or sometimes Aleppo pepper, before being stored in clean glass jars to eat plain with bread, or to make into a salad with tomatoes, onion, and olive oil to serve as part of a mezze spread. I still remember the taste of my aunt's *shanklish*, creamy and piquant, and absolutely exquisite. Most *shanklish* nowadays, at least that which is sold commercially, is actually made from labneh mixed with salt and Aleppo pepper and covered with za'atar with practically no fermented flavor.

SHANKLISH SALAD
SALATET SHANKLISH

This salad is one of my favorite mezze, but you need to find really good *shanklish* for it to be tasty, or you need to make your own *shanklish*. A few years ago I found a Syrian couple in London who made *shanklish* the way it should be made, but their venture did not last long. I guess they couldn't make it pay or they were hampered by regulations, which is a shame. I make my own in sunny Sicily, where I have a terrace to put the cheese out to dry. It is a little time-consuming and I have to watch out for the birds, but I cover the balls of cheese with cheesecloth and the birds leave them alone.

SERVES 4 TO 6

1 ball shanklish (about 7 ounces/200 g), crumbled

2 medium firm-ripe tomatoes (7 ounces/200 g total), seeded and cut into small cubes

1 small red onion (2 ounces/60 g), finely chopped

2 or 3 sprigs fresh thyme, leaves only (optional)

¼ cup (60 ml) extra-virgin olive oil, plus more for serving

Pita Bread (page 4), for serving

Put all the ingredients except the pita in a bowl and mix well. Transfer to a salad bowl and serve with more olive oil and pita bread.

PANEER

This is the South Asian version of the Levantine *qarisheh* on page 000 except that once the milk has curdled and been strained of all the whey, it is pressed into a block, which is then cut into squares or rectangles and used in various dishes, such as the Paneer Makhni (opposite) or the Spinach with Paneer (page 421).

MAKES 1 BLOCK (ABOUT 9 OUNCES/250 G)

2 quarts (2 liters) whole milk
2 tablespoons lemon juice

Put the milk in a saucepan and bring to a boil over medium heat. As soon as the milk comes to a boil, add the lemon juice—you can also use vinegar, but I prefer lemon juice. When the milk separates and starts to curdle, take it off the heat and strain it through cheesecloth. The whey will take a few hours to drain away completely, at which stage tighten the cheesecloth around the curds and place in a square mold on a plate. Weight down the curds to let them set into a block. This should take less than an hour.

PANEER MAKHNI

SERVES 4 TO 6

8 medium tomatoes (1¾ pounds/800 g total), quartered
¼ cup (60 ml) vegetable oil
4 green cardamom pods
6 whole cloves
1 cinnamon stick
6 cloves garlic, minced to a fine paste
2 inches (5 cm) fresh ginger, peeled and finely minced
2 small green chilies, thinly sliced
One 7-ounce (200 g) block paneer, store-bought or homemade (opposite), halved lengthwise
1½ teaspoons Kashmiri chili powder (see page 515)
Sea salt
A few sprigs cilantro, most of the bottom stems discarded, finely chopped
1 teaspoon Garam Masala 1 (page 361)
4 dried fenugreek leaves
2 tablespoons honey
¼ cup (60 ml) whole milk
Indian Flatbread (page 30), for serving

1. Puree the tomatoes in a food processor. Transfer to a large pot and bring to a boil over medium heat. Reduce the heat to medium-low and let bubble gently until it has reduced by one-quarter; this should take 20 to 30 minutes.

2. Meanwhile, heat 1 tablespoon of the oil in a deep sauté pan over medium heat. Add the cardamom, cloves, cinnamon stick, garlic, and ginger and sauté until fragrant. Add the green chilies and sauté for a couple of minutes more.

3. Add the reduced tomato sauce to the sauté pan and let bubble gently while you fry the paneer.

4. Heat the remaining oil in a skillet over medium heat until hot. Slide the paneer slices into the pan. Sprinkle with half the chili powder and season with salt to taste and pan-fry until golden, about 3 minutes. Flip over, season with the remaining chili powder and salt to taste and pan-fry until golden. Take out of the pan and cut into medium cubes.

5. Add the cilantro, garam masala, fenugreek leaves, and honey to the tomato sauce and mix well. Add the paneer cubes to the sauce. Let bubble for a couple more minutes, then stir in the milk. (If not serving the dish immediately, do not stir in the milk until you reheat just before serving.) Let bubble for a few seconds and serve hot with bread.

YOGURT DRINK

AYRAN

Ayran is one of the most refreshing drinks made with yogurt. It is called *doogh* or *dugh* in Iran and Azerbajian, *ayran* in Turkey and the rest of the Levant, and *lassi* in India and Pakistan. *Ayran* or lassi are often served as alcohol-free drinks with roast meat, kebabs, or biryani, and when lassi is made sweet, it is served on its own. I give three variations here: a plain Turkish *ayran* (with a variation for *doogh*), a sweet lassi, and a mango lassi. The best *ayran* I have ever had was in Konya, in Turkey, at a place that only served *firni kebab* (lamb cooked in fat in big copper dishes in wood-fired ovens) together with *ayran*. Their *ayran* was sour and frothy, slightly salty, and incredibly refreshing, a perfect accompaniment to the fatty roast lamb. As we finished our meal, a sporty-looking young man sitting across from us—I was with Nevin Halici, the grande dame of Turkish cooking—started asking Nevin questions about me in Turkish, finishing with a marriage proposal. She mischievously relayed everything he said to me so that I understood the conversation when I would have preferred not to, because at the end I had to graciously decline his offer, through Nevin of course. The exchange was very amusing, and the gentleman wouldn't let us go without offering us a second round of *ayran* despite my not having accepted his extravagant proposal.   SERVES 4

2 cups (500 g) sheep
  yogurt (or goat or
  cow's milk yogurt)
4 to 6 ice cubes
Sea salt

Put the yogurt, 1½ cups (375 ml) water, ice cubes, and salt to taste in a blender and process until frothy. Serve with more ice cubes if you want your ayran to be more chilled, although if you start out with refrigerated yogurt and water, your ayran will be chilled enough. Pour into 4 glasses and serve.

DOOGH: To turn your *ayran* into Iranian *doogh*, add ½ to 1 teaspoon dried mint, or very finely chopped fresh mint (1 to 2 teaspoons) to taste.

MANGO YOGURT DRINK

MANGO LASSI

INDIA | PAKISTAN | BANGLADESH

The best time to prepare this is obviously during mango season. Alphonso mangoes are my favorite, but honey mangoes also work well. Avoid those that are stringy, and chill all your ingredients before preparing the lassi. This way when you make and serve the lassi it will already be chilled. And here you would do well to use a rather loose yogurt so the drink is not too dense. If it turns out too thick, loosen it with a little milk or water.

SERVES 4

Pulp from 4 Alphonso or honey mangoes (about 1½ cups/310 ml)
1⅓ cups (340 g) whole-milk yogurt
2 tablespoons raw cane sugar
Ice cubes (optional)

Combine the mango pulp, yogurt, and sugar in a blender or food processor and process until the mixture is foamy. Divide among 4 glasses and serve cold. You can add a couple of ice cubes in each glass if you want the lassi to be very chilled.

SWEET YOGURT DRINK
SWEET LASSI

Sweet lassi is usually consumed in India, Pakistan, and Bangladesh between meals or when guests come to visit. When I was in Pakistan recently, I stopped at a lassi vendor and watched him whisk his lassi with a special wooden implement called a *madani*, which has a long, thick handle and a round bottom block carved with wings so that when it is twirled inside the drink, it whisks it the same way as if you were using an electric beater. Even though lassi vendors whisk their lassi by hand, they are amazingly quick and efficient at producing a lot of froth, furiously twirling the *madani* handle in between the palms of their hands with the whisk part inside the bulbous metal lassi jar, spinning one way and the other in quick succession until a thick foam covers the drink, at which point the vendor pours the lassi into either tin or plastic cups. You can also make a sweet lassi with mango (see page 172), but if you do, be sure to use less sugar than in the classic Indian/Pakistani version. For a savory lassi, omit the sugar and cardamom and, if you want, add a pinch of salt and cumin to the yogurt, and process as below. Or make *ayran* or *doogh* (page 171); it's more or less the same.

SERVES 4

2 cups (500 g) sheep yogurt
¼ cup (60 g) raw cane sugar
Seeds from 4 green cardamom pods, coarsely ground
Ice cubes (optional)

Put the yogurt, 1⅓ cups (325 ml) cold water, the sugar, and cardamom in a food processor and process until you have a nice foam floating over the lassi. Serve in 4 glasses. Add a couple of ice cubes to each glass if you want your lassi extra cold and serve immediately.

COOKED YOGURT SAUCE

LABAN MATBOOKH

Cooking with yogurt is very common in Lebanon, Syria, and Jordan, as well as in Turkey and parts of Southern and Central Asia. Goat yogurt is the most stable yogurt to use in cooking, but it is safer to use a stabilizer when boiling yogurt, regardless of the type. Many use cornstarch and/or egg. I like to use only egg, as cornstarch tends to make the yogurt sauce coarser. Ideally you should cook the dish and serve it immediately as the sauce risks curdling during reheating, especially if done too quickly and if the sauce is allowed to boil hard. This sauce is the base for several dishes and can be flavored with mint or cilantro depending on what you are using it for.

SERVES 4 TO 6

2 tablespoons (30 g) unsalted butter

½ bunch cilantro (about 3½ ounces/100 g), most of the bottom stems discarded, finely chopped, or ¼ bunch mint (2 ounces/50 g), leaves stripped off the stems, finely chopped (or 3 tablespoons finely crumbled dried mint)

4 large cloves garlic, minced to a fine paste

4 cups (1 kg) yogurt

1 organic egg

1. Melt the butter in a skillet over medium heat. Add the chopped fresh herb of choice (or dried mint) and garlic and sauté for 1 minute, or until the herb has wilted. Take off the heat.

2. Whisk the yogurt and egg together in a large heavy saucepan. Bring to a boil over medium heat, stirring constantly (or else the yogurt will curdle). When the yogurt has come to a boil, reduce the heat to low and let simmer for 3 minutes, still stirring.

3. Add the herb-garlic mixture and set aside to use with the recipes on pages 179 and 181–183.

FESTIVE JORDANIAN LAMB in YOGURT over a Bed of RICE and BREAD

MANSAF

JORDAN

Mansaf is a typical Bedouin dish that comes from Hebron in the West Bank. It is served at large family gatherings, for celebrations, or simply to honor special guests. Traditionally it was made with a whole lamb, with the lamb's head proudly placed in the middle of the dish to indicate that the animal had been slaughtered for the occasion; but nowadays, it is more often than not made with a shoulder, a leg, or shanks. The meat is cooked in a yogurt sauce made with *jameed*, or dried yogurt.

Jameed is how Bedouins preserve the milk from their goats. To make it, the yogurt is drained in cotton sacks to remove the whey and salted every day until it thickens. The sacks are regularly rinsed with water on the outside to get rid of every trace of whey. The strained yogurt is then rolled into balls (either round or with a pointed top) and put to dry in the shade (if dried under direct sun, the *jameed* will be yellow instead of white) until the balls of *jameed* are rock hard to the core, after which they are stored away.

Jameed is mixed with water to reconstitute it before being used in in this dish. You can also make *mansaf* with fresh yogurt, although the flavor will not be as sour (the fermentation process gives *jameed* a particular flavor that imparts a faintly sour taste to the lamb as it cooks). I personally use a mixture of *jameed* for the sour flavor and fresh yogurt for creaminess. I have adapted the recipe below from one I found in a small Arabic cookbook, *The Palestinian Kitchen*. In the original recipe, the lamb is cooked in the yogurt-*jameed* mixture from the outset, but the yogurt can curdle during such long cooking, so I boil the lamb separately, then finish it in the yogurt sauce. While the flavor may not be quite so intense, the consistency of the sauce is creamier. You can also make *mansaf* with chicken but the dish will not be as celebratory as when made with lamb.

SERVES 6

Recipe continues

4 lamb shanks (3 pounds 5 ounces/1.5 kg total)
1 medium onion (about 5 ounces/150 g), peeled
1 cinnamon stick
Sea salt
2 jameed balls (each about the size of a tennis ball), soaked overnight in 3 cups (750 ml) water (see Note)
4 cups (1 kg) Greek yogurt
1 teaspoon ground allspice
1 teaspoon ground cinnamon
1 teaspoon finely ground black pepper
Good pinch of saffron threads
7 tablespoons (105 g) unsalted butter
2½ cups (500 g) Calasparra or Egyptian rice, rinsed under cold water and drained

FOR SERVING
⅔ cup (100 g) pine nuts
⅔ cup (100 g) blanched almonds
2 loaves handkerchief bread (page 6)
A few sprigs flat-leaf parsley, most of the bottom stems discarded, finely chopped

1. Put the shanks in a large pot and cover with water. Add the onion and cinnamon stick and bring to a boil over medium-high heat, skimming the froth from the surface. Reduce the heat to medium-low, season with salt to taste, cover, and simmer for 1 hour, or until the meat is tender.

2. Meanwhile, knead the *jameed* in its soaking water to help it dissolve completely. Strain the liquid into a large pot in case there are still little pellets of undissolved *jameed*. Add the Greek yogurt and bring to a boil over medium heat, stirring constantly to prevent the yogurt from curdling. Stir in the allspice, cinnamon, black pepper, and saffron. Remove from the heat as soon as the yogurt comes to a boil. Cover the pan with a clean kitchen towel and keep warm.

3. Melt the butter in a small pot and add the rice, stirring it in the butter until well coated. Add 4 cups (1 liter) water and season with salt to taste. Bring to a boil, then reduce the heat, cover, and simmer for 10 to 15 minutes, or until the rice is tender and the water is fully absorbed. Wrap the lid in a clean kitchen towel and replace over the rice.

4. Meanwhile, preheat the oven to 425°F (220°C).

5. Spread the pine nuts and almonds on separate nonstick baking sheets and toast in the oven until they turn golden brown (5 to 6 minutes for the pine nuts, 7 to 8 minutes for the almonds). Remove from the oven.

6. Remove the cooked lamb from the broth and take the meat off the bone. Drop the boiled lamb into the yogurt sauce and place the pan over low heat. Bring to a simmer, stirring all the time, adding a ladle or two of broth until you have a sauce the consistency of light cream. Taste and adjust the seasoning if necessary.

7. To serve, lay the bread over a large round serving platter. Spread the rice over the bread, then arrange the meat over the rice. Ladle as much yogurt sauce as you would like over the meat and rice without making the dish soupy. Pour any leftover sauce into a sauceboat. Garnish with the toasted nuts and serve immediately.

NOTE: *If dried jameed is not available, use 1½ cups (355 ml) prepared jameed stock or soup.*

LAMB SHANKS in YOGURT

LABAN EMMOH

In Arabic, *laban emmoh* means "the milk of its mother," and this dish is named this because the meat is cooked in the milk of the ewe—well, actually yogurt, but yogurt starts out as milk. It is one of my favorite dishes and I often make and serve it in the summer because the sauce is light and somewhat refreshing even if it is eaten hot. And I can imagine a similar dish being very much what early Muslims ate, as the meat and milk from their flocks was pretty much all they had, together with dates.

SERVES 6

4 lamb shanks (3 pounds 5 ounces/1.5 kg total)
Sea salt
16 baby onions (14 ounces/400 g total), peeled
Cooked Yogurt Sauce (page 175)
Lebanese/Syrian Vermicelli Rice (page 241) or bread, for serving

1. Put the shanks in a large pot. Add 5 cups (1.25 liters) water and bring to a boil over medium heat, skimming the froth from the surface. Cover the pot and let bubble gently for 1 hour, or until the meat is very tender. Add 1 tablespoon sea salt and the baby onions and let simmer for 10 more minutes, or until the onions are just firm-tender.

2. Meanwhile, make the cooked yogurt sauce through step 2, setting the herb-garlic mixture aside. For the yogurt, use a pot large enough to eventually hold the cooked shanks and onions. Keep the sauce warm while the meat finishes cooking.

3. When the meat and onions are done, return the yogurt sauce to medium-low heat and stir until it starts simmering. Add the meat and onions and stir in the reserved herb-garlic mixture. Add ¼ cup (60 ml) meat broth and simmer, stirring gently so as not to undo the onions, for 3 to 5 more minutes, until the onions are just tender.

4. Serve hot with the vermicelli rice or with good bread.

GRILLED EGGPLANT PUREE and MINCED MEAT in TOMATO SAUCE

BATERSH

I remember first having this dish, a specialty of Hama, in Syria, in the delightful courtyard of an Ottoman house converted into a restaurant in what was left of the old quarter of Hama—the father of the current president destroyed much of the city to quell an uprising by the Muslim Brotherhood. *Batersh* is a delightful dish, rather similar to the Turkish *hunkar begendi*, except that in the Turkish version, the meat is cut into chunks and the eggplant puree is fluffier.   SERVES 4

FOR THE EGGPLANT PUREE
4 large eggplants
   (2¼ pounds/1 kg total)
2 cloves garlic, minced to
   a fine paste
⅓ cup (90 g) yogurt
⅓ cup (80 ml) tahini
Sea salt

FOR THE MEAT TOPPING
3 tablespoons (45 g)
   unsalted butter
1 pound 2 ounces (500 g)
   lean ground lamb, from
   the shoulder or leg
One 14-ounce (400 g)
   can Italian chopped
   tomatoes
2 tablespoons tomato
   paste
Sea salt and finely ground
   black pepper

FOR SERVING
A few sprigs flat-leaf
   parsley, most of the
   stems discarded, finely
   chopped
2 ounces (60 g) pine nuts,
   toasted in a hot oven
   for 5 to 7 minutes, until
   golden brown
Pita Bread (page 4) or
   Saj Bread (page 6)

1. To make the eggplant puree: Prick the eggplants with the tip of a knife in a few places and char over an outdoor grill, over a gas burner, or under the broiler until the skin is blackened and the eggplants are very soft, about 20 to 25 minutes on each side. (I normally char the skin over a gas flame to get the smoky flavor, then I put the eggplants to roast in a hot oven for 30 minutes or so to cook them through; this way I avoid the mess of the flying charred skin all over the gas burner and I still get a smoky taste.)

2. Halve the grilled eggplants lengthwise and scoop the flesh out of the skin. Put in a sieve to drain off the excess liquid. Transfer the eggplant flesh to a shallow bowl and mash with a potato masher or with a fork. Add the garlic, yogurt, and tahini. Season with salt to taste and mix well. Taste and adjust the seasoning if necessary. Keep warm.

3. To make the meat topping: Melt the butter in a deep skillet over medium heat. Add the lamb and sauté, breaking up any lumps, until it has lost all traces of pink. Add the chopped tomatoes, tomato paste, and ¼ cup (60 ml) water. Season with salt and pepper to taste and let bubble gently for 15 minutes or so, until the sauce has thickened and there is no excess liquid. Keep hot.

4. To serve, spread the eggplant puree over a serving platter, raising the edges so that you can spoon the minced meat inside the edge. Sprinkle the chopped parsley all over the edges and the toasted pine nuts over the meat. Serve immediately with bread.

KIBBEH BALLS in MINTY YOGURT SAUCE

KIBBEH LABNIYEH

This is one of my favorite Lebanese/Syrian dishes, although I prefer the Lebanese version because of the added mint. The Syrian one is plain without any herbs, and most people stabilize the yogurt with cornstarch whereas few people in Lebanon do this. Instead, they use one or more eggs depending on the quantity of yogurt, which makes for a lighter, more refined texture.   SERVES 4

Kibbeh balls from Kibbeh in Sumac Sauce (page 132)
Cooked Yogurt Sauce (page 175)
Sea salt

1. Prepare the kibbeh balls as directed and put them uncooked in the freezer while you make the yogurt sauce.

2. Make the herb-garlic mixture as directed in step 1 of the cooked yogurt sauce recipe, using fresh mint in the herb-garlic mixture. Set the mint-garlic mixture aside.

3. Make the yogurt sauce as directed in step 2, and once the yogurt has boiled, drop in the barely frozen kibbeh balls, reduce the heat to low, and simmer for 5 minutes, stirring occasionally—do this gently so that you do not break the kibbeh balls. Stir in the mint-garlic mixture and simmer for a couple of minutes more.

4. Serve hot, preferably as soon as it is ready (see Note) in soup plates with spoons to scoop up the sauce.

NOTE: *You can make this ahead and reheat it, but as with all dishes cooked in yogurt, you have to be careful not to let the yogurt curdle during reheating. You need to reheat over low heat and stir very regularly at the beginning and all the time at the end as the yogurt is about to boil.*

LEBANESE DUMPLINGS in YOGURT SAUCE

SHISH BARAK

These dumplings are time-consuming to make and I usually prepare a whole batch to put in the freezer so that I only need to make the yogurt sauce on the day I plan to serve *shish barak*, thus avoiding hours in the kitchen making the dumplings. You can do the same or you can use store-bought Turkish *manti*, which are the Turkish version of these dumplings, and cook them in your own yogurt sauce. Obviously ready-made is not as good as homemade, so here is a recipe to make them. I have found a similar recipe for this dish in a fifteenth-century Syrian cookery book, *Kitab al-Tibakhah* (the *Book of Cookery*), written by a legal scholar from Damascus, Ibn al-Mabrad or Ibn al-Mubarrad: "Shushbarak: You take minced meat and stuff it in dough rolled out like cut *tutmaj* [unfilled dough cooked in yogurt]. It is cooked in water until done. Then take off the fire and put yogurt, garlic and mint in it." This recipe hasn't changed much since. The Turkish version, which is called *manti,* is made by first boiling or baking the dumplings, then serving them with fresh yogurt spooned all over, whereas the Lebanese cook the dumplings in the yogurt sauce.

SERVES 4 TO 6

FOR THE DOUGH
1½ cups (175 g) unbleached all-purpose flour, plus more for rolling out
Sea salt

FOR THE STUFFING
1 small onion (3½ ounces/100 g), finely chopped
¼ teaspoon ground allspice
⅛ teaspoon ground cinnamon
⅛ teaspoon finely ground black pepper
Sea salt
5 ounces (150 g) lean ground lamb

TO FINISH
Cooked Yogurt Sauce (page 175)
Lebanese/Syrian Vermicelli Rice (page 241), for serving
Dried rose petals, for garnish

1. To make the dough: Mix the flour and a pinch of salt in a bowl. Make a well in the center and add ⅓ cup plus 2 tablespoons (110 ml) water to the well. Gradually bring in the flour and mix until you have a rough dough.

2. Transfer the dough to a lightly floured work surface and knead for 3 minutes. Shape the dough into a ball, invert the bowl over the dough, and let rest for 15 minutes. Knead for 3 more minutes, until you have a smooth, malleable, but rather firm dough. Cover with a damp cloth and let rest while you make the filling.

3. To make the filling: Put the onion in a medium bowl. Season with the allspice, cinnamon, pepper, and salt to taste and firmly rub the seasonings into the onion with

your fingers until it softens. Add the lamb and mix with your hands until well blended with the onion. Taste and adjust the seasoning if necessary (see Note, page 115).

4. To make the dumplings: Sprinkle a little flour all over a large freezerproof platter and have it on hand to put the meat dumplings on it. Divide the dough into two balls. Flatten one slightly, dip both sides in the flour, shake off the excess flour and roll out into a large round about ⅛ inch (3 mm) thick. Use a 2-inch (5 cm) round pastry cutter to cut the dough into as many disks as you can, starting from the very edge and working your way around the outside then the inside. If you do not have a pastry cutter, use a thin-edged glass. Pick up the dough scraps, knead it into a small ball, and let it rest to make more dumplings once you have finished the first batch.

5. Turn the disks over. Lift one and lay it on the fingers of one hand. Place ¼ teaspoon stuffing in the center, and fold the dough over the filling to form a half-moon. With your free thumb and index finger pinch the edges tightly together into a thin flat edge. Fold the half-moon-shaped dumpling until the tip ends of the half-moon meet, pinch them well together, and stand the curled dumpling on the floured platter—the dumplings for shish barak should look like tortellini but with a flat rim. Continue making the dumplings and arranging them neatly on the platter until you finish both dough and filling.

6. Put the dumplings in the freezer until you need them. This should stiffen them a little and prevent their shape from being spoiled by handling when you drop them into the yogurt sauce. (If you are freezing them for later use, wait until they have frozen before covering them with plastic wrap so you don't squash them.)

7. Prepare the yogurt sauce as directed, but keep the cilantro-garlic mixture separate. Take the dumplings out of the freezer and carefully drop them into the simmering yogurt. Bring back to a simmer and stir in the cilantro-garlic mixture. Simmer for 5 more minutes, or until the dumplings are done.

8. Sprinkle with a few dried rose petals and serve immediately as is or with Lebanese vermicelli rice.

TURKISH DUMPLINGS with GARLICKY YOGURT

MANTI

The main difference between *manti* and *shish barak* (page 182) is in the shape of the dumplings—tiny and square for *manti* and just small and round for *shish barak*—and the yogurt sauce, which is only warmed up and seasoned for *manti* but cooked for *shish barak*. These two differences result in very distinct dishes, even if the concept is the same. I am not sure how Turkish cooks manage to make dumplings that are smaller than the nail on your little finger, which is the criterion for those learning to make them, especially for young Turkish brides. I for one am not eligible to marry a Turk as my *manti* are bigger than my little fingernail. Fortunately, the size does not affect the taste. Some people bake their *manti* before ladling the yogurt onto it. I like the silky texture of boiled *manti*.

SERVES 6

FOR THE DOUGH
2 cups (240 g)
   unbleached all-purpose
   flour, plus more for
   rolling out the dough
½ teaspoon fine sea salt
1 organic egg

FOR THE FILLING
9 ounces (250 g) lean
   ground lamb
1 medium onion
   (5 ounces/150 g),
   grated on the fine side
   of a grater

A few sprigs flat-leaf
   parsley, most of the
   stems discarded, finely
   chopped
½ teaspoon finely ground
   black pepper
Sea salt

TO FINISH
4 cups (35 ounces/1 kg)
   Greek yogurt
4 cloves garlic, minced to
   a fine paste
Sea salt
4 tablespoons (60 g)
   unsalted butter
1 teaspoon pul biber or
   Aleppo pepper

1. To make the dough: Mix the flour and salt in a bowl and make a well in the center. Add the egg and ⅓ cup (80 ml) water and gradually bring in the flour. Knead until you have a rough dough.

2. Transfer to a lightly floured work surface and knead for 3 minutes. Shape the dough into a ball, invert the bowl over the dough, and let rest for 15 minutes. Knead the dough for 3 more minutes. Roll into a ball and cover with a damp towel. Let rest while you prepare the filling.

3. To make the filling: Combine the ground lamb, onion, parsley, pepper, and salt to taste (see Note, page 115) in a bowl. Mix with your hands, kneading the mixture, both to mix it well and make it smoother.

4. Form the manti: Divide the dough into 4 equal portions and roll each into a ball. Place one ball on a lightly floured work surface and cover the others. Roll out the dough as thinly as you can. Cut it into strips 1½ inches (3.5 cm) wide, then cut the strips crosswise into 1½-inch (3.5 cm) squares. Put a little meat stuffing in the middle of each square and either fold into triangles (which was the shape the Ottomans made) or shape them how they are made these days by lifting 2 opposite corners of the square and pinching them together, then lifting the other two corners so you have a kind of pouch with 4 angles. Pick up the dough scraps, knead together, then shape into a ball. Let it rest while you roll out another ball of dough to make more dumplings. Continue in the same way until you have used all the dough, including the scraps that you rerolled, and the filling. You should end up with 120 tiny dumplings—if you find it tedious to make these so small, make the squares bigger to make about 40 larger dumplings.

5. Bring a large pot with water to a boil over medium heat. Add salt to taste. Meanwhile, heat the yogurt in a double boiler until very warm. Add the garlic and salt to taste and keep warm.

6. Melt the butter in a skillet over medium heat. When the butter starts sizzling, add the *pul biber*. Keep over very low heat.

7. Drop the *manti* into the boiling water and cook for 5 to 7 minutes. Drain well and transfer to a serving dish.

8. To serve, pour the warm yogurt all over and drizzle the *pul biber* butter over the yogurt. Serve immediately.

FRESH ALMONDS in YOGURT SAUCE

YOĞURTLU ÇAĞLA AŞI

The recipe below comes from Filiz Hosukoglu, my great friend and guru for all things culinary in the Turkish city of Gaziantep. One day, after she'd seen my post online on fresh green almonds that can be eaten whole, she commented on how they cook them in yogurt in Turkey and when the nut inside is not yet fully formed. Within a month or so, the shell hardens and becomes inedible but is not yet so hard as to need cracking with a nutcracker. At this stage, the inner nut is fully formed and is the only edible part, along with the inner skin of course.   SERVES 4 TO 6

2 tablespoons extra-
  virgin olive oil
10½ ounces (300 g)
  lamb, cut into ½-inch
  (1 cm) cubes
Sea salt
4 cups (1 liter) boiling
  water
1 pound 5 ounces
  (600 g) fresh green
  almonds, halved, the
  soft immature kernels
  removed, rinsed
⅓ cup (60 g) cooked
  chickpeas, well rinsed if
  canned

FOR THE SAUCE
1½ cups (375 g) strained
  yogurt
1 organic egg

TO FINISH
2 tablespoons (30 g)
  clarified butter
½ teaspoon finely ground
  black pepper
½ tablespoon safflower
  (see Note)
Good bread, for serving

1. Put the oil in a large pot over medium-high heat. Add the meat and a little salt. Sauté the meat until it has browned, about 5 minutes. Add the boiling water, reduce the heat, and let simmer for 30 minutes, or until the meat is tender.

2. Add the almond halves. (If the almonds are not fresh enough, blanch them first for 3 to 4 minutes to remove the acidic taste. You will be able to tell how fresh and tender they are if you taste one raw.) Cook for 30 more minutes, or until the fresh almonds are tender. Add the chickpeas and turn off the heat.

3. To make the sauce: Mix the yogurt with the egg in a separate pot. Place over medium-low heat and start stirring until the yogurt becomes hot enough to almost burn your little finger. (This is how Filiz's grandmother used to describe the desired heat for the yogurt.) If the yogurt reaches a higher temperature or is allowed to boil without stirring, it will curdle. Add 2 to 3 tablespoons hot meat broth two or three times to the yogurt mixture to bring it to the same temperature as the broth.

4. Add the hot yogurt sauce to the meat, chickpeas, and fresh almonds. Cover and keep on very low heat—you do not want it to bubble, just to stay hot.

5. When ready to serve, combine the clarified butter, black pepper, and safflower in a skillet and place over medium heat. Wait until the butter starts sizzling. As soon as that happens, transfer the yogurt, meat, and almonds to a serving bowl. Drizzle the sizzling safflower butter all over the top. Serve immediately with good bread.

NOTE: *Safflower is known as "bastard saffron," and unscrupulous vendors in Egypt and other Middle Eastern countries often sell it as saffron to unsuspecting customers.*

SPINACH and YOGURT SPREAD
SPINACH BORANI

It is said that the word *borani* comes from the name of Poorandokht, the daughter of a Sassanian king who was the first woman to rule Persia more than thirteen hundred years ago. She was apparently so keen on yogurt that various dishes using yogurt were created for her, and called *poorani* after her. Later, it was changed to *borani*. True story or not, *borani* refers to dishes cooked with yogurt. There are many variations, but they more or less follow the same principle of frying onions until caramelized, adding the vegetable of choice and the yogurt, and garnishing with saffron water and sometimes chopped walnuts.

SERVES 4

2 tablespoons extra-virgin olive oil

1 medium onion (5 ounces/150 g), halved and cut into thin wedges

1 pound (450 g) spinach (preferably baby spinach)

¼ teaspoon ground turmeric

½ cup (125 g) labneh (see page 188)

Sea salt

Pinch of saffron threads, soaked in 1 tablespoon water

Iranian Flatbread (page 9), for serving

1. Heat the oil in a large deep skillet or sauté pan over medium heat. Add the onion and cook, stirring regularly, until soft and golden, about 10 minutes. Add the spinach and turmeric and cook for a few minutes, still stirring regularly, until the spinach has wilted but not completely melted.

2. Transfer the mixture to a sieve to let the excess liquid drain off. Once the spinach has cooled and the excess liquid has drained, transfer to a bowl. Add the yogurt and salt to taste and mix well.

3. Transfer to a shallow serving bowl and make grooves here and there. Drizzle the saffron water into the grooves and serve with the bread.

LABNEH and TARRAGON DIP
LABNEH BIL-TARKHUN

Labneh is very easy to make. Just spoon your choice of yogurt—I alternate between sheep and goat yogurt—into a double layer of cheesecloth and let it drain for a few hours. The whey will drain off the yogurt and you will be left with creamy labneh, which you can have plain drizzled with very good olive oil and sprinkled with za'atar or use to make dips like the one below, which I discovered at Khawali restaurant in Damascus, back in the days when Syria was a peaceful country. The dip is a gorgeous pastel green color and it has an intriguing flavor, a combination of the subtle sour tang of labneh and the heady aroma of crushed tarragon.   SERVES 6

2 ounces (60 g) fresh
  tarragon sprigs
1 small clove garlic,
  coarsely chopped
Sea salt
1½ cups (375 g) labneh
Extra-virgin olive oil, for
  garnish
Coarse sea salt and
  toasted sesame seeds,
  for garnish (optional)
Good bread, for serving

1. Strip the tarragon leaves off the stems and put in a mortar along with the garlic and a little salt. Crush with a pestle until totally pulverized and creamy.

2. Put the labneh in a bowl. Stir in the tarragon-garlic mixture. Taste and adjust the seasoning if necessary.

3. Spread the dip onto a serving platter, making grooves here and there. Drizzle olive oil into the grooves and sprinkle with a little coarse sea salt and toasted sesame seeds if you feel like it. Serve with bread for dipping.

EGGPLANT and YOGURT SPREAD
BORANI-E BÂDENJÂN

IRAN

This is a wonderful dip with a subtle flavor of caramelized onion and saffron and a silky texture offset by the lovely crunch of the walnut garnish.

SERVES 4

2 large eggplants
   (1 pound 2 ounces/
   500 g)
¼ cup (60 ml) extra-
   virgin olive oil
1 medium onion
   (5 ounces/150 g),
   halved lengthwise and
   cut into thin wedges
1 clove garlic, minced to a
   fine paste
Sea salt and finely ground
   black pepper
½ cup (125 g) labneh
Pinch of saffron threads,
   soaked in 1 tablespoon
   water
⅓ cup (50 g) walnuts,
   coarsely chopped
Iranian Flatbread (page
   9), for serving

1. Preheat the broiler to high.

2. Prick the eggplants in several places with the tip of a knife and place under the hot broiler. Broil for 30 to 40 minutes, turning them halfway through, until the skin is charred and the flesh is very soft. Halve the grilled eggplants lengthwise. Scoop out the flesh and place in a colander for about 20 minutes to drain off the excess liquid. Mash the eggplants.

3. Heat the olive oil in a skillet over medium-high heat. Add the onion and cook until soft and lightly golden, about 5 minutes. Add the garlic and sauté for another minute or so. Add the mashed eggplants and season with salt and pepper to taste. Cook for another 5 minutes, stirring occasionally. Take off the heat and let cool.

4. Stir the strained yogurt into the cooled mixture. Transfer to a serving dish. Drizzle with the saffron water and sprinkle the chopped walnuts all over. Serve with the bread.

YOGURT and ELEPHANT GARLIC DIP
MAST-O MUSIR

Yogurt is always served as a refreshing side with curries, kebabs, rice, or baked kibbeh, either plain or with a garnish. Here it is mixed with rehydrated dried elephant garlic (known as *musir* in Farsi) to produce a rather pungent side to serve with kebabs. In kebab restaurants in Iran, you just order the kebab you want then go to a buffet laid on the side to help yourself to yogurt with *musir* or cucumbers, fresh herbs, and crudités before returning to your table to wait for your kebabs to be served with rice.

SERVES 4 TO 6

3½ ounces (100 g) dried Persian elephant garlic
2 cups (500 g) yogurt
Sea salt and finely ground black pepper
Iranian Flatbread (page 9)

1. Put the garlic in a small pot. Add water to cover and bring to a boil over high heat. Reduce the heat to low and let simmer for 20 minutes. Drain and rinse under cold water. Spread over a clean kitchen towel to dry. Finely chop the garlic.

2. Put the yogurt in a bowl. Add the chopped garlic. Season with salt and pepper to taste. Serve slightly chilled with the bread.

YOGURT and CUCUMBER DIP
MAST-O KHIYAR

Here is the cucumber variation of the Yogurt and Elephant Garlic Dip (above). SERVES 4 TO 6

2 cups (500 g) goat or Greek yogurt
1 clove garlic, minced to a fine paste
3 tablespoons dried mint, plus more for garnish
3 Armenian cucumbers, coarsely grated and drained
Sea salt

Mix the yogurt, garlic, and dried mint. Add the cucumber and season with salt to taste. Taste and adjust the seasoning. Transfer to a serving bowl. Garnish with a little dried mint and serve.

AZERBAIJANI YOGURT SOUP

DOVGA

AZERBAIJAN

You can turn this soup into a summery dish by omitting the meatballs and chilling the soup once it has cooled down. When served cold, *dovga* is usually offered at the end of a rich meal, a little like a palate cleanser. And when served hot, it is usually offered as a first course, or even a light meal.

SERVES 4

7 ounces (200 g) lean ground lamb
Sea salt and finely ground black pepper
½ cup (100 g) dried chickpeas, soaked overnight in plenty of water with ½ teaspoon baking soda

4 cups (1 kg) Greek yogurt
1 organic egg
¼ cup (50 g) short-grain rice, rinsed and drained
1 ounce (30 g) fresh chervil, most of the bottom stems discarded, finely chopped

1 ounce (30 g) fresh cilantro, most of the bottom stems discarded, finely chopped
1 ounce (30 g) fresh dill, most of the bottom stems discarded, finely chopped
1 ounce (30 g) fresh mint, leaves stripped off the stems, finely chopped

1 ounce (30 g) fresh flat-leaf parsley, most of the bottom stems discarded, finely chopped
Handful of spinach leaves, thinly sliced
2 sprigs celery tops, finely chopped
2 mini leeks, thinly sliced

1. Put the lamb in a bowl and season with salt and pepper to taste (see Note, page 115). Mix well and shape into tiny meatballs, the size of large marbles. Keep in the fridge to firm them up.

2. Drain and rinse the soaked chickpeas. Put in a pot with water to cover and bring to a boil over medium heat. Reduce the heat to medium-low, cover and simmer for 45 minutes, or until tender but not mushy. Drain well.

3. Put the yogurt in a heavy pot. Add the egg and mix well. Add 2 cups (500 ml) water and the rice and bring to a boil over medium heat, stirring all the time. Add the chopped herbs, spinach, celery tops, leeks, and the chickpeas and bring back to a boil, stirring all the time.

4. Gently stir in the meatballs. Reduce the heat to low and let bubble very gently, stirring frequently, for 10 to 15 minutes, or until the rice and meat are done. Take off the heat and add salt to taste. Serve the soup hot or warm.

RICE, GRAINS, PASTA & LEGUMES

EATING RICE

MAACHEY BHAATEY BANGAALE

—AN OLD BENGALI SAYING

DELICATELY SHEATHED,

WRAPPED

IN PAPERY HUSK—

I LOVE THE FEEL AND

ELEGANCE OF LONG SLENDER

RICE GRAINS—

THEIR SEDUCTION

AND CHARM,

THEIR AROMA AND SHAPE—

THEIR FINE FLAVOR

AND

THE DEEP VIRGIN TASTE.

—SUDEEP SEN

Rice is the most important crop in the world, with more than three billion people relying on it as a staple. Muslims may have first learned about rice from the Persians of the Sassanid empire when they defeated them in 635. Or they could have learned about rice in the Indian Sind province, which they conquered in 711. In either case, Muslims were growing rice more or less throughout the territories they had conquered and ruled over by the year 1000. Until then, wheat had been their staple, and you still find a noticeable division among Muslim countries between those relying on grain—such as Turkey, Lebanon, Syria, Jordan, and Egypt—and those that rely mostly on rice and/or noodles—such as the Arabian Gulf, Iran, India, Pakistan, and Northern China.

Long-grain rice is the preferred type in Iran, Afghanistan, the Arabian Gulf, India, and Pakistan, while short-grain is favored by Malaysians, Indonesians, and Levantines. Rice was first grown in China and from there it was taken to countries like India and Sri Lanka. It is reputed to have been brought to West Asia and Greece in 300 BC by the army of Alexander the Great.

Wheat, on the other hand, was the first crop to be domesticated in the Fertile Crescent, a region that encompasses Turkey, Lebanon, Syria, and Jordan. It is of course milled to produce flour for bread, but it is also used whole in both sweet and savory dishes, and it is parboiled and cracked to produce bulgur, which for a long time was the "rice" of that region. And in the spring, some of it is harvested green and burned in the fields to produce frikeh. Most of North Africa has couscous as a main staple after bread. Legumes are one of the most ancient foods. They're eaten throughout the Muslim world, and chickpeas and lentils are essential ingredients in most Muslim countries. As for pasta, it is mostly in the form of dumplings, dough cooked in a meat and vegetable sauce like in *marguga* (page 76), or vermicelli cooked with rice.

The recipes I have included in this chapter are mostly for main courses, although there are a few for side dishes.

SLOW-COOKED BIRYANI

DUMPUKHT BIRYANI

Dumpukht in Lucknow or *dumpokht* in Hyderabad describes a way of slow-cooking in an airtight pot (*handi*), which can be earthenware or metal. The word comes from the Persian—*dum* meaning "breathe in" and *pukht* meaning "to cook." The method is traditionally associated with the Awadh region of India, once ruled by the Muslim Nawabs with the origins of *dumpukht* assigned to the reign of Nawab Asaf Udd-Daulah, who ruled from 1748 to 1797.

I learned to make this biryani in the garden of Begum Mirza (Begum is a title given to noble-women deriving from the word *Bey*, the title given to noblemen) in Hyderabad, and even though the Begum was quite old and not so mobile, she had organized a perfect *mise en place* and was very precise and attentive to details as she proceeded through each step of the biryani. Begum Mirza used mutton, which means goat in India, saying it is the preferred meat there; but goat in India seems to be a lot more tender than goat in England or even America, so I am suggesting lamb. As I watched the Begum cover the raw marinated meat with the uncooked rice, I wondered how the meat was going to cook in the same time as the rice. She assured me it would, explaining that the green papaya she had added to the meat marinade was a natural tenderizer. The Begum also did something very interesting at the very end. She took a piece of charcoal and held it with tongs over the gas fire. When it started turning into a glowing ember, she put it in with the rice to give it a smoky flavor. I had never seen anything like it done before. She didn't leave it for too long, just a few minutes to smoke the biryani. As she scooped the biryani out of the pot and onto the serving platter, I was surprised to see that both rice and meat had cooked perfectly. Then, when I started eating, I found the meat to be very tender and the rice wonderfully fragrant, having absorbed the flavors of the subtle marinade as well as the smoky flavor of the burning piece of charcoal. Perfectly exquisite.

SERVES 6 TO 8

FOR THE MARINATED MEAT
4 small onions (14 ounces/400 g total), grated on the fine side of a grater
1 tablespoon finely minced green papaya
Seeds from 2 black cardamom pods
1 tablespoon black peppercorns
1 teaspoon cumin seeds
6 whole cloves
Good pinch of saffron threads
2¼ pounds (1 kg) boneless lamb shoulder or leg, cut into medium chunks
Sea salt
2 cups (500 g) yogurt

FOR THE BIRYANI
2½ cups (500 g) long-grain rice, soaked for 15 minutes in lightly salted water
2 cups (500 g) yogurt
Sea salt
½ cup (125 g) ghee or unsalted butter, melted, plus 2 tablespoons (30 g), melted, for the rice
½ cup (125 ml) whole milk

1. To marinate the meat: Mix the onions, green papaya, and spices in a large bowl. Add the meat and season with salt to taste (see Note, page 115). Mix well. Add the yogurt, mix again, and let marinate for at least 2 hours, preferably longer.

2. To make the biryani: Drain and rinse the rice and put in a bowl. Add the yogurt, ⅔ cup water (160 ml), and salt to taste.

3. Put the marinated meat in the bottom of a large pot. Pour the ½ cup melted ghee over the meat. Add the rice and 1 cup (250 ml) water. Wrap the lid with a clean kitchen towel and place over the pot. Wrapping the lid stops the steam from the rice from falling back, which keeps the rice fluffy and the grains separate. Place the pot over medium-high heat and bring to a boil, for about 5 minutes. Reduce the heat to low and let simmer gently for 20 minutes.

4. Uncover the pan and sprinkle the 2 tablespoons melted ghee over the rice, along with the milk. Place the lid back over the pan and cook for another 15 minutes, or until the meat is completely tender and the rice has absorbed all the liquid and is tender and fluffy. Serve immediately.

HYDERABADI BIRYANI

INDIA

Also known as *katchi biryani*, this is quite different from the Dumpukht Biryani (page 198), which is also from Hyderabad. Here, the meat is cooked and the rice parboiled before being combined, whereas in the *dumpukht* version, the meat and rice cook together (which works surprisingly well). This biryani is very close to the Persian polows, although in Iran, the meat is usually layered in between the rice and not buried underneath it. This and most other biryanis make perfect one-pot meals that are fairly simple to prepare. They also have the advantage of keeping well if left over very low heat until you are ready to serve them.

SERVES 6 TO 8

Good pinch of saffron threads
½ cup (125 ml) whole milk

FOR THE MARINATED MEAT
½ cup (125 ml) vegetable oil
4 medium onions (1 pound 5 ounces/ 600 g total), halved and cut into thin wedges

1 inch (2.5 cm) fresh ginger, peeled and finely minced
6 cloves garlic, minced to a fine paste
1 tablespoon finely minced green papaya
2¼ pounds (1 kg) boneless lamb shoulder or leg, cut into medium chunks
10 mild green chilies, seeded and pureed

¼ bunch cilantro (2 ounces/50 g), most of the bottom stems discarded, finely chopped
A few sprigs fresh mint, leaves stripped off the stems, finely chopped
1 teaspoon Indian Biryani Masala (page 362)
2 cups (500 g) yogurt
Juice of 3 limes
Sea salt

FOR THE BIRYANI
Sea salt
3¼ cups (650 g) long-grain rice, soaked for 30 minutes in lightly salted water, drained
2 tablespoons (30 g) ghee or unsalted butter, melted

1. Put the saffron to steep in the milk.

2. To marinate the meat: Heat the oil in a large skillet over medium heat. Add the onions and fry, stirring regularly, until golden brown, about 10 minutes. Let cool slightly, then puree in a food processor.

3. Mix the ginger, garlic, and papaya in a large bowl. Add the meat and mix well. Let sit for about 15 minutes—the green papaya acts as a tenderizer. Add the onion puree, green chili puree, cilantro, mint, masala, yogurt, lime juice, and salt to taste. Let the meat marinate for at least 2 hours, preferably longer in the refrigerator.

4. To make the biryani: Bring 4 quarts (4 liters) water to a boil in a large pot over high heat. Add 4 tablespoons sea salt and the drained rice. Bring back to a boil and let the rice boil for 3 minutes, or until the hard core is just softened. Drain in a colander and rinse under cold water. Let the rice drain off any excess water while you start cooking the meat.

5. Put the meat and the marinade in a large pot and place over medium-high heat. Cook, stirring constantly, until the yogurt starts bubbling. Add 1 cup (250 ml) water and bring back to a boil. Reduce the heat to very low and spread the parboiled rice over the meat. Cover the pan with the lid wrapped in a clean kitchen towel to make sure it fits snugly over the biryani. Let steam for 30 minutes, then sprinkle the saffron milk and melted ghee over the rice. Cover the pan again, and let steam for another 15 minutes, until the meat is done and the rice is very fluffy.

6. Transfer the meat and rice to a serving platter without mixing them so you have different colors. Serve immediately.

AWADHI BIRYANI

Awadhi cuisine was developed in Lucknow during the time of the Nawabs, who ruled the state of Awadh from 1722 to 1856, when the last Nawab was imprisoned by the Company of India before being sent into exile in Calcutta (or Kolkota as it is now known). The Nawabs were fine gourmets, and their cooks, known as *bawarchis*, prepared incredibly refined dishes. They also invented the *dum* method of cooking, where dishes were completely sealed in their terra-cotta cooking pots and placed over a low fire to cook slowly. This biryani is one of the glories of this cuisine and the rice is made more interesting by being cooked in spiced water before being layered with the cooked meat.

SERVES 4 TO 6

FOR THE MARINATED MEAT
2 medium onions (10½ ounces/300 g total), finely chopped
1 inch (2.5 cm) fresh ginger, peeled and finely minced
3 cloves garlic, minced to a fine paste
1 teaspoon ground coriander
1 teaspoon Kashmiri chili powder
1 teaspoon Garam Masala 1 (page 361)
Juice of 1 lime
1 cup (250 g) yogurt
1 pound 2 ounces (500 g) boneless lamb shoulder or leg, cut into medium chunks
Sea salt

1. To marinate the meat: Put the onions, ginger, garlic, spices, lime juice, and yogurt in a large bowl and mix well. Add the lamb and salt to taste and mix again. Let marinate for at least 2 hours, preferably longer in the refrigerator.

2. To make the rice: Rinse the rice under cold water, then soak it for 1 hour in lightly salted water. Meanwhile, put the whole spices in a large heatproof measuring cup and add the boiling water. Let sit until it is time to use with the rice.

3. Melt the ghee or butter in a pot over medium heat. Drain the rice, add to the pot, and sauté for a couple of minutes. Add the saffron and strain the spice water over the rice. Bring to a boil, then reduce the heat to low, cover, and let simmer for 10 minutes. Take off the heat. Wrap the lid with a clean kitchen towel and replace over the pot. Let steam while you cook the meat.

4. To finish: Combine the ghee, onions, and cardamom pods in a pot and place over medium heat. Sauté until the onions are soft and translucent, about 3 minutes. Add the marinated lamb and sauté the meat for a few minutes. Then reduce the heat to low, cover the pot, and let the lamb cook slowly for 30 minutes, or until tender.

5. Meanwhile, put the saffron in a small bowl. Add the hot milk and the *kewra* and let infuse until you are ready to use it.

FOR THE RICE

2½ cups (500 g) basmati rice

1 cinnamon stick

3 black cardamom pods

3 green cardamom pods

6 black peppercorns

6 whole cloves

1 teaspoon fennel seeds

4 cups (1 liter) boiling water

5 tablespoons (75 g) ghee or unsalted butter

Good pinch of saffron threads

TO FINISH

3 tablespoons (45 g) ghee or unsalted butter

3 medium onions (1 pound/450 g total), finely chopped

2 green cardamom pods, smashed

Good pinch of saffron threads

½ cup (125 ml) milk, heated

1 teaspoon kewra (pandanus flower extract)

6. When the meat is done, take off the heat unless the sauce is too runny, in which case increase the heat to high and boil hard until the excess liquid has evaporated. You want the sauce to be very thick and rather dry.

7. Take a clean pot large enough to hold both the rice and meat. Spread one-quarter of the rice over the bottom. Lay one-third of the meat over the rice. Repeat this layering two more times, finishing with rice. Sprinkle the saffron-infused milk over the rice. Wrap the lid of the pot with a clean kitchen towel and place over the pot. Place over very low heat and let steam for about 30 minutes. Serve immediately.

CALCUTTA BIRYANI

INDIA

When I was in Calcutta, now known as Kolkota, my friend Bipasha Ghosh, who is Bengali, recommended we take a culinary walking tour of the city's food, both on and off the street, with the lovely Iftekhar Ahsan of Calcutta Walks. We explained to Iftekhar that I was mainly interested in Muslim foods and he took us on a spectacular tasting tour, culminating at the Royal India Hotel (*hotel* in India means "restaurant") to taste both their biryani and *chaap* (smashed mutton—which actually means goat—chops half braised, half fried in their own fat). It was the first time I had tasted a biryani with next to nothing in it, just potatoes, but it was so flavorful that we had to order another plate even though we were already pretty full. There are several stories behind the Calcutta Biryani and why it is made with potatoes. All refer to the last ruler of Lucknow, Wajid Ali Shah, who found himself in exile with his court in Calcutta. On that same trip, I met with the last ruler's great-great-grandson Shahanshah Mirza and his lovely wife, Fatima, and Shahanshah's version was that the Nawab liked to experiment with food and had given his chefs carte blanche as to how they made biryani, so they added potatoes, which he liked. Another theory is that the chefs used potatoes instead of meat because the ruler was impoverished. Either way, the "potato" biryani at Royal India is absolutely superb. At the Royal, they don't cook meat with the rice. Instead, you order their "potato" biryani together with *chaap*. It was one of the best biryanis I had while in India, together with that cooked by chef Gulam Qureshi at Dum Pukht restaurant in New Delhi where I was taken by Vir Sanghvi and his wife, Seema, for an extraordinary tasting menu.

SERVES 6 TO 8

⅓ cup (80 ml) vegetable oil, plus more for browning the lamb

3 medium onions (1 pound/450 g total), halved and cut into thin wedges

6 whole cloves

1 teaspoon black peppercorns

1 cinnamon stick

1 teaspoon caraway seeds

2 bay leaves

1 inch (2.5 cm) fresh ginger, peeled and minced to a fine paste

4 cloves garlic, minced to a fine paste

2¼ pounds (1 kg) boneless lamb shoulder or leg, cut into medium chunks

1 teaspoon Kashmiri chili powder

Sea salt

3 medium tomatoes (10½ ounces/300 g total), peeled and finely chopped

1 cup (250 g) yogurt

8 medium new potatoes (1 pound 2 ounces/ 500 g total), scrubbed clean

2½ cups (500 g) long-grain rice

2 good pinches of saffron threads

1 tablespoon (15 g) ghee or unsalted butter

1. Heat the oil in a large sauté pan over medium heat. Add the onions and sauté until lightly golden, about 5 minutes. Add the cloves, peppercorns, cinnamon stick, ½ teaspoon of the caraway seeds, and 1 of the bay leaves and stir for a minute or so. Add the ginger and garlic and sauté until fragrant.

2. Heat a little oil in a pot over medium heat. Add the chunks of lamb and cook until browned. Add to the onion and spices together with the chili powder. Season with salt to taste. Add the tomatoes and cook for 5 minutes, or until the tomatoes have softened. Add the yogurt and cook, stirring continuously, until the yogurt starts bubbling gently. Add ½ cup (125 ml) water, cover the pan, and cook over low heat for about 30 minutes, or until the lamb is just tender.

3. Add the potatoes and cook for another 20 minutes, or until both meat and potatoes are done. Check the liquid in the pan. There should be a little sauce left by the time both meat and potatoes are done as you will be adding it to the rice.

4. Meanwhile, rinse the rice and soak it for 20 minutes in lightly salted cold water. Drain the rice and put in a separate pot. Add the saffron, ghee, and 2 cups (500 ml) water. Season with salt to taste and bring to a boil over medium heat. Reduce the heat to medium-low and let the rice simmer for 6 to 8 minutes, or until it has absorbed the water and is almost done.

5. Spread the remaining ½ teaspoon caraway seeds over the bottom of a clean pot and add the remaining bay leaf. Add the parboiled rice to the pot, and cover with the meat, potatoes, and sauce. Wrap the lid of the pot with a clean kitchen towel and place snugly over the pot. Place over medium-high heat and let cook for 3 minutes, then reduce the heat to as low as you can and let steam for another 15 minutes, or until the rice is completely done and fluffy and the meat is very hot. Serve immediately.

MALABAR CHICKEN BIRYANI

INDIA

The Muslims from the northern part of Kerala are known as Moplahs and they are mostly descendants of Arab traders who intermarried with local women. Their cuisine is quite distinctive apart from sharing the same dependence on rice, which in this region is short-grain rather than the long-grain used in the rest of India. One of the best times to sample Moplah cuisine is during festive occasions, and in particular wedding ceremonies, which are particularly festive there. The ceremony lasts several days, and each day is devoted to a different ritual, such as henna night or the night of the wedding proper. Each ritual has its own foods, and biryani is always served on the night of the wedding. You can make the biryani below by frying the chicken first or you can make it by sautéing it with the sauce, which is what I prefer to do. This biryani is somewhat mellow compared to others unless you add one or two hot chilies. Also the rice here is fully cooked before being added to the chicken whereas in most other biryanis it is parboiled, drained, then put to steam with the meat and/or sauce.

SERVES 4 TO 6

Good pinch of saffron threads

2 tablespoons rose water

½ cup (125 g) ghee or vegetable oil

4 small onions (about 14 ounces/400 g total), halved and cut into thin wedges

2 ounces (60 g) mild green chilies, finely minced

2 inches (5 cm) fresh ginger, peeled and finely minced

6 cloves garlic, minced to a fine paste

½ teaspoon poppy seeds, finely crushed

2 poussins or Cornish hens, quartered, or 1 whole chicken (3 pounds 5 ounces/ 1.5 kg), cut into 8 pieces

⅔ cup (180 g) yogurt

Sea salt

Juice of 1 lime, or to taste

A few sprigs cilantro, most of the bottom stems discarded, coarsely chopped

A few sprigs mint, leaves stripped off stems, coarsely chopped

⅓ cup (50 g) cashews, coarsely chopped

⅓ cup (50 g) golden raisins, soaked for a couple hours in water

2½ cups (500 g) long-grain rice

1 teaspoon Garam Masala 1 (page 361)

1. Put the saffron to soak in the rose water.

2. Heat half the ghee in a large pot over medium heat. Add half the onions and sauté until soft and golden, about 5 minutes. Add the chilies, ginger, garlic, and poppy seeds and sauté for a couple more minutes, or until fragrant. Add the poussins and sauté for a few minutes, or until browned. Add the yogurt and ¼ cup (60 ml) water. Season with salt to taste. Reduce the heat to medium-low and simmer over low heat for 15 minutes. Add the lime juice and herbs and another ¼ cup (60 ml) water and let simmer for another 15 minutes, or until the poussins are done and the sauce has thickened.

3. Meanwhile, heat the remaining ghee in a pot over medium heat. Add the remaining onions and sauté until lightly caramelized, about 7 minutes. Add the cashews and sauté for 3 minutes or so, or until lightly golden. Drain the golden raisins and add to the pot. Sauté for a couple of minutes more. Remove with a slotted spoon to a plate.

4. Rinse the rice under cold water. Drain well and add to the pot. Sauté in the oil for a couple of minutes, then add 2½ cups (625 ml) water and bring to a boil. Reduce the heat to low and simmer for 10 to 15 minutes, or until the rice is done and has absorbed all the water. Take off the heat.

5. Return the pot with the poussins to low heat. Sprinkle ¼ teaspoon of the garam masala over the poussins, then fluff the rice with a fork and spread one-third over the poussins. Sprinkle 2 teaspoons saffron rose water over the rice. Spread half the onion-cashew-raisin mixture on top. Sprinkle ¼ teaspoon garam masala all over and cover with another one-third of the rice. Sprinkle with 2 teaspoons saffron rose water, the remaining onion-cashew-raisin mixture and another ¼ teaspoon garam masala and cover with the remaining rice. Sprinkle the remaining saffron rose water and garam masala over the rice. Wrap the lid with a clean kitchen towel and cover the pot with it.

6. At this point, you can finish the rice in a hot oven for 15 minutes (traditionally they place hot coals on the lid to have heat from both below and above) or you can leave it over very low heat for about 20 minutes.

7. Transfer to a serving platter, arranging the poussins on top of the rice. Serve hot.

EMIRATI BIRYANI

This Emirati biryani is different from most of the Indian and Pakistani ones in that it is made with a spicy meatless sauce, which is layered in between the rice, and is usually served with roast meat. If you are not keen on highly spicy flavors, simply tone down the spices in the recipe to your taste, or even do away completely with the chili and cayenne pepper, which is what gives the sauce its heat. Serve with any roast meat, fish, or poultry; it goes brilliantly with Baby Goat Roast (page 94).

SERVES 6 TO 8

Good pinch of saffron
   threads
¼ cup (60 ml) water

FOR THE SAUCE
¼ cup (60 ml)
   vegetable oil
3 small onions
   (10½ ounces/300 g
   total), halved and cut
   into thin wedges
9 ounces (250 g) green
   Turkish Marmara
   peppers (you can use
   regular green bell
   peppers but they

are thicker), halved
   lengthwise, seeded,
   and thinly sliced
   crosswise
4 dried bay leaves
4 firm-ripe tomatoes
   (14 ounces/400 g
   total), halved and
   thinly sliced
Sea salt
1½ teaspoons green
   cardamom pods
1½ teaspoons black
   peppercorns
1½ teaspoons whole
   cloves

1 small dried hot chili
1 cinnamon stick
1 tablespoon b'zar
   (Arabian Spice Mixture,
   page 366)
1 tablespoon ground
   turmeric
1½ teaspoons ground
   cumin
1 teaspoon finely ground
   black pepper
½ teaspoon cayenne
   pepper
2 dried limes, halved

FOR THE RICE
Sea salt
2 tablespoons
   vegetable oil
2½ cups (500 g) basmati
   rice, soaked for about
   2 hours in lightly salted
   water
2 bay leaves
4 green cardamom pods
4 black peppercorns
4 whole cloves
1 cinnamon stick

1. Put the saffron threads in the water and set aside to soak.

2. To make the sauce: Heat the oil in a skillet over medium heat. Add the onions, peppers, and bay leaves and cook until very soft and translucent, about 10 minutes. Add the tomatoes, salt to taste, cardamom, peppercorns, cloves, hot chili, and cinnamon stick and continue cooking over low heat for about 30 minutes, until the vegetables are very soft and the sauce concentrated. Add the ground spices and dried limes and simmer, stirring occasionally, for another 10 minutes. You may have to add a little water at this stage if the sauce is sticking but be careful not to add too much. The sauce needs to be very concentrated.

3. To parboil the rice: Put 4 quarts (4 liters) water in a large pot. Add 2 tablespoons salt and the oil and bring to a boil over medium heat. Drain the rice and add to the boiling water, together with the whole spices. Boil for 3 minutes. Remove from the heat and drain. Rinse under cold water.

4. In the bottom of a clean round pot, spread one-quarter of the sauce. Spoon one-quarter of the parboiled rice over it. Sprinkle with a little saffron water. Repeat this layering three more times. Wrap the lid of the pot with a clean kitchen towel. Place over the pot and let the rice steam over very low heat for about 20 minutes, or until it is completely tender and steaming hot. As you serve the rice, the sauce will have colored and flavored some of it and you will have a lovely mix of white rice, some saffron colored, and some moistened by the sauce.

INDONESIAN KEBULI BIRYANI

When I visited Indonesia to research recipes for this book, I had tremendous help from William Wongso, the country's foremost celebrity chef. William took me on a food frenzy tour in Medan, together with Indra Halim, the town's most famous foodie, and other foodie friends Gio and her husband, Jalaluddine, and their son, Didi. We were spoiled for good recommendations as to where to have all kinds of delectable Muslim specialties. I also met Tanya Alwi, the owner of the delightful Maulana hotel on the island of Banda Neira in Indonesia through James Oseland, former editor of *Saveur* magazine. With Tanya I explored Ambon and Banda Neira, both part of the Maluku islands in Indonesia, where Tanya's hotel is right on the water, across from nutmeg plantations. She arranged for me to taste different local specialties, including *kebuli biryani* (I guess named after Kabul in Afghanistan, perhaps because the dish originated there). Initially, Tanya had asked her cook to make the biryani with chicken, but I was keen on having it the way they would traditionally, with baby goat. The meat was surprisingly tough for such a small animal, but the dish was delicious and here is Tanya's cook's recipe.

SERVES 4 TO 6

2 tablespoons vegetable oil
5 small shallots (3½ ounces/100 g total), very finely chopped
3 cloves garlic, minced to a fine paste
1 inch (2.5 cm) fresh ginger, peeled and minced to a fine paste

2 inches (5 cm) fresh turmeric, minced to a fine paste
1 tablespoon ground coriander
1 teaspoon ground caraway seeds
½ teaspoon ground anise seeds
1 cinnamon stick
4 whole cloves

½ nutmeg
2 green cardamom pods
2 stalks lemongrass, white part only
5 kaffir lime leaves
2 bay leaves
1 teaspoon sea salt
1 pound 2 ounces (500 g) mutton (meaning goat) or beef, cut into medium chunks, or bone-in chicken parts

5 cups (1 kg) long-grain rice
3 tablespoons raisins
3 tablespoons fried onions
6 cups (1.5 liters) coconut cream
2 tablespoons (30 g) ghee or unsalted butter

1. Heat the oil in a large pot over medium heat. Add the shallots and garlic and sauté until golden. Add the ginger, turmeric, coriander, caraway, and anise and sauté for a minute or so. Add the cinnamon stick, cloves, nutmeg, cardamom, lemongrass, citrus leaves, bay leaves, and salt and continue sautéing until very fragrant. Add the meat and cook until browned.

2. Rinse the rice under cold water until the water runs pretty clear, then add the rice to the pot and sauté with the spices and meat for a couple of minutes. Add the raisins, fried onions, and coconut cream, reduce the heat to a simmer, and cook for 10 minutes, until the coconut cream starts bubbling.

3. Reduce the heat to as low as you can get it. Wrap the lid of the pot with a clean kitchen towel. Replace over the pot and let the rice steam for 45 minutes, until the liquid is fully absorbed and the rice is fluffy.

4. Add the ghee and gently stir it into the rice and meat as you transfer them to a serving platter. Serve hot.

SAUDI SHRIMP "RISOTTO"

MASHBUSS RUBYAN

Mashbuss, makbuss, or *kabsah* are different names for more or less the same rice and meat (or fish or seafood or poultry) dish, a classic of the Arabian Gulf, also known in Dubai as *foga* (meaning "over" because the rice is cooked over the meat or fish element of the dish). *Mashbuss* originated in Yemen but it has become so much a part of the Arabian Gulf's culinary repertoire—with slight variations depending on where you are—that no one ever mentions its origins. The recipe below is for the Saudi version of shrimp *mashbuss* (for a Qatari version that is quite different, see page 215). A Saudi woman chef, Rajaa Merani, who I was helping modernize a Saudi menu for a restaurant, gave me this recipe as well as the Saudi Lamb Kabsa (page 219).   SERVES 6

Pinch of saffron threads
¼ cup (60 ml) rose water

FOR THE SHRIMP
2¼ pounds (1 kg)
   shell-on shrimp
1 small onion
   (3½ ounces/100 g),
   quartered
1 teaspoon ground
   turmeric
1 cinnamon stick
½ teaspoon black
   peppercorns
2 whole cloves
2 green cardamom pods,
   smashed
Sea salt

FOR THE SAUCE
¼ cup (60 ml)
   vegetable oil
3 large onions (1 pound
   5 ounces/600 g total),
   finely chopped
1 clove garlic, minced to a
   fine paste
½ inch (1 cm) fresh
   ginger, peeled and
   minced to a fine paste
1 fresh red or green chili,
   finely chopped
1½ teaspoons b'zar
   (Arabian Spice Mixture,
   page 366)
1 teaspoon ground dried
   limes

1 teaspoon ground
   turmeric
¼ teaspoon ground
   cardamom
½ bunch cilantro (about
   3½ ounces/100 g),
   most of the bottom
   stems discarded, finely
   chopped
Sea salt

FOR THE RICE
Sea salt
½ teaspoon black
   peppercorns
2 whole cloves
2 green cardamom pods,
   smashed

2½ cups (500 g) basmati
   rice, soaked for
   2 hours in 2 quarts
   (2 liters) water with
   2 tablespoons salt

**FOR ASSEMBLY AND
SERVING**
3 tablespoons vegetable
   oil, plus more for the
   onion
1 large onion (7 ounces/
   200 g), halved
   lengthwise and cut into
   thin wedges
Saudi "Salsa" (page 429)

1. Put the saffron to steep in the rose water.

2. To cook the shrimp: Put 6 cups (1.5 liters) water in a saucepan. Add the onion, turmeric, cinnamon stick, peppercorns, cloves, and cardamom and bring to a boil over medium heat. Season with salt, then add the shrimp and poach for 1 minute. Drain the shrimp and let them cool for a few minutes before peeling them.

3. To make the sauce: Heat the oil in a large skillet over medium heat. Add the onions and sauté until very soft and golden. Add the garlic, ginger, chili, and ground spices and mix well. Stir in the shrimp and cilantro. Add salt to taste and mix well. Add 1 tablespoon of the saffron rose water and take off the heat.

4. To parboil the rice: Put 2 quarts (2 liters) water and 1 tablespoon salt in a large pot and bring to a boil over high heat. Add the peppercorns, cloves, and cardamom. Drain the rice and add to the pan. Boil for 3 minutes. Drain the rice.

5. To assemble the *mashbuss*: Put 3 tablespoons vegetable oil and 1 tablespoon saffron-rose water in a saucepan over medium-high heat. Let the oil and saffron-rose water sizzle a little before spooning half the rice into the pan. Spread the shrimp and sauce over the rice and cover with the rest of the rice. Sprinkle with the remaining saffron-rose water. Wrap the lid with a clean kitchen towel and place over the pan. Reduce the heat to low and let the rice steam for 30 to 40 minutes, until completely fluffy.

6. Meanwhile, heat a little oil in a skillet. Add the onion and fry, stirring regularly, until crisp and golden brown, about 10 minutes. Remove with a slotted spoon into a sieve and shake to get rid of any excess oil.

7. Transfer the rice and shrimp to a serving dish. Garnish with the crisp onions and serve hot with the Saudi "salsa."

QATARI SHRIMP "RISOTTO"

MASHBUSS RUBYAN

This shrimp *mashbuss* is quite different from the Saudi version (page 213), fresher in taste and simpler to make. The shrimp in the Arabian Gulf are large and sweet and quite fabulous. Unfortunately cooks there have a tendency to overcook them, whereas I like mine barely cooked. So I have changed the recipe slightly and I suggest sautéing them quickly first, then steaming them with the rice at the very end to get the flavors to meld without the risk of overcooking. Ideally you need to use fresh shell-on shrimp, which you peel and rinse at home. Most cooks suggest removing the vein on the back of the shrimp, but I don't worry too much about it, preferring to leave the shrimp as they are without slitting them open to pull out the vein. You can also leave the shrimp unpeeled as I have done in the photograph of the recipe for a more beautiful presentation, although it will make for messier eating. The recipe remains the same for unpeeled shrimp.

SERVES 4 TO 6

- 4 tablespoons (60 g) unsalted butter
- 2¼ pounds (1 kg) large shrimp, peeled and rinsed
- ⅓ cup plus 1 tablespoon (100 ml) extra-virgin olive oil
- 3 medium onions (1 pound/450 g total), finely chopped

- 3 curry leaves
- 1 teaspoon ground turmeric
- 2 teaspoons b'zar (Arabian Spice Mixture, page 366)
- 1 tablespoon ground dried limes
- 3 or 4 whole cloves

- 2 medium tomatoes (7 ounces/200 g total), diced into small cubes
- 3 tablespoons tomato paste
- A few sprigs flat-leaf parsley, most of the stems discarded, finely chopped
- A few sprigs cilantro, most of the stems

- discarded, finely chopped
- 3 cloves garlic, minced to a fine paste
- 2 cups (400 g) basmati rice, soaked for 30 minutes in 2 quarts (2 liters) water with 1 tablespoon salt
- Sea salt

1. Melt the butter in a skillet over medium heat. Add the peeled shrimp in the butter for 2 minutes over medium heat. Take off the heat.

2. Heat the olive oil in a large pot over medium heat. Add the onions and and sauté until golden, about 5 minutes. Add the curry leaves, turmeric, *b'zar*, ground limes, cloves, tomatoes, tomato paste, herbs, and garlic and stir for a minute or so.

3. Add 2 cups (500 ml) water and bring to a boil. Drain the rice and add to the pan. Season with salt to taste. Reduce the heat to low and let simmer for 10 minutes. Arrange the shrimp over the rice. Wrap the lid with a clean kitchen towel and replace over the pot. Steam the rice and shrimp for 10 more minutes.

4. Stir the shrimp into the rice while fluffing it with a fork. Transfer to a serving platter and serve hot.

QATARI CHICKEN and RICE

MASHKHUL D'JAJ

I am fortunate to count Aisha al-Tamimi, Qatar's best-known celebrity chef, as one of my great friends in Doha. She and her sister, Mariam el-Abdallah, who was Qatar's first TV chef, taught me almost all I know about Qatari cuisine when I worked with them on developing a food culture program for the National Museum of Qatar. I spent days in both their kitchens learning how to prepare various Qatari dishes, including this one. I love it, not only for its simplicity but also for the lovely and different textures it combines, as well as the fact that it constitutes a complete meal, as with so many of the rice dishes in this chapter that combine rice with meat and some-times vegetables. You can also make it with lamb shanks. If you decide to use lamb, cook the meat for 30 minutes longer than the chicken, possibly even longer depending on the size and quality of the shanks.

SERVES 6 TO 8

FOR THE GARNISH
Vegetable oil, for frying
2 medium onions (10½ ounces/300 g total), halved and cut into thin wedges
1⅓ cups (200 g) blanched almonds

FOR THE MASHKHUL
1 organic or free-range chicken (3 pounds 5 ounces/1.5 kg), cut into 8 pieces
Sea salt
Vegetable oil, for frying
2 medium potatoes (10½ ounces/300 g total), cut into medium wedges

1 large eggplant (9 ounces/250 g), halved lengthwise, then cut into wedges
4 medium onions (1 pound 5 ounces/ 600 g total), finely chopped
1 green bell pepper, sliced into long strips
3 cups (600 g) basmati rice, soaked for 1 hour in lightly salted water
1 teaspoon ground cardamom
1 teaspoon ground cinnamon
1 teaspoon ground coriander

1 teaspoon ground cumin
1 teaspoon ground fennel
1 teaspoon Qatari Biryani Masala (page 362)
1 teaspoon ground turmeric
4 black dried limes, inside pulp only (seeds and peel discarded)
1 small clove garlic, minced to a fine paste
½ inch (1 cm) fresh ginger, peeled and minced to a fine paste
2 medium tomatoes (7 ounces/200 g total), quartered and thinly sliced

A few sprigs flat-leaf parsley, most of the stems discarded, finely chopped
A few sprigs cilantro, most of the stems discarded, finely chopped

TO COLOR THE RICE
3 tablespoons (45 g) ghee or clarified butter
1 teaspoon ground turmeric
Good pinch of saffron threads, soaked in ¼ cup (60 ml) rose water

Recipe continues

1. Preheat the oven to 450°F (230°C).

2. To make the garnish: Pour 1 inch (2.5 cm) vegetable oil into a skillet and heat over medium heat until hot. Add the sliced onion and fry, stirring regularly, until crisp and golden, about 10 minutes. Remove to a sieve and shake off the excess oil.

3. Toast the almonds in the hot oven for 6 to 7 minutes, or until golden brown.

4. To make the *mashkul*: Put the chicken pieces in a large pot, cover with 2 quarts (2 liters) water, and bring to a boil over medium heat, skimming the froth from the surface. Add salt to taste and cook the chicken for 30 minutes, until tender.

5. Meanwhile, heat 1 inch (2.5 cm) vegetable oil in a skillet over medium heat until sizzling. Add the potatoes and fry, turning them halfway through, until golden all over and cooked through, about 10 minutes. Remove to a plate lined with several layers of paper towels to drain. Add the eggplant and fry, turning them halfway through, until golden all over, about 8 minutes. Remove to several layers of paper towels to drain. Add a little more oil and add the chopped onions. Sauté over medium heat until golden brown, about 10 minutes. Remove to a plate. Add the bell pepper and sauté until softened, about 10 minutes. Remove to the plate with the onions.

6. When the chicken is done, remove it from the broth. Remove the skin if you prefer it without. Keep hot.

7. Drain the soaked rice and drop it into the broth. Cook at a boil for 8 to 10 minutes, or until done. Drain and keep hot.

8. Put a little oil in a large skillet to cover the bottom of the pan and add the ground spices and place over medium heat. Stir for a few seconds until fragrant. Add the cooked chicken and sauté for a minute or two, then remove the chicken. Add the sautéed onion-pepper mixture to the pan, along with the dried lime pulp, garlic, ginger, and tomatoes. Cook for a few minutes, then add the parsley and cilantro, along with the fried eggplant and potatoes. Stir and cover. Keep hot while you color the rice.

9. Heat the ghee and turmeric in a small frying pan over medium heat. When it is hot, add the saffron-rose water. Sprinkle the saffron ghee over the cooked rice and mix lightly to get a mix of white and yellow rice.

10. Spread one-third of the rice over a serving dish, cover with half the chicken still on the bone, then the vegetables. Cover with another one-third of the rice. Spread the remaining chicken and vegetables over the rice and cover with the remaining rice. Garnish with the caramelized onions and toasted almonds. Serve hot.

SAUDI LAMB KABSA

KABSA BIL-LAHM

Kabsa is *the* national dish of Saudi Arabia, prepared at all kinds of gatherings, from simple family meals to special occasions. It can be made with chicken, lamb, or seafood. As for the rice, it can be cooked with the broth in which the meat is cooked, or parboiled and put to steam on top of the meat or fish. Either way, *kabsa* is a sumptuous classic rice dish. Garnish the dish with crisp fried onions or toasted nuts or serve as is.

SERVES 4 TO 6

3 tablespoons vegetable oil

2 medium onions (10½ ounces/300 g total), halved and cut into thin wedges

1 green chili, halved lengthwise and seeded

½ inch (1 cm) fresh ginger, peeled and minced to a fine paste

1 tablespoon tomato paste

1 pound 10 ounces (750 g) bone-in lamb (shoulder, shanks, or ribs)

Sea salt

3 medium carrots (10½ ounces/300 g total), peeled and julienned

3 medium tomatoes (10½ ounces/300 g total), peeled and seeded—2 cut into thin wedges and 1 processed into a puree

2 teaspoons ground cumin

2 teaspoons finely ground black pepper

1 teaspoon ground cardamom

¼ teaspoon ground cinnamon

1 stick cinnamon

2½ cups (500 g) long-grain rice, rinsed

1. Heat the oil in a pot over medium heat. Add the onions and chili and sauté until the onions are lightly golden. Add the ginger and tomato paste and stir for a minute or so. Add the meat and salt to taste and sauté for a few minutes, or until the meat is browned.

2. Add the julienned carrots and tomato wedges and sauté for 3 to 4 minutes. Add the pureed tomato, the ground and whole spices, and 4 cups (1 liter) water. Season with salt to taste. Bring to a boil, then cover the pan and let bubble gently on medium-low heat for 1 hour, or until the lamb is tender.

3. Remove the lamb to a plate and keep warm. Drop the rice into the broth. Add a little more salt. Cover the pot, reduce the heat to low, and let simmer for 10 to 15 minutes, or until the rice has absorbed all the liquid. Take off the heat. Wrap the lid with a clean kitchen towel and replace over the pot. Let sit for 5 minutes.

4. Fluff up the rice with a fork before transferring to a serving platter. Place the lamb over the rice and serve hot—some people crisp up and brown the lamb under a hot broiler before serving with the rice; if you like this idea, you can do it while the rice is cooking.

EMIRATI RICE and MEAT

AYSH WA LAHM

The first time I went to the United Arab Emirates, I had the incredible fortune of being invited on a culinary tour by Sheikha Bodour Al-Qasimi, the ruler's daughter. It all happened by chance. I had tweeted that I was on my way there, and Sheikha Bodour tweeted back offering to introduce me to her country's culinary riches. I was thrilled, as I knew very little about Emirati food. The only Gulf country I was familiar with was Kuwait and I knew that the food there was quite different. Sheikha Bodour organized amazing meals, as well as a cookery demonstration at Sharjah's Heritage Center that was followed by a lunch at which I tried many dishes, including the one below, which can be considered one of their most festive dishes. We had it with a whole baby goat, but I adapted the recipe and scaled it down to four lamb shanks. If you want to make it with a baby goat, simply double the quantities.   SERVES 4 TO 6

4 lamb shanks (3 pounds 5 ounces/1.5 kg total)
1 large onion (7 ounces/200 g), quartered
4 dried golden limes, pierced with a sharp knife in several places
2 cinnamon sticks
6 green cardamom pods
2 bay leaves
1 tablespoon b'zar (Arabian Spice Mixture, page 366)

1 teaspoon finely ground black pepper
¼ teaspoon ground turmeric
Good pinch of saffron threads
Sea salt
4 cups (800 g) long-grain rice, rinsed under cold water, soaked for 30 minutes in lightly salted water

FOR THE GARNISH
¼ cup (60 ml) vegetable oil
4 medium onions (1 pound 5 ounces/600 g total), finely chopped
Good pinch of saffron threads
⅔ cup (100 g) golden raisins, soaked for 2 hours in cold water
½ teaspoon ground dried lime

½ teaspoon ground cardamom
¼ teaspoon ground cinnamon
1 cup (200 g) dried chickpeas, soaked overnight in plenty of water with ½ teaspoon baking soda, rinsed, drained, and cooked until tender but not falling apart

1. Put the lamb shanks in a large pot, cover well with water, and bring to a boil over medium heat, skimming the froth from the surface. Add the onion, dried limes, whole spices, ground spices, saffron, and salt to taste, being careful not to oversalt as you will eventually be cooking the rice in the broth. Cover the pot, reduce the heat to medium-low, and let simmer for 1½ to 2 hours, or until the lamb is very tender. Remove the meat from the broth and arrange on a baking dish (you will eventually be roasting it in the oven to color and crisp it up).

2. Preheat the oven to 450°F (230°C).

3. Drain the rice and put it in a clean pot. Strain the cooking broth of the meat and measure out 5¼ cups (1.25 liters). Add to the rice and bring to a boil over medium heat. Reduce the heat to low, cover the pot, and cook for 10 minutes, or until the rice is tender. Take it off the heat. Wrap the lid with a clean kitchen towel and replace over the pot.

4. Place the meat in the hot oven for 15 to 20 minutes to color and crisp it up.

5. Meanwhile, make the garnish: Heat the vegetable oil in a large skillet over medium heat. Add the onions and sauté for a few minutes, then add 1 tablespoon water and the saffron threads. Sauté for 5 more minutes, then add another 1 tablespoon water. Repeat twice more at 5-minute intervals, stirring regularly so that the onion colors evenly, until the onion is golden. Add the raisins and ground spices and continue sautéing until the onion is golden brown, 5 more minutes. Add the cooked chickpeas and stir until the chickpeas are hot and well blended with the other ingredients. Taste and adjust the seasoning if necessary, then take off the heat.

6. Transfer the rice to a serving platter. Place the roasted meat over the rice then spoon the garnish all over and serve hot.

QATARI FESTIVE RICE and CHICKEN

MASHBUSS EL-EID BADDAWI

Here is another recipe that I learned to make with Aisha al-Tamimi, my great friend and Qatari celebrity chef extraordinaire. I have tweaked her recipe by reducing the amount of tomato paste she uses in the chicken marinade. Aisha serves this dish for large family gatherings, normally for Friday lunch, or when she invites people over for formal occasions. It looks great on the table with its mixed garnish and colored eggs. I helped her present it in London during a series of cooking demonstrations she did at Books for Cooks for Qatar/UK, an initiative of the Qatari government where they partner with a different country every year to offer exchanges of cultural programs, exhibitions, and so on. Most of the audience that night was learning about and tasting Qatari food for the first time and they were all wowed by this elaborate and exquisite rice dish.

SERVES 4 TO 6 PEOPLE

FOR THE SEASONING MIXTURE
3 large tomatoes
   (1 pound 5 ounces/
   600 g total), peeled
   and processed in a food
   processor to a puree
2 medium red onions
   (10½ ounces/
   300 g total), very finely
   chopped
1 stalk celery, halved
½ inch (1 cm) fresh
   ginger, peeled and
   minced to a fine paste
1 small clove garlic,
   minced to a fine paste
¼ cup (60 ml)
   vegetable oil
1 green chili, halved
   lengthwise and seeded
3 black dried limes,
   pierced with a sharp
   knife here and there

½ medium green bell
   pepper, quartered
1 tablespoon ground
   turmeric
1½ teaspoons b'zar
   (Arabian Spice Mixture,
   page 366)
1½ teaspoons ground
   coriander
1½ teaspoons ground
   cumin
¾ teaspoon ground
   fennel
½ teaspoon ground
   cardamom
½ teaspoon ground
   cinnamon
3 whole cloves
3 green cardamom pods
1 cinnamon stick
¼ teaspoon red pepper
   flakes
Sea salt

FOR THE CHICKEN AND RICE
1 whole chicken
   (3 pounds 5 ounces/
   1.5 kg), quartered
4 cups (1 liter) boiling
   water
A few sprigs flat-leaf
   parsley, most of the
   stems discarded, finely
   chopped
A few sprigs cilantro,
   most of the stems
   discarded, finely
   chopped
2 sprigs fresh dill, fronds
   only, finely chopped
2½ cups (500 g) basmati
   rice, rinsed under cold
   water, soaked for 30
   minutes in water to
   cover by 1 inch (2.5 cm)
   with 1 tablespoon salt

FOR THE MARINADE
Pinch of saffron threads
2 tablespoons rose water
¼ cup (60 g) tomato
   paste
Juice of 1 lemon, or to
   taste
2 tablespoons extra-
   virgin olive oil
½ teaspoon Dijon
   mustard
½ teaspoon cayenne
   pepper
½ teaspoon ground
   turmeric

Recipe continues

½ cup (100 g) blanched
    almonds
Vegetable oil, for frying
2 medium onions
    (10½ ounces/300 g
    total), halved and cut
    into thin wedges
1 tablespoon unbleached
    all-purpose flour
2 medium carrots,
    coarsely grated
⅓ cup (50 g) golden
    raisins
¼ cup (50 g) yellow split
    peas, boiled for
    20 minutes, until
    tender and drained
4 hard-boiled eggs,
    peeled
4 black dried limes, inside
    pulp only (seeds and
    peel discarded)
1 teaspoon ground cumin
½ teaspoon ground
    coriander
½ teaspoon ground
    turmeric
¼ teaspoon b'zar
    (Arabian Spice Mixture,
    page 366)
⅛ teaspoon ground
    cardamom
⅛ teaspoon ground
    cinnamon
⅛ teaspoon ground
    fennel

1. To make the seasoning mixture: In a large bowl, mix the pureed tomatoes, onions, celery, ginger, garlic, oil, chili, black limes, bell pepper, the ground spices, whole spices, pepper flakes, and salt to taste. Aisha recommends mixing all the ingredients in one bowl so that you can add them all at once and won't forget any.

2. To cook the chicken: Put the chicken in a large pot and add the boiling water. Bring to a boil over medium heat, skimming the froth from the surface. Add the seasoning mixture, cover the pan, and let bubble for 30 minutes.

3. Preheat the oven to 400°F (200°C).

4. Pull the cooked chicken pieces out of the pot with a slotted spoon and place on a baking sheet. Add the fresh herbs to the pot and bring back to a boil. Drain and rinse the rice and add to the boiling liquid in the pot. Cover and cook the rice for 10 minutes. Remove from the heat. Wrap the lid with a clean kitchen towel and replace over the rice.

5. To make the marinade: Put the saffron to steep in the rose water for 15 minutes in a medium bowl. Then add the tomato paste, lemon juice, olive oil, mustard, cayenne, and turmeric. Rub the mixture into the cooked chicken, coating it all over. Place the chicken pieces in the hot oven and roast for 15 minutes, or until crisp and golden.

6. To prepare the garnish: Spread the almonds on a baking sheet and toast them in the oven for 6 to 7 minutes, or until golden brown.

7. Pour 2 inches (5 cm) of oil into a deep skillet and heat over medium heat until hot (if you drop a piece of bread in the oil, the oil should immediately bubble around it). Toss the onions with the flour and deep-fry them until golden brown and crisp, about 10 minutes—watch them at the end so that they don't burn. Drain in a sieve and shake off the excess oil to keep them crisp.

8. Heat 2 tablespoons vegetable oil in a skillet over medium heat. Add the grated carrots, raisins, cooked split peas, eggs, dried lime pulp, fried onions, almonds, and ground spices and mix well. Sauté for 5 minutes, until the carrots have softened and the mixture is well blended.

9. Transfer the rice to a large serving platter. Lay the chicken pieces over the rice and garnish with the fried onion and nut mixture. Serve immediately.

YEMENI CHICKEN "RISOTTO"

YEMENI MANDI

The first time I had *mandi* was in Syria at Palmyra, a fabulous Roman site in the middle of the desert once ruled by Queen Zenobia in the third century. A Frenchman built a fascinating hotel right on the edge of the ruins in the early 1900s and called it the Zenobia Hotel. It must have been magnificent then and I guess for a while longer, although sadly not by the time I got to know it. The only magnificent thing left was the setting, with its spectacular views of the ruins from some of the rooms and the most amazing terrace overlooking the ruins and at times unbelievable sunsets. I always included Palmyra on the itinerary of my culinary tours, not only for the ruins but also to let the group sample the chef's *mandi*. The dish comes from Yemen, where they make it by roasting a whole lamb in a *tannur* oven (see page 2), which they then serve over a luxurious rice flavored with saffron, nuts, and raisins. But the Palmyra *mandi* was made with lamb shanks and roasted in a regular oven, and the yellow color of the rice came from turmeric and not saffron. Still, my groups and I enjoyed it—that is, until I had *mandi* at a specialist *mandi* restaurant in Dubai where the cooks were Yemeni. The rice there was flavored with saffron and enriched with ghee while the meat was cooked in a *tannur* oven—although it was a shoulder and ribs and not a whole lamb—and was far superior to the Syrian version. *Mandi* has now been adopted by most Arab countries and you find it throughout the Middle East. The recipe below is closer to the *mandi* I had in Dubai except that it is made with chicken. You can use lamb shanks instead (see Note).

SERVES 4

FOR THE CHICKEN
4 teaspoons Yemeni
    Mandi Spice Mixture
    (page 364)
Juice of 1 lemon
Good pinch of saffron
    threads

Sea salt
1 whole organic chicken
    (3 pounds 5 ounces/
    1.5 kg), quartered
2 tablespoons
    vegetable oil

FOR THE RICE
1 tablespoon (15 g)
    unsalted butter
1 small onion
    (3½ ounces/100 g),
    finely chopped
4 green cardamom pods
4 whole cloves

6 black peppercorns
1 small tomato
    (2½ ounces/75 g),
    seeded and finely diced
1½ cups (300 g) basmati
    rice, rinsed under cold
    water
Sea salt

Recipe continues

1. To marinate the chicken: Combine the mandi spice mixture, lemon juice, and saffron in a large bowl. Add 2 tablespoons water and salt to taste and mix well. Let steep for 15 minutes. Add the chicken pieces and toss them in the marinade. Let marinate for at least 2 hours, preferably longer in the refrigerator.

2. Heat the oil in a large deep skillet over medium heat. When the oil is hot, add the chicken and brown on all sides, about 5 minutes. Reduce the heat to low, cover, and slowly roast for 30 minutes. Remove the chicken to a plate. Pour the cooking juices into a large jug.

3. To make the rice: Melt the butter in a pot over medium heat. Add the onion and sauté until lightly golden, about 5 minutes. Add the whole spices and stir for a couple of minutes. Then add 1⅔ cups (410 ml) water to the jug with the chicken cooking juices. Stir well and add to the pot, along with the tomato and rice. Add salt to taste and bring to a boil. Reduce the heat to low, cover, and simmer for 15 minutes. Uncover and place the chicken pieces over the rice. Wrap the lid with a clean kitchen towel and replace over the pot. Take off the heat and let sit for 5 minutes. Serve hot.

NOTE: *To make the* mandi *with lamb, use 2 shanks if they are very large or 4 if they are a regular size. Depending on the size and quality of the shanks, you will need to cook them for at least 30 minutes longer than the chicken.*

SWEET-SAVORY RICE

MUHAMMAR

There are two ways of making this sweet-savory rice, another classic from the Arabian Gulf, normally served with fried or grilled fish. One way is to caramelize sugar before adding water and parboiling the rice in the sweet water, then finishing the rice by steaming it with a little butter or ghee and saffron-rose water. The other method is to sweeten the rice with date syrup, which is what was done traditionally. I like the flavor of date syrup and the recipe below, which was given to me by Mariam al-Abdallah, who was Qatar's first celebrity chef, calls for date syrup. Mariam cooks the rice by the absorption method—i.e., in just enough water so the rice absorbs it fully—but you can also parboil the rice (see Note). Be sure to get the right date syrup. Some are very thick and dark and they do not produce a great result. Instead try to find a light golden date syrup. Serve with the Arabian Spiced Fried Fish (page 345) or any other fish dish that strikes your fancy and will go with the sweet-savory flavors of *muhammar*.   SERVES 4 TO 6

1 cup (250 ml) date syrup

2 cups (500 ml) boiling water

4 cardamom pods, smashed

1 cinnamon stick

2½ cups (500 g) basmati rice, soaked for 30 minutes in 2 quarts (2 liters) water and 1 tablespoon salt

Sea salt

3 tablespoons vegetable oil

1 tablespoon ground cardamom

Good pinch of saffron threads, steeped in ¼ cup (60 ml) rose water

1. Put the date syrup in a large pot in which you will be cooking the rice. Add the boiling water, cardamom pods, and cinnamon stick and place over medium heat. Bring to a boil, then drain the rice and add to the pot. Stir the rice, bring back to a boil, and then reduce the heat to low and cover the pot. Let simmer for 10 minutes, or until the liquid is fully absorbed—check after 10 minutes and taste for salt; add more if necessary.

2. Meanwhile, heat the oil in a small pan over medium heat.

3. When the rice is done, sprinkle the hot oil over the rice and sprinkle the ground cardamom and saffron-rose water all over. Use a fork to mix the rice and fluff it up. Wrap the lid with a clean kitchen towel and let the rice steam over very low heat for 10 more minutes. Fluff it up again with a fork and serve hot.

NOTE: *You can also parboil the rice in a lot of water, then drain it and return to the pan to let it steam over very low heat. To do so, increase the amount of date syrup by ½ cup (125 ml) and add 5¼ cups (1.25 liters) water to parboil the rice for 3 minutes. Drain the rice and instead of the oil in the recipe, add a little ghee or butter to a clean pan and add the drained rice. Place over very low heat and steam the rice for 20 minutes. Sprinkle a little saffron-rose water over the rice at the end.*

SAUDI FISH "RISOTTO"
SAYYADIYAT SAMAK

SAUDI ARABIA

This is the Saudi version of *sayadiyeh,* a classic Lebanese dish (see page 230), but made with *hamour*, which is the most popular fish in the Gulf. The Lebanese version is quite different, both in look (brown from the caramelized onion broth) and in flavor. The different spicing and the tamarind sauce for the Saudi version give an interesting tart flavor to the dish. Make sure you ask your fishmonger to give you heads for your stock. Using them will make the stock so much tastier. Fish heads are usually discarded in the West so you should be able to get them for free. SERVES 6 TO 8

FOR THE FISH STOCK
¼ cup (60 ml) vegetable oil
4 medium onions (1 pound 5 ounces/ 600 g total), finely chopped
3 cloves garlic, minced to a fine paste
1 medium tomato (3½ ounces/100 g), quartered
2 fish heads
4 green cardamom pods

4 whole cloves
1 cinnamon stick
½ teaspoon ground cumin
½ teaspoon finely ground black pepper
Sea salt

FOR THE TAMARIND SAUCE
About 1 cup (200 g) seedless tamarind paste, soaked for 30 minutes in 1½ cups (375 ml) hot water

½ teaspoon ground coriander
½ teaspoon finely ground black pepper
Sea salt
1 tablespoon finely chopped cilantro

FOR THE "RISOTTO"
2½ cups (500 g) basmati rice, soaked for 1 hour in lightly salted water
2 tablespoons tomato paste

TO FINISH
3 pounds 5 ounces (1.5 kg) white fish steaks
Sea salt and finely ground black pepper
Vegetable oil, for pan-frying the fish
½ cup (75 g) blanched almonds, toasted in a hot oven for 7 minutes, for garnish

1. To make the fish stock: Heat the oil in a large skillet over medium heat. Add the onions and cook, stirring regularly, until the onions are caramelized and have turned golden brown, about 10 minutes. Add the garlic and stir for a minute or so. Transfer to a food processor. Add the tomato and blend until smooth.

2. Transfer the tomato-onion puree to a saucepan. Add the fish heads, 4 cups (1 liter) water, whole spices, cumin, pepper, and salt to taste. Bring to a boil over medium heat, then reduce the heat to medium-low and simmer for 30 minutes, until the stock has reduced by a quarter. Take off the heat. Discard the fish heads and strain the stock into a clean pot.

3. To make the tamarind sauce: Mash the tamarind paste in the water, then push through a sieve set over a bowl, pressing on the pulp to extract as much tamarind sauce as possible. Add the coriander, pepper, salt to taste, and cilantro. Mix well.

4. To make the "risotto": Drain the rice and add to the pot of stock. Add the tomato paste and bring to a boil over medium heat. Reduce the heat to medium-low and let simmer for 10 minutes, or until the rice is done and has completely absorbed the liquid. Wrap the lid with a clean kitchen towel and replace over the pot. Let steam over very low heat for 10 more minutes.

5. To finish: While the rice is cooking, season the fish steaks with salt and pepper to taste. Pour enough oil to cover the bottom of a large skillet and place over medium-high heat until the pan is very hot. Slide the fish in skin side down and fry for 2 to 3 minutes, until the skin is crisp and golden. Flip and fry on the other side for another 2 to 3 minutes, until the fish steaks are just done. If the fish steaks don't fit in the pan at once, you may have to cook them in two batches. In that case, between batches wipe the pan clean and add a little more oil.

6. Transfer the rice to a serving platter. Arrange the cooked fish steaks over the rice. Garnish with the toasted almonds and serve immediately with the tamarind sauce.

LEBANESE FISH and CARAMELIZED ONION "RISOTTO"

SAYADIYEH

LEBANON

In this *sayadiyeh,* the rice has the loveliest golden brown color because of the stock made with caramelized onions, and the flavor is pretty straightforward with only lemon wedges served with the "risotto." SERVES 4 TO 6

1 pound 2 ounces (500 g) white fish heads
2¼ pounds (1 kg) white fish fillets or steaks
Sea salt
Vegetable oil, for frying
4 medium onions (1 pound 5 ounces/ 600 g total), halved and cut into thin wedges
2 cups (400 g) Calasparra or bomba rice, rinsed and soaked for 30 minutes in lightly salted water
½ teaspoon ground cumin
½ teaspoon finely ground black pepper
2 ounces (60 g) pine nuts
1 lemon, cut into wedges

1. Put the fish heads in a pot. Add 3½ cups (875 ml) water and bring to a boil over medium heat, skimming the froth from the surface. Reduce the heat to medium-low and let bubble gently for 15 minutes, until the stock has reduced slightly.

2. Pat the fish dry with paper towels and rub lightly with salt. Pour ½ inch (1 cm) vegetable oil into a large nonstick skillet and heat over medium heat until hot (if you drop a piece of bread in the oil, the oil should immediately bubble around it). Fry the fish for 1 minute on each side to seal it. Remove with a slotted spoon and drain on several layers of paper towels.

3. Pour 1 inch (2.5 cm) oil into the pan and heat over medium heat until hot (if you drop a piece of bread in the oil, the oil should immediately bubble around it). Add the onions and fry until golden brown, being careful not to let them burn, about 10 minutes. Remove with a slotted spoon to a sieve and gently shake the sieve to get rid of any excess oil and let the onions become crisp.

4. Strain the fish head stock into a clean pot and add three-quarters of the fried onions, reserving the rest for garnish. Bring the stock to a boil and let simmer for 10 to 15 minutes, or until it has taken on the color of the onions. Reserving the onions in the sieve, strain the broth into a clean stockpot. Transfer the onions to a food processor and puree, then stir back into the stock.

5. Preheat the oven to 400°F (200°C).

6. Bring the stock to a boil over medium heat. Drain the rice and add to the pot together with any loose fish flakes from the fried fish. Season with the cumin, pepper, and salt to taste. Reduce the heat to low, cover, and let simmer for 15 minutes, or until the rice is tender and the liquid absorbed.

7. Meanwhile, spread the pine nuts on a baking sheet and toast in the hot oven for 5 to 6 minutes, or until golden brown.

8. Place the fried fish fillets on top of the cooked rice. Wrap the lid with a clean kitchen towel and replace over the pot. Let steam over low heat for a few more minutes or until the fish is just done.

9. Transfer gently to a serving dish, making sure the fish sits on top of the rice. Scatter the reserved crispy onion slices and toasted pine nuts all over the fish and rice. Serve hot with the lemon wedges.

BENGALI VEGETABLE "RISOTTO"

BENGALI KHICHDI

There are many ways of preparing *khichdi, khichri,* or *khichuri,* from the simplest version with only rice and mung dal to *bhoutik,* considered to have "supernatural" properties, with added spinach, bitter gourd, potatoes, and peas. *Bhoutik* was Chitrita Bhanerji's family winter recipe, as she explains in her book *Bengali Cooking.* The *khichdi* recipe below could become "supernatural" if you add a little spinach and bitter gourd, but I like it as it is. Like many of the rice dishes in this chapter, it makes a perfect one-pot vegetarian meal (although you can easily change that by serving it with fried fish). You can also add the Indian Fried Eggplant (page 419). **SERVES 6**

1 cup (200 g) mung dal
¼ cup (60 ml) mustard oil
2 large potatoes (14 ounces/400 g total), cut into medium cubes
1 cup (225 g) cauliflower florets

1 teaspoon cumin seeds
2 bay leaves
4 whole cloves
1 cinnamon stick
3 green cardamom pods
2 dried red chilies
1 teaspoon ground cumin
½ teaspoon Kashmiri chili powder

1 inch (2.5 cm) fresh ginger, peeled and minced to a fine paste
1 large tomato (7 ounces/200 g), finely chopped
½ cup (75 g) fresh or frozen petits pois

1 cup (200 g) Calasparra or Thai fragrant jasmine rice, rinsed and soaked for 30 minutes in 2 cups (500 ml) water
1 teaspoon ground turmeric
½ teaspoon Garam Masala 1 (page 361)
Sea salt

1. Put the mung dal in a large karahi (a thick, deep, round cooking pot not quite as wide as a wok) and dry-roast it over medium heat until it starts darkening. Transfer to a plate.

2. Add the mustard oil to the karahi, increase the heat to high, and heat the oil until it starts smoking. Reduce the heat to medium and let the oil cool slightly and stop smoking. Add the potatoes and cauliflower, and sauté until they start coloring. Remove to a plate.

3. Add the cumin seeds to the pot and sauté for a minute or so. Add the bay leaves, cloves, cinnamon stick, cardamom pods, and whole red chilies and sauté for a couple of minutes. Reduce the heat to low, then add the ground cumin, chili powder, and minced ginger and sauté for a minute or so. Add the chopped tomato and sauté for 3 to 4 minutes, until the chopped tomato softens.

4. Return the toasted mung dal to the pot and sauté for 3 minutes. Add 2 cups (500 ml) water, cover the pot, and increase the heat to medium-high. When the water starts bubbling, add the sautéed potatoes and cauliflower and the petits pois. Replace the lid and let bubble gently for 5 minutes. Drain the rice and add it to the pot along with the turmeric, garam masala, and salt to taste, mixing well. Cover and cook, stirring occasionally, until the rice and dal are very soft, 10 to 15 minutes. You may need to add more water if the dish gets too dry. Taste and adjust the seasoning if necessary.

KOSHARI

The food of the revolution! This is how *koshari* is now described in Egypt, but before the uprising of the people against Mubarak, when thousands gathered in Tahrir Square, relying on *koshari* for sustenance, it was one of Egypt's most loved national dishes, by poor and rich alike. The poor ate it on the street, off beautiful carts decorated with colored glass—these are becoming rarer now, replaced by stainless steel carts—and the rich ate it at home or in busy restaurants that serve only *koshari*, like Hind in modern Cairo and Abu Tareq in downtown Cairo. *Koshari* is a multilayered dish consisting of a mixture of rice/vermicelli, lentils, and pasta that could very well be a descendant of the Bengali Khichdi (page 232). It is served topped with a spicy tomato sauce, cooked chickpeas, and crisp caramelized onions, and it is an incredibly satisfying and delicious dish that is fairly simple to prepare, although you need several pans to make it. In Egypt, they have two tomato sauces, one that is plain and the other, called *shatta*, that is very spicy. I combine both in a rather spicy tomato sauce, pepped up with a naga jolokia chili (ghost pepper), one of the hottest chilies in the world, but you can use a milder chili such as Aleppo pepper, in which case increase the quantity to 1 teaspoon.

SERVES 4 TO 6

FOR THE TOMATO SAUCE
3 tablespoons extra-virgin olive oil
1 small onion (3½ ounces/100 g), finely chopped
2 cloves garlic, minced to a fine paste
Two 14-ounce (400 g) cans Italian chopped tomatoes
¼ teaspoon naga jolokia (ghost pepper) flakes
Sea salt

FOR THE KOSHARI
Sea salt
1¼ cups (125 g) elbow macaroni
2 tablespoons extra-virgin olive oil, plus more for the macaroni
1 cup (200 g) brown lentils, soaked for 1 hour in water to cover
1 ounce (30 g) vermicelli, broken in 1-inch (2.5 cm) pieces if not already broken
1 cup (200 g) bomba or Calasparra rice

FOR THE GARNISH
Vegetable oil, for deep-frying
2 large onions (14 ounces/400 g total), halved and thinly sliced
½ cup (100 g) dried chickpeas, soaked overnight in plenty of cold water with ½ teaspoon baking soda, drained, rinsed, and boiled in fresh water until tender but not mushy

1. To make the tomato sauce: Heat the oil in a saucepan over medium heat. Add the onion and fry until golden, about 5 minutes. Add the garlic and stir for another minute or so. Add the chopped tomatoes and chili flakes and season with salt to taste. Let bubble gently for about 25 minutes, or until the sauce is reduced. Keep hot.

2. To make the *koshari*: In a medium pot of boiling salted water, cook the macaroni for 2 minutes less than the package directions. Drain and toss with a little olive oil to stop it from sticking.

Recipe continues

3. Drain the lentils and put in a saucepan with water to cover by 1 inch (2.5 cm). Bring to a boil over medium heat, then reduce the heat to medium-low and let simmer for 10 minutes, or until tender but not mushy—some lentils will take longer to cook; test them after 10 minutes and if they need longer, let them cook for up to an extra 15 minutes.

4. Meanwhile, heat the 2 tablespoons olive oil in a pot over medium heat. Add the vermicelli and sauté, stirring all the time, until golden brown, about 7 minutes. Rinse the rice under cold water and add to the pot and sauté for a few seconds. Add 1⅔ cups (410 ml) water and salt to taste. Bring to a boil, then reduce the heat to low and let simmer for 10 minutes, until the liquid is absorbed and the rice is tender.

5. Drain the lentils and add to the rice together with the macaroni (see Note). Taste and adjust the salt if necessary. Then wrap the lid with a clean kitchen towel and replace over the pan.

6. To make the garnish: Pour 1 inch (2.5 cm) vegetable oil into large skillet and heat over medium heat until hot (if you drop a piece of bread in the oil, the oil should immediately bubble around it). Drop the sliced onions into the oil and fry, stirring every now and then, until golden brown, about 10 minutes. The onions need to get to a deep color for them to be crisp, but be careful not to let them burn. Remove with a slotted spoon to a sieve and shake off the excess oil—this will make them really crisp.

7. Transfer the *koshari* to a serving platter. Spoon the tomato sauce over the center and garnish with the chickpeas and crispy onions. Serve hot.

NOTE: *You can also leave everything separate, mixing a little of the lentils in with the rice, and serve the dish in layers the way they do in Egypt.*

ZANZIBARI COCONUT RICE
WALI WA NAZI

ZANZIBAR

The way coconut milk is made in Zanzibar—and elsewhere like India or Indonesia, for that matter—is quite fascinating. First you need to grate fresh coconuts, which in Zanzibar is done with a specialized piece of equipment: a wooden stool on which the cook sits with a metal grater attached to its side. The cook places a bowl underneath the grater part, then takes coconut halves and rubs them back and forth against the teeth of the grater to release the flesh. Once she (home cooks are almost always women) has enough grated coconut, she adds water and mixes it with the coconut before she starts squeezing it to extract the milk. The first squeezing produces the thick coconut milk, or coconut cream as it is often sold, then more water is added and the coconut squeezed again for a thinner milk, and finally she may do it a third time for a really diluted result. Obviously this is not practical in the West, so you need to buy coconut milk—or, to be more accurate, coconut cream—in cans. Those that specify 25 percent fat are the thick coconut milk or cream. If you can't find lower-fat ones, mix the coconut cream with water (2 parts milk to 1 part water) to make thin coconut milk. This rice cooked in coconut milk has a lovely flavor and goes well with fish, such as the Zanzibari Grilled Fish (page 348) or curries.   SERVES 4 TO 6

1⅔ cups (425 ml) thin coconut milk

1⅔ cups (425 ml) coconut cream

2 cups (400 g) long-grain rice, soaked for 30 minutes in lightly salted water

Sea salt

Put both the coconut milk and cream in a pot and bring to a boil over medium heat. As soon as the coconut milk has come to a boil, drain the rice and drop it into the milk. Add salt to taste. Reduce the heat to low, cover, and let the rice simmer for 10 to 15 minutes, or until it has absorbed all the liquid. Take off the heat. Wrap the lid with a clean kitchen towel and replace over the pot. Let the rice steam for a few minutes.

AFGHANI VERMICELLI RICE I
RESHTA PULAU I

Cooking rice with noodles goes back many centuries and you find the word *reshta*, which means thread in Iranian, in medieval cookbooks. There are two versions to this rice. One is the simple one below, whereas the more complicated meat version is in the following recipe. Both are intriguing because of the sweet/savory element. The plainer one is wonderful served with grilled or roasted meats or stews while the meat version makes for a very sophisticated one-pot meal. I have adapted both from recipes in Helen Saberi's *Afghan Food & Cookery*. Many of the Persian *khoresht* (see pages 158 to 163) are perfect accompaniments to this rice, as are some curries.

SERVES 4 TO 6

2½ cups (500 g) long-grain rice, rinsed and soaked for 30 minutes in lightly salted water
Sea salt
½ cup (125 ml) vegetable oil
9 ounces (250 g) vermicelli, broken into 1-inch (2.5 cm) pieces
1 cup (200 g) raw cane sugar
Good pinch of saffron threads
¼ cup (40 g) slivered pistachios
¼ cup (40 g) slivered almonds

1. Drain the rice. Put 6 cups (1.5 liters) water in a large pot and bring to a boil over medium-high heat. Add 1 tablespoon salt and the drained rice and boil for 3 minutes. Drain the rice. Reserving one-quarter of the rice, transfer the remainder of it to a Dutch oven (or other ovenproof pot). Wrap the lid with a clean kitchen towel. Place over the pot and set aside.

2. Heat ¼ cup (60 ml) of the oil in a skillet over medium heat. Add the vermicelli and sauté for a few minutes stirring all the time, or until lightly browned. Take off the heat.

3. Preheat the oven to 300°F (150°C).

4. Put the sugar in a medium saucepan and add a scant 1 cup (225 ml) water. Place over medium-high heat and let bubble until you have a thin syrup. Add the fried vermicelli, saffron, pistachios, and almonds. Set a sieve or colander in the sink. Put a large spoonful of the reserved rice into the sieve and add a large spoonful of the vermicelli and nut mixture. Continue building the layers until you finish both the reserved rice and the nut/syrup mixture. Most of the syrup will drain away so don't worry about the rice becoming too sweet.

5. Mix the remaining ¼ cup (60 ml) oil with ⅓ cup (80 ml) water and a little salt and pour over the rice in the Dutch oven. Stir once, then place the vermicelli rice on one side of the plain rice without stirring it in. Unwrap the lid and place it back over the pot. Transfer the Dutch oven to the hot oven and let the rice steam for 45 minutes.

6. To serve, remove the vermicelli rice to a plate. Transfer the plain rice to a large serving platter. Scatter the vermicelli rice over the top and serve hot.

LEBANESE / SYRIAN VERMICELLI RICE

REZZ BIL-SH'AYRIYEH

LEBANON | SYRIA

Also known as *rezz mufalfal* (a term found in medieval Arab cookbooks meaning that grains of rice cook separately and not sticking together), this rice is a slight variation on plain rice, with added toasted vermicelli. In Lebanon, people normally serve vermicelli rice with meats or vegetables cooked in yogurt or in tahini sauce, while plain rice is served with regular stews (*yakhni*), but there is no absolute rule as to which rice is served with what. If you want to make plain rice, simply omit the vermicelli.

SERVES 6

1 cup (200 g) bomba or
  Calasparra rice
2 tablespoons (30 g)
  unsalted butter
1 ounce (30 g) vermicelli,
  broken into 1-inch
  (2.5 cm) pieces
Sea salt

1. Rinse the rice in several changes of cold water.

2. Melt the butter in a medium pot over medium heat. Add the vermicelli and fry, stirring continually, until golden brown, about 7 minutes. Add the rice and mix well.

3. Add 1⅔ cups (410 ml) water and season with salt to taste. Bring to a boil. Reduce the heat to low, cover, and let simmer for 15 minutes, or until the rice is tender and the water is fully absorbed. Take off the heat. Wrap the lid with a clean kitchen towel. Replace over the pot and let the rice steam for 5 minutes. Serve hot.

AFGHANI VERMICELLI RICE II
RESHTA PULAU II

This vermicelli rice is a savory meat version of Afghani Vermicelli Rice I (page 238). It is a little like a biryani but with added vermicelli. I love the way Afghans put the garnishes of rice dishes on the side of the rice, then spread them over the rice instead of layering them so that they are mixed into the rice. The result is pretty much the same as with biryani but the presentation differs.

SERVES 4 TO 6

Good pinch of saffron
    threads
1 tablespoon rose water
⅓ cup (80 ml) plus
    3 tablespoons
    vegetable oil
1 medium onion
    (5 ounces/150 g), finely
    chopped
1 pound 10 ounces
    (750 g) lamb, cut into
    1-inch (2.5 cm) cubes
½ teaspoon ground
    cinnamon
Sea salt and finely ground
    black pepper
3½ ounces (100 g)
    vermicelli, broken into
    1-inch (2.5 cm) pieces
⅓ cup (50 g) golden
    raisins, soaked for a
    couple hours in cold
    water
¼ cup (40 g) slivered
    pistachios
¼ cup (40 g) slivered
    almonds
2½ cups (500 g) long-
    grain rice, rinsed and
    soaked for 30 minutes
    in lightly salted water

1. Put the saffron to steep in the rose water plus 1 tablespoon water.

2. Heat ⅓ cup (80 ml) of the oil in a pot over medium heat. Add the onion and sauté until golden brown, about 10 minutes. Add the lamb and sauté until browned. Add the cinnamon and salt and pepper to taste. Barely cover the meat with water and bring to a boil. Reduce the heat to low and let simmer for about 45 minutes, or until the meat is tender and the sauce has become quite thick.

3. Meanwhile, heat 2 tablespoons of the oil in a skillet over medium heat. Add the vermicelli and sauté until golden brown, about 7 minutes. Be careful not to burn it. Heat the remaining 1 tablespoon oil in a small pan over medium heat and sauté the golden raisins and nuts for 2 to 3 minutes, until the raisins have puffed up a little.

4. Preheat the oven to 300°F (150°C).

5. Put 6 cups (1.5 liters) water in a large pot and bring to a boil over medium-high heat. Add 1 tablespoon salt. Drain the rice and add to the boiling water and boil for 3 minutes. Drain and transfer half the rice to a Dutch oven (or other ovenproof pot). Add the vermicelli and mix with the rice. Spread the meat and its juices (see Note) over the rice/vermicelli mix. Cover with half the remaining rice. Then mix what's left of the rice with the saffron rose water and place over one side of the rice in the pot. Spoon the raisins and nut mixture onto the other side. Cover the Dutch oven, transfer to the oven, and let steam for 45 minutes.

6. To serve, spoon out the saffron rice and golden raisins and nut mixture onto a small plate. Spoon the top layer of rice onto a serving platter. Spread the meat over the rice and cover with the bottom layer of rice. Scatter the saffron rice and golden raisins and nut mixture over the plain rice and serve hot.

NOTE: *The meat juices should be about ⅔ cup (160 ml). If you have less juice, do not worry. If you have more and the rice ends up being too wet, increase the heat to high for a few minutes to let the liquid evaporate. Be careful not to let the bottom scorch.*

PLAIN IRANIAN RICE

POLOW

Rice is an important staple throughout much of the Muslim world, but there is one country where rice is practically revered, and that is Iran, where you find stores that sell only rice, several types, as well as rock salt, which is essential for cooking rice. If you were to enter a rice merchant's shop in Qazvin, an important market town in Gilan, you would find the rice displayed in big sacks lined up in the shop window, with labels informing clients of the type, the price, and whether it is local—rice is grown in Iran, mainly in the province of Gilan on the Caspian shore. And often, you will find customers sipping tea in small glasses, which the vendor will have ordered from a nearby teahouse, while leisurely inspecting the rice before buying it. The way they do this is by plunging their hands into the bag to lift some of the rice, which they then let run through their fingers to study the grain, whether it's broken (a no-no unless they are making rice pudding) or intact. They will then ask the vendor how long the rice has been aged. The first time I overheard such a conversation (translated to me), I was astonished. I didn't know then that rice had to be aged! The best Iranian rice is called *domesiah*, which means "black end," a name given to the rice because it has a black tip. It is rare to find *domesiah* now in Iran, and practically impossible to buy it outside the country. The Iranian stores in London don't even stock Iranian rice today, selling instead Pakistani or Indian long-grain rice, both basmati and other types.

The secret to a good Iranian rice dish is to first rinse the rice, then let it soak in lightly salted water for up to 2 hours before draining it and parboiling it for 2 to 3 minutes, just enough to break the hardness. After that, it is put to steam over very low heat until it forms a *tah-dig*, or golden crust—the prize part of Persian rice—while the rest of the rice becomes incredibly fluffy. You can prepare it plain as here or make the *sabzi polow* (Herbed Polow, page 245), a typical rice dish for Nowruz (Iranian New Year), or the Lentil Polow (page 246), to name but a few of the variations.

As for the *tah-dig*, you can make it in different ways—the name is a combination of two words, *tah*, which means "bottom," and *dig*, which means "pot." I like to make a plain rice *tah-dig*, with just rice, oil, and saffron water, but you can also make a *tah-dig* by simply lining the pan with a thin layer of thinly sliced potatoes or lavash before you add the first layer of rice.

Serve this polow with the dish of your choice, either kebabs or *khoresht*.   SERVES 4 TO 6

Good pinch of saffron
   threads
2½ cups (500 g) basmati
   rice
Sea salt
⅓ cup (80 ml) vegetable
   oil
4 tablespoons (60 g)
   unsalted butter, melted

1. Put the saffron to soak in 2 tablespoons water.

2. Rinse the rice in several changes of cold water, then put in a large bowl. Pour enough water to cover the rice by about two fingers. Add 2 tablespoons salt and let soak for 2 hours.

3. Thirty minutes before the rice is done soaking, bring 2 quarts (2 liters) water to a boil in a large pot. Drain the rice and add to the boiling water along with 2 tablespoons salt. Bring back to a boil and cook for 3 minutes. The rice should be "al dente." Drain the parboiled rice in a colander and rinse under cold water. Let drain.

4. Put the oil and half the saffron water in a large clean pot with a heavy bottom and place over medium heat. When the oil starts sizzling, sprinkle a good layer of rice all over the bottom, about ¾ inch (2 cm) thick. Then add the rest of the rice, building it into a pyramid so that it does not stick to the sides. Make a hole in the center and pour in the melted butter and the remaining saffron water. Wrap the lid with a clean kitchen towel, cover the pot tightly, and leave over medium heat for about 4 minutes. Reduce the heat to very low and let the rice steam for 1 hour or so, or until the bottom becomes very crisp and golden brown—you may not succeed on the first try as it takes some practice to figure out how low a setting you need to cook the rice that long without burning it, but you will soon get the hang of it.

5. Take the pot off the heat and place the bottom on a very cold surface or in iced water to loosen the crust or *tah-dig*. Scoop out the saffron-colored rice from the center of the rice and transfer to a small bowl. Transfer the rest of the rice to a serving platter, taking care not to disturb the *tah-dig*. Scatter the saffron-colored rice all over. Then, remove the *tah-dig* and break it into pieces. Arrange the *tah-dig* all around the rice and serve hot.

COOKING RICE IN IRAN

There are three main ways of cooking rice in Iran, not counting the different garnishes. In one, called *polow*, rice is parboiled and then steamed over very low heat until it forms a crust on the bottom. In another, called *kateh*, rice is cooked with the absorption method and left long enough over low heat that it forms a crust both on the bottom and sides. And for the third, called *tahchin*, rice is parboiled and then mixed with yogurt and egg and baked in the oven so that it becomes like a cake with a crusty outside and the rice fluffy inside. Of course, you can add meat or a vegetable garnish to any of these three methods, although *kateh* is more often than not made plain.

RICE with FAVA BEANS
BÂGHÂLI POLOW

Serve this *polow* with the kebab or *khoresht* of your choice.

SERVES 4 TO 6

2½ cups (500 g) basmati rice

Good pinch of saffron threads

⅓ cup (80 ml) vegetable oil

7 ounces (200 g) fresh dill, bottom stems discarded, finely chopped

1¾ cups (350 g) shelled and peeled fresh or frozen fava beans

4 tablespoons (60 g) unsalted butter, melted

1. Soak, parboil, and rinse the rice as directed in steps 2 and 3 of Plain Iranian Rice (page 242).

2. Put the saffron to soak in 2 tablespoons water.

3. Put the vegetable oil and half the saffron water in a large clean pot and place over medium heat. When the oil starts sizzling, spread a good layer of rice all over the bottom, about ¾ inch (2 cm) thick. Cover with a layer of dill and a layer of fava beans. Then spread another layer of rice over the beans and dill, keeping the rice away from the edges. Carry on alternating the layers, building the mixture in the shape of a pyramid, until all is used up, but ending with a layer of rice. Make a hole in the middle of the pyramid and pour in the melted butter and remaining saffron water. Wrap the lid of the pot with a clean kitchen towel, cover the pot tightly, and leave over medium heat for 4 minutes. Then reduce the heat to very low and let the rice, beans, and dill steam for 1 hour or so, or until the bottom layer of rice has become very crisp and golden brown—you may not succeed on the first try as it takes some practice to figure out how low a setting you need to cook the rice that long without burning it, but you will soon get the hang of it.

4. When the rice is ready, place the bottom of the pot on a very cold surface or in iced water to loosen the crust or *tah-dig* (as it is known in Persian). Scoop out the saffron-colored rice from the center of the rice and transfer to a small bowl. Spoon the rest onto a serving platter, taking care not to disturb the *tah-dig*. Scatter the saffron-colored rice all over the rice. Then remove the *tah-dig* from the pan and break it into pieces. Arrange these around the rice and serve hot.

HERBED POLOW

SABZI POLOW

In Iran, people buy their *sabzi* (see page 160) ready-mixed, even ready-chopped from the market. Unfortunately, there isn't such a thing in the West, but do not despair because you can easily make your own *sabzi* by mixing equal quantities of flat-leaf parsley, cilantro, dill, chives or leeks, scallions, and even spinach if you want. In some regions like in Gilan, the *sabzi* contains local wild herbs. You can add sorrel if you want, or even wild chicory. Or you can buy dried *sabzi* from Iranian stores and use half the weight indicated below, in the same way. *Sabzi polow* is a must for the celebrations of Nowruz, the Iranian New Year, and is usually served with Iranian Herb Omelet (page 400) and fried fish.

SERVES 4 TO 6

2½ cups (500 g) basmati rice

Good pinch of saffron threads

12 ounces (350 g) sabzi (mixed fresh herbs; see page 160), finely chopped

½ teaspoon powdered dried fenugreek

1 clove garlic, finely chopped

Sea salt

⅓ cup (80 ml) vegetable oil

4 tablespoons (60 g) unsalted butter, melted

1. Soak, parboil, and rinse the rice as directed in steps 2 and 3 of Plain Iranian Rice (page 242).

2. Put the saffron to soak in 2 tablespoons water.

3. Mix the *sabzi* with the dried fenugreek and garlic and season with a little salt in a small pot.

4. Put the vegetable oil and half the saffron water in a large pot and place over medium heat. When the oil starts sizzling, spread a good layer of rice over the bottom, about ¾ inch (2 cm) thick. Spread half the *sabzi* mixture over the rice and cover with half the remaining rice. Spread the remaining *sabzi* mixture and cover with the rest of the rice, building the mixture in the shape of a pyramid. Make a hole in the center and pour in the melted butter and the remaining saffron water. Wrap the lid with a clean kitchen towel, cover the pot tightly, and leave over medium heat for 4 minutes. Reduce the heat to very low and let the rice and herbs steam for 50 minutes to 1 hour, or until the bottom becomes very crisp and golden brown. You may not succeed on the first try, as it takes some practice to figure out how low a setting you need to cook the rice that long.

5. When the rice is ready, take off the heat and immediately place the bottom of the pot on a very cold surface or in iced water to loosen the crust (*tah-dig* as it is known in Persian). Transfer the rice to a serving platter, taking care not to disturb the *tah-dig*.

LENTIL POLOW

ADDAS POLOW

It was on one of my last trips to Iran that I met Feridoonjan (adding *jan* at the end of someone's name forms the diminutive, like saying dear Feridoon), a splendid-looking man with a fabulous long gray mustache, which he curls over his cheeks. Feridoon is also a splendid cook and the first time I met him, at my friend Ali Farboud's mother's place, he had just finished cooking a lentil *polow*, which Ali's mother immediately invited us to taste. It was exquisite. Feridoon did not garnish his lentil *polow* with dates as I am doing here, but I love the sweet-savory note the dates give to each bite, while the caramelized onions provide a nice crunch. Serve on its own or with roast lamb or chicken.   SERVES 4 TO 6

2½ cups (500 g) basmati rice
Good pinch of saffron threads
¾ cup (150 g) brown lentils, soaked for 1 hour in cold water
⅓ cup (80 ml) vegetable oil, plus more for frying
⅔ cup (100 g) pitted dates, halved lengthwise
1 large onion (7 ounces/200 g), halved and cut into thin wedges
Heaping ⅓ cup (50 g) golden raisins, soaked for 1 hour in cold water
Sea salt
4 tablespoons (60 g) unsalted butter, melted

1. Soak, parboil, and rinse the rice as directed in steps 2 and 3 of Plain Iranian Rice (page 242).

2. Put the saffron to soak in 2 tablespoons water.

3. Drain the lentils and put them in a pot. Cover well with water and bring to a boil over medium heat. Reduce the heat to medium-low and let bubble gently for 10 minutes, or until the lentils are just barely tender. They continue to cook with the rice and any slight bite they may still have will soften (and you don't want them to go mushy).

4. Heat a little vegetable oil in a skillet over medium heat. Add the dates and sauté until they start glistening.

5. Heat 3 tablespoons vegetable oil in another skillet over medium heat. Add the onion and fry until golden brown, about 10 minutes. Be careful not to let it burn or it will taste bitter. Transfer to a sieve and shake a few times to get rid of any excess oil. The onions should be crisp.

6. Put the ⅓ cup (80 ml) vegetable oil and half the saffron water in a large clean pot and place over medium heat. When the oil starts sizzling, spread a good layer of rice over the bottom, about ¾ inch (2 cm) thick. Spread half the lentils and golden raisins over the rice, season with salt to taste, and cover with half the remaining rice. Spread the remaining lentils and golden raisins, season with salt to taste, and cover with the rest of the rice. The layered rice should be in the shape of a pyramid. Make a hole in the middle of the pyramid and pour in the melted butter and remaining saffron water. Gently put the dates over one side of the rice. Wrap the lid with a clean kitchen towel and place over the pot. Reduce the heat to very low and let steam for 50 minutes to 1 hour until a nice crust (or *tah-dig* as it is known in Persian) forms on the bottom—you may not succeed on the first try, as it takes some practice to figure out how low a setting you need to cook the rice that long without burning it, but you will soon get the hang of it.

7. When the rice is ready, place the bottom of the pan on a very cold surface or in iced water to loosen the *tah-dig*. Remove the dates to a small plate. Transfer the rice to a serving platter, taking care not to disturb the *tah-dig*. Remove the *tah-dig* and arrange around the rice. Scatter the dates over the rice, then the crispy onions and serve hot.

BAKED RICE CAKE with LAMB
TAHCHIN-O BARREH

Tahchin is one of the ultimate party dishes, not only because the presentation is so appealing, but also because the rice stays hot under the crust, making it an ideal dish for a buffet spread. I still remember my first taste of it in Tehran at Nasrine Faghih's home. I was there researching Iranian food, and Nasrine, an old friend from when I lived in Paris, had arranged for me to cook with one of her friends, Minou, and her cook, Mariam. I had had rice cakes before, both in Kuwait (where they are known as *bardalof*) and in London, cooked by the late Zaha Hadid, who was also a great friend and had perfected the crust.

In the Iranian version, the parboiled rice is mixed with yogurt and egg, then cooked meat (as here) or chicken before being put in a baking dish and baked. You can make it plain, or with greens. It is perfectly delicious, and the crust is less difficult to achieve than *tah-dig* because the oven temperature is easier to regulate than that of most stovetop burners. The baking dish you use will also affect the result. A good nonstick solid metal cake pan with medium-high (4-inch/10 cm) straight sides is perfect for *tahchin*. In Iran they have a special pot they swear by, but I have yet to get one.

SERVES 4 TO 6

Good pinch of saffron threads

8 tablespoons vegetable oil

1 medium onion (5 ounces/150 g), halved and cut into thin wedges

9 ounces (250 g) lean lamb from the leg or shoulder, diced into 1-inch (2.5 cm) cubes

Sea salt

⅔ cup (175 g) yogurt

2 organic eggs

1¾ cups (350 g) long-grain rice, rinsed and soaked for 2 hours in lightly salted water

1. Put the saffron threads to steep in 2 tablespoons water.

2. Put 2 tablespoons of the oil, the onion, and lamb in a sauté pan and place over low heat. Barely cover with water. Season with a little salt and let cook slowly, stirring regularly, for 1 to 1½ hours, until tender. Let cool.

3. Put the yogurt and eggs in a large mixing bowl and mix well. Add the saffron water and salt to taste and mix again. Drain the lamb and onions if there is still any liquid in the pan and add to the saffron-yogurt-egg mixture. Let marinate for 2 hours at least, preferably overnight in the refrigerator.

4. Preheat the oven to 300°F (150°C).

5. Put 6 cups (1.5 liters) water in a large pot and bring to a boil over medium heat. Add 1½ tablespoons salt. Drain the rice and add to the boiling water and let boil for 3 minutes. Drain well. Rinse under cold water. Drain well again and add to the yogurt and lamb, together with the remaining 6 tablespoons oil. Mix well.

6. Transfer the rice mixture to a 9-inch (17.5 cm) round nonstick baking dish with medium-high (4-inch/10 cm) sides. Level the top and cover with foil. Bake for 2 hours, or until the rice is tender and completely crusty on the bottom and sides. Let sit in the pan for 5 minutes, then invert onto a round serving platter and serve hot.

JEWELED RICE

MORASA POLOW

There are many good books on Persian cuisine but none are as thorough, informative, and brilliant as the late Margaret Shaida's *Legendary Cuisine of Persia*. Despite being English, Margaret became totally immersed in the Iranian way of life after she married into an Iranian family. The recipes in her book are incredibly accurate and completely foolproof. I befriended her at the Oxford Symposium of Food and Cookery and learned much of what I know about Persian food from her and her book, and of course from my travels to Iran. The recipe below is adapted from one in her book. Jeweled rice is thus named because of the jewel-like ingredients added to the rice, which provide a delightful combination of sweet and savory flavors and contrasting textures. It is Iran's ultimate rice dish, served at special occasions to honor important guests or to mark significant events, both religious and secular.

A truly regal dish as its name implies, it makes a wonderful accompaniment to a plain roast chicken, or fish, or leg of lamb, elevating the meal to something special. In Iran, this rice is also served with fried chicken, although the Iranian version of fried chicken is quite different from America's Southern version. Still there is no reason why you can't make your Southern fried chicken more festive and exotic by serving it with this jeweled rice. Some people make the *tah-dig* (crust) here by mixing the rice with yogurt and saffron water, but I like to keep mine plain. You can also make a *tah-dig* by laying a single lavash over the bottom of the pot or very thinly sliced potatoes before layering the rice over it.

SERVES 4 TO 6

Good pinch of saffron
    threads
2½ cups (500 g) Iranian
    or basmati rice
Sea salt
3 tablespoons plus ⅓ cup
    (80 ml) vegetable oil

1 pound 10 ounces
    (750 g) carrots, peeled
    and julienned
8 tablespoons raw cane
    sugar
Peel of 3 unwaxed
    organic oranges (see
    Note, page 252), cut
    into very thin julienne
    sticks

⅓ cup (50 g) slivered
    almonds, soaked for
    1 hour in cold water
⅓ cup (50 g) slivered
    pistachios, soaked for
    1 hour in cold water
¼ cup (40 g) barberries
    (zereshk)

⅓ cup (50 g) dried
    currants, soaked for
    1 hour in cold water
    and drained
1 teaspoon Advieh (page
    363)
4 tablespoons (60 g)
    unsalted butter, melted

1. Put the saffron to soak in ¼ cup (60 ml) water.

2. Rinse the rice under cold water and place in a large bowl. Add enough cold water to cover it by two fingers. Stir in 2 tablespoons salt and let soak for 2 hours.

3. Heat 2 tablespoons of the oil in a large skillet over medium heat. Add the carrots and sauté for 10 minutes. Sprinkle 1 tablespoon sugar over the carrots and add 1 tablespoon saffron water and 2 tablespoons water. Reduce the heat to low, cover, and cook for 3 to 4 minutes, until there is no more liquid in the pan. Take off the heat. Cover with a clean kitchen towel—you do not want the carrots to continue cooking—and set aside.

4. Place the orange peel in a small pan. Cover with water and place over medium heat. Bring to a boil, then drain the peel. Repeat a couple more times to get rid of any bitterness. Drain.

5. Drain the almonds and pistachios.

6. Put the remaining 7 tablespoons sugar in a medium pan. Add ⅓ cup (80 ml) water and place over low heat. Stir every now and then until the sugar has dissolved but not colored. Add the orange peel and most of the drained almonds and pistachios, reserving a few for garnish, and boil for a minute or so. Drain (discard the syrup) and set aside.

Recipe continues

7. Heat 1 tablespoon of the oil in a small skillet over medium heat. Add the barberries and sauté for a couple of minutes until they turn a bright red—be careful not to burn them. (Some barberries are very dark in which case they will not turn red but don't worry about this. They will still be good.)

8. Bring 2 quarts (2 liters) water to a boil in a large pot. Drain the rice and add to the boiling water. Add 2 tablespoons salt. Bring back to a boil and cook for 2 to 3 minutes, just long enough to break the hardness of the grain. Drain the rice.

9. Wipe the pot clean and place over medium heat. Add the remaining ⅓ cup (80 ml) oil and half the remaining saffron water. As soon as the saffron water starts sizzling, spread one-third of the rice in an even layer over the bottom. Spread half the carrots over the rice. Spread half of the orange/nut mixture, barberries, drained currants, and *advieh* over the carrots. Cover with another one-third of the rice, trying to pile the rice in a pyramid so that it does not stick to the sides. Spread the remaining carrots, orange/nut mixture, barberries, drained currants, and *advieh* over the rice and cover with the rest of the rice.

10. Pour the butter and the remaining saffron water over the rice. Wrap the lid in a clean kitchen towel. Cover the pot tightly and leave over medium heat for 4 minutes. Then reduce the heat to very low and let the rice steam for 50 minutes to 1 hour, until it forms a perfect crust (known as *tah-dig*).

11. Just as the rice is about to be ready, prepare some iced water in your sink. Take the pan off the heat and dip the bottom in the iced water to loosen the crust. Mix the rice a little in the pan, fluffing it up, then spoon it onto a serving platter, taking care not to disturb the *tah-dig*. Scatter the reserved nuts all over. Remove the *tah-dig* from the pan and break it into medium pieces. Arrange them around the rice and serve hot.

NOTE: *You can also use ½ cup (75 g) dried orange peel, which you can find in Persian stores.*

FESTIVE SWEET-SAVORY RICE

MUTTHANJAN PULAU

PAKISTAN

Here is the Pakistani/Indian version of the Persian Jeweled Rice (page 250). Persian cuisine is the mother cuisine of the Muslim world—the Abbasid Caliphs who oversaw the expansion of their empire favored Persian chefs and had them in their court as well as wherever they invaded, expanding the influence of Persian cooks far and wide, both eastward and westward. Of course, recipes changed over the centuries and some are completely different from how they started, sometimes only keeping the name and sometimes losing this too. *Mutthanjan* has the sweet-savory element of jeweled rice although it is actually sweeter and headier as far as seasonings are concerned. It also has added meat. It is a very festive dish, served at special occasions, such as Eid and weddings, and can be made much sweeter, but I prefer a subtle combination of sweet and savory. Many people do away with the meat to make it as a sweet, but it was traditionally made with meat, so I am sticking to tradition.

SERVES 6 TO 8

FOR THE MILK/ALMOND MIXTURE
4 cups (1 liter) whole milk
½ cup (75 g) ground almonds

FOR THE SAFFRON MILK/KEWRA INFUSION
Good pinch of saffron threads
2 tablespoons whole milk
2 tablespoons kewra (pandanus flower extract)

FOR THE LAMB AND STOCK
1 pound 10 ounces (750 g) boneless lamb shoulder or leg, cut into medium chunks
8 whole cloves
4 green cardamom pods
1 black cardamom pod
1 cinnamon stick

¼ nutmeg
1 teaspoon black peppercorns
2 bay leaves
2 shards of blade mace
1 medium onion (5 ounces/150 g), quartered
4 cloves garlic, peeled but whole
Sea salt
1 tablespoon ghee or unsalted butter
¼ cup (60 ml) vegetable oil
2 medium onions (10½ ounces/300 g total), halved and cut into thin wedges
½ inch (1 cm) fresh ginger, peeled and finely chopped
½ cup (125 g) yogurt, whisked

1 teaspoon garam masala
1 teaspoon ground coriander
½ teaspoon cayenne pepper

FOR THE RICE
2½ cups (500 g) long-grain rice, soaked for 30 minutes in lightly salted water
1 tablespoon ghee
Sea salt

FOR THE MUTTHANJAN
2 tablespoons vegetable oil
⅔ cup (100 g) golden raisins, soaked for a couple hours in cold water and drained
⅓ cup (50 g) pistachios, soaked for a couple hours in cold water and drained

½ to 1 cup (50 to 100 g) powdered sugar, to taste
Juice of 2 limes

FOR THE MEATBALLS
9 ounces (250 g) lean ground lamb, from the shoulder or leg
2 tablespoons chana dal (split yellow peas), soaked for 1 hour in cold water and drained
½ teaspoon cayenne pepper
Sea salt
2 to 3 green chilies, seeded and very thinly sliced
Vegetable oil, for frying
Edible gold leaves

Recipe continues

1. To make the milk/almond mixture: Put the milk in a medium nonstick saucepan and bring to a boil over medium-low heat—be careful not to let it boil over—then reduce the heat to very low and let the milk bubble very gently, stirring regularly, until it has reduced by three-quarters and has become quite thick and slightly golden. This will take about 1 hour. Add the ground almonds and mix well.

2. For the saffron milk/*kewra* infusion: Put the saffron in a small bowl. Add the milk and *kewra* and let infuse while you prepare the rest of the dish.

3. To prepare the lamb and stock: Put the lamb in a large pot. Add 5¼ cups (1.25 liters) water. Tie 4 cloves, the whole spices, onion, and garlic in cheesecloth and add to the pot along with salt to taste. Bring to a boil over medium-high heat, skimming any froth from the surface. Reduce the heat to medium and let bubble gently for 1 hour, or until the meat is tender. Strain the stock (discard the cheesecloth bag). Set the meat aside and keep hot. Measure out 2½ cups (625 ml) stock and place in a large pot.

4. Heat the ghee and remaining 4 cloves in a small pan over medium heat. Sauté until fragrant. Add to the stock. Set the pot of stock aside.

5. Heat the vegetable oil in a large skillet over medium heat. Add the onions and sauté until lightly golden. Add the lamb, ginger, yogurt, garam masala, coriander, and cayenne and cook, stirring regularly, and adding a couple of tablespoons water, for 10 to 15 minutes, or until the meat has browned and the sauce is reduced. Set aside.

6. To cook the rice: Drain the rice and add to the reserved stock in the pot. Bring to a boil over medium heat. Add the ghee and salt if necessary and reduce the heat to low. Cook the rice for 10 minutes, or until it has absorbed all the stock and is barely tender. Take off the heat. Wrap the lid with a clean kitchen towel and replace over the pot.

7. To put the *mutthanjan* together: Pour the oil into a large pot and spread half the lamb over the bottom. Cover the meat with one-third of the rice. Spread half the milk/almond mixture over the rice. Top with the remaining lamb, half the drained raisins and pistachios. Sprinkle half the sugar and lime juice and cover with another one-third of the rice. Spread the remaining milk/almond mixture over the rice, then the remaining raisins, pistachios, sugar, and lime juice. Cover with the last of the rice. Sprinkle the saffron milk/*kewra* infusion all over the top. Wrap the lid of the pot with a clean kitchen towel, cover, and place the pot over medium-high heat. Leave for 3 minutes, then reduce the heat to very low and let the rice steam for 20 to 30 minutes, or until it is steaming hot and completely tender.

8. Meanwhile, to make the meatballs: Put the ground meat and chana dal in a medium skillet and add ½ cup (125 ml) water. Place over medium heat and season with the cayenne and salt to taste. Cook for 20 to 30 minutes, until the dal is completely tender and the water has evaporated. Transfer to a food processor and process to a fine paste. Transfer to a medium mixing bowl and add the sliced chilies. Mix well using your hands.

9. Lightly wet your hands and shape the meat into small meatballs. Place a medium skillet over medium heat and pour in enough oil to cover the bottom. Add the meatballs and sauté until browned, about 3 minutes.

10. Transfer the rice and lamb chunks to a serving platter. Press the sautéed meatballs into the rice all around the edges leaving the center plain. Lay a piece of gold leaf over each meatball and dot a few pieces of gold leaf in the middle of the rice. Serve hot.

INDONESIAN YELLOW RICE

NASI KUNING

When *nasi kuning* is served at special occasions, it is pressed into a cone and inverted on the plate and as such it is called *tumpeng*. The cone of yellow rice is served surrounded with a selection of vegetable, meat, and/or fish dishes as well as the obligatory crackers. *Nasi kuning* is not only reserved for special meals. I have had it for breakfast in Ambon, in the living room of a street vendor who had set up her stall on her porch—there are many places like hers in Indonesia with vendors cooking their specialty in their kitchen, then setting up their stall on their porch and selling the food from there. Customers either take the food away wrapped in paper lined with banana leaf to insulate it or they eat it in the vendor's living room off plastic plates. Some rooms are converted into mini restaurants with tables or counters along the wall and chairs, while others are left exactly as when the family uses them with customers sitting on the cook's sofas and using the coffee tables to rest their plates on—it's a wonderful way to eat and communicate with the other diners. I found Indonesian people to be among the most charming and gentle people I have met on my travels and it was never a problem talking with anyone, provided they spoke English, that is; or if I happened to be with someone who could translate, which fortunately was most of the time. Serve with either of the fish curries on pages 321 and 324.

SERVES 4 TO 6

2½ cups (500 g) Thai
  jasmine rice
1 cup (250 ml) coconut
  cream
½ inch (1 cm) fresh
  turmeric, grated on the
  fine side of a grater
2 teaspoons ground
  coriander
1 teaspoon lemon juice
Sea salt

1. Rinse the rice under cold water. Drain and put in a medium pot.

2. Mix together the coconut cream, turmeric, and coriander in a large mixing bowl, then add to the rice. Add the lemon juice and 1½ cups (375 ml) water. Season with salt to taste and bring to a boil over medium heat.

3. Reduce the heat to low and simmer for 10 to 15 minutes, or until the rice is tender and the liquid fully absorbed. Serve hot.

INDONESIAN FRIED RICE

NASI GORENG

Nasi goreng is Indonesian fried rice, flavored with chili sambal, shrimp paste, kecap manis (sweet Indonesian soy sauce), and palm sugar. You can add what you want to the rice, but traditionally it is made simply with scallions and fresh chilies and served for breakfast with a fried egg. It is incredibly addictive and I couldn't have enough when I was in Indonesia. I got so used to their savory breakfasts that could have easily been lunch or dinner that I had to make myself some once I was back home! The rice Indonesians like to use is fragrant jasmine, but you can also use basmati. You could turn this *nasi goreng* into a full one-pot meal by adding shredded chicken, or shrimp or strips of beef or lamb. Count on 7 ounces (200 g) of meat and sauté it before adding the egg and adjusting the seasonings at the end.

SERVES 2

¼ cup (60 ml) vegetable oil

1 tablespoon shrimp paste (terasi)

4 cloves garlic, minced to a fine paste

2 organic eggs, beaten

1 cup (200 g) Thai jasmine rice, boiled in twice the amount of water until tender and the liquid fully absorbed

1 tablespoon kecap manis (Indonesian sweet soy sauce)

2 green chilies, seeded and thinly sliced (optional)

1 bunch scallions (2 ounces/50 g), thinly sliced

3 tablespoons Chili and Tomato Sambal (page 372), plus more for serving

Sea salt and finely ground black pepper

FOR THE EGG GARNISH

2 tablespoons vegetable oil

2 organic eggs

Sea salt

Chili pepper flakes

1. Heat the oil in a wok or a deep skillet over medium heat. Add the shrimp paste and sauté for a minute or so. Transfer to a small plate. Add the garlic to the pan and cook for a couple of minutes, or until golden, making sure you do not let it burn. Add the beaten eggs and let them cook undisturbed a little as if it were a frittata, then start stirring them to break them up in pieces. You want the egg to brown on the bottom to release the aroma, as William Wongso, Indonesia's foremost celebrity chef, explained to me. Remove half the egg to a plate.

2. Add half the rice to the egg remaining in the pan (this is being done a half at a time because if you overpack the pan, the rice will not fry properly). Stir for a couple of minutes until the rice starts to heat up and toast a little. Add ½ tablespoon of the kecap manis and mix until it is completely blended with the rice. Add half the shrimp paste and mix well. By now, the rice should have turned a lovely golden reddish brown color.

3. Add half the chilies (if using) and half the scallions and mix until they are well blended. Add half the sambal and mix well. Taste before adding salt and pepper to

taste. Remove to a plate and keep hot while you fry the remaining rice in the same way. Then add the already fried rice to the pan and keep on a very low flame while you fry the eggs for the garnish.

4. To make the egg garnish: Heat the oil in a small skillet over medium heat. When the oil is hot, break the eggs into the pan and fry for 3 to 4 minutes, or until the edges are crisp and the white is done but the yolk still runny. Season the eggs with salt and a light sprinkling of pepper flakes.

5. To serve, transfer the fried rice to a serving platter. Place the fried egg garnish over the rice and serve with more chili sambal for those who want to have more.

AZERBAIJANI SWEET-SAVORY RICE

SUDLU PLOV

This is another interesting sweet-savory rice, this time from Azerbaijan, where they cook the rice in milk and flavor it with saffron, dark raisins, and dates. My nephew happened to marry an Azerbaijani girl and we all went to their lavish wedding reception in Baku, which they followed the next day with an equally lavish lunch, with a huge buffet of all kinds of Azerbaijani dishes that reminded me of what people ate in the '50s, with half the dishes drowning in commercial mayonnaise. Somehow, they didn't think it would be more interesting to have local dishes rather than Soviet dishes and I wish they'd had this rice with a whole roast lamb and a few salads instead of the rather unappetizing Russian salads and smoked fish and so many other practically inedible dishes. I have used tiny dried raisins from southeastern Turkey here as they contrast nicely with the saffron-colored rice; also I find their drier texture more suitable than the plumper golden raisins. Serve with the Arabian Spiced Fried Fish (page 345).   SERVES 4 TO 6

Good pinch of saffron
    threads
¼ cup (60 ml) rose water
2 cups (400 g) long-grain
    rice, rinsed and well
    drained
1 cup (150 g) dark raisins
3 cups (750 ml) whole
    milk
1 stick plus 3 tablespoons
    (175 g) unsalted butter
1 tablespoon raw cane
    sugar
Sea salt
12 pitted dates, quartered
    lengthwise

1. Put the saffron threads to steep in the rose water and ¼ cup (60 ml) water.

2. Put the rice and raisins in a medium saucepan. Add the milk, butter, sugar, and saffron rose water. Add salt to taste. Bring to a boil over medium-low heat, being careful not to let the milk boil over, then reduce the heat to simmer, cover, and cook for 7 minutes, or until the rice has absorbed almost all the milk. Stir in the dates.

3. Wrap the lid with a clean kitchen towel and cover the pan—the towel helps to absorb the steam. Turn the heat down to very low and let the rice cook for another 7 minutes, or until it is tender and the milk is fully absorbed.

COUSCOUS with SEVEN VEGETABLES

KSEKSÛ BIDAWI

MOROCCO

Friday is couscous day all over Morocco, and this couscous with seven vegetables is what families will gather around every Friday at lunchtime. The classic vegetables are carrots, zucchini, cabbage, pumpkin, turnips, fava beans, and tomatoes to enrich the cooking broth, but you can use eggplant if you want or potatoes or sweet potatoes or whatever is in season or takes your fancy. I often use baby vegetables for a prettier presentation, but normal-size vegetables are what everyone uses in Morocco. The presentation may be less dainty, but if they are cut well and not overcooked, they will look just as attractive.

SERVES 6

FOR THE COUSCOUS
2½ cups (500 g) fine or medium couscous (not instant)
Sea salt
1 tablespoon extra-virgin olive oil
2 tablespoons (30 g) unsalted butter, melted

FOR THE MEAT AND BROTH
½ cup (100 g) dried chickpeas, soaked overnight in plenty of water with ¼ teaspoon baking soda

1 pound 2 ounces (500 g) boneless lamb, neck fillets or meat from the shanks
Good pinch of saffron threads
2 medium onions (10½ ounces/300 g total), quartered
One 14-ounce (400 g) can chopped tomatoes
1 teaspoon finely ground black pepper
Sea salt
3 tablespoons extra-virgin olive oil

4 tablespoons (60 g) unsalted butter

TO FINISH
1 small conehead (pointed) cabbage, damaged outer leaves discarded, quartered
5 ounces (150 g) baby carrots
5 ounces (150 g) baby zucchini
5 ounces (150 g) baby turnips
5 ounces (150 g) frozen, unpeeled fava beans

A few sprigs flat-leaf parsley, most of the bottom stems discarded, finely chopped
A few sprigs cilantro, most of the bottom stems discarded, finely chopped
⅓ cup (50 g) golden raisins
¼ teaspoon red pepper flakes, or to taste
Harissa (page 370), for serving

1. To start the couscous: Put the couscous in a large shallow bowl. Measure ⅔ cup (160 ml) water into a small measuring cup and add 1 teaspoon salt. Stir until the salt is diluted, then with your hand, sprinkle the water onto the couscous, little by little, raking it with your fingers to allow it to absorb the water evenly. When you have used up all the water, add the olive oil and mix well, rubbing any lumps with your hands to break them up. Put the couscous in the top half of a couscoussière. (If you don't have

Recipe continues

one, line with cheesecloth a metal colander that will fit over the pot you will use to cook the meat and broth. The pot should be deep enough that the colander doesn't touch the broth underneath.)

2. To start the meat and broth: Drain and rinse the chickpeas and put them in the bottom half of the couscoussière (or a large pot). Add the meat, saffron, onion, tomatoes, and 6 cups (1.5 liters) water. Add the pepper and salt to taste and bring to a boil. Cook for 45 minutes, or until both the meat and chickpeas are just tender. Add the olive oil and 4 tablespoons (60 g) butter.

3. Continue cooking the couscous: Place the top part of the couscoussière (or colander) with the couscous in it on top of the broth. Cover and let steam for 15 minutes. Remove the top part of the couscoussière (or colander) and cover the pot. Let the meat and chickpeas continue to cook. Tip the steamed couscous into the shallow bowl and sprinkle with another ⅔ cup (160 ml) water, this time using a wooden spoon to stir the couscous as you sprinkle (unless your hands can stand the heat, which Moroccan cooks seem to be able to!). Once all the water is incorporated and there are no lumps, add the 2 tablespoons (30 g) melted butter. Mix well. Cover the bowl and let sit to allow the couscous to fluff up, while you finish the meal.

4. Add the cabbage to the bottom half of the couscoussière (or the pot) and cook for 15 minutes. Add the carrots, zucchini, turnips, fava beans, herbs, raisins, and pepper flakes to the broth. Return the couscous to the top half of the couscoussière (or the colander), place over the broth, and let steam uncovered for 15 minutes, or until the meat and vegetables are tender.

5. To serve, pile the steamed couscous in the shape of a pyramid in a large shallow serving bowl. Flatten the top and arrange the meat on top and the vegetables around the sides. Pour the broth into a sauceboat and serve hot, with harissa on the side for those who like their couscous spicy.

SOUTH ASIAN MEAT, LEGUMES, and WHEAT "PORRIDGE"

PAKISTANI/INDIAN HALEEM

PAKISTAN | INDIA

Here is the Pakistani/Indian version of *h'risseh* (see page 266). There are slight variations between the Pakistani and Indian *haleems*—not to mention regional variations in each country, with Hyderabadi *haleem* being one of the most famous—but the differences are not that great, so I have simplified and am giving one general recipe here as an example of a South Asian *haleem* (see Note). It is a lot spicier and more complex than the Levantine *h'risseh*, the Arabian *h'riss*, or the Iranian *haleem*.

Haleem is sold on the street all year long and it is also prepared for both the month of Ramadan and the month of Muharram. You can see it being made on the street in India, in huge cauldrons placed over wood fires, and it is a spectacle to behold. The cauldrons are massive and the amounts of meat and grain used are astonishing, as is the labor required to prepare the dish in such huge quantities. Fortunately, the quantities in this recipe are just enough to feed a family, and apart from the stirring at the end to mash the ingredients into one another, the process is very simple. Most people use a hand blender now to mash the ingredients, but I prefer the texture achieved by stirring the mixture by hand.

SERVES 6 TO 8

¼ cup (60 ml) vegetable oil

2 medium onions (10½ ounces/300 g total), halved and cut into thin wedges

1 pound 10 ounces (750 g) boneless lamb leg or stewing beef or veal, cut into medium chunks

2 inches (5 cm) fresh ginger, peeled and minced to a fine paste

6 cloves garlic, minced to a fine paste

2 bay leaves

½ cup (15 g) dried rose petals

1 tablespoon allspice berries

1 tablespoon ground allspice

1 tablespoon ground cumin

1 tablespoon Kashmiri chili powder

1 teaspoon ground turmeric

2 cups (400 g) wheat berries, soaked overnight in cold water

1 cup (200 g) hulled barley, soaked overnight in cold water

1 cup (200 g) chana dal (split yellow peas), soaked for 1 hour in cold water

1 cup (200 g) red lentils

4 tablespoons (60 g) ghee or unsalted butter

Sea salt

FOR THE GARNISH

Vegetable oil, for frying

2 large onions (14 ounces/400 g total), halved and cut into thin wedges

Ghee (optional), melted

2 lemons, quartered

Handful of cilantro leaves

2 green chilies, seeded and thinly sliced

Naan (optional; page 24), for serving

1. Heat the ¼ cup (60 ml) oil in a large pot over medium heat. Add the onion and fry, stirring regularly, until golden, about 5 minutes. Add the meat and sauté until it has browned, 4 to 5 minutes. Add the ginger and garlic and stir for a minute or so. Add the bay leaves, dried rose petals, and spices and stir for a couple of minutes.

2. Drain the grains and dal and add them to the meat and onions (see Note) together with the red lentils. Add 2 quarts (2 liters) water and bring to a boil. Add the ghee, cover, reduce the heat to low, and simmer for 1 hour, stirring regularly. Add 1 cup (250 ml) water and continue simmering for another hour, stirring very regularly, until the meat is very tender and the grains and legumes have dissolved into a thick porridge-like mixture. Add salt to taste.

3. Meanwhile, to make the garnish: Pour 1 inch (2.5 cm) vegetable oil into a large skillet and heat over medium heat until hot (if you drop a piece of bread in the oil, the oil should immediately bubble around it). Add the sliced onion and fry, stirring regularly, until golden brown, about 10 minutes. Be careful not to burn the onions. Transfer to a sieve and shake to drain off the excess oil and keep the onion wedges crisp.

4. Once the *haleem* is cooked, it needs to be mashed, either by hand or with a hand blender.

Hand method: With a wooden spoon, beat the meat, grains, and legumes in the pot until the meat disintegrates completely into the mashed-up porridge.

Blender method: Use a hand blender, as many do in both Pakistan and India, to process the grains and meat into a thick porridge-like texture. Use the blender in pulses as you want the *haleem* to retain a little texture.

5. Transfer the *haleem* to a large shallow round or oval serving bowl. If desired, sprinkle a little ghee over the *haleem*, then garnish with the lemon quarters along the edges of the bowl. Scatter the fried onions in a circle or oval (depending on the bowl) inside the edges of the *haleem*. Mix the cilantro with the chilies and scatter in the middle. Serve hot with or without naan.

NOTE: *There are two ways of making* haleem*. Some people cook the grains and legumes separately from the spiced meat/onion mixture, then finish everything together. I have chosen the simpler option of cooking everything together, which some cooks do as well.*

WHEAT and MEAT "PORRIDGE"
H'RISSEH

LEBANON

H'risseh, harissa, or *h'riss* in the Arab world, *keskek* in Turkey, *bokoboko* in Zanzibar, or *haleem* in Pakistan, India, and Iran—these are all different names for more or less the same dish made with meat and grain (and in the case of *haleem*, also legumes) that is slow-cooked for so long that the ingredients dissolve into a thick porridge. In Lebanon, *h'risseh* is served at 'Ashura, the tenth day of the month of Muharram marking the death anniversary of the Prophet's grandson, Hussein bin Ali, as an alms dish to share with those less fortunate. Its origins are reputed to go back to the sixth century during the time of Persian king Khosrow. The Muslims discovered it when they conquered Persia some hundred years later, and as with Tharid (page 85), it became a favorite of the Prophet's. In Iran it is eaten for breakfast, in India it is street food, in Pakistan it is served at main meals, usually lunch, and in Lebanon, Syria, and Turkey, the same.

It can be made with either chicken or lamb. Ideally, you should cook the meat on the bone, then take it out to discard the bones before returning it to the pot. On the street in India, they cook, bone, and mash the meat before adding it to the grain and legumes. The recipe changes from one country to another, with Pakistan and India using a lot more spices, whereas the Levantine version is fairly plain. Also it is one of those seminal Muslim dishes that is associated with both 'Ashura and Ramadan. For instance, in Lebanon, *h'risseh* is prepared in huge vats during Muharram to give out to those in need, as well as to neighbors, family, and friends. In the Gulf, *h'riss* is an essential dish during the month of Ramadan, and in some mosques you will find hugh pots of *h'riss* in the courtyard ready to serve to whomever wishes to have some. I give recipes for two other versions: Pakistani/Indian Haleem (page 264) and Persian Haleem (page 268).   SERVES 4 TO 6

1 whole chicken (3 pounds 5 ounces/ 1.5 kg) or 1 small lamb leg (ask your butcher to skin and trim the leg of most of its fat and cut it into medium chunks, still on the bone)

2½ cups (300 g) wheat berries or barley

2 cinnamon sticks

½ teaspoon ground allspice

¼ teaspoon Lebanese 7-Spice Mixture (page 358)

¼ teaspoon finely ground black pepper

Sea salt

6 tablespoons (90 g) unsalted butter, plus 3 tablespoons (45 g) for finishing

1. Put the chicken or lamb in a large pot and add 2 quarts (2 liters) water. Bring to a boil over medium-high heat, skimming any froth from the surface. Reduce the heat to medium and add the wheat (or barley) and cinnamon sticks. Cover the pot and cook for 1 hour, stirring occasionally, or until the chicken is done—the lamb will take about 30 minutes longer.

2. Lift the chicken or lamb out of the pot and discard the cinnamon sticks. Reduce the heat to low and let the grain simmer while you take the meat off the bone. Discard the chicken skin or most of the fat off the lamb and shred the meat into small pieces.

3. Return the meat to the pot. Add the allspice, 7-spice mixture, pepper, salt to taste, and 6 tablespoons (90 g) of the butter. Cover and continue simmering for about 30 minutes, stirring regularly, until the grain is cooked. If you find that the *h'risseh* is getting too dry, add a little water, although not too much because you should end up with a thick porridge-like mixture.

4. Once the grain is very tender, reduce the heat to very low. Then start stirring the mixture with a wooden spoon, cutting into the meat pieces to shred them further. You want the meat to disintegrate into the wheat. You can also pulse it with a hand blender, but be careful not to process it too much. Remove from the heat. Taste and adjust the seasoning if you need to and keep the pot covered until serving.

5. Melt 3 tablespoons of the butter in a small frying pan over medium heat until the butter starts sizzling and colors lightly, 3 to 4 minutes.

6. Pour the *h'risseh* into a large shallow serving bowl. Make grooves here and there. Pour the browned butter into the grooves. Serve hot.

PERSIAN MEAT and WHEAT "PORRIDGE"

PERSIAN HALEEM

It was in Rasht, in the Gilan province of Iran, where I was researching an article on Iranian food that I first tried Persian *haleem*. It is quite different from the Pakistani/Indian version (see page 264), with no legumes and a lot fewer seasonings. Rasht is not so far from Tehran and we got there in the morning just in time for breakfast. We found a rather kitsch pink café—the walls had been painted pink, and on each table there were plastic pink tulips—to have breakfast. As I peeked through a door that opened onto the courtyard, I found a burly man sitting on a stool by a huge copper pot placed over a low gas fire. He was bent over the pot, holding a long wooden paddle and stirring and beating whatever was in the pot. I got closer to him and realized he was cooking *haleem*, which he'd been stirring for hours. Luckily for me and my friend Ali Farboud, who took the Iranian pictures in this book, the *haleem* was just about ready and we asked if we could have some. It was delectable, with the grain and meat completely melded into a thick porridge-like mixture. I was surprised to find him still beating the *haleem* by hand with a wooden paddle as most people nowadays use a hand blender to pulverize the meat and grain. The texture of the hand-beaten *haleem* is superior, but if you don't have the time, or the energy, to beat the *haleem* by hand, use a hand blender in pulses to mash it.

SERVES 4

2 small lamb shanks
(1 pound 10 ounces/
750 g total)
⅓ cup (50 g) dried
chickpeas, soaked
overnight in plenty of
cold water with
¼ teaspoon baking
soda

1 medium onion
(5 ounces/150 g),
coarsely chopped
½ teaspoon ground
turmeric
¼ teaspoon finely ground
black pepper

1¼ cups (250 g) wheat
berries, soaked
overnight in cold water
Sea salt

FOR THE GARNISH
4 tablespoons (60 g)
ghee or unsalted
butter, melted
Ground cinnamon
(optional)
Raw cane sugar
(optional)

1. Put the meat in a large pot. Drain and rinse the chickpeas and add to the meat. Add water to cover by 1½ inches (3.5 cm). Bring to a boil over medium heat, skimming any froth from the surface. Add the onion, turmeric, and pepper and let bubble gently for 1 hour 30 minutes.

2. Meanwhile, put the drained wheat in a medium pot and add water to cover by 2 inches (5 cm). Place over medium heat and bring to a boil. Then reduce the heat to medium-low and cook, covered, for at least 2 hours, until very tender, checking on the water so that it doesn't dry up.

3. Reserving the broth, drain the meat, onions, and chickpeas. Set the chickpeas aside in a small saucepan to use as a garnish and cover with a little broth so that you can reheat them. On a cutting board, take the meat off the bone. Trim off any fat and cartilage and shred the meat. You can also process it or, if you have the energy, pound it in a mortar with a pestle, which is how it was done traditionally. Transfer the onions and meat to a mixing bowl.

4. When the wheat is done, uncover the pan and skim any husks that have floated to the surface. Reduce the heat to low and start stirring the wheat to help it disintegrate. Keep stirring until the wheat and cooking liquid become like a thick soup. Scoop a little out and mix with the meat and onions. Then pour the meat-onions-wheat mixture into the wheat and keep stirring until the meat, onions, and wheat are well blended and you have a somewhat stretchy "porridge."

5. Transfer to a large shallow serving bowl. Drain the chickpeas and scatter them over the *haleem* before pouring the melted ghee or butter over the top. Sprinkle with a little ground cinnamon and cane sugar (if using) and serve hot, with more cinnamon and sugar if desired.

QATARI CHICKEN "PORRIDGE"
QATARI MADHRUBA

Madhruba means "beaten" in Arabic, and the dish is a kind of savory porridge made with cracked wheat (*jerish*). The flavorings are fresh with both fresh tomatoes and tomato paste used in the dish, adding both color and flavor, together with the ever-present garlic and ginger pastes that must be a South Asian influence. I learned to make *madhruba* with Aisha al-Tamimi, Qatar's foremost celebrity chef, and the first thing she did after organizing her mise en place was to dry-sauté the chicken to get rid of the off flavor that chicken usually has. (You won't need to do this if you buy good organic chicken. And don't wash it as she does. Washing chicken presents more risk of salmonella with contaminated droplets of water flying here and there on your counter.) Aisha uses black dried limes instead of pale ones in dishes where the color does not matter, saying they are more flavorful.

SERVES 8

¼ cup (60 ml) vegetable oil

1 medium onion (5 ounces/150 g), finely chopped

1 dried red chili pepper, left whole

1 whole chicken (3 pounds 5 ounces/ 1.5 kg), cut into 8 pieces

4 black dried limes, pulp only (seeds and peel discarded)

1 inch (2.5 cm) fresh ginger, peeled and minced to a fine paste

1 clove garlic, minced to a fine paste

1 tablespoon b'zar (Arabian Spice Mixture, page 366)

1 tablespoon ground turmeric

1 teaspoon ground coriander

1 teaspoon ground cumin

½ teaspoon ground cardamom

½ teaspoon ground cinnamon

½ teaspoon ground fennel

1 star anise

½ cup (125 g) tomato paste

4 large tomatoes (1 pound 5 ounces/ 600 g total), peeled and pureed in a food processor

3 cups (600 g) jerish (coarsely cracked wheat), soaked overnight in plenty of cold water

1 cup (200 g) basmati rice, soaked for 1 hour in lightly salted water

½ green bell pepper, trimmed, deseeded, and cut into medium wedges

A few sprigs flat-leaf parsley, most of the bottom stems discarded, coarsely chopped

A few sprigs cilantro, most of the bottom stems discarded, coarsely chopped

3 sprigs fresh dill, bottom stems discarded, coarsely chopped

1. Heat the vegetable oil in a large pot over medium heat. Add the onion and chili pepper and sauté until golden, about 5 minutes, stirring occasionally.

2. Add the chicken, dried lime pulp, ginger, and garlic. Add the spices, tomato paste, and pureed tomatoes. Drain the *jerish* and rice and add them to the pot. Add the green pepper and herbs. Cover with 2 quarts (2 liters) water and bring to a boil. Reduce the heat to low, cover, and let simmer, stirring every now and then, for 1 hour 30 minutes, or until the liquid is absorbed but without the grain and rice becoming too dry—if the grain is getting too dry, add a little water. Serve hot.

SWEET COUSCOUS

SEFFA

Moroccans have a course called *avant les desserts* (meaning "before the desserts" in French) and this sweet couscous is served at the end of the meal, not so much as a dessert but as a semisweet finish before the fruit and mint tea are brought in. I have had it like this, but I actually prefer it for breakfast, even if none of my Moroccan friends would approve. *Seffa* is normally prepared with the finest grade couscous, which is not available precooked—not to mention that hardly anyone in Morocco would use precooked. Also called "instant," precooked couscous is the type where you pour boiling water over it and let it sit until it absorbs the water. North Africans like their couscous very fluffy and the only way to achieve that is to make it the traditional way, by steaming it at least twice. Some steam their couscous up to five times, but this may be going too far. Twice is good for me and I never do anything else. I buy my couscous from Moroccan stores that import it from Morocco. Though instant couscous is convenient, the texture is never as good; and in the case of *seffa*, the difference is even more noticeable than when couscous is served with meat and/or vegetables.

SERVES 6 TO 8

2½ cups (500 g) fine or medium couscous (not instant)

Sea salt

1 tablespoon extra-virgin olive oil

1 cup (150 g) blanched almonds

4 tablespoons (60 g) unsalted butter, at room temperature

3 tablespoons (30 g) powdered sugar, plus more for dusting and serving

Ground cinnamon, for garnish and serving

1. Prepare the couscous as in step 1 of Couscous with Seven Vegetables (page 261), steaming it twice over plain water.

2. Preheat the oven to 450°F (220°C).

3. Spread the almonds on a baking sheet and toast in the hot oven for 7 to 8 minutes, until golden brown. Let cool, then coarsely grind two-thirds of the almonds in a food processor. You will use the remaining whole almonds for garnish.

4. When the couscous is ready to serve, add the softened butter and powdered sugar to the hot couscous and mix well. Tip half of the couscous into a medium-size, shallow serving bowl and spread the ground almonds evenly over it. Sprinkle with a little more powdered sugar and cover with the remaining couscous. With the back of a wooden spoon, form the couscous into the shape of a pyramid. Sprinkle a little ground cinnamon into 4 thin lines fanning out from the top all the way down to the bottom. Line the whole almonds in between the lines of cinnamon. Serve hot, with more powdered sugar and cinnamon for those who like it.

SWEET-SAVORY COUSCOUS with CHICKEN

KSEKSÛ TFAYA

MOROCCO

This couscous is a lot more festive than the regular seven-vegetables version (see page 261). It is usually made with chicken, but you can easily make it with beef or lamb (see Note). *Tfaya* is the name of the sweet-savory onion sauce spread over the meat that is served with the couscous. The dish is usually prepared for weddings, which in Morocco last for three days. One of the days is called henna day, when female family members and friends of both the bride and groom gather to have their hands and feet decorated with henna; and of course, they also feast while together. This dish is served on that occasion.

SERVES 4 TO 6

FOR THE COUSCOUS
2½ cups (500 g) fine or medium couscous (not instant)
Sea salt
1 tablespoon extra-virgin olive oil
2 tablespoons (30 g) unsalted butter, melted

FOR THE CHICKEN AND BROTH
1 whole chicken (3 pounds 5 ounces/ 1.5 kg)
½ cup (100 g) dried chickpeas, soaked overnight in plenty of cold water with ½ teaspoon baking soda

2 medium onions (10½ ounces/300 g total), finely chopped
A few sprigs cilantro and flat-leaf parsley tied together
1 cinnamon stick
Good pinch of saffron threads
4 whole cloves
½ teaspoon ground ginger
½ teaspoon finely ground black pepper
¼ cup (60 ml) extra-virgin olive oil
Sea salt

FOR THE TFAYA
5 large onions (2¼ pounds/1 kg total), halved lengthwise and cut into thin wedges
2 tablespoons smen, ghee, or unsalted butter
1 tablespoon raw cane sugar
Good pinch of saffron threads
½ teaspoon ground cinnamon
½ teaspoon ground ginger
½ teaspoon ground turmeric

½ teaspoon finely ground black pepper
1⅓ cups (200 g) golden raisins, soaked for a couple of hours in cold water and drained
2 tablespoons orange blossom water

FOR THE GARNISH
⅔ cup (100 g) blanched almonds, toasted in a hot oven for 7 to 8 minutes until golden brown

1. To start the couscous: Prepare the couscous as in step 1 of Couscous with Seven Vegetables (page 261). Put the couscous in the top half of a couscoussière. (If you don't have one, line with cheesecloth a metal colander that will fit over the pot you will use to cook the chicken in; the pot should be deep enough that the colander won't touch the chicken.)

2. To start the chicken and broth: Put the chicken in the bottom half of the couscoussière (or in the large pot). Rinse and drain the chickpeas and add to the chicken together with the onions, herbs, and spices. Add 3 cups (750 ml) water and bring to a boil over medium heat. Add the oil and cover. Let bubble gently for 30 minutes. Remove the cover, then place the top part of the couscoussière (or the colander) with the couscous in it on top of the pot, cover, and steam for 20 minutes. Turn the chicken over in the broth.

3. Meanwhile, to make the *tfaya*: Combine the sliced onions, ½ cup (125 ml) water, the *smen*, sugar, and spices in a large skillet. Place over low heat and cook, stirring regularly, for about 30 minutes. Add the drained golden raisins and cook, stirring very regularly, for about 30 minutes longer, or until the onion has softened and become caramelized and there is no sauce to speak of in the pan. Add the orange blossom water and take off the heat. Keep warm.

4. After the couscous has steamed for 20 minutes, tip the couscous into a large bowl and sprinkle with ⅔ cup (160 ml) water, stirring with a wooden spoon as you sprinkle. Once all the water is incorporated, and there are no lumps, add the 2 tablespoons (30 g) melted butter. Mix well. Cover the bowl and let sit to allow the couscous to fluff up.

5. Add salt to taste to the chicken—by then the chickpeas should have cooked and the salt will no longer harden their skin. Return the couscous to the couscoussière (or colander) and set over the chicken to steam for another 10 to 15 minutes.

6. Tip the couscous onto a large serving platter. Smooth the edges while raising them to make a pyramid, then make a large dip in the center for the chicken—you can press a soup plate in the middle of the couscous to make the dip.

7. Take the chicken out of the broth and cut into four pieces. Arrange these in the dip in the middle of the couscous. Use a slotted spoon to scoop out the chickpeas and spread them over the chicken. Spoon a little broth all over the chicken, then spread the *tfaya* over the chicken. Garnish with the toasted almonds and serve immediately with more broth on the side.

NOTE: *Use the same weight in lamb shanks or 2¼ pounds (1 kg) stewing beef or veal cut into medium chunks. Allow a little more time to cook the meat than it takes for chicken.*

MOROCCAN COUSCOUS
with MONKFISH
KSEKSÛ BEL HÛT

MOROCCO

You find this couscous in coastal areas, prepared with whatever fish is available in the market. I like to use monkfish as it can take prolonged cooking unlike most other fish, but you can also cook the sauce up to three-quarters of the way before adding a more delicate fish.   SERVES 4 TO 6

Two 28-ounce (800 g) cans whole peeled Italian tomatoes
⅓ cup (80 ml) extra-virgin olive oil
1¾ pounds (800 g) monkfish tail, boned (keep the bone) and cut into 6 or 8 pieces
Unbleached all-purpose flour, for dredging

3 medium onions (1 pound/450 g total), halved lengthwise and cut into thin wedges
3 cloves garlic, minced to a fine paste
1 tablespoon fresh thyme leaves
¼ bunch flat-leaf parsley (2 ounces/50 g), most of the bottom stems discarded, finely chopped

1½ teaspoons ground cumin
1 teaspoon paprika
¼ teaspoon red pepper flakes, or to taste
Sea salt
2 tablespoons (30 g) unsalted butter
Pinch of saffron threads

FOR THE COUSCOUS
2½ cups (500 g) couscous

Sea salt
1 tablespoon extra-virgin olive oil
2 tablespoons (30 g) unsalted butter, melted

FOR THE DRESSING
A handful of fresh basil leaves
Sea salt
3 tablespoons extra-virgin olive oil

1. Drain the tomatoes (reserve the juice for another use, which can be stored in a glass jar or bowl in the refrigerator, covered, for a couple of days), discard the seeds, and coarsely chop.

2. Pour the olive oil in the bottom half of the couscoussière. (If you don't have one, use a large pot that can hold a metal colander for steaming the couscous in.) Place over medium-high heat and when the oil is hot—dip a piece of bread in it, if the oil immediately bubbles around it, it is ready—dip the monkfish pieces in flour and fry for 2 minutes on each side. Remove to a plate.

3. Sauté the onions in the same oil until lightly golden, about 5 minutes. Add the garlic and sauté for a minute or so, then add the chopped tomatoes together with the fish bone, the thyme leaves, parsley, cumin, paprika, and pepper flakes. Add 3 cups (750 ml) water and season with salt to taste. Bring to a boil, then add the butter and saffron. Reduce the heat to medium and let bubble gently, uncovered, while you prepare the couscous.

4. Prepare the couscous as in step 1 of Couscous with Seven Vegetables (page 261). Put the couscous in the top half of the couscoussière (or a colander lined with cheesecloth). Set over the tomato sauce, cover, and steam for 20 minutes. Take the couscous off the heat and tip the couscous into a large bowl. Sprinkle with ⅔ cup (160 ml) water, stirring with a wooden spoon as you sprinkle. Once all the water is incorporated, and there are no lumps, add the 2 tablespoons (30 g) melted butter. Mix well. Cover and allow to fluff up.

5. Stir the sauce and continue cooking it, covered, for another 15 minutes, or until it becomes quite thick. Then reduce the heat to low and add the fish. Return the couscous to the couscoussière (or colander), set over the sauce, cover, and steam for another 10 to 15 minutes, or until both the fish and couscous are done.

6. Meanwhile, make the dressing: Pound the basil leaves with a little sea salt in a mortar (if you don't have a mortar, chop the basil leaves very finely) and add the olive oil. Mix well.

7. Tip the couscous into a large shallow serving bowl. Add the dressing and mix well. Arrange the couscous into the shape of a pyramid and flatten the top.

8. Remove the fish steaks from the tomato sauce and arrange over the couscous. Spoon a little tomato sauce over the fish and serve hot with more sauce on the side. You can spike the additional sauce with more pepper flakes if you like.

TUNISIAN FISH COUSCOUS

Many years ago in Tunisia, I visited a cooking school not far from Sidi Bou Said, a charming town overlooking the sea where the houses are white and blue, the same brilliant azure blue as the sea. It was an enchanting place, as was the restaurant of the cooking school, which overlooked the sea. We were served a fish couscous that was one of the best I have ever had, spicier than the Moroccan Couscous with Monkfish (page 274), with a thinner broth that was more like a soup. The couscous I had in the cooking school restaurant was fairly plain apart from it being quite spicy, and it was made with only fish whereas the one below has an added fruit element in the form of quince, making it very seasonal. The slightly sweet/sour quince adds an interesting note to the spicy tomato broth.

SERVES 4 TO 6

FOR THE COUSCOUS
2½ cups (500 g) fine or medium couscous (not instant)
Sea salt
1 tablespoon extra-virgin olive oil
2 tablespoons (30 g) unsalted butter, melted

FOR THE FISH BROTH
Sea salt
2¼ pounds (1 kg) sea bream or sea bass fillets
½ cup (125 ml) vegetable oil
1 tablespoon tomato paste, diluted in 1 cup (250 ml) water

½ cup (100 g) dried chickpeas, soaked overnight in plenty of cold water with ½ teaspoon baking soda
½ teaspoon Tunisian B'harat (page 366)
1½ teaspoons cayenne pepper
½ teaspoon finely ground black pepper

2 tablespoons smen or unsalted butter
⅓ cup (50 g) golden raisins
1 large quince (7 ounces/200 g), peeled and cut into thick wedges
Harissa (page 370), for serving

1. To start the couscous: Prepare the couscous as in step 1 of Couscous with Seven Vegetables (page 261).

2. To make the fish broth: Lightly salt the fish and set aside. Put the oil in the bottom half of a couscoussière. (If you don't have one, use a large pot that can hold a lined metal colander for steaming the couscous in.) Place over medium heat. Add the diluted tomato paste. Drain and rinse the chickpeas and add to the pot together with the *b'harat*, cayenne, and black pepper. Bring to a boil, then reduce the heat to medium-low and let bubble gently, covered, for about 15 minutes. Add 4 cups (1 liter) water, increase the heat to medium, and bring back to a boil.

3. Put the couscous in the top of the couscoussière (or a colander lined with cheesecloth) and place over the bubbling broth. Let steam gently for 20 minutes. Tip the couscous into a large bowl and sprinkle with ⅔ cup (160 ml) water, stirring with a wooden spoon as you sprinkle. Once all the water is incorporated, and there are no lumps, add the 2 tablespoons (30 g) melted butter. Mix well. Cover and allow to fluff up.

4. Add the *smen* to the broth, along with the raisins, quince, and fish. Add salt to taste. Return the couscous to the top of the couscoussière (or colander), set over the broth, cover, and steam for another 20 minutes.

5. Transfer the couscous to a shallow serving bowl and shape it into a pyramid. Flatten the top, making a dip in the center. With a slotted spoon, remove the fish, quince, chickpeas, and golden raisins from the broth and place in the dip in the center of the couscous. Spoon a little of the broth over the fish and put more broth in a medium bowl. Serve hot with the broth on the side and harissa for those who like it.

LEBANESE COUSCOUS
with CHICKEN
MOGHRABBIYEH 'ALA D'JAJ

LEBANON

Often wrongly called Israeli couscous, *moghrabbiyeh*, which means "North African" in Arabic, is the Lebanese version of the North African *m'hammsa*, which is the larger grain couscous. In Lebanon, you can buy *moghrabbiyeh* dried or you can buy it freshly made, but in the United States only the dried variety is available. Unlike the many variations of North African couscous, which is served either sweet or with different meats or vegetables, *moghrabbiyeh* is always prepared in the same way and the only variation is that some people serve it with both chicken and lamb, while others make it with only chicken. And in Tripoli, in the north of Lebanon, *moghrabbiyeh* is made into a sandwich, but only with chickpeas and baby onions. This version uses both chicken and lamb, but you can also make it with one or the other. If using only one type of meat, just under 4½ pounds (2 kg) is needed. The flavor will not change, except if you use lamb only, it will be more meaty.

SERVES 4 TO 6

1 whole chicken
   (3 pounds 5 ounces/
   1.5 kg)
10½ ounces (300 g) lamb
   meat from the shanks,
   cut into medium pieces

2 cinnamon sticks
Sea salt
½ teaspoon ground
   cinnamon, plus more as
   needed

16 baby onions, peeled
   (about 1 pound
   2 ounces/500 g total)
2½ cups (500 g) dried
   moghrabbiyeh
4 tablespoons (60 g)
   unsalted butter

⅓ cup (75 g) canned
   chickpeas, drained and
   rinsed
¼ teaspoon finely ground
   black pepper

1. Put the chicken in a large pot. Add 5¼ cups (1.25 liters) water. Put the lamb in a medium pot and add 2½ cups (625 ml) water. Place each pot over medium-high heat and bring to a boil. As the water is about to boil, skim any froth from the surface, then add 1 cinnamon stick and 1 tablespoon salt to the chicken and 1 cinnamon stick, 1½ teaspoons salt, and the ½ teaspoon ground cinnamon to the lamb. Reduce the heat to medium under both pots and let bubble gently for 1 hour. Fifteen minutes before the chicken is done, add the baby onions. Cover and cook for 10 minutes, or until both chicken and onions are tender.

2. Meanwhile, in a medium pot of boiling water, cook the *moghrabbiyeh* over medium heat for 10 minutes. Drain. Melt the butter in a large pot over low heat. Add the cooked *moghrabbiyeh* and sauté in the butter until well coated.

3. Add the chickpeas and about ½ cup (125 ml) chicken broth to the *moghrabbiyeh* and sauté over medium heat, stirring all the time. Keep adding a little more broth and cooking the *moghrabbiyeh* as if it were a risotto until it is done to your liking and most of the broth is absorbed.

4. Drain the chicken and onions, collecting the broth in a medium bowl. Drain the lamb, discarding the broth or reserving it for another use stored in a covered glass jar or bowl in the freezer. Add the onions and lamb to the *moghrabbiyeh*. Mix carefully. Taste and adjust the seasoning, adding the pepper and more cinnamon and salt if necessary.

5. Transfer the chicken to a carving board and cut into 4 or 8 pieces. Keep warm.

6. Transfer the *moghrabbiyeh* to a large serving platter. Arrange the chicken pieces on top. Serve hot with more broth on the side.

SPICY NOODLES
with SHRIMP
MIE ACEH

I visited Banda Aceh, the capital of the province of Aceh in Indonesia, during Ramadan, which was great on the one hand and not so on the other. Great because every afternoon *takjil* (Ramadan snacks) vendors would line designated streets to sell a whole range of snacks and drinks that people bought to break their fasts. Breaking the fast in Indonesia is called *buka puasa* or "opening the fast"—and unlike other Muslim countries that favor breaking the fast with dates or soup such as *harira* (Moroccan Chickpea and Lamb Soup, page 295), Indonesians like sweet or savory snacks that they buy from vendors or caterers rather than making them at home. Almost all the markets I went to were heaving with people buying either *takjil* or ready-made dishes to take home to break their fasts. Also, the restaurants I went to were absolutely packed for both *buka puasa* as well as later into the night. There was one amazing café that had excellent coffee—Indonesia is a country of serious coffee drinkers—and a noodle vendor stationed outside taking orders for noodles that he then sent to the tables. You could order the noodles with shrimp or crab and it was where I had the following recipe with crab. The version I give here is made with shrimp as it is simpler to prepare at home.

SERVES 4 TO 6

FOR THE CHILI PASTE
5 small shallots (3½ ounces/100 g total), peeled
3 cloves garlic, peeled
4 fresh mild red chilies, seeded
½ inch (1 cm) fresh turmeric, peeled
Seeds from 4 green cardamom pods

1 teaspoon cumin seeds, toasted
1 teaspoon black peppercorns

FOR THE NOODLES
3 tablespoons vegetable oil
3 scallions, thinly sliced
4 cloves garlic, thinly sliced
5 ounces (150 g) peeled shrimp

1 medium tomato (3½ ounces/100 g), seeded and cut into ⅓-inch (1 cm) cubes
2 cups (500 ml) vegetable stock (homemade or using organic bouillon cubes)
1 small leek, thinly sliced
2 inches (5 cm) celery heart, thinly sliced
1 teaspoon apple cider vinegar

Sea salt
3½ ounces (100 g) cabbage, thinly sliced
2 ounces (60 g) bean sprouts
14 ounces (400 g) fresh yellow noodles
2 tablespoons soy sauce

FOR THE GARNISH
Shrimp crackers
Pickled cucumber

1. To make the chili paste: Put all the ingredients for the chili paste in a food processor or spice grinder and process until you have a fine paste. In Indonesia, cooks grind everything in a wide stone or earthenware mortar using a horizontal pestle that they roll over the ingredients to grind them (rather than beating down on them as in a bowl-style mortar).

2. To make the noodles: Heat the oil in a wok over medium-high heat. Add the scallions and garlic and sauté for a couple of minutes, then add the chili paste. Sauté until fragrant. Add the shrimp and tomato and sauté for a couple more minutes.

3. Add the stock, leek, celery, and vinegar and season with a little salt. Let the stock bubble, stirring very regularly, until reduced by half, about 1 hour.

4. Add the cabbage and bean sprouts and cook for a couple more minutes before adding the noodles and soy sauce. Cook, stirring constantly, until both vegetables and noodles are done, a couple more minutes. Taste and adjust the seasoning if necessary.

5. Transfer to a serving bowl and serve hot with shrimp crackers and pickled cucumber.

SALIM'S PASTA SAUCE

CHINA

I got the following recipe from Fuchsia Dunlop, the author of many brilliant books on regional Chinese cuisines, who explained, "The Uyghurs, like the Italians, are pasta specialists, and their geographical location on the ancient bridge between China and the West is strikingly apparent in their pasta cookery. Their hand-pulled noodles connect them with the Muslims who live scattered across northern China. . . ." And with Carolyn Phillips, author of *All Under Heaven*, I tried shaved noodles. It's mesmerizing to see them being made, but it's a specialist's job, and I am suggesting you use regular noodles.

SERVES 4 TO 6

Vegetable oil, for cooking
1 pound (450 g) boneless lamb leg, thinly sliced
2 tablespoons Turkish mild red pepper paste
1 inch (2.5 cm) fresh ginger, peeled and finely chopped
1 clove garlic, finely chopped
4 baby leeks, sliced crosswise at an angle

5 Chinese garlic chives, cut into ¾-inch (2 cm) sections
1 medium red bell pepper, cut into small squares
1 medium green bell pepper, cut into small squares
1 small zucchini, sliced fairly thinly lengthwise, then cut into small squares

10½ ounces (300 g) green cabbage or spring greens such as chard or spinach, shredded
2 large tomatoes (10½ ounces/300 g total), finely chopped
1 tablespoon tomato paste
1⅔ cups (375 ml) meat or vegetable stock

1 teaspoon dark soy sauce
Sea salt and finely ground black pepper

FOR THE NOODLES
Sea salt
3½ ounces (100 g) dried noodles per person or 5 ounces (150 g) fresh noodles per person (depending on how many you plan to serve, for a maximum of 6)

1. Heat ¼ cup (60 ml) oil in a wok until smoking. Add the lamb and stir-fry until the pieces separate and the oil is clear again. Add the pepper paste and stir-fry briefly. Add the ginger, garlic, and leeks and stir-fry until fragrant.

2. One at a time, and stir-frying after each addition, add the garlic chives, bell peppers, zucchini, and cabbage. Add the tomatoes and tomato paste.

3. Barely cover the ingredients with stock and bring to a boil. Add the soy sauce and season with salt and pepper to taste. Reduce the heat and simmer until everything is just cooked. Set aside and allow to cool slightly while you prepare the noodles of your choice.

4. To make the noodles: Bring a large pot of salted water to a boil. Add the noodles and cook to a minute less than called for in the package instructions for the dried and 1 to 2 minutes for the fresh. Drain the noodles.

5. Divide the noodles equally among individual bowls, spoon an equal amount of sauce over each, and serve hot.

CLASSIC BALALEET

A typical Arabian sweet-savory breakfast dish, *balaleet* is also served to guests as part of *fuala*, the Qatari/Emirati equivalent of the English tea spread, a selection of sweet, savory, and sweet-savory dishes served to visitors in between meals with Arabian coffee, *karak* (see page 507), tea, and soft drinks. Offering *fuala* is also a way of entertaining without having to go to the trouble of preparing a full meal. You can make *balaleet* by first toasting the vermicelli then boiling it, or you can boil it straightaway and add turmeric to the boiling water to give the *balaleet* color. The recipe below is for the turmeric version (see Note).

SERVES 6 TO 8

Good pinch of saffron threads
¼ cup (60 ml) rose water
1 tablespoon ground turmeric
1 teaspoon ground cardamom

1 pound (450 g) vermicelli, broken into 1-inch (2.5 cm) pieces

4 tablespoons (60 g) ghee or unsalted butter, melted
¼ cup (50 g) raw cane sugar

Sea salt
4 organic eggs, beaten
¼ teaspoon finely ground black pepper
¼ teaspoon ground coriander

1. Put the saffron to steep in the rose water.

2. Preheat the oven to 200°F (100°C).

3. Put 2 quarts (2 liters) water, the turmeric, and cardamom in a large saucepan and bring to a boil over medium-high heat. Add the vermicelli and cook for 3 minutes. Drain the vermicelli and put in a medium oven-to-table dish. Add the melted ghee, sugar, saffron rose water, and a little sea salt and mix well.

4. Put the dish, uncovered, in the hot oven and bake for 20 to 30 minutes, or until the vermicelli has lost any excess liquid.

5. Meanwhile, heat a medium nonstick skillet over medium heat and when it is hot, add the beaten eggs. Season with salt to taste. Add the pepper and coriander and make a rather dry, thin frittata.

6. Place the frittata on top of the vermicelli. Serve hot.

NOTE: *If you want to make the toasted vermicelli* balaleet*, before adding the vermicelli to the boiling water, toast it in a skillet in a little vegetable oil over medium heat, stirring constantly until the vermicelli is golden brown, about 7 minutes. Omit the turmeric.*

UMM SAEED'S BALALEET

QATAR | UNITED ARAB EMIRATES | BAHRAIN

This recipe for *balaleet* is very different from the classic one on page 283. I learned to make it from Umm Saeed, an amazing woman caterer in Al-Ayn, one of the United Arab Emirates near Abu Dhabi, who runs a huge kitchen where her chefs cook meals for hundreds at a time. She uses Thai rice noodles instead of regular vermicelli, and because the noodles are white, you end up with a lovely mix of plain white noodles and saffron-colored ones. Umm Saeed also hard-scrambles the eggs instead of making them into a thin frittata to end up with an egg "crumble," which mixes nicely with the noodles, adding more flavor and texture.

SERVES 4 TO 6

FOR THE SCRAMBLED EGGS
¼ cup (60 ml) vegetable oil
1 small red onion (3½ ounces/100 g), finely chopped
Pinch each of ground cinnamon, curry powder, and finely ground black pepper
1 small green chili, seeded and finely chopped
4 organic eggs, beaten
Sea salt
½ teaspoon ground cardamom
¼ teaspoon ground cinnamon
¼ teaspoon curry powder
¼ teaspoon finely ground black pepper
¼ teaspoon ground turmeric
A good pinch of saffron threads soaked in 2 teaspoons water

FOR THE NOODLES
14 ounces (400 g) Thai rice noodles
2 bay leaves
4 green cardamom pods
4 whole cloves
1 cinnamon stick
2 tablespoons vegetable oil
1 cup (200 g) raw cane sugar
Good pinch of saffron threads soaked in 2 tablespoons water

1. To make the scrambled eggs: Heat the oil in a medium skillet over medium heat. Add the onion, pinches of spices, and green chili and fry until golden, about 5 minutes.

2. Season the beaten eggs with salt to taste, then add the cardamom, cinnamon, curry powder, pepper, turmeric, and saffron water and pour into the pan. Scramble until well done and crumbly. Take off the heat.

3. To make the noodles: Soak the rice noodles in water for 10 minutes. Cut them in half and drain.

4. Fill a large pan with water and add the bay leaves, cardamom pods, cloves, cinnamon stick, and vegetable oil. Bring to a boil and add the rice noodles. Wait for the water to boil again, then drain the noodles. Place the noodles in a bowl, add the sugar, and mix well. Let sit for 5 minutes.

5. Spread one-third of the noodles over the bottom of a pot. Sprinkle a quarter of the saffron water over the noodles, then spread a third of the scrambled eggs over the noodles. Make two more layers in the same way until you have used up the noodles, scrambled eggs, and saffron water, sprinkling the last quarter of the saffron water over the top of the noodles. Wrap the lid of the pot with a clean kitchen towel. Cover and place over very low heat. Let the noodles steam for 10 minutes. Serve hot or warm.

BULGUR and NUT CAKES

BATIRIK

There are few Lebanese dishes that do not have their equivalent in the Turkish culinary repertoire, with the Turkish version always being different from the Lebanese, and often plainer. This recipe is more or less the equivalent of the southern Lebanese vegetarian tomato kibbeh or *kibbet banadurah*, except that the Turkish version here is prettier, a little more elaborate, and just as healthy. These bulgur and nut cakes, or as a friend of mine likes to call them raw veggie burgers, are the perfect answer for vegetarians: nourishing without being boring, easy to make, and totally natural.

SERVES 4 TO 6

¾ cup (150 g) fine bulgur
1 teaspoon tomato paste
3 firm-ripe tomatoes
  (10½ ounces/300 g
  total), peeled, seeded,
  and finely chopped
1 medium onion
  (5 ounces/150 g),

halved lengthwise and
  cut into thin wedges
1 ounce (30 g) grated
  green bell pepper
  (2 tablespoons)
⅔ cup (100 g) pistachios,
  finely ground (see
  Note)

1 teaspoon pul biber
  (or Aleppo pepper)
1 tablespoon finely
  chopped flat-leaf
  parsley
1 tablespoon finely
  chopped fresh
  marjoram
Sea salt

FOR THE GARNISH
1 medium tomato,
  seeded and sliced into
  8 thin disks
½ green bell pepper,
  finely diced

1. Put the bulgur in a large mixing bowl. Add the tomato paste and tomatoes and use your hands to mix well.

2. Add the onion and bell pepper and knead until well blended. Add the pistachios and mix again until well blended. Add the pepper and herbs and season with salt to taste. Mix well.

3. Divide the mixture into 8 equal portions and shape into flat patties. Arrange the tomato slices in a circle on a serving platter. Place a bulgur cake on each. Make a small pile of diced bell pepper in the middle of each cake. Serve immediately.

NOTE: Batirik *can also be made with tahini instead of pistachios. Omit the pistachios and use ⅓ cup plus 1 tablespoon (100 ml) tahini, adding it when you would have added the pistachios. The tahini version is richer and not as pretty but just as delicious.*

BULGUR "RISOTTO" with CHICKPEAS and LAMB

BULGUR BI-DFEENEH

LEBANON | SYRIA

I still remember the excitement when I lived in Beirut and my mother would make us bulgur *bi-dfeeneh* for lunch. It was, and still is, one of my favorite dishes and before rice became common, most Levantine people would rely on bulgur as their main staple, apart from bread, using it to stuff vegetables, to serve as a side dish cooked with tomatoes, or to make as a one-pot dish cooked with meat and chickpeas, as in the recipe below. Rural folks still favor bulgur over rice. I use lamb shanks here because the bones add richness to the stock that is eventually absorbed into the grain, but you can also make this with boneless lamb shoulder or leg or neck fillets. SERVES 4 TO 6

4 tablespoons (60 g) unsalted butter

4 lamb shanks (about 3 pounds 5 ounces/ 1.5 kg total)

1 medium onion (5 ounces/150 g), finely chopped

⅔ cup (135 g) dried chickpeas, soaked overnight with ½ teaspoon baking soda

2 cinnamon sticks

1¼ cups (250 g) coarse bulgur

½ teaspoon ground cinnamon

1 teaspoon ground allspice

¼ teaspoon Lebanese 7-Spice Mixture (page 358)

¼ teaspoon finely ground black pepper

Sea salt

1¾ cups (16 ounces/ 450 g) Greek yogurt, for serving

1. Melt the butter in a large pot over medium heat and brown the shanks. Remove to a plate, then add the chopped onion and sauté until the onion is soft and lightly golden, about 5 minutes. Return the shanks to the pot.

2. Drain the chickpeas and rinse under cold water. Add to the meat and onion. Sauté for a couple of minutes, to coat them in butter, then add 6⅓ cups (1.5 liters) water and the cinnamon sticks. Cover, reduce the heat to medium-low, and let bubble gently for 1 hour, or until the chickpeas and meat are tender. At this point you can keep the shanks as they are. Or you can take them out to take the meat off the bone. Return the meat to the pan and discard the bones.

3. Discard the cinnamon sticks. Add the bulgur and season with the ground cinnamon, allspice, 7-spice mixture, pepper, and salt to taste. Reduce the heat to low and simmer for about 25 minutes, or until the bulgur is tender and the liquid is fully absorbed. Take off the heat. Wrap the lid in a clean kitchen towel, put it back over the pot, and let steam for a few minutes.

4. Serve hot with the yogurt on the side.

CHICKEN and LAMB with FRIKEH

FRIKEH 'ALA D'JAJ WA LAHMEH

LEBANON | SYRIA | JORDAN

Frikeh, the grain of the moment, is wheat that has been harvested still green, burned in the fields, then threshed before being sun-dried and cracked. It has a wonderful smoky flavor because some of the grains get charred in parts during burning. You find frikeh in Syria, Lebanon, Jordan, Turkey, and Egypt. The Syrian and Jordanian frikeh are the same, coarsely cracked with burned bits and a strong smoky flavor. But most Lebanese farmers harvest the wheat a little later and often leave it whole, while Egyptian and Turkish farmers harvest it very green and don't burn it as much. Regardless, wherever you eat it, it is a wonderful grain and a must-add to your larder.   SERVES 4 TO 6

1 small whole chicken (2¼ pounds/1 kg), quartered
2 small lamb shanks (1 pound 11 ounces/ 750 g)
1 medium onion (5 ounces/150 g), peeled

2 cinnamon sticks
Sea salt
2 tablespoons (30 g) unsalted butter
1 cup (200 g) frikeh
½ teaspoon ground allspice

½ teaspoon ground cinnamon
¼ teaspoon Lebanese 7-Spice Mixture (page 358)
¼ teaspoon finely ground black pepper

¼ cup (40 g) blanched almonds, toasted in a hot oven for 6 to 7 minutes, until golden brown
2 cups (17 ounces/ 500 g) Greek yogurt, for serving

1. Put the chicken and lamb in a large pot and add 6⅓ cups (1.5 liters) water. Bring to a boil over high heat, skimming the froth from the surface. Add the onion, cinnamon sticks, and salt to taste. Reduce the heat to medium, cover, and let bubble gently for 45 minutes, until the meat is tender.

2. Remove the chicken and lamb to a plate. Strain the stock and measure out 2½ cups (625 ml) to cook the frikeh. Pour the remaining stock into a clean saucepan, add the meat, and place over very low heat to keep hot.

3. Melt the butter in a medium pot over medium heat. Add the frikeh and stir until it is well coated with the butter. Add the reserved stock, season with the spices and salt to taste, and bring to a boil. Reduce the heat to low and simmer for 30 minutes, or until the stock is absorbed and the frikeh is tender. Take off the heat. Wrap the lid in a clean kitchen towel, replace over the pot, and let steam for a few minutes.

4. Transfer the frikeh to a serving platter. Arrange the chicken pieces and lamb over the frikeh. Scatter the toasted almonds all over and serve hot, with the yogurt on the side.

LAMB SHANKS with CHICKPEAS and WHEAT

HERGMA

MOROCCO

A classic *hergma*, which is a hearty breakfast Moroccan people eat on the street, is usually made with calves' feet or sheep's trotters. I love it with trotters, but I am not sure most of my readers are too keen on their gelatinous texture, so I am replacing the trotters (see Trotters with Chickpeas and Wheat, below) with lamb shanks. And even though Moroccans have *hergma* for breakfast, I have never been able to sit down to it early in the morning. The sight of the huge enamelware dishes filled with greasy trotters early in the day is a bit of a turnoff. Fortunately, people also make it at home for lunch and I still remember an exquisite *hergma* I had with friends in Casablanca many years ago. They had used sheep's trotters, which are more delicate than calf's feet. Their version was supremely sophisticated and not at all greasy like that of street vendors. Serve the dish hot with good bread and a refreshing salad.

SERVES 4 TO 6

4 lamb shanks (3 pounds 5 ounces/1.5 kg total)
⅓ cup (80 ml) extra-virgin olive oil

1¼ cups (250 g) dried chickpeas, soaked overnight in plenty of water with 1 teaspoon baking soda

1 cup (200 g) wheat berries
4 whole cloves garlic
2 tablespoons ground cumin

½ teaspoon red pepper flakes
2 tablespoons paprika
Sea salt

1. Put the shanks in a large pot. Add 3 quarts (3 liters) water and bring to a boil over medium-high heat, skimming the froth from the surface. Then add the olive oil. Drain and rinse the chickpeas and add to the pot along with the wheat berries, garlic, cumin, and pepper flakes. Reduce the heat to medium-low, cover, and simmer for 1½ hours, stirring occasionally, or until the meat, chickpeas, and wheat are tender. By then, the broth should have reduced to a silky sauce. If the sauce is still runny, uncover the pot and boil hard for a few minutes until reduced.

2. Add the paprika and salt to taste. Taste and adjust the seasoning if necessary. Serve hot.

TROTTERS WITH CHICKPEAS AND WHEAT: For those of you who like the idea of trotters, simply substitute them for the shanks: one calf's foot or 8 sheep's trotters for the quantities given in the recipe. Cook them for 1 hour before you add the chickpeas and wheat. You also need to add more water, possibly an extra 2 cups (500 ml), but add 1 cup (250 ml) at a time, so that you don't end up with a sauce that is too thin.

ZANZIBARI SWEET NOODLES
TAMBI

ZANZIBAR

These sweet noodles are an essential "break fast" during Ramadan. Most Zanzibaris break their fast with a few dates, spiced tea or porridge, and a serving of these noodles, which they eat with their hand. No easy feat! The noodles can be prepared in one of two ways: either toasted until golden, then boiled and sweetened or boiled in sweetened milk or water. I like the toasted version as it has a more interesting flavor, but the plain version is also lovely. Zanzibaris use locally made fresh noodles that are a cross between spaghetti and pici, thicker than regular spaghetti and thinner than pici. They are found everywhere in the markets during Ramadan and can be bought fresh or sun-dried. It is unlikely you will find them outside Zanzibar; and in the various Zanzibari cookbooks I looked at, the authors recommend substituting vermicelli. You can also use angel hair spaghetti, known as capellini, which is even closer to what I had in Zanzibar. SERVES 6 TO 8

Good pinch of saffron
  threads
½ cup (125 ml) whole
  milk
3 tablespoons vegetable
  oil

4 ounces (120 g)
  angel hair spaghetti
  (capellini), broken into
  2- to 3-inch (5 to
  7.5 cm) pieces

½ cup (100 g) raw cane
  sugar
1 tablespoon ground
  cardamom

2 tablespoons golden
  raisins
2 tablespoons slivered
  almonds

1. Put the saffron to steep in the milk.

2. Preheat the oven to 300°F (180°C).

3. Heat the oil in a large pot over medium heat. Add the broken spaghetti and sauté, stirring constantly, until the pasta is golden brown—the pasta needs to be dark enough in color to stay brown as it boils, but be careful not to burn it.

4. Add the saffron milk, sugar, cardamom, and golden raisins to the pasta and bring to a boil. Watch the milk as it nears the boiling point so as not to let it boil over. Once the milk has started to bubble, reduce the heat to low and let simmer for 7 minutes, or until the pasta is al dente, stirring regularly to make sure the pasta is not sticking. Transfer to a medium-size oven-to-table dish and place in the oven for 10 minutes, or until the pasta has completely absorbed the milk and softened completely. (They don't like their pasta al dente in Zanzibar!) Scatter the slivered almonds all over the pasta and serve hot.

EGYPTIAN SPLIT LENTIL SOUP

SHORBAT 'ADASS

No Egyptian can imagine a menu that doesn't include lentil soup, but their version is different from Lebanese and Syrian soups because they use split lentils, whereas the others use brown or green lentils. Both versions are delicious. (See Lebanese Lentil Soup, opposite page.) SERVES 4 TO 6

2½ cups (500 g) red lentils, rinsed

2 medium onions (10½ ounces/300 g total)—1 quartered and 1 finely chopped

2 medium tomatoes, peeled, seeded, and coarsely chopped

1 medium carrot, cut into medium chunks

1 medium zucchini, cut into medium chunks

4 tablespoons extra-virgin olive oil

1 teaspoon ground cumin

Juice of 1 lemon, or to taste

Sea salt

FOR GARNISH
A few sprigs cilantro
Lemon wedges

1. Put the lentils in a large pot. Add the quartered onion, the tomatoes, carrot, and zucchini. Add 4 cups (1 liter) water and bring to a boil over medium heat. Add 2 tablespoons of the oil and the cumin and cook for 20 minutes.

2. Meanwhile, heat the remaining 2 tablespoons oil in a medium skillet over medium heat. Add the chopped onion and cook until golden brown, about 10 minutes.

3. Add the fried onion (and the oil from the pan) to the lentils and simmer for 10 more minutes, until very tender. Take off the heat. Add the lemon juice and salt to taste and blend, either in a food processor or with a hand blender.

4. Serve hot, garnished with cilantro and more lemon for those who would like it.

LEBANESE LENTIL SOUP

SHORBET 'ADASS

This soup is essentially the same in Lebanon and Syria except for the spices that flavor it, cinnamon for the Lebanese version and cumin for the Syrian. Serve with toasted pita bread or pita fried in olive oil.

SERVES 4

2 cups (400 g) brown lentils, soaked for 30 minutes in cold water

¼ cup (60 ml) extra-virgin olive oil

2 medium onions (10½ ounces/300 g total), finely chopped

1 teaspoon ground cinnamon or ground cumin

Sea salt and finely ground black pepper

1. Drain the lentils and put in a large pot. Add 2½ quarts (2.5 liters) water and bring to a boil over high heat. Reduce the heat to medium, stir, and let bubble gently for 45 minutes to 1 hour, or until tender.

2. Meanwhile, heat the olive oil in a large skillet over medium heat. Add the onions and cook, stirring regularly, until the onions are golden brown, about 10 minutes.

3. Take the lentils off the heat and let cool for about 10 minutes before pureeing in a food processor or with a hand blender. Return the pureed lentils to the pan. Add the fried onions together with their oil. Season with the cinnamon (or cumin if you prefer), and salt and pepper to taste. If the soup is more like a puree than a thick soup, add a little water to have a looser consistency. Do not make it too runny, though, as the soup is meant to be thick. Let simmer for 10 more minutes. Taste and adjust the seasoning if necessary. Serve hot or warm.

TUNISIAN CHICKPEA SOUP

LABLABI

TUNISIA

A typical winter street food in Tunisia, this warming soup is served over bread, garnished with harissa and cumin. It is very simple to prepare, but you need to plan for it a day ahead by putting the chickpeas to soak.

SERVES 6

1½ cups (300 g) dried chickpeas, soaked overnight in plenty of water with 1 teaspoon baking soda (see Note)

¼ cup (60 ml) extra-virgin olive oil, plus more for serving

Juice of 1 lemon, or to taste

1 tablespoon Harissa (page 370), plus more for garnish

5 cloves garlic, minced to a fine paste

1 tablespoon ground cumin, plus more for garnish

Sea salt

2 to 4 slices day-old bread, cut into bite-size pieces

2 lemons, cut into wedges

1. Drain and rinse the chickpeas. Put in a large pot with 5¼ cups (1.25 liters) water and bring to a boil over medium-high heat, skimming off the white foam. Reduce the heat to low, cover, and simmer for 1 hour, or until the chickpeas are tender but not mushy.

2. When the chickpeas are done, add the oil, lemon juice, harissa, garlic, cumin, and salt to taste. Simmer for a few more minutes.

3. Divide the bread among 6 individual soup bowls—how much you put in depends on your taste and how thick you want your soup to be. Taste and adjust the seasoning of the soup before ladling it onto the bread. Place a knob of harissa in the middle of each bowl of soup. Drizzle a little olive oil all around and sprinkle a little cumin all over. Serve very hot with the lemon wedges.

NOTE: *Don't neglect to add the baking soda: It helps soften the chickpeas and shorten their cooking time. Without the baking soda, the chickpeas will take 2 hours, possibly longer, to cook.*

MOROCCAN CHICKPEA and LAMB SOUP

HARIRA

Harira is Morocco's national soup and the first nourishment Moroccans take when they break their fast during Ramadan. Throughout that month, people replace the dates with *sh'bakkiyah*, a crisp fried pastry that is dipped in syrup. Serve with dates or *sh'bakkiyah*: both offer an intriguing sweet contrast to the slightly tart soup.   SERVES 6

⅓ cup (75 g) dried chickpeas, soaked overnight in plenty of water with ½ teaspoon baking soda

7 ounces (200 g) lean lamb, cut into small cubes

1 medium onion (5 ounces/150 g), halved lengthwise and cut into thin wedges

A few sprigs flat-leaf parsley, most of the stems discarded, finely chopped

¾ teaspoon finely ground black pepper

¼ teaspoon ground ginger

Pinch of saffron threads

One 14-ounce (400 g) can chopped tomatoes

2 tablespoons (30 g) unsalted butter

2 ounces (50 g) broken vermicelli

A few sprigs cilantro, most of the stems

discarded, finely chopped

1 tablespoon tomato paste

Juice of 1 lemon, or more to taste

4 tablespoons unbleached all-purpose flour

Sea salt

1. Drain and rinse the chickpeas. Spread them onto a clean cloth. Cover them with another cloth and, with a rolling pin, crush them lightly to split them in half and loosen their skins. Peel and discard the skins.

2. Put the peeled split chickpeas into a large pot. Add the lamb, onion, parsley, pepper, ginger, saffron, tomatoes and their juice, and 2 quarts (2 liters) water. Bring to a boil over medium heat. Add the butter, then cover the pot and let bubble for 1 hour.

3. Add the vermicelli, cilantro, tomato paste, and lemon juice and reduce the heat to low. Mix the flour with ⅔ cup (160 ml) water and slowly pour into the soup, stirring constantly to prevent lumps from forming. The soup should thicken to a velvety consistency at the end of cooking. Add salt to taste and simmer for a couple more minutes. Taste and adjust the seasoning if necessary. Serve very hot.

LENTIL, CHICKPEA, and BEAN SOUP

SHORBAH MAKHLUTAH

LEBANON

This is a hearty soup from the mountains of Lebanon, which can be served hot, warm, or at room temperature. It is a wonderful combination of grain, legumes, and rice that provides all the nutrition needed in one meal to those who don't eat meat.　　SERVES 4 TO 6

¾ cup (150 g) brown lentils

¼ cup (50 g) dried cannellini beans, soaked overnight in plenty of water with ¼ teaspoon baking soda

⅓ cup (75 g) dried chickpeas, soaked overnight in plenty of water with ½ teaspoon baking soda

⅔ cup (160 ml) extra-virgin olive oil

2 medium onions (10½ ounces/300 g total), finely chopped

2 tablespoons coarse bulgur

2 tablespoons short-grain white rice

2 teaspoons ground cinnamon or cumin

2 teaspoons ground allspice

½ teaspoon finely ground black pepper

Sea salt

1. Put the lentils in a large pot. Drain and rinse the soaked beans and chickpeas under cold water and add to the lentils. Add 9½ cups (2.25 liters) water, cover, and bring to a boil over medium-high heat. Reduce the heat to medium and let bubble gently, covered, for 1 hour, or until the legumes are tender.

2. Meanwhile, heat the olive oil in a large skillet over medium heat. Add the onions and sauté until golden, about 5 minutes. Rinse the bulgur and rice in several changes of cold water, drain and set aside.

3. When the legumes are ready, add the bulgur, rice, and fried onions (with their oil). Season with the cinnamon (or cumin), allspice, pepper, and salt to taste and simmer for 15 minutes, until all the ingredients are tender. Adjust the soup consistency to your taste. If it is too thin, boil for a little longer; if too thick, add a little boiling water. Boil for a couple more minutes, then take off the heat. Taste and adjust the seasoning if necessary. Serve hot, warm, or at room temperature.

MEAT, BEANS, and TOMATO STEW

FASSULIAH BIL-LAHMEH

You can prepare this wonderful, warming dish with either fresh beans when in season or with dried ones. I use cannellini or navy beans, but you can easily use lima beans for a creamier consistency—they tend to break more easily hence making the sauce thicker.   SERVES 4

4 tablespoons (60 g) unsalted butter

1 pound 2 ounces (500 g) boneless lamb shoulder, trimmed of excess fat, cut into medium chunks

1 large onion (7 ounces/200 g), halved, sliced into medium-thin wedges

9 ounces (250 g) dried cannellini or navy beans (see Note), soaked overnight in plenty of water with 1 teaspoon baking soda

3½ ounces (100 g) tomato paste

1 teaspoon ground allspice

1 teaspoon ground cinnamon

½ teaspoon finely ground black pepper

¼ teaspoon freshly grated nutmeg

Sea salt

Cooked rice or bread, for serving

1. Melt the butter in a large pot over medium heat. Add the meat and stir it to brown all over. Remove the meat to a plate. Add the onion to the pot and cook, stirring occasionally, until soft and translucent, 3 to 4 minutes. Return the meat to the pot and add 4 cups (1 liter) water. Bring to a boil and as the water is about to boil, skim the froth from the surface. Cover and let bubble gently for 15 minutes.

2. Drain and rinse the beans. Add to the meat and onion and let bubble gently, covered, for 45 more minutes, or until the beans are tender.

3. Dilute the tomato paste with a little water and stir into the broth. Season with the allspice, cinnamon, pepper, nutmeg, and salt to taste. Cover and cook for 10 more minutes, or until the sauce has thickened and the beans and meat are done. Taste and adjust the seasoning if necessary. Serve hot with rice or bread.

NOTE: *When in season use 1 pound 2 ounces (500 g) fresh borlotti beans. In step 1, cook the meat for 30 minutes. Then add the fresh beans and cook for 30 minutes, or until tender. Continue to step 3. The rest of the recipe is the same.*

IRANIAN POMEGRANATE SOUP

ÂSH-E ANÂR

IRAN

I've had this soup, a winter specialty from Tabriz in Iran, as street food in a bustling café in Tajrish market in Tehran, and I've had it for tea in the hushed tearoom of the grand Shah Abbasi hotel in Afghanistan. Of course the hotel version was more refined than the street version, but both were totally delicious. It is not the quickest soup to make but it is well worth trying for its richness and its intriguing sweet-savory flavor. Serve with *barbari* (Iranian Flatbread, page 9) or any other good bread.

SERVES 6

FOR THE SOUP
2 tablespoons extra-virgin olive oil
1 medium onion (5 ounces/150 g), halved lengthwise and cut into thin wedges
½ teaspoon ground turmeric
½ teaspoon ground cinnamon
⅔ cup (125 g) short-grain white rice, soaked for 30 minutes in cold water

⅔ cup (125 g) yellow split peas, soaked for 30 minutes in cold water
Sea salt and finely ground black pepper

FOR THE MEATBALLS
8 ounces (250 g) lean ground lamb
1 medium onion (5 ounces/150 g), grated on the fine side of a grater

Sea salt and finely ground black pepper

TO FINISH
1 bunch flat-leaf parsley (7 ounces/200 g), most of the bottom stems discarded, finely chopped
¾ bunch cilantro (5 ounces/150 g), most of the bottom stems discarded, finely chopped

¼ bunch mint (2 ounces/50 g), leaves stripped off the stems, finely chopped
1 bunch scallions (2 ounces/60 g), thinly sliced
⅓ cup (80 ml) pomegranate molasses
2 tablespoons raw cane sugar
2 tablespoons extra-virgin olive oil
1 teaspoon dried mint

1. To start the soup: Heat the 2 tablespoons of oil in a large pot over medium heat. Add the onion and fry, stirring occasionally, until lightly golden, about 5 minutes. Add the turmeric and cinnamon and mix well. Drain the rice and split peas and add to the pot along with 8½ cups (2 liters) water. Season with salt and pepper to taste and bring to a boil. Reduce the heat to medium-low and cover the pot. Let bubble while you prepare the meatballs.

2. Meanwhile, to make the meatballs: Put the ground lamb and grated onion in a medium mixing bowl and season with salt and pepper to taste. Mix well.

3. Lightly moisten your hands with a little water and pinch off a little meat to shape into a meatball the size of a regular marble. Drop the meatball into the simmering soup and continue making the meatballs and dropping them into the soup until you have used up all the meat. Cover the pot, reduce the heat to low, and let simmer for 30 minutes.

4. Add the herbs and scallions to the soup and simmer for another 30 minutes, until all the ingredients are cooked and the soup has become concentrated. Stir in the pomegranate molasses and sugar. Taste and adjust the seasoning if necessary.

5. Just before serving, heat the olive oil in a small skillet, add the dried mint, and let sizzle for a couple of minutes, or until fragrant.

6. Transfer the soup to a tureen. Drizzle the mint-flavored oil over the top and serve hot.

FUL MEDAMMES

EGYPT | SYRIA

Ful medammes is the Egyptian breakfast par excellence, enjoyed by poor and rich alike, on the street or at home. Often, people take a pot to their local street *ful medammes* vendor to have him fill it with *ful* to eat in the comfort of their home. I give here both the classic Egyptian version and a Syrian one I used to have in Aleppo at Hajj Abdo's simple corner café in the heart of the city's Christian quarter. His remains the best I have ever had.

SERVES 4

FOR THE FUL
2 cups (400 g) dried large
  fava beans, soaked
  overnight in plenty of
  water with 1 teaspoon
  baking soda
Sea salt

**FOR EGYPTIAN-STYLE
FUL**
3 cloves garlic, minced to
  a fine paste
Sea salt

Extra-virgin olive oil
1 medium firm-ripe
  tomato (3½ ounces/
  100 g), cut into small
  cubes
2 to 3 scallions, thinly
  sliced, to taste
A few sprigs flat-leaf
  parsley, most of
  the bottom stems
  discarded, finely
  chopped

½ teaspoon ground
  cumin
Lemon wedges
Pita bread, for serving

FOR SYRIAN-STYLE FUL
½ cup (125 ml) tahini
1 clove garlic, minced to a
  fine paste
Juice of 1 lemon, or to
  taste

2 tablespoons Aleppo
  or Turkish red pepper
  paste, diluted with
  3 tablespoons water
  (optional)
Extra-virgin olive oil, for
  drizzling
Pita bread, for serving
Sliced tomatoes and
  scallions, for serving

1. To start the *ful*: Drain and rinse the favas under cold water. Put in a large pot and add 4 cups (1 liter) water. Bring to a boil over medium heat, then reduce the heat to low and simmer for 2½ to 3 hours, until the beans are very tender and the cooking water has thickened. Check after 1 hour or so to make sure the beans are not drying out. If they are, add a little boiling water. Don't add too much as you will not be draining the cooked beans at the end. Once done, add salt to taste—you do not want to do this until the very end, otherwise the skins will harden.

2. To serve the *ful* Egyptian style: Mash the beans coarsely inside the pot, then spoon them into a large serving bowl. Mix in the garlic and more salt if needed. Wipe the sides of the bowl clean, then drizzle all over with olive oil. Pile the diced tomato in the center, then the scallions, then the parsley. Sprinkle the cumin all around the edges over the beans and serve with the lemon wedges and pita bread.

3. To serve the *ful* Syrian style (like Hajj Abdo): Mix the tahini, garlic, and lemon juice, then gradually add ¾ cup (180 ml) water until the tarator is like heavy cream. You will notice the tahini thickening at first but don't worry, it will loosen as you go. Pour the tarator into a large serving bowl. Add the hot beans. If desired, spoon a little diluted pepper paste all over the top. Drizzle with olive oil. Serve immediately with pita bread, tomatoes, and scallions.

NIGERIAN BREAKFAST FRITTERS

AKARA

NIGERIA

Akara are interesting Nigerian fritters made with peeled black-eyed peas and are a typical breakfast, served with hot bread or a kind of savory jelly made with cornstarch called *agidi*. Serve the fritters on their own or with hot bread. SERVES 4 TO 6

2 cups (400 g) dried black-eyed peas, soaked overnight in cold water and peeled (see Note)

½ red bell pepper, cut into chunks

1 medium onion (5 ounces/150 g), coarsely chopped

1 habanero chili

1 organic vegetable bouillon cube

Vegetable oil, for deep-frying

Sea salt (optional)

1. Put the peeled black-eyed peas, the bell pepper, the onion, habanero, the bouillon cube, and ¼ cup (60 ml) water in a food processor and process until you have a thick, coarse batter. Transfer to a large mixing bowl.

2. Pour 2 inches (5 cm) oil into a medium deep skillet to deep fry the fritters and heat over medium-low heat. You don't want the oil to be too hot, otherwise the fritters will not cook through. Test the oil by dropping a little batter in it; if the oil immediately bubbles around it, then it's ready. Using a large tablespoon, drop as many tablespoons of batter into the hot oil as will fit comfortably in the pan. Fry on both sides until golden all over. Transfer to a sieve lined with paper towels.

3. Serve hot with sea salt for those who would like the fritters saltier.

NOTE: *To easily peel the black-eyed peas, bash them lightly and put them in bowl full of water; rub with your hands to loosen the skins, which you can then skim as they float to the surface.*

LENTIL KIBBEH

MERCIMEKLI KOFTE

When one mentions kibbeh, people immediately think about the meat version (see page 129), but there are many vegetarian versions, in Turkey, Syria, and South Lebanon to name but a few. The following recipe comes from a wonderful Turkish home cook, Belgin, who does cookery demonstrations for my culinary groups in her kitchen before she serves them her exquisite dishes in her dining room. Because I love to snack on them while waiting for the other dishes to be ready, I always ask her to start with this *kofte*. (Confusingly, the Turks call kibbeh *kofte* whereas the Lebanese use the word *kofte* to describe a ground meat, herb, and onion mixture that can be either grilled, stewed, or baked.)

SERVES 4 TO 6

1 cup (200 g) red lentils
Heaping ¾ cup (175 g) fine bulgur
⅓ cup (80 ml) extra-virgin olive oil
2 medium onions (10½ ounces/ 300 g total), very finely chopped
½ cup (100 g) Turkish red pepper paste
½ cup (100 g) tomato paste
1 teaspoon ground cumin
Sea salt

TO FINISH
4 Little Gem lettuces, for serving
Olive oil, for drizzling
A few sprigs flat-leaf parsley, finely chopped, for garnish

1. Rinse the lentils under cold water, then put in a medium pot. Add 2 cups (500 ml) water and bring to a boil over medium heat. Reduce the heat to low and simmer, covered, for 30 minutes, or until the lentils are tender and mushy and the water almost evaporated. Add the bulgur and mix well. Cover the pot.

2. Heat the olive oil in a medium skillet over medium heat. Add the onions and cook, stirring regularly, until the onion is very soft and golden. Add the pepper paste and tomato paste and mix well.

3. Transfer the lentil/bulgur mixture to a large mixing bowl. Add the fried onions and with your hand (wear a glove as the mixture will turn your hand red) mix to a smooth paste. Add the cumin and season with salt to taste and mix again, adding a little water if the mixture is too stiff to shape easily. Taste and adjust the seasoning if necessary.

4. To finish, arrange lettuce leaves in a rosette on a round platter. Pinch off one piece of kibbeh mixture the size of a large walnut and shape it into an oval patty. Press your fingers into it to leave indents and place inside one lettuce leaf. Continue shaping the kibbeh in the same way and placing each on a lettuce leaf. Drizzle each kibbeh with a little olive oil and sprinkle with a little parsley. Serve immediately.

CANNELLINI BEANS, DILL, and EGGS
BAGHALI GHATOG

I like to use Rancho Gordo cannellini beans for this recipe as they are quite similar to those I saw being used in Iran, which are larger than regular cannellini. Also they peel easily, that is if you have the patience to spend the time peeling the beans one by one. I remember one particular stall in the market in Rasht, in Gilan in northern Iran, where they cooked *baghali ghatog*. The wife was slaving over the large pan stirring the eggs into the bean and dill mixture while the husband was peeling the beans one by one for the next batch. They were both quite old and I marveled at their dedication and energy making batch after batch of this wonderful vegetarian dish for people to eat there and then or for them to take home to eat with their families. Serve hot with *barbari* or lavash bread, or even plain rice.

SERVES 4

1 cup (200 g) dried cannellini beans, soaked overnight in plenty of water with ½ teaspoon baking soda

7 tablespoons (100 g) unsalted butter

4 cloves garlic, minced to a fine paste

½ teaspoon ground turmeric

4 cups (200 g) chopped fresh dill

Good pinch of saffron threads

Sea salt and finely ground black pepper

4 organic eggs

1. Drain and rinse the beans. Peel them one by one by nicking one corner to break the skin before peeling or squeezing it off.

2. Melt the butter in a large deep skillet over medium heat. Add the garlic and when it starts sizzling and is fragrant, stir in the turmeric.

3. Add three-quarters of the dill and the beans and sauté for a minute or two. Add 2 cups (500 ml) water along with the saffron and bring to a boil. Reduce the heat to low, cover, and simmer for 45 minutes. Add the remaining dill and continue simmering until the beans are tender, about 15 minutes. Uncover the pan and reduce the sauce if it is still too thin. Season with salt and pepper to taste.

4. Make 4 shallow depressions in the beans for the eggs. Break an egg into each depression and season the eggs with salt and pepper. Cook until the eggs are done to your liking. Serve hot.

THE CHICKEN THAT FLEW

D'JAJA TARAT

The rather amusing name of this Moroccan vegetarian dish refers to a chicken having flown out of the pot. The cooking time for the chickpeas varies depending on how old they are, and more important whether they have been soaked with baking soda in the water or not. If the chickpeas are not soft enough after you have cooked them for the time given below, add more boiling water (about half the amount given) and cook for another 15 minutes, or until tender.   SERVES 4

5 ounces (150 g) dried chickpeas, soaked overnight in plenty of cold water with ½ teaspoon baking soda
Pinch of saffron threads
1 large sweet potato (14 ounces/400 g), peeled and cut into medium chunks
1 medium onion (5 ounces/150 g), halved lengthwise and cut into thin wedges
¼ bunch cilantro (2 ounces/50 g), most of the bottom stems discarded, finely chopped
2 tablespoons extra-virgin olive oil
Sea salt and finely ground black pepper

1. Drain and rinse the chickpeas well and put in a medium pot. Add the saffron and 3 cups (750 ml) water. Bring to a boil over medium-high heat, skimming the froth from the surface. Reduce the heat to medium-low. Cover the pot and cook for 30 minutes, or until the chickpeas are tender but not mushy.

2. Add the sweet potato, onions, cilantro, and olive oil. Season with salt and pepper to taste. Cover and cook for 10 more minutes, or until the sweet potatoes are tender and the water is completely evaporated. Serve hot, warm, or at room temperature.

CHICKPEA FLOUR FRITTERS
KABAB HOMMUS

"Kabab" immediately conjures up grilled meat or Syrian meatballs, so when a Qatari friend was telling me about *kabab hommus* being essential Iftar food, I wondered how you could grill chickpeas (*hommus* in Arabic). She then explained them to me and I asked my friend Aisha al-Tamimi, Qatar's foremost celebrity TV chef, to show me how to make them. They are basically fritters made with chickpea flour and with pureed tomatoes for a more intense flavor, not to mention the herbs and seasonings. They are simple and quick to make, and scrumptious for Iftar or any other time.

SERVES 6

FOR THE TAMARIND SAUCE
⅓ cup (60 g) seedless tamarind paste
1 small green chili, thinly sliced
A handful of mint leaves, finely chopped
1 tablespoon white vinegar

FOR THE FRITTERS
2 cups (250 g) chickpea flour
1 tablespoon all-purpose flour

½ teaspoon baking powder
1 teaspoon ground coriander
1 teaspoon ground cumin
1 teaspoon ground turmeric
½ teaspoon ground fennel
½ teaspoon red pepper flakes
½ teaspoon dried mint
1 organic egg

4 scallions, thinly sliced
½ inch (1 cm) fresh ginger, peeled and minced to a fine paste
1 green chili, thinly sliced
½ bunch flat-leaf parsley, most of the bottom stems discarded, finely chopped
½ bunch cilantro (3½ ounces/100 g), most of the bottom stems discarded, finely chopped

2 or 3 sprigs fresh dill, bottom stems discarded, finely chopped
1 cup (50 g) chopped chives or fresh green garlic
4 large tomatoes (1¾ pounds/800 g total), pureed
Sea salt

Vegetable oil, for deep-frying

1. To make the tamarind sauce: Put the tamarind paste in a medium mixing bowl. Add 1 cup (250 ml) water and whisk until the paste is completely dissolved. Stir in the chili, mint, and vinegar.

2. To prepare the fritters: Mix together the chickpea flour, all-purpose flour, baking powder, ground spices, pepper flakes, dried mint, the egg, scallions, ginger, chili, fresh herbs, pureed tomatoes, and salt to taste, to make the batter. If the batter is too thick, add a little water.

3. Set a wire rack in a rimmed baking sheet. Pour 2 inches (5 cm) of oil into a deep skillet and heat over medium heat until hot (if you drop a piece of bread in the oil, the oil should immediately bubble around it). Use a large ice cream scoop or ¼-cup (60 ml) measure to drop the batter into the hot oil. Drop as many as will fit comfortably and fry until golden on both sides, about 3 minutes on each side. Transfer to the rack to let the excess oil drain off. Serve hot with the tamarind sauce.

THE SEA

EATING FISH

I USE MY FINGER-TIPS

TO PRY OPEN,

FEEL, AND SENSE

THE HIDDEN TASTE

OF FISH—

ITS FLESH AND SCALES,

ITS COARSENESS

AND GLOSS,

ITS GEOMETRY,

ITS MUSCLE-BONE

AND TONE—

GENTLY, I RELISH IT ALL.

—SUDEEP SEN

In Arabic, fish is known as *samak* (plural of *samaka*), but in Morocco, fish is known as *hût*, also an Arabic word, which in classical Arabic-speaking countries (Moroccan is a mix of Arabic and Berber) generally refers to whales and other large fish. Another little-known Arabic word for fish is *nûn*, from the Accadian *nunu*. What is interesting though is that there is no mention of fish in the Qur'an, probably because the first Muslims were desert people living in land-locked Mecca, and later in Medina—until they set off on their conquests and started contending with Christians, for nearly eight centuries, for primacy in the Mediterranean. From there, Muslims sailed to conquer further lands, many of which were coastal. As they settled in these coastal regions, the fruit of the sea became as important to them as meat and dairy were to early Muslims.

In the Arabian Gulf, where the first Muslim conquests took place, no meal is considered complete without fish on the table. Fish markets are plentiful, both covered and by the waterside where fishermen offload their freshly caught fish to sell directly to customers. In

many of the markets, there is a special section where you can have your fish scaled, gutted, and cut the way you want. Some markets even have a kitchen area where you can take your newly purchased fish to be cooked to either eat there and then or take home to share with your family or friends.

The most prized fish in the Arabian Gulf is *hamour* (reef cod), which you can find in all sizes. In the Levant, sea bass and red mullet are king, whereas in North Africa, people like both freshwater and saltwater fish. Trout is plentiful in Morocco to the point that it was once shunned by the Berbers as not worth having. And shad, another fish favored by Moroccans, is fished in lakes, rivers, and the sea. In fact, Moroccans are fortunate to have both the Mediterranean to the north and the Atlantic to the west to provide them with all kinds of different fish. Even then, you will not find as much of a variety in their fish recipes as you do in either their meat or vegetable recipes.

This applies to the rest of the Muslim world. Nowhere do you find a large number of fish recipes, mainly because fish is so prized that often cooks simply fry or grill it to serve with a dipping sauce or a condiment and, of course, rice or bread depending on the country. The fish is often marinated before frying or grilling, or simply rubbed with salt and lemon and sometimes a spice mixture. The marinades obviously vary from one country to the other. In Libya, the fish is marinated in a strongly flavored cumin and garlic marinade whereas in the Arabian Gulf, it is rubbed with a heady mix of spices, known as *b'zar* (see page 366), which is mixed differently for fish from that used for meat and vegetable dishes. North Africans use a marinade known as chermoula, which is made with fresh herbs, while Indonesians use a variety of sambals.

This is not to say there are no elaborate fish dishes. The Iranian *mâhi tu-por* (Baked Stuffed Fish, page 312) is served at weddings, while the Lebanese *samkeh harrah* (*bil-Kuzbarah* and *bil-Tahineh*, pages 315 and 316) is considered a splendid dish; and in Senegal, the main family dish is a stew of fish and vegetables, served on rice cooked in the same sauce the fish and vegetables were cooked in. Regardless, the treatment of fish is on the whole kept simple.

BAKED STUFFED FISH

MÂHI TU-POR

IRAN

This is probably Iran's most festive fish dish, which comes from the north of the country. In this recipe, the fish is stuffed with a dried fruit and nut mixture and bathed in a lemony saffron sauce before being baked. It is one of my favorite party dishes, and I usually serve it as the Iranians do, with Polow, the plain Iranian rice speckled with saffron (see page 242). Sometimes, I use individual fish, but the wow factor is lost with small fish, so I always try to source a beautiful large fish as indicated below. Let the fish come to room temperature before baking it so that you can time it to cook perfectly.

SERVES 4 TO 6

Good pinch of saffron
  threads
1 large (4½ pounds/2 kg)
  white-fleshed fish—cod,
  sea bass, or hamour
  (reef cod)—scaled,
  gutted, and cleaned,
  but head and tail left on
Sea salt
7 tablespoons (100 g)
  unsalted butter, plus
  more for the baking dish
½ cup (75 g) dried
  apricots, soaked for
  1 hour in boiling water
½ cup (75 g) prunes,
  soaked for 1 hour in
  boiling water
½ cup (75 g) golden
  raisins, soaked for
  1 hour in boiling water
½ cup (75 g) walnuts,
  finely chopped
1½ tablespoons
  pomegranate molasses
Finely ground black
  pepper
Juice of 1 lemon, or to
  taste
Plain Iranian Rice (page
  242), for serving

1. Put the saffron to steep in 2 tablespoons water.

2. Pat the fish dry inside and out with paper towels and rub the inside with a little salt. With a little butter, grease a baking dish large enough to hold the fish comfortably. Preheat the oven to 400°F (200°C).

3. Drain the dried fruit. Very finely chop the apricots and prunes. Combine all the fruit in a large mixing bowl with the walnuts and pomegranate molasses and season with a little salt and pepper, just enough to offset the sweetness of the fruit. Mix well.

4. Stuff the fish with the fruit/nut mixture. Flap the sides of the fish over the stuffing and place in the greased baking dish.

5. Melt the 7 tablespoons butter in a small saucepan and stir in the lemon juice and saffron water. Pour over the fish and bake for 35 to 40 minutes, basting from time to time, until the fish just barely flakes—you don't want to overcook the fish otherwise it will become rubbery. Let sit for 5 minutes, then carefully transfer to a serving platter. Pour the sauce all over. Serve hot with the rice.

BAKED SEA BASS with TOMATOES and OLIVES

DAR'I M'SLALLA

You can use either saltwater or freshwater fish for this recipe as long as you choose a fish with a firm white flesh. Let the fish come to room temperature before baking so that you can time it to cook perfectly. Also, use ripe but firm tomatoes to achieve both an optimal flavor and texture—tomatoes are the main accompaniment, so they need to be perfect. Serve with good bread.

SERVES 4

2 whole sea bass or other similar fish (about 1 pound 12 ounces/ 800 g each), scaled, gutted, and rinsed
Chermoula (page 342)
A few sprigs flat-leaf parsley
4 large firm-ripe vine tomatoes (1 pound 12 ounces/800 g total), cut into medium-thick slices
Sea salt
10½ ounces (300 g) green olives, pitted (don't use already pitted, pit your own)

1. Pat the fish dry with paper towels and place on a large platter. Rub it all over with the chermoula, inside and out. Let marinate for at least 2 hours, preferably longer, in the refrigerator.

2. Preheat the oven to 425°F (220°C).

3. Spread the parsley over the bottom of an oven-to-table baking dish large enough to hold both fish. Lay the marinated fish in the dish and cover with the sliced tomatoes. Season with salt to taste and pour any chermoula still in the dish over the tomatoes. Roast for 25 minutes, or until the fish is done to your liking—I like mine just done so that it stays very moist.

4. Blanch the pitted olives in boiling water for 5 minutes. Drain well and arrange them around the fish for the last 10 minutes of roasting. Take out of the oven and let sit for 5 minutes before serving.

MOROCCAN GREY MULLET STUFFED with SWISS CHARD

HÛT M'AMMAR BEL SILQ

MOROCCO

Moroccans who live by the sea tend to prefer fish to meat whereas those living inland don't consume much fish, which makes sense given Moroccan cooks' insistence on both seasonality and freshness of ingredients. In the old days, cooks baked their fish in ashes, often stuffing it beforehand with rice, couscous and dates, potatoes, or greens like in this recipe. Serve with good bread.

SERVES 4 TO 6

4 grey mullets (about 14 ounces/400 g each) or 2 mullets (2 pounds/900 g each)
Chermoula (page 342)
1 pound 12 ounces (800 g) Swiss chard, both leaves and stems, sliced into ½-inch (1 cm) strips
7 ounces (200 g) purple or Kalamata olives, halved and pitted
A few sprigs flat-leaf parsley

1. Pat the fish dry with paper towels and place on a large platter. Then rub with the chermoula both inside and out. Let marinate for at least 2 hours, preferably longer, in the refrigerator.

2. Put the sliced Swiss chard and halved olives in a steamer basket and steam for 15 to 20 minutes, or until the chard is just done. Mix well. Remove the steamer basket, cover with a clean kitchen towel, and let the chard and olives cool. (There is no need to season the chard as the fish marinade will eventually flavor it.)

3. Preheat the oven to 425°F (220°C).

4. Cover the bottom of an oven-to-table baking dish large enough to hold all the fish with the parsley. Fill each fish with as much Swiss chard as it will take (see Note), not forgetting the head cavity, and lay the fish on the parsley. Pour any chermoula that is left in the dish over the fish and roast for 20 to 25 minutes for the 4 smaller fish, or 25 to 30 minutes for the 2 large fish. Let sit for 5 minutes before serving.

NOTE: *If there is any Swiss chard left over, heat it gently with a little extra-virgin olive oil and serve it alongside the fish.*

SPICY BAKED FISH with HERBS and NUTS

SAMKEH HARRAH BIL-KUZBARAH

LEBANON

Samkeh harrah is a specialty from Tripoli in north Lebanon. There are two ways of preparing it: one with just fresh herbs, nuts, and tomatoes as here, and the other is tahini-based with added herbs and nuts (see Samkeh Harrah bil-Tahineh, page 316). Both versions are delightful, with this recipe having fresher flavors. In this recipe (which is my mother's), I like to use individual fish instead of fillets. Serve with good bread and a green salad.

SERVES 4

4 whole sea bream or sea bass (about 14 ounces/400 g each), scaled, gutted, and rinsed
Sea salt

FOR THE HERB STUFFING
⅓ cup (50 g) pine nuts, ground medium fine
⅓ cup (50 g) walnuts, ground medium fine

8 cloves garlic, minced to a fine paste
2 bunches cilantro (14 ounces/400 g), most of the bottom stems discarded, finely chopped
1 medium onion (5 ounces/150 g), finely chopped

1 medium tomato (3½ ounces/100 g), seeded and cut into 1/4-inch (6 mm) dice
1 teaspoon ground cumin
1 teaspoon ground coriander
½ teaspoon cayenne pepper
¼ teaspoon finely ground black pepper

Sea salt
Juice of 2 lemons, or to taste

½ cup (125 ml) extra-virgin olive oil, plus more for greasing the baking sheet

1. Pat the fish dry with paper towels and lightly rub with a little salt, inside and out.

2. To make the herb stuffing: Put the ground nuts in a large bowl. Add the garlic, cilantro, onion, and tomato. Season with the spices and salt to taste, then add the lemon juice and olive oil. Mix well. Taste and adjust the seasoning if necessary.

3. Preheat the oven to 350°F (180°C). Grease a large baking sheet with a little olive oil.

4. Put as much stuffing as you can inside each fish, making sure you don't have any stuffing spilling out. Lay the fish on the baking sheet. Wrap any leftover stuffing in foil and place next to the fish or on another baking sheet.

5. Bake for 25 to 35 minutes, or until the fish is just done. Let cool and serve at room temperature.

SPICY BAKED FISH in a TAHINI, HERB, and NUT SAUCE

SAMKEH HARRAH BIL-TAHINEH

LEBANON

At the Silver Shore restaurant in Tripoli, they prepare this fish using a large sea bass that feeds four, but I suggest making it with fish fillets, which are easier to eat with the sauce with no need to pick out any bones or discard the skin.

SERVES 4 TO 6

⅓ cup (50 g) pine nuts

⅔ cup (100 g) walnuts

1 cup (250 ml) tahini

8 cloves garlic, minced to a fine paste

Juice of 3 lemons, or to taste

Vegetable oil, for frying

2¼ pounds (1 kg) white fish fillets (4 to 6 pieces)

⅓ cup (80 ml) extra-virgin olive oil

2 medium onions (10½ ounces/300 g total), finely chopped

1 medium red bell pepper, finely chopped

½ bunch cilantro (3½ ounces/100 g), most of the bottom stems discarded, finely chopped

1 tablespoon ground coriander

1 teaspoon Aleppo pepper

½ teaspoon ground cumin

Sea salt

1. Preheat the oven to 425°F (220°C).

2. Spread the pine nuts and walnuts on separate nonstick baking sheets and toast in the hot oven for 5 to 6 minutes, or until golden brown. Transfer the pine nuts to a small bowl. Wait until the walnuts have cooled, then chop them coarsely.

3. Put the tahini in a large mixing bowl and add the garlic. Add the lemon juice and start mixing it in. At first you will notice the tahini thickening instead of thinning, but do not worry, it will eventually thin out as you add more liquid. Slowly add ¾ cup (180 ml) water, stirring all the time until you have a sauce the consistency of heavy cream. Set the tahini sauce aside.

4. Place a large skillet over medium heat and pour in enough vegetable oil to cover the bottom. When the oil is hot, slide the fish fillets into the pan, skin side down, and cook for 3 to 5 minutes, or until the skin is crisp and golden and the fish just done. You don't need to flip the fish as it will finish cooking in the tahini sauce. Transfer to a plate.

5. Wipe the pan clean. Heat the olive oil over medium heat. Add the onion and bell pepper and sauté until the onion is golden and the pepper completely softened, 7 to 10 minutes. Add the cilantro and stir until wilted. Add the ground walnuts, coriander, Aleppo pepper, cumin, and salt to taste. Add the tahini sauce and let it bubble gently for 3 to 4 minutes, stirring regularly, until you see a little oil rise to the surface.

6. Slide the cooked fish into the sauce, skin side up, and gently shake the pan to coat the fish with the sauce. Let simmer for a couple of minutes, until the fish has finished cooking. Transfer to a serving platter. Garnish with the toasted pine nuts and serve hot or warm.

BANGLADESHI FISH HEAD "RISOTTO"

BANGLADESH

Here is another favorite fish head dish, from Bangladesh this time. It starts out as a curry, that is until you add the rice to cook it in the sauce, at which point you can consider the dish as the Bangladeshi equivalent of risotto. It is quite different from the Indonesian version (see Indonesian Fish Head Curry, page 321) in that the sauce is made with tomatoes rather than with coconut cream. The fish head used here comes from *rui* or *rohu*, a kind of carp found in Southeast Asia. I doubt you will be able to source it in the West, so ask your fishmonger for sea bass or hake heads, or even plain carp heads if he has any. You could also try to buy whole carp from an Asian supermarket, where they keep fish in tanks, and use the heads for this recipe while reserving the bodies for fish soup. I have adapted this recipe from one in Shawkat Osman's *Bangladeshi Cuisine*.

SERVES 4

2 rui or rohu fish heads
1 teaspoon ground turmeric
Sea salt
Vegetable oil, for shallow-frying
⅔ cup (160 ml) mustard oil
1 tablespoon cumin seeds
5 bay leaves

10 green cardamom pods, lightly smashed
2 cinnamon sticks
10 whole cloves
1 large onion (7 ounces/ 200 g), grated on the fine side of a grater
12 cloves garlic, minced to a fine paste

2 inches (5 cm) fresh ginger, peeled and minced to a fine paste
10 medium firm-ripe tomatoes (2¼ pounds/1 kg total), peeled, seeded, and cut into wedges
2 tablespoons ground coriander

1 tablespoon red chili powder
2 teaspoons ground cumin
Juice of 1 small lemon
1 cup (200 g) kalijira or Thai fragrant rice, soaked for 30 minutes in lightly salted water
A few sprigs cilantro, leaves only, for garnish

1. Pat the fish heads dry with paper towels and lightly rub with the turmeric and a little salt.

2. Set a wire rack in a rimmed baking sheet. Pour ½ inch (1 cm) vegetable oil into a large deep skillet and heat over medium heat until hot—test with a piece of bread; if the oil immediately bubbles around it, then it is ready. Add the fish heads and fry on both sides for 3 to 5 minutes until crisp and golden brown. Remove to the wire rack to drain off any excess oil.

Recipe continues

3. Heat the mustard oil in a wok over high heat. Add the cumin seeds and stir for a few seconds, then add the bay leaves, cardamom, cinnamon, and cloves and let sizzle for a minute or so. Add the onion, garlic, and ginger and stir with the spices until fragrant. Add the tomatoes and mix well.

4. Add the ground spices, lemon juice, 2 tablespoons water, and salt to taste. Cook, stirring frequently, until the oil rises to the sides, about 10 minutes. Add the fried fish heads and stir into the sauce to coat them well. Drain the rice and add to the wok. Add enough water to just cover the rice. Reduce the heat to low. Cover the wok and let simmer gently for 15 to 20 minutes, or until the rice has absorbed the sauce and is tender. Remove from the heat. Wrap the lid with a clean kitchen towel and replace over the wok. Let sit for a few minutes.

5. Transfer the fish heads and rice to a serving platter, discarding both bay leaves and cinnamon sticks. Garnish with the cilantro and serve hot.

INDONESIAN FISH HEAD CURRY

GULAI KEPALA IKAN

INDONESIA

You find fish head curry throughout Southeast Asia. I tasted the following version in Medan in Indonesia, at a restaurant specializing in fish head curry where I was taken by the wonderful William Wongso, Indonesia's foremost celebrity chef, and his equally wonderful friend Indra Halim, who owns a mini food and coffee empire in Medan. The fish head was big and fleshy with lots of meat on it and this is what you need to ask your fishmonger for—the biggest and meatiest fish head he has available. Most fish heads go into the recycling bin in Europe and America so it shouldn't be difficult sourcing one from a good fishmonger. Serve this with plain rice or Indonesian Yellow Rice (page 257).

SERVES 4

1 large sea bass or other whitefish head (about 1 pound 5 ounces/ 600 g)
Juice of 1 lime
Sea salt

FOR THE SPICE PASTE
10 small shallots (7 ounces/200 g total), peeled
5 cloves garlic, peeled
5 fresh red chilies

1 medium tomato (3½ ounces/100 g)
1 inch (2.5 cm) fresh turmeric, peeled
2 teaspoons ground coriander
1 teaspoon raw cane sugar
1 teaspoon sea salt

FOR THE SAUCE
3 tablespoons vegetable oil

5 bilimbi (see Glossary) or star fruit, cut crosswise into slices ¼ inch (6 mm) thick
1 teaspoon seedless tamarind paste
3 bay leaves
2 stalks lemongrass, white part only, smashed
2 inches (5 cm) fresh galangal, peeled and minced to a fine paste

2 inches (5 cm) fresh ginger, peeled and minced to a fine paste
2 cups (500 ml) coconut cream
1 firm-ripe medium tomato (about 3½ ounces/100 g), finely diced
3½ ounces (100 g) long beans, stringed and cut into 1-inch (2.5 cm) lengths

1. Pat the fish head dry with paper towels, then rub with the lime juice and a little salt. Let sit for 1 hour.

2. To make the spice paste: If you have a mortar and pestle, grind the ingredients for the spice paste in the mortar together. Otherwise use your food processor to make the paste.

3. To make the sauce: Heat the oil in a large deep skillet over medium heat. Add the spice paste and cook, stirring constantly, for a couple of minutes. Add the bilimbi, tamarind paste, bay leaves, lemongrass, galangal, and ginger and cook, still stirring, for a minute or so. Add 2 cups (500 ml) water, the coconut cream, and the fish head. Let bubble gently until the sauce has reduced by half, about 30 minutes.

4. Add the tomato and long beans and cook for another 10 minutes, or until the beans are done. Serve hot.

INDONESIAN CRAB CURRY

KETAM MASAK NANAS

There is a debate about whether Muslims are allowed to eat seafood. According to the Hanafī school of jurisprudence, only *samak* (which means "fish" in Arabic) is allowed, but other Muslim jurists do not see crabs or shrimp as *haram* (forbidden), and given how plentiful they are in the Arabian Gulf and in other parts of the Muslim world, those who think they are *haram* must be in the minority. Serve this with plain rice or Indonesian Yellow Rice (page 257) and Indonesian shrimp crackers.   SERVES 4

FOR THE COCONUT PASTE
½ cup (100 g) grated fresh coconut
10 small shallots (7 ounces/200 g total), peeled
4 cloves garlic, peeled
½ inch (1 cm) fresh ginger, peeled

FOR THE CURRY
¼ cup (60 ml) vegetable oil
2 tablespoons ground coriander
2 teaspoons cayenne pepper
1 teaspoon ground turmeric

1 stalk lemongrass, smashed
2 medium crabs (3 pounds 5 ounces/ 1.5 kg), boiled and chopped in half
2 cups (500 ml) coconut cream

½ medium slightly underripe pineapple, peeled, halved lengthwise, and cut across into 8 wedges
Sea salt

1. To make the coconut paste: Toast the grated coconut in a medium nonstick skillet over medium heat, stirring constantly, until the coconut is golden, 7 to 10 minutes. Transfer to a food processor and let cool before adding the shallots, garlic, and ginger. Process until you have a fine paste.

2. To make the curry: Heat the vegetable oil in a large pot over medium heat. Add the coconut paste, ground spices, and lemongrass and cook, stirring very regularly, until fragrant. Add the crab pieces and mix well with the sauce. Add the coconut cream and bring to a boil. Add the pineapple and salt to taste, then reduce the heat to low and simmer for about 10 minutes, or until a little oil rises to the surface. Taste and adjust the seasoning if necessary. Serve hot.

INDONESIAN FISH CURRY
GULAI

Indonesian chilies, known as *lombok*, have a mild heat and can be used in abundance to make the various sambals and chili pastes essential to Indonesian food. Those available in the West are either mild or too fiery. Use the mild ones with one or two fiery chilies to re-create the mild heat so typical of Indonesian chili pastes. You can also buy excellent Indonesian ready-made pastes to use in curries and other dishes. Serve this curry with plain rice or Indonesian Yellow Rice (page 257) and shrimp crackers.

SERVES 4 TO 6

2¼ pounds (1 kg) tilapia or other similar fish, cut into steaks or big chunks
Juice of 1 lemon
Sea salt

FOR THE CHILI PASTE
5 mild fresh red chilies
1 bird's eye chili

3 small shallots, peeled
5 cloves garlic, peeled
1 teaspoon ground turmeric
½ teaspoon shrimp paste (terasi)
1 inch (2.5 cm) fresh ginger, peeled
1 inch (2.5 cm) fresh turmeric, peeled

FOR THE CURRY
3 tablespoons vegetable oil
2 bay leaves
1 stalk fresh lemongrass, halved lengthwise and smashed
1½ cups plus 2 tablespoons (400 ml) coconut cream

2 teaspoons seedless tamarind paste, diluted with 2 tablespoons water
Sea salt

Vegetable oil, for pan-frying the fish

1. Pat the fish dry with paper towels, then rub it with the lemon juice and a little salt.

2. To make the chili paste: Put all the ingredients for the chili paste in a food processor (see Note) and process until you have a fine paste.

3. To make the curry: Heat the 3 tablespoons vegetable oil in a wok or a wide deep pan over medium heat until hot. Add the chili paste and fry, stirring regularly, until fragrant. Add the bay leaves and lemongrass and stir for a minute or so. Add the coconut cream, tamarind water, and season with salt to taste. Let bubble gently until a little oil rises to the surface, 10 to 15 minutes.

4. Meanwhile, place a large skillet over medium heat, pour in enough oil to cover the bottom, and heat until the oil is hot. Working in batches, slide the fish into the pan and sear on both sides until crisp and golden, 2 to 3 minutes on each side. Transfer to a plate. In between batches, wipe the pan clean and add more oil.

5. Add the pan-fried fish to the sauce and let simmer for 10 minutes. Serve hot.

NOTE: *Indonesian cooks use a shallow mortar with a horizontal pestle to grind the ingredients for the chili paste rather than beat down on them, but many also use a food processor.*

FISH KIBBEH

KIBBET SAMAK

North Lebanon is home to the Sunnis whereas most of the Shias hail from the southern part of the country, and this fish kibbeh is a Sunni northern specialty that is not often seen in other regions. You can prepare it in one large pie, as it is done traditionally, or you can shape it into 4 to 6 smaller pies depending on how large you want your individual portions to be.   SERVES 4

FOR THE STUFFING
⅓ cup (80 ml) extra-virgin olive oil
2 medium onions (11 ounces/300 g total), halved and cut into thin wedges
⅓ cup (50 g) pine nuts

¼ teaspoon finely ground black pepper
Sea salt

FOR THE KIBBEH
¼ bunch cilantro (2 ounces/50 g), most of the bottom stems discarded

1 pound 2 ounces (500 g) skinless whitefish fillets
1 medium onion (5 ounces/150 g), peeled and quartered
Grated zest of ½ unwaxed orange or lemon

½ teaspoon ground cinnamon
¼ teaspoon finely ground black pepper
Sea salt
¾ cup (150 g) fine bulgur

TO FINISH
Extra-virgin olive oil

1. To make the stuffing: Put the oil, sliced onions, and pine nuts in a medium skillet and place over medium heat. Sauté, stirring regularly, until the onion is soft and golden and the pine nuts have colored slightly, 5 to 7 minutes. Season with the pepper and salt to taste and mix well.

2. To make the kibbeh: Put the cilantro, fish, and quartered onion in a food processor and process until you have a somewhat smooth mixture. Transfer to a large mixing bowl. Add the citrus zest, cinnamon, pepper, and salt to taste.

3. Rinse the bulgur under cold water and drain well. Add to the fish. Using your hands, mix until you have a smooth mixture. Pinch off a piece, pan-fry it to taste, and adjust the seasoning if necessary.

4. Preheat the oven to 350°F (180°C). Grease a 10-inch (25 cm) round baking dish with a little olive oil.

5. Divide the fish kibbeh into two equal portions. Layer and decorate the kibbeh as per steps 6, 7, and 8 of Kibbeh bil-Saniyeh (page 130). Drizzle a little olive oil over the top and bake for 15 to 20 minutes, or until done to your liking. Serve hot or warm.

FISH in TAHINI SAUCE

SAMAK BIL-TAHINI

LEBANON

My grandmother made the ultimate *samak bil-tahini*. She used whole fish and cooked the fish in the sauce long enough for it to absorb its flavor. But as much as I loved her recipe, I use fish fillets or steaks so as not to worry about picking out the bones. And I often use black cod, which is not only unorthodox, but also extravagant. Still, it works brilliantly with the sauce (a simpler, milder version than the sauce for Spicy Baked Fish in a Tahini, Herb, and Nut Sauce, page 316). If you find black cod too expensive, use sea bream fillets or any other white saltwater fish, although pike also works well here. And unlike my grandmother, I cook my fish separately so as not to overcook it, slipping the cooked fillets into the sauce at the very last minute. You could flake the fish into the sauce, which is what some Lebanese cooks do, in which case the dish is known as *tajen*, from the word *tajine*.

SERVES 4 TO 6

½ cup (125 ml) tahini
2 cloves garlic, minced to a fine paste
Juice of 1½ lemons, or to taste
4 tablespoons extra-virgin olive oil
1 pound (450 g) whitefish fillets, cut into 4 or 6 pieces
3 medium onions (1 pound/450 g total), halved lengthwise and cut into thin wedges
1 teaspoon ground cumin
Sea salt
Finely ground black pepper
2 tablespoons pine nuts, toasted

1. Put the tahini in a medium bowl. Add the garlic, then slowly add the lemon juice, stirring all the time—at first you will notice the tahini becoming quite thick despite the fact you are adding liquid, but do not worry, it will thin out as you add more liquid. Gradually add ¾ cup (180 ml) water, still stirring, until you have a thin creamy sauce.

2. Heat 1 tablespoon of the olive oil in a large nonstick skillet over medium-high heat until hot. Slide the fish pieces into the pan, skin side down, and cook for 2 to 3 minutes, until the skin is crisp and golden. Turn the fish over and cook for another minute or so, until it is just done. Remove to a plate and wipe the pan clean.

3. Add the remaining 3 tablespoons oil to the pan. Add the onions and cook, stirring regularly, until soft and golden, 5 to 7 minutes. Add the tahini sauce. Season with the cumin and salt and pepper to taste. Mix well. Let bubble for 3 to 5 minutes, stirring every now and then, until you see a little oil rising to the surface.

4. Take the sauce off the heat and slide the fish fillets into it. Gently shake the pan back and forth to coat the fish with the sauce. Taste and adjust the seasoning if necessary. Remove to platter and serve warm or at room temperature garnished with the toasted pine nuts.

FISH YASSA

NIGERIA

Here is a lovely Nigerian recipe for a spicy marinade that is used to marinate fish, then cooked and served as a sauce to go with either grilled or fried fish.

SERVES 4 TO 6

2¼ pounds (1 kg) whitefish steaks
Sea salt and finely ground black pepper

FOR THE MARINADE
Juice of 2 lemons
½ cup (125 ml) vegetable oil
4 cloves garlic, minced to a fine paste
1 tablespoon Dijon mustard
½ teaspoon paprika
½ teaspoon red pepper flakes, plus more for serving
6 medium onions (2 pounds/900 g total), halved lengthwise and cut into thin wedges

White rice, for serving
Lemon wedges, for serving

1. Pat the fish steaks dry with paper towels and rub with a little salt. Grind a little pepper over the steaks and let sit while you prepare the marinade.

2. To make the marinade: Whisk the lemon juice, oil, garlic, mustard, paprika, and pepper flakes together in a large bowl. Add the sliced onions and mix well.

3. Add the fish to the marinade and mix well to coat the fish all over with the marinade. Let marinate, covered, for at least 2 hours, preferably longer, in the refrigerator.

4. Remove the fish from the marinade and place on a large platter. Transfer the marinade to a large deep skillet and place over low heat. Cook, stirring regularly, for 30 to 45 minutes, until the onion is completely softened and caramelized to a golden brown color. Add ¼ cup (60 ml) water halfway through so that the onion softens completely before starting to caramelize.

5. Now you have three choices as to how to cook the fish steaks: grilled or broiled—in which case prepare a charcoal fire in an outdoor grill or preheat the broiler to high—or pan-fried. Whichever method you use, cook the fish until done to your liking.

6. Slip the cooked fish into the skillet of marinade and cook for a couple of minutes to allow the fish to absorb the flavor of the onion. Serve hot with plain rice, together with lemon wedges and more pepper flakes for those who want their fish spicier.

INDONESIAN FRIED FISH

PECEL LELE

Indonesia is a collection of more than seventeen thousand islands. Wherever you go you will not be far from the water. When I traveled there, I visited several islands, with the most enchanting being Banda Neira, once a rich Dutch nutmeg outpost. There, I stayed in Tanya Alwi's gorgeous if somewhat crumbling hotel, right on the water. Sadly, I spent only one night, and that evening there was no fish on the menu because Tanya had organized a goat feast for me (page 94). But my first meal in Indonesia, straight off the plane, was at a wonderful fish restaurant in Jakarta. I can't remember if I had the fried fish (for which I give a recipe below) that night, but I remember that one of my favorite dishes that evening was pomfret cooked in a delectable spicy sauce with stinky beans, which look like green colored almonds and taste a bit like fresh almonds. It was a totally new ingredient to me, like so many others on that trip. Unfortunately, you cannot find it easily abroad so I am not giving a recipe for that fish dish, whereas you can make the one below easily without having to source any special ingredients.

SERVES 4

FOR THE FRIED FISH
4 whole red snappers
   (10½ ounces/
   300 g each), gutted and
   rinsed, slashed across
   on the diagonal on both
   sides at two or three
   intervals
Juice of ½ lemon, or to
   taste
1 tablespoon ground
   coriander

2 cloves garlic, minced to
   a fine paste
Sea salt

**FOR THE CHILI
SAMBAL**
Vegetable oil, for frying
2 medium tomatoes
   (7 ounces/200 g total),
   quartered
1 medium red bell pepper,
   quartered
3 mild red chilies,
   trimmed but not
   seeded

1 bird's eye chili, seeded
   and quartered
4 cloves garlic
10 small shallots
   (7 ounces/200 g total),
   halved
6 blanched almonds
1 inch (2.5 cm) fresh
   turmeric, minced to a
   fine paste
Juice of ½ lemon, or to
   taste
Sea salt

TO FINISH
Vegetable oil, for frying
2 tomatoes, thinly sliced
   crosswise
Cucumber, thinly sliced
Onion, sliced thinly into
   rings
Leaves from a few sprigs
   basil
White rice or Indonesian
   Fried Rice (page 258),
   for serving

1. To prepare the fish: Pat the snapper dry with paper towels. Then mix the lemon juice, coriander, garlic, and salt to taste. Rub the marinade into the fish. Let sit while you prepare the sambal.

2. To make the chili sambal: Put a large skillet or wok over medium heat. Drizzle a little oil over the bottom and when the oil is hot, add the tomatoes, bell pepper, chilies, garlic, shallots, and almonds. Stir the ingredients until softened and slightly colored, 5 to 7 minutes. Transfer to a food processor. Add the turmeric, lemon juice, and salt to taste and process until almost completely pulverized.

3. To finish: Wipe the pan clean, put 3 tablespoons oil in it, and return to medium heat. Pour the sambal into the pan and let it bubble until it thickens slightly, stirring regularly, 7 to 10 minutes. Take off the heat.

4. Set a wire rack in a rimmed baking sheet. Pour 2 inches (5 cm) oil into a large deep skillet and heat over medium heat until hot—test by dropping a piece of bread in it; if the oil immediately bubbles around the bread, it is ready. Slide the fish into the oil and fry 3 to 5 minutes on each side, until the skin is crisp and the flesh is just cooked. Remove to the wire rack to drain off any excess oil.

5. To serve, alternate the slices of tomato, cucumber, and onion all around the edge of a serving platter. Arrange the fried fish in the center and sprinkle basil leaves over the salad garnish. Serve immediately with the sambal and white rice or fried rice.

ALGERIAN FISH CAKES

OJEIJAT AL-HÛT

I wonder if these fish cakes are not a remnant from Algeria's French colonial days. They are remarkably plain for an Algerian recipe. Regardless, they are delicious, and make a lovely light meal served with a green salad. They are also great for picnics.

SERVES 4

10½ ounces (300 g) potatoes, peeled and cut into medium chunks

Sea salt

14 ounces (400 g) whitefish fillets

¼ lemon

6 tablespoons (90 g) unsalted butter, plus more for frying the fish cakes

3 medium onions (1 pound/450 g total), grated on the fine side of a grater

A few sprigs flat-leaf parsley, most of the bottom stems discarded, finely chopped

3 organic eggs, beaten

1 teaspoon red pepper flakes

Finely ground black pepper

Vegetable oil, for shallow-frying

All-purpose flour, for dredging

1. Put the potatoes in a medium pot and add water to cover by 2 inches (5 cm). Bring to a boil over medium heat, add 1 tablespoon salt, and cook for 20 to 25 minutes, or until completely tender but not falling apart. Drain and mash. Keep covered with a clean kitchen towel.

2. Put the fish and the lemon in a small pot. Add water to cover and bring to a boil over medium heat. Add 1 tablespoon salt and let the water bubble gently for about 3 minutes, or until the skin comes off easily and the fish flakes easily. Remove the fish from the water and discard the skin. Flake the fish and place the flakes on a plate. Drain off any excess liquid from the plate.

3. Meanwhile, melt 3 tablespoons of the butter in a large skillet over medium heat. Add the grated onion and cook, stirring very often, until lightly golden, 4 to 5 minutes. Be careful not to let the onion burn or it will be bitter. Add the parsley and stir for a few seconds more.

4. Put the mashed potatoes in a medium pot and add the remaining 3 tablespoons butter. Place over medium heat and stir the mash until the butter has melted and is fully incorporated. Transfer to a large mixing bowl. Add the flaked fish, the fried onion and parsley, beaten eggs, pepper flakes, and salt and pepper to taste. Mix well. Shape the fish cakes into disks 2½ inches (6 cm) across by 1¼ inches (3 cm) thick and place on a platter.

5. Set a fine-mesh wire rack in a rimmed baking sheet. Place a large skillet over medium heat and pour in enough vegetable oil to cover the bottom. Put some flour in a shallow bowl and season with salt and pepper to taste. When the oil is hot, dip the fish cakes into the seasoned flour on both sides. Shake off the excess flour and slip into the hot oil. Fry 2 to 3 minutes on each side, until golden. If your pan is not large enough to cook all the cakes at once, work in batches, wiping the pan clean and adding more oil in between each one. Remove the cakes to the wire rack to drain off any excess oil. Serve hot.

EGYPTIAN FERMENTED FISH

FESIKH

EGYPT

Fesikh or *feseekh* is a fermented fish that is beloved by Egyptians, although not by most other people, who find it too pungent. I rather like it, but in small quantities. *Fesikh* is served during the Sham-El-Nessim festival, a spring celebration that dates back to the time of the Pharaohs. It is prepared by a specialist known as a *fasakhani* who uses grey mullet—*fesikh* can be toxic if not prepared and stored properly. People eat it with *aysh baladi* (thick whole wheat pita), diced onions, and lemon juice. I am not giving a recipe for how to make it here as it is not so easy (nor so safe) to prepare if you are not familiar with the process. But it is worth knowing about, and if you can source it, try it. The larger the fish, the better the *fesikh* because of the fat content. It is made by first soaking the fish to get rid of all traces of blood. Then it is put to dry in the sun or in the sand, before being salted and fermented.

IRANIAN/ARABIAN FISH SAUCE

MEHYAWA OR MAHYAWA

IRAN | UNITED ARAB EMIRATES | BAHRAIN

Mehyawa—a fish sauce that is made by seasoning salted anchovies with various spices such as cumin, coriander, and cumin seeds to achieve a rather thick dark brown sauce and then fermenting them—originally comes from Iran. It was brought to the Arabian Gulf by the Arab Huwala and Ajam communities who migrated there. It is an acquired taste for those not familiar with it, just like Asian fermented fish sauces. In the Gulf, people have it spread over Regag (page 16) or over flatbread before laying a fried egg on top. It is very salty and a little goes a long way, but it is well worth having if you can find a good source for it. Gulf Arabs seem to favor that which is made in Bahrain. According to Charles Perry, the foremost expert on Arab medieval cookery, the name looks like the Persian word for fish with a suffix that usually means a kind of stew, such as the *mastawa* of Uzbekistan and the *goshtaba* of Kashmir.

FRIED MUSSEL BROCHETTES

MIDYE TAVA

TURKEY

Mussels are one of Turkey's most typical street foods. You can buy them stuffed (see page 340), often beautifully arranged over metal trays lined with old newspaper, or you can have them fried, stuffed in a fat baguette with tarator drizzled all over them. The vendor threads the mussels on wooden skewers then dips them in water, then flour for what seems like a hundred times to build up a nice coat before dropping them into a huge pan full of hot oil. Fresh anchovies are also prepared and fried in the same way.

You need a very large skillet to fry skewers, so if you don't have one, simply fry the mussels without threading them on skewers (see Note). I am not so keen on dipping the mussels in water, then flour, so instead I use a light batter to have more delicate mussel fritters. The batter recipe I give here comes from Bill Briwa, who worked at the French Laundry before joining the teaching staff of the CIA in St. Helena, Napa, California. Serve with a salad of your choice and good bread.

SERVES 4 TO 6

FOR THE BATTER
1½ cups (175 g)
   unbleached all-purpose
   flour
Just under ⅓ cup (50 g)
   cornstarch
½ tablespoon baking
   soda
1 tablespoon salt
1¼ cups (310 ml)
   sparkling water

TO FINISH
45 large mussels,
   steamed and shucked
   (or 36 fresh anchovies)
Vegetable oil, for deep-
   frying
Salt
Turkish Tarator (page
   337)
Lemon wedges

1. To make the batter: Whisk together the flour, cornstarch, bakng soda, and salt in a bowl wide enough to accommodate a skewer. Whisk in the sparkling water until the mixture is smooth.

2. Thread the mussels onto 8 or 12 medium (7 inch/17.5 cm) bamboo skewers—2 skewers per person.

3. Set a fine-mesh wire rack in a rimmed baking sheet. Pour 2 inches (5 cm) vegetable oil into a large skillet (see Note) and heat over medium heat until hot (if you drop a piece of bread in the oil, the oil should immediately bubble around it).

4. Drop a few skewers in the batter. Stir them to coat evenly, then remove one by one, wait a little for the excess batter to slip off, and drop into the hot oil. Fry for 30 seconds or so on each side, or until golden all over. Remove with tongs to the wire rack to drain off the excess oil. Sprinkle with more salt if necessary. Skim the oil clean in between each batch so as not to have burning bits of batter clinging to the fritters. Serve hot with tarator sauce and lemon wedges.

NOTE: *If your pan is not large enough for the skewers, drop individual mussels in the batter. Stir them to coat evenly, then remove them one by one, wait a little for the excess batter to slip off, and drop into the hot oil. Fry in the same way as the skewers. Remove with a slotted spoon to the wire rack and sprinkle with more salt if necessary.*

SHRIMP BROCHETTES

SHRIMP MISHKAKI

Mishkaki is the name given to grilled meat or fish in Oman and Zanzibar, which was once part of the Sultanate of Oman. The marinade for these shrimp brochettes can also be used for fish or meat. The tamarind gives the shrimp a lovely tart flavor and the tomato moistens them as they grill. Serve with good flatbread and a salad of your choice or plain rice.   SERVES 4 TO 6

½ teaspoon seedless tamarind paste, diluted with 2 tablespoons water

2 cloves garlic, minced to a fine paste

1 inch (2.5 cm) fresh ginger, peeled and minced to a fine paste

1 large tomato (7 ounces/200 g), pureed in a food processor

2 tablespoons vegetable oil

Sea salt and finely ground black pepper

2¼ pounds (1 kg) large shrimp, peeled

1. Put the tamarind paste, garlic, ginger, pureed tomato, oil, and salt and pepper to taste in a large bowl. Mix well, then add the shrimp and mix again. Let marinate for 2 hours at least, preferably longer, in the refrigerator.

2. Prepare a charcoal fire in an outdoor grill or preheat the broiler to high.

3. Thread the shrimp onto 8 or 12 skewers (2 skewers per person). Grill or broil for 2 to 3 minutes on each side depending on how large the shrimp are and how well cooked you like them. I like mine slightly underdone. Serve hot.

SWORDFISH BROCHETTES

QOTBANE DEL HOOT

In Morocco, cooks cut both meat and fish for brochettes in very small pieces, but you can cut the swordfish to the size you prefer. Just remember to increase the cooking time accordingly. You can replace the swordfish with monkfish, tuna, or any other dense-fleshed fish. Marinating and grilling fish the Moroccan way makes for delicious quick summer meals and of course, the brochettes will be even more delectable if grilled over a charcoal fire. Serve with good bread and a salad of your choice.

SERVES 4 TO 6

¼ bunch flat-leaf parsley (2 ounces/50 g), most of the bottom stems discarded, finely chopped

2 cloves garlic, minced to a fine paste

2 teaspoons ground cumin

2 teaspoons paprika

¼ teaspoon red pepper flakes

Sea salt

1 pound 10 ounces (750 g) swordfish, cut into 1-inch (2.5 cm) cubes

1. In a bowl large enough to hold the fish, mix the parsley, garlic, cumin, paprika, pepper flakes, and salt to taste. Add the fish and mix well. Let marinate for at least 2 hours, preferably longer, in the refrigerator.

2. Prepare a charcoal fire in an outdoor grill or preheat the broiler to high.

3. Thread the pieces of fish onto 8 or 12 long skewers (2 skewers per person). Grill or broil the brochettes as near the heat as you can for 2 to 3 minutes on each side, or until the fish is done to your liking. Don't cook it too long or it will become rubbery. Serve hot.

MACKEREL TARATOR

USKUMRU BALIGI TARATORU

Here, a Turkish-style tarator (which is made with nuts) is spooned over poached mackerel. The same sauce is also served with fried mussels or anchovies (see Fried Mussel Brochettes, page 332). Serve with good bread.

SERVES 4

2 medium mackerel
  (about 2¼ pounds/
  1 kg in total)
Sea salt
1 bay leaf
2 lemon wedges
Turkish Tarator (recipe
  follows)
A few sprigs flat-leaf
  parsley, most of the
  stems discarded, finely
  chopped
1 teaspoon pul biber

1. Pat the fish dry with paper towels before rubbing them with salt inside and out. Put them in a fish poacher. Add the bay leaf and lemon wedges and add water to barely cover. Bring to a boil over medium heat. Turn the heat off as soon as the water has come to a boil. Let the fish sit in the hot water for 10 minutes. Then, gently lift them out of the water. Discard the heads and skin and if you can manage it, fillet the fish in 4 whole pieces. If not, don't worry. Just take off the bone and transfer to a serving dish. Make sure you don't leave bones in the fish.

2. Spread the tarator over the fish. Sprinkle the chopped parsley all over, then the pul biber. Serve warm or at room temperature. Or, if you want to serve it later, cover with plastic wrap and refrigerate. Simply remember to take it out of the refrigerator about an hour before serving.

TURKISH TARATOR

Tarator is a sauce or a dip usually served with fish or seafood, but I sometimes like to serve it as a dip with crudités. It differs substantially depending on whether you have it in Lebanon and Syria, where it is made with tahini, or in Turkey where it is made with nuts. There is actually a Lebanese tarator that is made with pine nuts and served with fish, but it is rare to find it nowadays, I guess because pine nuts have become so expensive.

If you have the patience and energy, make this dip by pounding the ingredients in a large mortar with a pestle. The texture will be finer.

1½ cups (225 g) hazelnuts or walnuts, soaked for 1 hour in lots of boiling water

3 to 4 slices (use more for a thicker tarator) soft white bread, crusts discarded

2 large cloves garlic, peeled

⅔ cup (160 ml) extra-virgin olive oil

Juice of 1½ lemons, or to taste

Sea salt

Drain the nuts and put in a food processor together with the bread, garlic, and 1 teaspoon water. Blend until smooth, then start drizzling in the olive oil while still processing. When the oil is completely absorbed, add the lemon juice and salt to taste. Taste and adjust the seasoning if necessary. Transfer to a medium bowl and serve with the Fried Mussel Brochettes (page 332) or spoon over the Mackerel Tarator (opposite page). You can also keep it in the refrigerator, stored in a hermetically sealed container, for a couple of days. You may need to add a little oil or liquid before serving in case it becomes too thick.

PICKLED SWORDFISH

KILIC BALIGI TURSUSU

Most Muslim coastal countries have their own way of preserving fish, with drying being the most common; but Turks also pickle fish. When treated this way, the fish keeps for only a couple of weeks in the refrigerator. And if left at room temperature, it will last for only 2 or 3 days. This recipe goes back to Ottoman times when it was served as part of a mezze spread. SERVES 6 TO 8

Good pinch of saffron threads

2½ cups (625 ml) apple cider vinegar

3 swordfish steaks (about ½ pound/225 g each)

Sea salt

⅓ cup (80 ml) extra-virgin olive oil

1 teaspoon ground cardamom

1 teaspoon ground cloves

1 tablespoon dried currants

1 tablespoon pine nuts

1 tablespoon black peppercorns

6 cloves garlic, quarterered lengthwise

A couple of handfuls fresh or dried bay leaves, and if possible (optional) a few bitter orange or lemon leaves

2 tablespoons honey

1. Put the saffron to steep in ½ cup (125 ml) of the vinegar.

2. Pat the fish steaks dry with paper towels, then rub with a little salt. Heat the olive oil in a large skillet over medium heat until hot. Slip the swordfish into the pan and fry 3 to 4 minutes on each side, until lightly golden. Remove to a plate.

3. Mix the ground cardamom and cloves in a small bowl. Mix the currants, pine nuts, and peppercorns in another small bowl. Have the garlic at hand, ready to use.

4. Line an 8-inch (20 cm) round dish that is 4 inches (10 cm) deep with a few bay leaves and a couple citrus leaves if you are using them. Place a swordfish steak on the leaves. Sprinkle with one-third of the cardamom/clove mixture. Scatter one-third of the currant/pine nuts/peppercorn mixture and one-third of the cut garlic. Repeat the layering two more times. Cover with a final layer of leaves.

5. Pour the remaining 2 cups (500 ml) vinegar into a small saucepan. Add the honey and bring to a boil over medium heat. Let bubble for a couple of minutes, then take off the heat. Let cool before adding the saffron vinegar. Mix the pickling solution well.

6. Put the fish dish on a large rimmed plate to catch the pickling solution that will spill over as you weight the fish. Pour the pickling solution over the fish, being careful not to displace the bay leaves. Invert a plate over the fish and place a weight on the plate. The excess vinegar will overflow and this is how it should be. Refrigerate or place in a cool place. The fish will be ready after 2 or 3 days, and it will last for up to 10 days if kept in an airtight container in a cool place or the refrigerator. Serve as part of a mezze spread.

FISH in TAMARIND SAUCE
SAMAK BIL HUMMAR

SAUDI ARABIA

This is an interesting and simple Saudi sweet and sour sauce to serve with plain roasted or poached fish. I usually roast the fish in the oven, the way they do in Saudi Arabia, but you can also poach it, although make sure you pat it very dry before serving it with the sauce. And you can also cook it on an outdoor grill or in a grill pan.   SERVES 6

4 ounces (120 g) seedless tamarind paste, soaked for 1 hour in 2 cups (500 ml) boiling water

¼ cup (60 ml) extra-virgin olive oil, plus more for brushing

4 medium onions (1 pound 5 ounces/ 600 g total), very finely chopped

6 cloves garlic, minced to a fine paste

2 medium tomatoes (about 7 ounces/ 200 g total), seeded and finely diced

1 teaspoon ground coriander

½ teaspoon ground cumin

¼ teaspoon ground cinnamon

Sea salt and finely ground black pepper

6 whitefish fillets (3 pounds 5 ounces/ 1.5 kg total)

White rice, for serving

Saudi "Salsa" (page 429), for serving

1. Preheat the oven to 400°F (200°C).

2. Mash the tamarind paste into the soaking water, then strain through a sieve set over a medium bowl to catch the juice, pushing on the pulp to extract as much flavor as you can. Set aside.

3. Heat the oil in a large skillet over medium heat. Add the onions and sauté, stirring regularly, until golden, about 5 minutes. Add the garlic and stir for a minute or so before adding half the tomatoes, the coriander, cumin, cinnamon, salt to taste, and 1 teaspoon pepper. Cook for a few minutes, until the tomatoes have softened.

4. Add the tamarind juice and cook for 20 minutes, stirring regularly, until the sauce has thickened. Add a little water (up to 1 cup/250 ml) if the sauce is becoming too dry.

5. Meanwhile, oil a baking sheet and put the fish, skin side down, on it. Brush the fish with oil and season with salt and pepper to taste. Roast for 10 to 15 minutes, or until the fish is done to your liking.

6. Gently transfer the fish to a serving platter. Spoon the sauce over the fish but without completely covering it. Garnish with the remaining diced tomatoes. Serve hot with the rice and salsa.

STUFFED MUSSELS

MIDYE DOLMASI

The first time I tried these stuffed mussels was when I spotted them beautifully displayed by a street vendor near the Pera Palace hotel in Istanbul where I was staying. I was intrigued. I had never had them before. They were a revelation—exquisite and completely unexpected as street food given how much time they take to prepare, not to mention how sophisticated the recipe is. And yet you find them sold cheaply on the street, usually by older men who I suspect prepare them at home, or perhaps have their wives make them while they take care of selling them. I actually never found out as I don't speak Turkish and I have yet to find a stuffed mussel vendor who speaks another language! The mussels you buy in Turkey are very large and work perfectly for stuffing. They need to be stuffed raw so that the rice becomes enclosed on both sides by the flesh of the mussel, but opening them takes some real skill, and it is important to know where to insert the knife, which I explain below, so that you immediately cut into the muscle that opens and closes the shell.

SERVES 4

FOR THE STUFFING
¼ cup (60 ml) extra-virgin olive oil
2 small onions (7 ounces/200 g), finely chopped
1 tablespoon pine nuts
½ cup (100 g) Calasparra rice or other short-grained rice, soaked in warm water for 30 minutes

1 tablespoon golden raisins
1½ tablespoons tomato paste
¼ teaspoon ground allspice
¼ teaspoon ground cinnamon
¼ teaspoon paprika
⅛ teaspoon cayenne pepper

⅛ teaspoon ground cloves
2 to 3 sprigs flat-leaf parsley, most of the bottom stems discarded, finely chopped
2 to 3 sprigs dill, bottom stems discarded, finely chopped
Sea salt and finely ground black pepper

FOR THE MUSSELS
About 40 large mussels; in Turkey they use mussels about 2 inches (5 cm) long (see Note)
2 lemons, cut into wedges

1. To prepare the stuffing: Heat the oil in a saucepan over medium heat. Add the onions and pine nuts and cook, stirring occasionally, until lightly golden, 5 to 7 minutes. Drain the rice and add to the pan. Mix in the raisins, tomato paste, ground spices, fresh herbs, and salt and pepper to taste. Add 1 cup (250 ml) water and bring to a boil. Reduce the heat to low, cover, and simmer for 8 to 10 minutes, or until the water is fully absorbed and the rice is just barely tender. Take off the heat. Wrap the lid with a kitchen towel and replace over the pan. Let cool.

2. To prepare the mussels: Pull out and discard the beards (if there are any) and rinse the mussels under cold water—do not put them in a bowl to soak or else they will die. Lay a mussel on a kitchen towel on your work surface and insert the tip of a small but solid sharp knife in between the shells at the nerve end, which is at the slanted hinged end of the mussel. Slide the knife downward and all around the shell until you cut into the muscle. This will allow you to open the mussel easily while keeping the two halves attached. Open the rest of the mussels the same way, making sure you do not rush or you will either break the shells or hurt yourself with the knife.

3. Stir the stuffing with a fork to fluff it up, then fill each mussel with 1 teaspoon or more of it, depending on how large they are. Gently close them, wiping away any grains of rice sticking out, and arrange in 2 or 3 layers in a flat steamer basket. Weight down the stuffed mussels with a plate and steam for 20 to 25 minutes, until the mussels are cooked and the rice stuffing is tender. Pull the steamer basket out of the steamer and let the mussels cool before serving at room temperature with wedges of lemon to squeeze onto the stuffing. If you have any rice stuffing left over, add a little water and finish cooking it on the stove. Serve on the side.

NOTE: *If you can't find large mussels, change the dish to a pilaf. Prepare twice the amount of rice stuffing and cook it completely. Then steam the mussels. Take them off shell, and place them half inside the cooked rice here and there.*

SARDINES CHERMOULA
HÜT BEL CHERMOULA

MOROCCO

Sardines chermoula are the quintessential street food in Morocco, even in the parts that are far from the sea where people don't usually eat fish. These are a staple of almost every street food vendor. I usually ask my fishmonger to butterfly the sardines and if your fishmonger is good, he will do it for you. Serve with good bread and the salad of your choice. SERVES 4 TO 6

2¼ pounds (1 kg) fresh sardines, butterflied
Chermoula (recipe follows)
Unbleached all-purpose flour, for dredging
Sea salt and finely ground black pepper
Vegetable oil, for frying

1. Pat the sardines dry with paper towels. Lay them skin side down on your work surface, and spread a little chermoula over half of the sardines. Then lay the remaining sardines over those spread with chermoula, skin side up, as if you were making sandwiches with the chermoula as the filling. Transfer the sardines to a large platter and let them sit for at least 2 hours, preferably longer, in the refrigerator to absorb the flavors of the chermoula.

2. Put enough flour to dredge the sardines in a soup plate or a wide shallow bowl and season with a little salt and pepper. Dip each sardine "sandwich" into the flour on both sides. Place on a plate.

3. Set a fine-mesh wire rack in a rimmed baking sheet. Pour 2 inches (5 cm) vegetable oil into a large skillet and heat over medium heat until hot (if you drop a piece of bread in the oil, the oil should immediately bubble around it). Working in batches, slip in as many sardines as will fit comfortably in the pan and fry for 1 to 2 minutes on each side, or until crisp and golden. Remove with a slotted spoon to the rack to drain off excess oil. Serve hot, warm, or at room temperature.

CHERMOULA

MAKES ABOUT 1 CUP (250 ML)

5 cloves garlic, minced to a fine paste
1 small onion (3½ ounces/100 g), grated on the fine side of a grater

½ bunch cilantro (3½ ounces/100 g), most of the bottom stems discarded, finely chopped

1 teaspoon ground cumin
½ teaspoon paprika
¼ teaspoon red pepper flakes

¼ cup (60 ml) extra-virgin olive oil
Juice of 2 lemons, or to taste
Sea salt, to taste

Put all the ingredients in a medium bowl and mix well. Taste and adjust the seasoning if necessary. You can store this, covered, in the refrigerator for a day.

FISH STEWED in SPICY CORIANDER

SAMKEH HARRAH MATBOOKHAH

This is a homely Lebanese way of preparing fish that is typical in Sunni coastal communities. Most Arabs tend to overcook both meat and fish, so I have changed the traditional recipe slightly to avoid it. I also use the unorthodox and rather extravagant black cod to prepare this dish, but you can replace it with sea bream or sea bass, which is what Lebanese cooks use.   SERVES 4

2¼ pounds (1 kg) whitefish fillets or steaks
Sea salt
Vegetable oil, for shallow-frying
Unbleached all-purpose flour, for dredging
Finely ground black pepper
½ cup (125 ml) extra-virgin olive oil
4 medium onions (1 pound 5 ounces/ 600 g total), finely chopped
8 cloves garlic, minced to a fine paste
2 bunches cilantro (14 ounces/400 g), most of the bottom stems discarded, finely chopped
1 teaspoon ground cumin
½ teaspoon ground coriander
½ teaspoon Aleppo pepper, or to taste
1 cup (250 ml) lemon juice, or to taste

1. Pat the fish pieces dry with paper towels and lightly rub with salt. Let sit for 30 minutes to soak up the salt.

2. Set a fine-mesh rack in a rimmed baking sheet. Place a large nonstick skillet over medium heat and pour in enough vegetable oil to cover the bottom. Heat over medium heat until the oil is hot (if you drop a piece of bread in the oil, the oil should immediately bubble around it). Put enough flour to dredge the fish in a soup plate or a wide shallow bowl and season with salt and pepper to taste. Dip the fish pieces into the flour on both sides to lightly coat them, shaking off any excess flour. Working in batches, put in as many fish pieces as can fit comfortably in the pan, skin side down, and fry for 1 minute on each side to set the coating and seal the fish. In between batches, wipe the pan clean and add more oil. Remove with a slotted spoon and place on the rack to drain any excess oil.

3. Heat the olive oil in a wide, deep sauté pan over medium heat. Add the onions and sauté, stirring regularly, until soft and golden, about 5 minutes. Add the garlic and sauté for a minute or so. Add the cilantro, cumin, coriander, and Aleppo pepper and stir for another minute, or until the cilantro is wilted. Add the lemon juice and salt and pepper to taste and bring to a boil. Let bubble for 5 minutes.

4. Reduce the heat to medium-low and slip the fried fish into the lemony cilantro sauce. Cover and let simmer for 3 to 5 more minutes, or until the fish is done to your liking and the sauce has thickened. Serve warm or at room temperature.

ARABIAN SPICED FRIED FISH

SAMAK MEQLI

ARABIAN GULF

This is a typical recipe from the Arabian Gulf where many people cannot conceive of lunch without fish on the table. Often, restaurants will have both fish and meat for diners to choose from. This fried fish is particularly good served with the Sweet-Savory Rice on page 227, as the fish's spicy marinade provides a delectable contrast to the sweetish rice.   SERVES 4

FOR THE MARINADE
3 cloves garlic, minced to a fine paste
½ inch (1 cm) fresh ginger, minced to a fine paste
1 tablespoon b'zar (Arabian Spice Mixture, page 366)

¼ teaspoon ground turmeric
¼ teaspoon finely ground black pepper
Sea salt
Juice of ½ lemon

FOR THE FISH
4 whole sea bream (about 10½ ounces/

300 g each), or 2 Thai snappers (1 pound 3 ounces/550 g each), scaled and gutted, fins removed (but not the heads or tails)
Sea salt
Unbleached all-purpose flour, for dredging

Finely ground black pepper
B'zar (Arabian Spice Mixture, page 366)
Vegetable oil, for shallow-frying

FOR SERVING
Lime or lemon wedges
Sweet-Savory Rice (page 227)

1. To make the marinade: Mix the garlic, ginger, *b'zar*, turmeric, black pepper, a little sea salt, and the lemon juice in a small bowl.

2. To prepare the fish: Pat the fish dry with paper towels, then make 2 or 3 diagonal slashes across the flesh on both sides. Rub the fish with a little salt inside and out and let it sit for 5 minutes.

3. Dividing evenly, rub the marinade all over the fish, inside and out and into the slashes. Put in a dish and let the fish absorb the flavors for 30 minutes, or longer if you have the time.

4. Put a little flour on a plate and season it with a little salt, pepper, and *b'zar*.

5. Set a wire rack in a rimmed baking sheet. Pour about ½ inch (1 cm) oil into a large skillet and heat over medium-high heat until hot (if you drop a piece of bread in the oil, the oil should immediately bubble around it). Working in batches, dip each fish into the seasoned flour on both sides, shaking off the excess, then slide in as many fish as will comfortably fit in the pan and fry for 2 to 3 minutes on each side, or until the skin is crisp and golden and the fish is just cooked through. Remove with a slotted spoon to the wire rack to drain off any excess oil.

6. Serve hot with the lime or lemon wedges and the rice.

ARABIAN "RAVIOLI" with FISH
GABBOOT AL-BOWALIEL

I first tasted this dish in Kuwait. It was prepared with meat, whereas this version, which is common in other parts of the Arabian Gulf, is made with fish. The dumplings for *gabboot* are time consuming to prepare but worth the effort. *Bowaliel* is plural for *baloul*, Arabic for "baby shark," and this dish is named after the fish that is normally used to make it. You can also use *hamour*, another fish typical of the Arabian Gulf, or any other white-fleshed saltwater fish. SERVES 6 TO 8

FOR THE "RAVIOLI" DOUGH
1½ cups (180 g) unbleached all-purpose flour, plus more for kneading and shaping
1 packet (7g/ 2¼ teaspoons) instant (fast-acting) yeast
¼ teaspoon sea salt
1½ teaspoons vegetable oil

FOR THE STUFFING
¼ cup (50 g) dried mung beans, soaked overnight in plenty of cold water
Sea salt
Pinch of saffron threads
2 teaspoons rose water
1 medium onion (5 ounces/150 g), finely chopped
2 teaspoons vegetable oil

1 clove garlic, minced to a fine paste
½ teaspoon ground dried lime
1 small green chili
½ teaspoon b'zar (Arabian Spice Mixture, page 366)
½ teaspoon ground cardamom
A few sprigs cilantro, most of the bottom stems discarded, finely chopped

FOR THE FISH
4 cloves garlic, minced to a fine paste
½ inch (1 cm) fresh ginger, minced to a fine paste
1 tablespoon b'zar (Arabian Spice Mixture, page 366)

Sea salt
Juice of ½ lemon or 1 lime
3 pounds 5 ounces (1.5 kg) thick (2-inch/ 5 cm) fish steaks: cut from baloul (baby shark), hamour, or any white-fleshed saltwater fish, such as grouper or halibut
Vegetable oil, for shallow-frying

FOR THE FISH SAUCE
3 tablespoons vegetable oil
1 medium onion (5 ounces/150 g), finely chopped
2 medium tomatoes (8 ounces/200 g total), finely chopped
1 small green chili, thinly sliced into rings

4 tablespoons tomato paste
4 cups (1 liter) boiling water
1 cinnamon stick
3 pale dried limes, pricked here and there
2 tablespoons seedless tamarind paste, soaked for 1 hour in ½ cup (125 ml) boiling water
1 teaspoon b'zar (Arabian Spice Mixture, page 366)
1 teaspoon ground coriander
1 teaspoon ground cumin
1 teaspoon finely ground black pepper
Sea salt

A few sprigs cilantro, for garnish

1. To make the "ravioli" dough: Mix the flour, yeast, and salt in a large bowl and make a well in the center. Add the oil and ½ cup (125 ml) warm water to the well and gradually bring in the flour, mixing it in until you have a rough dough.

2. Transfer the dough to a lightly floured work surface and knead for 3 minutes. Invert the bowl over the dough and let rest for 15 minutes. Knead the dough for 3 more minutes, then shape into a ball. Cover with a damp kitchen towel and let rest for 30 minutes.

3. To make the stuffing: Drain and rinse the mung beans. Put them in a small pot. Add water to cover and bring to a boil over medium heat. Cook until tender, 25 to 35 minutes. Drain and sprinkle with salt to taste. Put the saffron to steep in the rose water. Put the onion in a small pot and place over medium heat. Stir it constantly until it starts coloring and sticking to the bottom of the pan. Sprinkle it with a little water and continue stirring it until golden. Add the oil (this inverted way of cooking the onion is very traditional and still popular in the Gulf), then add the garlic, ground dried lime, chili, and the drained beans. Add the saffron rose water, *b'zar*, cardamom, and cilantro and mix well. Taste and adjust the seasoning if necessary. Let cool.

4. To prepare the fish: Mix together the garlic, ginger, *b'zar*, salt to taste, and the lemon juice. Measure out 1 teaspoon of the marinade and set aside (for the sauce) and rub the fish inside and out with the remainder. Let sit for 30 minutes.

5. To form the "ravioli," roll out the dough to a thickness of 1/16 inch (1.5 mm), then use a 1½-inch (3.8 cm) round pastry cutter to cut out as many rounds as you can. You should have about 50.

6. Place ½ teaspoon stuffing in the center of each round of dough and fold into a half-round, stretching the dough a little and pressing on the edges to seal them. Line a baking sheet with wax paper. Lightly sprinkle it with flour and arrange the "ravioli" on the sheet.

7. To make the fish sauce: Heat the oil over medium heat in a wide saucepan large enough to take both fish and "ravioli." Add the onion and cook, stirring regularly, until golden, about 5 minutes. Add the reserved 1 teaspoon marinade, tomatoes, and chili. Cover and let bubble for a couple of minutes.

8. Dissolve the tomato paste in the boiling water and add to the pan together with the cinnamon stick and dried limes. Cover the pan and let bubble for 10 minutes.

9. Mash the tamarind paste in the water and strain the liquid, pressing on the pulp to extract as much flavor as you can. Add the tamarind water to the sauce along with the spices and salt to taste. Let bubble gently for about 20 minutes.

10. Meanwhile, fry the marinated fish: Set a wire rack in a rimmed baking sheet. Place a large skillet over medium heat and pour in enough vegetable oil to cover the bottom. When the oil is hot, add the fish and cook 2 minutes on each side, or until just done. In between batches, wipe the pan clean and add more oil. Transfer the fried fish to the wire rack to drain off any excess oil.

11. Drop the "ravioli" into the bubbling tomato sauce and cook, stirring gently, for 5 minutes. Then add the fried fish and let the sauce bubble for a few more minutes. Taste and adjust the seasoning if necessary.

12. Transfer to a serving bowl. Garnish with chopped cilantro and serve hot.

ZANZIBARI GRILLED FISH in COCONUT SAUCE

SAMAKI WA KUPAKA

ZANZIBAR

The food markets in Zanzibar are quite spectacular, bustling with life and produce. And the fish on display in the fish section is always fresh, caught locally by fishermen going out to sea in the most beautiful sailboats. Here is a Zanzibari way to make grilled fish more exciting by serving it with a creamy, spicy sauce. You can use one big fish as is done traditionally, or you can use small individual ones. If you opt for the smaller fish, adjust the cooking time to 5 minutes or so on each side. And if you don't have a charcoal grill, which is what Zanzibaris would use, or access to a broiler, you can cook the fish on a stovetop grill pan.   SERVES 4 TO 6

1 large white snapper (4½ pounds/2 kg), with head and tail on, scaled, gutted, and rinsed

8 cloves garlic, minced to a fine paste

8 mild green chilies, seeded and minced to a fine paste

Sea salt

6⅓ cups (1.5 liters) coconut cream

1 inch (2.5 cm) fresh ginger, peeled and minced to a fine paste

1 teaspoon ground cardamom

Finely ground black pepper

3 limes—2 cut in wedges and 1 sliced into very thin wheels

Indian Flatbread (page 30) or Zanzibari Coconut Rice (page 237), for serving

1. Pat the fish dry with paper towels. Take a long skewer and thread it through the fish, along the vertebrae—this will keep the fish straight during grilling.

2. Mix the garlic and chili pastes in a small bowl, adding a little salt. Rub the fish with half the mixture both inside and out. Let the fish marinate in a large platter while you cook the coconut sauce.

3. Prepare a charcoal fire in an outdoor grill (which is what they would do in Zanzibar) or preheat the broiler to high.

4. Put the coconut cream in a large saucepan. Add the remaining garlic/chili paste, the ginger paste, cardamom, and salt and pepper to taste. Bring to a boil over medium heat, then reduce the heat to medium-low and let it bubble gently, stirring occasionally, until the sauce has thickened, about 30 minutes. Keep hot.

5. Grill or broil the fish for 15 minutes or so on each side until just done. You don't want to overcook it or else it will turn rubbery.

6. Transfer the grilled fish to a large serving platter. Spoon the hot coconut sauce all over it. Arrange the lime wedges around the fish, and lay the thinly sliced lime in a line down the middle of the fish. Serve hot with flatbread or coconut rice.

SENEGALESE FISH STEW
THIEBOU DIEUNNE

One of Senegal's quintessential dishes, this fish stew is served at least once a week at gatherings. It can be considered the Senegalese rice version of the Moroccan seven-vegetable couscous that is a fixture of Friday lunch throughout Morocco. It is a tasty, slightly spicy dish and makes for a very satisfying one-pot meal. I suggest making it with four individual fish, although many Senegalese will make it with fish steaks, pushing the marinade (*rof*; see Note, page 351) into slits made in them. Using fish steaks makes for easier eating, while using whole fish makes for a prettier presentation. Either way, it is a lovely dish and a delightful, unusual way to prepare fish.

SERVES 4

FOR THE ROF
2 cloves garlic, peeled
¾ bunch flat-leaf parsley (about 5 ounces/ 150 g), bottom stems discarded
1 small onion (3½ ounces/100 g), quartered
1½ teaspoons Aleppo pepper
Finely ground black pepper

FOR THE FISH
4 whole grouper or sea bream (about 9 ounces/250 g each), scaled and gutted
Sea salt

FOR THE SAUCE
¼ cup (60 ml) vegetable oil
1 medium onion (5 ounces/150 g), finely chopped
1 small green bell pepper, sliced into thin strips
1 cup (200 g) tomato paste
2 medium tomatoes (7 ounces/200 g total), processed into a puree
Sea salt
1 whole Scotch bonnet pepper
2 tablespoons Thai fish sauce

Finely ground black pepper

TO FINISH
2 medium wedges green cabbage
2 small turnips, peeled and quartered
4 Japanese eggplants (7 ounces/200 g total), halved lengthwise
½ butternut squash, peeled and cut into medium chunks
1 small yuca (cassava) root, about 3 inches (7.5 cm) long, peeled and cut into chunks

1 large carrot, halved lengthwise and cut crosswise into chunks
Salt and finely ground black pepper
3½ ounces (100 g) okra, trimmed
1 teaspoon seedless tamarind paste
1 cup (200 g) bomba rice, rinsed and soaked for 30 minutes in lightly salted water
2 limes, cut into wedges

1. To make the *rof*: In Senegal, *rof* is made in a mortar and pestle, but it's easier and quicker to use a food processor. Put all the ingredients for the *rof* in a food processor and pulse a few times until you have a coarsely chopped mixture.

2. To prepare the fish: Pat the fish dry inside and out with paper towels, then lightly rub them with salt, again inside and out. Make 2 diagonal slits on one side of each fish and place a little *rof* in the slits. Put the fish on a large platter and spread the remaining *rof* over them. Let marinate while you prepare the sauce.

Recipe continues

3. To make the sauce: Heat the vegetable oil in a large deep sauté pan over medium heat. Add the onion, bell pepper, tomato paste, and pureed tomatoes and stir for a minute or so, then reduce the heat to low and cook, stirring regularly, for about 15 minutes, or until the onion and pepper have softened and the tomato sauce has changed color.

4. Add 2½ cups (625 ml) water and salt to taste and mix well. Increase the heat to medium-low and let the sauce bubble gently for about 30 minutes, until you see a little oil rising to the surface.

5. Stir in the Scotch bonnet, fish sauce, and black pepper to taste, then slip the fish into the sauce and let simmer for about 10 minutes, or until the fish is done to your liking. Carefully remove the fish to a platter and keep warm.

6. To finish: Add the cabbage, turnips, eggplants, squash, yuca, and carrot to the sauté pan and season with salt and more pepper to taste. Bring back to a boil, then reduce the heat to low and let simmer, covered for 15 minutes. Add the okra and tamarind paste and simmer for another 5 to 10 minutes, or until all the vegetables are firm-tender.

7. With a slotted spoon, transfer the vegetables to a platter. Spoon a little of the sauce over the vegetables, also over the fish. Keep both warm in a low oven or by covering them with foil while you cook the rice.

8. Return the sauce in the sauté pan to medium heat. Drain the rice and stir into the sauce. Bring the sauce to a boil, then reduce the heat to low and simmer the rice for 10 minutes, or until it has absorbed all the sauce and is tender.

9. Transfer the rice to a large serving platter. Lay the fish in the middle and arrange the vegetables all over the rice. Serve hot with the lime wedges.

NOTE: Rof *is the Senegalese equivalent of Italian gremolata, a mildly spicy herb paste made with onion, garlic, and parsley that is used to flavor fish by inserting it into deep slits made in the fish.*

SPICY BABY SHARK
JASHEED

Jasheed is a typical dish from the Arabian Gulf, made with baby shark, which is plentiful in the Gulf. If you can't find baby shark, use Atlantic mackerel or Pacific halibut and prepare in the same way. Be careful not to let the fish dry out as you cook it. I tried it in many different places and only once did I have it moist, in a totally unpromising café in Fujairah, one of the seven emirates. The café was attached to a catering kitchen where we had been filming for my "The Chef Discovers" show that aired on Abu Dhabi TV several years ago. The chef was showing my co-presenter, the poet Tarek El Mehyas, and me how to prepare various Emirati dishes including *jasheed*, and the owner invited us to taste his dishes. His *jasheed* was by far the best I had tried and the following recipe approximates his. *Jasheed* is normally served with rice, but it is also lovely wrapped in pita bread, or spread over toasted bread to have an Arabian version of bruschetta. SERVES 4 TO 6

FOR THE FISH
1 teaspoon ground turmeric
4 black peppercorns
1 cinnamon stick
2 green cardamom pods
2¼ pounds (1 kg) baby shark fillets (or mackerel or halibut)
Sea salt

FOR THE SAUCE
2 tablespoons ghee or unsalted butter
1 medium onion (5 ounces/150 g), finely chopped
2 cloves garlic, minced to a fine paste
3 pale dried limes, halved
½ bunch cilantro (3½ ounces/100 g), most of the bottom stems discarded, finely chopped
1 small green chili, thinly sliced
2 teaspoons b'zar semach (Arabian Fish Spice Mixture, page 368)
¼ teaspoon ground cardamom
¼ teaspoon ground cinnamon
¼ teaspoon ground cumin
¼ teaspoon finely ground black pepper
Sea salt

White rice garnished with crispy fried onions or Pita Bread (page 4), for serving

1. To prepare the fish. Put the turmeric, peppercorns, cinnamon, cardamom, and 3 cups (750 ml) water in a saucepan and bring to a boil over medium heat. Add the fish and salt to taste and let bubble gently for 20 minutes, or until the skin peels off the fish easily. Drain well. Skin the fish and flake it into small pieces.

2. To make the sauce: Melt the ghee in a large sauté pan over medium heat. Add the onion and sauté, stirring regularly, until golden, about 5 minutes. Add the garlic and dried lime and sauté for a minute or so. Add the cilantro and sliced chili, then the flaked fish and mix well. Cook until the mixture is fairly dry, then add the *b'zar semach*, cardamom, cinnamon, cumin, black pepper, and salt to taste. Reduce the heat to low and cook for a few more minutes, or until there is no liquid in the pan. Taste and adjust the seasoning if necessary. Serve with rice or wrapped in a pita.

EMIRATI FISH in an ONION and TOMATO SAUCE
SEMACH AL HASHO

Traditionally, this dish is served with the *muhammar* (Sweet Savory Rice, page 227). Gulf cooks normally use whole *safi* (emperor or rabbit fish), a kind of flatfish with a firm flesh, for this recipe, but I doubt you will find *safi* outside the Gulf. So, I suggest you use whole sea bream. If you prefer not to have to deal with the skin and bones of whole fish, use fish fillets or steaks. Swordfish would also work well here, as would monkfish or cod.   SERVES 4

4 whole sea bream or pomfrets (about 10½ ounces/300 g each), or 2¼ pounds (1 kg) fish fillets or steaks
Sea salt

FOR THE SAUCE
4 tablespoons ghee or unsalted butter
3 large onions (1 pound 5 ounces/600 g total), halved lengthwise and cut into thin wedges

3 medium tomatoes (10½ ounces/300 g total), thinly sliced
1 tablespoon tomato paste
1 teaspoon b'zar semach (Arabian Fish Spice Mixture, page 368)

1 tablespoon golden raisins, soaked for a couple of hours in hot water and drained
Sea salt

Vegetable oil, for pan-frying the fish
Sweet Savory Rice (page 227), for serving

1. Pat the fish dry with paper towels and lightly rub with salt inside and out. Let sit while you make the sauce.

2. To make the sauce: Melt the ghee in a large sauté pan over medium heat. Add the onions and cook, stirring regularly, until soft and golden, about 5 minutes. Add the tomatoes, tomato paste, *b'zar semach*, and drained golden raisins. Add ½ cup (125 ml) water and season with salt to taste. Cook for about 15 minutes, until the tomatoes have softened and you have a nice thick sauce. Take off the heat.

3. Set a wire rack in a rimmed baking sheet. Place a large skillet over medium heat and pour in enough vegetable oil to cover the bottom. Heat the oil over medium heat until hot (to test it, drop a piece of bread in the oil; if it immediately bubbles around it, it is ready). Slip in the fish and fry for 3 to 5 minutes on each side, until crisp and golden and just done. Transfer to the wire rack to drain off any excess oil. In between batches, wipe the pan clean and add more oil.

4. To finish, slip the fish into the sauce and return the pan to the heat. Let the sauce bubble for a few minutes. Serve hot with the rice.

SPICES, SPICE MIXTURES & SPICE PASTES

The Arabs had control over the spice trade long before the advent of Islam, and they kept this control after they converted to Islam, using the trade to start spreading their new religion beyond Arab lands along the spice trade routes. The spice trade was their main vehicle for spreading Islam—the other was violent conquest, although this was more in the early days. And when the Prophet Muhammad came into conflict with the powerful Quraish tribe in Mecca, who were people of his own family, it was a commercial relationship, again through the spice trade, that led the people of Medina (then known as Yathrib) to extend an invitation to the Prophet to take refuge with them.

Later, after Muhammad died and was succeeded by the Rashidun (meaning "rightly guided caliphs"), the Arabs expanded their trade and spices became even more important commodities. Not only were they not perishable and easy to carry over long distances, but spices were also very sought after, both for the taste they imparted to food and the fact that some spices could be used to preserve food.

Spices and spice mixtures are essential to the cooking in practically the entire Muslim world, whether in Asia, Africa, or Europe. Almost every Muslim majority country has its own spice mixtures, with some being very complex—like the Moroccan ras el-hanout with more than twenty-five spices in the mixture—to others such as the Tunisian *b'harat,* which is simply two spices, one of them being a fragrant flower. Each country can be associated with one or more spices. No dish in the Arabian Gulf would be complete without cardamom, whereas the Levant's flavors are cinnamon, allspice, and black pepper. You wouldn't find a kitchen in Iran without a stock of saffron, nor one in Morocco for that matter; many of these countries' dishes are infused with the unmistakable taste of saffron. Ginger could be considered the flavor of India and Pakistan, not to mention the amazing garam masalas that are used to enhance both rice dishes and curries, as well as side dishes and the fillings in samosas. Chili is the spice of Indonesia, Malaysia, and most of Muslim Africa.

In this chapter, I give recipes for essential spice mixtures, condiments, and sauces.

LEBANESE 7-SPICE MIXTURE

SABE' BHARAT

This is a Lebanese/Syrian mixture that varies slightly from one spice merchant to another, or from one butcher to another—many like to make their own—and even from family to family if they make their own. You can buy it premade, either in a package or loose from a *mahmassa* (which translates as "roaster," but is a term to describe spice merchants), where they roast, grind, and mix their own spices. Obviously the one from a *mahmassa* will be better and fresher than prepacked commercial brands even if some of these are pretty good. You can also mix your own following the recipe below, which is my mother's, or have the spice merchant prepare the mixture to your own recipe. In prewar Aleppo, I used to buy Lena Antaki's Syrian 7-spice mixture from one of the Hilali spice merchants in the old souk, sadly completely destroyed now. I never wrote down her recipe, but it is headier than the Lebanese mixture and I remember it including galangal, and actually being made with more than seven spices.

MAKES ABOUT ¼ CUP (25 G)

1 tablespoon finely ground black pepper
1 tablespoon ground allspice

1 tablespoon ground cinnamon

1 teaspoon ground coriander
1 teaspoon ground cloves

1 teaspoon ground ginger
1 teaspoon freshly grated nutmeg

Mix all the spices well in a medium bowl. Transfer to an airtight container and store away from both heat and light.

DRIED HERB and BULGUR MIXTURE
TAHWICHEH OR KAMMOUNEH

LEBANON

Kammouneh (meaning "made with cumin") or *tahwicheh* (meaning "foraged") is more of an herb and spice mixture than just a spice mixture. It is specific to south Lebanon and, when prepared with fresh herbs such as marjoram, basil, mint, and parsley, it is known as *tahwicheh* while, when made with dried herbs, it is known as *kammouneh*. Both mixtures also include dried rosebuds, spices, bulgur, and onions. The mixture can be used as a spread over ground meat, or it can be mixed with the meat. When the *tahwicheh* or *kammouneh* is spread over the ground meat, the dish is known as *malseh* and when mixed in, it is known as *kibbeh frakeh*. MAKES ABOUT 2 CUPS (250 G)

1 tablespoon cumin seeds
1 small onion
    (3½ ounces/100 g),
    quartered
¼ bunch flat-leaf parsley
    (2 ounces/
    50 g), bottom stems
    discarded

1 ounce (30 g) marjoram,
    leaves stripped off the
    stems
Small handful of basil
    leaves, plus more for
    garnish

Small handful of mint
    leaves
2 dried rosebuds, petals
    only
Zest of ½ unwaxed
    lemon

Zest of ½ unwaxed
    orange
½ cup (100 g) fine bulgur,
    rinsed under cold water
    and drained
Sea salt and finely ground
    black pepper

Put the cumin seeds, onion, herbs, and rosebuds in a food processor and process until very fine. Transfer to a large bowl. Add the lemon and orange zest and bulgur. Season with salt and pepper to taste and mix well. Store in a cool dark place in a hermetically sealed jar. Use with minced meat as explained below.

NOTE: *The quantities I give above are enough for 10½ ounces (300 g) freshly ground lean lamb. (And please don't buy preground meat, which will be too fatty. Also, you will not know which cut has been used.) Ideally, the meat to use for* kibbeh *should come from the top part of the leg. You can ask your butcher to mince it for you or if you have a meat grinder, you can mince it yourself using the fine attachment on the meat grinder and passing the meat twice through it. Once you have minced the meat, put it in a food processor, add salt to taste and 3 or 4 ice cubes, and process for a few seconds to make the meat really smooth. Scoop it out and spread on a platter. Spread the* tahwicheh *over the meat, leaving the edges free for* malseh, *or mix it with the meat and spread the mixture on a platter for* frakeh. *It is very important that you do either immediately before serving as the minced meat will change color very quickly and become less pink.*

GARAM MASALA

Garam masala is the spice mix Indians, Pakistanis, and Bangladeshis use in their cooking. There are many different garam masalas. In fact, most cooks keep their spices in a beautiful round box inside which are individual containers for each spice, and whenever they cook, they have the box at hand to use as much of each spice as they need to make their own mix. Here, I give three versions to use to your taste. There isn't that much difference among them, just a change in proportions and a few extra spices from one to the other. They can be used interchangeably in the recipes calling for garam masala depending on which mix you like best. The method is the same for all three in that you need to toast the spices before grinding them. I keep all three and alternate their use depending on what I feel like on the day.

GARAM MASALA 1

MAKES ABOUT 1¼ CUPS (125 G)

¼ cup (25 g) anise seeds

¼ cup (25 g) caraway seeds

¼ cup (25 g) cumin seeds

2 tablespoons green cardamom pods

2 tablespoons whole cloves

2½ cinnamon sticks

2½ whole nutmegs

6 shards blade mace

GARAM MASALA 2

MAKES ABOUT ¼ CUP (25 G)

1 tablespoon black peppercorns

1 tablespoon cumin seeds

1 teaspoon whole cloves

12 green cardamom pods

6 black cardamom pods

1 cinnamon stick

1 star anise

½ whole nutmeg

2 shards blade mace

6 bay leaves

GARAM MASALA 3

MAKES ABOUT 3 CUPS (300 G)

⅔ cup (50 g) green cardamom pods

½ cup (50 g) cumin seeds

½ cup (50 g) fennel seeds

⅓ cup (25 g) black cardamom pods

⅓ cup (25 g) whole cloves

⅓ cup (50 g) black peppercorns

1 tablespoon whole cubeb pepper

⅓ cup (25 g) black stone flower or patthar ke phool (see Glossary)

3 cinnamon sticks

1 whole nutmeg

5 shards blade mace

5 bay leaves

Stir the spices in a large nonstick skillet over medium heat for a minute or two, or until fragrant. Let cool, then transfer to a spice grinder and grind until fine. Store airtight in a glass jar and keep in a cool dark place for up to one year.

INDIAN BIRYANI MASALA

INDIA

This masala recipe is used specifically in biryanis. MAKES ABOUT 1 CUP (100 G)

2 tablespoons coriander seeds

1 tablespoon black cumin seeds (shahi jeera)

1½ teaspoons whole cloves

¾ teaspoon fennel seeds

½ teaspoon black peppercorns

3 green cardamom pods

1 black cardamom pod

2 cinnamon sticks

1 star anise

½ whole nutmeg

2 shards blade mace

1½ medium black stone flowers or patthar ke phool (see page 000)

1 small bay leaf

Stir the spices in a large nonstick skillet over medium heat for a minute or two, or until fragrant. Let cool, then transfer to a spice grinder and grind all the ingredients together. Store in an airtight jar kept in a dark cool place for up to one year.

QATARI BIRYANI MASALA

QATAR

This masala is specific to Qatar. It was given to me by Aisha al-Tamimi, Maryam Abdallah's sister, who has taken over Maryam's mantle as Qatar's foremost celebrity chef—Maryam was Qatar's first-ever TV chef. Both Maryam and Aisha have taught me most of what I know about the food and culinary heritage of their country as well as how to cook many of their wonderful dishes.

MAKES ABOUT 1½ CUPS (150 G)

¼ cup (12 g) coriander seeds

1 tablespoon whole cloves

1½ teaspoons fennel seeds

1 teaspoon black peppercorns

6 green cardamom pods

4 cinnamon sticks

2 star anise

1 whole nutmeg

4 shards blade mace

1 bay leaf

Grind all the ingredients together and store in an airtight jar kept in a dark cool place for up to one year, possibly longer.

ADVIEH

The word *advieh* comes from the Arabic word for medicines (*adwiyeh*) and in Iran, it describes a spice mixture that is a little like the Indian garam masala. In fact, garam masala is derived from the Persian words *garm*, meaning "hot," and *masaleh*, meaning "ingredients." There are different regional *adviehs*, such as one from the Persian Gulf used in hearty dishes, another from the Central Provinces used in delicate dishes, and a fragrant one like the one below that is used to add a luxurious touch to rice dishes, including Jeweled Rice (page 250). MAKES ABOUT ½ CUP (50 G)

⅓ cup (50 g) pistachios, coarsely ground

2 tablespoons raw cane sugar

2 tablespoons ground cinnamon

1 teaspoon ground cardamom

1 teaspoon ground dried rose petals

Good pinch of saffron threads, ground

Mix all the ingredients together in a medium bowl and transfer to a glass jar. Store airtight in a dark place for up to one year, possibly longer. I usually keep mine in the freezer.

RAS EL-HANOUT

MOROCCO

Meaning "the head of the shop," ras el-hanout is probably the most complex of all spice mixtures in this book. In her excellent book, *Les Secrets de Cuisine en Terre Marocaine*, the late Zette Guinaudeau-Franc lists no fewer than twenty-seven spices that go in the making of ras el-hanout. Unfortunately, Guinaudeau-Franc does not give a recipe and I doubt one can re-create the complex mixture that you can buy at good spice merchants in the medina in Fez or Marrakesh, so my advice is to source a good mix and to use it sparingly. In Morocco, ras el-hanout is used in game tagines, and in some sweet-savory dishes like M'ruziyah on page 149. It is also used to season Moroccan Kefta (page 110) and the tagine that goes into Moroccan Pigeon Pie (page 37).

YEMENI SPICE MIXTURE
YEMENI HAWAYEJ

YEMEN

Hawayej means "gathered stuff" in Yemen and describes a spice mixture that is mainly used for soups.

MAKES ABOUT 1¼ CUPS (125 G)

¼ cup (35 g) black peppercorns
⅓ cup (15 g) coriander seeds

⅓ cup (30 g) cumin seeds
2 tablespoons green cardamom pods

1 teaspoon whole cloves
5 teaspoons ground turmeric

2 teaspoons ground cinnamon

Toast the whole spices in a large nonstick skillet over medium heat, stirring constantly, until fragrant. Let cool, then transfer to a food processor or spice grinder and process until finely ground. Transfer to a bowl. Stir in the turmeric and cinnamon. Store airtight in a glass jar and keep it in a cool dark place for up to one year, possibly longer.

YEMENI MANDI SPICE MIXTURE
HAWAYEJ MANDI

YEMEN

This is a fairly simple spice mixture used in *mandi*, one of the Middle East's most popular dishes. *Mandi* is originally from Yemen but is now found throughout the Arabian Gulf and as far north as Syria.

MAKES JUST UNDER 1 CUP (90 G)

¼ cup (20 g) green cardamom pods

¼ cup (20 g) whole cloves

4 teaspoons black peppercorns
2 whole nutmegs

8 bay leaves
2 tablespoons ground ginger

Put the whole spices and bay leaves in a food processor or spice grinder and process until finely ground. Transfer to a medium bowl and add the ground ginger. Mix well. Store airtight in a glass jar and keep it in a cool dark place for up to one year, possibly longer.

SOMALI SPICE MIXTURE

SOMALIA

A slightly more complex mix than that for Yemeni *mandi* (see opposite page at bottom), this is used in Somali stews and soups.

MAKES ABOUT 1¼ CUPS (125 G)

½ cup (50 g) cumin seeds
½ cup (25 g) coriander seeds

2 tablespoons black peppercorns
1 tablespoon broken-up cinnamon bark

1 tablespoon green cardamom pods
1 teaspoon cloves

2 tablespoons ground turmeric

Toast the whole spices in a large skillet over medium heat, stirring constantly, until fragrant. Let cool, then transfer to a food processor or spice grinder and process until finely ground. Transfer to a large bowl and add the ground turmeric. Mix well. Store airtight in a glass jar and keep it in a cool dark place for up to one year, possibly longer.

BERBERE SPICE MIXTURE

ETHIOPIA | ERITREA | SOMALIA

An essential mix in Ethiopian, Eritrean, and Somali cooking, this mixture is rather subtle despite the number of spices used; and even though the cayenne pepper is the dominant spice, its heat is offset by the paprika.

MAKES ABOUT ¾ CUP (75 G)

½ teaspoon black peppercorns
½ teaspoon cumin seeds
¼ teaspoon cardamom seeds

¼ teaspoon coriander seeds
¼ teaspoon fenugreek seeds
2 whole cloves

¼ cup (30 g) cayenne pepper
¼ cup (30 g) paprika
¼ teaspoon ground turmeric

½ teaspoon ground ginger
¼ teaspoon ground cinnamon

Toast the whole spices in a medium skillet over medium heat, stirring constantly, for 2 to 3 minutes, until fragrant. Let cool, then transfer to a spice grinder or mini food processor. Process until fine, then transfer to a medium bowl. Add the ground spices and mix well. Store airtight in a glass jar and keep it in a cool dark place for up to one year, possibly longer.

ARABIAN SPICE MIXTURE
B'ZAR

ARABIAN GULF

B'zar is an indispensable spice mixture in the Arabian Gulf, and shortly before Ramadan most households will get busy preparing their *b'zar* to last them not only the month of Ramadan but also the whole year. This recipe comes from my delightful friend, Maryam Abdallah, who was the first celebrity Qatari TV chef. I often eat at her home when I am in Doha and both she and her sister Aisha al-Tamimi, Qatar's foremost celebrity chef, have taught me to make many Qatari dishes. The following recipe was handed down by their mother. Maryam buys her spices whole in the souk. She washes them at home and puts them out to dry in the sun before grinding them. She then portions them in bags, which she keeps in the freezer to take out when she needs to.

MAKES ABOUT 1½ CUPS (200 G)

- ½ cup (75 g) black peppercorns
- ½ cup (50 g) cumin seeds
- ½ cup (25 g) coriander seeds

- 2 tablespoons whole cloves
- 2 tablespoons broken Ceylon cinnamon sticks

- 2 tablespoons green cardamom pods
- 2 tablespoons small dried red chilies
- 2 whole nutmegs

- 2 heaping tablespoons ground ginger
- 2 tablespoons ground turmeric

Put the whole spices in a food processor or spice grinder and process until finely ground. Transfer to a large bowl and add the ground ginger and turmeric. Mix well. Store airtight in a glass jar and keep it in a cool dark place for up to one year, possibly longer.

TUNISIAN B'HARAT

TUNISIA

B'harat means "spices" in Arabic and this Tunisian mixture is a simple 50/50 mélange of dried rosebuds and cinnamon that is used in both baking and cooking. You do not need a recipe here. Just grind as many rosebuds (removing the core and stem if any and just using the petals) as you need and mix with an equal quantity of ground cinnamon. Store in a cool dark place in a hermetically sealed glass jar.

ARABIAN SPICE MIXTURE for DESSERTS

BHARAT AL-HELOU

It is not often that you see spice mixtures used in sweets, but here is one from the Arabian Gulf. In fact, many Arabian sweets are flavored with spices such as cinnamon, or cardamom and/or saffron, not to mention fragrant waters and sometimes mastic (see pages 447 and 451), giving them an intriguing exotic taste.

MAKES 2¼ CUPS (225 G)

½ cup (50 g) cumin seeds
½ cup (75 g) black peppercorns

2 tablespoons green cardamom pods
2 tablespoons whole cloves

3 whole nutmegs
½ cinnamon stick
1 tablespoon ground fenugreek

½ cup (50 g) ground ginger
2 tablespoons ground turmeric

Grind the whole spices in a spice grinder or a food processor until very fine. Transfer to a large bowl and add the fenugreek, ground ginger, and turmeric. Mix well. Store in an airtight glass jar and keep it in a cool dark place for up to one year, possibly longer.

MOROCCAN SALT AND CUMIN MIXTURE

MOROCCO

Like Tunisian B'harat (opposite page), this is a simple mixture of two ingredients in a ratio of 1:1. In this case it's salt and cumin, to be served with *mechoui* and kebabs. Store in a cool dark place in a heremetically sealed glass jar.

ARABIAN FISH SPICE MIXTURE

B'ZAR SEMACH

ARABIAN GULF

This *b'zar* is used specifically in fish dishes. It is a lot less complex than the one used for meat or vegetables but equally tasty. Gulf Arab cooks often use both *b'zar* and single spices to season their dishes to end up with a rather complex seasoning.

MAKES ABOUT 1 CUP (100 G)

½ cup (50 g) cumin seeds
½ cup (25 g) coriander
    seeds

2 tablespoons ground
    cinnamon
1 tablespoon finely
    ground black pepper

1 tablespoon ground
    ginger

1 tablespoon ground
    turmeric

Toast the cumin and coriander seeds in a large nonstick skillet over medium heat, stirring constantly, until fragrant. Let cool, then transfer to a spice grinder and process until finely ground. Transfer to a large bowl. Add the ground cinnamon, pepper, ginger, and turmeric and mix well. Store in an airtight jar and keep it in a cool dark place for up to one year, possibly longer.

DUKKAH

EGYPT

In Egypt, where dukkah (also spelled *duqqa* or *doqqa*) originates, people have it for breakfast or as a snack, using *aysh baladi* (thick pita made with whole wheat flour) or *shami* (the same pita but made with all-purpose flour) to dip into the mixture. Dukkah has now become global, with chefs and home cooks sprinkling it over grilled vegetables or meat or fish, as well as on salads.

MAKES ABOUT 8 CUPS (800 G)

1¼ ounces (40 g) fine sea
    salt
4 cups (200 g) coriander
    seeds, toasted

1⅓ cups (200 g) unsalted
    roasted peanuts

1⅓ cups (200 g) unsalted
    roasted chickpeas
1 cup (40 g) dried mint

¾ cup (125 g) toasted
    sesame seeds

Put all the ingredients in a food processor and process until coarsely ground. Store in an airtight glass jar and keep in a cool dark place for up to one year, possibly longer.

YEMENI CILANTRO CHUTNEY

Z'HOUG

Z'houg is a Yemeni relish or chutney and, as with dukkah, it has entered the mainstream in the West with chefs featuring it on their menus to go with grilled meats or as a spread in sandwiches, which is how it is used in Yemen, a little like the French use butter. I sometimes use it as a dip or even as a marinade. You can use green chilies here instead of red ones, but be sure to use a mix of mild and hot chilies so that the *z'houg* is not too fiery.   MAKES 2 CUPS (500 ML)

4 ounces (125 g) mild red chilies, seeded and cut into chunks
4 ounces (125 g) hot red chilies, seeded and cut into chunks

5 cloves garlic, peeled
½ bunch cilantro (3½ ounces/100 g), leaves stripped off the stems

½ bunch flat-leaf parsley (3½ ounces/100 g), leaves stripped off the stems
1 teaspoon ground cumin
¼ teaspoon ground cardamom

1 teaspoon salt
1 teaspoon finely ground black pepper
2 tablespoons extra-virgin oil

Put the chilies and garlic in a food processor and grind until coarse. Add the herbs, spices, salt, pepper, and oil and continue processing until you have a lightly textured paste. Transfer to a glass jar with a tight-fitting lid. This chutney will keep in the refrigerator for about 2 weeks.

HARISSA

In Tunisia, harissa is served as a dip, drizzled with olive oil, and often garnished with canned tuna and olives. It is a fixture of most main meals, brought to the table with bread before any other food is served. The chilies used for harissa in Tunisia are very mild and I usually bring back some when I visit, but if I don't have any I use a mixture of dried Mexican guajillo and árbol chilies to approximate the mild heat of Tunisian harissa.

MAKES 2 CUPS (500 ML)

5 ounces (150 g) dried
   guajillo chilies
½ ounce (15 g) dried
   árbol chilies
Boiling water
¼ cup (25 g) caraway
   seeds
10 cloves garlic, peeled
Sea salt
Extra-virgin olive oil, for
   covering the harissa

1. Pull the stems off the chilies. Shake out and discard the seeds. Rinse the chilies under cold water, then soak them in boiling water for about 30 minutes.

2. Put the caraway seeds in a food processor and process for a minute or so, then add the garlic and a little salt and process until the garlic is almost completely minced.

3. Drain the chilies. Add to the garlic and caraway seeds and add more salt to taste—the harissa needs to be salted enough without tasting salty. Process until you have a lightly textured paste—the chilies should not be completely pulverized.

4. Taste and add more salt if necessary. Spoon into a 1-pint (500 ml) glass jar. Pour in enough olive oil to completely cover the surface of the harissa. This will help preserve it—make sure you top up the oil every time you use some of the harissa. Well covered in oil, harissa will keep for months in the refrigerator.

SPICY SHRIMP SAMBAL
SAMBAL TERASI

INDONESIA

Sambal is to Indonesians and Malaysians what harissa is to North Africans, an essential chili paste that is used as a sauce or dip as well as in cooking—except that there are endless variations on sambal. There is, however, a problem with making sambal in the West, and that is that the main type of mildly hot chilies used in Indonesia, known as *lombok*, are not easily available abroad. You can approximate the flavor by sourcing mild red chilies or making a mix of both mild and hot, remembering that the sauce should not be fiery and is used more like a condiment, to be eaten with boiled rice and/or curries and to flavor soups. I have even used red bell pepper and one or two bird's eye chilies to add some heat. In Indonesia, you can watch women in the markets pulling the stems off the chilies so that cooks can grind them straightaway without having to trim them. And even today, and almost universally in Indonesia, Indonesian cooks grind the ingredients for sambal in a large wide stone or earthenware mortar using a horizontal stone or wooden pestle. In the three weeks I was there, I saw only one cook using a food processor. All the others whom I met and watched ground the sambal ingredients in a mortar with a pestle. Serve this sambal with plain or fried rice, or a curry of your choice. You can also serve it with grilled meat or fish.

MAKES ABOUT ⅔ CUP (160 G)

5 mild red chilies,
  trimmed
1 bird's eye chili, trimmed
1 small shallot, peeled
1 medium tomato
  (3½ ounces/100 g),
  quartered
1 tablespoon shrimp
  paste (terasi)
2 teaspoons chopped
  palm sugar or brown
  sugar
Sea salt
Juice of 3 limes

Put the chilies, shallot, tomato, shrimp paste, and palm sugar in a food processor and process until you have a slightly textured paste. Transfer to a medium mixing bowl. Add salt to taste and the lime juice. Mix well. Store in an airtight glass jar in the refrigerator where it will keep for a couple of days.

CHILI and TOMATO SAMBAL
SAMBAL BAJAK

This sambal comes from Java and unlike the Spicy Shrimp Sambal (page 371), it is cooked slightly to produce a darker, richer mixture.

MAKES ABOUT 1 CUP (250 G)

5 fresh mild red chilies, seeded and sliced into rings
2 bird's eye chilies
6 small shallots (4½ ounces/125 g total), peeled and quartered

1½ teaspoons chopped palm sugar
2 tablespoons vegetable oil
2 bay leaves
2 stalks fresh lemongrass, smashed

½ inch (1 cm) fresh galangal, peeled and cut in very thin julienne
1 teaspoon tamarind paste, diluted in 2 tablespoons water

¼ teaspoon freshly grated nutmeg
Sea salt

1. Put the chilies, shallots, and palm sugar in a food processor and process until you have a fine paste.

2. Put the vegetable oil, chili/shallot paste, bay leaves, lemongrass, and galangal in a medium skillet and place over medium heat. Sauté, stirring all the time, until the mixture has darkened somewhat. Add the diluted tamarind paste, nutmeg, and salt to taste and simmer for another minute or so. Let cool, then discard the bay leaves and lemongrass before serving. This sambal will keep for a few days, either in the refrigerator or in another cool place, stored in an airtight container.

FRESH CHILI and TOMATO SAMBAL

SAMBAL DABU-DABU

INDONESIA

This sambal is commonly served with grilled fish and it can be made fresh, a little like a salsa, or the ingredients can be quickly sautéed for a slightly more intense flavor. If you can't find lime basil, use regular Mediterranean basil.   MAKES 2 CUPS (400 G)

3 mild red chilies, seeded and sliced into rings
1 or 2 bird's eye chilies (depending on how spicy you want your sambal), seeded and sliced into rings
3 medium tomatoes (10½ ounces/300 g total), peeled, seeded, and cut into small cubes
3 small shallots (2 ounces/60 g total), finely chopped
2 sprigs lime basil, leaves only, coarsely chopped
Juice of 2 limes
Sea salt

Put all the ingredients in a large mixing bowl. Season with salt to taste and mix well before serving. Serve immediately, or within 24 hours.

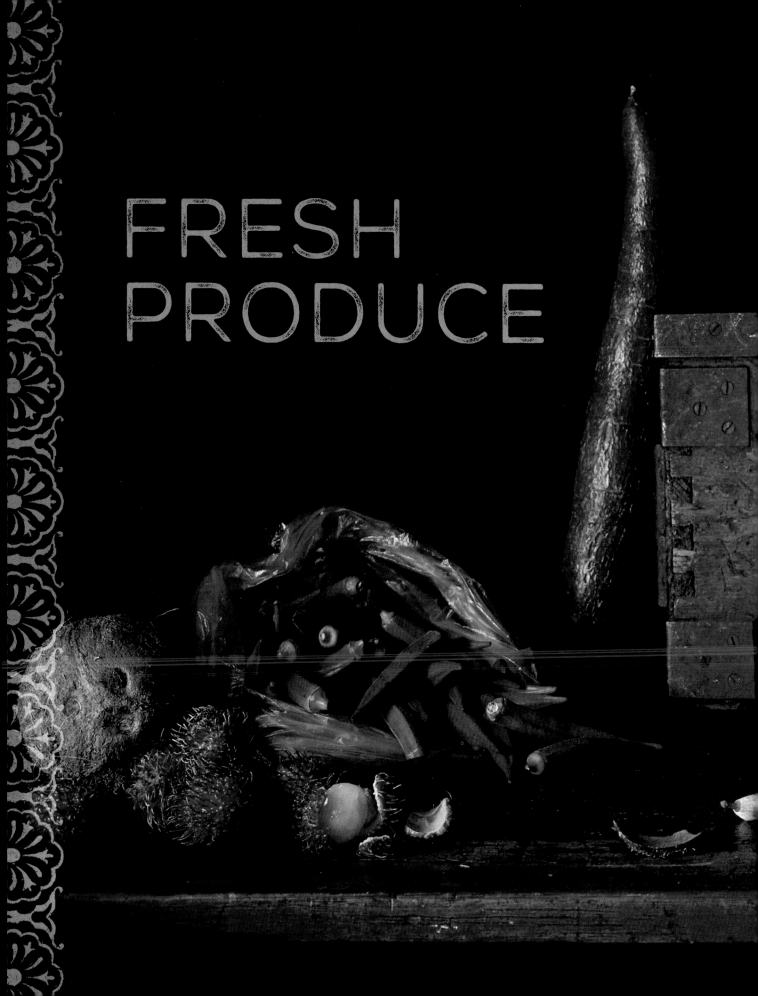

FRESH
PRODUCE

The early Muslims couldn't have had much access to fresh produce. They lived in a very harsh climate in an oasis in the desert with very little rainfall, extremely hot summers, and not much fertile land. Their early diet must have consisted primarily of meat and dairy, dates (of course), and wheat, as well as some local seasonal produce such as the desert truffle.

As they spread their religion beyond the Arabian Gulf and started conquering new, more fertile lands such as Syria and Iraq, they ruled over lush countries that not only had an abundance of fresh produce, but also culinary traditions on how to cook that produce, much of it new to them; and just as important, they also learned how to preserve the produce for the fallow winter months when there was less growing in the fields. And with the conquest of Iran, they also acquired great chefs. The Abbasids, whose seat of power was in Baghdad, favored Persian chefs, and as they conquered yet more countries they took those chefs along, expanding the influence of Persian cooking all the way to North Africa and beyond. With the advent of the Ottoman Empire, with its magnificent court and spectacular kitchens at the Topkapi Palace, the Muslim culinary repertoire expanded even farther, both with new dishes and novel interpretations of old ones.

One example of Persian dishes being adopted by the Ottomans is stuffed vegetables, possibly the most glorious group of dishes from that part of the world. Stuffed vegetables are said to have originated in Iran, but the modern Iranian repertoire concentrates mainly on grape leaves. These are cooked in different sauces. However, in Turkey, Lebanon, and Syria (not to mention Jordan and Palestine), almost everything can be stuffed, from the common zucchini to the seasonal quince, taking in melons, eggplants, cabbage, and carrots to name but a few. Many of those vegetables are dried at the end of summer so that they can be used in winter. I could have devoted the whole chapter to stuffed vegetables alone given the variety, but I include a limited but typical selection here, together with a selection of other dishes making use of typical seasonal produce.

TABBOULEH

LEBANON | SYRIA | JORDAN | PALESTINE

Now that tabbouleh has gone global, it has become one of the most commonly misinterpreted salads. The most typical mistake is adding too much bulgur. Then there are those who add cucumber, or worse, cilantro, both absolute no-nos. Of course there are variations from region to region or even family to family, but a few golden rules apply. One, it is an herbs and tomato salad, *not* a grain salad, so the proportion of bulgur to the herbs and tomatoes is minimal. Second, all the herbs should be cut by hand. Don't even entertain the idea of chopping the herbs in a food processor. You will end up with a mushy salad that will oxidize more quickly than if you cut your herbs into thin slivers using a very sharp knife. And lastly, use firm but ripe tomatoes. In Lebanon, most people like their tabbouleh very juicy, but I like mine rather dry and crisp, and I drain off the juice before adding the tomatoes to the herbs. I also use less lemon juice, but this is a question of taste. Also important is the quality of the bulgur. Use a fine granulation, which means that you don't need to soak it. Just rinse and drain it and let it sit to fluff up before using.   SERVES 4 TO 6

Scant ¼ cup (30 g) fine bulgur

6 firm-ripe medium tomatoes (1 pound 5 ounces/600 g total), cut into small cubes

1 bunch scallions (2 ounces/50 g)

2 bunches flat-leaf parsley (14 ounces/ 400 g total), most of the bottom stems discarded

⅓ bunch mint (2½ ounces/75 g), leaves stripped off the stems

¼ teaspoon ground cinnamon

½ teaspoon ground allspice or Lebanese 7-Spice Mixture (page 358)

¼ teaspoon finely ground black pepper

Sea salt

Juice of 1 lemon, or to taste

⅓ cup (80 ml) extra-virgin olive oil

4 Little Gem lettuces, washed and quartered

1. Rinse the bulgur in several changes of cold water. Drain well and let sit in a medium bowl. Stir every now and then with a fork to help it fluff up.

2. Put the diced tomatoes in a small bowl and set aside while you prepare the scallions and herbs. Finely slice the scallions and place over the tomatoes. Use a razor-sharp knife to chop the herbs and gather as much as you can handle in a bunch, then slice the herbs very thinly to end up with nice, crisp, thin slivers.

3. Drain the tomatoes of their juice and transfer the tomatoes and scallions to a large bowl. Add the herbs. Sprinkle the bulgur all over, then season with the cinnamon, allspice or 7-spice mixture, and pepper. Add salt to taste. Add the lemon juice and olive oil and mix well. Taste and adjust the seasoning if necessary.

4. Serve immediately with the quartered lettuce on the side. In the Levant, diners use the lettuce leaves to scoop the tabbouleh instead of a spoon or fork and eat them both together.

WHITE TABBOULEH
TABBOULEH BAIDAH

I am not sure where this version of tabbouleh comes from. Initially, I assumed it was a winter version from days long past, but tomatoes are summer vegetables, so my guess was wrong. Then I thought it was possibly a regional variation, but I have yet to find another reference to it outside the recipe I initially found in Ibrahim Mouzannar's *Lebanese Cuisine*. I have adapted his recipe to make it lighter on the bulgur as well as the olive oil. And, unlike him, I use fine bulgur and have replaced the paprika he suggests using with Aleppo pepper to give the salad a nice kick.

SERVES 4 TO 6

½ cup (100 g) fine bulgur
1 conehead (pointed) cabbage (1 pound 2 ounces/500 g), outer damaged leaves discarded, very finely shredded

2 bunches scallions (3½ ounces/100 g total), thinly sliced
1 bunch mint (7 ounces/200 g), leaves stripped off

the stems, chopped medium fine
14 ounces (400 g) cherry tomatoes, quartered
Juice of 1 lemon, or to taste

⅓ cup (80 ml) extra-virgin olive oil
1 teaspoon Aleppo pepper, or to taste
Sea salt

1. Rinse the bulgur under cold water. Drain and set aside to fluff up—let sit for about 10 minutes while you prepare the other ingredients. Stir with a fork every now and then to separate the grains.

2. Put the cabbage, scallions, mint, and tomatoes in a large bowl. Add the bulgur, lemon juice, and oil. Season with the Aleppo pepper and salt to taste. Mix well. Taste and adjust the seasoning if necessary. Serve immediately.

TURKISH BULGUR SALAD

KISSIR

TURKEY

Kissir is the Turkish version of tabbouleh, except that in *kissir*, bulgur is the main ingredient and in tabbouleh, it is the herbs and tomatoes that are. You can also dress *kissir* with pomegranate molasses for an intriguing sweet and sour flavor (see Note).

SERVES 4 TO 6

1 cup (200 g) fine bulgur
¾ cup plus 1 tablespoon (200 ml) boiling water
2 small Spanish onions (7 ounces/200 g total), very finely chopped

5 firm-ripe medium tomatoes (1 pound 2 ounces/500 g), seeded and cut into ½-inch (1 cm) cubes
½ small green bell pepper, diced into small cubes

A few sprigs flat-leaf parsley, most of the bottom stems discarded, finely chopped
¼ cup (60 ml) extra-virgin olive oil

1 teaspoon Aleppo pepper
3 tablespoons lemon juice
2 tablespoons mild Turkish red pepper paste, or spicy to taste
Sea salt

1. Put the bulgur in a large bowl and add the water a few spoonfuls at a time, stirring it in. Cover with a kitchen towel and let sit for 15 minutes.

2. Add the onions to the bulgur and mix well. Stir in the tomatoes, bell pepper, parsley, olive oil, Aleppo pepper, lemon juice, pepper paste, and salt to taste. Taste and adjust the seasoning if necessary. Serve immediately.

NOTE: *To make this with pomegranate molasses, omit both the lemon juice and pepper paste and replace with 1½ tablespoons pomegranate molasses.*

MIXED HERB and TOASTED BREAD SALAD

FATTOUSH

LEBANON | SYRIA | JORDAN | PALESTINE

There are endless variations of fattoush, both in how it is seasoned and in the way it is prepared. Some families, like my mother's, make fattoush without lettuce, with only the herbs (leaving the leaves whole); and the salad is dressed with just sumac and olive oil. Others chop the herbs, add shredded lettuce, and use lemon juice, olive oil, and garlic in the dressing. Some let the bread soak in the dressing before mixing the salad, while others are keen on keeping the bread crisp as long as possible. In Syria, the bread is fried instead of toasted, which has the advantage of keeping the bread crisp and the disadvantage of making the salad heavier. Regardless of all the variations, fattoush remains an essential salad for breaking the fast during the month of Ramadan in both Lebanon and Syria.

SERVES 6

1 medium pita bread, split horizontally into 2 disks, toasted in a hot oven until golden brown, broken into bite-size pieces
3 tablespoons ground sumac
⅓ cup (80 ml) extra-virgin olive oil

2 Little Gem lettuces (14 ounces/400 g total), outer damaged leaves discarded, cut across into ½-inch (1 cm) strips
2 bunches scallions (3½ ounces/100 g total), thinly sliced
6 mini cucumbers (10½ ounces/300 g total), halved

lengthwise and cut crosswise into medium-thin half-moons
10½ ounces (300 g) cherry tomatoes, quartered
1 bunch flat-leaf parsley (7 ounces/200 g), most of the bottom stems discarded, coarsely chopped

½ bunch mint (3½ ounces/100 g), leaves stripped off the stems, coarsely chopped
½ bunch purslane (3½ ounces/100 g), leaves only
Sea salt

1. Put the pieces of toasted bread in a medium mixing bowl. Sprinkle the sumac over the bread. Add the oil and mix well. This will stop the bread from sogging up quickly after it is mixed with the salad. Taste the bread to see if it is salty. Some sumac has a little salt mixed in.

2. Put the lettuces, scallions, cucumbers, tomatoes, parsley, mint, and purslane in a large salad bowl. Add the seasoned toasted bread and mix well. Add salt to taste. Taste and adjust the seasoning if necessary. Serve immediately.

INDONESIAN VEGETABLE and EGG SALAD

GADO GADO

When I visited Indonesia, half of my time there happened to be during Ramadan when street vendors seem to multiply, selling all kinds of snacks and dishes to those fasting and not having the time to cook at home. In Banda Aceh, I went to one street where most of the vendors specialized in the sweet snacks (*takjil*) and drinks that people break their fast with, but one cart had gado gado (*gado* means "mix" and *gado gado* means "mixes," because this salad is made of so many different ingredients). The vendor had his ingredients piled in different mounds inside the cart with a wide mortar to one side, which he used to grind batch after batch of the seasoning ingredients for the salad, which is eaten as a snack or as a meal. The version I give here is served with a peanut-based dressing, whereas on some islands, the dressing has a coconut cream base.   SERVES 2 TO 4

FOR THE DRESSING
1½ cups (225 g) raw peanuts
6 mild red chilies, trimmed
1 bird's eye chili, trimmed
¼ teaspoon shrimp paste (terasi)
1 tablespoon seedless tamarind paste, diluted with 2 tablespoons water

2 tablespoons palm sugar, grated
Sea salt

FOR THE SALAD
2 medium potatoes, boiled, peeled, and cut into medium-thin rounds

2 hard-boiled organic eggs, peeled and cut into wedges
5 ounces (150 g) cauliflower florets, cooked until crisp-tender
5 ounces (150 g) cabbage, finely shredded and blanched

5 ounces (150 g) asparagus beans, cut into medium pieces, cooked until crisp-tender
1 small cucumber, peeled and thinly sliced
5 ounces (150 g) tempeh, sliced into 4 portions, shallow-fried in vegetable oil

1. Preheat the oven to 450°F (220°C).

2. To make the dressing: Spread the peanuts on a nonstick baking sheet. Toast in the hot oven for 7 to 8 minutes, or until golden brown. Let cool, then process in a food processor until finely chopped. Transfer to a medium bowl.

3. Put the chilies and shrimp paste in the food processor and process until you have a fine paste. Add to the peanuts. Strain the tamarind paste into a small bowl and add to the peanuts and chili paste. Add the palm sugar and ⅔ cup (160 ml) water and season with salt to taste. Mix well. Taste and adjust the seasoning if necessary.

4. To assemble the salad: Arrange the ingredients on a serving platter, making a separate mound of each ingredient, and add a few crackers. Serve with the dressing on the side.

SCRAMBLED EGG
and EGGPLANT DIP

MIRZA GHASSEMI

There are many versions of *mirza ghassemi*. I don't think I had it tasting the same from one home or restaurant to another. A Gilaki specialty (meaning from the northern province of Gilan in Iran), *mirza ghassemi* is a delightful half dip, half spread that is ideal for those who do not eat meat, as it combines eggs for protein with eggplants and tomatoes for freshness. It is found throughout the country both in homes and restaurants. Iranian cooks normally use vegetable oil, but I prefer to use olive oil.

SERVES 4 TO 6

Pinch of saffron threads

3 large eggplants (2 pounds/ 900 g total)

¼ cup (60 ml) extra-virgin olive oil

4 cloves garlic, minced to a fine paste

½ teaspoon ground turmeric

4 medium tomatoes (14 ounces/400 g total), peeled, seeded, and coarsely chopped

Sea salt and finely ground black pepper

3 organic eggs, lightly beaten

Barbari or lavash bread, for serving

1. Put the saffron to soak in 1 tablespoon water.

2. Preheat the oven to 400°F (200°C).

3. Prick the eggplants in several places and place on a baking sheet. Bake for 45 minutes to 1 hour, or until very soft, turning them halfway through. Cut the eggplants in half and scoop the flesh out. Place in a sieve to let the excess liquid drain away. Mash the eggplant with a potato masher—you do not want to do this in a food processor as the mashed eggplant needs to retain some, albeit soft, texture.

4. Heat the oil in a large skillet over medium-high heat. Add the garlic and stir for a minute or so, until the garlic starts sizzling and is fragrant. Add the turmeric and mix well. Add the tomatoes and cook until the tomatoes have softened and reduced to a thick sauce, 15 to 20 minutes.

5. Add the mashed eggplant and sauté for a few minutes, or until all the excess liquid has evaporated. Season with salt and pepper to taste.

6. Stir the beaten eggs into the eggplant/tomato mixture. Continue stirring until the eggs have set to your liking. It is important not to have any liquid left in the pan. Add the saffron water and mix well. Taste and adjust the seasoning. Cover the pan loosely with a clean kitchen towel. Let cool. Transfer to a serving dish. Serve warm or at room temperature with bread.

ONION and PARSLEY SALAD

LEBANON | SYRIA | JORDAN | PALESTINE | TURKEY

This salad is used as a bed for grilled meat and poultry throughout the Levant. The dressing varies slightly from country to country. In Turkey, cooks use only sumac, while in Egypt they favor lemon juice. In Syria and Lebanon, the seasoning combines both. I learned to soak the onion in boiling water from Sami Tamimi, Ottolenghi's partner, to slightly soften it and, more important, to take away some of the sharpness. You can chop the parsley or you can leave the leaves whole, that is if the parsley is not overgrown. I normally chop mine unless I buy parsley imported from Lebanon, Syria, or Jordan where they pick it quite young, in which case I leave it whole.

Serve this with your choice of grilled meat by spreading the salad on a pita or any other flatbread, then laying the grilled meat on top.

SERVES 4

2 medium onions (10½ ounces/ 300 g total), halved lengthwise and cut into thin wedges

¼ bunch flat-leaf parsley (2 ounces/50 g), most of the bottom stems discarded, coarsely chopped

1 to 2 tablespoons ground sumac, to taste

1 tablespoon lemon juice

1 to 2 tablespoons extra-virgin olive oil, to taste

Salt and finely ground black pepper

Soak the onions in 2 cups (475 ml) hot water for 5 minutes. Drain and spread to dry on a clean kitchen towel, then transfer to a medium mixing bowl. Add the parsley, sumac, lemon juice, olive oil, and salt and pepper to taste and mix well. Taste and adjust the seasoning if necessary.

EGGPLANT in TOMATO SAUCE

IMAM BAYILDI

The name of this dish is almost always wrongly translated as "the imam fainted," but according to Nevin Halici, my guru for all things culinary in Turkey, it cannot be the right translation as no Turkish imam would faint when presented with a dish made with two of the most basic ingredients in Turkey. Whatever the name actually means, imam bayildi is one of the great Turkish dishes. You can make it using Japanese eggplants as suggested in the recipe below, or you can use larger eggplants (four for the quantities listed below), which you need to halve lengthwise and fry before filling and cooking as below. The large eggplants may take a little longer to fry.   SERVES 4 TO 6

FOR THE EGGPLANTS
12 Japanese eggplants
   (about 3 ounces/85 g
   each)
Vegetable oil, for deep-
   frying

FOR THE STUFFING
3 tablespoons extra-
   virgin olive oil
4 medium onions
   (1 pound 5 ounces/
   600 g total), halved
   lengthwise and cut into
   thin wedges
6 cloves garlic, finely
   chopped
2 medium tomatoes
   (7 ounces/200 g),
   halved and thinly sliced
1 teaspoon tomato paste
A few sprigs flat-leaf
   parsley, most of
   the bottom stems
   discarded, finely
   chopped
Sea salt

1. To prepare the eggplants: Trim off the stem and peel off the calyx (cap) at the top of the eggplants. Peel the eggplants lengthwise to create a striped effect.

2. Pour 2 inches (5 cm) vegetable oil into a large skillet and heat over medium-high heat until hot (if you drop a piece of bread in the oil, the oil should immediately bubble around it). Working in batches, drop in as many eggplants as will fit comfortably in the pan and fry for 8 to 10 minutes, turning them over every now and then, until they are soft and golden brown all over. Gently remove them with a slotted spoon onto several layers of paper towels to drain off the excess oil.

3. To make the stuffing: Heat the oil in a large sauté pan over medium-high heat. Add the onion and cook, stirring occasionally, until the onion is soft and translucent, 5 to 7 minutes. Add the garlic and stir for a minute or so. Add the tomatoes and tomato paste and cook for 3 to 5 minutes, until the tomatoes have softened. Add ⅔ cup (160 ml) water, the parsley, and salt to taste. Simmer for 10 more minutes, until the sauce has thickened.

4. Preheat the oven to 350°F (180°C).

5. Make a lengthwise slit down each eggplant to make a pocket, taking care not to cut through to the other end. Gently prise each open and line them up in a shallow oven-to-table dish. Spoon as much onion/tomato filling as you can inside each eggplant, piling a little more on top to form a shallow mound.

6. Pour a little water to cover the bottom of the baking dish and bake for 30 to 40 minutes, or until the eggplants are soft. Let cool to room temperature and serve straight from the pan, or carefully transfer to a serving dish.

MOROCCAN STEAMED EGGPLANT SALAD

ZA'LUK

MOROCCO

Moroccan starters are made up of a dizzying array of what are described as *salades variées* (varied salads), most of which are more like side dishes than salads as we understand them. Many are cooked vegetable dishes, one of the most famous being *za'luk*. Some cooks use a lot more eggplant than tomatoes and others a good balance of both, which is how this recipe is.

SERVES 4 TO 6

2 large eggplants
   (14 ounces/ 400 g
   total), peeled
   lengthwise in strips,
   cut into 2-inch (5 cm)
   cubes
3 cloves garlic, peeled
   but whole
¼ cup (60 ml) extra-
   virgin olive oil
Two 14-ounce (400 g)
   cans whole peeled
   tomatoes, drained,
   seeded, and coarsely
   chopped
½ bunch cilantro
   (3½ ounces/100 g),
   most of the bottom
   stems discarded, finely
   chopped
½ teaspoon ground
   cumin
Juice of ½ lemon, or to
   taste
½ teaspoon paprika
¼ teaspoon red pepper
   flakes
Sea salt

1. Put the eggplant cubes and whole garlic in a steamer basket and steam for about 30 minutes, or until very soft.

2. Put the olive oil in a sauté pan. Add the chopped tomatoes, cilantro, and cumin and mix well. Place over medium-high heat and cook, stirring occasionally, for about 15 minutes, or until the juices have evaporated and the sauce looks fresh and chunky.

3. Mash the steamed eggplant and garlic with a fork or a potato masher—don't use a food processor or else the eggplant will become too mushy. The salad should have a soft but chunky texture.

4. Add the mashed eggplant and garlic to the tomato sauce along with the lemon juice, paprika, and pepper flakes. Season with salt to taste and mix well. Let simmer over low heat for another 10 minutes, stirring regularly, until there is no excess liquid in the pan. Taste and adjust the seasoning if necessary. Serve at room temperature.

SMOKY EGGPLANT DIP

BABA GHANNUGE

Together with hummus, this is the classic mezze dip that in Lebanon is called *baba ghannuge* and in Syria *mutabbal*. There is this rather puzzling habit in the Muslim world to switch names of dishes from one country to another: for example, the word *tagine* in Tunisia is a kind of frittata but in Morocco it is a stew. *Mutabbal* in Lebanon describes a grilled eggplant salad, which in Syria is called *baba ghannuge*, and at the beginning, when I was less aware of these quirks in naming dishes, I would get annoyed in Syrian restaurants thinking I had ordered one dish only to be presented with another.

SERVES 4 TO 6

FOR THE DIP
6 large eggplants (about 9 ounces/250 g each)
¼ cup (60 ml) tahini
1 to 2 cloves garlic, minced to a fine paste
Juice of 1½ lemons, or to taste
Sea salt

FOR SERVING
Fresh pomegranate seeds (ideally sour pomegranate)
Extra-virgin olive oil
Flatbread

1. Position a rack as close to the heat as you can (without the eggplant touching the heating element) and preheat a broiler to very high.

2. Prick the eggplants in several places to stop them from bursting. Place on a nonstick baking sheet and broil for 20 to 25 minutes on each side. The skins should become somewhat charred—this will give the dip the smoky flavor that is so typical.

3. Remove the broiled eggplants to a large cutting board. Cut each in half and scoop out the flesh. Place the flesh in a sieve and let sit for 30 minutes or so to drain the excess liquid.

4. Mash the eggplant in a large wide bowl, using a fork or a potato masher—do not use a food processor; the dip should have some texture. Add the tahini, garlic, lemon juice, and salt to taste. Mix well. Taste and adjust the seasoning if necessary.

5. Transfer to a medium shallow serving bowl and make grooves here and there. Garnish the peaks with pomegranate seeds and drizzle a little olive oil in the grooves. Serve with good bread.

MARIO HADDAD'S FATTOUSH

LEBANON

As much as I like my mother's fattoush, my favorite version is the one below, which I learned from Mario Haddad, a member of the Lebanese Academy of Gastronomy and the owner of the brilliant Falamanki, one of the coolest café/restaurants in Beirut. His recipe uses components of all the different variations and his seasoning mixes lemon juice with vinegar and sumac, pomegranate molasses, garlic, and even dried mint to produce a vibrant salad that is quite unique in flavor.

SERVES 6

FOR THE DRESSING

2 teaspoons sumac soaked for 15 minutes in 2 teaspoons warm water, plus more for tartness

1 small clove garlic, minced to a fine paste

4 teaspoons apple cider vinegar

Juice of 1 small lemon (see Note)

4 teaspoons pomegranate molasses

½ teaspoon dried mint

Sea salt

3 tablespoons extra-virgin olive oil

FOR THE SALAD

2 medium pita breads, split horizontally into disks, toasted in a hot oven until golden brown, and broken into bite-size pieces

3 tablespoons extra-virgin olive oil

10½ ounces (300 g) cherry tomatoes, quartered

3 mini cucumbers (4 ounces/120 g total), halved lengthwise and thinly sliced crosswise

4 Little Gem lettuces or 1 large romaine lettuce (1 pound/450 g), sliced crosswise into medium-thin strips

1 bunch scallions (2 ounces/50 g), thinly sliced

1 bunch flat-leaf parsley (7 ounces/200 g), leaves stripped off the stems

½ bunch mint (3½ ounces/100 g), leaves stripped off the stems

½ bunch purslane (3½ ounces/100 g), leaves stripped off the stems

1. To make the dressing: Put the sumac and its water, the garlic, vinegar, lemon juice, pomegranate molasses, and dried mint in a medium bowl. Mix well, then add salt to taste. Slowly add the olive oil until well blended. Taste and adjust the tartness to your taste.

2. To make the salad: Put the pieces of toasted bread in a large salad bowl and pour the olive oil over the bread. Toss together. (Coating the bread in olive oil makes it stay crisp longer by delaying the absorption of the moisture from the salad vegetables and the dressing.) Add the tomatoes, cucumbers, lettuce, scallions, parsley, mint, and purslane. Add the dressing and mix well, taking care not to bruise the vegetables or herbs. Taste and adjust the seasoning if necessary. If the fattoush is not tart enough, add a little more sumac.

NOTE: *At Falamanki, the chef uses about 1 tablespoon verjuice instead of lemon juice.*

STUFFED GRAPE LEAVES
Cooked on a Bed of LAMB CHOPS
MEHSHI WARAQ 'ENAB MA' KASTALETTAH

LEBANON | SYRIA | JORDAN | PALESTINE

This is the Lebanese/Syrian version of stuffed grape leaves cooked on a bed of lamb chops, and when done, the stuffed leaves are inverted onto a platter to form a cake with the lamb chops on top. It is one of the Levant's most festive dishes, always prepared when people receive honored guests or for special celebrations. When unripe green gage plums come into season in April/May, the dish can also include these for an extra sour note, already provided by the lemon juice added to the cooking liquid. A word of advice: Allow plenty of time to prepare this dish as it is fairly time-consuming, especially if you are not familiar with rolling stuffed grape leaves. In Iran, the rice is cooked prior to using in the stuffing, whereas in Lebanon it is not, so when you are rolling the leaves, roll the leaf loosely around the stuffing to allow room for the rice to expand. SERVES 4

FOR THE STUFFING
Scant ⅔ cup (125 g) Egyptian or Calasparra rice, rinsed
7 ounces (200 g) lean ground lamb
½ teaspoon ground allspice
¼ teaspoon ground cinnamon
¼ teaspoon finely ground black pepper
Sea salt

FOR THE LAMB CHOPS
8 thin lamb chops (1 pound 7 ounces/ 650 g total), most of the fat trimmed
Sea salt
1 cinnamon stick

FOR THE STUFFED GRAPE LEAVES
7 ounces (200 g) fresh or preserved medium grape leaves
Sea salt
Juice of 1 lemon, or to taste
1¾ cups (16 ounces/ 450 g) Greek yogurt, for serving

1. To make the stuffing: Put the rice in a large mixing bowl. Add the ground lamb and 2 tablespoons water. Season with the allspice, cinnamon, pepper, and salt to taste and mix well—we do it by hand to make sure the rice is well blended with the meat. Taste and adjust the seasoning if necessary.

2. To prepare the lamb chops: Put the lamb chops in a medium pot, and add water to cover by 2 inches (5 cm). Bring to a boil over medium heat, skimming the froth from the surface. Add a little salt and the cinnamon stick. Cover the pot and cook for 15 minutes, until they are just done. Lift the chops out and reserve the broth for later. Choose a pot with straight sides that's large enough to hold the chops in a tight, even layer over the bottom. Arrange the lamb in the pot.

Recipe continues

3. To make the stuffed grape leaves: If you are using fresh grape leaves, put them in a colander and run boiling water over them. This will soften them and make them easier to roll. If you are using preserved leaves, rinse them under cold water, at least a couple of times, to get rid of the briny taste.

4. Take a grape leaf and cut away the stem, if any, then lay flat on your work surface, smooth side down with the stem end nearest to you. Arrange from ½ to 1½ teaspoons stuffing, depending on the size of the leaf, in a thin raised line across the stem end of the leaf, about ½ inch (1 cm) away from the edge and more or less the same distance from the sides. Fold the sides over the rice, in a line that slightly tapers toward the bottom, then fold and tuck the stem end over the stuffing and roll neatly but loosely, to leave enough space for the rice to expand during cooking.

5. Place the rolled grape leaf, with the loose end down, on the lamb chops, starting from the side of the pot. Continue filling, rolling, and arranging the grape leaves, side by side, doing layer after layer, and not packing them too tightly, until you have finished both leaves and stuffing. (If you have any leftover stuffing, cook it as a side dish: Put it in a small pan, add an equal amount of water, and cook for 15 to 20 minutes, or until tender.)

6. Pour enough reserved broth over the rolled leaves so it just barely covers them—if you do not have enough broth, add water. Add salt to taste and swirl the stock around to dilute the salt. Put an overturned heatproof plate over the leaves to stop them from unrolling during cooking and cover the pan. Bring to a boil over medium-high heat, then reduce the heat to medium and let bubble gently for 45 minutes. Add the lemon juice and cook for another 15 minutes. It is a good idea to test one grape leaf before you take them off the heat, to make sure that the rice is cooked.

7. Remove from the heat and let the stuffed grape leaves sit, covered, for about 15 minutes. Wearing heatproof gloves, hold the leaves back with the plate covering and pour off the cooking juices into a medium bowl. Remove the plate. Invert a big round flat serving platter over the top of the pot. Hold it firmly against the pot with the palm of one hand. Then, slide the pot slowly over the edge of the counter and support it with your other hand. Lift the pot up and quickly turn it upside down. Slide the platter back onto your kitchen counter and slowly lift the pot off to uncover a cake of grape leaves topped with juicy lamb chops. (If you find this operation too cumbersome, simply spoon the rolled leaves out, a few at a time and arrange them in neat layers on a serving platter. Arrange the lamb chops over the stuffed leaves or around them.)

8. Baste with some of the cooking juice and serve immediately with a bowl of yogurt on the side.

IRANIAN STUFFED GRAPE LEAVES

DOLME-YE BARG-E MO

Dolma in Turkish, *dolme* in Persian, and *mehshi* in Arabic are all names to describe stuffed vegetables, said to have originated in Persia. Mīrzā ' Alī-Akbar Khan Āšpaz-bāšī, chef to the court of Nāṣer-al-Dīn Shah (1264–1313/1848–95—the first set of dates are for the hijri or Muslim calendar), recorded *dolma* as a category of Persian cuisine and gave recipes for stuffing grape leaves, cabbage leaves, cucumbers, eggplants, apples, and quince. They are one of the crowning glories of Levantine and Iranian cooking and no menu for a special meal, either celebratory or casual, would be complete without at least one type present at the table.

This recipe is for the Iranian version of stuffed grape leaves, where the stuffing is heavy on herbs and the stuffed leaves are cooked in a tamarind sauce. You can also cook them with lemon juice or verjuice (see Variation, page 396), and in early spring, consider layering a few green gage plums here and there between the rolled leaves for an extra special tartness.

SERVES 6 TO 8

FOR THE STUFFING
1 cup (200 g) short-grain rice, rinsed
½ teaspoon ground turmeric
Sea salt
Heaping ¼ cup (60 g) yellow split peas
3 tablespoons vegetable oil
2 large onions (14 ounces/400 g total)—1 grated and the other halved lengthwise and cut into thin wedges
1 pound 2 ounces (500 g) lean ground lamb
1¼ bunches flat-leaf parsley (9 ounces/ 250 g), most of the bottom stems discarded, finely chopped
A few sprigs tarragon, leaves stripped off the stems, finely chopped
A few sprigs marjoram, leaves stripped off the stems
A few sprigs dill, bottom stems discarded, finely chopped
½ teaspoon ground cinnamon
¼ teaspoon ground cloves
¼ teaspoon ground ginger
Sea salt and finely ground black pepper

FOR THE SAUCE
⅔ cup (120 g) seedless tamarind paste
4 tablespoons (60 g) unsalted butter, melted

FOR THE GRAPE LEAVES
Vegetable oil
60 brine-packed grape leaves, soaked in hot water to get rid of the saltiness, plus a few extra for lining the pan

1. To make the stuffing: Put the rice in a medium pot and add water to cover by 1½ inches (3 cm). Add the turmeric and 1 tablespoon sea salt. Bring to a boil over medium heat and cook for 3 minutes. Drain.

2. Put the split peas in a small pot and add water to cover by 1½ inches (3 cm). Bring to a boil over medium heat, then reduce the heat and let bubble gently for about 30 minutes, or until tender but not mushy. Drain.

Recipe continues

3. Heat the oil in a large skillet over medium heat. Add the sliced onion and let sizzle, then reduce the heat and fry, stirring occasionally, until the onion is soft and golden. Add the ground lamb and stir, breaking up any lumps, until the meat is no longer pink. Mix in the boiled rice, split peas, chopped herbs, ground spices, and salt and pepper to taste.

4. To make the sauce: Put the tamarind paste in a medium bowl. Add 1 cup (250 ml) hot water and let sit while you roll the grape leaves, stirring from time to time to help the paste dissolve in the water. Then strain through a fine-mesh sieve and mix with the melted butter.

5. To stuff the grape leaves: Now comes the time-consuming part. Drizzle a little oil over the bottom of a medium pot and line the bottom with a layer of loose grape leaves. Take a grape leaf, cut away the stem, if any, and lay it flat on your work surface, smooth side down with the stem end nearest to you. Depending on how big the leaf is, spread 2 to 3 teaspoons stuffing in a thin raised line across the leaf, about ½ inch (1 cm) away from the beginning of the stem and a little more distance short from either side. Fold the sides over the rice, in a line that slightly tapers toward the bottom, then fold the stem edge over the stuffing and roll neatly to completely encase the stuffing. Place the rolled grape leaf, with the loose end down on the grape leaves lining the bottom of the pot, starting from the side of the pan. Continue filling, rolling, and arranging the grape leaves, side by side, doing one layer after the other, and not packing them too tightly, until you have finished both leaves and stuffing.

6. Pour the tamarind sauce over the grape leaves and invert a plate over the grape leaves to weight them down and stop them from unfolding as they cook. Cover the pot and place over medium heat. Bring to a boil, then reduce the heat to low and let simmer for about 1 hour, or until the leaves and filling are tender. It is a good idea to taste one stuffed leaf before taking the pot off the heat to make sure it is done. Serve hot.

STUFFED GRAPE LEAVES WITH LEMON OR VERJUICE: Replace the tamarind sauce with this: Soak a good pinch of saffron in 2 tablespoons water in a small saucepan for 15 minutes. Add 4 tablespoons butter and place over low heat. Let simmer for 5 minutes. Combine ¾ cup (180 ml) lemon juice or verjuice, and ¼ cup (50 g) raw cane sugar, and add to the saffron/butter mixture. Mix well, then add to the stuffed grape leaves the same way as with the tamarind sauce and cook as directed.

STUFFED GRAPE LEAVES WITH POMEGRANATE SAUCE: Replace the tamarind sauce with this: Soak a good pinch of saffron in 2 tablespoons water in a small saucepan for 15 minutes. Add 4 tablespoons butter and place over low heat. Let simmer for 5 minutes. Mix 1 cup (250 ml) water with ½ cup (125 ml) pomegranate molasses. Add to the saffron/butter mixture. Mix well and add to the stuffed grape leaves the same way as with the tamarind sauce and cook as directed.

THE LORD OF STUFFED VEGETABLES

SHEIKH EL-MEHSHI

This dish is considered to be the most elegant of all stuffed vegetable dishes as indicated by its Arabic name, which translates as "the lord of stuffed vegetables." Use small Japanese eggplants for a beautiful presentation. *Sheikh el-mehshi* is said to have originated in the Aleppo/Damascus region and was made with greens. It is one of Ottoman cuisine's most famous dishes, going back to the eighteenth century. Serve the eggplants with plain rice.   SERVES 4

FOR THE STUFFING
⅓ cup (50 g) pine nuts
3 tablespoons (45 g)
   unsalted butter
5 ounces (150 g) ground
   lean lamb
½ teaspoon ground
   allspice
¼ teaspoon ground
   cinnamon
¼ teaspoon finely ground
   black pepper
Sea salt

FOR THE EGGPLANTS
12 Japanese eggplants,
   each about 4 inches
   (10 cm) long, with
   the stems on
   (1¾ ounces/50 g each)
Vegetable oil, for deep-
   frying

1. Preheat the oven to 450°F (220°C).

2. To make the stuffing: Spread the pine nuts on a nonstick baking sheet and toast in the oven for 5 to 7 minutes, or until golden brown. Keep the oven on, but reduce the temperature to 350°F (180°C).

3. Melt the butter in a medium skillet over medium heat. Add the lamb and cook until it loses all traces of pink. Keep mashing and stirring it with a wooden spoon or fork so that it separates well and does not form lumps. Take off the heat. Season with the allspice, cinnamon, pepper, and salt to taste. Add the toasted pine nuts and mix well. Taste and adjust the seasoning if necessary.

4. To prepare the eggplants: Trim the stems of the eggplants back to about ½ inch (1.25 cm) above the calyxes (caps). Peel the eggplants in lengthwise stripes about ½ inch (1.25 cm) wide.

5. Pour 2 inches (5 cm) vegetable oil into a large deep skillet and heat over medium heat until hot—test by dropping a piece of bread in it; if the oil immediately bubbles around it, it is ready. Fry the eggplants until golden all over. Remove with a slotted spoon and drain on several layers of paper towel.

6. Take one eggplant and with a small knife, slit it lengthwise down the middle—the peeled section will cut more easily—no more than halfway into the flesh. Gently pry the eggplant open and press on the flesh inside to form a pocket in which you will put 1 tablespoon meat stuffing. Place in a deep oven-to-table baking dish and fill the rest of

Recipe continues

Two 14-ounce (400 g) cans whole peeled tomatoes, drained and finely chopped

¼ teaspoon ground allspice

¼ teaspoon ground cinnamon

⅛ teaspoon finely ground black pepper

Sea salt

the eggplants in the same way. If there is any leftover stuffing, spread it on the bottom of the dish between the eggplants.

7. To make the tomato topping: Season the chopped tomatoes with the allspice, cinnamon, pepper, and salt to taste.

8. Spread the tomato sauce evenly all over the bottom of the baking dish in between the eggplants. Bake for 40 minutes, or until the tomatoes have softened and most of their juice has evaporated. Serve hot.

YOGURT SAUCE: There is an interesting northern variation in which the tomato topping is replaced with a yogurt sauce. Make the meat mixture and stuff the eggplants as directed. Arrange the eggplants in a wide sauté pan that will take the stuffed eggplants in one layer and is deep enough to also take the yogurt sauce. Omit the tomato mixture. Make the Cooked Yogurt Sauce (page 175), but use 3 tablespoons dried mint instead of a fresh herb. Mix the mint and garlic into the cooked yogurt and pour it hot over the eggplants. Simmer over very low heat for 10 minutes. (This version is cooked on the stovetop instead of baking, because the yogurt may curdle in the oven.)

IRANIAN HERB OMELET
SABZI KUKU

Kuku is a more elaborate version of a Spanish omelet, made with different fillings from green beans to this amazing herb version that is served for Nowruz (Persian New Year). *Sabzi* means "herbs" in Iranian and usually people buy the herbs ready-mixed and often chopped to order in the market, but you will have to make your own mix here in the West.

SERVES 4

Pinch of saffron threads

4 walnut halves, coarsely chopped

1 teaspoon dried barberries (zereshk)

1 bunch flat-leaf parsley (7 ounces/200 g), most of the bottom stems discarded, finely chopped

1 bunch cilantro (7 ounces/200 g), most of the bottom stems discarded, finely chopped

3 bunches scallions (5 ounces/150 g total), thinly sliced

½ teaspoon dried powdered fenugreek leaves

8 organic eggs

2 teaspoons unbleached all-purpose flour

1 teaspoon baking powder

Sea salt and finely ground black pepper

2 tablespoons vegetable oil

1. Put the saffron to steep in 2 teaspoons water.

2. Put the walnuts, barberries, herbs, scallions, and dried fenugreek in a large mixing bowl and mix well. Break the eggs into a medium mixing bowl and beat well. Add the saffron water, flour, and baking powder and mix well. Pour over the herbs. Season with salt and pepper to taste.

3. In a 6-inch (17.5 cm) round nonstick skillet (you don't want to use too large a pan as you need your omelet to be at least an even 1 inch [2.5 cm] high), heat the oil over medium heat until hot. Pour in the egg mixture and shake slightly from side to side to even out the mixture. Reduce the heat to low, cover, and let cook gently for about 25 minutes, or until the omelet has risen well. Invert a plate over the pan and invert the omelet onto it. Slide it back into the pan and cook, uncovered, for another 10 to 15 minutes, until browned on both sides and cooked through.

4. Gently transfer to a serving platter and serve hot or let cool to serve at room temperature.

IRAQI STUFFED ONIONS
DOLMA BASSAL

The best onions to use here are the elongated ones with a yellow or white skin. The red ones are the right flavor or shape but the color is too red and will not be as pretty as the white onions, which eventually end up a lovely brown color, from both the caramelization and the pomegranate molasses in the stuffing. It is one of my favorite *dolma* dishes, and I still remember the first time I had it in Kuwait, at a friend's beach house. His mother had cooked and sent the onions over together with other delightful Iraqi delicacies. She was Iraqi and had married my friend's father who was a Kuwaiti diplomat posted to Iraq, where they lived many years; and in their home, both Kuwaiti and Iraqi dishes were de rigueur at every meal.

SERVES 6 TO 8

FOR THE STUFFING
1½ cups (300 g) Egyptian or Calasparra rice, rinsed and soaked for 30 minutes in lightly salted water
1 small onion (3½ ounces/100 g), finely chopped

1 medium tomato (3½ ounces/100 g), cut into small cubes
½ cup (125 ml) extra-virgin olive oil
Juice of 2 lemons, or to taste
1 bunch flat-leaf parsley (7 ounces/200 g), most of the bottom stems discarded, finely chopped

A few sprigs mint, leaves stripped off the stems, finely chopped
⅓ cup (80 ml) pomegranate molasses
½ teaspoon ground turmeric
1 teaspoon finely ground black pepper
Sea salt

TO ASSEMBLE
15 large elongated onions (3½ ounces/100 g each), peeled
2 potatoes, peeled and cut into medium-thin slices
Sea salt

3½ cups (900 g) Greek yogurt, for serving

1. To make the stuffing: Drain the rice and transfer to a large mixing bowl. Add the onion, tomato, olive oil, lemon juice, parsley, mint, pomegranate molasses, turmeric, pepper, and salt to taste. Mix well.

2. To stuff the onions: Trim the top and bottom of each onion making sure you cut off the root part completely so that you can easily separate the layers once you have blanched them. Cut halfway through the onion lengthwise, just to the center. This way you can peel the layers one by one without tearing them. Fill a large pot with water and add the onions. Place over medium heat and bring to a boil. Reduce the heat to low and let simmer for 15 to 20 minutes, or until the onions have completely softened but are not mushy. Drain and let cool enough to handle.

3. Line a large pot in which you will cook the stuffed onions with the potatoes and sprinkle the potatoes with a little salt.

4. Mix the stuffing again, then separate the layers of onion and very gently place 1 to 3 teaspoons of stuffing in each, closing the onion over the stuffing. Reserve the last skinny layers to line the bottom of the pot. Remember that the rice will expand during cooking so don't fill the onion too much. Each filled onion should resemble a mini rugby ball. Place the filled onions fairly tightly side by side in the pot, making two or three layers, depending on the size of your pot. Once done, pour a little water into the stuffing bowl and swirl it around to extract the last of the juices and pour over the stuffed onions.

5. Add enough water to barely cover the onions. Sprinkle with salt to taste, then place an inverted heatproof plate over the stuffed onions to stop them from unrolling. Bring to a boil over medium heat, then cover, reduce the heat to medium-low, and let bubble gently for about 1 hour, until the filling is done. It is a good idea to taste one stuffed onion before taking the pot off the heat to make sure it is done.

6. Serve hot with the yogurt on the side.

STUFFED CABBAGE LEAVES
MEHSHI MALFUF

In Syria this dish is simply called *malfuf*, which in Arabic means both "cabbage" and "rolled," an apt name. A word of advice here. Cabbage leaves are prone to break while raw and they tear easily after they are blanched, so be gentle as you prise them free. If you can find one, use a flat-head cabbage: The leaves are more tender and they will make nicer stuffed leaves. You can use the same stuffing with *qara'* (*Cucurbito pepo* or *C. lagenaria*), a type of marrow related to zucchini (see Variation).

SERVES 4 TO 6

FOR THE STUFFING
½ cup (100 g) Egyptian or Calasparra rice
5 ounces (150 g) lean ground lamb
2 medium tomatoes (7 ounces/200 g total)
¼ teaspoon ground cinnamon

½ teaspoon ground allspice
½ teaspoon finely ground black pepper
Sea salt

FOR THE CABBAGE
1 head cabbage (about 3¼ pounds/1.5 kg), preferably a flat-head cabbage

2 medium tomatoes (7 ounces/200 g total), cut into medium-thin slices
3 or 4 lamb bones (optional)
Sea salt

TO FINISH AND SERVE
7 large cloves garlic, minced to a fine paste

1 tablespoon ground dried mint
2 tablespoons lemon juice
Sea salt

1¾ cups (16 ounces/ 450 g) Greek yogurt, for serving

1. To make the stuffing: Rinse the rice under cold water. Drain and put in a large mixing bowl. Add the ground lamb, then squeeze the fresh tomatoes with your hands over the meat and rice, extracting as much juice and pulp as you can. Line the bottom of the pot in which you will cook the stuffed leaves with the skins. Season with the cinnamon, allspice, pepper, and salt to taste and mix well. Taste and adjust the seasoning if necessary.

2. To prepare the cabbage leaves: Cut off the cabbage leaves, one by one, cutting as close to the core as you can. Gently remove each, making sure you do not break them. Discard any damaged outer leaves.

3. Fill a large pot with boiling water and salt to taste, place over high heat, and bring back to a boil. Plunge in a few leaves and blanch for 2 to 3 minutes, or until the leaves have softened. Carefully remove with a slotted spoon to a colander. Put a few more in the pot. Add more boiling water if necessary. Blanch and drain as with the first batch and continue until you have blanched all the leaves.

4. Shave the thick ribs off the leaves without breaking the leaves and if some leaves are too big to make a medium roll, cut them across in two, taking where the rib thins down

to become pliable as the dividing line. Pile the leaves one on top of the other on your work surface with the glossy sides down.

5.   Line a large pot with the cabbage ribs, then the sliced tomatoes and the bones if you are using them—they will make the sauce richer.

6.   To stuff the leaves: Lay one cabbage leaf at a time on your work surface, glossy side down, and with the cut side nearest to you. Spread 1 to 1½ teaspoons stuffing depending on the size of the leaf in a thin raised line across the leaf, about ½ inch (1 cm) inside the edge nearest to you and the same distance from the other edges. Roll the leaf over the stuffing fairly loosely in order to leave enough room for the rice to expand during cooking. Lift and place onto the bones and tomatoes, loose side down.

7.   Continue filling, rolling, and arranging the leaves, side by side, doing one layer at a time until you have finished both leaves and stuffing. If you have any leftover leaves, simply lay them over the rolled ones. If you have any leftover stuffing, cook it as a side dish: Put it in a small pan, add an equal amount of water, and cook for 15 to 20 minutes, or until tender.

8.   Pour some water in the empty stuffing bowl, swirl it around to extract the last bits of flavoring, and pour over the stuffed leaves until you barely cover them. Add salt to taste, bearing in mind that the stuffing is already seasoned, and place an overturned heatproof plate over the leaves to stop them from unrolling during cooking. Bring to a boil over medium-high heat, then cover, reduce the heat to medium-low, and let bubble gently for 30 minutes, until it is time to add the garlic/mint mixture.

9.   Put the garlic, mint, and lemon juice in a small bowl. Add salt to taste, and mix well. Uncover the pot and remove the plate covering the cabbage leaves. Stir the garlic and mint mixture into the cooking juices, tilting the pot to bring enough juice to the surface. Taste to check if you need to add any more salt. Cover and continue cooking for another 15 to 20 minutes, until both cabbage leaves and filling are tender. It is a good idea to taste one stuffed leaf to make sure it is done before taking the pot off the heat. Let sit for a few minutes off the heat.

10. Gently lift the stuffed leaves—you might have to use two spoons for the long-rolled leaves so as not so break them—onto a serving platter. Pour some sauce into a sauceboat and serve hot with a bowl of yogurt on the side.

STUFFED QARA': For this recipe, choose 8 to 10 small *qara'*, about 8 inches (20 cm) long, with a lovely pale green color that indicates freshness. Cut off and discard the stem ends, leaving most of the narrow top end on, and cut the bottoms of the marrows. Peel the skin off and use a corer to core the marrow from the wide bottom end, leaving walls about ⅛ inch (3 mm) thick. Rinse the cored marrows under cold water, and let drain. Make the stuffing as directed. Fill up to three-quarters of the marrow, leaving enough space for the rice to expand during cooking. Cook and finish as for the stuffed cabbage.

VEGETARIAN STUFFED SWISS CHARD

MEHSHI SILQ BIL-ZEYT

LEBANON | SYRIA

Traditionally this vegetarian stuffing includes chickpeas, which are soaked overnight, then skinned and split. I don't like their crunchy bite, finding it an unpleasant contrast to the melting rice and velvety leaves, and I make mine without. I even made my mother stop using them! In South Lebanon, they leave out the lemon juice and olive oil and increase the amount of sumac to 3 tablespoons. You can replace the Swiss chard with grape leaves, in which case the dish will be known in both Syria and Turkey as *yalanci* ("fake" in Turkish): Use 7 ounces (200 g) preserved or fresh grape leaves for the amount of stuffing below. The stuffed grape leaves are more commonly prepared and they are an indispensable addition to any mezze spread. They are time-consuming to make but well worth the effort. Practiced chefs can roll a whole potful of grape leaves in no time, using a particular way of bunching up the leaf around the filling and rolling it in seconds. I have yet to acquire this knack and because they take so long to make, I usually make mine a day ahead. In fact, they taste better the day after. You can use the same stuffing to stuff eggplants, zucchini, peppers, or tomatoes.

SERVES 4

FOR THE STUFFING
¾ cup (150 g) short-grain rice
3 firm-ripe medium tomatoes (10½ ounces/300 g total), cut into ¼-inch (6 mm) dice
1 bunch scallions (2 ounces/50 g), thinly sliced

½ bunch flat-leaf parsley (3½ ounces/100 g), most of the bottom stems discarded, coarsely chopped
¼ bunch mint (2 ounces/50 g), leaves stripped off the stems, coarsely chopped
2 heaping tablespoons ground sumac

½ teaspoon ground allspice or Lebanese 7-Spice Mixture (page 358)
¼ teaspoon ground cinnamon
¼ teaspoon finely ground black pepper
Juice of 1 large lemon, or to taste

½ cup plus 2 tablespoons (150 ml) extra-virgin olive oil
Sea salt

TO FINISH
2 bunches Swiss chard (2¼ pounds/1 kg total)
1 large tomato, thinly sliced
Sea salt

1. To make the stuffing: Rinse the rice under cold water. Drain well and put in a large mixing bowl. Add the tomatoes, scallions, parsley, and mint. Add the sumac, allspice, cinnamon, pepper, lemon juice, and olive oil. Season with salt to taste. Mix well. The stuffing should look more or less like a rice tabbouleh. Taste and adjust the seasoning if necessary.

2. To prepare the Swiss chard: Cut off the stems of the chard and set aside. Then cut across the top third of a leaf, taking where the central rib becomes thin and pliable as the dividing line. Then from the remaining piece of leaf, slice out and remove the thick rib, to create two more pieces of chard leaf. The pieces should make rolls measuring from 3 to 6 inches (8 to 15 cm) long. Some leaves may be too small to cut in three, in which case simply cut them in half, again taking where the rib becomes thin as the dividing line. Shave off the back of the thick rib of the bottom parts without breaking the leaf and reserve the stems and ribs to line the bottom of the pot. Arrange the cut leaves, smooth side down, in neat layers inside a colander. Then run boiling water over them to soften them. Let drain.

3. Line the bottom of a large pot—big enough to hold the stuffed leaves—with the stems and ribs from the chard leaves and the tomato slices.

4. To stuff the Swiss chard leaves: Remove any damaged leaves and lay them over the stems and tomato slices in the pan. Then, take one leaf and lay it, smooth side down, on your work surface with the cut side nearest to you and the veins running away from you. Spread 1 teaspoon stuffing (or more depending on the size of the leaf) in a long, thin, slightly raised line, along the side nearest to you, about ½ inch (1 cm) in from the edge and the same distance from the sides. Fold the narrow strip over the stuffing and roll into a flat, loosely packed roll to leave enough space for the rice to expand during cooking. Flatten the edges and carefully lift the rolled leaf and lay over the tomatoes with the loose side down. Continue stuffing, rolling, and arranging the stuffed leaves side by side, forming one layer at a time, until you have used up both leaves and stuffing. If you have leftover leaves, use them to cover the rolled ones. If you have any stuffing left over, make it into a side dish: Put it in a small pan with twice the amount of water and cook over low heat for 15 to 20 minutes, or until tender.

5. Pour enough water into the pot to barely cover the stuffed leaves and add a little salt, bearing in mind that the stuffing is already seasoned. Place an overturned heatproof plate over the leaves to stop them from unrolling during cooking. Bring to a boil over medium-high heat, then cover, reduce the heat to medium, and let bubble gently for 45 minutes, or until the stuffed leaves are done. Two-thirds of the way through cooking, taste the broth to check the salt content, adding more if necessary. It is a good idea to taste one stuffed leaf before taking the pot off the heat to make sure it is done. Remove from the heat and let cool.

6. Gently transfer the leaves to a serving platter—I usually pick them up with my fingers to keep them intact. Serve at room temperature.

EGYPTIAN MULUKHIYAH

MULUKHIYAH MASRIYAH

In Egypt, from where *mulukhiyah* (Jew's mallow in English) originates, people eat it as a soup, either on its own, or with rice, meat, and pickled onions. It is one of Egypt's national dishes, loved by rich and poor alike. I personally prefer the Lebanese or Saudi versions (see pages 409 and 434), having started out by hating *mulukhiyah* because of its mucilaginous texture. Then, my mother taught me how to minimize it by boiling the leaves for a very short time. The Egyptians, on the other hand, love the texture of *mulukhiyah*. They also believe it is a superfood, enhancing immunity among other good things. The main difference between the Egyptian and Lebanese versions, apart from the accompaniments, is that in Egypt, *mulukhiyah* is flavored with a garlic and ground coriander *taqliyah* (a kind of soffrito), whereas in Lebanon, cilantro is also added to the *taqliyah*. Serve the dish with Lebanese/Syrian Vermicelli Rice (page 241) on the side.   SERVES 4 TO 6

FOR THE CHICKEN AND BROTH
1 whole chicken
　(3 pounds 5 ounces/
　1.5 kg)
2 bay leaves
4 green cardamom pods,
　smashed
1 small onion
　(3½ ounces/100 g),
　peeled
Sea salt

FOR THE SOUP
Vegetable oil, for frying
10 cloves garlic, minced
　to a fine paste
2 teaspoons ground
　coriander
Sea salt
Juice of 1 small lemon, or
　to taste
One 17.6-ounce
　(500 g) package frozen
　mulukhiyah, thawed

1. To cook the chicken and make the broth: Put the chicken in a large pot. Add water to cover and bring to a boil over medium-high heat, skimming the surface. Add the bay leaves, cardamom pods, onion, and salt to taste. Cook for 45 minutes to 1 hour, or until the chicken is done. Remove the chicken from the broth and transfer to a plate. Joint the chicken into 8 parts and put in a medium pan. Pour a little broth over it. Cover the pan and keep warm, either over very low heat or in a warm oven. Strain the broth and measure out 2 cups (500 ml).

2. To make the soup: Heat 2 tablespoons vegetable oil in a small skillet over medium heat. Add the garlic, coriander, and salt to taste and cook for a couple of minutes, stirring occasionally, until the garlic is golden. Add the lemon juice and take off the heat.

3. Pour the reserved broth into a medium pot and bring to a boil. Add the thawed *mulukhiyah* and cook for 5 minutes, then add the garlic/coriander mixture and mix well. Taste and adjust the seasoning if necessary. Take off the heat.

4. Heat ½ inch (1 cm) vegetable oil in a large frying pan over medium heat. Quickly fry the chicken joints to brown them.

5. Serve the chicken alongside the soup and the rice.

LAMB SHANKS with MULUKHIYAH

MULUKHIYAH 'ALA LAHM

LEBANON

The mere mention of *mulukhiyah* transports me back to prewar Beirut summers when I used to spend my days lazing at the St. Georges beach—the St. Georges was the ritziest hotel in Beirut in those days, and as it was right on the sea, it had an elegant beach attached to it where *le tout* Beirut could be seen taking in the sun, water-skiing, or dining in the beach restaurant. One of the restaurant's star daily specials was *mulukhiyah*. On that given day, the restaurant would fill up, not only with the habitués—the beach was membership only—but also with nonmembers invited by their member friends to feast on this elaborate preparation. I hated the slimy texture of *mulukhiyeh* then and stayed by the pool while everyone went to lunch. Later, when I started to write about food, my mother shared the secrets for how to avoid the "sliminess." First, it is essential to pick the leaves off the stems without leaving any stems on them because that is where the mucilaginous substance lurks. Then, the lemon juice should be added to the broth before the leaves; and finally and just as important, it is essential not to overboil the leaves, otherwise they sink in the broth.

This can be made with dried, frozen, or fresh *mulukhiyah*. The dried leaves will taste quite different from the frozen and both are in my opinion inferior to the fresh leaves. So, try to source fresh *mulukhiyah* if you can. It is a good idea to prepare the fresh leaves before starting to cook the meat.

SERVES 6 TO 8

FOR THE LAMB
4 lamb shanks (3 pounds 5 ounces/1.5 kg total)
2 medium onions (10½ ounces/300 g total), peeled
2 sticks cinnamon
1 tablespoon sea salt

FOR THE MULUKHIYAH
3½ ounces (100 g) dried mulukhiyah leaves, or 1 pound 5 ounces (600 g) frozen

mulukhiyah, or 1 pound 5 ounces (600 g) fresh leaves on the stem
6 tablespoons (90 g) unsalted butter
10 cloves garlic, minced to a fine paste
1 bunch cilantro (7 ounces/200 g), most of the bottom stems discarded, finely chopped

½ teaspoon ground coriander
Juice of 2 lemons, or to taste
1 teaspoon ground allspice
½ teaspoon ground cinnamon
½ teaspoon finely ground black pepper
Sea salt

FOR SERVING
½ cup (125 ml) apple cider vinegar
1 large red onion, very finely chopped
2 medium pita breads, split horizontally into disks, toasted and broken into bite-size pieces
Lebanese/Syrian Vermicelli Rice (page 241)

Recipe continues

1. To cook the lamb: Put the shanks in a large pot. Add 7½ cups (1.75 liters) water and bring to a boil over medium-high heat, skimming the froth from the surface. Add the onions, cinnamon sticks, and salt. Reduce the heat to medium-low and let simmer for 1 hour, or until the shanks are done.

2. To prepare the *mulukhiyah*: For dried: Crumble the leaves with your hands and discard the stems if any. For frozen: Take them out of the freezer 30 minutes before you are ready to drop them into the broth to let them defrost. For fresh: Pick the leaves off the stems, making sure you do not leave any stem on them. Wash and dry them in a salad dryer, then spread them onto clean kitchen towels so that they dry completely. Chop the leaves into very fine slivers (see Note), doing this in small batches so as not to bruise them, and use a razor-sharp knife to slice them into ¹⁄₁₆-inch (1.6 mm) slivers. Place in a large bowl and cover with a clean kitchen towel until you are ready to use them.

3. Melt the butter in a medium skillet over medium heat. Add the garlic, cilantro, and ground coriander and sauté for a minute or so, until the cilantro has wilted but not turned brown. Take off the heat.

4. Reserving the broth, pull the meat and boiled onions out of the pot. Place the meat in a large bowl and cover. Put the onions in a smaller bowl. Discard the cinnamon sticks. Mash the onions into a puree and mix with the garlic/cilantro mixture. Measure out 5¼ cups (1.25 liters) of the meat broth and pour into a clean large pot.

5. Bring the broth to a boil over medium heat. Add the lemon juice, then the chopped (or whole) *mulukhiyah*. Season with the allspice, cinnamon, pepper, and salt to taste and bring back to a boil. Stir in the garlic/cilantro mixture and let bubble gently: 10 minutes if using dried leaves, 2 to 3 minutes if using frozen, and 5 minutes if using fresh leaves. Do not boil any longer as the *mulukhiya*h will sink in the broth and not stay suspended in it.

6. To serve, transfer the shanks to a cutting board and pick the meat off the bones, discarding any skin and fat. Tear the meat into bite-size pieces and transfer to a medium serving dish. Keep warm.

7. Put the vinegar in a small serving bowl. Add the chopped onion and mix well. Put the toasted bread in another medium serving dish and the rice in another. Pour the *mulukhiyah* into a soup tureen.

8. *Mulukhiyah* is a composite dish and it is served in soup plates with each diner making the layers to his/her taste by first spreading a few pieces of toasted bread on the plate, then spooning a little rice over the bread, scattering a few pieces of meat on top, and covering generously with *mulukhiyah*. The onion/vinegar mixture is drizzled over the top and can be omitted, but it gives the mixture a nice kick.

NOTE: *You can also use the leaves whole as they do in the South and drop them as they are in the broth, which will obviously save you a fair amount of time.*

CAULIFLOWER
in TOMATO SAUCE
CHOU-FLEUR BIL-TAMATEM

This is a very simple dish that could be easily changed into a *chakchouka* by spreading the finished dish in a large frying pan and placing over medium heat. Once the tomato sauce and cauliflower are hot, make 4 dips at equal distances and break four eggs in the dips. Let bubble gently until the eggs are done to your liking. Serve hot.   SERVES 4

Two 14-ounce (400 g)
   cans whole peeled
   tomatoes, drained,
   seeded, and coarsely
   chopped
3 cloves garlic, minced to
   a fine paste
2 tablespoons extra-
   virgin olive oil
1 teaspoon paprika
Sea salt and finely ground
   black pepper
1 cauliflower (1 pound
   7 ounces/650 g),
   broken into small
   florets

1. Put the tomatoes in a medium pot. Add ½ cup (125 ml) water, the garlic, olive oil, paprika, and salt and pepper to taste. Bring to a boil over high heat and let bubble for about 5 minutes, until the tomatoes have softened and the liquid has slightly reduced.

2. Add the cauliflower, reduce the heat to medium, cover, and cook for another 7 to 10 minutes, until the cauliflower is done to your liking and the sauce is very thick. If the tomato sauce is not thick enough, uncover the pan and boil for a few more minutes to reduce it. Serve hot, warm, or at room temperature.

VEGETABLE CURRY

Many people in India have this curry for breakfast with plain rice or a slice of bread. A wonderful start to the day! Traditionally, you would use fresh coconut to make the base for the curry, but it can be difficult to source in the West. You can re-create it by rehydrating dried shredded coconut, which is what I suggest below, or you can buy frozen grated coconut. In either case, let the coconut drain really well before toasting it.

SERVES 2

½ cup dried shredded coconut, soaked for up to 1 hour in ½ cup (125 ml) water until completely rehydrated
4 tablespoons (60 g) ghee or unsalted butter
3 dried red chilies
2 tablespoons coriander seeds
4 whole cloves
10 black peppercorns
One 2-inch (5 cm) cinnamon stick
2 medium onions (7 ounces/200 g total)—1 thinly sliced and 1 finely chopped
½ teaspoon mustard seeds
½ teaspoon cumin seeds
¼ teaspoon ground turmeric
¼ teaspoon asafetida powder (optional)
1 bay leaf
1 blade mace
Sea salt
1 pound (450 g) diced mixed vegetables (carrots, potato, sweet potato, yam, green beans, and peas)
1 teaspoon lime juice, or to taste
White rice, for serving

1. Drain the coconut, then squeeze it in your hands to extract as much of the liquid as possible. Melt 1 tablespoon of the ghee in a medium skillet over medium heat. Add the coconut and sauté for 5 minutes, or until lightly golden. Transfer to a small food processor.

2. In the same skillet, toast the whole red chilies and coriander seeds for a couple of minutes. Add the cloves, peppercorns, and cinnamon and toast for another minute or so. Add to the coconut along with the sliced onion and ½ cup (125 ml) water and process until you have a smooth mixture.

3. Heat the remaining 3 tablespoons ghee in a large heavy pot over medium heat. Add the mustard seeds, cumin seeds, turmeric, and asafetida (if using). Stir for a minute, then add the bay leaf and chopped onion and fry, stirring occasionally, until the onion is golden brown, about 10 minutes. Add the coconut/spice mixture and mace and fry, stirring regularly, for about 10 minutes, until you have a thick sauce.

4. Add 2½ cups (625 ml) water and salt to taste and bring to a boil before adding the vegetables in the order of their cooking time. First cook hard vegetables (such as carrots, potatoes, sweet potatoes, and yams) for 5 minutes, then add softer vegetables (such as green beans and peas). Simmer, uncovered, over low heat, for another 5 to 7 minutes, or until the vegetables are done. Add the lime juice just before taking off the heat. Serve hot with rice.

FAVA BEAN SALAD

SHLADA DEL FUL

In Morocco, they make this salad without peeling the fava beans, but I like to peel them for a prettier and fresher presentation. You can also prepare this salad with garden peas.   SERVES 4

1 pound 2 ounces (500 g)
    fresh or frozen shelled
    fava beans
3 tablespoons extra-
    virgin olive oil
1 small onion
    (3½ ounces/100 g),
    halved lengthwise and
    cut into thin wedges
Sea salt
¼ bunch cilantro
    (2 ounces/50 g), most
    of the bottom stems
    discarded, finely
    chopped
1 teaspoon paprika
Juice of ½ lemon, or to
    taste
½ preserved lemon, peel
    only, cut into thin strips

1. In a large pot of boiling water, blanch the fava beans for 2 to 3 minutes. Drain and rinse under cold water, then peel them and discard the skins.

2. Heat the oil in a medium skillet over medium heat. Add the onion and sauté until soft and lightly golden, about 5 minutes. Add the fava beans and ⅓ cup (80 ml) water, salt to taste, and bring to a boil. Cook, uncovered, stirring regularly, for 5 minutes, or until the fava beans have just softened without going mushy and without losing their beautiful green color.

3. Add the cilantro, paprika, and lemon juice and cook for another couple of minutes, or until the sauce is completely reduced. Transfer to a medium serving dish and garnish with the strips of preserved lemons. Serve hot, warm, or at room temperature.

INDIAN FRIED EGGPLANT
BEGUN BHAJA

INDIA

This is a lovely variation on plain fried eggplant, with a mildly spicy flavor that makes them a perfect accompaniment to the Bengali Khichdi (page 232) or any grilled fish, meat, or poultry. They also make a scrumptious vegetarian sandwich wrapped in flatbread. SERVES 4 TO 6

2 teaspoons Kashmiri
   chili powder
1 teaspoon ground
   turmeric
Sea salt
2 large eggplants
   (1 pound 2 ounces/
   500 g total), cut into
   medium thick rounds
¼ cup (60 ml)
   mustard oil

1. Put the chili powder, turmeric, and a little salt in a small bowl and mix well. Spread on a plate.

2. Dip both sides of each eggplant slice in the spice mix and shake off any excess—this is best done as soon as you cut the eggplant.

3. Set a wire rack in a rimmed baking sheet. Heat the mustard oil in a large skillet over medium heat until really hot (test by dropping a piece of bread into the oil; if it immediately bubbles around it, it is ready). Add as many eggplant pieces as will fit comfortably into the pan (see Note) and fry until golden brown on both sides, 2 to 3 minutes on each side. Transfer to the wire rack to drain off any excess oil. When done, the eggplants should be crisp on the edges and soft and silky on the inside. Serve hot, warm, or at room temperature.

NOTE: *It's best to fry the eggplants all in one go, otherwise there will be masala residue in the pan that will burn and stick to any subsequent batch. If your skillet is not large enough, wipe it clean after the first batch and use fresh mustard oil to fry the second batch.*

WILD ENDIVE in OLIVE OIL
HINDBEH BIL-ZEYT

Italian *cicoria* or *hindbeh* is available from Middle Eastern stores in summer. The type I buy in Sicily comes in long bunches, with thin stems and wide leaves that are kind of serrated with pointed ends where they branch off and it is slightly different from that available in Lebanon. That said, the taste is pretty much the same and it makes a wonderful mezze dish that also has the advantage of being supremely healthy.

SERVES 4

2¼ pounds (1 kg) Italian cicoria or wild endive
Sea salt
½ cup (125 ml) extra-virgin olive oil
4 medium onions (about 14 oz/400 g total), halved and cut into thin wedges
Lemon wedges, for garnish

1. Wash and drain the *cicoria*. Trim the bottoms of the stems and cut into pieces 2½ inches (6 cm) long.

2. Set up a large bowl of ice and water. Fill a large pan with water and bring to a boil over medium-high heat. Add salt to taste (I like to add enough salt so that I don't need to salt the greens after). Add the *cicoria*, return to a boil, and let bubble for 5 minutes, until just cooked. Drain the *cicoria* and dunk in the iced water.

3. Heat the olive oil in a large skillet over medium heat. Add the onions and fry, stirring occasionally, until the onion turns a rich golden brown, being mindful not to let it burn, about 10 minutes. With a slotted spoon, transfer three-quarters of the onion to a sieve to drain any excess oil and crisp up. Leave the rest in the pan.

4. Squeeze the cooked *cicoria* dry, then loosen the leaves and put them in the pan with the fried onion and oil. Sauté over medium heat for a couple of minutes, stirring regularly, until the *cicoria* is well blended with the oil and onion. Transfer to a serving platter. Scatter the crispy onion all over. Serve at room temperature with lemon wedges.

SPINACH with PANEER
PALAK PANEER

INDIA | PAKISTAN

There are many ways of making this northern Indian dish. You can blanch the spinach whole and cream it, or you can chop it and blanch it to use as is, or you can quickly sauté the spinach, either whole or chopped, before adding the paneer. As for the paneer, you can pan-fry it before adding to the spinach or add it as is. My favorite is to sauté the spinach whole, drain it if there is any excess liquid, then pan-fry the paneer separately and add it at the very end to combine crisp with creamy. That said, all versions are just as delicious and you can choose the one to your taste.

SERVES 4 TO 6

1 tablespoon vegetable oil
14 ounces (400 g) baby spinach
1 tablespoon ghee
½ teaspoon cumin seeds
1 medium onion (about 5 ounces/150 g), finely chopped

1 small green chili, seeded and thinly sliced
½ inch (1 cm) fresh ginger, peeled and minced to a fine paste
1 clove garlic, minced to a fine paste
½ teaspoon Kashmiri chili powder

2 teaspoons ground coriander
3 medium tomatoes (10½ ounces/300 g total), peeled, seeded, and processed into a puree
Sea salt
5 ounces (150 g) paneer, cut into medium cubes

1 tablespoon heavy cream
¼ teaspoon garam masala (grind 1 clove, 1 green cardamom pod, and ½ cinnamon stick)
Pinch of crumbled dried fenugreek leaves
White rice or roti, for serving

1. Heat the oil in a large skillet over medium-high heat until hot. Add as much spinach as you can fit into the pan, remembering that it will wilt very quickly, and sauté until just wilted, 3 to 4 minutes. You may have to do this in several batches, adding a little more oil in between batches. Place the cooked spinach in a colander to drain off any excess liquid.

2. Melt the ghee in a deep sauté pan over medium heat. When the ghee is hot, add the cumin seeds and let them sizzle. Add the onion and chili and sauté until the onion is golden brown, about 10 minutes. Add the ginger and garlic and sauté for a minute or so. Then stir in the Kashmiri chili powder and coriander.

3. Add the tomato puree and salt to taste and let bubble for 5 minutes or so, until thickened. Add the drained spinach. Mix well and cook for 5 more minutes. Add the paneer. Mix well. Reduce the heat to low, cover, and cook for a couple of minutes, until everything is well blended. Add a little water if the mixture is too dry and taste for salt. Increase the heat to medium and cook for about 10 minutes, until the spinach is done and there is hardly any sauce left. Add the cream, garam masala, and the crumbled fenugreek leaves and mix well. Cook for a couple more minutes. Transfer to a serving dish and serve hot with rice or roti.

IRANIAN PICKLED EGGPLANTS

TORSHI-YE BÂDENJÂN

There are two ways of making Iranian eggplant pickles. This one, where the eggplants are kept whole and stuffed with an herb mixture, and another with the eggplants mashed and mixed with herbs, garlic, and chili. You can use other vinegars, but wine or any other type of alcohol is forbidden in Islam, so they only use white or apple cider vinegar. MAKES ONE 1-QUART (1-LITER) JAR

15 Japanese eggplants (1¾ ounces/50 g each)

1¼ bunches flat-leaf parsley (9 ounces/ 250 g total), most of the bottom stems discarded, finely chopped

1¼ bunches cilantro (9 ounces/250 g total), most of the bottom stems discarded, finely chopped

4 teaspoons dried mint

4 teaspoons dried basil

10 cloves garlic, minced to a fine paste

2 teaspoons plus 2 tablespoons sea salt

2 teaspoons nigella seeds

1 teaspoon coriander seeds

4 small green chilies

2 cups (500 ml) apple cider vinegar

1. Stem the eggplants and remove the calyxes (caps).

2. Put the eggplants in a steamer basket and steam for 10 to 15 minutes, until soft but not mushy. Transfer to a colander and put a weighted bowl over them to press out any excess liquid. Let drain for 24 hours, then spread on paper towels—squeezing the eggplants dry will stop them from spoiling quickly.

3. Put the fresh and dried herbs in a large mixing bowl. Add the garlic and 2 teaspoons of the salt. Mix well.

4. Make a lengthwise slit down the eggplants making sure you don't cut through them. Gently pry them open and fill each with as much of the herb mixture as you can fit in the opening. Close each eggplant, wipe it clean, and lay flat in a sterilized 1-quart (1-liter) canning jar. When you have done one layer, sprinkle a little of the remaining salt, nigella, and coriander seeds all over. Add 2 of the chilies, then make a second layer and a third dividing the remaining salt, nigella, and coriander seeds as well as the 2 chilies equally between the layers. Pack the jar tightly, then pour the cider vinegar over the eggplants to cover completely. Add any remaining salt. Close tightly and gently shake back and forth to distribute the salt. Store in a cool, dark place. The pickled eggplant will be ready within 2 to 3 weeks.

TURKISH PICKLED GREEN ALMONDS

ÇAĞLA TURŞUSU

Some cooks use a pure vinegar solution to pickle both fruit and vegetables, but I prefer to dilute the vinegar with water as I find the pure vinegar solution too tart. There is a wonderful pickle store in Nisantasi, a well-heeled neighborhood in Istanbul, where they only sell pickles. The display is quite spectacular, with jars filled with fruit, vegetables, herbs, such as fresh thyme, and even fresh nuts stacked to the ceiling. They are famous throughout Turkey and beyond for having the best pickles, and they still work in an artisanal way with the family overseeing the production.

MAKES ONE 1-QUART (1-LITER) JAR

1 cup (250 ml) white or
   apple cider vinegar
2 teaspoons sea salt
1 pound 11 ounces (750 g)
   fresh green almonds

Put the vinegar in a large measuring cup. Add 2 cups (500 ml) water and the salt. Mix until the salt is dissolved. Wash the fresh almonds and drain well. Pack tightly in a sterilized 1-quart (1-liter) jar. Pour the pickling solution over the almonds to cover them. Close the jar and store in a cool, dark place. The pickled almonds will be ready within 5 days to a week.

PINK PICKLED TURNIPS
KABISS LEFT

This pickling solution for Lebanese/Syrian pickles, which are less tart than either Iranian or Turkish, can be used with the vegetable of your choice, from cabbage to cucumber to green tomatoes. Pickled turnips are probably the most famous of Lebanese/Syrian pickles, mainly for their beautiful pink color imparted by the added beet. Sadly these days most people, especially those commercial pickle makers, use artificial coloring for a psychedelic rather than vibrant pink. At home though, they are still colored naturally with beet. Be mindful to store the jars in a dark spot, as light will cause the color to fade. The taste will not be affected much, but the presentation will no longer be attractive.

MAKES ONE 1-QUART (1-LITER) JAR

⅔ cup (160 ml) grape vinegar
2 tablespoons sea salt
1 teaspoon sugar
1 pound 2 ounces (500 g) small turnips
1 small beet, washed, unpeeled, and quartered
1 fresh chili (optional)

1. Put the vinegar, salt, and sugar in a spouted pitcher or large measuring cup. Add 1¼ cups (310 ml) water and mix until both salt and sugar are completely dissolved.

2. Wash and dry the turnips, then trim the stem and root ends and pull out any thin roots on the skin.

3. If the turnips are very small, make one deep incision down the middle from the root end stopping about ¼ inch (6 mm) short of the stem end. If they are small to medium, cut into them every ½ inch (1 cm) from the root end to have thin slices, making sure you do not cut through to the other side.

4. Pack them into a sterilized 1-quart (1-liter) canning jar, interspersing the beet pieces, which will turn the white turnip a lovely pink color. Add the chili (if using). Pour the pickling solution over the turnips to cover them. Close the jar and store in a cool, dark place. They will be ready to consume within 2 to 3 weeks.

EGGPLANT with WALNUTS and GARLIC Preserved in OLIVE OIL

MAKDUSS

SYRIA

This is a wonderful Syrian way to preserve eggplants. In Syria, many use tiny white eggplants to make *bijou makduss* that can be eaten in one bite, but you can just as well make them with Japanese eggplants, which are more commonly available.

MAKES ONE 1-QUART (1-LITER) JAR

1 pound 10 ounces
 (750 g) Japanese
 eggplants
1 tablespoon coarse sea
 salt
2 heads garlic
 (3½ ounces/100 g
 total), separated into
 cloves and peeled
1 fresh red chili, seeded
1 teaspoon fine sea salt
⅔ cup (100 g) walnuts
Extra-virgin olive oil

1. Discard the eggplant stems and peel off the calyxes (caps), but without cutting into the eggplants. Put the eggplants in a large pot. Cover with boiling water and add the coarse salt. Place over medium-high heat, bring to a boil, and let bubble for 5 minutes. Drain and place in a colander. Weight down the eggplants to extract as much excess liquid as you can.

2. Put the garlic and trimmed chili in a food processor and add the fine salt. Process until nearly smooth. Add the walnuts and process until the walnuts are ground medium-fine. The filling should have a fine crunch.

3. Make a lengthwise slit down the middle of each eggplant, cutting halfway into the flesh—be careful not to cut through the other side. Gently prise the flesh open with your fingers to create a pocket for the filling. Press 1 teaspoon of the walnut-garlic mixture into the eggplant. Smooth the filling to level it with the eggplant, put on a plate, and fill the remaining eggplants in the same way.

4. Pack the eggplants in layers, filled side up, in a sterilized glass jar, arranging them snugly next to one another without crushing them. Cover with extra-virgin olive oil. Close the jar and store in a cool, dark place. They will be ready within 3 to 4 weeks.

LIME PICKLES

ACHAAR

INDIA/PAKISTAN

These are traditionally made with yellow limes, but I have also made them with small lemons and they worked out really well. Another type of lemon that would be eminently suitable is the Moroccan *doqq*, which has a thin skin.

MAKES THREE 1-PINT (500 ML) JARS

FOR THE PICKLES

15 yellow limes or small lemons with a thin skin, stem end cut but without cutting into the pulp, washed, and dried

3 cloves garlic, minced to a fine paste

½ teaspoon ground turmeric

¼ teaspoon ground fenugreek

⅓ cup (30 g) Kashmiri chili powder

½ cup (75 g) coarse sea salt

FOR THE TEMPERING

½ cup vegetable oil

3 dried red chilies

¾ teaspoon cumin seeds

¾ teaspoon mustard seeds

6 fresh curry leaves

¼ teaspoon asafetida powder

1. To make the pickles: Squeeze the juice from 5 limes into a small bowl and set aside. Cut the rest into 8 pieces each, by first halving crosswise, then cutting each half into 4 wedges. Remove the seeds and put in a large bowl. Add the garlic, turmeric, and fenugreek and mix well. Add the chili powder and salt and mix again. Add the lime juice. Mix again, then cover with plastic wrap and keep in the refrigerator for 3 days. As they are, these will last for a few months. You can serve them as is, or you can temper them by adding the tempering solution to serve after a few days. Once tempered, the limes will not last past 2 to 3 weeks.

2. To temper the limes (or lemons): Heat the oil in a medium skillet over medium heat until hot. Stir in the chilies, cumin seeds, and mustard seeds. Take off the heat as soon as the spices start to sizzle. Add the curry leaves and asafetida. They will sizzle as the oil will still be hot. Mix well and transfer to three sterilized 1-pint (500 ml) jars. Divide equally between the jars of pickled lime. The pickled lime will be ready in 5 days and will last about 2 to 3 weeks. Store in a cool, dark place or refrigerate.

GREEN MANGO PICKLE

AAM KA ACHAAR

INDIA | PAKISTAN

Pickle or relish, it is a moot point, but whatever you want to call this green mango "preserve," it is very easy to make and delicious served with plain rice and Vegetable Curry (page 415) or any other curry of your choice, or simply with grilled or roast meats. MAKES ONE 1-PINT (500 ML) JAR

1 large green mango, about 14 ounces (400 g), peeled and cut into medium cubes (about 2½ cups)
1 tablespoon salt
1 teaspoon fenugreek seeds
1 teaspoon nigella seeds
1 tablespoon ground coriander
1 tablespoon ground fennel
1 teaspoon Kashmiri chili powder
¼ teaspoon ground turmeric
2 tablespoons mustard oil

1. Put the diced mango in a medium mixing bowl. Add the salt and mix well. Let sit for 4 hours.

2. Mix the mango again and squeeze it dry over a small bowl, reserving the liquid for later. Spread the mango over a tray to let it dry. If you have access to a sunny table, leave it in the sun for 4 hours, otherwise let it dry overnight on your kitchen counter. You don't want the mango to become dried out, just drier and slightly shrunk.

3. While the mango is drying, add the spices to the reserved salt water and mix well.

4. When the mango is ready, add the spiced water together with the mustard oil and mix well. Pack in a sterilized 1-pint (500 ml) glass jar. Seal and store in a cool, dark place. The pickle/relish will be ready to eat within a week and will last for a few months.

SAUDI "SALSA"

DUGGUS

Also known as *daqqouss*, this relish is the Saudi equivalent of Mexican salsa even if it is lightly cooked. *Duggus* is served with a variety of dishes including Saudi Lamb Kabsa (page 219), which is Saudi Arabia's national dish, and the Saudi Meat Pies (page 47). And if you like spicy flavors, simply increase the amount of chili pepper given below.

MAKES JUST UNDER 1 CUP (SCANT 250 G)

1 tablespoon extra-virgin olive oil

1 clove garlic, minced to a fine paste

3 medium tomatoes (10½ ounces/300 g total), peeled and finely chopped

1 green chili, finely chopped

1 teaspoon tomato paste

Sea salt

1. Heat the oil in a shallow skillet over medium heat. Add the garlic and stir-fry until fragrant.

2. Add the tomatoes and chili. When the tomatoes start bubbling, add the tomato paste and ¼ cup (60 ml) water. Reduce the heat to medium-low. Let bubble gently for 5 minutes, stirring every now and then, until the "salsa" is slightly reduced. Add salt to taste. Take off the heat and let cool. You can keep this refrigerated for about 1 week.

FALAFEL

Originally from Egypt where they are known as *ta'miyah*, falafel are a typical street food throughout the Middle East and beyond now that they have gone global. For a perfect texture the soaked legumes need to be minced in a meat grinder using the finest attachment. According to Mohammed Antabli, chef owner of Al Waha restaurant in London, whose recipe this is, grinding them this way makes them fluffy and less pasty, as if they were minced in a food processor. However, not many cooks have a meat grinder and using a food processor will also yield a good result.

SERVES 4 TO 6

⅔ cup (3½ ounces/ 100 g) dried chickpeas, soaked overnight in plenty of water with ½ teaspoon baking soda

1⅓ cups (7 ounces/ 200 g) peeled split dried broad beans, soaked overnight in plenty of water with 1 teaspoon baking soda

5 large garlic cloves, peeled

1 small onion, peeled

¼ bunch cilantro (2 ounces/50 g)

1 teaspoon ground cumin

1 teaspoon ground allspice or Lebanese 7-Spice Mixture (page 358)

¼ teaspoon finely ground black pepper

⅛ teaspoon cayenne pepper

½ teaspoon baking soda, plus another ½ teaspoon to mix in just before frying

Sea salt

Vegetable oil for deep-frying

FOR THE GARNISH

Tahini Sauce (page 128)

Pink Pickled Turnips (page 424)

Sliced tomatoes

Chopped flat-leaf parsley

Flatbread, for serving

1. Drain and rinse the chickpeas and broad beans. Grind through a meat grinder with the finest blade attached, together with the garlic, onion, and coriander. If you don't have a grinder, process in a food processor until you have a fine paste.

2. Transfer the mixture to a bowl. Add the seasonings, ½ teaspoon baking soda, and salt to taste. Taste and adjust the seasoning if necessary. Cover and let rest for 30 minutes in the refrigerator.

3. Pour 2 inches (5 cm) of vegetable oil in a large frying pan and place over a medium heat. Mix the remaining ½ teaspoon baking soda in the falafel mix. When the oil is hot—drop in a piece of bread; if the oil immediately bubbles around it, it is ready—start shaping the falafel. If by hand, make rather shallow round patties measuring 1½ inches (3½ cm) in diameter and ¾ inch (1½ cm) thick. If you have a falafel mold, use the spatula part of the falafel shaper to scoop a little falafel mixture. Pack it into the mold, making sure you slide the lever down to make space. Fill the mold, then smooth the mixture down against its sides to make a mound. Hold the mold over the hot oil and

release the lever to pop the falafel into the oil. Be careful not to splash. Repeat the process until you have used up all the falafel mix, making sure you do not crowd the frying pan. You should end up with about 15 falafel balls. If you've shaped the falafel by hand, slide them into the oil. Fry for 3 to 4 minutes, stirring every now and then, until the falafel are golden brown all over. Remove with a slotted spoon onto several layers of paper towels to drain off the excess oil or place on a wire rack with a baking sheet underneath to collect the dripping oil.

4. Serve the falafel hot with the tahini sauce, vegetable garnishes, and good flatbread, either on their own or as part of a mezze spread.

HOMMUS

Hommus is a Levantine dip that has gone completely global, and as such the name has become generic to describe any kind of dip, whether made with chickpeas or not—*hommus* means "chickpeas" in Arabic. You can make it with dried chickpeas, which you'll need to soak overnight, or you can shorten the preparation considerably by using already cooked chickpeas preserved in salted water—I like those preserved in glass jars rather than cans. You will need about 2½ cups (400g) of preserved chickpeas, drained and rinsed before using. And for the ultimate hommus, you also need to peel the cooked chickpeas, not one by one but rather by rubbing them slightly against each other to loosen the skins, then either picking out the skins or running cold water while swirling the chickpeas with your hand to let the skins float to the surface so that you can skim them.

SERVES 4

Just over 1 cup (200 g) dried chickpeas, soaked overnight in plenty of water with 1 teaspoon baking soda
¾ cup (180 ml) tahini
Juice of 2 lemons, or to taste
2 garlic cloves, minced to a fine paste
Fine sea salt

FOR THE GARNISH
Aleppo pepper
Extra-virgin olive oil
Flatbread, for serving

1. Drain and rinse the chickpeas. Place them in a saucepan, cover well with cold water, and place over a medium-high heat. Bring to a boil, reduce the heat to low, and simmer, covered, for 1 to 1½ hours, or until very tender.

2. Drain the chickpeas, keeping some of the cooking water in case you need to thin the puree later. Put in a food processor together with the tahini, lemon juice, and garlic and process to a smooth puree. Transfer to a mixing bowl. If the dip is too thick, use a little of the cooking liquid to thin it down—the dip should be creamy but not runny. Taste and adjust the seasoning if necessary, then spoon into a shallow round or oval bowl. Spread across the dish, raising the dip slightly around the edges and in the center. Sprinkle the raised edges and the center with Aleppo pepper and drizzle a little olive oil in the groove inside the edges. Serve with good flatbread either on its own or as part of a mezze spread.

TAHINI SAUCE

TAHINA

If you walk around the old part of Cairo during Ramadan, you will find restaurants having already laid their tables for *iftar*, and if you are there close to sunset, you will also find diners sitting down, waiting for the muezzin—the chosen person at the mosque charged with leading the prayer five times a day, every day, and at special events—to announce the break of the fast as soon as the sun sets. On the table, there will be a plate of *tahina*, bread, juices, and water, as well as a salad and dates. People wait patiently until the cry of the muezzin announces the sun has finally set and even though they will not have eaten or drunk anything since sunrise, none of the seated people will rush to drink or eat anything. It all seems to happen very serenely, almost as if it were in slow motion. I never tire of watching how dignified the break of the fast is, even among the poor who gather around what in Egypt is called *ma'edat al-rahman,* which means "the table of the one who takes pity." These meals are subsidized by local businesses, rich patrons, and mosques, and anyone can sit at the meal provided, which, in Egypt, will always include *tahina*, a thick tahini sauce. In Egypt, it is served as a dip with *aysh* (Egyptian pita, which is thicker than the Lebanese/Syrian) for breaking the fast. You can also serve it with pita chips or a selection of crudités.

SERVES 4

½ cup (125 ml) tahini
Juice of 1 lemon, or to taste
1 small clove garlic, minced into a fine paste
Sea salt

Put the tahini in a medium mixing bowl and gradually, and alternately, add the lemon juice and ¼ cup (60 ml) water. Disconcertingly, the tahini will first thicken, despite the fact that you are adding liquid, but do not worry, it will soon start to thin out again. Keep stirring until the sauce has a consistency that is slightly thicker than double cream. Add the garlic and salt to taste and mix well. Taste and adjust the seasoning if necessary.

SAUDI MULUKHIYAH DIP

HARISSAH AL-MULUKHIYAH

Here is a very unusual Saudi dip made with *mulukhiyah* (the leaves of a plant commonly known as Jew's mallow). You can make it with fresh *mulukhiyah*, if it is available, or you can use dried *mulukhiyah*, which is what I did in the recipe.

SERVES 8

1 pound 2 ounces (500 g) boneless lamb leg or shoulder
4 green cardamom pods
2-inch (5 cm) piece galangal
6 black peppercorns
Sea salt
1 pound 2 ounces (500 g) dried

mulukhiyah, finely ground in a food processor
1¼ cups (300 ml) extra-virgin olive oil
4 medium onions (1 pound 5 ounces/ 600 g total), finely chopped
4 cloves garlic, minced to a fine paste

2 firm-ripe medium tomatoes (7 ounces/200 g total), cut into small cubes
2 tablespoons tomato paste
½ teaspoon ground cardamom
½ teaspoon ground cinnamon

½ teaspoon finely ground pepper
¾ cup plus 1 tablespoon (200 g) yogurt, plus more for garnish
Juice of 1 lemon, or to taste
Flatbread or pita chips, for serving

1. Put the lamb in a large pot, add 4 quarts (4 liters) water, and bring to a boil, skimming the froth from the surface. Add the whole spices and 2 tablespoons sea salt and cook for 1 hour, or until completely tender.

2. Fry the *mulukhiyah* in ½ cup plus 2 tablespoons (150 ml) of the olive oil in a large skillet over medium heat until fragrant, about 5 minutes.

3. Heat the remaining olive oil in a large skillet over medium heat. Add the onions and fry, stirring regularly, until golden, about 5 minutes. Add the garlic and tomatoes and mix well. Add the tomatoes and cook until the tomatoes are just wilted, about 5 minutes. Remove a little of the tomatoes to a plate to use for the garnish. Take off the heat.

4. When the meat is done, pull it out of the broth and place on a cutting board. Trim it of any fatty bits and finely shred it. Add the shredded meat to the tomato sauce and return to medium heat. Cook for a minute or so, then add the tomato paste and 1½ cups (350 ml) water. Cook for about 20 minutes, or until the water has reduced and the tomatoes have softened completely while still retaining some texture.

5. Stir in the *mulukhiyah* and ground spices. Stir in enough broth to make a thick puree. Add the yogurt and lemon juice, and simmer for 7 to 10 minutes. Transfer to a serving bowl.

6. To serve, drizzle a little yogurt in swirls over the top. Put the reserved tomatoes in the middle and serve with the flatbread of your choice or pita chips.

LEBANESE SPICY TOMATO "SALSA"

BANADURAH HARRAH

LEBANON

This is an unusual spicy dip that is delicious on its own with pita chips, or you can serve it as a side sauce with fried vegetables or grilled meat or fish. The sauce is cooked quickly to retain a certain freshness and texture, but you can cook it longer if you want it thicker. Just be careful not to let it burn.

SERVES 4 TO 6

3 tablespoons extra-virgin olive oil
2¼ pounds (1 kg) firm-ripe tomatoes, peeled, seeded, and cut into small cubes
3 cloves garlic, minced to a fine paste
1 teaspoon cayenne pepper
1 tablespoon dried mint
Sea salt

Heat the oil in a deep sauté pan over medium heat until hot. Add the tomatoes and garlic and cook, stirring regularly, for 5 minutes, until the tomatoes have softened. Stir in the cayenne, mint, and salt to taste and cook for another 5 minutes, stirring regularly, until you have a fresh, slightly chunky "salsa." Taste and adjust the seasoning. Transfer to a serving bowl and serve at room temperature.

DRIED OKRA SOUP
BAMYA CORBASI

TURKEY

This soup is a specialty of Konya, the home of Jalal al-Dinn Muhammad Rumi, the great Sufi master—the kitchen was very important in Sufi teaching, and the place where disciples learned to submit to Sufi tenets. I was in Konya recently and I had this soup on an almost daily basis. Normally, it is made with meat, but it can also be made vegetarian as my friend Filiz Hosukoglu, whose recipe this is, sometimes does, substituting eggplant and zucchini for meat. When okra is used for drying, it is picked when still tiny, strung on long threads, and then hung to dry. You can see the "necklaces" of dried okra in the markets, either piled high on vendors' stalls or hung in long strands. It is sold by weight and before you can use it, it needs to be boiled to rehydrate it. When doing this, it is a good idea to leave it on the string so that it is easy to fish out.

SERVES 4

1¾ ounces (50 g) dried okra

3 tablespoons extra-virgin olive oil

1 small onion (3½ ounces/100 g), finely chopped

2 cloves garlic, minced to a fine paste

7 ounces (200 g) lean lamb, diced into small cubes

2 teaspoons tomato paste

2 teaspoons mild Turkish red pepper paste

2 teaspoons pul biber

2 medium tomatoes (7 ounces/200 g total), peeled and finely chopped

Sea salt

Juice of 2 lemons, or to taste

Bread, for serving

1. Put the okra still on the string in a small pot. Add water to cover and bring to a boil over medium-high heat. Reduce the heat to medium-low and let bubble gently for 7 to 9 minutes, until the okra has plumped up and softened. Drain and let cool slightly before gently slipping the okra off the string.

2. Heat the olive oil in a medium pot over medium heat. Add the onion and cook, stirring regularly, until the onion is golden, about 5 minutes. Add the garlic and stir for a minute or so, then add the lamb and sauté for a couple of minutes to brown it. Stir in the tomato and pepper pastes. Add the pul biber, chopped tomatoes, 3 cups (750 ml) hot water, and salt to taste. Bring to a boil, then add the okra. Cover the pot and let bubble gently for about 20 minutes, until both meat and okra are tender. Add the lemon juice and continue cooking for another 5 minutes. Serve hot with good bread.

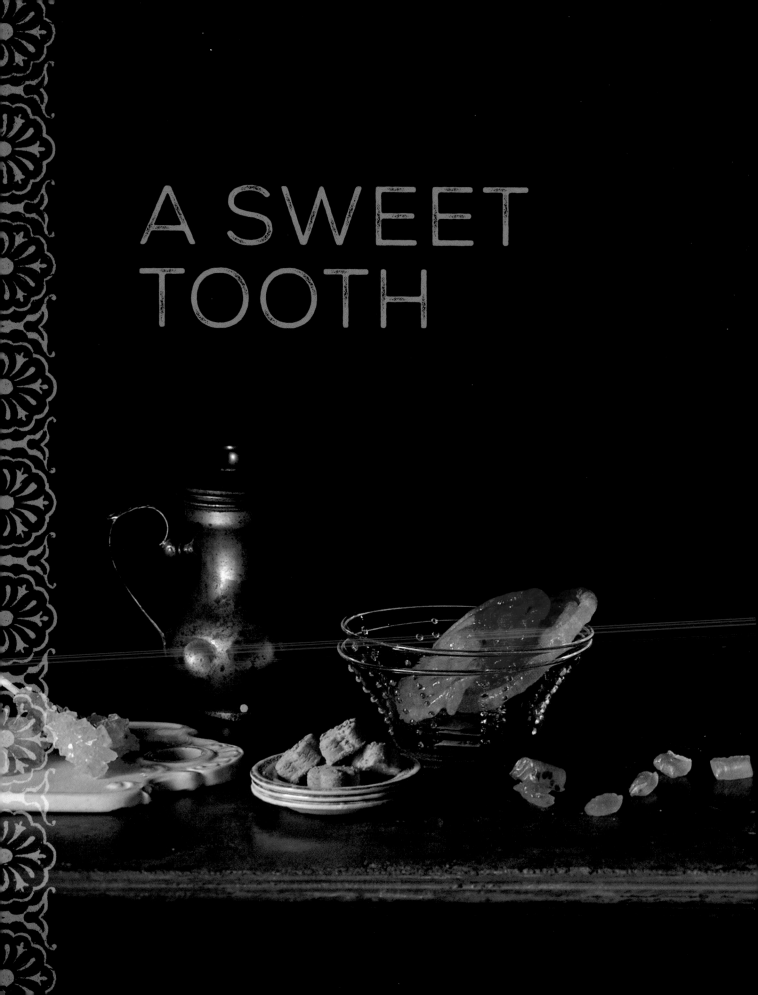

A SWEET TOOTH

Sweets are as important to Muslims as bread or rice. They are an essential part of Muslim hospitality, served with coffee or tea when visitors come, or simply enjoyed between meals with family or friends. In some countries in the Arab world, the sweets are very sweet, often soaked in sugar syrup, whereas in other places like Indonesia and Malaysia, sweet confections have a little added salt to achieve subtle sweet-savory flavors.

Sweets are also an essential part of Ramadan, the month of fast, as well as the two important feasts, Eid el-Fitr (the feast of breaking the fast) and Eid al-Adha (the feast of sacrifice) that follow. During that month, most Muslims will break their daily fast with something sweet, either a drink, snacks, or simply dates before they move on to *iftar*, which is the first meal of the night. Whichever it is, that sweet little something will help smooth the transition from the long day's fast into the night's feasting.

In the early days of Islam, desserts were sweetened with molasses from dates, grapes, or carob, or with honey. Then in the seventh century, the Arabs discovered sugar (from the Arabic word *sukkar*, derived from the Persian *shakar*) when they invaded Persia—sugarcane was originally grown in the tropical Far East, and was taken from there to India and China and on to Persia in the fifth century—and from there, to Egypt, North Africa, Sicily, Spain, and other places they conquered. In fact, Egypt remains the world's largest producer of cane sugar.

Specific sweets are associated with celebrations or special occasions—for instance, sugared almonds are merrily thrown at guests after a boy's circumcision. And when a baby is born, Muslim parents will make sure that the first taste they give their baby is sweet, often chewing on a piece of date and rubbing the juice on the baby's gums. The Prophet Muhammad is said to have carried out this practice, believing it helped to get the tiny digestive system going. There is even a tribe in Pakistan called Halwai, from *halva*, which means "sweet" in Hindi and Arabic. The Halwais were initially Hindu sweets makers who converted to Islam.

This chapter includes a selection of classic sweets from around the Muslim world, as well as sweets associated with particular religious occasions and various celebrations.

ALEPPINE BREAKFAST PORRIDGE

MA'MUNIYEH

SYRIA

Ma'muniyeh is a typical breakfast from Aleppo in Syria, a kind of sweet Syrian porridge, made with semolina and served with a stringy cheese called *jibneh m'challaleh* for a delightful sweet-savory combination to start the day. It is very simple to make, and with the exception of the cheese, it uses ingredients you might normally have on hand. The string cheese can be quite salty, so it is a good idea to soak it for a short while before using.

SERVES 4

3 tablespoons (45 g) unsalted butter or ghee
1 cup (175 g) semolina
½ cup (100 g) raw cane sugar
Ground cinnamon, for garnish
3½ ounces (100 g) stringy cheese (jibneh m'challaleh), rinsed, dried, and pulled apart in fine strings, for garnish

1. Melt the butter in a large skillet over medium heat. Add the semolina and stir constantly until the semolina has turned a golden color, 10 to 15 minutes.

2. Put the sugar and 4 cups (1 liter) water in a medium saucepan and bring to a boil over medium heat. Gradually add the toasted semolina and cook, stirring constantly, for a few minutes, or until you have a fairly thick mixture. Take off the heat. Cover the pan and let sit for 15 minutes.

3. Serve hot, sprinkled with cinnamon and with a little stringy cheese piled in the middle.

DRIED FRUIT and NUTS
in APRICOT LEATHER JUICE

KHOSHAF

LEBANON | SYRIA

Khoshaf gets its name from Persian—*khosh-ab* (good water)—suggesting that it probably originated in Persia, although you can find it with slight variations throughout the Levant. In this recipe, the water in which the dried fruit and nuts are soaked is sweetened with apricot leather (*qamar el-din*), but you can also sweeten it with a little raw cane sugar, or omit the sugar altogether and just have the little sweetness imparted by the dried fruit. SERVES 4

5¼ ounces (150 g) apricot leather

2 cups (500 ml) boiling water

⅔ cup (100 g) golden raisins

⅔ cup (100 g) whole dried apricots

¼ cup (40 g) blanched almonds, soaked for 2 hours in cold water

¼ cup (40 g) pistachios, soaked for 2 hours in cold water

¼ cup (40 g) walnuts, cut in half lengthwise to have quarters, soaked for 2 hours in cold water

¼ cup (40 g) pine nuts, soaked for 2 hours in cold water

4 teaspoons orange blossom water

1. Cut the apricot leather into medium pieces and put in a bowl. Add the boiling water and let sit for a while, until the leather has softened. Then, stir the apricot leather in the water until completely dissolved.

2. Rinse the raisins and dried apricots under cold water and add to the apricot leather water. Let sit for 2 hours, preferably longer, in the refrigerator to serve chilled.

3. Transfer the fruit and their soaking water to a large mixing bowl. Drain and rinse the nuts and add to the fruit—if you have the patience, peel the pistachios and walnuts before adding them for more vibrant colors. Add the orange blossom water. Taste and adjust the sweetness if necessary. Serve slightly chilled.

LEBANESE SWEET CHEESE "PIE"
KUNAFAH BIL-JEBN

LEBANON | SYRIA | JORDAN | PALESTINE | TURKEY

There is an ongoing debate about where *kunafah*, a sweet cheese "pie" usually eaten for breakfast, originated. Some claim Turkey as its country of origin, others swear it is Palestine, and others claim it is from Syria. There isn't enough research for us to tell for sure, but what is certain is that there are two main types of *kunafah*. In *kunafah Nabulsiyah*, from Palestine, the *kataifi* pastry—called "hair" pastry because it is made in very thin, long strands—is colored red and used as is (see Variation, page 446). The Lebanese version is known as *kunafah mafrukah* (meaning "rubbed"), because the strands of *kataifi* are buttered, then rubbed and rubbed until they become like fluffy breadcrumbs. Also the Lebanese version has no coloring. In Lebanon *kunafah* is made into a sweet sandwich by stuffing it inside the fat part of a sesame bread that looks like a handbag, with a handle and a fat pouch part, then drenching it and the inside of the bread in sugar syrup.

It is fairly simple to prepare and all you need is to buy *kataifi* fresh or frozen from a Middle Eastern store.

You can make this in the oven (as below) or on the stovetop (see Note, page 446). You can vary the cheese by using 1 pound (450 g) Arabic clotted cream (*qashtah*) and follow the instructions as below.

SERVES 4 TO 6

10½ ounces (300 g) akkawi (see Glossary) or fior de latte mozzarella (cow's milk mozzarella)

9 ounces (250 g) kataifi ("hair" pastry)

8 tablespoons (115 g) unsalted butter, cut into small cubes

¾ cup (180 ml) sugar syrup (page 454), cooled

---

1. A few hours ahead: Slice the cheese into thin slices, about ¼ inch (6 mm) thick, and put to soak in cold water. Change the water regularly until the cheese has lost all traces of saltiness—you will probably need to change the water up to ten times in the space of 2 to 3 hours.

2. Preheat the oven to 400°F (200°C).

3. Chop the pastry into pieces ½ inch (1 cm) long and transfer to a large skillet. Make a well in the center and add 7 tablespoons (100 g) of the diced butter to the well. Place over low heat, then, with your fingers, slowly rub the melting butter into the pastry until it is well coated and completely crumbled.

4. Grease a 9-inch (23 cm) round baking dish with the remaining 1 tablespoon (15 g) butter. Spread the shredded pastry across the dish in an even layer, pressing down hard with your hands. Bake for 10 to 15 minutes, or until golden brown.

5. Meanwhile, drain the cheese and pat it dry with paper towels. Take the pastry out of the oven and spread the cheese slices evenly over it. Return to the oven and bake for 10 more minutes, or until the cheese is melted.

Recipe continues

6. Brush a serving dish with a little sugar syrup so that the melting cheese does not stick and turn the pie over onto the dish to reveal the crisp golden pastry. Pour a little sugar syrup over the pastry and serve hot, with more syrup on the side.

NOTE: *Spread the cheese slices over the pastry before cooking and place the round baking dish over low heat. (Here it would be a good idea to use a copper dish, if you have one, as most other baking dishes will not go over the fire.) Cook for 20 to 30 minutes, turning the dish regularly to make sure the pastry browns evenly. By the time it is done, the pie should move in one block if you shake the dish from side to side.*

KUNAFAH NABULSIYAH: To make the Palestinian version of this dish, use a few drops food coloring to color the *kataifi* a reddish orange and mix it with the melted butter. Toss the pastry with the melted butter, but do not rub it. Use the remaining melted butter to brush the baking dish. The rest of the dish is the same.

KATAIFI

Some cookery writers have recently taken to describing *kataifi* as shredded phyllo. It is definitely *not* shredded phyllo. The pastry is made by dropping very thin strands of batter through tiny holes (either by hand with a cup-like implement with narrow funnels on the bottom or by machine through a trough lined with multiple narrow funnels) onto a hot metal plate. The batter is drizzled in a circular motion and the thin strands sizzle as soon as they hit the plate. These are immediately gathered into a figure eight and laid onto paper or linen towels to be later taken to the sweets makers for use in *kunafah* or other sweets such as *borma* or bird's nests, to name but a few.

MOROCCAN ALMOND SPIRALS
M'HANNCHA

MOROCCO

When home cooks plan to make *m'hanncha* at home, they will rarely make the *warqa*, the Moroccan equivalent of phyllo dough. Instead they will buy it at the market or at pastry shops, made by women who are *warqa* specialists; or they will ask the specialist *warqa* maker to come to their home to make it in situ. Unlike the Cornes de Gazelles (page 451), where you need to make the pastry as well as the almond paste, these are much quicker to prepare as you only have to make and shape the almond paste filling. Despite having the same flavor as that of *cornes de gazelle*, *m'hanncha* are different in that they are a lot crunchier, not to mention that the shape is also different. Moroccans will usually have a tray of sweets on which they will have different types, including these and the *cornes de gazelles* to offer with Mint Tea (page 503). They very rarely serve them as dessert, unless it is for a *diffa* (a word that means "invitation" and refers to a celebratory or special occasion meal).

MAKES ABOUT 20

FOR THE FILLING
3⅓ cups (500 g) blanched almonds, soaked for 1 hour in boiling water
1¼ cups (150 g) powdered sugar
¼ cup (60 ml) orange blossom water
2 tablespoons (30 g) unsalted butter, at room temperature
¼ teaspoon ground mastic (see Glossary)

FOR THE SPIRALS
20 sheets phyllo dough (measuring 7¼ x 12¾ inches/18 x 32 cm but more common are shorter sheets)
10 tablespoons (150 g) unsalted butter, melted

1. To make the filling: Drain the almonds well and spread to dry on a kitchen towel. Put the almonds and powdered sugar in a food processor and process until very finely ground. Add the orange blossom water, butter, and mastic and process until well blended.

2. Transfer the almond paste to a work surface and roll into a sausage shape. Divide into 20 equal pieces and shape each first into a ball, then into a long, thin sausage measuring 10¾ inches (27 cm) long. Cover with plastic wrap.

3. Preheat the oven to 400°F (200°C). Line a baking sheet with parchment paper or a silicone baking mat (or use a nonstick sheet).

4. To make the spirals: Lay a sheet of phyllo on a work surface with a long side facing you and brush with melted butter. Lay an almond "sausage" about ½ inch (1 cm) away from the edge nearer you and about 1 inch (2.5 cm) away from the ends. Fold the ½ inch (1 cm) of phyllo over the almond cylinder and roll, keeping the phyllo very close to the filling as you roll over it. Brush the roll with butter and, with the loose end down, fold one empty edge and start rolling into a coil, sliding the other empty edge under the coil. Transfer the coil to the baking sheet and press lightly on it to make sure it doesn't unroll during baking. Make the remaining coils the same way. Prick each with a toothpick here and there to stop the pastry from puffing.

5. Bake for 25 minutes, or until golden brown. Let cool on a wire rack. Serve at room temperature. These will keep in an airtight container for up to 1 week.

BAKLAVA

Baklava is a generic term describing a whole range of Middle Eastern sweets, such as *kol wa shkor* (translated as "eat and be grateful"), which are tiny pastries made with phyllo dough. They come as tiny rolls, or small squares, or little "baskets," all filled with ground nuts—pistachios, pine nuts, almonds, cashews, or walnuts. Another more limited range is a selection made with *kataifi* (or "hair" pastry; see page 446), which come in cylinders (*borma*), squares (*ballouriyeh*), or nests (*'esh el-bulbul*). These, too, are filled with nuts. A few baklava are fried but most are baked, and all are drenched in sugar syrup after baking or frying. The syrup is left plain in Turkey, while in Lebanon and Syria it is flavored with orange blossom and rose water. Syria is the land of baklava even if Turkish baklava is better known globally. Syrian baklava, which is the same as that made in Lebanon, is crunchier and less golden than its Turkish counterpart, and it is made smaller.

The recipe below is for the classic diamond-shaped baklava, but you can also make fingers (see Variation).

SERVES 6 TO 8

FOR THE SYRUP
Scant 1 cup (175 g) raw cane sugar
½ teaspoon lemon juice
1 teaspoon rose water
1 teaspoon orange blossom water

FOR THE FILLING
1⅓ cups (200 g) pistachios, pine nuts, or walnuts
½ cup (100 g) raw cane sugar
¾ teaspoon ground cinnamon
1 tablespoon orange blossom water
1 tablespoon rose water

1. To make the syrup: Put the sugar, lemon juice, and ¼ cup plus 1 tablespoon (75 ml) water in a small saucepan. Bring to a boil over medium heat, stirring every now and then, and let bubble for 3 minutes. Take off the heat and add the rose and orange blossom water. Let cool.

2. Preheat the oven to 400°F (200°C).

3. To make the filling: Process the nuts in a blender until medium fine. (Or, for a nicer texture, pack them loosely in a zip-seal plastic bag and use a rolling pin to crush or beat them.) Transfer to a medium mixing bowl. Add the sugar, cinnamon, and orange flower and rose water and mix well.

4. Brush a 7 x 12½-inch (18 x 32 cm) baking dish with a little melted butter. Spread one sheet of phyllo dough over the bottom and brush with melted butter. (Keep the remaining sheets covered with plastic wrap, then a kitchen towel to stop them from drying up.) Lay 5 more sheets of phyllo on top, brushing each with melted butter as you go, for a total of 6 layers.

TO ASSEMBLE
8 tablespoons (115 g)
  butter, melted
12 sheets phyllo dough
  (12½ x 7¼ inches/32 x
  18 cm)

5. Spread the nut filling evenly over the phyllo and cover with 6 more sheets of phyllo, making sure you brush each with melted butter. Pour any leftover butter onto the pastry and cut into medium-size diamonds or thin rectangles all the way through the filled pastry.

6. Bake for 20 to 25 minutes, or until crisp and golden. Remove from the oven and let sit for a couple of minutes before pouring the cooled syrup all over the baklava. Serve at room temperature. Baklava will keep for at least a couple of days if stored in an airtight container.

BAKLAVA FINGERS: Make the syrup and nut filling as directed. Halve the phyllo lengthwise for a total of 24 strips of phyllo. Keeping the unused phyllo covered while you work, make a stack of 6 strips of phyllo, brushing melted butter over each layer as you go. With a long side of the pastry facing you, spread a quarter of the nut filling in a thin raised line down the length of the pastry, close to the edge nearer to you. Roll into a long thin sausage. Cut the roll crosswise into 2-inch (5 cm) lengths. Repeat to make 3 more rolls. Arrange the pastries loose side down on a nonstick baking sheet (or one lined with parchment paper or a silicone baking mat), keeping the rolls close to one another. Bake and add the syrup as indicated above.

CARAWAY PUDDING

MEGHLI

Meghli is the sweet par excellence that is associated with newborns, especially with newborn boys. Lebanese home cooks make industrial quantities of *meghli* whenever new children are born. They keep some at home to serve those who come to congratulate them on the happy occasion and send out the rest to family and friends to share in the happiness. *Meghli* means "boiled" in Arabic, and the pudding does indeed need to boil, for a minimum of an hour, before it reaches the right consistency. Some people boil it for less time, but the resulting pudding is bland and watery. You can buy a ready-made *meghli* mix to which you add water and boil for less time. It is an acceptable alternative, but it is well worth your while making your own from scratch, even if it means time stirring the mixture until it thickens into the velvety fragrant custard-like mixture. It's traditional to sprinkle shredded coconut over the pudding, although I'm not so fond of it myself. If you would like to include it, simply sprinkle a little over the pudding before adding the nuts.

SERVES 4

⅔ cup (100 g) ground rice

2 tablespoons ground caraway seeds

1 tablespoon ground anise

1 teaspoon ground cinnamon

1 cup (200 g) raw cane sugar

FOR GARNISH

¼ cup (50 g) pine nuts, soaked in boiling water for a couple of hours

¼ cup (50 g) shelled walnuts, soaked in boiling water for a couple of hours

¼ cup (50 g) blanched almond halves, soaked in boiling water for a couple of hours

Put the ground rice in a large pot. Add 2½ quarts (2.5 liters) water. Add the ground caraway and anise and place over high heat. Bring to a boil, stirring constantly, and boil for 25 minutes, still stirring all the time. Reduce the heat to medium and cook for another 5 minutes, stirring as you go. Add the cinnamon and stir for another 20 minutes, then reduce the heat to medium-low, add the sugar, and stir for a further 10 minutes. Remove from the heat and pour into a single shallow serving bowl or into 4 or 6 individual ones, depending on their size. Let the pudding cool before garnishing with the drained nuts. Serve chilled or at room temperature.

CORNES DE GAZELLES
QA'B EL-GH'ZAL

The most elegant of all Moroccan pastries, *cornes de gazelles* (meaning "the horns of a female deer") are a labor of love as they are time-consuming to prepare. Still, they are definitely worth making. They are among the most elegant and most delicious of all North African sweet confections. They are the first treat I buy when I visit Morocco, and it is rare for a day to go by when I am there without having some, usually with mint tea. It is not often that you will find them prepared in the same delicate way in the West. Most of those you buy in pastry shops outside Morocco are too coarse with a very thick pastry and bland filling. The only way you are going to have them as delicate and tasty as those made in Morocco is by making them yourself, or by having them in a Moroccan home where they've been made.

MAKES ABOUT 20

FOR THE FILLING
1⅔ cups (250 g) blanched almonds, soaked for 1 hour in boiling water
½ cup plus 1 tablespoon (75 g) powdered sugar
2 tablespoons orange blossom water
1 tablespoon unsalted butter, at room temperature
¼ teaspoon ground mastic (see Glossary)

FOR THE DOUGH
1 cup (120 g) unbleached all-purpose flour
1 tablespoon unsalted butter, melted
2 tablespoons orange blossom water
Softened butter, for shaping

1. To make the filling: Drain the almonds and spread them to dry on a clean kitchen towel.

2. Put the almonds in a food processor along with the powdered sugar and process until very fine. Transfer to a bowl. Add the orange blossom water, butter, and mastic and mix with your hands until you have a homogeneous paste. Cover with a clean kitchen towel.

3. To make the dough: Put the flour in a shallow medium mixing bowl and make a well in the center. Add the melted butter and orange blossom water to the well and gradually add 3 tablespoons water, working the liquid into the flour with your hand.

4. Transfer the dough to a work surface and knead for 3 minutes. Shape the dough into a ball, invert the bowl over the dough, and let rest for 15 minutes. Knead for 3 more minutes, or until the dough is smooth and elastic and quite soft.

5. Divide the almond filling into 20 portions. Roll each into a ball, then into a small sausage about 4 inches (10 cm) long. Taper the ends of each almond roll.

6. Preheat the oven to 400°F (200°C).

7. Smear your pastry board, rolling pin, and hands with a little butter. Take a piece of dough and roll it out, turning it over once or twice, until very thin and about 5 inches (12.5 cm) wide. Carefully stretch the dough with your hands to widen and thin it a

Recipe continues

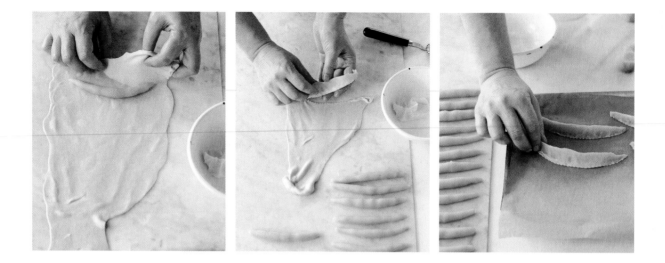

little more. With the 5-inch (12.5 cm) side facing you, place an almond paste sausage crosswise about ¾ inch (2 cm) up from the edge. Pull the dough up and over the sausage and press tightly around the almond roll, encasing it. Pinch the filling and dough along the top to make a ridge and at the same time, bend it into a crescent with pointed ends (like a gazelle horn). Press the dough together at the seam and cut, following the shape of the crescent, using a fluted pastry wheel. The crescent should measure about 4 inches (10 cm) long and 1¼ inches (3 cm) high. Prick with a toothpick in several places on both sides, to stop it from puffing up, and place on a nonstick baking sheet (or a regular baking sheet lined with parchment paper or a silicone baking mat). Repeat to make 20 crescents.

8. Bake for 10 minutes, or until they are barely colored. Transfer the pastries to a wire rack to cool before serving. They will keep for at least 1 week in an airtight container.

SEMOLINA CAKE
BASBOUSSA

Basboussa in Egypt, *nammoura* in Lebanon, *h'risseh* in Syria, and *revani* in Turkey—all of these names describe a simple sponge cake made with semolina and yogurt and drenched in sugar syrup. The Syrian version is topped with a mixture of pistachios, almonds, walnuts, and cashews; the other versions are garnished with almonds or pine nuts. Egyptian *basboussa* is typical street food, especially during Ramadan, whereas the others are mainly everyday sweets, and often made at home even if you can find them at sweets makers. In fact, it is one of very few sweets that people prefer to make at home than buy from a sweets maker.

SERVES 6 TO 8

FOR THE SYRUP
1¾ cups (350 g) raw cane sugar
1 teaspoon lemon juice
2 teaspoons rose water
2 teaspoons orange blossom water

FOR THE CAKE
1¼ cups (225 g) semolina flour (choose the regular grade, not the fine)
¼ cup (50 g) raw cane sugar
6 tablespoons (90 g) unsalted butter, at room temperature
1¾ cups (450 g) yogurt
¼ teaspoon baking soda
Tahini, for the baking dish
⅓ cup (50 g) blanched almonds

1. To make the syrup: Put the sugar, lemon juice, and ½ cup plus 2 tablespoons (150 ml) water in a saucepan. Bring to a boil over medium heat, stirring every now and then, then let bubble for 3 minutes. Take off the heat. Add the rose and orange blossom water and let cool.

2. To make the cake: Put the semolina, sugar, and softened butter in a large mixing bowl and work together with a spatula until well blended. Add the yogurt and baking soda and mix until you have a firm cake batter.

3. Grease an 8 x 1½-inch (20 x 3.5 cm) round baking dish with a little tahini (or use a nonstick one) and spread the batter evenly across the dish. Flatten it gently with a spatula. Cover with a clean kitchen towel and let rest for 3 hours.

4. About 20 minutes before you are ready to bake the cake, preheat the oven to 400°F (200°C).

5. Cut the uncooked cake into 2-inch (5 cm) squares and press one blanched almond in the middle of each square. Bake for 40 minutes, or until golden.

6. Remove from the oven and pour the cooled syrup all over. Let the cake stand for 30 minutes to soak up the syrup. If you think the amount of syrup is excessive, reduce the quantity to your taste. Bear in mind that the cake will take time to absorb the syrup and although it may look as if it is swimming in it to start, it will eventually fully absorb it. Serve at room temperature.

SYRIAN H'RISSEH: If you want to make the Syrian version, make the cake as directed through step 4. In step 5, just before putting the cake in the oven, do not cut the cake; just cover it with 1 cup (150 g) mixed pistachios, walnuts, and cashews, gently pressing them into the top of the batter. Bake as directed.

RAMADAN DATE COOKIES
QRASS BIL-TAMR

LEBANON | SYRIA

Ramadan is the most important month in the Islamic calendar, a time for fasting during the day and feasting after sunset and until sunrise. During that whole month, sweets occupy an important place in people's lives. They are offered to guests who come to visit after sunset, or they are snacked on throughout the night before the fast starts again at sunrise. They are also taken to family and/or friends during the nightly visits—social life increases considerably during Ramadan—and these date-filled cookies are a typical Ramadan sweet, together with the nut versions called ma'mul (see page 458), filled with pistachios or walnuts and shaped differently for people to tell which is which. They are time-consuming to make but well worth the effort. If you can't find store-bought date paste, substitute with an equal amount of pitted dates and process these with the cinnamon and butter in your food processor until they turn into a smooth paste.

The cookies are shaped with the use of a special mold that traditionally was carved out of wood but is now more often than not made in plastic. I still have my mother's molds, which—though I could easily replace them as there are still young men who carve them by hand in the souk of Damascus in Syria—I guard jealously as they have acquired a lovely patina over the years.

MAKES ABOUT 40

FOR THE DOUGH
2 cups (350 g) semolina
¼ cup plus 1 tablespoon (50 g) all-purpose flour, plus more for rolling the dough
¼ teaspoon instant (fast-acting) yeast
¼ cup (50 g) baker's sugar or superfine sugar
1 stick plus 2 tablespoons (150 g) unsalted butter, at room temperature
3 tablespoons orange blossom water
3 tablespoons rose water

1. To make the dough: Mix the semolina, all-purpose flour, yeast, and sugar in a large mixing bowl. Add the softened butter and, with the tips of your fingers, work it in until fully incorporated. Add the orange blossom and rose water and knead until the dough is smooth and elastic. Roll the dough into a ball and place seam side down on your lightly floured counter. Cover with a very damp cloth and let rest for 1½ hours in a cool place.

2. To make the date filling: Put the date paste in a bowl. Add the cinnamon and gradually add the melted butter, working it in by hand until you have a smooth, soft paste. Pinch off a small piece and shape it into a disk 1½ inches (3.5 cm) in diameter and about ¼ inch (6 mm) thick. Place on a plate and make the remaining disks until you have used up all the paste. You should end up with 40 date disks. Cover with plastic wrap.

3. Preheat the oven to 400°F (200°C).

Recipe continues

FOR THE DATE FILLING
12 ounces (350 g) dried
　　date paste
½ teaspoon ground
　　cinnamon
2 tablespoons (30 g)
　　unsalted butter, melted

4. To make date-filled cookies: Pinch off a piece of dough and roll into a ball the size of a walnut. Flatten it on your palm until you have a 3-inch (7.5 cm) disk that is about ¼ inch (6 mm) thick. Lay a date disk in the middle of the dough and flap the dough over the date to cover it. Pinch the edges together—the date disk should be covered with an even layer of dough. Lightly press into the round flat mold that is used for the date-filled cookies, then turn the mold over and tap the top edge lightly against a table while holding your other hand underneath to catch the cookie as it falls out of the mold. Slide the cookie onto a nonstick baking sheet, or one lined with parchment paper or a silicone baking mat. Make the remaining cookies in the same way. You should end up with 40 date cookies.

5. Bake for 15 to 18 minutes, or until lightly golden. Transfer to a wire rack to cool. Serve or pack in an airtight container where they will keep for 2 weeks.

RAMADAN NUT-FILLED COOKIES

MA'MUL BIL-JOZ AW BIL-FISTOQ

These nut-filled cookies are made with special molds called *tabe'*. If making the nut filling with pistachios, use the oval and pointed mold; if using walnuts, the round and pointed mold. Or if you don't have the molds, you can shape these inside a small tea strainer or by hand.   MAKES 30

Dough from Ramadan Date Cookies (page 455)

1¼ cups (175 g) walnuts or pistachios, ground medium fine

¼ cup (50 g) superfine sugar

½ teaspoon ground cinnamon

1½ teaspoons rose water

1½ teaspoons orange blossom water

Powdered sugar, for dusting

1. Make the dough as directed

2. Put the ground nuts in a medium mixing bowl. Add the sugar and cinnamon and mix well. Then add the rose and orange blossom water and mix again.

3. Preheat the oven to 400°F (200°C).

4. To make cookies: Pinch off a small piece of dough and roll it into a ball the size of a walnut. Place it in the cup of your hand and with your index finger, burrow into it to shape it into a hollow cone—be careful not to pierce the bottom. The cone walls should be about ¼ inch (6 mm) thick. Fill the pastry cone with 1 teaspoon walnut or pistachio filling and pinch the dough together to close it over the filling. Carefully shape the filled pastry into a ball and lightly press into the ma'mul, leaving the pinched side on the outside so that when you invert the pastry, it is on the bottom. Invert the mold and tap it lightly against your work surface holding your hand underneath to catch the cookie that falls out. Slide the cookie onto a nonstick baking sheet, or one lined with parchment paper or a silicone baking mat. Fill and shape the remaining dough in the same way. You may have to scrape the inside of the mold every now and then in case some pastry has stuck to it. You should end up with about 30 nut-filled pastries, each measuring about 2 inches (5 cm) wide at the bottom and 1¼ inches (3 cm) high at the tip.

5. Bake for 15 to 18 minutes, or until lightly golden. Transfer to a wire rack to cool. Dust with powdered sugar. Serve or pack in an airtight container where they will keep for 2 weeks.

DATE HALVA

BATHITH

Gulf Arabs don't have a huge range of sweets. Mostly halvas, fritters, and puddings, with many either made with dates or served with date syrup. It is not surprising really as their cuisine has for a long time been more about survival, given the harsh desert living conditions before the discovery of oil made them wealthy. This halva, which is a typical Arabian Gulf sweet, combines both dates and nuts. It can be made crumbly to serve as a kind of granola, or it can be made soft so that it can be molded in the same ma'mul molds used for the Ramadan Nut-Filled Cookies (page 458). Both versions are delightful, although the presentation of the latter is more elegant.

SERVES 4 TO 6

1¼ cups (150 g) white whole wheat flour

2½ cups (375 g) pitted dates

4 tablespoons (60 g) unsalted butter

¼ cup (60 ml) rose water

½ teaspoon ground cardamom

½ teaspoon ground cinnamon

¼ cup (30 g) walnuts, coarsely chopped

¼ cup (30 g) blanched almonds, coarsely chopped

1. Put the flour in a large skillet and toast over medium heat, stirring constantly, until lightly colored, 10 to 15 minutes. Let cool.

2. Put the dates in a large pot and heat over medium heat, stirring constantly, until they start to mash up. Add the toasted flour and mix well. Stir in the butter, then the rose water and spices. Mix well, then stir in the nuts until well blended. Serve warm or at room temperature.

NOTE: *If you are going to mold the halva, you need to use ½ cup (60 g) less flour and add 2 extra tablespoons (30 g) butter and 1 extra tablespoon rose water. Mix well. Then pinch off enough to make a ball the size of a walnut. Press the ball of date halva into the ma'mul mold following the directions in the Ramadan Nut-Filled Cookies (page 458). Serve at room temperature.*

DATE "FUDGE"

RANGINA

Rangina is originally an Iranian dessert known as *ranginak* (meaning "colorful") and named thus because of the slivered pistachios and almond garnish. The recipe below comes from my friend Aisha al-Tamimi, Qatar's foremost celebrity chef. She sometimes makes her *rangina* as below and other times she makes the flour halva a little thicker to fill the dates with it, then she thins down what's left with a little more melted butter to drizzle over the dates. She uses fresh dates whereas Iranians use their own dates, which are darker and softer and a lot riper. I like both versions although when *rangina* is made with fresh dates, you get a lovely contrast between the crunch of the fresh fruit and the melting softness of the halva. However, fresh dates are not always available—the season is in late summer to early fall—so, use Iranian dates the rest of the year, and follow the traditional method of pouring the halva in between and over the dates as in the recipe below. Serve with regular or mint tea, Arabian or Turkish coffee, or the drink of your choice.

SERVES 6 TO 8

⅔ cup (100 g) walnut halves, cut in half lenthwise

1 tablespoon slivered almonds

1 pound (450 g) Iranian or Barhi dates

1⅔ cups (250 g) unbleached all-purpose flour

2 sticks plus 1½ tablespoons (250 g) unsalted butter, melted

1 tablespoon slivered pistachios

1. Preheat the oven to 450°F (220°C).

2. Spread the walnuts and almonds on two separate baking sheets and toast in the hot oven for 4 to 5 minutes. Check on the almonds after 3 minutes in case they are coloring too fast. Take out of the oven and let cool.

3. Carefully pit the dates and gently insert a quarter walnut inside each. Press on the ends to close the dates and lay them neatly in a serving dish, leaving a little space between each.

4. Toast the flour in a large skillet over medium heat, stirring all the time, until the flour turns golden. Gradually stir the melted butter into the flour, stirring all the time until you have a smooth loose paste.

5. Pour this flour halva over and between the dates making sure you fill the gaps. Sprinkle the slivered pistachios and toasted almonds all over. Or you can pour the halva over the serving dish and set the dates into it like in the opposite picture. Let set. Serve at room temperature.

TURKISH FLOUR HALVA
UN HELVASI

TURKEY

Unlike complicated halvas such as tahini halva (see sidebar below), flour halva is much simpler and quicker to prepare. Here is the Turkish version that has added pine nuts, whereas the Iranian version has saffron. Both are delectable and when home cooks prepare halva, in Turkey and in Iran, they will often make more than they need so that they can send it out to their neighbors, friends, or family. Sharing halva is an absolute must during 'Ashura, the day commemorating the killing of Hussein, the Prophet Muhammad's grandson.   SERVES 6

1 stick plus 2 tablespoons (150 g) unsalted butter
¼ cup (50 g) pine nuts
1¼ cups (150 g) unbleached all-purpose flour
1 cup plus 2 tablespoons (225 g) superfine sugar

1. Melt the butter in a large heavy skillet. Add the pine nuts and flour and stir over low heat until golden. This may take as long as 45 minutes, but it needs to be done to get the nutty taste that is typical of a good halva.

2. Ten minutes before the flour is ready, put the sugar and 1⅔ cups (400 ml) water in a medium saucepan and place over medium-high heat. Bring to a boil. Let the syrup bubble for a couple of minutes, then add to the flour, stirring quickly and constantly to avoid lumps. Continue stirring until the mixture starts sticking to the pan. Take off the heat and let sit, covered, for 15 minutes. Transfer to a serving dish and serve warm.

HALVA

Halva in Turkey is the special occasion sweet par excellence, associated with both joyous and sad occasions. Making it allows people to come together—it takes constant stirring and more than one person will be in the kitchen taking turns stirring the flour or semolina halva; and at funerals a gathering over the preparation of a symbolic food lets people grieve together. There are many different types of halva. Some are made with flour, others with semolina, and others with tahini, although the latter is the preserve of specialized halva makers as it is too difficult and arduous to make at home.

The tahini halva makers I visited in Aleppo pressed their own tahini, which by itself is a complicated process—sesame seeds are first roasted, then soaked, then hulled, then finally pressed to produce tahini. Then they have to prepare the *natef*, a rather miraculous confection made with soapwort root that is like a soft meringue and finally, they have to mix the tahini with the *natef*, churning, then beating, then kneading it before it is finally tahini halva, which can be left plain or mixed with nuts or even chocolate now.

CHICKPEA FLOUR HALVA

KHABISS AL-NAKHI

This halva comes from the Arabian Gulf and it is made with chickpea flour instead of wheat flour for a slightly different texture, and of course flavor. It is ideal for those who cannot have wheat. Whether made with wheat or chickpea flour, halva is associated with 'Ashura and funerals, although it is served as dessert at joyous occasions as well or as part of *fuala* (a simple spread of savory and sweet offerings) when guests come to visit.   SERVES 4 TO 6

Pinch of saffron threads
¼ cup (60 ml) rose water
Scant 2 cups (250 g) chickpea flour
1½ teaspoons ground cardamom
1¼ cups (250 g) raw cane sugar
1 cup (250 ml) boiling water
1 stick (125 g) unsalted butter, melted
2 tablespoons slivered pistachios or chopped pistachios

1. Put the saffron to steep in the rose water.

2. Toast the chickpea flour in a large skillet over medium heat, stirring constantly, until fragrant, about 8 minutes. Be careful not to burn the flour or else it will taste bitter. Add the ground cardamom. Mix well and remove from the heat.

3. Put the sugar in a medium saucepan, melt over medium heat, and cook until it turns golden, about 10 minutes. (As with the flour, be careful not to let the sugar burn. It is better to undercook the caramel than to risk burning it.) As soon as the sugar is ready, carefully and slowly add the boiling water. The caramel will bubble furiously and splatter as you add the water, so make sure you keep your face well away from the pan and wear protective gloves as you stir the water into the caramel.

4. Return the chickpea flour to medium heat. Add the melted butter and whisk until well blended. Then add the caramel water, stirring all the time and mix well. Reduce the heat to very low and cover the pan. Let steam for about 15 minutes, stirring occasionally, until the halva is smooth. Remove from the heat and add the saffron rose water.

5. Transfer the halva to a large shallow serving bowl and scatter the slivered pistachios over the top. Serve warm, or soon after making.

CARROT HALVA

GAJAR HALWA

In South Asia cooks also make halva with carrots, adding a little *khoya*, but if not available, use heavy cream, or even better clotted cream. SERVES 6 TO 8

¼ cup (40 g) almonds, split into halves

⅓ cup (50 g) cashews, split into halves

6 tablespoons (90 g) ghee or unsalted butter

12 medium carrots (1¾ pounds/800 g total), grated on the fine side of a grater

1 cup (200 g) raw cane sugar

4 tablespoons crumbled khoya (see Glossary) or clotted cream

Seeds from 2 green cardamom pods, coarsely ground

1 tablespoon golden raisins

1. Preheat the oven to 450°F (220°C).

2. Spread the almond and cashew halves on a baking sheet and toast in the hot oven for 6 to 7 minutes, or until golden brown. Remove from the oven and let cool.

3. Heat 4 tablespoons (60 g) of the ghee in a large sauté pan over medium heat. Add the grated carrots and cook, stirring regularly, for about 15 minutes, or until the carrots are just tender. Add the sugar and *khoya* and cook for 5 more minutes, until the sugar is melted and the mixture is well blended. Add the remaining 2 tablespoons (30 g) ghee, the cardamom, raisins, and toasted nuts and mix well. Serve hot, warm, or at room temperature.

DATE-FILLED PASTRIES
MAQRUD

TUNISIA

These luscious pastries come from Kairouan in Tunisia. They are usually shaped with a special stamp that both flattens the dough and etches a pattern on it. It is unlikely you will find this stamp outside of Kairouan, but don't let this stop you from making the pastries as you don't really need it. All you have to do once you have filled them is to simply flatten them with your fingers, then make a pattern by pressing the side of a box grater on the flattened dough. The pastries may not end up as perfectly shaped as those made with the special stamp, but the taste will be just as good. *Maqrud* are another Ramadan specialty, sold on the street throughout the medina during that month, and at specialized vendors the rest of the year.

MAKES ABOUT 24

FOR THE DOUGH
Pinch of saffron threads, crushed to a fine powder with a small mortar and pestle
1½ cups (225 g) fine semolina
⅛ teaspoon fine sea salt
¼ teaspoon baking soda
2 tablespoons extra-virgin olive oil
All-purpose flour, for rolling the dough

FOR THE HONEY SYRUP
Scant 1 cup (175 g) raw cane sugar
4 tablespoons (60 g) honey

FOR THE FILLING
¾ cup (120 g) pitted dates
1 tablespoon extra-virgin olive oil
⅛ teaspoon ground cinnamon
Grated zest of ½ orange

Vegetable oil, for deep-frying

1. To make the dough: Steep the saffron in ½ cup (125 ml) warm water in a small bowl for 15 minutes.

2. Mix together the semolina, salt, and baking soda in a large bowl. Make a well in the center. Add the saffron water and olive oil to the well and gradually bring in the semolina until you have a rough dough.

3. Transfer the dough to a lightly floured work surface and knead until you have a smooth, malleable dough. Shape into a ball. Cover with plastic wrap and let rest on your kitchen counter for 15 minutes.

4. To make the honey syrup: Put the sugar, honey, and ¾ cup (180 ml) water in a saucepan and bring to a boil over medium heat, stirring occasionally. Let boil for 3 minutes. Remove from the heat and let cool.

5. To make the filling: Put the dates in a food processor and pulse until coarsely chopped. Add the olive oil, cinnamon, and orange zest and process until you have a smooth paste.

6. Divide the filling into 6 equal portions. Shape each portion into a cylinder about ¾ inch (2 cm) thick and 2 inches (5 cm) long and set on a plate or baking sheet. Cover with plastic wrap.

7. Line a baking sheet with parchment paper or a silicone baking mat (or use a nonstick sheet).

8. Divide the dough into 6 equal portions and shape into balls. Roll one ball of dough into an oval about 4 inches (10 cm) long, 2 inches (5 cm) wide, and ½ inch (1 cm) thick. Place a date cylinder along the length of the oval, centered over one half. Fold the other half to enclose the filling. Then, using a *maqrud* stamp, your fingers, or the fine-holed side of a box grater, flatten the filled dough to an even ½ inch (1 cm) thickness. With a knife, trim the edges, and cut the dough at an angle into diamonds with sides about 1 inch (2.5 cm) long. You should get 4 diamonds from each cylinder. Lay these on the baking sheet. Repeat with the remaining dough and filling.

9. Place a fine-mesh wire rack in a rimmed baking sheet. Set the honey syrup near the stove. Pour 2 inches (5 cm) vegetable oil into a medium deep skillet and heat over medium heat until hot (if you drop a piece of bread in the oil, the oil should immediately bubble around it). Working in batches, drop in as many pastries as will comfortably fit in the pan. Fry for 2 to 3 minutes on each side, or until golden brown all over. Remove the pastries from the oil with a slotted spoon and immediately drop into the syrup. Turn a few times in the syrup to coat them well, then transfer to the wire rack to drain off the excess syrup. Let cool before transferring to a serving platter; or store in an airtight container to serve later. They will keep for a few days.

IRAQI DATE COOKIES
AL-KELAIJAH

These Iraqi date cookies are an absolute must for Eid, both Eid il-Futr, which immediately follows Ramadan, and Eid al-Adha, the feast of the sacrifice, which is a few months after. They are also prepared for special occasions, such as weddings or other celebrations; and even if prepared in huge quantities, as for a feast, none are wasted, because they last a long time. The recipe below is for date-filled ones, but *kelaijahs* can also be filled with walnuts or almonds or sesame seeds.

MAKES 36

FOR THE DOUGH
2 good pinches of saffron threads
¼ cup (60 ml) rose water
1 organic egg, beaten
3¾ cups (450 g) unbleached all-purpose flour
1 packet (7g/ 2¼ teaspoons) instant (fast-acting) yeast
1 teaspoon fine sea salt
¼ teaspoon Arabian Spice Mixture for Desserts (page 367)
2 sticks (250 g) unsalted butter, melted and cooled
¼ cup (60 ml) whole milk

FOR THE FILLING
1½ cups (225 g) pitted dates (Barhi, Medjool, or any other soft type)
3 tablespoons (45 g) unsalted butter, at room temperature
1 teaspoon ground cardamom

FOR GARNISH
⅓ cup (50 g) sesame seeds

1. To make the dough: Put 1 pinch of the saffron to steep in the rose water and mix the other pinch with the beaten egg in a small bowl. Cover the beaten egg with plastic wrap so that it doesn't dry while you mix and rest the dough.

2. Put the flour, yeast, salt, and spice mixture in a large bowl and mix well. Make a well in the center and add the melted butter and saffron rose water. Using the tips of your fingers, bring in the flour to mix with the butter and rose water. Then add the milk and ¼ cup (60 ml) water and mix to form a smooth, supple dough. Shape the dough into a ball. Cover with plastic wrap and let sit on your counter for 30 minutes.

3. To make the filling: Put the dates, butter, and cardamom in a food processor and process until you have a smooth paste. Transfer to a medium bowl.

4. Preheat the oven to 350°F (180°C). Line a baking sheet with parchment paper or a silicone baking mat (or use a nonstick sheet).

5. To make the cookies: Divide the dough into 36 equal pieces and roll each piece into a ball the size of a walnut. Take one ball of dough and place it in the cup of one hand. With your index and middle fingers flatten the dough into a disk on the palm of your hand, then cup your hand to hold it as if it were a shell. Take 1 teaspoon date filling and place it in the middle of the dough. Seal the joints and shape into a ball. Flatten the ball into a disk measuring 2½ inches (6 cm) in diameter. At this point, you can give the disk a concave shape or leave it as is. Place on the baking sheet and finish making the *kelaijahs*.

6. Brush the *kelaijahs* with the saffron-flavored beaten egg and sprinkle with sesame seeds. Bake for 20 to 25 minutes, or until crisp and lightly golden. Let cool on a wire rack before serving or storing in an airtight container. They will keep for at least 1 week.

PISTACHIO ICE CREAM
BOOZA 'ALA FISTUQ

Arabic, Turkish, and Iranian ice creams have a completely different texture from that of Italian gelato or other Western ice creams. In many cases, there isn't even cream in the mixture, simply milk that is thickened with salep, a powder ground from the dried tubers of orchids that grow in Turkey and Iran. I love the thick stretchy texture that salep gives to ice cream, which makes you feel as if you are chewing on it rather than letting it melt in your mouth. However, it is almost impossible to get salep outside of the Middle East and you may need to make this ice cream with cornstarch. If you find salep, make sure it is good-quality pure salep, which is grayish in color, and slightly flecked. The whiter the powder, the more likely it is mixed with cornstarch.

MAKES JUST OVER 4 CUPS (1 LITER)

⅔ cup (100 g) pistachios

4 cups (1 liter) whole milk

1 cup (200 g) raw cane sugar

1 tablespoon salep or 2 tablespoons cornstarch

1¼ cups (300 ml) crème fraîche

3 tablespoons rose water

½ teaspoon ground mastic (see Glossary)

1. Place the pistachios very loosely in a zip-seal plastic bag. Seal and place on a cutting board. With a rolling pin, beat on the pistachios to crack them. Break the nuts unevenly with some large pieces and others very small.

2. Put the milk and sugar in a large pot and bring to a boil over medium heat and at the same time, add the salep, little by little and in very small quantities, whisking all the time—if you do not do this, you will get lumps in the milk. If you are going to use cornstarch, mix it with a little milk and add as you put the milk over the heat, whisking all the time as with the salep. After the milk starts boiling, carry on whisking for 10 to 15 minutes, or until the milk has thickened.

3. Remove from the heat and transfer to a large measuring cup or a large bowl with a spout. Add the crème fraiche, crushed pistachios, and rose water and whisk until the cream is fully incorporated. Add the mastic little by little, quickly whisking it in the mixture. Mix well. Let cool, then refrigerate to chill so that it takes less time to churn it into ice cream.

4. Churn the mixture in an ice cream maker following the manufacturer's instructions. (If you don't have an ice cream maker, pour the mixture in a freezer container and place in the freezer. Whisk every hour or so, for 6 to 8 hours, or until the ice cream has reached the desired consistency.) Serve as is or scatter a few dried rose petals over the ice cream before serving.

SAFFRON ICE CREAM: To turn this ice cream into a saffron one, with or without the pistachios, sprinkle 2 or 3 good pinches of saffron threads into the milk and let them steep in the milk for 30 minutes. Then make the ice cream as directed.

DATE ICE CREAM

BUZA 'ALA-TAMR

Before sugar became commonly available, dates were an important sweetener in Arabia, and even though this date ice cream must be a recent addition to the Arabian culinary repertoire, it makes use of dates as the main sweetener just as they did at the advent of Islam and for long after. This means a lot less sugar in the ice cream, which makes it ideal for those who need to cut down on sugar but still want something sweet. **MAKES 1½ QUARTS (1.5 LITERS)**

2 tablespoons (20 g) cornstarch, or 1 tablespoon salep (see Note)

4 cups (1 liter) whole milk

½ cup (100 g) raw cane sugar

2 tablespoons rose water

2 teaspoons ground cardamom

3 cups (450 g) pitted dates (Khlass or Barhi)

1 cup (250 ml) double cream or crème fraîche

Slivered or coarsely ground pistachios, for garnish

1. Whisk the cornstarch into ¼ cup (60 ml) of the milk in a small mixing bowl and have at hand. Put the remaining 3¾ cups (940 ml) milk and sugar in a medium pot and place over medium heat. Slowly add the cornstach/milk mixture (see Note), whisking all the time. Bring to a boil, still whisking. Let bubble for about 10 minutes while still whisking. Take off the heat and add the rose water and cardamom. Cover with a clean kitchen towel and let cool.

2. Put the dates in a food processor. Add the thickened milk and process until the mixture is creamy. Transfer to a large measuring cup with a 2-quart (2-liter) capacity and whisk in the cream. Cover with plastic wrap and refrigerate until well chilled.

3. Churn the mixture in an ice cream maker following the manufacturer's instructions. Serve garnished with slivered or coarsely crushed pistachios.

NOTE: *If you are going to use salep, add it little by little as you are bringing the milk to a boil, then continue as with the cornstarch.*

PAKISTANI/INDIAN ICE CREAM
KULFI

Kulfi is the Indian/Pakistani version of Arab ice cream, also made without egg but with reduced milk, for a "crumbly" texture rather than creamy, but with an intense dairy flavor, not to mention the taste of cardamom. Kulfi molds come in different sizes, and they are made in the shape of cones with flat tips and screw-on lids so that the mixture does not spill out as it freezes. If you can't get ahold of any kulfi molds, use conical Popsicle molds. They may not be the exact shape but they are close enough. SERVES 4 TO 6 (DEPENDING ON THE SIZE OF THE MOLDS)

Pinch of saffron threads

4 cups (1 liter) whole milk

¼ cup (60 g) crème fraîche or khoya (see Glossary)

½ cup (100 g) raw cane sugar

1 tablespoon slivered pistachios, plus more for garnish

1 tablespoon slivered almonds

Seeds of 4 green cardamom pods, coarsely ground

1. Put the saffron to steep in 2 tablespoons of the milk.

2. Put the remaining milk in a medium pot and bring to a boil over medium heat. Add the cream, reduce the heat to low, and let the milk and cream bubble gently, stirring very regularly so as not to let the bottom burn, until reduced by half.

3. Add the sugar and slivered nuts and mix well. Let bubble for 5 more minutes, then take off the heat and add the cardamom. Let cool completely before ladling into kulfi molds and freezing for 4 to 5 hours. Halfway through, insert a solid bamboo stick into each kulfi.

4. To take the kulfi out of the molds, plunge the molds for a second or two in hot water, then unmold. Serve garnished with slivered pistachios.

SAFFRON KULFI: Omit the nuts. Increase the saffron to 2 pinches.

CREAM or WALNUT SWEET "HAND PIES"

QATAYEF

Qatayef are like English crumpets, but made thinner so that they can be filled with *qashtah* (Arabic clotted cream) or walnuts and fried until crisp and golden before being dipped in syrup. They are also served unfried, half filled with *qashtah*, drizzled with sugar syrup, and finished with a pretty garnish of Orange Blossom Jam (page 502). Like many other sweets, they are a must for Ramadan. During that month, many sweets makers set up colorful tents outside their stores to make industrial quantities of *qatayef* right on the street, both for show and to meet the increased demand. Most home cooks in the Middle East buy the pancakes ready-made to fill and fry at home, but I also give you the recipe for how to make them—it is not so easy to find them in the West, except at Syrian or Lebanese sweets makers, and often only during Ramadan.

MAKES 12 SMALL PANCAKES

Sugar syrup from page 454

FOR THE BATTER
1 cup (120 g) unbleached all-purpose flour
Heaping ½ teaspoon instant (fast-acting) yeast
¼ teaspoon fine sea salt

1. Make the sugar syrup following the instructions on page 454.

2. To make the batter: Put the flour, yeast, and salt in a large bowl and mix well. Add ⅔ cup (160 ml) water and mix until you have a smooth batter. Cover with plastic wrap and let sit for 1 hour, or until the batter has doubled in size and its surface has become quite bubbly.

3. Make your filling of choice.

4. To cook the pancakes: Brush a large nonstick skillet with a little oil and heat over medium heat. Scoop out a heaping tablespoon of batter and drop into the skillet, spreading it, either with the back of the ladle or by shaking the pan from side to side, to have a round about 3 inches (7.5 cm) in diameter and ¼ inch (6 mm) thick. Drop as many pancakes as will fit comfortably in the pan without letting them touch. Cook on one side only until the top is completely pockmarked with holes, and the bottom is lightly golden. Remove to a clean kitchen towel and finish making the remaining pancakes in the same way. Let cool.

5. To assemble, lay a pancake on one hand. Arrange 1 tablespoon filling in a line down the middle, staying clear of the edges, and fold the pancake up into a half-moon enclosing the filling. Pinch the edges firmly together so that they don't open during frying and lay on a platter. Finish filling the pancakes.

FOR THE FILLING (CHOOSE ONE)

1½ cups (375 g) Arabic clotted cream (see Glossary)

7 ounces (200 g) coarsely ground walnuts, 1 tablespoon raw cane sugar, ¼ teaspoon ground cinnamon, and 1 tablespoon orange blossom water (stirred together)

Vegetable oil, for frying

6. Set a fine-mesh wire rack in a rimmed baking sheet. Have the sugar syrup near the stove. Pour 2 inches (5 cm) vegetable oil into a large skillet and heat over medium heat until hot (if you drop a piece of bread in the oil, the oil should immediately bubble around it). Slide in as many filled pancakes as can fit comfortably in the pan and fry for 2 to 3 minutes on each side, or until golden brown all over. Remove with a slotted spoon and drop into the sugar syrup. Turn in the syrup until well coated, then transfer to the wire rack to let the excess syrup drain off. Repeat with the remaining pancakes and serve within the hour. They are at their crunchiest and most delicious served immediately after frying.

SWEET-SALTY CASSAVA CAKES
GETUK LINDRI

Indonesian sweets are never very sweet and often they are also slightly salty. These cakes are a case in point, with a little salt added to the cassava before mixing with the sugar syrup.

SERVES 4 TO 6

½ cup (100 g) raw cane sugar

1 tablespoon vanilla sugar

1 pound 2 ounces (500 g) yuca (cassava), peeled and cut into chunks

4 tablespoons (60 g) unsalted butter

Sea salt

Natural yellow and green food coloring

1 cup (75 g) desiccated shredded coconut, for garnish

1. Put the raw sugar, vanilla sugar, and ⅔ cup (150 ml) water in a small saucepan and stir over medium heat until the sugar is completely dissolved. Let cool.

2. Put the yuca in a steamer basket and steam for about 30 minutes, or until very soft. Transfer to a large bowl and while still hot, mash with the butter, adding a little salt, until you have a smooth puree.

3. Slowly add the sugar syrup and carry on mashing until you have a very smooth puree. Taste and adjust the seasoning if necessary—there needs to be a good balance between sweet and salty.

4. Divide in half and add one of the food colorings to each part. Use a sheet of plastic wrap to roll each piece into a log about 1¼ inches (3 cm) thick. Slice crosswise into disks about ¾ inch (2 cm) thick and arrange on a large platter in a rosette shape. You can also shape them into a square, scoring the top to create a pattern.

5. Steam the shredded coconut in a bamboo steamer or a steamer basket lined with cheesecloth for 10 to 15 minutes, or until softened. Sprinkle the steamed grated coconut over the cassava cakes and serve warm or at room temperature.

MALAYSIAN PANDAN BALLS
KLEPON/ONDE ONDE

INDONESIA | MALAYSIA

Klepon in Indonesia and *onde onde* in Malaysia, these sweet-salty rice flour balls filled with palm sugar and garnished with shredded coconut are totally addictive. I first had them in Banda Aceh, at Mita Sugesty's house. It was Ramadan and even though the family was all fasting, Mita insisted that I should taste her mother's *klepon*, which she made there and then for me to see how they were prepared. Mita's mother used fresh pandan leaf to color her cakes but you may not find this, in which case use pandan paste, and if neither is available, use a natural green food coloring to impart the pale green color that is so typical of these rice balls.   SERVES 4 TO 6

1 pandan leaf or 2 to 3
  drops pandan paste
1⅔ cups (250 g)
  glutinous rice flour
½ teaspoon fine sea salt,
  plus more for sprinkling
1 cup (150 g) crumbled
  palm sugar
1 cup (75 g) desiccated
  shredded coconut, for
  garnish

1. Break the pandan leaf (if you have it) in two and put it to steep in 1 cup (250 ml) water. Add the pandan paste drops and stir until the water is a deep green. Remove pandan leaf, if using.

2. Mix the rice flour and salt in a large mixing bowl and make a well in the center. Add the pandan-colored water little by little and mix until you have a soft, pastel-green dough.

3. Pinch a little dough and roll into a ball the size of a walnut. With a finger, make an indent in the middle of the ball of dough and put 1 teaspoon of crumbled palm sugar in the hole. Pinch the dough together to close and roll again into a ball, making sure there are no gaps from which the palm sugar can ooze out as you boil the *klepon*. Place on a large platter and make the remaining *klepon* in the same way.

4. Put the coconut in a bamboo steamer or a steamer basket lined with cheesecloth and steam for 10 to 15 minutes, or until softened. Spread on a medium platter to make a bed of shredded coconut to place the *klepon* on. Sprinkle very lightly with salt.

5. Bring a medium pot of water to a boil. Working in batches, drop as many balls of *klepon* as will fit comfortably in the pot and boil for 4 to 5 minutes, or until the balls float. When they do, let them boil for another 30 seconds or so, then transfer to the bed of shredded coconut. Roll the balls to coat with coconut and remove to a large serving platter.

6. Serve warm while the palm sugar is still melted inside.

INDIAN/PAKISTANI MILK RICE PUDDING

KHEER

There are variations on milk pudding in almost every single Middle Eastern and South Asian country. Some variations are slight, while others are more substantial, and some puddings are more elegant than others but all will be tasty. The one below is the Indian/Pakistani version, where the milk is thickened with rice, and has added nuts and raisins. Most other versions are plain and have a silkier texture, and the flavorings range from spices to fragrant waters.

SERVES 4

1 tablespoon ghee or unsalted butter

4 cups (1 liter) whole milk

¼ cup (50 g) basmati rice, rinsed, soaked for 30 minutes in cold water, and drained

⅓ cup (75 g) raw cane sugar

1 tablespoon slivered pistachios, plus more for garnish

1 tablespoon slivered almonds, plus more for garnish

4 cashews, coarsely chopped, plus more for garnish

1 tablespoon golden raisins

Seeds of 2 cardamom pods, coarsely ground

Pinch of saffron threads

Sea salt

Melt the ghee or butter in a medium pot over medium heat. Add the milk and bring to a boil. Add the drained rice and let bubble, stirring regularly, for 10 minutes, or until the rice is tender. Add the sugar, nuts, and golden raisins and let bubble for another 10 minutes. Add the cardamom, saffron, and a pinch of salt and let cook for another 15 minutes or so, or until the milk has reduced to a creamy consistency. Take off the heat and transfer to one large serving bowl or 4 individual bowls. Serve warm or at room temperature, garnished with more nuts.

SAFFRON LEBANESE/SYRIAN MILK PUDDING

MUHALLABIYEH BIL-ZA'FARAN

This Lebanese/Syrian version of milk pudding is very different from the South Asian one. Redolent with orange blossom and rose water as well as the intriguing flavor of mastic, this pudding is my favorite. Normally it is made thicker, but I prefer to use less cornstarch for a softer, more luxurious texture. I also flavor it with saffron to make it even more sumptuous, but you can leave the saffron out for a more traditional version.

SERVES 4 TO 6

4 cups (1 liter) whole milk
Good pinch of saffron threads
4½ heaping tablespoons (50 g) cornstarch
¾ cup (150 g) baker's sugar or superfine sugar
2 teaspoons orange blossom water
2 teaspoons rose water
¼ teaspoon ground mastic (see Glossary)
2 tablespoons slivered pistachios, for garnish

1. Put 3½ cups (875 ml) milk in a saucepan and add the saffron. Let steep for 30 minutes while you prepare your ingredients. The saffron needs this time to flavor the milk before you start making the *muhallabiyeh*.

2. Whisk the cornstarch with the remaining ½ cup (125 ml) milk.

3. Add the sugar to the saffron milk and place the pan over medium heat. Whisk the cornstach milk into the pan and continue whisking as you bring the milk to a boil. As soon as the milk starts boiling, reduce the heat to low and continue whisking for another 10 to 15 minutes, or until the milk has thickened. Take off the heat.

4. Add the orange blossom and rose water, then add the mastic and quickly whisk it in. Pour into one large shallow serving bowl or into individual bowls. Let cool, then refrigerate until well chilled. Serve chilled, garnished with slivered pistachios.

INDONESIAN BLACK RICE PUDDING

BUBUR PULUT HITAM

Like milk puddings, rice puddings change from one Muslim country to another, usually with slight variations—until you get to Indonesia and Malaysia where the rice used is black and glutinous and it needs soaking for a few hours before using. Instead of dairy milk, both Indonesians and Malaysians use coconut cream, but as a sauce rather than a liquid for cooking the rice. As for longans, they are a sweet, juicy fruit related to lychees. When longans are dried, their white flesh turns almost black.

SERVES 4

FOR THE RICE PUDDING
¾ cup (150 g) black glutinous rice, soaked overnight in cold water and drained
2 pandan leaves, knotted, plus extra for garnish (optional)
2½ ounces (75 g) rock sugar (see Note)
1 ounce (30 g) palm sugar (see Note)
2 ounces (60 g) dried longans (optional)

FOR THE COCONUT SAUCE
1 cup (250 ml) coconut cream
1 teaspoon salt

1. Put 6 cups (1.5 liters) water into a medium pot and add the drained rice. Bring to a boil over medium heat. Drop the knotted pandan leaves (if using) into the rice. Reduce the heat to medium-low, cover the pot, and let bubble gently until the rice opens up and expands, about 1 hour.

2. Add the two sugars and the dried longans (if using) and let simmer, uncovered, for another 25 minutes, still stirring very regularly.

3. Meanwhile, make the coconut sauce: Put the coconut cream and salt in a small saucepan and bring to a boil over medium heat. Take off the heat and keep warm.

4. Divide the hot rice pudding into 4 individual bowls, drizzle one-quarter of the warm coconut sauce over each, and serve immediately. If you have managed to get pandan leaves, cut four pieces into a nice shape and spike one in each bowl for a traditional presentation.

NOTE: *If you can't get rock sugar or palm sugar, substitute an equal amount of brown sugar.*

MOROCCAN RICE PUDDING
ROZZ B'LEHLIB

Rice puddings are common throughout the Middle East although they vary slightly from one country to another. In Turkey, saffron is added and no milk is used, whereas in Lebanon you have orange blossom and rose water as the main flavorings. The Moroccan version here is cooked longer and only flavored with orange blossom water. It is also softer and more velvety and fragrant and possibly more delightful than the Lebanese, Syrian, or Egyptian versions. SERVES 4

¾ cup (150 g) short-grain white rice
¼ teaspoon sea salt
2 tablespoons (30 g) unsalted butter
2½ cups (625 ml) whole milk
⅓ cup (75 g) powdered sugar
2 tablespoons orange blossom water
⅓ cup (50 g) blanched almonds, toasted for 6 to 7 minutes in a hot oven until golden brown

1. Rinse the rice under cold water and put in a medium pot. Add 1½ cups (375 ml) water and the salt and bring to a boil over medium-high heat. Add the butter, reduce the heat to low, cover, and simmer for 15 minutes, or until the water is almost completely absorbed.

2. Uncover, add the milk and sugar, increase the heat to medium, and bring to a boil. Reduce the heat to medium-low and let bubble gently, uncovered, stirring the rice regularly so that it does not stick, for 5 minutes, or until the rice pudding has the consistency of runny porridge.

3. Take off the heat and add the orange blossom water. Pour into a shallow serving bowl or individual bowls. Let cool. Garnish with the toasted almonds and serve at room temperature.

SYRIAN/LEBANESE RICE PUDDING

REZZ BIL-HALIB

For this rice pudding, the rice is cooked with less milk than the Moroccan version for a slightly less creamy pudding, and rose water is also added for a more fragrant flavor.   SERVES 4 TO 6

1 cup (200 g) short-grain white rice, rinsed under cold water and drained

1¼ cups (310 ml) whole milk, plus more as needed

½ cup (100 g) raw cane sugar

1 teaspoon rose water

1 teaspoon orange blossom water

Slivered pistachios, for garnish

1. Put the rice in a medium pot with 2 cups (500 ml) water and bring to a boil over medium heat. Reduce the heat to low and cook the rice, covered, for 20 minutes, stirring occasionally, or until the rice has absorbed all the water.

2. Add the milk and bring to a boil. Add the sugar and simmer, uncovered, stirring very regularly so that the rice doesn't stick or dry up, for 20 more minutes, or until the texture is like that of custard. Add a little more milk if you think it is becoming too dry.

3. Remove the pot from the heat and mix in the rose water and orange blossom water. Pour the rice pudding into a big shallow serving bowl or individual bowls. Let cool. Serve at room temperature, garnished with slivered pistachios.

TURKISH SAFFRON RICE PUDDING

ZERDE

TURKEY

This rice pudding must be a direct descendant of the Iranian *sholeh zerd*, both as far as the name is concerned and the way it is made, except that Iranians also add oil or butter to theirs whereas Turks don't use any fat but add a few slivered nuts for texture.   SERVES 6

Good pinch of saffron
   threads
¼ cup (60 ml) rose water
½ cup (100 g) Calasparra
   or other short-grain
   rice
¾ cup (150 g) superfine
   sugar
1 tablespoon slivered
   almonds
1 tablespoon slivered
   pistachios, plus more
   for garnish
Pomegranate seeds, for
   garnish (if in season)

1. Put the saffron threads to soak in the rose water.

2. Rinse the rice under cold water and put in a medium pot. Add 6 cups (1.5 liters) water and bring to a boil over medium heat. Add the sugar and let simmer, covered, for about 30 minutes, or until the rice has expanded and is very soft.

3. Add the nuts and the saffron rose water and simmer, covered, for another 5 minutes, or until the rice is like a thin porridge. It will thicken as it sits.

4. Pour into 6 individual bowls or one large serving bowl and let cool. Serve at room temperature garnished with more slivered pistachios and pomegranate seeds if you have them.

SWEET FRITTERS

You find sweet fritters throughout the Muslim world from Zanzibar (where they are called *kaimati*) to Saudi Arabia (where they go by the name of *loqmat al-qadi* or "the bite of the judge") to Lebanon and Syria (*'uwwamat* or "floating") to Turkey (*loqma* or "bite") to the Arabian Gulf (*l'geimat* or "bites"). In Pakistan, the fritters are made differently, mainly with dried or powdered milk, and are known as *gulab jamun*—from the Persian, *gol* ("flower") and *ab* ("water"), while *jamun* is a Hindi-Urdu word for a fruit that has the same shape as the milk fritters.

There are slight variations between the Levantine and Arabian fritters with some being crisper and sweeter while the Arabian ones are softer and less sweet with added saffron and cardamom. The South Asian version is quite a lot softer because of the milk solids and as a result a lot more syrupy. I am giving recipes for the most distinctive variations (see pages 488 and 489).

SAFFRON-FLAVORED FRITTERS
L'GEIMAT

ARABIAN GULF

Traditionally, *l'geimat* are served drizzled with date syrup, but many Arabian cooks sweeten them with a sugar syrup flavored with saffron and cardamom. You can also serve these drizzled with date syrup.

SERVES 6 TO 8

FOR THE FRITTERS
1 cup (120 g) unbleached all-purpose flour
1 cup (120 g) white whole wheat flour
1 teaspoon instant (fast-acting) yeast
1 tablespoon sugar
¼ teaspoon fine sea salt
½ cup (125 g) yogurt
1 organic egg
Sugar Syrup (recipe follows)

Vegetable oil, for deep-frying

1. To make the fritters: Mix both flours, the yeast, sugar, and salt in a large bowl. Add the yogurt and ½ cup (125 ml) water. Add the egg and mix until you have a very loose dough or a very thick batter. Cover with plastic wrap and let rest for at least 3 hours, preferably overnight.

2. Set the sugar syrup near the stove. Pour 2 inches (5 cm) vegetable oil into a large skillet and heat over medium heat until very hot (if you drop a piece of bread in the oil, the oil should immediately bubble around it). Use one of the different ways of forming round fritters (see Forming Round Fritters on page 491), then drop the fritters in the hot oil and fry them until golden brown all over, stirring all the time to color them evenly, 7 to 10 minutes. Remove to a sieve to let the excess oil drain. Serve immediately or soon after frying, drizzled with sugar syrup.

SUGAR SYRUP

2 cups (400 g) raw cane sugar
¼ teaspoon ground cardamom
1 small cinnamon stick
A pinch of saffron threads
1 tablespoon lemon juice

Put the sugar in a medium pot and add 1 cup (250 ml) water. Add the cardamom, cinnamon stick, saffron, and lemon juice and bring to a simmer over low heat. Let simmer for 30 minutes, stirring every now and then, until you have a thick syrup. Take off the heat. If you are not going to use the syrup straightaway, store it in an airtight glass jar in the refrigerator, where it will last for a few days.

SAUDI SWEET FRITTERS
LOQMAT AL-QADI

SAUDI ARABIA

Here is the Saudi version of sweet fritters, which seems to combine almost all aspects of the Lebanese/Syrian and Arabian versions (see pages 490 and 486).   SERVES 6 TO 8

1 cup (120 g) unbleached
    all-purpose flour
2 tablespoons whole milk
    powder
2 tablespoons cornstarch
2 tablespoons raw cane
    sugar
1 teaspoon baking
    powder
1 tablespoon instant
    (fast-acting) yeast
1 teaspoon fine sea salt
1 teaspoon ground
    cardamom
1 teaspoon ground
    cinnamon
2 tablespoons yogurt
1 organic egg
Sugar Syrup (page 486)
Vegetable oil, for deep-
    frying

1. To make the batter: Put the flour, powdered milk, cornstarch, sugar, baking powder, yeast, salt, cardamom, and cinnamon in a large mixing bowl and mix well. Then add the yogurt and the egg and mix a little bit before adding ½ cup (125 ml) water. Mix well. Then with your hand beat the thick batter or loose dough until it is smooth. This is a very traditional technique that you will find used from Egypt to Zanzibar to develop the gluten in very loose doughs until the dough becomes smooth, which will take a few minutes. Cover the batter with plastic wrap and let rest for 30 minutes.

2. Meanwhile, make the sugar syrup as directed. Set the syrup by the stove.

3. Pour 2 inches (5 cm) oil into a large skillet and heat over medium heat until very hot (if you drop a piece of bread in the oil, the oil should immediately bubble around it). Grease your right hand with a little oil and do the same with a teaspoon. Pick up a handful of dough with your oiled hand and squeeze a little ball through your clenched fist. Scoop the ball with the oiled teaspoon and drop into the hot oil. Repeat the process until you have dropped enough balls of dough to fit comfortably in the pan. Fry until golden brown all over, 7 to 10 minutes, stirring very regularly so that they color evenly. Drain on paper towels, then drop the fritters into the syrup. Stir for a minute or so, then remove to a large shallow bowl and serve immediately. These are best eaten soon after frying as they tend to go soggy rather quickly.

SOUTH ASIAN SWEET MILK FRITTERS

GULAB JAMUN

INDIA | PAKISTAN

Possibly the best known of South Asian sweets, these round fritters are similar to *'uwwamat* (Lebanese/Syrian Round Fritters, page 490) or *l'geimat* (Saffron-Flavored Fritters, page 486), but they are made very differently, having a base of milk solids rather than flour, and as a result they absorb a lot more syrup, which results in a spongy rather than crisp fritter. SERVES 6 TO 8

FOR THE SYRUP
1 cup (200 g) raw cane sugar
4 green cardamom pods, smashed
1 teaspoon kewra (pandanus flower extract)

FOR THE FRITTERS
1 cup (80 g) nonfat powdered milk
1½ teaspoons unbleached all-purpose flour
¾ teaspoon semolina
1 teaspoon baking powder
Sea salt
1 small egg
½ teaspoon vegetable oil
¼ cup (60 ml) whole milk

Vegetable oil, for deep-frying

1. To make the syrup: Put the sugar and ¾ cup (180 ml) water in a medium saucepan. Add the cardamom pods and bring to a boil over medium heat. Let bubble for about 5 minutes. Take off the heat and add the *kewra*.

2. To make the fritters: Put the powdered milk, flour, semolina, baking powder, and a pinch of salt in a medium bowl and mix well. Add the egg, vegetable oil, and milk and mix until you have a smooth dough. Let the dough rest for 10 minutes. Divide the dough into 16 equal portions and roll each into a ball the size of a walnut.

3. Pour 2 inches (5 cm) vegetable oil into a large deep skillet and heat over medium heat until hot (if you drop a piece of bread in the oil, the oil should immediately bubble around it). Working in batches, drop as many balls as will fit comfortably in the pan and fry, stirring frequently, until golden brown all over, 3 to 5 minutes—because of the milk sugars, these color quickly. Scoop with a slotted spoon and place on a plate for a few minutes—if you drop them too hot in the sugar syrup they may lose their shape—then drop into the sugar syrup. Let them soak up the syrup for 5 to 10 minutes, stirring occasionally. Remove with a slotted spoon to a shallow serving bowl. Serve soon after, at room temperature.

LEBANESE/SYRIAN ROUND FRITTERS

'UWWAMAT

I used to visit Syria very regularly before the uprising and in each city I had one or more favorite food spots. One of those in Damascus was in Souk el-Tanabel (Souk of the Lazy People). I loved the souk itself for the displays of vegetables prepared by women in their homes during the night so that they could be fresh in the shops the following morning. But it was one sweets stall that drew me back to the souk every time I visited the city because the sweets maker had the most extraordinary technique for making *'uwwamat*. He stood a few feet away from his gigantic frying vat, next to a large tub in which he had the loose *'uwwamat* dough. He worked incredibly quickly, dipping his left hand, then a small spoon in water before grabbing a chunk of dough in his wet hand. He would squeeze a little ball of dough through his clenched fist and, with the spoon, he scooped the dough and flicked it into the hot oil. He never missed and the dough never stuck to the spoon. He was there morning and evening, making hundreds of these small round fritters, and I would stand and watch, mesmerized by the spectacle. Most other *'uwwamat* makers simply stood over their skillets, dropping the dough straight into it. I had never seen anyone flicking it from a distance the way he did. Not only did he have a masterful technique, but his fritters were also exquisite and always crisp as he seemed to sell them as soon as he made them—*'uwwamat* are best eaten soon after they have been fried. He obviously knew he was the best because written in big letters at the front of his stall was a sign proclaiming him as Malak al-'Uwwamat—"King of the Round Fritters"!

SERVES 4 TO 6

1¼ cups (150 g) unbleached all-purpose flour
1¼ cups (300 g) yogurt
½ teaspoon baking soda
Twice the amount of Lebanese sugar syrup on page 454
Vegetable oil, for deep-frying, and to dip the spoon in

1. Put the flour in a large bowl. Add the yogurt and baking soda and whisk until you have a smooth batter. Cover with plastic wrap and let rest for 45 minutes.

2. Make the syrup as directed. Keep the syrup near the stove.

3. Pour 2 inches (5 cm) oil into a large deep skillet and heat over medium heat until very hot (if you drop a piece of bread in the oil, the oil should immediately bubble around it). Dip a dessert spoon in a little cold oil, fill it with batter, and drop this ball of batter into the hot oil. Drop in as many balls as will fit comfortably in the pan and fry them, stirring to brown them evenly, until golden all over, 5 to 7 minutes. Drain on paper towels, then drop into the syrup. Turn them in the syrup a few times and transfer to a serving dish. Serve soon after frying for an optimal texture.

FORMING ROUND FRITTERS

You can form round fritters in one of several ways:

1. Wet your hand and with the tips of your fingers pinch off bits of dough, adding them to the oil to fry and puff up to the size of an apricot.

2. Wet your hand, grab a handful of the soft dough, invert your clenched fist over the oil, and squeeze enough dough from between your thumb and index finger to have the same size ball, though this method is difficult and requires practice.

3. An easier method is to grab a handful of dough in the palm of your wet hand, then close your hand and squeeze the dough out from between your thumb and index finger so that you can scoop it with a wetted spoon to drop into the hot oil to have the same size round fritter.

4. Use a pastry bag with a large plain tip and pipe the fritters into the oil.

ANISEED FRITTERS

MA'CARUN

LEBANON

Ramadan is the month of sweets. Wherever you go during that month and for Eid after, you will find abundant displays of sweets and, in Lebanon and Syria, these anise seed fritters will be prominently displayed, piled high on large metal trays, next to pyramids of baklava and neat lines of *qatayef*. The sweets serve two purposes after this month's day-long fasts. The first is to restore energy quickly to all those who have had no food or drink pass through their lips from sunrise to sundown, while the second is to take them as presents when visiting with family and/ or friends and neighbors—Ramadan is when people exchange the most visits, not to mention that each family will keep beautiful trays of sweets at home ready to be passed around with coffee and tea.

MAKES 20

1½ cups (275 g) fine semolina

¼ teaspoon instant (fast-acting) yeast

1 teaspoon ground anise seeds

¼ teaspoon ground cinnamon

3 tablespoons extra-virgin olive oil

All-purpose flour, for shaping the dough

Twice the amount of Lebanese sugar syrup on page 454

Vegetable oil, for deep-frying

1. Put the fine semolina, yeast, ground anise seeds, and cinnamon in a large bowl and mix well. Make a well in the center and add the olive oil to the well. Work it in with your fingertips until fully incorporated. Add ½ cup (125 ml) plus 2 tablespoons water and knead with your hands until you have a firm, elastic dough. Shape the dough into a ball. Place on a lightly floured work surface. Cover with a damp cloth and let rest for 45 minutes.

2. Meanwhile, prepare the sugar syrup as directed. Set the syrup near the stove.

3. Divide the dough into 20 equal portions and shape each into a fat sausage, about 2½ inches (7 cm) long. Place a dough roll against a perforated surface, like the bottom of a colander or the fine side of a box grater, and with your fingers press the dough down and roll it toward you to create a knobbly pattern and a groove as the ends meet. Place, groove side down, on a platter and continue making a pattern on the remaining dough rolls in the same way until you have shaped all 20 pieces.

4. Pour 2 inches (5 cm) vegetable oil into a large deep skillet and heat over medium heat until hot (if you drop a piece of bread in the oil, the oil should immediately bubble around it). Working in batches, drop in as many dough rolls as will fit comfortably in the pan and fry until golden brown all over, 7 to 10 minutes. Remove with a slotted spoon and immediately drop into the sugar syrup. Let the fritters soak up the syrup until just before the second batch is ready, then lift them out onto a medium serving platter before dropping in the second batch of fritters. Finish doing the rest of the *ma'carun* in the same way. Serve at room temperature. These are really best soon after they have been fried as they tend to lose their crunch fairly quickly.

TURKISH MIXED NUT, DRIED FRUIT, and LEGUMES DESSERT

ASURE

Asure is prepared on the feast day of Noah's escape from the flood in the first month of the Muslim calendar. Those living in the countryside will usually make it with whatever they have growing in their fields, or in their neighbors', most of which they will have picked and dried themselves, while city folks will buy the necessary ingredients in the bazaar. *Asure* is also prepared to commemorate 'Ashura on the tenth day of Muharram, which is when the Prophet's grandson, Hussein bin Ali, was martyred in the battle of Karbala.

SERVES 8

½ cup (100 g) wheat berries, rinsed

¼ cup (30 g) dried chickpeas, soaked overnight in plenty of water with ½ teaspoon baking soda

¼ cup (30 g) dried cannellini beans soaked overnight in plenty of water with ½ teaspoon baking soda

¼ cup (30 g) dried fava beans soaked overnight in plenty of water with ½ teaspoon baking soda

¼ cup (50 g) short-grain white rice, soaked overnight in cold water

4 dried figs, soaked overnight in cold water

6 dried apricots, soaked overnight in cold water

2 tablespoons golden raisins, soaked overnight in cold water

2 tablespoons (30 g) unsalted butter

1 cup (200 g) raw cane sugar

⅓ cup (50 g) hazelnuts, coarsely ground

1 tablespoon cornstarch

½ cup (125 ml) whole milk

⅓ cup plus 1 tablespoon (100 ml) rose water

FOR GARNISH

1 teaspoon ground cinnamon

1 teaspoon toasted sesame seeds

1 teaspoon nigella seeds

⅓ cup (50 g) walnut quarters, toasted and coarsely chopped

Pomegranate seeds (if in season)

1. The night before: Put the wheat in a large pot and add 2 quarts (2 liters) water. Place over medium heat and bring to a boil. Take off the heat. Cover with a kitchen towel and let sit overnight.

2. Set up the chickpeas, beans, fava beans, rice, and dried fruit to soak in separate medium bowls.

3. The following day: Return the wheat to the heat and simmer, covered, for about 1 hour, or until tender. Drain and rinse the chickpeas, cannellini beans, and fava beans. In separate small pots, cook the beans for 45 minutes, or until tender but not mushy. Peel all the beans, if you have the patience.

Recipe continues

4. Drain the dried fruit and chop both the figs and apricots into small pieces the size of the plumped-up golden raisins.

5. Drain the rice and add to the cooked wheat, along with the dried fruit. Add the butter and bring back to a boil. Add the peeled chickpeas, cannellini beans, and fava beans and simmer for 10 minutes. Add the sugar in three or four different batches (according to Nevin Halici whose recipe I have adapted here, the wheat will harden if you add the sugar all at once). Add the hazelnuts and simmer for another 15 minutes, stirring all the time so that the mixture does not stick, until the *asure* has thickened and become like a textured porridge. Quickly whisk the cornstarch into the milk and add to the pan. Stir until the *asure* starts bubbling again. Take off the heat and add the rose water.

6. Pour the *asure* into a large serving bowl and sprinkle with the ground cinnamon, sesame seeds, and nigella seeds. Scatter the walnuts and pomegranate seeds all over and serve hot, warm, or at room temperature.

LEBANESE WHEAT and MIXED NUT PORRIDGE

S'NAYNIYAH

S'nayniyah is the Lebanese version of *asure* (Turkish Mixed Nut, Dried Fruit, and Legumes Dessert, page 495), except that it is associated with the appearance of a baby's first teeth and is prepared to offer to visitors coming to congratulate the proud parents, who will also send out bowls of *s'nayniyeh* to family and friends to let them know the exciting news! SERVES 4 TO 6

1¼ cups (250 g) wheat berries or hulled barley, soaked overnight

1 tablespoon anise seeds, wrapped in cheesecloth

FOR SERVING

Raw cane sugar

8 to 12 teaspoons orange blossom water

8 to 12 teaspoons rose water

⅓ cup (50 g) pine nuts, soaked for 1 hour in boiling water

⅓ cup (50 g) walnuts, cut in half lengthwise, soaked for 1 hour in boiling water (and peeled if you have the patience)

⅓ cup (50 g) blanched almond halves, soaked for 1 hour in boiling water

1. Drain the wheat (or barley) and put together with the parcel of anise seeds in a large pot. Add 6 cups (1.5 liters) water and bring to a boil over high heat, skimming the froth from the surface. Cover and boil hard for 10 minutes. Reduce the heat to medium-low and let bubble gently for another 10 minutes, then turn the heat to low and simmer for 40 minutes, or until tender but not mushy. Discard the anise seeds parcel.

2. Ladle into individual bowls, adding to each bowl sugar to taste and 2 teaspoons each of orange blossom and rose water. Mix well. Drain the soaked nuts and pat dry with paper towels before scattering a little of each over the wheat. Serve hot.

PUMPKIN HALVA

ASSIDAT AL-BOBAR

UNITED ARAB EMIRATES

Pumpkin in classical Arabic is *yaqtin* or *laqtin*, but in the Emirates where they speak a slightly different Arabic, pumpkin is referred to as *al-bobar* and this pumpkin "halva" is a perfect example of the sweet-savory desserts that are so typical of that part of the Muslim world.   SERVES 6 TO 8

1 pound 10 ounces
    (1.25 kg) pumpkin,
    peeled and cut into
    medium cubes
1½ cups (175 g)
    unbleached all-purpose
    flour
¾ cup (150 g) raw cane
    sugar
½ teaspoon crushed
    saffron
Pinch of saffron threads
¾ teaspoon ground
    cardamom
1 tablespoon rose water
2 tablespoons (30 g)
    Emirati ghee or clarified
    butter, plus more for
    brushing and drizzling

1. Put the pumpkin pieces in a large pot and add 2 cups (500 ml) water. Bring to a simmer over medium-low heat and cook, covered, 15 to 20 minutes, until the pumpkin softens completely and absorbs most of the water.

2. Meanwhile, toast the flour in a large skillet, stirring constantly, until the nutty aroma rises, 7 to 10 minutes. Be careful not to let the flour burn or it'll taste bitter.

3. Mash the pumpkin with a potato masher or a large fork, while still in the pot. Add the sugar to the pot and stir until completely dissolved. Add the crushed saffron, saffron threads, cardamom, and rose water. Mix well.

4. Gradually add the toasted flour and mix well until you have a smooth mixture. Add the ghee and mix well. Brush with more ghee. Place the lid over the pot and keep warm.

5. To serve the "halva" the traditional way, spread it in a large shallow bowl and brush with ghee. If you want a prettier presentation, use two spoons to make quenelles. Arrange these in a rosette on a large platter and drizzle with a little ghee. Then, pile pretty edible flowers in the middle and serve warm or at room temperature.

SUGARED ALMONDS

NOQL-E-BADOMI

AFGHANISTAN

Sugared almonds are very much part of any celebration, whether it is Eid or weddings or circumcision rituals. And of course you can buy them ready-made with the icing dyed in different pastel colors—pink, sky blue, or green—or white. If you want to tint these, add a drop or two of your choice of natural food coloring to the syrup before coating the almonds. You can also make this with toasted chickpeas (see Variation). SERVES 6 TO 8

3⅓ cups (500 g) blanched almonds
2½ cups (500 g) raw cane sugar
1 teaspoon ground cardamom

1. Preheat the oven to 400°F (200°C).

2. Spread the almonds on a baking sheet and toast in the preheated oven for 6 to 7 minutes, or until golden brown.

3. Put the sugar, ¾ cup (180 ml) water, and cardamom in a medium skillet and bring to a boil over medium heat. Let bubble for 2 minutes, until the syrup thickens slightly.

4. Put half the toasted almonds in a large skillet and place over low heat. Add the syrup, tablespoon by tablespoon, to the skillet and after adding each tablespoon of syrup, shake the almonds to coat them evenly. After adding about half the syrup, stir the nuts with a spoon as they will no longer easily shake in the pan. By the time you have used half of the syrup, the almonds should have become completely white or whatever color you have chosen. Transfer the sugared almonds to a large serving bowl or a container and repeat the process with the remaining almonds and syrup. Serve as a sweet snack or with dessert. Store in an airtight glass jar where they will keep for a week, possibly longer.

SUGARED CHICKPEAS: Replace the almonds with 3½ cups (500 g) roasted chickpeas, which you can buy already toasted from a Middle Eastern store. Just make sure they are unsalted.

GRAPE LEATHER

PESTIL

This recipe comes from my great friend Filiz Hosukoglu in Gaziantep, Turkey, where they make this grape leather (*pestil*), more or less the same way my aunt used to make it in Mashta el-Helou in Syria. The time to make *pestil* is September when the grapes have ripened and are ready to be picked. Here is Filiz's description of how her grandmother made *pestil*: "The grapes are brought home, washed, then transferred into a rectangular-shaped container (called *sal*) made of stone or wood. White soil (a kind of soil with 50 to 90 percent calcium carbonate) is spread over the grapes. This white soil decreases the acidity of the grape juice and helps it to settle. Mostly men with wooden sabots on their feet press the grapes to get the juice out." When I read Filiz's note, it immediately brought back childhood memories of when my aunt made *malban* (the Arabic name for *pestil*) and how she allowed us children to trample the grapes. I personally don't remember men participating in the making of *malban*. It was only my mother, my aunt, and our female cousins—in those long gone days there were only family members living in Mashta el-Helou—who every summer set about making industrial quantities of *malban*. Once the juice was strained, it was boiled and skimmed off. I can still see my mother and aunt in the courtyard tending to a huge pot in which they boiled the grape juice. They kept stirring the juice until it reached the desired consistency, then they poured it over white sheets and spread it thinly using an implement similar to a plasterer's trowel. Before doing this, they gave each of us children a soup bowl full of the boiled-down grape juice, which we wolfed down in no time before swarming around my mother and aunt to watch them spread the concentrated juice. It took a couple of days for the juice to dry and become "leather," at which point everyone went back to work, peeling the grape leather off the sheets, cutting it into squares, and folding it like handkerchiefs before being stored in wooden boxes to use in winter months. This *malban* was our sweet snack of choice wrapped around walnut halves. Here is Filiz's recipe, which you can make in your kitchen, spreading the thickened juice on silicone baking mats instead of cotton sheets. *Pestil* lasts a whole year, until the next grape season.

SERVES 8 TO 10

4 tablespoons wheat
  starch
2 tablespoons raw cane
  sugar
2 tablespoons grape
  molasses (pekmez)

1. Mix the wheat starch with 2 cups (500 ml) water in a medium saucepan. Add the sugar and grape molasses and bring to a boil over medium heat, stirring constantly. Reduce the heat to medium-low and let bubble gently for about 15 minutes, until the mixture is very creamy.

2. Spread the *pestil* with a spatula over ½ sheet pan lined with a silicone baking mat. Let dry either in a very low oven or on your kitchen counter. Once dry, cut into large squares and fold like handkerchiefs to serve. Store in a closed container in a cool place where they will keep for one year, possibly longer.

GRAPE JUICE PUDDING

FRESH BASTIK

Here is a recipe from Filiz's mother, which she served when she had unexpected guests and didn't have anything sweet in the house to offer them. It is delicious and quick to prepare.   SERVES 6

1 cup (120 g) wheat starch
2½ quarts (2.5 liters) grape juice from fresh sweet white grapes
Pistachio slivers and/or walnut halves, for garnish

1. Put the wheat starch in a medium bowl. Add 1 cup (250 ml) water and whisk together until well blended. Put the grape juice in a large pot and place over medium heat. Whisking constantly, slowly add the wheat starch mixture. Bring to a boil, stirring or whisking constantly so as not to have lumps as well as to avoid the juice sticking to the bottom of the pot. Let bubble gently for at least 15 minutes, or until the juice has thickened and coats a spoon thickly.

2. Pour into 6 individual shallow bowls. Garnish with slivered pistachios and walnut halves and serve hot, at room temperature, or chilled.

ORANGE BLOSSOM JAM

MORABBA AL-ZAHR

You need to live in an area that grows oranges to be able to make this jam. I normally pick my blossoms in Sicily, but in Lebanon you can buy them in the market when they are in season. The jam is incredibly beautiful, with the white blossoms turning a pastel pink because of the added natural colorant. In Lebanon, where sweets makers use the jam to garnish cream-filled sweets, the jam is colored a violent red, which I find a little too intense, not to mention completely un-natural. The delightful, subtle floral flavor of the blossoms makes this jam a perfect topping for delicate cheeses like ricotta

MAKES TWO ½-PINT (250 ML) JARS

2¼ pounds (1 kg) orange blossoms

4 cups (800 g) raw cane sugar

A few drops of natural red food coloring

½ cup (125 ml) lemon juice

1. Pick the petals cleanly off the blossoms, trying not to tear them. Put them in a medium saucepan and cover the blossoms with water to about ¾ inch (2 cm). Bring to a boil over medium heat and continue to boil for 30 minutes, until they have softened but still retain their shape. Drain and rinse under cold water, then let soak in a fresh bowl of water.

2. Put the sugar and 6 cups (1.5 liters) water in a medium saucepan and bring to a boil over medium heat. Add the coloring and simmer for 30 minutes, until the syrup has slightly thickened. Let cool.

3. Drain the petals well and add to the syrup. Let soak for 24 hours in a cool place or the refrigerator. Drain the petals in a sieve set over a clean medium saucepan to collect the syrup. Place the syrup over medium heat and boil for 10 minutes, then add the petals and let bubble gently for 10 more minutes. Add the lemon juice and let bubble for another 10 minutes, until the petals have become translucent and have turned a lovely pastel orangey pink color.

4. Transfer the jam to two sterilized ½-pint (250 ml) jars and cover with wax paper. Close the jars and let the jam cool before keeping in a cool place or the refrigerator where it will keep for a year, until blossom season comes around again. Serve as a garnish over creamy sweets or as with any other jam.

MINT TEA

SHAY NA'NA'

MOROCCO | TUNISIA

The making of mint tea in Morocco is surrounded with ritual, with the task of making and serving it falling to the man of the house. And if the tea maker is a stickler for quality, he will always use pieces of sugar hacked from a cane sugar loaf wrapped in gorgeous purple paper to sweeten the tea. He will also add the sugar to the pot rather than to the individual cups. That said, you don't really need to do either to produce an excellent mint tea.

SERVES 4

2 teaspoons green tea leaves
3 tablespoons raw cane sugar
¼ bunch mint (2 ounces/50 g)

1. Rinse a teapot with boiling water, then discard the water and add the tea leaves. Add a little boiling water and swirl around a bit before draining the water (this was done traditionally to rinse the tea of any impurities, but there is no need for this now except to stick to tradition).

2. Add 3 cups (750 ml) boiling water to the tea and stir in the sugar. Crush the mint a little with your hands, then add to the pot. Push the mint down into the liquid with a spoon. Let infuse for a few minutes before serving in traditional Moroccan tea glasses, which are small and narrow and often made of colored glass that is beautifully decorated with paint and/or gold.

TURKISH COFFEE

QAHWA

Whenever you are offered Turkish coffee in Lebanon, Syria, Jordan, or Palestine, you will be asked how you like it. If you want your coffee without sugar, you will ask for it to be *murr* (meaning "bitter" in Arabic). If you like it a little sweet, you will ask for it to be *wassat* (meaning "medium" in Arabic) or *mazbout* (meaning "correct" in Arabic), and if you want it really sweet, you will ask for it to be *helou* (meaning "sweet" in Arabic). I know only one of the Turkish words describing the degrees of sweetness, and that is *sada*, which means "plain" or "without sugar."

Turkish coffee is always "cooked" to the taste of the guest, except when there is a funeral or a sad or solemn occasion when only bitter coffee is served.

1. To prepare coffee medium-sweet, measure 1 teaspoon of very finely ground Turkish coffee and ½ teaspoon sugar for each demitasse (about ¼ cup) coffee cup of water. If you want it sweet, increase the quantity of sugar to 1 teaspoon. Put the water in the *rakweh* (a special coffee pot with a protruding flat spout to make pouring the coffee easy) or in a small saucepan, preferably with a spout. Place over medium heat and bring to a boil. Once the water has come to a boil, stir in the coffee and sugar, reduce the heat to low, and wait until the coffee foams up. Take off the heat as soon as it starts rising, let settle, then return to the heat. Remove as soon as the coffee foams up again and repeat another two or three times, until there is no more foam. Some people like their coffee foamy and they take it off the heat after the first or second foaming.

2. If you don't have the specific small, narrow cups with a handle that are used for Turkish coffee, use espresso or demitasse cups. Arrange the cups on a tray, then pour the coffee into them and pass the tray around to the guests. Rural people also use round cups with no handle in which they pour a very small amount of bitter coffee, which they call *shaffeh* (meaning "one sip"). These cups are the same ones used for the Arabian Coffee (opposite page).

ARABIAN COFFEE

QAHWA

Hospitality is an absolute must among believers in Islam who are reminded by the Prophet Muhammad of the high status of those who treat their guests well. He said, "Let the believer in God and the Day of Judgment honor his guest," thus making hospitality a right rather than a gift, and as such the duty to supply it is a duty to God. And the first sign of hospitality in Arabia, where Islam came into being, is coffee. The coffee served in the Arabian Gulf differs slightly from one country to the next but all versions are made with very lightly roasted beans and are flavored with spices such as saffron and cardamom. It is also "cooked" longer, making it a very different coffee from the Turkish version. Serving it is also different from the way Turkish coffee is served and it follows a ritual. When the coffee is ready, it is poured in a *dalla*, a large jug with a prominent spout and a lid to keep the coffee hot. The coffee pourer holds the small handleless coffee cups stacked in the right hand and the *dalla* in the left and goes around pouring a little coffee, less than half of the cup, and handing a cup to each guest. The guest keeps the cup in his/her hand and unless he/she shakes the cup from one side to the other to indicate he/she has had enough, the host will keep refilling the cup. Throughout the coffee drinking, the cup should stay in the drinker's hand. If the guest places it on the table, it means he/she has a request to make and will not drink the coffee until an answer is received.

SERVES 8 TO 10

2 tablespoons ground Arabian coffee
2 tablespoons ground cardamom
A few threads of saffron

1. Bring 4 cups (1 liter) water to a boil in a pot. Add the coffee and simmer for 5 minutes.

2. Add the ground cardamom and saffron to the thermos (*dalla*). Pour the coffee (grounds and all) into the thermos. Let sit for 5 to 10 minutes for the grounds to settle.

3. Serve in the traditional cups.

ARABIAN or INDIAN MILKY TEA

KARAK/CHAI

Chai in India and *karak* in the Arabian Gulf are two names for the same cardamom-flavored and heavily sweetened milky tea. When I was in India, I stopped at chai vendors whenever I passed by one to have some chai, never worrying about the hygiene because they had a wonderful system of disposable terra-cotta cups. Once you drank your tea, either you or the vendor would throw the small terra-cotta cup onto a heap of broken cups. Far more ecological than using disposable paper cups, even if I didn't really get to the bottom of how they recycled them. MAKES 2 CUPS

3 green cardamom pods, smashed

1 inch (2.5 cm) fresh ginger, smashed

2½ teaspoons Assam tea leaves

2½ teaspoons raw cane sugar

¾ cup plus 1 tablespoon (200 ml) whole milk

Put ⅓ cup plus 1 tablespoon (100 ml) water in a saucepan with a pouring spout. Add the cardamom and ginger and bring to a boil over medium heat. Add the tea and sugar and let bubble for 1 minute or so. Add the milk and bring to a boil. As soon as the milk threatens to boil over, remove the pan from the heat. Let the milk settle and return the pan to the heat. Again let it almost boil over and remove from the heat. Repeat once more, then strain into two cups. Pour the *karak* from high up into one cup and again into the other so as to aerate it. You can also transfer the *karak* to a thermos to keep hot for serving later or to a teapot to serve more elegantly. Serve hot.

ACKNOWLEDGMENTS

With every book that I write, I add to the list of wonderful people from around the world who have helped with my research; on top of that list are my faithful friends who never tire of letting me tap in to their expertise, contacts, or whatever else I need. And, of course, my beautiful mother, Laurice Helou, is ever present with her encyclopedic knowledge of Lebanese foodways.

The list of those I would like to thank for this book is long, but first I need to thank Nicole Aragi, my agent in New York, who immediately loved the concept, and my publisher Dan Halpern, who commissioned the book soon after he read the proposal. Then as the book progressed, Gabriella Doob, who was a dream editor; Rachel Meyers, a great production editor; Suet Chong and Renata De Oliveira, who did a wonderful job designing the interior; and Sara Wood, who created a lovely jacket. Thank you, too, to Miriam Parker and copy editor Kate Slate.

In London, my thanks go to my agent Caspian Dennis, and to another dream team with whom I worked on the recipe photographs. Kristin Perers shot the beautiful photographs in her equally beautiful studio with the help of her assistants, Sam Harris and Sophie Bronze, and her son, Ben Cook, who always helped when he was around. Claire Ptak was a great partner in cooking and styling the recipes. And Domingues Pinto (or Mida as we all call her), my wonderful housekeeper, helped us prep and clean without ever complaining about the heavy workload. Also Victoria Allen at Props Ltd for her wonderful collection of props, some of which we used in the photographs.

I also owe special thanks to Amy Dencler, head chef at Chez Panisse and tester extraordinaire, for testing almost all the recipes in the book in her American kitchen. And young Chiara Bosco, who was a delightful recipe-testing assistant in Trapani, and her parents, Agata and Gino, and sisters, Francesca and Anna, for being willing tasters.

My thanks to Helen Saberi for letting me use some of the recipes from her Afghan cookbook, *Noshe Djan*; Carolyn Phillips, for allowing me to use her Uighur Scallion Pancakes recipe from *All Under Heaven*; and Fuchsia Dunlop, for giving me her Kashgar kebabs and noodles recipes and for always being there whenever I had questions about Muslim Chinese food or needed help with my Muslim China trip. I am also grateful for the help of Evan Sung and Pierre Thiam for my trip to Senegal.

And now for those I met or connected with on my travels. In Muscat, Felicia Campbell introduced me to various chefs and showed me around; Matthew Teller introduced me to Riyadh Al-Balushi, who very kindly sent me suggestions. Also Pallavi and Ekta at the Chedi hotel.

In Zanzibar, Fatma Alloo invited me for *futari* (breaking of the fast during Ramadan) and talked to me about Zanzibari cuisine. Everyone at Emerson Spice and Emerson Hurumzi, including Katia and Len, for their gracious welcome. Farid Bawazir, for being a great guide, and Haji, my driver. Nadine Toukan was the perfect traveling companion. Simai and his family let us spend the day with them while his mother, sister, and cousin prepared the food for *futari*, which we then shared with them. Bi Nasra and her daughter, both famous Zanzibari cooks, and Amir A. Mohamed, author of *Zanzibar Traditional Cookery*, spoke with me about Zanzibari food. And Said El-Geithy was our guide the first couple of days we were there. Also Rashid, from Emerson Spice, who graciously invited me to join him and his family for *futari* before I left.

In the Emirates, I must first thank Sheikha Bodour bint Sultan al-Qasimi, for inviting me to Sharjah on a culinary tour that included a day spent with the lovely ladies of the Sharjah Heritage Centre to learn how to prepare typical Emirati dishes and sweets and for an amazing evening at her grandmother's farm, where another group of wonderful ladies from Khorfakkan, a seaside town, cooked and baked typical Emirati dishes and breads. When on a later trip to the United Arab Emirates, Sheikha Bodour gave me a baby camel so I could cook the hump—you can't get just a camel hump, it has to come with the camel! It fell to Amani al-Ali, director of Sheikha Bodour's Executive Office, to accompany me to the slaughterhouse to watch the baby camel being butchered. Marwa al-Aqroubi, now president of the United Arab Emirates Board on Books for Young People, but then still in Sheikha Bodour's Executive Office, accompanied me to an extraordinary breakfast prepared by the ladies at the Heritage Centre and later sent me the recipe for one of their most festive dishes, *aysh wa lahm*. Arwa Lootah invited me to her home to watch her mother cook *foga*, and Amira al-Khaja brought me delicious homemade cookies and *mehyawa*. And Moza Hantoush, who on my last visit to Dubai organized the opportunity for me to sample an amazing meal cooked by @maalatha, one the Emirates' best-known caterers. Finally, Sheikha Hoor bint Sultan al-Qasimi, for introducing me to Imane Fares to help with my trip to Senegal.

In India, Bobby and Bipasha Gosh made me fall in love with India all over again. On my first trip, Bipasha was my near-constant companion in Calcutta, where we went on an amazing Muslim food tour with Iftekhar Ahsan of Calcutta Walks. And when I got to New Delhi, Bobby introduced me to Vir and Seema Sangvi, who took me to Dum Pukht restaurant where chef Gulam Qureshi prepared a feast that included *nargisi kebab*, a dish that had eluded me during my trip. Also, Bipasha introduced me to Anup and Peali Gupta. On my second trip, Bobby and Bipasha graciously received me in their home in New Delhi and again introduced me to great friends. They took me to various restaurants, and in Mumbai, where we first met, they had organized a complete food blow-out starting with an amazing Kashmiri feast laid out by Aditi Dugar and Prateek Sadhu of Masque restaurant. Aditi brought the most exquisite saffron rice cooked by her mother, and Prateek and his wife, Aashina, cooked the rest. Then Anirban Blah organized a meal for us at the Bohri Kitchen, a remarkable supper club set up by Munaf Kapadia and his mother, Nafisa. Anirban also took me and Bipasha to the Bombay Canteen, where chef Thomas Zacharias spoiled us with a stunning tasting menu. And, finally, Bobby and Bipasha's cook Dhirendra showed me how to prepare different breads.

Also in India, thanks go to Mr. Mukherjee and my driver, Samim, in Calcutta. Simon Parkes connected me from London with Ankur Roy Chowdhury and Rudrangshu Mukherjee, who both very kindly talked to me about Muslim food in India. Masood Parvez at the Royal India Hotel, for taking me to the back of the house and letting me photograph in the kitchen. Joe Roberts connected me from London with Shahanshah and Fatima Mirza in Calcutta, who were a fount of knowledge about Awadhi cuisine—Shahanshah is a direct descendant of the ruler of Awadh Nawab Wajid Ali Shah.

In Lucknow, Nawab Jafar Mir Abdullah received me graciously in his special reception room full of family heirlooms.

Allan Jenkins connected me from London with Bomti Iyengar in Calcutta and Jonty Rajagopalan in Hyderabad, as well as Begum Mirza and her daughter, Parveen. Begum Mirza showed me how to make biryani while Jonty took me on a fascinating culinary tour of Hyderabad, during which we stumbled on an amazing spectacle where dozens of huge cauldrons were set over woodfire inside which bubbled curries that were being prepared for the month of Muharram to distribute to those in need. And Bomti hosted me in his fascinating home for a home-cooked Bengali lunch.

Anubhav Sapra of Delhi Food Walks was the perfect guide through the lanes of Old Delhi, making me taste the most marvelous Muslim delicacies.

Chef Manish Mehrotra at Indian Accent cooked me the most exquisite meal in New Delhi, and chef Vikram Roy gave me my first taste of Kashmiri food when he took me to Chor Bizarre.

And my thanks to Marryam Reshii, who on my first trip arranged for me to eat at a Kashmiri caterer in Delhi to taste typical Muslim Kashmiri dishes and on my second trip accompanied me to Kashmir. She was not only a perfect travel companion, but also an amazing guide to the culinary delights of Kashmir, starting with a splendid tea at Roohi Nazki's tea salon, Chai Jai, where we sampled Kashmir's version of harissa. Then we spent a memorable day with Marryam's sister-in-law, Baji, watching her cook a feast for us, and in between we visited a private house where Fayez Waza and his men were preparing a spectacular *wazwan* (a multicourse meal for weddings or other celebrations) for one daughter's wedding.

And, finally, Sudeep Sen, for sending me some of his poems to include in the book.

In Pakistan, Razi Ahmed not only invited me to the Lahore Literary Festival, but also hosted me in his beautiful family home, where every morning I had a wonderful time with his mother, Saira, over breakfast, learning the secrets of perfect paratha, roti, aloo, and other typical breakfast fare. My thanks also to Razi's uncle Shawkat and Shawkat's wife, Marina. Nuscie Jamil had me over to lunch for delicious home-cooked food. And Momina Aijazuddin; her mother, Shehnaz; and her father, Aijaz, took me to the market and also had me over for another delicious home-cooked meal. Also thank you to Kamila Shamsie and her mother, Muneeza Shamsie.

In Indonesia, William Wongso was instrumental in my having an incredibly productive and delightful trip. Olivia Wongso, William's daughter, invited me to my first proper Indonesian meal, together with Santhi Serad, Ade Putri Pramadita, Erna Setyowati and her husband Zamil, and Putri R. Mumpuni, at a typical fish restaurant where I discovered one of my favorite Indonesian ingredients, the stinky bean or *Parkia speciosa*, which was used in a dressing for fried pomfret.

Thanks to William I had great guides in each of the places I visited after Jakarta. He joined me in Medan, together with Indra Halim and the lovely Tahari family, Jamal Uddine, Gio, and their son Didi, all of whom knew Medan's food inside out. For three days we indulged in a total food frenzy sampling almost all that Medan had to offer. And on our last day, we were joined by the amazingly tattooed Rahung Nasution.

From Medan I went to Banda Aceh, where I was taken in charge by Mita Sugesty and Fathur Maulana Iben'z. Mita and Fathur were the perfect guides to the culinary delights of Banda Aceh, and Mita also took me to her parents who cater big parties. Even though it was Ramadan, they prepared a delicious lunch for me.

My last stop in Indonesia was Padang, where I was looked after by the very sweet Uda Dian Anugraph, who adopted me as his second mom.

And my first stop was on the eastern side, in two of the Malukku islands, Ambon and Banda Neira, where I was looked after by Tanya Alwi, whom I met through James Oseland. Tanya in turn introduced me to Mey, who became my guide and translator in Ambon, while Tanya hosted me in her hotel on Banda Neira and arranged for me to watch her cooks prepare a *buka puasa* (breaking the fast) meal featuring a baby goat that was killed for the occasion.

In China, my thanks go to Mei Zhang, founder of Wild China. Mei comes to my aid in China and elsewhere whenever I need it. Lillian Chou accompanied me to Uighur country and was my translator where she could. (Uighurs have their own language that has roots in both Turkish and Persian languages with many Arabic words, which unfortunately I couldn't distinguish.)

In Turkey, I am indebted to Nevin Halici, the grande dame of Turkish cooking and a walking encyclopedia on the foodways of her country, and Filiz Hosukoglu, for all things culinary in Gaziantep. Mustafa Ozguler and his brother, Murat, for their wonderful hospitality and advice every time I am in Gaziantep. And Talat Cagdas and his father and grandfather, for their hospitality at Imam Cagdas and letting me go behind the scenes to watch the kebabs and baklava being made. Thanks also to Hande Bozdogan, founder of the Istanbul Culinary Institute and my guru for Turkish food, and Osman Guldemir.

In Lebanon, I am grateful to many friends who contributed in different ways. Jacquot Ayoub, for always taking me to the most interesting foodie places. Mona Zaatari, for her amazing cooking. Huda Barudi, Mona's sister, for her all-around knowledge. Ziad Ghorly, for his advice on various Shi'a culinary customs and dishes, and Omar Fahreldinne, for bringing me the best-ever orange blossom jam. And, finally, Chirine Maktabi, for inviting me to a spectacular Iranian feast, and her son Sherif, for finding me a first edition of Margaret Shaida's *Legendary Cuisine of Persia*.

In Qatar, Aisha al-Tamimi and her sister, Maryam Abdallah, for teaching me practically everything I know about Qatari cooking, and Nadia Mohamed Saleh, whom I worked with at the National Museum of Qatar on a food culture program.

In Iran, my thanks to Nasrine Faghih for having me stay more than once in her beautiful home in Tehran, and getting her cook, Maryam, and the late Minou Saberi to cook a real feast for me to see how various Iranian dishes are prepared. Ali Farboud, for letting me use some of his great photographs and for traveling with me to Rasht, Isfahan and Feridoonjan's village outside Tehran, where Feridoon cooked an amazing meal for us that we shared with his family. Also Alimo Nafisi, who was my first guide in Iran, for taking me to the wonderful Tajrish market and other places in Tehran. And to Amir Amirani, who introduced me to various friends there.

In Senegal, Noura Khochman and her son Karim, for hosting me at Noura's home and making me taste their white *thiebou dieune* (rice with fish), Senegal's classic family dish. Fatou Mboup, for taking me to her great friends, Billo and Abdoul Mbaye, for an exquisite Friday lunch of *thiebou yapp* (rice with meat). Fatou also very kindly took me around Marche Tilene.

In Morocco, I would like to thank Mina Hamouchi and her family, for hosting me to various delicious meals; Mortada Chami, the charming owner of the wonderful Stylia restaurant, who always invites me to dine with him when I am in Marrakesh so that he can make me taste many exquisite Moroccan dishes; and he always lets me go into the kitchen to watch his ladies cook and make *warqa*. Choumicha Chafay, Morocco's foremost TV celebrity chef, and her husband, Karim, for hosting me graciously in Casablanca and making me taste the best *melwi* ever (a generic term that covers a whole range of flatbreads and pancakes, as Choumicha explained to me). In fact, Choumicha is always on the ready whenever I need advice on various Moroccan dishes. Also Tara Stevens, for taking me around the medina in Fez to look at the produce and taste all kinds of delicious street food and sweets. And Hafed, my sweet driver, for taking me to the Wednesday souk and letting me use his smart phone as a hotspot.

And, finally, in London, Sameer Khan, who gave me a whole lot of spices from his native Pakistan; Alastair Hendy and Liz Hasell, for letting me use some of their photographs; and Saad Bahbahani, for information on various Shiaa culinary customs in Kuwait. Also Aleksandar Taralezhkov, for bringing us his wonderful yogurt with skin the way it was once made when we were doing the photographs for the book. And in Belgium, Victoria Frolova, for telling me about a precious little book on Malabar Muslim cooking. I would also like to thank my adoptive sister in Oakland, Roberta Klugman, who always receives me warmly in her home and lets me and Amy test recipes in her kitchen.

I would also like to apologize to those I have failed to mention due to my memory not being what it used to be.

GLOSSARY

In these days of global cooking, combined with immediate and accessible Internet, the need for glossaries is less pressing, not to mention that most home cooks are now more familiar with exotic ingredients than ever before. I am still providing a select glossary for those ingredients that may not be on some home cooks' radar as well as those that may be familiar but are different from one country to another.

FRESH INGREDIENTS

ASPARAGUS BEANS
Also known as yardlong or snake beans, these grow in the warmer parts of South and Southeast Asia and in southern China. You normally find them in Indian or Asian stores, but if they are not available, you can use green beans.

BILIMBI
A sour fruit growing on a tree also known as a cucumber tree or tree sorrel, *bilimbi* is like a small light-green cucumber with a very sour taste. It is used fresh or dried to add tart flavor to various Indonesian and Malaysian dishes, and it is closely related to star fruit. You can interchange them, although the flavor of star fruit is a lot less sour than that of *bilimbi*.

CHILIES
Finger-length chilies are used extensively in Indonesia and Malaysia. The green and red versions are the same chili, with the unripe green chili turning red as it ripens. These chilies are very mild when green, and a little hotter when red although they are still mild enough to be used in industrial quantities in some sambals. If you can't source them, a good alternative is to use red bell peppers (preferably organic because they are less watery) for both color and texture, adding one or more bird's eye chilies depending on the quantity to give a little heat.

CURRY LEAVES
Described as sweet neem leaves in most Indian languages, these leaves from the curry tree, which is native to India and Sri Lanka, are used in curries, usually fried with onions in the first stages of the preparation. They are also fried by themselves to use as garnish.

GALANGAL
A root from four different plants that belong to the ginger family, galangal is an essential ingredient in Indonesian cooking. In fact, you often see it in the markets sold by the same vendors who sell ginger and turmeric roots, and often all three are used in dishes.

GRAPE LEAVES
Stuffed grape leaves are one of the glories of Middle Eastern dishes and when made with fresh leaves, the result will be superior than when using preserved leaves. Unfortunately, the season for fresh grape leaves is short—they need to be picked young and tender. Freezing the leaves is a good option, but if you don't have access to fresh grape leaves to freeze, use vacuum-preserved leaves. They are better than those that are preserved in brine, mainly because they are not salted. However, if you are going to use those in brine, be sure to rinse them well before using; and when you come to seasoning them, remember that there will always be residual saltiness from the brine. You can also buy them dried and reconstitute them by soaking in water, but they can easily break when dried and you may find that there is a fair amount of waste in each package of dried leaves.

GREEN PAPAYA
This meat tenderizer is essential in India, but it may not be necessary for meat bought in the United States or Europe as most of it will either come from young animals (as in lamb or veal) or, if it is beef, it will have been properly aged. That said, do use it if you can source it in Indian or Asian stores.

JAPANESE EGGPLANTS

These come in different colors and sizes, but it is the small, elongated dark-purple eggplants that are used throughout the Middle East in stuffed vegetables. Egyptians also use the white ones for stuffing, while in Syria they choose very small dark-purple or white eggplants to make *makduss* (see page 426).

MULUKHIYAH

Mulukhiyeh, mulukhiyah, or *mlukhiyah* are the leaves of *Corcorus olitorius*, commonly known as Jew's mallow. In Egypt, where *mulukhiyah* originated, the leaves are used to make a rather tart soup that is served on its own, or with rice and chicken. In Lebanon, a soupy sauce made with *mulukhiyah* tops a composite dish made up of layers of toasted bread, rice, chicken, and/or lamb, garnished with finely chopped onions soaked in vinegar. Like okra (in fact, okra is called *mlukhiyah* in Morocco), *mulukhiyah* releases a mucilaginous substance that makes it somewhat slimy, but you can minimize this by boiling the leaves for a short time so that it stays suspended in the broth. You can buy *mulukhiyah* fresh in season, or you can buy it dried or frozen.

PANDAN LEAVES

These are long glossy leaves used in Indonesian and Malaysian desserts to both color and flavor them. Pandan is also used in India and Bangladesh to flavor rice dishes, and the water distilled from the plants' flower, *kewra*, is also used in cooking. You can buy them fresh in Asian stores; or you can buy an extract (which probably has green food coloring).

SHALLOTS

In Indonesia, where they use an extraordinary amount of shallots, you can buy them already peeled. The shallots there are very small. For the purpose of the recipes in this book, my suggestion is to use normal shallots, bearing in mind that one normal-size shallot would be the equivalent of at least two Indonesian ones. You can also use very small red onions.

DRIED, FERMENTED, AND PROCESSED INGREDIENTS

BARBERRIES (ZERESHK)

Barberries are pleasantly sour berries that are dried and used in Persian cooking. You can buy them red or dark depending on how they have been processed. The red ones offer a prettier contrast and turn an even brighter red when quickly sautéed in oil. They are used in soups, stews, rice dishes, and in the famous Iranian Herb Omelet (page 400). The berries are also said to have medicinal qualities and in Persian poetry, teardrops are likened to barberries.

DRIED LIMES

There are two types of dried limes, black and pale. Some people favor the black ones whereas others go for the light ones. The black ones are definitely stronger in flavor, and they will color sauces more pronouncedly than the light ones, so do not use them if you are looking to make a light-colored sauce. And make sure you pierce the dried limes with the point of a sharp knife here and there before adding to the pot so that the flavor can be released during cooking. You can buy these in ground form in Persian stores, often wrongly labeled as ground lemons when they should be ground dried limes.

JAMEED

Jameed are dried balls of yogurt that are an essential ingredient in the Jordanian dish *mansaf* (see page 177). The Iranian equivalent is called *kashk*, and if you can't buy *jameed*, I suggest you use store-bought *kashk*, which comes in cartons or jars under the name of *jameed* soup or *jameed* soup starter.

KACHNAR

The flower of the orchid tree, this is used when in season in various dishes including a *kachnar* curry where the buds are cooked with onion and yogurt and various spices to produce a dish prized not only for its seasonality but also for its health-giving qualities.

KHOYA/KHOA/MAWA/MALAI

A dairy product made by boiling full-fat cow or buffalo milk down to the milk solids to become the "ricotta" of India, Pakistan, Bangladesh, and Nepal. *Khoya* is sold either as curds or pressed into beautiful cakes that are stamped with the maker's name. It is used the way we use cream, to enrich both sweet and savory dishes.

MOGHRABBIYEH

Mistakenly labeled in the United States as Israeli couscous, the word *moghrabbiyeh* in Arabic means "from North Africa," and it describes a large-grain couscous

SYRUPS, SAUCES, AND PASTES

CAROB MOLASSES (DIBSS AL-KHARRUB)

Thick and dark carob molasses is extracted from carob pods. The long pods are picked when dark and ripe and are taken to a special press to extract their juice. *Dibss al-kharrub* is served with pita bread as a sweet dip and can be eaten alone or mixed with tahini to tone down the sweetness and make it richer. The ripe pods are also chewed on as a sweet snack, a favorite among Mediterranean children, especially when picked straight off the tree.

DATE SYRUP (DIBSS AL-RUMMAN)

A syrup extracted from dates, date syrup could be considered the honey of the Arabian Gulf. Drizzled over fritters or used to sweeten rice or cakes, it adds a lovely sweet yet not cloying taste to whatever you are using it with. Some syrups are thick and dark while others are lighter both in color and consistency, and I suggest you use the latter if you can find it.

KECAP MANIS (INDONESIAN SWEET SOY SAUCE)

This is a sweet soy sauce that is thicker than regular soy sauce and a lot sweeter because of the palm sugar that is added to the *Aspergillus wentii* molds that are mixed in with a fermented paste made of boiled soybeans, roasted grain, salt, and water. Spices such as star anise, coriander, cloves, cinnamon, and black pepper are often also added to the sauce.

POMEGRANATE MOLASSES OR SYRUP

A ubiquitous seasoning in Syrian and Iranian cooking, pomegranate molasses or syrup is made by boiling down the juice from the seeds of sweet sour pomegranates (called *Abu Luffan* in Arabic) until it becomes dark and thick. Pomegranate molasses has an intriguing sweet and sour flavor, and it is also used throughout the rest of the Levant.

TAMARIND (TAMR HINDI)

Tamarind is a rather sour fruit in the shape of a pod, which grows longer in Asia than in Africa and the West Indies. The pulp is soaked in water and the resulting juice is widely used to impart a tart flavor to a variety of dishes. Pure tamarind juice is sold on the street in countries such as Syria and others in the Middle East.

TERASI (SHRIMP PASTE)

Made from small shrimp that are dried and pounded with various spices, shrimp paste is a dense, pungent ingredient that is first heated to release the flavor, then mixed into sambals and various dishes to impart an unmistakable fishy flavor that can be overwhelmingly salty if you use too much. Be sparing in its use and stick to the quantities stated in the recipes.

OTHER INGREDIENTS

AKKAWI CHEESE

This is a semi-fresh white cheese used to make the Lebanese Sweet Cheese "Pie" (page 444). If you cannot source it, use mozzarella made with cow's milk as it is less wet than buffalo mozzarella, and make sure you pat it dry before using.

ARABIC CLOTTED CREAM (QASHTAH)

Arabic clotted cream is produced by pouring whole milk in a large shallow pan and placing the pan over low heat with the heat concentrated in one corner where the milk starts bubbling, pushing the skin away. As the skin forms, it is skimmed and placed into plastic buckets like those used for ricotta to let the excess liquid drain away leaving only a very thick layered cream that does not melt when used in dessert making. You need an inordinate amount of milk to produce the cream.

COCONUT MILK/COCONUT CREAM

In most countries where coconut milk is used, cooks make it themselves by grating fresh coconuts with a special implement—it is hard to grate coconuts—then adding water and pressing on the pulp to extract the milk. The first pressing produces the creamiest coconut milk, with the second and third pressings producing one that is more diluted. There are different qualities and I suggest you look for coconut cream to use with the recipes in the book.

WARQA/MALSUQA/BRIK

This is the North African equivalent of phyllo dough except that *warqa* (in Morocco, meaning "leaf") or *malsuqa* (in Tunisia, meaning "stuck") is actually very quickly cooked against a hot plate called a *tobsil*. It is used to make *briouats* and b'stilla. The commercial version is called *brik* and it is a lot thicker than that made by specialists. In the recipe for b'stilla (see page 37). I suggest using fewer sheets than you would with the handmade *warqa* you can buy in the markets in Morocco.

UTENSILS AND EQUIPMENT

MA'MUL MOLDS (TABE')

These beautiful molds—traditionally carved out of wood but now also molded from plastic—are used to shape filled cookies that are a mainstay of both Ramadan and Eid. They come in three shapes: a round flat one for date-filled ma'mul, a round domed one for those filled with pistachios or walnuts depending on the region (or even family), and an oval domed one for those also filled with pistachios or walnuts, depending on the region or even the family. The trick to using these molds successfully is in making the cookies the right size so that they completely fit the mold without any overhang.

SMALL GRINDER FOR SPICES

Making your own spice mixtures is not only very rewarding but also yields better results than using the ready-packaged spice mixtures—unless you go to a spice vendor who makes his own mixtures (more often than not, they are men; women mix their own spices for home use). So, my suggestion is to buy a small electric coffee grinder that you use only for spices to make your own mixtures, and also to grind single spices for a fresher stock.

SMALL GRINDER FOR GARLIC, GINGER, AND OTHER FRESH INGREDIENTS

Get yourself a small electric coffee grinder to grind garlic and ginger and even turmeric, all of which are essential to Indian cooking as well as the cooking of the Arabian Gulf. Or make sure that your food processor comes with a small bowl for these as you mostly need them in smaller quantities.

MORTAR AND PESTLE

Most cooks in Indonesia grind chilies and other ingredients for sambal and for peanut sauces in a wide stone or earthenware mortar using a horizontal pestle. Only a few use a food processor. It is not so easy sourcing Indonesian mortars and pestles in the West, but any kind would work if you want to grind your ingredients by hand. And even if traditional cooks don't like using food processors, there is nothing wrong in you doing so to save time and effort. The result may not be as smooth as grinding the ingredients by hand, but it will be good enough for you to use in any of the recipes here.

INDEX

Note: Page references in *italics* indicate photographs.

A

Aceh-Style Goat Curry, 154–55, *155*
Advieh, 363
Afghani Sikh Kebabs, 123
Afghani Vermicelli Rice I, 238
Afghani Vermicelli Rice II, 240, *241*
Aleppine Breakfast Porridge, 442
Algerian Fish Cakes, 330
Almond(s)
    Afghani Vermicelli Rice I, 238
    Afghani Vermicelli Rice II, 240, *241*
    Awadhi Chicken Korma, 150–51, *151*
    Carrot Halva, 465
    Cornes de Gazelles, 451–52, *453*
    Date Halva, 459
    Dried Fruit and Nuts in Apricot Leather Juice, 443
    Festive Jordanian Lamb in Yogurt over a Bed of Rice and Bread, *176*, 177–78
    Fresh, in Yogurt Sauce, 186
    Green, Turkish Pickled, 423
    Iranian Stuffed Whole Lamb, 96–97
    Jeweled Rice, 250–52, *251*
    Lebanese Wheat and Mixed Nut Porridge, 497
    Moroccan Pigeon Pie, *36*, 37–39
    Moroccan Rice Pudding, 482
    Qatari Chicken and Rice, 216–18, *217*
    Spirals, Moroccan, 447
    Sugared, 499
    Sweet Couscous, 271
    Sweet-Savory Couscous with Chicken, 272–73
    Sweet-Savory Lamb Tagine for Eid el-Kbir, 149
    Zanzibari Sweet Noodles, 291
Aniseed
    Fritters, 492, *493*
    Garam Masala, 361

Apricot Leather Juice, Dried Fruit and Nuts in, 443
Apricots
    Baked Stuffed Fish, 312
    Dried Fruit and Nuts in Apricot Leather Juice, 443
    Iranian Stuffed Whole Lamb, 96–97
    Turkish Mixed Nut, Dried Fruit, and Legumes Dessert, *494*, 495–96
Arabian Coffee, 505
Arabian Date Bread, 20
Arabian Fish Spice Mixture, 368
Arabian/Iranian fish sauce, about, 331
Arabian Meat and Vegetable Stew over Crispy Bread, *84*, 85–86
Arabian or Indian Milky Tea, *506*, 507
Arabian Pancakes, 17
Arabian "Pasta" with Meat and Vegetables, 76–77
Arabian "Ravioli" with Fish, 346–47
Arabian Spiced Fried Fish, 345
Arabian Spice Mixture, 366
Arabian Spice Mixture for Desserts, 367
Ashura, xiii
Awadhi Biryani, 202–3, *203*
Awadhi Chicken Korma, 150–51, *151*
Azerbaijani Sweet-Savory Rice, 260
Azerbaijani Yogurt Soup, 193

B

Baklava, 448–49
Baklava Fingers, 449
Balaleet
    Classic, 283
    Umm Saeed's, 284, *285*
Bangladeshi Fish Head "Risotto," *318*, 319–20
Barley
    Lebanese Wheat and Mixed Nut Porridge, 497
    South Asian Meat, Legumes, and Wheat "Porridge," 264–65

    Wheat and Meat "Porridge," 266–67
Bean(s). *See also* Chickpea(s)
    Cannellini, Dill, and Eggs, 303
    Couscous with Seven Vegetables, 261–63, *262*
    Egyptian-Style Ful Medammes, 300
    Falafel, 430–31
    Fava, Rice with, 244
    Fava, Salad, 416, *417*
    Indonesian Vegetable and Egg Salad, *384*, 385
    Iranian Mixed-Herb Lamb Stew, 160–61
    Lentil, and Chickpea Soup, 296
    Meat, and Tomato Stew, 297
    Syrian-Style Ful Medammes, 300
    Turkish Mixed Nut, Dried Fruit, and Legumes Dessert, *494*, 495–96
Beef. *See also* Veal
    Indonesian Kebuli Biryani, 210–11, *211*
    Meat Filling for North African Bread, 65
    Meat Satay, 111
    Saudi Meat Pies, 46–48, *47*
Bengali Vegetable "Risotto," 232–33
Berbere Spice Mixture, 365
Berber Meat Bread, 49–51, *50*
Biryani
    Awadhi, 202–3, *203*
    Calcutta, 204–5
    Chicken, Malabar, 206–7
    Emirati, 208–9
    Hyderabadi, 200–201
    Indonesian Kebuli, 210–11, *211*
    Slow-Cooked, 198–99, *199*
Biryani Masala
    Indian, 362
    Qatari, 362
Black-eyed peas
    Nigerian Breakfast Fritters, 301
Boreks, Turkish Meat, 60–61, *61*

Bread-based dishes
  Arabian Meat and Vegetable Stew over Crispy Bread, *84*, 85–86
  Arabian "Pasta" with Meat and Vegetables, 76–77
  The Bread of the Harem, 88
  Egyptian Bread "Pudding," 89
  Egyptian Fattah, 81
  Lebanese Lamb Fatteh, 80
  Saudi Eggplant Fatteh, 78
  Saudi Meat Fatteh, 79
  Syrian Fatteh, 82–83, *83*
Bread-based salads
  Mario Haddad's Fattoush, 391
  Mixed Herb and Toasted Bread Salad, 382, *383*
Breads, filled and topped. *See* Filled and topped breads and pies
Bread(s). *See also* Pancakes
  Date, Arabian, 20
  Indian Flatbread, 30
  Iranian Flatbread, 9
  in Islamic cuisine, 2–3
  Kashgar Multilayered Non, 34
  M'lawwah, 18
  Moroccan, 11–12, *13*
  multilayered, creating, 23
  Multilayered, North African, *14*, 15–16
  Naan, 24–25, *25*
  Paratha, 21–23, *22*
  Pita, 4–5, *5*
  Regag, 16
  resting dough between kneading, 2–3
  and Rice, a Bed of, Festive Jordanian Lamb in Yogurt over, *176*, 177–78
  Rolls, Senegalese, *74*, 75
  Saj, 6–7, *7*
  Sesame, Zanzibari, 28–29
  Sheermal, 23
  Tannur, 7
  Turkish Flatbread, 10
  Uzbek Flatbread, 32–33, *33*
  Yemeni, 18, *19*
Bulgur
  Baked Kibbeh, 129–31, *131*
  and Dried Herb Mixture, 359
  Fish Kibbeh, 325
  Grilled Syrian Kibbeh, 135
  in Islamic cuisine, 197
  Kibbeh Balls in Minty Yogurt Sauce, 181

Kibbeh Balls with Quince in a Fresh Pomegranate Sauce, 136–37
Kibbeh in Sumac Sauce, 132–34
Lentil Kibbeh, 302
and Nut Cakes, 286
"Risotto" with Chickpeas and Lamb, 287
Salad, Turkish, 381
Tabbouleh, 378, *379*
White Tabbouleh, 380

C

Cabbage
  Couscous with Seven Vegetables, 261–63, *262*
  Indonesian Vegetable and Egg Salad, *384*, 385
  Leaves, Stuffed, 404–5
  Salim's Pasta Sauce, 282
  White Tabbouleh, 380
Cake, Semolina, 454
Calcutta Biryani, 204–5
"Calzone," Turkish, 62–63
Camel hump, roasting a, 100–101
Camel Meatballs, Saudi, 102–3, *103*
Caraway
  Garam Masala, 361
  Harissa, 370
  Pudding, 450
Cardamom
  Arabian Coffee, 505
  Arabian or Indian Milky Tea, *506*, 507
  Garam Masala, 361
  Pakistani/Indian Ice Cream, *472*, 473
  Sweet Savory Rice, 227
  Sweet Yogurt Drink, 174
  Yemeni Mandi Spice Mixture, 364
  Zanzibari Savory Doughnut, *26*, 27
  Zanzibari Sweet Noodles, 291
Carrots
  Arabian Meat and Vegetable Stew over Crispy Bread, *84*, 85–86
  Arabian "Pasta" with Meat and Vegetables, 76–77
  Carrot Halva, 465
  Couscous with Seven Vegetables, 261–63, *262*
  Egyptian Split Lentil Soup, 292
  Jeweled Rice, 250–52, *251*
  Olives, and Preserved Lemon, Poussin Tagine with, *142*, 143

Qatari Festive Rice and Chicken, 222–24, *223*
Saudi Lamb Kabsa, 219
Cashews
  Carrot Halva, 465
  Syrian H'risseh, 454
Cassava Cakes, Sweet-Salty, 476
Cauliflower
  Bengali Vegetable "Risotto," 232–33
  Indonesian Vegetable and Egg Salad, *384*, 385
  in Tomato Sauce, 412, *413*
Cheese
  Aleppine Breakfast Porridge, 442
  Kunafah Nabulsiyah, 446
  Paneer, 168
  Paneer Makhni, 169
  and Parsley Filling for Fatayer, 57
  "Pie," Lebanese Sweet, 444–46, *445*
  shanklish, about, 165
  Shanklish Salad, 166, *167*
  Spicy, Filling for Fatayer, 57
  and Spinach Filling for "Calzones," 63
  Spinach with Paneer, 421
Chermoula, 342, *343*
Cherry, Sour, Sauce, Meatballs in, 138, *139*
Chicken
  Arabian "Pasta" with Meat and Vegetables, 76–77
  Biryani, Malabar, 206–7
  Curry, Pakistani, 156–57
  Egyptian Mulukhiyah, 408
  Indonesian Kebuli Biryani, 210–11, *211*
  Iranian, in Walnut and Pomegranate Sauce, 153
  Kebabs, 125
  Korma, Awadhi, 150–51, *151*
  and Lamb with Frikeh, 288, *289*
  Lebanese Couscous with, 278–79
  Mishkaki, 121
  "Porridge," Qatari, 270
  and Rice, Qatari, 216–18, *217*
  and Rice, Qatari Festive, 222–24, *223*
  "Risotto," Yemeni, 225–26
  Satay, *112*, 113
  Sweet-Savory Couscous with, 272–73

Tagine with Olives and Preserved Lemons, 140–41
Wheat and Meat "Porridge," 266–67
Chickpea Flour
  Fritters, 306, *307*
  Halva, 464
Chickpea(s)
  Azerbaijani Yogurt Soup, 193
  The Chicken That Flew, *304*, 305
  Couscous with Seven Vegetables, 261–63, *262*
  Dukkah, 368
  Emirati Rice and Meat, 220–21
  Falafel, 430–31
  Fresh Almonds in Yogurt Sauce, 186
  Hommus, 432
  in Islamic cuisine, 197
  Koshari, 234–36, *235*
  and Lamb, Bulgur "Risotto" with, 287
  and Lamb Soup, Moroccan, 295
  Lebanese Couscous with Chicken, 278–79
  Lebanese Lamb Fatteh, 80
  Lentil, and Bean Soup, 296
  Persian Meat and Wheat "Porridge," 268–69
  Soup, Tunisian, 294
  Sugared, 499
  Sweet-Savory Couscous with Chicken, 272–73
  Tunisian Fish Couscous, 276–77
  Turkish Mixed Nut, Dried Fruit, and Legumes Dessert, *494*, 495–96
  and Wheat, Lamb Shanks with, 290
  and Wheat, Trotters with, 290
Chilies
  Chili and Tomato Sambal, 372
  Fresh Chili and Tomato Sambal, 373
  Harissa, 370
  Indonesian Fish Curry, 324
  Indonesian Fried Fish, 328–29
  Indonesian Vegetable and Egg Salad, *384*, 385
  Yemeni Cilantro Chutney, 369
Chutney, Yemeni Cilantro, 369
Cilantro
  Chermoula, 342, *343*
  Chutney, Yemeni, 369
  Cooked Yogurt Sauce, 175

Fish Stewed in Spicy Coriander, 344
Iranian Herb Omelet, 400, *401*
Spicy Baked Fish with Herbs and Nuts, 315
Cinnamon
  Advieh, 363
  Garam Masala, 361
  Lebanese 7-Spice Mixture, 358
  Lebanese Lentil Soup, 293
  Lentil, Chickpea, and Bean Soup, 296
  Tunisian B'harat, 366
Cloves
  Garam Masala, 361
  Lebanese 7-Spice Mixture, 358
  Qatari Biryani Masala, 362
  Yemeni Mandi Spice Mixture, 364
Coconut
  Indonesian Black Rice Pudding, 480, *481*
  Malaysian Pandan Balls, 477
  Rice, Zanzibari, 237
  Sauce, Zanzibari Grilled Fish in, 348
  Sweet-Salty Cassava Cakes, 476
Coffee
  Arabian, 505
  Turkish, 504
Cookies
  Date, Iraqi, 468
  Date, Ramadan, 455–56, *457*
  Nut-Filled, Ramadan, 458
Coriander
  Arabian Fish Spice Mixture, 368
  Arabian Spice Mixture, 366
  Dukkah, 368
  Indian Biryani Masala, 362
  Indonesian Yellow Rice, *256*, 257
  Lebanese 7-Spice Mixture, 358
  Qatari Biryani Masala, 362
  Somali Spice Mixture, 365
  Yemeni Spice Mixture, 364
Cornes de Gazelles, 451–52, *453*
Cornish hens
  Chicken Kebabs, 125
  Chicken Tagine with Olives and Preserved Lemons, 140–41
  Malabar Chicken Biryani, 206–7
  Poussin Tagine with Carrots, Olives, and Preserved Lemon, *142*, 143
Couscous
  Fish, Tunisian, 276–77
  Lebanese, with Chicken, 278–79

Moroccan, with Monkfish, 274–75
in North African cuisine, 197
with Seven Vegetables, 261–63, *262*
Sweet, 271
Sweet-Savory, with Chicken, 272–73
Crab Curry, Indonesian, 322, *323*
Cream or Walnut Sweet "Hand Pies," 474–75, *475*
Cucumber(s)
  Mario Haddad's Fattoush, 391
  Mixed Herb and Toasted Bread Salad, 382, *383*
  and Yogurt Dip, 192
Cumin
  Arabian Fish Spice Mixture, 368
  Arabian Spice Mixture, 366
  Arabian Spice Mixture for Desserts, 367
  Dried Herb and Bulgur Mixture, 359
  Garam Masala, 361
  Indian Biryani Masala, 362
  Lamb Stewed with, 148
  Lentil, Chickpea, and Bean Soup, 296
  and Salt Mixture, Moroccan, 367
  Somali Spice Mixture, 365
  Tunisian Chickpea Soup, 294
  Yemeni Spice Mixture, 364
Curry
  Chicken, Pakistani, 156–57
  Crab, Indonesian, 322, *323*
  Fish, Indonesian, 324
  Fish Head, Indonesian, 321
  Goat, Aceh-Style, 154–55, *155*
  Vegetable, *414*, 415

D

Dairy products, 164–65
Date(s)
  Azerbaijani Sweet-Savory Rice, 260
  Bread, Arabian, 20
  Cookies, Iraqi, 468
  Cookies, Ramadan, 455–56, *457*
  -Filled Pastries, 466–67
  "Fudge," 460, *461*
  Halva, 459
  Ice Cream, 470, *471*
  Lentil Polow, 246–47
  Ramadam Bread, 44–45
  types of, xii

Date syrup
    Sweet-Savory Rice, 227
Dill, Cannellini Beans, and Eggs, 303
Dips
    Eggplant, Smoky, 390
    Eggplant and Yogurt Spread, *190,*
        191
    Harissa, 370
    Hommus, 432
    Labneh and Tarragon, 188, *189*
    Lebanese Spicy Tomato "Salsa,"
        435
    Mulukhiyah, Saudi, 434
    Saudi "Salsa," 429
    Scrambled Egg and Eggplant,
        386
    Spinach and Yogurt Spread, 187
    Tahini, 102
    Tamarind, 102
    Turkish Tarator, 337
    Yogurt and Cucumber, 192
    Yogurt and Elephant Garlic, 192
Doogh, 171
Doughnuts, Zanzibari Savory, *26, 27*
Drinks
    Arabian Coffee, 505
    Arabian or Indian Milky Tea, *506,*
        507
    Doogh, 171
    Mango Yogurt, 172, *173*
    Mint Tea, 503, *503*
    Turkish Coffee, 504
    Yogurt, *170,* 171
    Yogurt, Sweet, 174
Dukkah, 368
Dumplings
    Arabian "Ravioli" with Fish,
        346–47
    Lebanese, in Yogurt Sauce, 182–83,
        183
    Turkish, with Garlicky Yogurt,
        184–85

E

Eggplant
    Arabian "Pasta" with Meat and
        Vegetables, 76–77
    Dip, Smoky, 390
    Fatteh, Saudi, 78
    Fried, Indian, *418,* 419
    Grilled, Puree and Minced Meat in
        Tomato Sauce, 180
    Kibbeh in Sumac Sauce, 132–34
    and Lamb Stew, Iranian, 162
    Lamb Tagine with, 146

The Lord of Stuffed Vegetables,
    397–99, *398*
Pickled, Iranian, 422
Pide, 59
Qatari Chicken and Rice, 216–18,
    217
Salad, Moroccan Steamed, 389
and Scrambled Egg Dip, 386
Senegalese Fish Stew, 349–51, *350*
Syrian Fatteh, 82–83, *83*
in Tomato Sauce, 388
with Walnuts and Garlic Preserved
    in Olive Oil, 426
and Yogurt Spread, *190,* 191
Egg(s)
    Briouats, 40–41, *41*
    Cannellini Beans, and Dill, 303
    Classic Balaleet, 283
    Indonesian Fried Rice, 258–59,
        259
    Iranian Herb Omelet, 400, *401*
    Moroccan Pigeon Pie, *36,* 37–39
    Qatari Festive Rice and Chicken,
        222–24, *223*
    "Scotch," Indian, 118–20, *119*
    Scrambled, and Eggplant Dip, 386
    Umm Saeed's Balaleet, 284, *285*
    and Vegetable Salad, Indonesian,
        384, 385
Egyptian, fermented fish, about, 331
Egyptian Bread "Pudding," 89
Egyptian Fattah, 81
Egyptian Mulukhiyah, 408
Egyptian Split Lentil Soup, 292
Egyptian-Style Ful Medammes, 300
Eid al-Adha, xiii, 92
Eid al-Fitr, xiii, 92
Emirati Biryani, 208–9
Emirati Fish in an Onion and Tomato
    Sauce, 353
Emirati Rice and Meat, 220–21

F

Falafel, 430–31
Fatayer
    Lebanese, 52–57, *53*
    Syrian, *53,* 55–57
Fattah, Egyptian, 81
Fatteh
    Eggplant, Saudi, 78
    Lamb, Lebanese, 80
    Meat, Saudi, 79
    Syrian, 82–83, *83*
Fattoush, Mario Haddad's, 391
Filled and topped breads and pies

Berber Meat Bread, 49–51, *50*
Egg Briouats, 40–41, *41*
Eggplant Pide, 59
Ground Meat Pide, 58–59
Indian Meat Breads, 69–70, *70*
Indonesian Multilayered Bread,
    66–68, *67*
Lebanese/Syrian Savory Pastries,
    52–57, *53*
Moroccan Pigeon Pie, *36,* 37–39
North African Filled Bread, 64–65
Ramadam Bread, 44–45
Saudi Meat Pies, 46–48, *47*
Southern Lebanese Za'atar "Pizza,"
    42–43, *43*
Turkish "Calzone," 62–63
Turkish Meat Boreks, 60–61, *61*
Uighur Scallion Pancakes, 71–73,
    72
Fish
    Arabian "Ravioli" with, 346–47
    Baked Sea Bass with Tomatoes and
        Olives, 313
    Baked Stuffed, 312
    Cakes, Algerian, 330
    and Caramelized Onion "Risotto,"
        Lebanese, 230–31
    Couscous, Tunisian, 276–77
    Curry, Indonesian, 324
    Emirati, in an Onion and Tomato
        Sauce, 353
    fermented, Egyptian, about,
        331
    Fried, Arabian Spiced, 345
    Fried, Indonesian, 328–29
    in Islamic cuisine, 310–11
    Kibbeh, 325
    Mackerel Tarator, 336
    Moroccan Couscous with
        Monkfish, 274–75
    Moroccan Grey Mullet Stuffed
        with Swiss Chard, 314
    Pickled Swordfish, 338
    "Risotto," Saudi, 228–29
    Sardines Chermoula, 342, *343*
    Spice Mixture, Arabian, 368
    Spicy Baby Shark, 352
    Spicy Baked, in a Tahini, Herb, and
        Nut Sauce, 316, *317*
    Spicy Baked, with Herbs and Nuts,
        315
    Stew, Senegalese, 349–51, *350*
    Stewed in Spicy Coriander, 344
    Swordfish Brochettes, 334, *335*
    in Tahini Sauce, 326

in Tamarind Sauce, 339
Yassa, 327
Zanzibari Grilled, in Coconut
   Sauce, 348
Fish Head Curry, Indonesian, 321
Fish Head "Risotto," Bangladeshi, *318,*
   319–20
Fish sauce, Iranian/Arabian, about, 331
Frikeh, Chicken and Lamb with, 288,
   289
Fritters
   Aniseed, 492, *493*
   Chickpea Flour, 306, *307*
   Nigerian Breakfast, 301
   Round, Lebanese/Syrian, 490–91
   Saffron-Flavored, 486, *487*
   sweet, about, 485
   Sweet, Saudi, 488
   Sweet Milk, South Asian, 489
Fruit. *See specific fruits*
"Fudge," Date, 460, *461*
Ful Medammes, 300

G
Garam Masala, 361
Garlic
   Chermoula, 342, *343*
   Elephant, and Yogurt Dip, 192
   Harissa, 370
   Turkish Dumplings with Garlicky
      Yogurt, 184–85
   and Walnuts, Eggplant with,
      Preserved in Olive Oil, 426
Ginger
   Arabian or Indian Milky Tea, *506,*
      507
   Arabian Spice Mixture for Desserts,
      367
   Lebanese 7-Spice Mixture, 358
Goat
   Baby, Roast, 94–95, *95*
   Curry, Aceh-Style, 154–55, *155*
   Indonesian Kebuli Biryani, 210–11,
      211
   Indonesian Multilayered Bread,
      66–68, *67*
Grains. *See also* Barley; Bulgur; Rice;
   Wheat
   Chicken and Lamb with Frikeh,
      288, *289*
   in Islamic cuisine, 197
Grape Juice Pudding, 501
Grape Leather, 500
Grape Leaves
   Iranian Stuffed, 395–96

Stuffed, Cooked on a Bed of Lamb
   Chops, 392–94, *393*
Greens. *See also* Cabbage; Lettuce;
   Spinach
   Moroccan Grey Mullet Stuffed
      with Swiss Chard, 314
   Vegetarian Stuffed Swiss Chard,
      406–7
   Wild Endive in Olive Oil, 420
Grey Mullet, Moroccan, Stuffed with
   Swiss Chard, 314

H
Halva
   about, 463
   Carrot, 465
   Chickpea Flour, 464
   Date, 459
   Flour, Turkish, *462,* 463
   Pumpkin, 498
"Hand Pies," Cream or Walnut Sweet,
   474–75, *475*
Harissa, 370
Hazelnuts
   Turkish Mixed Nut, Dried Fruit,
      and Legumes Dessert, *494,*
      495–96
   Turkish Tarator, 337
Herbed Polow, 245
Herb(s). *See also specific herbs*
   Dried, and Bulgur Mixture, 359
   Filling for North African Bread, 65
   Mixed, and Toasted Bread, 382,
      383
   Omelet, Iranian, 400, *401*
Hommus, 432
Hyderabadi Biryani, 200–201
Hyderabadi Kebab, 116

I
Ice Cream
   Date, 470, *471*
   Pakistani/Indian, *472,* 473
   Pistachio, 469
   Saffron, 469
   Saffron Kulfi, 473
Indian Biryani Masala, 362
Indian Flatbread, 30
Indian Fried Eggplant, *418,* 419
Indian Galawati Kebabs, 114–15, *115*
Indian Meat Breads, 69–70, *70*
Indian or Arabian Milky Tea, *506,* 507
Indian/Pakistani Ice Cream, *472,* 473
Indian/Pakistani Milk Rice Pudding, 478
Indian "Scotch Egg," 118–20, *119*

Indonesian Black Rice Pudding, 480,
   481
Indonesian Crab Curry, 322, *323*
Indonesian Fish Curry, 324
Indonesian Fish Head Curry, 321
Indonesian Fried Fish, 328–29
Indonesian Fried Rice, 258–59, *259*
Indoniesian Kebuli Biryani, 210–11, *211*
Indonesian Multilayered Bread, 66–68,
   67
Indonesian Vegetable and Egg Salad,
   384, 385
Indonesian Yellow Rice, *256,* 257
Iranian/Arabian fish sauce, about, 331
Iranian Chicken in Walnut and
   Pomegranate Sauce, 153
Iranian Flatbread, 9
Iranian Ground Meat Kebabs, 124
Iranian Herb Omelet, 400, *401*
Iranian Lamb and Eggplant Stew, 162
Iranian Mixed-Herb Lamb Stew,
   160–61
Iranian Pickled Eggplants, 422
Iranian Pomegranate Soup, 298–99,
   299
Iranian Rice, Plain, 242–43
Iranian Stuffed Grape Leaves, 395–96
Iranian Stuffed Whole Lamb, 96–97, *97*
Iranian Yellow Split Pea Stew, 158–59
Iraqi Date Cookies, 468
Iraqi Stuffed Onions, 402–3

J
Jam, Orange Blossom, 502
Jameed, 165
Jordanian Lamb in Yogurt, Festive,
   over a Bed of Rice and Bread, *176,*
   177–78

K
Kabsa, Saudi Lamb, 219
Kafta, Lebanese, 109
Kandili, xiii
Kashgar Kebabs, 122
Kashgar Multilayered Non, 34
Kashk, 165
Kataifi
   about, 446
   Kunafah Nabulsiyah, 446
   Lebanese Sweet Cheese "Pie,"
      444–46, *445*
Kefta, Moroccan, 110
Kibbeh
   Baked, 129–31, *131*
   Balls in Minty Yogurt Sauce, 181

Balls with Quince in a Fresh
Pomegranate Sauce, 136–37
Fish, 325
Grilled Syrian, 135
Lentil, 302
in Sumac Sauce, 132–134
Kishk, 164–65
Koshari, 234–236, *235*
Kunafah Nabulsiyah, 446

L

Labneh
about, 164
Eggplant and Yogurt Spread, *190,*
191
Filling for Fatayer, 56
Spinach and Yogurt Spread, 187
and Tarragon Dip, 188, *189*
Lamb
Afghani Sikh Kebabs, 123
Afghani Vermicelli Rice II, 240, *241*
Arabian Meat and Vegetable Stew
over Crispy Bread, *84,* 85–86
Awadhi Biryani, 202–3, *203*
Azerbaijani Yogurt Soup, 193
Baby Goat Roast, 94–95, *95*
Baked Kibbeh, 129–31, *131*
Baked Rice Cake with, *248,* 249
Berber Meat Bread, 49–51, *50*
Calcutta Biryani, 204–5
and Chicken with Frikeh, 288, *289*
and Chickpeas, Bulgur "Risotto"
with, 287
and Chickpea Soup, Moroccan, 295
Chops, Stuffed Grape Leaves
Cooked on a Bed of, 392–94,
393
Couscous with Seven Vegetables,
261–63, *262*
Dried Okra Soup, *436,* 437
and Eggplant Stew, Iranian, 162
Egyptian Fattah, 81
Emirati Rice and Meat, 220–21
Fatteh, Lebanese, 80
Festive Sweet-Savory Rice,
253–55, *254*
Fresh Almonds in Yogurt Sauce,
186
Grilled Eggplant Puree and Minced
Meat in Tomato Sauce, 180
Grilled Syrian Kibbeh, 135
Hyderabadi Biryani, 200–201
Hyderabadi Kebab, 116
Indian Galawati Kebabs, 114–15,
115

Indian Meat Breads, 69–70, *70*
Indian "Scotch Egg," 118–20, *119*
Indonesian Multilayered Bread,
66–68, *67*
Iranian Ground Meat Kebabs,
124
Iranian Pomegranate Soup,
298–99
Iranian Stuffed Grape Leaves,
395–96
Iranian Yellow Split Pea Stew,
158–59
Kabsa, Saudi, 219
Kashgar Kebabs, 122
Kibbeh Balls in Minty Yogurt
Sauce, 181
Kibbeh Balls with Quince in a Fresh
Pomegranate Sauce, 136–37
Kibbeh in Sumac Sauce, 132–34
Lebanese Couscous with Chicken,
278–79
Lebanese Dumplings in Yogurt
Sauce, 182–83, *183*
Lebanese Kafta, 109
Lebanese Kebabs, *107,* 108
Liver, Grilled, 117
The Lord of Stuffed Vegetables,
397–99, *398*
Meat, Beans, and Tomato Stew,
297
Meatballs in Sour Cherry Sauce,
138, *139*
Meat Filling for North African
Bread, 65
Meat Satay, 111
Mixed-Herb Stew, Iranian, 160–61
Moroccan Kefta, 110
Moroccan Meatballs with Rice, 147
Moroccan Meat Kebabs, 105
Moroccan Mechoui, 104
Persian Meat and Wheat
"Porridge," 268–69
Quince Stew, 163
Salim's Pasta Sauce, 282
Saudi Meat Fatteh, 79
Saudi Meat Pies, 46–48, *47*
Saudi Mulukhiyah Dip, 434
Shanks in Yogurt, 179
Shanks with Chickpeas and Wheat,
290
Shanks with Mulukhiyah, 409–11,
410
Shawarma Sandwich, *126,* 127–28
Shoulder, Saudi Roast, on a Bed of
Fragrant Rice, 98–99, *99*

Slow-Cooked Biryani, 198–99, *199*
South Asian Meat, Legumes, and
Wheat "Porridge," 264–65
Stewed with Cumin, 148
Stuffed Cabbage Leaves, 404–5
Syrian Fatteh, 82–83, *83*
Tagine, Sweet-Savory, for Eid el-
Kbir, 149
Tagine with Eggplant, 146
Tagine with Potatoes and Peas,
144, *145*
Turkish Dumplings with Garlicky
Yogurt, 184–85
Turkish Kebabs, 106, *107*
Turkish Meat Boreks, 60–61, *61*
Wheat and Meat "Porridge,"
266–67
Whole, Iranian Stuffed, 96–97, *97*
in Yogurt, Festive Jordanian, over
a Bed of Rice and Bread, 176,
177–78
Lebanese Couscous with Chicken,
278–79
Lebanese Dumplings in Yogurt Sauce,
182–83, *183*
Lebanese Fatayer, 52–57, *53*
Lebanese Fish and Caramelized Onion
"Risotto," 230–31
Lebanese Kafta, 109
Lebanese Kebabs, *107,* 108
Lebanese Lamb Fatteh, 80
Lebanese Lentil Soup, 293
Lebanese 7-Spice Mixture, 358
Lebanese Spicy Tomato "Salsa," 435
Lebanese Sweet Cheese "Pie," 444–46,
445
Lebanese/Syrian Milk Pudding, Saffron,
479
Lebanese/Syrian Rice Pudding, 483
Lebanese/Syrian Round Fritters,
490–91
Lebanese/Syrian Vermicelli Rice,
241
Lebanese Wheat and Mixed Nut
Porridge, 497
Legumes. *See also* Bean(s); Chickpea(s);
Lentil(s); Yellow Split Pea(s)
Bengali Vegetable "Risotto,"
232–33
in Islamic cuisine, 197
Nigerian Breakfast Fritters, 301
Lemon(s)
Chermoula, 342, *343*
Preserved, and Olives, Chicken
Tagine with, 140–41

Preserved, Carrots, and Olives, Poussin Tagine with, *142,* 143
Lentil(s)
    Chickpea, and Bean Soup, 296
    in Islamic cuisine, 197
    Kibbeh, 302
    Koshari, 234–36, *235*
    Polow, 246–47
    Soup, Lebanese, 293
    South Asian Meat, Legumes, and Wheat "Porridge," 264–65
    Split, Soup, Egyptian, 292
Lettuce
    Mario Haddad's Fattoush, 391
    Mixed Herb and Toasted Bread Salad, 382, *383*
Lime Pickles, 427

M

Mackerel Tarator, 336
Malabar Chicken Biryani, 206–7
Malaysian Pandan Balls, 477
Mango
    Green, Pickle, 428
    Yogurt Drink, 172, *173*
Meat. *See also* Beef; Camel; Goat; Lamb; Veal
    Ground, Pide, 58–59
Meatballs
    Camel, Saudi, 102–3, *103*
    Moroccan, with Rice, 147
    in Sour Cherry Sauce, 138, *139*
Mechoui, Moroccan, 104
Milk Fritters, South Asian Sweet, 489
Milk Pudding, Saffron Lebanese/Syrian, 479
Milky Tea, Arabian or Indian, *506,* 507
Mint
    Cooked Yogurt Sauce, 175
    Doogh, 171
    Dukkah, 368
    Kibbeh Balls in Minty Yogurt Sauce, 181
    Mixed Herb and Toasted Bread Salad, 382, *383*
    Tea, 503, *503*
    White Tabbouleh, 380
M'lawwah, 18
Monkfish, Moroccan Couscous with, 274–75
Moroccan Almond Spirals, 447
Moroccan Bread, 11–12, *13*
Moroccan Chickpea and Lamb Soup, 295

Moroccan Couscous with Monkfish, 274–75
Moroccan Grey Mullet Stuffed with Swiss Chard, 314
Moroccan Kefta, 110
Moroccan Meatballs with Rice, 147
Moroccan Meat Kebabs, 105
Moroccan Mechoui, 104
Moroccan Pigeon Pie, *36,* 37–39
Moroccan Rice Pudding, 482
Moroccan Salt and Cumin Mixture, 367
Moroccan Steamed Eggplant Salad, 389
Mulukhiyah
    Dip, Saudi, 434
    Egyptian, 408
    Lamb Shanks with, 409–11, *410*
Mussel(s)
    Brochettes, Fried, 332
    Stuffed, 340–41

N

Naan, 24–25, *25*
Nigella seeds
    Kashgar Multilayered Non, 34
    Uzbek Flatbread, 32–33
Nigerian Breakfast Fritters, 301
Noodles. *See also* Vermicelli
    Salim's Pasta Sauce, 282
    Spicy, with Shrimp, 280–81
    Sweet, Zanzibari, 291
    Umm Saeed's Balaleet, 284, *285*
North African Filled Bread, 64–65
North African Multilayered Breads, *14,* 15–16
Nutmeg
    Garam Masala, 361
    Lebanese 7-Spice Mixture, 358
Nut(s). *See also* Almond(s); Peanuts; Pine nuts; Pistachio(s); Walnut(s)
    Egyptian Bread "Pudding," 89
    Gajar Halwa, 465
    Mixed, Dried Fruit, and Legumes Dessert, Turkish, *494,* 495–96
    Syrian H'risseh, 454
    Turkish Tarator, 337

O

Okra, Dried, Soup, *436,* 437
Olives
    Carrots, and Preserved Lemon, Poussin Tagine with, *142,* 143
    Moroccan Grey Mullet Stuffed with Swiss Chard, 314
    and Preserved Lemons, Chicken Tagine with, 140–41

and Tomatoes, Baked Sea Bass with, 313
Omelet, Iranian Herb, 400, *401*
Onion(s)
    Caramelized, and Fish "Risotto," Lebanese, 230–31
    Egg Briouats, 40–41, *41*
    Eggplant in Tomato Sauce, 388
    Fish Yassa, 327
    Kashgar Multilayered Non, 34
    Koshari, 234–36, *235*
    Lamb Shanks in Yogurt, 179
    Lebanese Couscous with Chicken, 278–79
    Lebanese Kebabs, *107,* 108
    and Parsley Salad, 387
    Stuffed, Iraqi, 402–3
    Sweet-Savory Couscous with Chicken, 272–73
    and Tomato Sauce, Emirati Fish in an, 353
    Uzbek Flatbread, 32–33
    Wild Endive in Olive Oil, 420
Orange(s)
    Blossom Jam, 502
    Jeweled Rice, 250–52, *251*

P

Pakistani Chicken Curry, 156–57
Pakistani/Indian Ice Cream, *472,* 473
Pakistani/Indian Milk Rice Pudding, 478
Pancakes
    Arabian, 17
    Cream or Walnut Sweet "Hand Pies," 474–75, *475*
    Savory, 31
    Scallion, Uighur, 71–73, *72*
    Somali, 8
Pandan Balls, Malaysian, 477
Paneer, 168
    Makhni, 169
    Spinach with, 421
Paratha, 21–23, *22*
Parsley
    and Cheese Filling for Fatayer, 57
    Iranian Herb Omelet, 400, *401*
    Mario Haddad's Fattoush, 391
    Mixed Herb and Toasted Bread Salad, 382, *383*
    and Onion Salad, 387
    Tabbouleh, 378, *379*
Pasta. *See also* Couscous; Dumplings; Noodles; Vermicelli
    in Islamic cuisine, 197

Pastries
  Baklava, 448–49
  Cornes de Gazelles, 451–52, *453*
  Date-Filled, 466–67
  Moroccan Almond Spirals, 447
Peanuts
  Chicken Satay, *112,* 113
  Dukkah, 368
  Indonesian Vegetable and Egg
    Salad, *384,* 385
  Meat Satay, 111
Peas and Potatoes, Lamb Tagine with,
  144, *145*
Peppercorns
  Arabian Spice Mixture, 366
  Arabian Spice Mixture for Desserts,
    367
  Garam Masala, 361
  Yemeni Spice Mixture, 364
Peppers. *See also* Chilies
  Salim's Pasta Sauce, 282
Persian Meat and Wheat "Porridge,"
  268–69
Pickle, Green Mango, 428
Pickled Eggplants, Iranian, 422
Pickled Green Almonds, Turkish, 423
Pickled Swordfish, 338
Pickled Turnips, Pink, 424, *425*
Pickles, Lime, 427
Pide
  Eggplant, 59
  Ground Meat, 58–59
"Pie," Lebanese Sweet Cheese, 444–46,
  445
Pies, savory. *See* Filled and topped
  breads and pies
Pineapple
  Indonesian Crab Curry, 322, *323*
Pine nuts
  Baklava, 448–49
  Dried Fruit and Nuts in Apricot
    Leather Juice, 443
  Festive Jordanian Lamb in Yogurt
    over a Bed of Rice and Bread,
    176, 177–78
  Lebanese Wheat and Mixed Nut
    Porridge, 497
  Spicy Baked Fish in a Tahini, Herb,
    and Nut Sauce, 316, *317*
  Spicy Baked Fish with Herbs and
    Nuts, 315
Pistachio(s)
  Advieh, 363
  Afghani Vermicelli Rice I, 238
  Afghani Vermicelli Rice II, 239

Baklava, 448–49
The Bread of the Harem, 88
Bulgur and Nut Cakes, 286
Dried Fruit and Nuts in Apricot
  Leather Juice, 443
Festive Sweet-Savory Rice,
  253–55, *254*
Ice Cream, 469
Iranian Stuffed Whole Lamb,
  96–97
Jeweled Rice, 250–52, *251*
Ramadan Nut-Filled Cookies, 458
Syrian H'risseh, 454
Pita Bread, 4–5, *5*
Polow
  Herbed, 245
  Lentil, 246–47
Pomegranate
  Sauce, Fresh, Kibbeh Balls with
    Quince in a, 136–37
  Soup, Iranian, 298–99, *299*
  and Walnut Sauce, Iranian Chicken
    in, 153
Porridge
  Aleppine Breakfast, 442
  Wheat and Mixed Nut, Lebanese,
    497
"Porridge"
  Chicken, Qatari, 270
  Meat, Legumes, and Wheat, South
    Asian, 264–65
  Meat and Wheat, Persian, 268–69
  Wheat and Meat, 266–67
Potato(es)
  Algerian Fish Cakes, 330
  Arabian Meat and Vegetable Stew
    over Crispy Bread, *84,* 85–86
  Arabian "Pasta" with Meat and
    Vegetables, 76–77
  Bengali Vegetable "Risotto,"
    232–33
  Calcutta Biryani, 204–5
  The Chicken That Flew, *304,* 305
  Filling for "Calzones," 63
  Indonesian Vegetable and Egg
    Salad, *384,* 385
  Iranian Yellow Split Pea Stew,
    158–59
  and Peas, Lamb Tagine with, 144,
    145
  Qatari Chicken and Rice, 216–18,
    217
  Sweet, Quail Tagine with, 152
Poultry. *See* Chicken; Cornish hens;
  Poussin(s); Quail

Poussin(s)
  Chicken Kebabs, 125
  Chicken Tagine with Olives and
    Preserved Lemons, 140–41
  Malabar Chicken Biryani, 206–7
  Tagine with Carrots, Olives, and
    Preserved Lemon, *142,* 143
Pudding
  Black Rice, Indonesian, 480, *481*
  Caraway, 450
  Grape Juice, 501
  Milk, Saffron Lebanese/Syrian, 479
  Milk Rice, Indian/Pakistani, 478
  Rice, Moroccan, 482
  Rice, Syrian/Lebanese, 483
  Saffron Rice, Turkish, *484,* 485
Pumpkin
  Arabian "Pasta" with Meat and
    Vegetables, 76–77
  Halva, 498

Q

Qara, Stuffed, 405
Qatari Biryani Masala, 362
Qatari Chicken and Rice, 216–18, *217*
Qatari Chicken "Porridge," 270
Qatari Festive Rice and Chicken,
  222–24, *223*
Qatari Shrimp "Risotto," *214,* 215
Quail
  Moroccan Pigeon Pie, *36,* 37–39
  Tagine with Sweet Potatoes, 152
Quince
  Kibbeh Balls with, in a Fresh
    Pomegranate Sauce, 136–37
  Stew, 163
  Tunisian Fish Couscous, 276–77

R

Raisins
  Afghani Vermicelli Rice II, 240, *241*
  Azerbaijani Sweet-Savory Rice,
    260
  Baked Stuffed Fish, 312
  Couscous with Seven Vegetables,
    261–63, *262*
  Dried Fruit and Nuts in Apricot
    Leather Juice, 443
  Egyptian Bread "Pudding," 89
  Emirati Rice and Meat, 220–21
  Festive Sweet-Savory Rice,
    253–55, *254*
  Lentil Polow, 246–47
  Malabar Chicken Biryani, 206–7

Qatari Festive Rice and Chicken, 222–24, *223*
Quail Tagine with Sweet Potatoes, 152
Sweet-Savory Couscous with Chicken, 272–73
Sweet-Savory Lamb Tagine for Eid el-Kbir, 149
Tunisian Fish Couscous, 276–77
Zanzibari Sweet Noodles, 291
Ramadam, about, xii–xiii
Ramadam Bread, 44–45
Ramadan Date Cookies, 455–56, *457*
Ramadan Nut-Filled Cookies, 458
Ras el-hanout, about, 363
"Ravioli," Arabian, with Fish, 346–47
Regag, 16
Rice
    Awadhi Biryani, 202–3, *203*
    Azerbaijani Sweet-Savory, 260
    Bangladeshi Fish Head "Risotto," *318*, 319–20
    a Bed of Fragrant, Saudi Roast Lamb Shoulder on, 98–99, *99*
    Bengali Vegetable "Risotto," 232–33
    Black, Pudding, Indonesian, 480, *481*
    and Bread, a Bed of, Festive Jordanian Lamb in Yogurt over, *176*, 177–78
    Cake, Baked, with Lamb, *248*, 249
    Calcutta Biryani, 204–5
    and Chicken, Qatari, 216–18, *217*
    and Chicken, Qatari Festive, 222–24, *223*
    Coconut, Zanzibari, 237
    cooking methods, in Iran, 243
    Egyptian Fattah, 81
    Emirati Biryani, 208–9
    with Fava Beans, 244
    Festive Sweet-Savory, 253–55, *254*
    Fried, Indonesian, 258–59, *259*
    Herbed Polow, 245
    Hyderabadi Biryani, 200–201
    Indonesian Kebuli Biryani, 210–11, *211*
    Iranian Stuffed Grape Leaves, 395–96
    Iranian Stuffed Whole Lamb, 96–97
    Iraqi Stuffed Onions, 402–3
    in Islamic cuisine, 197
    Jeweled, 250–52, *251*
    Koshari, 234–36, *235*
    Lebanese Fish and Caramelized

Onion "Risotto," 230–31
    Lentil Polow, 246–47
    Malabar Chicken Biryani, 206–7
    and Meat, Emirati, 220–21
    Milk Pudding, Indian/Pakistani, 478
    Moroccan Meatballs with, 147
    Plain Iranian, 242–43
    Pudding, Moroccan, 482
    Pudding, Syrian/Lebanese, 483
    Pudding, Turkish Saffron, *484*, 485
    Qatari Chicken "Porridge," 270
    Qatari Shrimp "Risotto," *214*, 215
    Saudi Fish "Risotto," 228–29
    Saudi Lamb Kabsa, 219
    Saudi Shrimp "Risotto," 212–213
    Senegalese Fish Stew, 349–51, *350*
    Slow-Cooked Biryani, 198–99, *199*
    Stuffed Cabbage Leaves, 404–5
    Stuffed Grape Leaves Cooked on a Bed of Lamb Chops, 392–94, *393*
    Stuffed Mussels, 340–41
    Sweet-Savory, 227
    Turkish Mixed Nut, Dried Fruit, and Legumes Dessert, *494*, 495
    Vegetarian Stuffed Swiss Chard, 406–7
    Vermicelli, Afghani, I, 238
    Vermicelli, Afghani, II, 240, *241*
    Vermicelli, Lebanese/Syrian, 239
    Yellow, Indonesian, *256*, 257
    Yemeni Chicken "Risotto," 225–26
"Risotto"
    Bulgur, with Chickpeas and Lamb, 287
    Chicken, Yemeni, 225–26
    Fish, Lebanese, and Caramelized Onion, 230–231
    Fish, Saudi, 228–29
    Fish Head, Bangladeshi, *318*, 319–20
    Shrimp, Qatari, *214*, 215
    Shrimp, Saudi, 212–13
    Vegetable, Bengali, 232–33
Rosebuds
    Tunisian B'harat, 366
Rose water
    Azerbaijani Sweet-Savory Rice, 260
    Chickpea Flour Halva, 466
    Classic Balaleet, 283
    Date Halva, 459
    Iraqi Date Cookies, 468
    Turkish Saffron Rice Pudding, *484*, 485

S

Saffron
    -Flavored Fritters, 486, *487*
    Ice Cream, 469
    Kulfi, 473
    Lebanese/Syrian Milk Pudding, 479
    Rice Pudding, Turkish, *484*, 485
Saj Bread, 6–7, *7*
Salads
    Bulgur, Turkish, 381
    Fava Bean, 416, *417*
    Mario Haddad's Fattoush, 391
    Mixed Herb and Toasted Bread, 382, *383*
    Onion and Parsley, 387
    Shanklish, 166, *167*
    Steamed Eggplant, Moroccan, 389
    Tabbouleh, 378, *379*
    Vegetable and Egg, Indonesian, *384*, 385
    White Tabbouleh, 380
"Salsa"
    Saudi, 429
    Tomato, Lebanese Spicy, 435
Salt and Cumin Mixture, Moroccan, 367
Sambal
    Chili and Tomato, 372
    Fresh Chili and Tomato, 373
    Spicy Shrimp, 371
Sardines Chermoula, 342, *343*
Satay
    Chicken, *112*, 113
    Meat, 111
Sauces
    Pasta, Salim's, 282
    Tahini, 433
    Turkish Tarator, 337
    Yogurt, Cooked, 175
Saudi Camel Meatballs, 102–3, *103*
Saudi Eggplant Fatteh, 78
Saudi Fish "Risotto," 228–29
Saudi Lamb Kabsa, 219
Saudi Meat Fatteh, 79
Saudi Meat Pies, 46–48, *47*
Saudi Mulukhiyah Dip, 434
Saudi Roast Lamb Shoulder on a Bed of Fragrant Rice, 98–99, *99*
Saudi "Salsa," 429
Saudi Shrimp "Risotto," 212–13
Saudi Sweet Fritters, 488
Scallion(s)
    Iranian Herb Omelet, 400, *401*
    Pancakes, Uighur, 71–73, *72*

Sea Bass
    Baked, with Tomatoes and Olives, 313
    Indonesian Fish Head Curry, 321
    Spicy Baked Fish with Herbs and Nuts, 315
    Tunisian Fish Couscous, 276–77
Sea bream
    Arabian Spiced Fried Fish, 345
    Emirati Fish in an Onion and Tomato Sauce, 353
    Senegalese Fish Stew, 349–51, 350
    Spicy Baked Fish with Herbs and Nuts, 315
    Tunisian Fish Couscous, 276–77
Semolina
    Aleppine Breakfast Porridge, 442
    Aniseed Fritters, 492, 493
    Cake, 454
    Date-Filled Pastries, 466–67
    Ramadan Date Cookies, 455–56, 457
    Ramadan Nut-Filled Cookies, 458
Senegalese Bread Rolls, 74, 75
Senegalese Fish Stew, 349–51, 350
Sesame seeds
    Dukkah, 368
    Iraqi Date Cookies, 468
    Kashgar Multilayered Non, 34
    Uzbek Flatbread, 32–33
    Zanzibari Sesame Bread, 28–29
Shanklish, 165
Shanklish Salad, 166, 167
Shark, Spicy Baby, 352
Sheermal, 23
Shellfish
    Fried Mussel Brochettes, 332
    Indonesian Crab Curry, 322, 323
    Qatari Shrimp "Risotto," 214, 215
    Saudi Shrimp "Risotto," 212–13
    Shrimp Brochettes, 333
    Spicy Noodles with Shrimp, 280–81
    Spicy Shrimp Sambal, 371
    Stuffed Mussels, 340–41
Shrimp
    Brochettes, 333
    "Risotto," Qatari, 214, 215
    "Risotto," Saudi, 212–13
    Sambal, Spicy, 371
    Spicy Noodles with, 280–81
Somali Pancakes, 8
Somali Spice Mixture, 365
Soups
    Chickpea, Tunisian, 294

Chickpea and Lamb, Moroccan, 295
Dried Okra, 436, 437
Egyptian Mulukhiyah, 408
Lentil, Chickpea, and Bean, 296
Lentil, Lebanese, 293
Pomegranate, Iranian, 298–99, 299
Split Lentil, Egyptian, 292
Yogurt, Azerbaijani, 193
South Asian Meat, Legumes, and Wheat "Porridge," 264–65
South Asian Sweet Milk Fritters, 489
Southern Lebanese Za'atar "Pizza," 42–43, 43
Spice Mixtures
    Advieh, 363
    Arabian, 366
    Arabian, for Desserts, 367
    Berbere, 365
    Chili and Tomato Sambal, 372
    Dried Herb and Bulgur Mixture, 359
    Dukkah, 368
    Fish, Arabian, 368
    Fresh Chili and Tomato Sambal, 373
    Garam Masala, 361
    Harissa, 370
    Indian Biryani Masala, 362
    in Islamic cuisine, 356
    Moroccan Salt and Cumin, 367
    Qatari Biryani Masala, 362
    Ras el-hanout, about, 363
    Salt and Cumin, Moroccan, 367
    7-, Lebanese, 358
    Somali, 365
    Spicy Shrimp Sambal, 371
    Tunisian B'harat, 366
    Yemeni, 364
    Yemeni Mandi, 364
Spinach
    and Cheese Filling for "Calzones," 63
    Filling for Fatayer, 56
    with Paneer, 421
    and Yogurt Spread, 187
Split peas. See Yellow Split Pea(s)
Squash. See also Zucchini
    Arabian "Pasta" with Meat and Vegetables, 76–77
    Pumpkin Halva, 498
    Senegalese Fish Stew, 349–51, 350
Stews
    Fish, Senegalese, 349–51, 350

Lamb and Eggplant, Iranian, 162
Meat, Beans, and Tomato, 297
Meat and Vegetable, Arabian, over Crispy Bread, 84, 85–86
Mixed-Herb Lamb, Iranian, 160–61
Quince, 163
Yellow Split Pea, Iranian, 158–59
Sugar Syrup, 486, 487
Sumac
    Mario Haddad's Fattoush, 391
    Mixed Herb and Toasted Bread Salad, 382, 383
    Onion and Parsley Salad, 387
    Sauce, Kibbeh in, 132–34
Sweet Potatoes
    The Chicken That Flew, 304, 305
    Quail Tagine with, 152
Sweets
    Aleppine Breakfast Porridge, 442
    Aniseed Fritters, 492, 493
    Baklava, 448–49
    The Bread of the Harem, 88
    Caraway Pudding, 450
    Carrot Halva, 465
    Chickpea Flour Halva, 466
    Cornes de Gazelles, 451–52, 453
    Cream or Walnut Sweet "Hand Pies," 474–475, 475
    Date-Filled Pastries, 466–67
    Date "Fudge," 460, 461
    Date Halva, 459
    Date Ice Cream, 470, 471
    Dried Fruit and Nuts in Apricot Leather Juice, 443
    Egyptian Bread "Pudding," 89
    Grape Juice Pudding, 501
    Grape Leather, 500
    Indian/Pakistani Milk Rice Pudding, 478
    Indonesian Black Rice Pudding, 480, 481
    Iraqi Date Cookies, 468
    in Islamic cuisine, 440
    Lebanese Sweet Cheese "Pie," 444–46, 445
    Lebanese/Syrian Round Fritters, 490–91
    Lebanese Wheat and Mixed Nut Porridge, 497
    Malaysian Pandan Balls, 477
    Moroccan Almond Spirals, 447
    Moroccan Rice Pudding, 482
    Orange Blossom Jam, 502
    Pakistani/Indian Ice Cream, 472, 473

Pistachio Ice Cream, 469
Pumpkin Halva, 498
Ramadan Date Cookies, 455–56,
    457
Ramadan Nut-Filled Cookies, 458
Saffron-Flavored Fritters, 486, *487*
Saffron Ice Cream, 469
Saffron Kulfi, 473
Saffron Lebanese/Syrian Milk
    Pudding, 479
Saudi Sweet Fritters, 488
Semolina Cake, 454
South Asian Sweet Milk Fritters,
    489
Sugared Almonds, 499
Sugared Chickpeas, 499
Sweet-Salty Cassava Cakes, 476
Syrian/Lebanese Rice Pudding, 483
Turkish Flour Halva, *462,* 463
Turkish Mixed Nut, Dried Fruit, and
    Legumes Dessert, *494,* 495
Turkish Saffron Rice Pudding, *484,*
    485
Swiss Chard
    Moroccan Grey Mullet Stuffed
        with, 314
    Vegetarian Stuffed, 406–7
Swordfish
    Brochettes, 334, *335*
    Pickled, 338
Syrian Fatayer, *53,* 55–57
Syrian Fatteh, 82–83, *83*
Syrian H'risseh, 454
Syrian Kibbeh, Grilled, 135
Syrian/Lebanese Milk Pudding, Saffron,
    479
Syrian/Lebanese Rice Pudding, 483
Syrian/Lebanese Round Fritters, 490–91
Syrian/Lebanese Vermicelli Rice, 241
Syrian-Style Ful Medammes, 300
Syrup, Sugar, 486, *487*

T

Tabbouleh, 378, *379*
Tabbouleh, White, 380
Tagines
    Chicken, with Olives and Preserved
        Lemons, 140–41
    Lamb, Sweet-Savory, for Eid el-
        Kbir, 149
    Lamb, with Eggplant, 146
    Lamb, with Potatoes and Peas,
        144, *145*
    Poussin, with Carrots, Olives, and
        Preserved Lemon, *142,* 143

    Quail, with Sweet Potatoes, 152
Tahini
    Dip, 102
    Grilled Eggplant Puree and Minced
        Meat in Tomato Sauce, 180
    Herb, and Nut Sauce, Spicy Baked
        Fish in a, 315
    Hommus, 432
    Lamb Shawarma Sandwich, *126,*
        127–28
    Sauce, 433
    Sauce, Fish in, 326
    Smoky Eggplant Dip, 390
    Syrian-Style Ful Medammes, 300
Tamarind
    Chickpea Flour Fritters, 306, *307*
    Dip, 102
    Iranian Stuffed Grape Leaves,
        395–96
    Sauce, Fish in, 339
    Saudi Fish "Risotto," 228–29
Tannur Bread, 7
Tarator
    Mackerel, 336
    Turkish, 337
Tarhana, 165
Tarragon and Labneh Dip, 188, *189*
Tea
    Milky, Arabian or Indian, *506,*
        507
    Mint, 503, *503*
Tomato(es)
    Arabian "Ravioli" with Fish,
        346–47
    Bangladeshi Fish Head "Risotto,"
        318, 319–20
    Bulgur and Nut Cakes, 286
    Chickpea Flour Fritters, 306, *307*
    and Chili Sambal, 372
    Couscous with Seven Vegetables,
        261–63, *262*
    Dried Okra Soup, *436,* 437
    Egyptian Fattah, 81
    Egyptian Split Lentil Soup, 292
    Egyptian-Style Ful Medammes,
        300
    Emirati Biryani, 208–9
    and Fresh Chili Sambal, 373
    Indonesian Fried Fish, 328–29
    Iranian Lamb and Eggplant Stew,
        162
    Kibbeh in Sumac Sauce, 132–34
    Koshari, 234–36, *235*
    The Lord of Stuffed Vegetables,
        397–99, *398*

    Mario Haddad's Fattoush, 391
    Meat, and Beans Stew, 297
    Moroccan Couscous with
        Monkfish, 274–75
    Moroccan Steamed Eggplant
        Salad, 389
    and Olives, Baked Sea Bass with,
        313
    and Onion Sauce, Emirati Fish in
        an, 353
    Pakistani Chicken Curry, 156–57
    Paneer Makhni, 169
    Qatari Chicken "Porridge," 270
    Qatari Festive Rice and Chicken,
        222–24, *223*
    Salim's Pasta Sauce, 282
    "Salsa," Lebanese Spicy, 435
    Sauce, Cauliflower in, 412, *413*
    Sauce, Eggplant in, 388
    Sauce, Grilled Eggplant Puree and
        Minced Meat in, 180
    Saudi Lamb Kabsa, 219
    Saudi "Salsa," 429
    Senegalese Fish Stew, 349–51, *350*
    Shanklish Salad, 166, *167*
    Spinach with Paneer, 421
    Tabbouleh, 378, *379*
    Turkish Bulgur Salad, 381
    Turkish Kebabs, 106, *107*
    Vegetarian Stuffed Swiss Chard,
        406–7
    White Tabbouleh, 380
Trotters with Chickpeas and Wheat,
    290
Tunisian B'harat, 366
Tunisian Chickpea Soup, 294
Tunisian Fish Couscous, 276–77
Turkish Bulgur Salad, 381
Turkish "Calzone," 62–63
Turkish Coffee, 504
Turkish Dumplings with Garlicky
    Yogurt, 184–85
Turkish Flatbread, 10
Turkish Flour Halva, *462,* 463
Turkish Kebabs, 106, *107*
Turkish Meat Boreks, 60–61, *61*
Turkish Mixed Nut, Dried Fruit, and
    Legumes Dessert, *494,* 495–96
Turkish Pickled Green Almonds, 423
Turkish Saffron Rice Pudding, *484,*
    485
Turkish Tarator, 337
Turmeric
    Classic Balaleet, 283
    Indonesian Yellow Rice, *256,* 257

Turnips
    Couscous with Seven Vegetables,
        261–63, *262*
    Pink Pickled, 424, *425*
    Senegalese Fish Stew, 349–51, *350*

U

Uighur Scallion Pancakes, 71–73, *72*
Uzbek Flatbread, 32–33, *33*

V

Veal
    Quince Stew, 163
Vegetable(s). *See also specific
    vegetables*
    Curry, *414*, 415
    in Islamic cuisine, 376
    "Risotto," Bengali, 232–33
    Seven, Couscous with, 261–63,
        262
    Stuffed, The Lord of, 397–99, *398*
Vermicelli
    Classic Balaleet, 283
    in Islamic cuisine, 197
    Koshari, 234–36, *235*
    Rice, Afghani, I, 238
    Rice, Afghani, II, 240, *241*
    Rice, Lebanese/Syrian, 239

W

Walnut(s)
    Baked Stuffed Fish, 312
    Baklava, 448–49
    Date "Fudge," 460, *461*
    Date Halva, 459
    Dried Fruit and Nuts in Apricot
        Leather Juice, 443
    Eggplant and Yogurt Dip, *190*, 191
    and Garlic, Eggplant with,
        Preserved in Olive Oil, 426
    Iranian Stuffed Whole Lamb,
        96–97
    Lebanese Wheat and Mixed Nut
        Porridge, 497
    or Cream Sweet "Hand Pies,"
        474–75, *475*
    and Pomegranate Sauce, Iranian
        Chicken in, 153
    Ramadan Nut-Filled Cookies, 458
    Spicy Baked Fish in a Tahini, Herb,
        and Nut Sauce, 316, *317*

Spicy Baked Fish with Herbs and
    Nuts, 315
Syrian H'risseh, 454
Turkish Mixed Nut, Dried Fruit,
    and Legumes Dessert, *494*,
    495–96
Turkish Tarator, 337
Weddings, xiii
Wheat. *See also* Bulgur; Wheat berries
    Chicken and Lamb with Frikeh,
        288, *289*
    in Islamic cuisine, 197
    Qatari Chicken "Porridge," 270
Wheat berries
    Lamb Shanks with Chickpeas and
        Wheat, 290
    Lebanese Wheat and Mixed Nut
        Porridge, *494*, 495
    Persian Meat and Wheat
        "Porridge," 268–69
    South Asian Meat, Legumes, and
        Wheat "Porridge," 264–65
    Trotters with Chickpeas and
        Wheat, 290
    Turkish Mixed Nut, Dried Fruit,
        and Legumes Dessert, 494.
        495–96
    Wheat and Meat "Porridge,"
        266–67
Wild Endive in Olive Oil, 420

Y

Yellow Split Pea(s)
    Iranian Pomegranate Soup,
        298–99
    South Asian Meat, Legumes, and
        Wheat "Porridge," 264–65
    Stew, Iranian, 158–59
Yemeni Bread, 18, *19*
Yemeni Chicken "Risotto," 225–26
Yemeni Cilantro Chutney, 369
Yemeni Mandi Spice Mixture, 364
Yemeni Spice Mixture, 364
Yogurt. *See also* Labneh
    and Cucumber Dip, 192
    Doogh, 171
    dried and salted, 165
    Drink, *170*, 171
    Drink, Sweet, 174
    Egyptian Fattah, 81
    and Elephant Garlic Dip, 192

Festive Jordanian Lamb in, over a
    Bed of Rice and Bread, *176*,
    177–78
Garlicky, Turkish Dumplings with,
    184–85
Grilled Eggplant Puree and Minced
    Meat in Tomato Sauce, 180
Hyderabadi Biryani, 200–201
in Iranian cuisine, 164
jameed, 165
kashk, 165
kishk, 164–65
Lamb Shanks in, 179
Lebanese Lamb Fatteh, 80
made into cheese, 165
Mango Drink, 172, *173*
preserved, types of, 164–65
Sauce, Cooked, 175
Sauce, Fresh Almonds in, 186
Sauce, Lebanese Dumplings in,
    182–83, *183*
Sauce, Minty, Kibbeh Balls in, 181
Saudi Eggplant Fatteh, 78
Saudi Meat Fatteh, 79
shanklish, 165
Slow-Cooked Biryani, 198–99, *199*
Soup, Azerbaijani, 193
Syrian Fatteh, 82–83, *83*
tarhana, 165

Z

Za'atar "Pizza," Southern Lebanese,
    42–43, *43*
Zanzibari Coconut Rice, 237
Zanzibari Grilled Fish in Coconut Sauce,
    348
Zanzibari Savory Doughnut, *26*, 27
Zanzibari Sesame Bread, 28–29
Zanzibari Sweet Noodles, 291
Zucchini
    Arabian Meat and Vegetable Stew
        over Crispy Bread, *84*, 85–86
    Arabian "Pasta" with Meat and
        Vegetables, 76–77
    Couscous with Seven Vegetables,
        261–63, *262*
    Egyptian Split Lentil Soup, 292
    Salim's Pasta Sauce, 282
    Saudi Eggplant Fatteh, 78

HarperCollins books may be purchased for educational, business, or
sales promotional use. For information please e-mail the Special Markets
Department at SPsales@harpercollins.com.

FIRST EDITION

Designed by Renata De Oliveira

Large photographs by Kristin Perers

Small photographs by Anissa Helou, except for page 2 (right) by Alastaire
Hendy, and pages 161, 299, and 377 (top and bottom right) by Ali Farboud

Food and food styling by Anissa Helou and Claire Ptak

Map illustration by Mike Hall

Library of Congress Cataloging-in-Publication Data has been applied for.

ISBN 978-0-06-236303-9

18 19 20 21 22   LSC   10 9 8 7 6 5 4 3 2 1